EASING INTO MODERN HEBREW GRAMMAR
A User-friendly Reference and Exercise Book

by

Gila Freedman Cohen and Carmia Shoval

VOLUME I

EASING INTO MODERN HEBREW GRAMMAR
A User-friendly Reference and Exercise Book

by
Gila Freedman Cohen and Carmia Shoval

VOLUME I

THE HEBREW UNIVERSITY MAGNES PRESS, JERUSALEM

The publication of this book was made possible in part by a grant from
Keren Karev of the Andrea and Charles Bronfman Philanthropies.

Editorial advisor: Sharon Sokoler

Graphic design: Yossi Pinchuk

Illustrations: Gustavo Viselner – pp. 26, 254, 286-289, 309, 319, 320, 324, 536, 675
Ofer Shoval – pp. 346, 444, 502

Published by The Hebrew University Magnes Press
P.O. Box 39099, Jerusalem 91390
Fax 972-2-5660341
www.magnespress.co.il

ISBN 978-965-493-601-9
eBook ISBN 978-965-493-602-6

Printed in Israel
Layout: Irit Nachum, Art Plus

Contents

VOLUME II

PART FOUR: HOW ARE HEBREW SENTENCES BUILT?

Acknowledgments

We would like to express our appreciation to the following people:

Our students at the Rothberg International School of the Hebrew University. Over the course of our many years of teaching Modern Hebrew to non-native speakers, our students have often expressed the need for an accessible, user-friendly reference book in English. It is primarily with their needs in mind that we embarked on this project. It is our hope that *Easing into Modern Hebrew Grammar* will provide them with the kind of explanations they have sought.

Ms. Sharon Sokoler, who edited a large portion of the book and provided important guidelines for the presentation of the material. Sharon's experience and insight as a teacher of English as a foreign language and her linguistic sensitivity and extraordinary common sense made her help invaluable. We also thank Sharon for her patience over the years of work on the manuscript.

Our colleagues, Ms. Sarah Israeli and Ms. Hanna Maschler, who read our manuscript with attention to every detail, providing wise insights not only into the subject material, but also into its presentation. Our acknowledgement of their input "here and there" in the footnotes does not do justice to their contribution to this book. We thank them both for their wonderful generosity and constant encouragement.

Prof. Steven Fassberg of the Hebrew University and Dr. Uri Melammed of the Hebrew Language Academy, who graciously clarified various linguistic issues dealt with in the book, providing insights not available in published sources. We appreciate their time and moral support.

Ms. Ruth Almagor-Ramon of the Israel Broadcasting Authority and the Hebrew Language Academy and Ms. Ronit Gadish of the Hebrew Language Academy, both of whom willingly answered our many questions on usage and normativity.

Our colleagues at the Rothberg International School – instructors of Hebrew and English – with whom we often discussed linguistic issues covered in the book. Instructors in the Division of Hebrew Language Instruction often served as linguistic "informants," filling in questionnaires or answering questions related to usage.

Graphic designer, Mr. Yossi Pinchuk, whose comments and questions provided important food for thought and whose ideas and design made the book more readable. Illustrators, Mr. Gustavo Viselner and Ms. Ofer Shoval, who helped convey our ideas with light-hearted images. A special thank you to our indefatiguable layout artist, Ms. Irit Nachum of Art Plus, whose exactitude and patience made working on the technical aspects of the book bearable. Our thanks also to Mr. Haim Gross of Art Plus.

Dr. Aliza Yahav, Prof. Aharon Loewenschuss, Mr. Doug McGredy for their advice on various aspects of language and graphics.

Our colleague, Ms. Varda Yishai, director of the *Sfatarbut* Program of the Division of Hebrew Language Instruction (Rothberg International School, Hebrew University), who provided steadfast support for this project from an early stage.

We would like to express our gratitude to the Andrea and Charles Bronfman Philanthropies, whose generous contribution to the Division of Hebrew Language of the Rothberg International School supported the editing and publication of this book. We would also like to thank Mr. Hai Tsabar and Mr. Ram Goldberg of the Magnes Press of the Hebrew University for their support of this project and for their help in seeing it through to completion.

Finally, a word of heartfelt thanks to our families for their willingness to support us in this project in every way. To our children – Tamar and Daniel, Ofer and Yarden – and to Dan Shoval, who served also as a trusted linguistic advisor and tireless informant, and Jeremy Cohen, who provided both technical assistance and much-needed moral support and encouragement.

Introduction

Learning the grammar of any language can be challenging. We have written this book to help students of Modern Hebrew meet this challenge. Our primary audience is English-speaking students of Modern Hebrew who are looking for explanations of Hebrew grammar in **non-technical** English. We have tried to "ease" them into Hebrew grammar in ways that are described below. Our explanations are accompanied by examples in Hebrew (with English translations). In order to understand these examples, readers must be able to read Hebrew and must know some basic vocabulary and grammar.

What material is covered?

This book deals with a wide range of topics covered in **beginning and intermediate** Hebrew language courses.[1] We have not attempted to describe Modern Hebrew as a whole, but rather have clearly limited the topics discussed (e.g., the verb groups, the prepositions, the time words, the reason words, etc.) and the vocabulary used to the topics and vocabulary generally learned at the beginning and intermediate levels.

In our presentation of Hebrew grammar we focus on different kinds of **words** (e.g., nouns, verbs, adjectives), their functions, and the ways in which they are formed, written and pronounced. We also look at common ways in which these words join together with other words to form **phrases** and **sentences**, which ultimately create a written or oral "text."[2]

Aims and format

Easing into Modern Hebrew Grammar is designed to serve as a **user-friendly reference and exercise book**. Our intention is to engage the student and, to this end, we often use a **question-answer** (Q-A) format: We first present a Hebrew sentence or passage (with English translation) and then ask the reader a question about it. The answer to this question appears immediately below it. At frequent intervals we provide brief **summaries** of the material covered (called *Let's review*). A *Chapter summary* appears at the end of many chapters. The interim and chapter summaries are often followed by **exercises** (labeled *Want to see if you've understood?*), which enable the reader to check if the topic has been understood. Answers are provided at the end of each exercise.

---

1   Our division into levels is based on the division used at the Hebrew University and, obviously, may vary from institution to institution.
2   We also deal with various aspects of how sentences relate to one another in a larger text, but we do not discuss the structure of this text as such.

Readers searching for a specific grammar topic can refer not only to the **table of contents**, but also to the English **subject index** and the **Hebrew word index** at the end of the book. Both the *Preview* at the beginning of each chapter and the various summaries provide additional guidance.

The following **icons** and **headings** appear throughout the book:

 Preview – presents a list of the main topics discussed in the chapter.

 Be careful! – emphasizes a point that is a frequent source of mistakes.

 Did you know? – adds material that is related but either is not of paramount importance or is a clear digression from the topic under discussion.

 Let's review – provides an interim summary of the material taught.

 Chapter summary – summarizes the material examined in the chapter.

 Want to see if you've understood? – offers a short exercise of the material taught.

Near the end of the book, we have included five **appendices**. These include material that students often find helpful. (See the table of contents for details.)

Use of grammatical terms, comparisons to English and "simplification" of material

In this book we have tried to use only basic grammatical terms and have avoided using more technical terms often found in books on Hebrew grammar. We have included these technical terms (in English or Hebrew) either in parentheses or in the footnotes at the bottom of the page. In several cases we have used Hebrew terms (e.g., *beenyan, smeechoot*) instead of translating them into English. These terms are written in Latin letters, but not as transcriptions (which would be: *been-YAN* and *smee-CHOOT*). The usual translations of these terms are noted in parentheses or in the footnotes.

In order to make our explanations clearer, we have often compared and contrasted Hebrew and English. Since the differences between the languages are commonly a source of error, many of the contrasts are included in explanations labeled *Be careful!*.

Teachers and advanced students may notice that we have sometimes "simplified" grammatical material in order to make it easier for students to learn. We have noted blatant cases of such simplification in our footnotes. Here are three examples:

1. Syllable division

In this book we have based the division of words into syllables on the (fairly slow and clear) pronunciation of Hebrew by most native speakers today. Thus, a word like דְּבָרִים is regarded as having two syllables: *dva-REEM* (as opposed to the traditional division *de/va-REEM*). The word דִּיבֵּר is regarded as having the following two syllables: *dee-BER* (as opposed to the traditional *deeb-BER*).

2. Sounds and writing

In our description of Hebrew, we have tried to differentiate between the **sounds** of the language (*consonants* and *vowels*) and the recording of these sounds in **writing** (*letters, vowel signs*, etc.). However, at times we felt it necessary to blur this distinction; for example, we use the term *root letters* when we sometimes mean *root consonants*. We also say that *letters* are "pronounced" when, properly stated, *consonants* and *vowels* are "pronounced," and *letters* and *vowel signs* are "realized."

3. Describing sentences

When describing sentence structure, we often use the term *base clause* to refer to an independent or subordinating clause. We use the term *added clause* to refer to a dependent or subordinate clause. In addition, when speaking of sentences **without** a verb (e.g., יש לי ספר – I have a book, דויד ספורטאי – David is an athlete), we often say that these sentences are in the *present tense*, even though – technically speaking – only a **verb** has tense. We do this because these sentences are perceived as being in the present tense. Indeed, the English equivalents of these sentences contain a present tense verb.

Spelling and vowel signs

Hebrew has two systems of spelling. According to one system, the word for "he spoke" is spelled דִּבֵּר. In this system we add to the letters both vowel signs and other signs – such as the *dagesh* (a dot that is placed in a letter) or the dot on the letters שׁ and שׂ.[3] In grammar books this system is often called *defective spelling* (כְּתִיב חָסֵר). We have chosen to call this system *standard spelling*. The second system, called *full spelling* (כְּתִיב מָלֵא), dictates that this same word be spelled דיבר. The letter י has been added and no vowel signs are used.

In this book we spell words according to the *full spelling* system. This is the spelling used in most publications in Modern Hebrew today.[4] In addition, we often add some or all vowel signs to words in order to make their pronunciation clearer. We use the *dagesh* sparingly, adding it primarily to the letters ב, כ, פ (when they are pronounced *b, k* and *p*). However, in chapters

---

3   In Hebrew these signs are called סִימָנֵי נִיקּוּד. When we use the term *vowel signs* we refer also to the diacritical marks like the *dagesh*.
4   Today we find *vowel signs* used mainly in children's books and in poetry.

dealing with *patterns* of words (*adjectives*, *nouns* and *verbs*), we do sometimes add a *dagesh* to letters other than 'פ ,כ' ,ב in cases where the *dagesh* is a significant part of the form and where its absence (in 'א' ,ה' ,ח' ,ע' ,ר) may cause a change in pronunciation. Compare, for example, the *regular* verb לְהִיגָּמֵר *le-hee-ga-MER* and the verb לְהֵיעָלֵם *le-he-'a-LEM*, whose first *root letter* is 'ע.[5]

In almost all cases we follow the spelling rules set forth by the Hebrew Language Academy.[6] In some cases, however, we diverge from these rules in order to make pronunciation clearer. For example, in words such as the following, we add a 'ו or 'י: תוכנית (program) instead of תכנית, איתי (with me) instead of אתי and פירות (fruit) instead of פרות.

In the exercises we usually do not add vowel signs, and we do not expect students to add vowel signs to their answers. In the answers that we supply, however, we often add vowel signs in order to make the pronunciation of words clearer.

Describing language as formal and informal, correct and incorrect

Foreign language students are usually taught the fairly standard Hebrew spoken and written by educated speakers, and this is the language we have presented in this book. When we deal with more than one word or expression denoting the same thing, we try to point out differences in the level of formality or in ways or circumstances in which the words are used.

We use the following terms to note levels of informality and formality:

---

colloquial – typical of popular spoken Hebrew, often does not adhere to the traditional rules of grammar.

informal – typical of spoken Hebrew and of informal written language (letters to friends and family). Language in this register usually adheres to the rules of grammar.

formal – a word or expression for which a less formal alternative exists in everyday usage. This Hebrew is spoken in more formal contexts (for example, a conversation with a professor, a lecture to a class) and is written in formal letters or academic writing. Formal pronunciation is used today in news broadcasts and at formal public ceremonies.

literary – used only in very formal language or in literature.

---

5   See the chapter "Guttural Consonants: *Beenyaneem Pee'el, Poo'al* and *Neef'al*," pp. 480-482 for an explanation.

6   See the chapter "Hebrew Spelling: Selected Issues," pp. 654-669.

The Hebrew that is taught to learners – and is the subject of this book – usually adheres to the rules of grammar. However, Hebrew is alive and changing. Sometimes what is "correct" according to the rules of grammar (i.e., "normative") sounds either out of place or even incorrect. When – in everyday usage by educated speakers – a certain non-normative usage or pronunciation is very widespread, we note this fact either in the body of the text or in the footnotes. For example, we teach the normative form אֶתְכֶם and note that the form אוֹתְכֶם is commonly used in everyday speech. In some special cases, we have chosen to teach the non-normative form (e.g., כָּתַבְתֶם ka-TAV-tem), while noting the traditional form and pronunciation (כְּתַבְתֶם ktav-TEM or ke-tav-TEM) in small letters. The guiding principle in deciding what to teach our students is our desire that they not sound like *ulpan* students when they speak and write. However, we do want them to be **aware** of what is normative and non-normative and to sound like educated speakers of Hebrew.

In cases where we were unsure regarding normativity, we consulted the Hebrew Language Academy and other experts in the field. We have made it a point to keep abreast of the decisions made by the Hebrew Language Academy, and these are reflected in our presentation of material in this book. In questions of usage – regarding what sounds "right" or "acceptable" to a native speaker in a certain situation – we have not only relied on our own judgment, but also have consulted reliable native-speaker "informants." In addition, we have used the Internet as a source of information – though with the requisite caution.

Transcription of words in Latin letters

In addition to English translations, we often provide *transcriptions* that indicate in Latin letters how a Hebrew word is pronounced. Our transcriptions are based on the pronunciation of Hebrew by a large segment of the Israeli population. In this pronunciation there is no differentiation between א' and ע'; in addition, כ' (without a *dagesh*) and ח' are pronounced the same. The vowel signs ◌ and ◌ are both pronounced *eh*, but when ◌ is followed by י', as in בֵּית סֵפֶר, it is pronounced by some speakers *ei*: *beit SE-fer*. In such a case, we have included the transcriptions of two common pronunciations of the same word (*beit* and *bet*).

As mentioned above, we have divided words into syllables according to how they are pronounced in Israeli Hebrew. In words with more than one syllable, the stressed syllable is indicated by capital letters (e.g., יֶלֶד = *YE-led*).

Despite our desire to make our transcriptions as exact as possible, we are keenly aware of their limitations. There are certain common phenomena that we have not attempted to transcribe; for example, we transcribe the pronunciation of a word like הִסְבִּיר as *hees-BEER* – according to its written form – rather than *heez-BEER*, which reflects the more commonly heard pronunciation of this word.

Here are some special features of our transcriptions:

1. *Consonants*

We have chosen the following signs or letter combinations to transcribe the following sounds:

'   is used to indicate 'א and 'ע at the beginning of a word or syllable. It indicates the slight "catch in the throat" you can feel and hear before the first vowel in the English word *eye*, for example: אֲנִי = *'a-NEE* and עָסוּק = *'a-SOOK*. (This "catch in the throat" is not always realized by Hebrew speakers; nevertheless, we have always transcribed 'א and 'ע as ' at the beginning of a syllable.) When 'א and 'ע are at the end of a word like קָרָא = *ka-RA*, their presence is not indicated in the transcription.

ch   is used to indicate a sound like that in the name of the German composer *Bach*. This is the transcription we use for the sounds represented by the letters 'ח, 'כ (without a *dagesh*) and 'ך, thus: חֶדֶר = *CHE-der*, לִכְתוֹב = *leech-TOV*.

ts   is used to indicate the pronunciation ("realization") of 'צ (and 'ץ), as at the end of the English word *cats*, for example: צָרִיךְ = *tsa-REECH*.

sh   is used to indicate the sound we hear at the beginning of the English word *shirt*, as in שִׁיר = *SHEER*.

2. *Vowels*

The vowels in Hebrew are not identical in sound to English vowels (and, of course, the pronunciation of vowels in English varies from accent to accent).[7] Our transcription is as follows:

a   represents the sound indicated by ◌ָ, ◌ַ and ◌ֲ.[8] For example: בָּא is transcribed as *ba*. When we refer to this vowel sound alone (not as part of a word), we use the transcription *ah*. The *h* in this transcription is intended to help English speakers know how to pronounce the Hebrew *a* vowel correctly; it does not represent the sound *h* when it is used in the transcription of the vowel *ah*. It also does not represent the sound *h* in the transcriptions *eh* and *oh* discussed below.

Note: Even though the transcription of a word like בַּת would be clearer to English speakers if it were transcribed as *baht*, we have decided – for reasons of simplicity – that when the *ah*

---

7   For guidance on how to pronounce Hebrew vowels and consonants, see: "Sabra Sound: Learning to Pronounce Hebrew" on the Internet: http://hebrew-multimedia.huji.ac.il/sabrasound/index1.htm. This multimedia courseware was developed by Esther Delshad and Carmia Shoval of the Division of Hebrew Language Instruction (Rothberg International School, Hebrew Univ.) and Asher Laufer of the Phonetic Laboratory at the Hebrew University.

8   This is the *kamats gadol*. The *kamats katan*, which looks the same, is pronounced *oh*, as in תָּכְנִית (*toch-NEET*), but it is quite rare.

sound appears in a word, our transcription will be *bat*. (Note: This *a* should not be pronounced as it is in **English** words like *bat* and *cat*. This sound does not exist in Hebrew.)

e is used to transcribe the sound indicated by ◌ֶ, ◌ֵ and ◌ֱ. For example: סֵפֶר is transcribed as *SE-fer*. This *e* is transcribed as *eh* when it stands alone, i.e., not in the context of a word.

ee represents the sound indicated by ◌ִ in words like שִׁירָה: *shee-RA*.

o is used to transcribe the sound indicated by וֹ, ◌ֹ, ◌ָ (*kamats katan*) and ◌ֳ in words such as דוֹד (*DOD*), ראשׁ (*ROSH*), תָּכְנִית (*toch-NEET*) and אֳנִיָּה (*'o-nee-YA*). When we refer to this sound alone, we transcribe it as *oh*.

oo is used for the vowel sound indicated by וּ or ◌ֻ in words like סִיפּוּר (*see-POOR*) and בֻּשַּׁל (in full spelling: בּוּשַּׁל) (*boo-SHAL*).

When the vowels *ah* and *eh* are followed by a *y* sound, we use the following transcriptions:

ai – as in the English pronunciation of *Thailand*, for example: עָלַיי (*'a-LAI*).

ei – as in the English word *eight*, for example: עָלֵינוּ (*'a-LEI-noo*).

3. *Strong Dagesh* (דָּגֵשׁ חָזָק)

Since in today's pronunciation a *strong dagesh* does not cause a doubling or lengthening of a consonant, we do not transcribe a letter with a *strong dagesh* as a double letter. Thus, סִיפּוּר is transcribed as *see-POOR*.

4. *Mapeek* (מַפִּיק)

When words written with vowel signs require a *mapeek* (a dot in a final ה׳, as in אוֹתָהּ), we indicate it, but we do not transcribe it as *h* since speakers of Modern Hebrew do not pronounce it as such.

Abbreviations

The following abbreviations and special signs are used in this book:

m. – *masculine*
f. – *feminine*
s. – *singular*
pl. – *plural*
lit. – *literally*
* at the beginning of a word – indicates that the form is theoretical and does not exist in Hebrew.
Q – *question*
A – *answer*

PART ONE: BASIC CONCEPTS, PARTS OF SPEECH AND PHRASES

I. Basic Concepts

Let's begin easing into Modern Hebrew grammar by taking a look at the following two building blocks of the Hebrew language:

1. Root שׁוֹרֶשׁ
2. Pattern מִשְׁקָל

1. Root שׁוֹרֶשׁ

> ### Preview
>
> • *What is a root?*
>
> • *Root and meaning*
>
> • *Do all words with roots have at least three root letters?*
>
> • *Are all three root letters always present?*

• *What is a root?*

Here are three Hebrew words:

כָּתוּב	מִכְתָּב	כָּתַבְתִּי ◄
written	letter	I wrote

Q: Which **three letters** are common to them all? כ ת ב

A: The letters כ-ת-ב.

These three letters are called the *root* (שׁוֹרֶשׁ) of the word. The *root letters* are one of the basic building blocks of words.[1] As we see above, one root (כ-ת-ב in this case) may serve as a building

---

1   In grammar, we generally distinguish between *letters*, which are symbols used in **writing**, and *consonants* and *vowels*, which are **sounds**. For the sake of simplicity, in this book we usually use the term *root letters* (and not *root consonants*) when referring to the *root*.

block of a number of words. Most words in Hebrew, as in all Semitic languages, contain a **three-letter** root. Some roots contain four letters.
Here are some examples:

three-letter root ד-ב-ר:	דְּבָרִים	דִּבַּרְנוּ	דִּבּוּר
	things, words	we spoke	speech

three-letter root נ-ה-ג:	מַנְהִיג	נָהַגְנוּ	נָהָג
	leader	we drove	driver

four-letter root[2] צ-ל-צ-ל:	מְצַלְצְלִים	צִלְצוּל	צִלְצְלָה
	(we/you/they) are ringing	ringing	she rang

Do all words have roots?

Most Hebrew words have a root. Of those that do not, the most obvious are words of foreign (non-Semitic) origin. Here are some examples of rootless words:

סַנְהֶדְרִין	טֶלֶוִיזְיָה	אוֹטוֹבּוּס	אוּנִיבֶרְסִיטָה	פְּסִיכוֹלוֹגְיָה
Sanhedrin	television	bus	university	psychology

Want to see if you've understood?
Circle the two words in each set that contain the same root.
What is the shared root?

The shared root:

enter	ס-נ-כ	יְרִידָה	כְּנִיסָה, נִכְנַסְתִּי, .1
greet?	שׁלֹם	לְשַׁלֵּם	דִּבּוּר, תַּשְׁלוּם, .2
watch/guard	שׁמר	כְּתִיבָה	שָׁמוֹר, שְׁמִירָה, .3
exit	יצ3י	יְצִיאָה, יוֹצְאִים,	עוֹצְרִים, .4
telephone?	ט-פ-ל-נ	טִלְפַנְתִּי, לְטַלְפֵּן,	מְשַׁעֲמֵם, .5

Answers:

1. נכנסתי, כניסה – כ-נ-ס   2. תשלום, לשלם – ש-ל-מ   3. שמירה, שמור – ש-מ-ר
4. יוצאים, יציאה – י-צ-א   5. לטלפן, טלפנתי – ט-ל-פ-ן

---

2   There are even some rare roots with five letters, for example: (ס-נ-כ-ר-נ) לְסַנְכְרֵן (to synchronize).

• *Root and meaning*

Does the root convey a basic meaning?

Often the root conveys a basic meaning. For example, the three words כָּתוּב, מִכְתָּב, כָּתַבְתִּי all have something to do with *writing*. The root כ-ת-ב carries this basic meaning, while the vowels and consonants that are added to the root (in black) modify this meaning in some way.

Here are a few more of the many words containing the root כ-ת-ב:

כְּתוֹבֶת	כְּתוּבָּה	לְהִתְכַּתֵּב
address	Jewish marriage contract	to correspond with someone

These words, too, are in some way connected with writing.

Does the root always convey a basic meaning?

In order to answer this question, let's examine another set of words:

סִיפּוּר	סוֹפֵר	סֵפֶר
story	writer	book

Q: Do these words share the same basic meaning?

A: Yes. The basic meaning of this root involves *stories*: סִיפּוּר means *a story*, סוֹפֵר means *a person who writes stories (a writer)* and סֵפֶר means *something that may contain stories (a book)*.

But what about the following words with the same root?

לִסְפּוֹר	מִסְפָּר
to count	number

Q: Do these words share the same basic meaning as the first set?

A: Perhaps at one time they did, but today it seems that these two sets of words do **not** share the same basic meaning. In any case, knowing the meaning of סִיפּוּר (a story) does not help us learn the meanings of לִסְפּוֹר (to count) and מִסְפָּר (a number).

The lesson to be learned from this is: Looking for shared roots can often be very **helpful** in guessing or remembering meanings of words. However, you must beware! Sometimes the meanings of words from the same root evolve in such different ways that it is hard to see any shared meaning.

סיבוכים

complications
(via human calculation)

Words that seem to have the same root – but don't

When looking for shared roots, here's another point you should be aware of: Sometimes words may **look** as if they share a common root, but they really don't. Take, for example, the words אֹזֶן (ear) and מֹאזְנַיִם (scales for weighing). We might guess that these words all come from the same root: א-ז-נ and are "genetically" related. On the basis of linguistic evidence, however, we know that they actually came from different sources. This is why they do not share the same basic meaning.[3]

Let's review

◆ Most Hebrew words have three-letter roots (מִכְתָּב), but some have roots of four letters (צִלְצֵל) or, rarely, even more.

◆ Often a root has a **single** basic meaning, and all of the words that contain this root share this basic meaning (as in the case of כ-ת-ב).

◆ Sometimes a root may have **more than one** basic meaning (as in the case of ס-פ-ר).

◆ In some cases, words that appear to have the same root, but different meanings, actually come from roots that are not "genetically" related, but simply look the same (as in the case of א-ז-נ).

• *Do all words with roots have at least three root letters?*

It is believed that, originally, not all Hebrew words had three root letters.[4] Some had only **two**, for example:

יָד	בֵּן	דָּג	◄
hand	son	fish	

---

3 For a more in-depth but easy to understand explanation of this phenomenon, see Edward Horowitz, 1960, pp. 102-112.

4 For more on roots, see Edward Horowitz, 1960, pp. 22-41 and 299-317. For a scholarly treatment of two-letter roots, see Yehoshua Blau, 1971, vol. 16, p. 1581.

To this day, these small two-letter words have only two root letters. However, over the centuries, some of the two-letter roots were probably expanded to three. Thus, from the word דָּג (ד-ג) we get words like:

דַּיָּג (fisherman) (a י has been added to make the root ד-י-ג),

לָדוּג (to fish) (a ו has been added to make the root ד-ו-ג)

and דָּגִיג (a little fish) (with a doubled ג).[5]

Similarly, from the original two-letter root ק-צ we get expanded three-letter roots with related meanings, such as:

ק-צ-צ as in לִקְצוֹץ (to chop) (with a doubled צ),

ק-צ-ב as in קַצָּב (butcher), תַּקְצִיב (budget) (with an added ב),

and ק-צ-ר as in קָצִיר (harvest), קָצָר (short) (with an added ר).

• *Are all three root letters always present?*

Look at the following words:

מַפּוֹלֶת	מַפָּל	לְהַפִּיל
rockslide, avalanche	waterfall	to drop (something…)

Q: Which letters are common to them all?

A: Two letters only: פ-ל.

The third root letter in these words is missing. Since knowing the third letter can help us see links between these words and others in which the full root may appear, it would be very helpful to try to guess what the third root letter is.

One way to do this is to think of other words that contain פ-ל and also share the same basic meaning of *falling*. If we do so, we find words such as נָפַל (he fell) and נְפִילָה (a fall, falling). When we **drop** something, obviously it **falls**. Hence, we can correctly guess that the root of לְהַפִּיל (to drop), and also of מַפָּל (waterfall) and מַפּוֹלֶת (rockslide, avalanche), is the same as that of נָפַל (he fell) and נְפִילָה (a fall, falling), namely נ-פ-ל. You may have noticed that in the forms לְהַפִּיל, מַפָּל and מַפּוֹלֶת, the disappearance of the נ of the root is marked by a *dagesh* (dot) in the next letter: פּ.[6]

---

5 The root is listed as ד-ו-ג in Yaacov Choueka, 1997, p. 304 and as ד-ג-ה in Avraham Even-Shoshan, 2003, p. 2029.

6 For more details on the disappearing נ, see the chapter "Verbs Whose First Root Letter Is נ," pp. 490-503.

According to this same method of seeking out other words that are close in meaning and may be related, we can also find the root of a word like הֵקִים (established, set up). Here the two root letters ק-מ remind us of the verb לָקוּם (to get up, rise), whose root is ק-ו-מ. Hence, the root of הֵקִים is also ק-ו-מ.

An additional way of discovering the missing third letter of a root requires some knowledge of the basic patterns of words in Hebrew.[7] When a root letter is missing, certain changes may take place in the pattern of a word. Your awareness of these changes will increase as you learn more Hebrew.

Traditionally, roots that share certain characteristics are grouped together in *root groups* (גְּזָרוֹת) (sing.: גִּזְרָה). For more on the root groups, see the introduction to "Special Root Groups," pp. 488-489.

Let's review

♦ Most Hebrew words have three-letter roots. Sometimes only **two** of these three letters are visible, as in יִפּוֹל (he will fall) from the root נ-פ-ל.

---

7   Many of these patterns are discussed in the next chapter ("Pattern") and in the chapters "Patterns of Verbs," pp. 361-368, "How Are Hebrew Nouns Formed?" pp. 78-82 and "How Are Adjectives Formed?" pp. 138-147.

2. Pattern מִשְׁקָל

> ### *Preview*
> - *What is a pattern?*
> - *Representing word patterns*
> - *The names of patterns*
> - *Patterns and meaning*
> - *The importance of learning patterns*

• *What is a pattern?*

We have seen in the preceding chapter that the words סֵפֶר (book), סוֹפֵר (writer, scribe), סִיפּוּר (story) all share the same *root*: ס-פ-ר.

You might ask: What is it that makes words of the same root into **different** words with **different** meanings?

The answer is: their *patterns*.[1] A word pattern is made up of the following elements:

1. *Added vowels and consonants*

Let's look at two words with the same root: סִפֵּר (*see-PER*) and סֻפַּר (*soo-PAR*).

          he told   it was told

Q: In what way do the form and sound of these words differ?

A: When we write with *vowel signs*, as we have here, we can see that it is their vowels that make these two words different from each other. When we write these same words in *full spelling*[2] – סִיפֵּר and סופר – we can see the difference between the words even more clearly.

---

1   For more on patterns, see the chapters "Patterns of Verbs," pp. 361-368, "How Are Hebrew Nouns Formed?" pp. 78-82 and "How Are Adjectives Formed?" pp. 138-147.

2   For an explanation of *full spelling*, see the chapter "Hebrew Spelling: Selected Issues," pp. 654-667.

Now let's look at another word: מִסְפָּר (*mees-PAR*).

Q: What have we added to the root ס-פ-ר?

A: Here we have added מְ- (the "consonant + vowel" *mee*) to the beginning of the word, along with ָ (the vowel *ah*) in the second syllable.

Here's still another example of the root ס-פ-ר with different consonants and vowels added at the beginning, in the middle and at the end of the word: תִסְפּוֹרֶת (haircut).

The consonants and vowels that we add to the root are the main components of the word's pattern. However, as we will now see, they are not the **only** components of the pattern.

2. *Strong dagesh* (דָגֵשׁ חָזָק)

Here are two more words with the same root letters: סָפַר (*sa-FAR* he counted) and סַפָּר (*sa-PAR* barber). These words not only have the same letters, but also their vowels are pronounced the same in today's Hebrew.

Q: What, then, is the difference between these two words?

A: The פ׳ in the word סָפַר is pronounced as a soft sound *f* (*sa-FAR*), while in סַפָּר it is pronounced as a hard sound *p* (*sa-PAR*), indicated in writing by a dot (*dagesh*). This is a *strong dagesh* (דָגֵשׁ חָזָק) and is part of some word patterns.[3]

3. *The place of the stress* (הַטְעָמָה)

Now let's look at two words that share a different root: פ-ח-ד (*p-ch-d*). Read the following sentences:

הילד לא נכנס לברכה(כי)הוא פָּחַד מהמים.
pa-CHAD
The boy didn't go into the pool because he was afraid of the water.

הילד לא נכנס לברכה(בגלל)הפַּחַד שלו מהמים.
PA-chad
The boy didn't go into the pool because of his fear of the water.

---

3   Traditionally, a letter with a *strong dagesh* is transcribed as a double letter, e.g., *sappar*. Here we have written only one *p* because the consonant *p* is not doubled in today's pronunciation. For more on the *strong dagesh*, see the chapter "The Pronunciation of ב׳, כ׳, פ׳ and the *Dagesh*," pp. 624-625, 630-638.

The vowel sounds added to the root פ-ח-ד are the same in today's pronunciation (even though they are written with different vowel signs). Nevertheless, the patterns of these two words are **different**.

Q: In what way do these words **sound** different?

A: The *stress* in these words falls on different syllables: the stress in פַּחַד (*pa-CHAD*) is on the **second** syllable, whereas in פַּחַד (*PA-chad*) it is on the **first** syllable.

Every word has a stressed syllable, and the place of the stress is part of the word's pattern.

Let's review

◆ Many Hebrew words are built by inserting *roots* into certain *patterns*.

◆ Everything that is added to the root makes up the pattern: vowels (sometimes indicated by letters and sometimes not), consonants (always indicated by letters), the place of the *stress* and a *strong dagesh* (if there is one).

• *Representing word patterns*

In this book, we have chosen to represent word patterns with blanks or empty boxes in place of the root letters. The stressed syllable will be written in capital letters.

Here are some patterns and a few examples of each. Read the examples aloud so that you can hear the pattern:

1. The pattern of   סֵ פֶ ר   is   □ ֵ □ ֶ □,   as in: עֵ מֶ ק   חֵ לֶ ק   סֵ פֶ ל

               SE-fer   _E-_ e_   *'E-mek*   *CHE-lek*   *SE-fel*

               book   valley   part   cup

2. The pattern of   סו פֵ ר   is   □ □ ו □ ֵ,   as in: מו כֵ ר   שו מֵ ר   שו טֵ ר

               so-FER   _o-_ E_   *mo-CHER*   *sho-MER*   *sho-TER*

               writer   salesman   guard   policeman

3. The pattern of	סַפָּר *sa-PAR* barber	is	□ַ□ָ□, _a-_A_	as in:	חַיָּיל *cha-YAL* soldier	טַבָּח *ta-BACH* cook	גַּנָּב *ga-NAV* thief

4. The pattern of	מִסְפָּרָה *mees-pa-RA* hair salon, barber shop	is	מִ□□ָ□ָה *mee-_a-_A*	as in:	מִרְפָּאָה *meer-pa-'A* clinic	מִכְבָּסָה *meech-ba-SA* laundry, laundromat	מִסְעָדָה *mees-'a-DA* restaurant

5. The pattern of	סָפוּר *sa-FOOR* counted	is	□ָ□וּ□, _a-_OO_	as in:	שָׁמוּר *sha-MOOR* guarded, reserved	כָּתוּב *ka-TOOV* written	שָׁבוּר *sha-VOOR* broken

6. The pattern of	סָפַר *sa-FAR* he counted	is	□ָ□ַ□, _a-_A_	as in:	לָמַד *la-MAD* he studied, learned	כָּתַב *ka-TAV* he wrote	שָׁמַר *sha-MAR* he guarded

A pattern functions as a kind of mold into which different roots may be inserted. This is just one method of forming words in Hebrew. It is used for various *parts of speech*: nouns (1-4 above), adjectives (5) and verbs (6). Sometimes the **same** pattern may be used for **different** parts of speech. For example, pattern 2 above may be a noun (סוֹפֵר – a writer, שׁוֹמֵר – a guard), a present tense verb (סוֹפֵר – he counts, שׁוֹמֵר – he guards) or an adjective (מוֹשֵׁךְ – attractive).

• *The names of patterns*

In traditional grammar books, the root ק-ט-ל is often used instead of the root letters to refer to **noun** and **adjective** patterns (מִשְׁקָלִים). Thus, the pattern of מִסְפָּרָה and מִסְעָדָה is often called מִקְטָלָה (*meek-ta-LA*); the pattern of עִיפָּרוֹן and זִיכָּרוֹן is called קִיטָלוֹן (*kee-ta-LON*), and an adjective pattern like קָרוֹב and גָדוֹל is called קָטוֹל (*ka-TOL*).

Verb groups are usually referred to in a similar way, except that in referring to verbs, the letters פ-ע-ל are used in place of the root letters. These letters are inserted into the pattern of the **past tense הוא** form. Thus, the pattern of כָּתַב and שָׁמַר is called פָּעַל (*pa-'AL*), and the pattern of הִזְמִין and הִמְשִׁיךְ is called הִפְעִיל (*heef-'EEL*).

Verb groups such as *pa'al* and *heef'eel* are called בְּנְיָנִים (pronounced *been-ya-NEEM*). There are seven ***beenyaneem*** in Modern Hebrew. Each *beenyan* is actually a **group** of patterns, each used for a different tense or verb form. For example, *beenyan pa'al* includes the following patterns, among others:[4]

[handwritten annotations: "to guard", "write", "remember"]

The pattern of the infinitive – לִ□□וֹ□:	לִכְתּוֹב, לִזְכּוֹר, לִשְׁמוֹר
The pattern of the present tense – □וֹ□ֵ□:	כּוֹתֵב, זוֹכֵר, שׁוֹמֵר
The pattern of the past tense – □ָ□ַ□:	שָׁמַר, זָכַר, כָּתַב
The pattern of the future tense – יִ□□וֹ□:	יִכְתּוֹב, יִזְכּוֹר, יִשְׁמוֹר
The pattern of the command form – □ְ□וֹ□:	כְּתוֹב, זְכוֹר, שְׁמוֹר

[handwritten: יִזְכּוֹר / we will remember]

Let's review

♦ We can represent word patterns in one of two ways:

    1. by using blanks or empty boxes to indicate the root

    2. by using the letters ק-ט-ל for roots of nouns and adjectives and פ-ע-ל for roots of verbs. The patterns of some nouns and adjectives, particularly those with a strong connection to verbs (such as the adjective כָּתוּב – written) are named using the letters פ-ע-ל (called, in this case, פָּעוּל).

♦ To the root letters we add the additional elements of the pattern: vowels and consonants, syllable stress and the strong *dagesh*. For example:

The pattern of מִסְפָּרָה would be: *mee_-_a-_A* / מְ□□ָ□ָה or מִקְטָלָה,
and the pattern of נִכְנַס would be: *nee_-_A* / נִ□□ַ□ or נִפְעַל.

♦ Noun and adjective patterns are called *meeshkaleem* (מִשְׁקָלִים). The seven groups of verb patterns are called *beenyaneem* (בְּנְיָנִים).

---

4   For more on verb patterns (*beenyaneem*), see the chapter "Patterns of Verbs," pp. 361-368.

Want to see if you've understood?

Cross out the word that does not have the same pattern as the others. (The stressed syllable is written in larger letters.)

יֶלֶד YE-led	מֶלֶךְ ME-lech	תַּלְמִיד tal-MEED	דֶּגֶל DE-gel	1.
שׁוֹטֵר sho-TER	בּוֹקֶר BO-ker	שׁוֹמֵר sho-MER	חוֹקֵר cho-KER	2.
סָפְרוּ saf-ROO	נִיגּוּן nee-GOON	סִיפּוּר see-POOR	דִּיבּוּר dee-BOOR	3.
שָׁמַר sha-MAR	הֵזְמִין heez-MEEN	חָשַׁב cha-SHAV	עָמַד 'a-MAD	4.
מַזְלֵג maz-LEG	מַסְרֵק mas-REK	מַחְשֵׁב mach-SHEV	מִשְׁקָל meesh-KAL	5.
אָדוֹם 'a-DOM	לָבָן la-VAN	יָרוֹק ya-ROK	סָגוֹל sa-GOL	6.

Answers:

1. תַּלְמִיד   2. בּוֹקֶר   3. סָפְרוּ   4. הֵזְמִין   5. מִשְׁקָל   6. לָבָן

• *Patterns and meaning*

Many times, a certain pattern has a specific **meaning**. The following words all belong to the same pattern:

□ָ□וֹ□	סָגוֹל purple	כָּחוֹל blue	צָהוֹב yellow	יָרוֹק green	◄

The pattern □ָ□וֹ□ is the pattern of colors. But **not all** words for colors have this pattern (e.g., חוּם – brown, לָבָן – white), and **not all** words in this pattern are colors. For example, the following words are not:

מָתוֹק long	עָמוֹק deep	אָרוֹךְ sweet

But many colors **do** have this pattern, and if a word needs to be found for a new color, this is the pattern that is most likely to be used. For example, to describe the color of the peel of an eggplant (חָצִיל *cha-TSEEL*), a good choice, theoretically speaking, might be חָצוֹל (*cha-TSOL*).

We will deal more with patterns and their possible meanings in the individual chapters on nouns, adjectives and verbs.[5]

Let's review

- ◆ In many cases, certain patterns have a specific meaning (e.g., patterns indicating colors). However, not all words in a certain pattern will necessarily have this meaning.

• *The importance of learning patterns*

The most important reason for learning patterns is that they help us decipher words in a text that has no vowel signs. This includes deciding what **part of speech** a word is (noun, adjective, verb, etc.) and how to **pronounce** it. It also helps us guess what the word may **mean**.

We can see how this works by asking: How would we pronounce and understand the word צפר in the following sentence?

◄ דיברתי עם הצפר על הציפורים שראינו בטיול.

First, on the basis of the context, we know that צפר is a **noun,** since it denotes a **person**:

◄ דיברתי עם ה_____ על הציפורים שראינו בטיול.
I spoke with the _____ about the birds that we saw on the hike.

Now we can go through the noun patterns that we know. Three root letters with no added ו, י or ה could fit into a limited number of patterns. We will examine the most common of them:

1. צפר could be צֶפֶּר* (*TSE-fer*) like the word סֵפֶר (*SE-fer*).[6] Pattern: ☐ ☐ ☐ _ E-_ e_

2. It could be צָפָר* (*tsa-FAR*) like the word דָבָר (*da-VAR*). Pattern: ☐ ☐ ☐ _ a-_ A_

---

5 On nouns, see the chapter "How Are Hebrew Nouns Formed?" pp. 78-82; on adjectives, see the chapter "How Are Adjectives Formed?," pp. 138-147; on verbs, see the chapter "Patterns of Verbs," pp. 361-368.
6 Or, with the same sound, but slightly different vowel signs in Hebrew: צֶפֶר like the word מֶלֶךְ.

3. It could be צַפָּר (*tsa-PAR*) like the word סַפָּר (*sa-PAR*). Pattern: □ ִ □ _ *a-_ A_* (with a strong *dagesh* in the middle root letter)

Since we are looking for a word denoting a **person**, we can make an educated guess. The third pattern, □ ִ □ is often used for people in certain professions: סַפָּר (barber), חַיָּיל (soldier), טַבָּח (cook, chef).[7] This pronunciation seems to make the most sense: צַפָּר.

Not always is the most **logical** guess the **correct** one. In this case, however, the dictionary can tell us that it is. A צַפָּר is a bird-watcher, a bird expert, an ornithologist. (The word for bird – צִיפּוֹר – comes from the same root.)

If, upon checking the three most common patterns, we do not find the correct one, we can also make the following guesses:

4. It could be צַפֵּר* (*tsa-FER*) like the word חָבֵר (*cha-VER*). Pattern: □ □ ִ _ *a-_ E_*

5. It could be צְפָר* (*TSFAR*) like the word דְבַשׁ (*DVASH*). Pattern: □ ִ □ _ _ *A_*

Our knowledge of patterns and the process by which we apply that knowledge can help us become better not only at **guessing** the pronunciation and meaning of a word, but also at **remembering** new words that we encounter.

---

7   On noun patterns that tend to have one or more specific meanings, see the chapter "How Are Hebrew Nouns Formed?" pp. 78-82.

II. Nouns שְׁמוֹת עֶצֶם

Introduction

Words for tangible objects like סֵפֶר (a book), יֶלֶד (a child) and בַּיִת (a house) are *nouns*. Words for intangible things or abstract concepts and ideas, such as אַהֲבָה (love), דִיבּוּר (speech) and יַלְדוּת (childhood), are also nouns.

Nouns in Hebrew can be *singular* (סֵפֶר) or *plural* (סְפָרִים). They can be *indefinite* (סֵפֶר – **a** book) or *definite* (הַסֵפֶר – **the** book). Unlike English nouns, all Hebrew nouns have *gender*: they are either masculine or feminine (there is no neuter – "it" – category).[1] For example, the word סֵפֶר is masculine and the word מַחְבֶּרֶת (notebook) is feminine.

In this unit we will explain these matters more fully and will look at some exceptions as well. In a separate unit, we will deal with how the form of nouns change when they join with other nouns to form *smeechoot (construct) phrases* – as in עוּגַת שׁוֹקוֹלָד (chocolate cake).[2]

In this unit we will discuss the following topics:

1. **The Gender of Nouns**
2. **How Are Nouns Made Plural?**
3. **Definite and Indefinite Nouns**
4. **Nouns with Possessive Endings**
5. **How Are Hebrew Nouns Formed?**
6. **Segolate Nouns (יֶלֶד, סֵפֶר, בּוֹקֶר)**
7. **Verbal Nouns שְׁמוֹת פְּעוּלָה**

---

1   See the chapter "The Gender of Nouns," p. 27, note 20 for several exceptions.
2   See the chapter "*Smeechoot*," pp. 175-182.

1. The Gender of Nouns

Preview

- *Feminine nouns*
- *Masculine nouns*

Introduction

The word שיעור (lesson) is **masculine**, but הצגה (performance, show) is **feminine** – and so is תל אביב (Tel Aviv)! We are, of course, not talking about the things themselves, but only about the **words**. As a rule, every noun in Hebrew is either masculine (זָכָר) or feminine (נְקֵבָה).[1]

We can see why it is important to know the *gender* of a noun in Hebrew by looking at the following sentences:

II	I
1. השיעור **מתחיל** ב-8:00.	1. השיעור **מעניין**.
The lesson begins at 8 a.m.	The lesson is interesting.
2. ההצגה **מתחילה** ב-20:00.	2. ההצגה **מעניינת**.
The show begins at 8 p.m.	The show is interesting.
3. השיעורים **מתחילים** ב-8:00.	3. השיעורים **מעניינים**.
The lessons begin at 8 a.m.	The lessons are interesting.
4. ההצגות **מתחילות** ב-20:00.	4. ההצגות **מעניינות**.
The shows begin at 8 p.m.	The shows are interesting.

Q: How many different forms do the adjective מעניין (Column I) and the verb מתחיל (Column II) have?

A: Each has **four** different forms. In the sentences above, the forms of the adjective and the verb are determined by the noun that they refer to: by its *gender* (masculine or feminine) together with its *number* (singular or plural). Thus, in line 1, the noun שיעור is **masculine** and **singular** and so are the adjective (מעניין) and verb (מתחיל). In line 2, the noun הצגה

---

1 Several nouns, to be discussed below, are both masculine and feminine.

is also singular but **feminine**. Thus, the adjective and verb change to מעניינת and מתחילה. In line 3, the noun שיעורים is masculine but **plural**; thus, we get מעניינים and מתחילים. In line 4, הצגות is also plural but **feminine**; thus, the forms מעניינות and מתחילות are used.

From these sentences we can see that without knowing the gender (and number) of nouns, it is virtually impossible to form a correct Hebrew sentence.

This being the case, the obvious question is: How can we tell whether a noun is masculine or feminine?

In general, it is fairly easy to recognize feminine singular nouns. In the following section, we will learn the **signs** by which we can identify them. Once we know how to identify feminine nouns (and learn a list of exceptions), we can assume that all the rest are masculine. Masculine nouns are dealt with in detail in the section "Masculine nouns" below.

For a concise list of the signs of feminine and masculine nouns, see Appendix I, pp. 1007-1010.

• *Feminine nouns* ♀

In order to determine if a noun is feminine or masculine, we always check its **singular** – **not** its plural – form. We do this because the endings on plural nouns (ים-, ות- and יים-) tell us only that a noun is plural, and **not** whether it is feminine or masculine.

In this section, we will concentrate on the signs of singular nouns that are feminine. Most of these signs take the form of special **endings**. Others have to do with certain **characteristics** of the objects that these nouns represent (for example, the names of cities and countries are always feminine). Once we know how to identify feminine nouns, we can just assume that all the rest are masculine.[2]

The feminine endings

We can divide feminine endings into **two** basic types.

---

2   The lists of feminine nouns **without** a feminine ending presented in the second part of this section include most of the words learned in the beginning and intermediate levels of study. Advanced level students will need to add a number of additional words to make these lists complete.

1. *Final* הָ- *(-ah)*

Look at the endings of the following feminine nouns:

	יַלְדָה	מוֹרָה	שָׂפָה	דִירָה	גִינָה
ç	girl	teacher (*f.*)	language	apartment	garden

עוּגִיָּיה	לַחְמָנִיָּיה	עַגְבָנִיָּיה	סִפְרִיָּיה
cookie	roll	tomato	library

קָפֶטֶרְיָה	הִיסְטוֹרְיָה	פִּילוֹסוֹפְיָה	סוֹצְיוֹלוֹגְיָה
cafeteria	history	philosophy	sociology

Q: What do they all have in common?

A: They all end in הָ- (*-ah*), including those that end in יָּיה- (*-ee-YA*) and יָה- (*-ya*). This, indeed, is one sign of a feminine noun, since almost **all** words ending in הָ- are feminine. The word לַיְלָה (night), which is masculine, is a rare **exception**.

The feminine ending הָ- (*-ah*) is usually stressed. However, various nouns that originated in other languages and are now part of the Hebrew language have an unstressed הָ- ending. For example:

	חַסָה	פִּיתָה	טוּנָה	טְחִינָה	בִּירָה	הִיסְטוֹרְיָה
	CHA-sa	PEE-ta	TOO-na	TCHEE-na	BEE-ra	hees-TOR-ya
	lettuce	pita	tuna	techina	beer	history

Be careful! When we speak of words ending in הָ-, we mean הָ- (*-ah*) , and not any of the following:

1. Words ending in הֶ- or הֵ- (*-eh*). These words are **not** *feminine*.

masculine:		מוֹרֶה	מַחֲנֶה	שָׂדֶה	קָפֶה	תֵה
		male teacher	camp	field	coffee	tea

2. Words whose final root letter is א' or ע'. These words may **sound** feminine, but most of them are **not**.[3]

masculine:			צָבָא	מִבְטָא	מִמְצָא	מִקְרָא
			army	accent	finding, artifact	Bible

masculine:	צֶבַע	רֶגַע	מַדָע	שָׁבוּעַ	רוֹבַע	כּוֹבַע
	color	moment	science	week	quarter	hat

---

3   There are several words whose final א- is an alternative spelling of the feminine ending *-ah*. The final ה- is the preferred spelling today, as in: דוּגְמָא / דוּגְמָה, קוּפְסָא / קוּפְסָה.
                                             box   example

There **are** feminine nouns that end in ע'.[4] We can recognize them as feminine **not** because of their ending, but for other reasons, which will be discussed below.

Want to see if you've understood?

Circle the correct form of the adjective (masculine or feminine). Remember: an adjective always matches its noun in gender (*m./f.*) and number (*s./pl.*).[5]

	f. / m.			*f. / m.*	
5. שִׁיטָה	חדש / חדשה		1. כּוֹבַע	יָפֶה / יָפָה	
6. מַתָּנָה	יָפֶה / יָפָה		2. קוּפְסָה	שחור / שחורה	
7. צָבָא	מודרני / מודרנית		3. מַחֲנֶה	גדול / גדולה	
8. מִבְטָא	אמריקני / אמריקנית		4. רוֹבַע	עתיק / עתיקה	

Answers:

1. יָפָה 2. שחורה 3. גדול 4. עתיק 5. חדשה 6. יָפָה 7. מודרני 8. אמריקני

2. *Final* ת- *(-t)*

Now look at the endings of the following:

		מָסוֹרֶת tradition	כְּתוֹבֶת address	מַחְבֶּרֶת notebook	1. ◄
		צַלַּחַת plate	שַׁפַּעַת flu	מִקְלַחַת shower	2.
טַלִּית[6] tallit (tallis)	אַנְגְּלִית English	עִבְרִית Hebrew	סְטוּדֶנְטִית student (*f.*)	מְכוֹנִית car	3.
		סַבְלָנוּת patience	בְּרִיאוּת health	חֲנוּת store	4.
			חָמוֹת mother-in-law	אָחוֹת sister	5.

---

4 For example: צְפַרְדֵּעַ צֵלָע זְרוֹעַ אֶצְבַּע קַרְקַע. All of these words are feminine.
   frog   rib   arm   finger   ground

5 For an explanation of *matching (agreement)*, see the chapter "How Do Adjectives Behave?" pp. 126-130.

6 In Modern Hebrew, the word טַלִּית is feminine (we say: טַלִּית לְבָנָה, טַלִּית גְּדוֹלָה). The term טַלִּית קָטָן – a fringed garment worn by orthodox males under their clothing – was coined in medieval times, when many nouns that are feminine today were regarded as masculine. (Isaac Avinery, 1964, p. 215.)

Q: What is common to all these feminine (singular) nouns?

A: They all end in ת'.[7] Some end in תֶ- (מַחְבֶּרֶת), some in ַת (מִקְלַחַת), some in ִית- (מְכוֹנִית), some in וּת- (בְּרִיאוֹת) and, very rarely, in וֹת- (אָחוֹת).

In all the examples above, the ת' is **not** one of the root letters, but rather is **added onto** the root (as an ending).

Sometimes a final ת' appears to be an **original** part of a word and **not** an ending that has been added on. Many words with a final ת', as in the following examples, are feminine:

◄	דָת	כַּת	שַׁבָּת	מַחֲבַת	אוֹת	עֵת	דֶּלֶת	אֱמֶת[8]
	religion	sect	Sabbath	frying pan	letter of alphabet	time	door	truth

Be careful! Some very common words end in ת' but are **not** feminine. In these words the final ת' is always a **root** letter and **not** an added ending. The following words are masculine and should be memorized:

masculine:	אוֹת[9]	צֶוֶת	צֹמֶת	מָוֶת	זַיִת	בַּיִת	◄
	sign, indication	staff, crew	intersection	death	olive	house	

Words that have the same pattern as דִּיבּוּר, and whose roots end in ת', are also masculine, even though they **look** feminine:

masculine:	עִימוּת	שֵׁירוּת	◄
	confrontation	service	

---

7   The final ת-, and not the final הָ- (*-ah*), which we saw in the first section above, was actually the **original** feminine ending at an earlier stage of the languages. The final הָ- (*-ah*) evolved from the original תַ- (*-at*) in the following way:

	(3)	(2)	(1)
◄	ילדה ⇐	ילד ⇐	ילדת
	yal-da ⇐	yal-da ⇐	yal-dat

(1) The original form at an earlier stage of the language: *yal-dat*
(2) The final ת- (*-t*) dropped off and the word became *yal-da*.
(3) Since the system of writing vowel signs under the letter had not yet been invented, a final ה- was added to make clear that the word was to be pronounced with a final *-a* (*yal-da*).

8   Although the final ת' in the last two words – אֱמֶת and דֶּלֶת – **appears** to be part of the root, it is actually an added *ending (suffix)*. (The root of אֱמֶת is א-מ-נ; the root of דֶּלֶת is uncertain, perhaps ד-ל-י). The final ת' in all the other words listed here is part of their root.

9   Note that אוֹת meaning *sign* or *indication* is masculine, while the more common אוֹת meaning *a letter of the alphabet*, is feminine.

Be careful! Words that end in the letter 'ט may **sound** feminine, but they are **not**, as in:

	שֶׁקֶט	סָלָט	סֶרֶט	תַּפְרִיט	בָּלֶט	קוֹנְצֶרְט	עֵט
masculine:	silence	salad	film	menu	ballet	concert	pen

Let's review

◆ The two feminine endings are:

- A final ה-ָ, as in: עֲבוֹדָה, סִפְרִיָּיה, סוֹצְיוֹלוֹגְיָה.
An important **exception** is לַיְלָה (*LAI-la* night), which is masculine.

- A final ת-, as in: מַחְבֶּרֶת, מִקְלַחַת, מְכוֹנִית, חֲנוּת, אָחוֹת.

◆ Many words whose **root** ends in 'ת are feminine, such as: דָּת, כַּת, שַׁבָּת. Others are masculine and must be memorized (see examples above).

Want to see if you've understood?

Circle the correct form of the adjective (masculine or feminine).

f. / m.			*f. / m.*			*f. / m.*		
חזק / חזקה	צָבָא	9.	פתוח / פתוחה	דֶּלֶת	5.	שֶׁלֶט חדש / חדשה		.1
עתיק / עתיקה	דָּת	10.	ירוק / ירוקה	שָׂדֶה	6.	שָׁבוּעַ טוב / טובה		.2
חדש / חדשה	כְּתוֹבֶת	11.	לבן / לבנה	צֶבַע	7.	כַּפִּית גדול / גדולה		.3
טוב / טובה	צַוֶּות	12.	קטן / קטנה	חֲנוּת	8.	שָׂפָה קל / קלה		.4
חדש / חדשה	בַּיִת	13.						

Answers:

1. חדש 2. טוב 3. גדולה 4. קלה 5. פתוחה 6. ירוק 7. לבן 8. קטנה 9. חזק 10. עתיקה 11. חדשה
12. טוב 13. חדש

Grouping feminine nouns according to meaning

There are quite a few nouns that are feminine, yet they do **not** have a feminine ending. There is usually no special reason why these nouns are feminine – they just **are**. In order to help you remember them, we'll group them according to **meaning**.[10]

1. *Parts of the body (pairs and singles)*

a. *Paired parts with the ending ـַיים in the plural*

The words for many parts of the body (human and animal) are feminine, especially those that come in **pairs** and take the ending ـַיים (*-A-yeem*) in the plural:

קֶרֶן	כָּנָף	שׁוֹק	יָרֵךְ	לְחִי	צִיפּוֹרֶן	שֵׁן[12]	כָּתֵף	בֶּרֶךְ	רֶגֶל[11]	יָד	אוֹזֶן	עַיִן
קַרְנַיים	כְּנָפַיים	שׁוֹקַיים	יְרֵכַיים	לְחָיַיים	צִפּוֹרְנַיים	שִׁינַיים	כְּתֵפַיים	בִּרְכַּיים	רַגְלַיים	יָדַיים	אוֹזְנַיים	עֵינַיים
horn	wing	calf, drumstick	thigh	cheek	fingernail, toenail	tooth	shoulder	knee	leg, foot	hand	ear	eye

Note also that the word נַעַל (shoe) (plural: נַעֲלַיים) is feminine, too. נַעַל is one of the only nouns denoting a **manufactured** object that takes the ending ـַיים and is **feminine**.[13]

Be careful! There are also some nouns for paired parts of the body that are **masculine**. The most striking of these is, ironically: שָׁדַיים / שַׁד (a woman's breast).[14]

b. *Other parts of the body (without the ending ـַיים in the plural)*

The words for three more parts of the body that come in **pairs** (or in two sets) are also feminine.

זְרוֹעַ	צֵלַע	אֶצְבַּע
arm	rib	finger

---

10 Our division into groups of meaning is based on Mordechai Kashtan, 1982, pp. 39-42.

11 To be exact, רֶגֶל means *leg* and כַּף רֶגֶל means *foot*, but in everyday speech רֶגֶל is used for both. In another of its meanings (with the plural רְגָלִים), רגל refers to one of the three pilgrimage holidays: Sukkot, Pesach and Shavuot. In this usage, רֶגֶל is either feminine שָׁלוֹשׁ הָרְגָלִים or masculine שְׁלוֹשֶׁת הָרְגָלִים.

12 The plural of שֵׁן has a dual ending: שִׁינַיים, probably because we have **two sets** of teeth: the upper and the lower. This is true also of צִיפורניים: we have a set on each hand.

13 For examples, see the next section on masculine nouns.

14 Here are more examples of masculine nouns that denote paired parts of the body:

	masculine:	מוֹתֶן	קַרְסוֹל	עַפְעַף	נְחִיר
		מוֹתְנַיים	קַרְסוּלַיים	עַפְעַפַּיים	נְחִירַיים
		waist	ankle	eyelid	nostril

These nouns are less commonly encountered at the beginning and intermediate levels of language study than some of the feminine nouns mentioned above.

The plural forms of these nouns do **not** end in ־ִים. All three singular forms happen to end in ע'.

The words for the following parts of the body (which do **not** come in pairs) also happen to be feminine.

 בֶּטֶן   כָּרֵס (כֶּרֶס)   לָשׁוֹן   עֶצֶם[15]   נֶפֶשׁ[16]
belly   pot belly   tongue   bone   soul

Special case: The word פָּנִים (face), which is always plural in Hebrew, is both feminine **and** masculine in Modern Hebrew (we say both פָּנִים יָפִים / פָּנִים יָפוֹת).

Want to see if you've understood?

Circle the correct form of the adjective (masculine or feminine).

f. / m.			f. / m.			f. / m.	
מלא / מלאה	בטן	.9	ציפורן	ארוך / ארוכה	.5	אף	גדול / גדולה	.1
גדול / גדולה	ראש	.10	ברך	כואב / כואבת	.6	יד	גדול / גדולה	.2
			אוזן	קטן / קטנה	.7	זרוע	ארוך / ארוכה	.3
			לשון	אדום / אדומה	.8	פה	קטן / קטנה	.4

Answers:

‏1. גדול   2. גדולה   3. ארוכה   4. קטן   5. ארוכה   6. כואבת   7. קטנה   8. אדומה   9. מלאה   10. גדול

---

15 Note: When the word עֶצֶם means *thing*, it is masculine.
16 For the sake of convenience, we are categorizing the word נֶפֶשׁ as a part of the body, though obviously it is not.

2. *Geographical areas and related words*

The following words are feminine, and they, too, have **no** feminine ending.

תְּהוֹם	בְּאֵר	קַרְקַע	חָצֵר	גָּדֵר	כִּכָּר	דֶּרֶךְ	עִיר	אֶרֶץ	◄
city	well	ground, land	yard	fence	city square, traffic circle[17]	way	city	land, country	

3. *Cities and countries*

We have seen that the words עיר (city) and ארץ (country, land) are feminine and singular. So, too, are the **names** of cities and countries, no matter what form the actual name takes. Here are some examples:

		דַּמֶּשֶׂק	לוֹנְדּוֹן	נְיוּ יוֹרְק	תֵּל אָבִיב	יְרוּשָׁלַיִם	◄
cities:		Damascus	London	New York	Tel Aviv	Jerusalem	

		יַפָּן	סִין	אַרְצוֹת הַבְּרִית	מִצְרַיִם	יִשְׂרָאֵל	◄
countries:		Japan	China	the United States	Egypt	Israel	

A rare exception is הַוָּתִיקָן (the Vatican), which is **masculine**.[18]

---

17 כִּכָּר also means *a loaf (of bread)*.
18 See Rivka Bliboim, 1995, p. 22.

Want to see if you've understood?

Circle the correct form of the adjective (masculine or feminine).

f. / m.				*f. / m.*		
המודרני / המודרנית	מִצְרַיִם	7.		רחוק / רחוקה	אֶרֶץ	1.
ארוך / ארוכה	רחוב	8.		גדול / גדולה	עִיר	2.
היפֶה / היפָה	תל אביב	9.		נעים / נעימה	מקום	3.
ארוך / ארוכה	דרך	10.		העתיק / העתיקה	ירושלַיִם	4.
רחב / רחבה	כביש	11.		גבוה / גבוהה	גדר	5.
יקר / יקרה	קרקע	12.		חדש / חדשה	גבול	6.

Answers:

1. רחוקה   2. גדולה   3. נעים   4. העתיקה   5. גבוהה   6. חדש   7. המודרנית   8. ארוך   9. היפָה   10. ארוכה
11. רחב   12. יקרה

4. *Objects and forces in nature*

Nouns denoting objects and forces in nature are often feminine in Modern Hebrew.[19]

קֶרֶן	שֶׁמֶשׁ	רוּחַ	אֵשׁ	אֶבֶן
ray, horn	sun	wind, spirit	fire	stone

5. *Utensils*

Some words denoting utensils are feminine. Three of these are sharp objects:

מַחַט	חֶרֶב	סַכִּין[20]
needle	sword	knife

Two more, like סַכִּין, are used in dining:

כַּף	כּוֹס
soup spoon, large spoon, tablespoon	glass

---

19   Because some of these words (e.g., שמש, אש, רוח) are both feminine and masculine in the Bible, they may appear in modern **literary** texts as **either**, but in standard language they are **feminine**.

20   The word סַכִּין is both feminine and masculine in Modern Hebrew. We often say סַכִּין חדה, but also סַכִּין חד (a sharp knife). Several other words are also both feminine and masculine in Modern Hebrew, for example: מַטְבֵּעַ קטן / קטנה (a small coin) and פָּנִים יפים / יפות (a pretty face).

Want to see if you've understood?
Circle the correct form of the adjective (masculine or feminine).

	f. / m.			f. / m.			f. / m.	
חזק / חזקה	אש	9.	מיוחד / מיוחדת	צלחת	5.	גדול / גדולה	כוס	1.
גדול / גדולה	כף	10.	קטן / קטנה	מזלג	6.	מעניין / מעניינת	אבן	2.
אדום / אדומה	עט	11.	חד / חדה	מחט	7.	גדול / גדולה	סלע	3.
חזק / חזקה	רוח	12.	חם / חמה	שמש	8.	גבוה / גבוהה	הר	4.

Answers:

1. כוס גדולה   2. אבן מעניינת   3. סלע גדול   4. הר גבוה   5. צלחת מיוחדת   6. מזלג קטן   7. מחט חדה
8. שמש חמה   9. אש חזקה   10. כף גדולה   11. עט אדום   12. רוח חזקה

6. *Animals and humans*

Up until now we have been looking at nouns that denote objects with no **biological** gender (for example: eye, city, spoon). In the case of animals, the biological gender (male / female) is **almost always** indicated by the form of the animal's name, thus:

	סוּס	חָתוּל	כֶּלֶב
male animals (their names usually have **no** ending):	horse	cat	dog
	⇕	⇕	⇕
female animals (their names usually have a feminine ending):	סוּסָה	חֲתוּלָה	כַּלְבָּה

Unfortunately, this is **not always** the case. For example, the names of the following **female animals** are totally different from those of their male counterparts:

	חֲמוֹר	תַּיִשׁ
male animals:	donkey (*m.*)	billy goat
	⇕	⇕
female animals:	אָתוֹן	עֵז
	donkey (*f.*)	nanny goat

The words עֵז and אָתוֹן are feminine (we say עֵז גדולה, אתון קטנה), but they have **no** feminine ending.

In the human realm, the word אֵם (mother) is feminine but has **no** feminine ending, thus:

➤ דליה היא אֵם מסורה.   Dalia is a devoted mother.

Here is an additional problem pertaining to words for animals: some animals have only **one name**, which is shared by **both** the male and the female of the species. In the following cases, the shared name happens to be feminine:

The bird sang all day.	◄ הַצִּיפּוֹר שרה כל היום.
A green frog jumped into the pool.	צְפַרְדֵּעַ ירוקה קפצה לבריכה.

In these cases, if we want to make clear that we are referring to a **male**, we say:

A bird of the male sex sat on the tree.	◄ ציפור **ממין זכר** ישבה על העץ.
A frog of the male sex jumped into the pool.	צפרדע **ממין זכר** קפצה לבריכה.

7. *The letters of the alphabet*

The names of all the letters of the alphabet are feminine (as is the word אוֹת – letter). Thus, we say, for example:

הנו"ן נופלת.	מֵ"ם סופית	◄ אָלֶ"ף גדולה
The *noon* drops out.	final *mem*	a big *'alef*

8. *The word* פַּעַם

"Once" and for all: the word פַּעַם (a time, once) is feminine.

זאת הפעם האחרונה.	◄ פעם אחת
This is the last time.	one time

Let's review

In order to determine if a noun is feminine or masculine, we always check its **singular** form.

♦ Most singular feminine nouns have one of the following **feminine endings**:

- Final הָ- (-*ah*)
- Final ת- (-*t*)

♦ Singular feminine nouns that do **not** have these endings can be memorized according to the following categories:

- Many parts of the body (paired and not paired)
- Some geographical areas and related words
- Names of cities and countries
- Some objects and forces in nature
- Some utensils
- Some animals
- Letters of the alphabet
- The word פעם

Want to see if you've understood?

Choose the correct form (masculine or feminine) of the missing word.

Note: The nouns in this exercise are plural. In order to determine whether they are feminine or masculine, first make them singular (see the answers for help).

7. אנתרופולוגים חוקרים תרבויות _____.
(עתיקים / עתיקות)

1. האבנים בכותל _____ מאוד.
(גדולים / גדולות)

8. המקומות האלה _____.
(שמורים / שמורות)

2. הסלטים האלה _____.
(טעימים / טעימות)

9. אם אתה לא מצליח, תנסה דרכים _____.
(אחרים / אחרות)

3. האוזניים שלי _____.
(כואבים / כואבות)

10. אלה היו שבועות _____.
(קשים / קשות)

4. הכוסות האלה לא _____.
(נקיים / נקיות)

11. דן, שים את השולחנות ה _____ פה!
(קטנים / קטנות)

5. ליונתן יש כתפיים _____.
(רחבים / רחבות)

12. ביקרנו בערים _____.
(מעניינים / מעניינות)

6. בבניין שלנו יש דירות _____.
(יפים / יפות)

Answers:

1. גדולות (אבן גדולה)   2. טעימים (סלט טעים)   3. כואבות (אוזן כואבת)   4. נקיות (כוס נקייה)
5. רחבות (כתף רחבה)   6. יפות (דירה יפה)   7. עתיקות (תרבות עתיקה)   8. שמורים (מקום שמור)
9. אחרות (דרך אחרת)   10. קשים (שבוע קשה)   11. קטנים (שולחן קטן)   12. מעניינות (עיר מעניינת)

• *Masculine nouns* ♂

Almost all the nouns that don't have a feminine ending and are not listed under one of the categories in the previous section are masculine.[21]

The following endings may help you identify masculine nouns:

1. *Nouns ending in* ־ֶה *and* ה ֵ

Nouns ending in ה- may be feminine or masculine. When their vowel is ־ָה (*-ah*), they are *feminine*.[22] When a final 'ה is preceded by *eh*, it is masculine.

	תֶה	קָפֶה	שָׂדֶה	מַחֲנֶה	מוֹרֶה	*masculine:*
	tea	coffee	field	camp	male teacher	

---

21 We are speaking here of the nouns learned by most intermediate level students. A number of additional nouns usually learned at the advanced level can be added to the lists in the preceding section on feminine nouns.

22 Except for לַיְלָה, which is masculine.

2. *Nouns ending in* וֹ-

Nouns that end in וֹ- are almost always masculine.

masculine:	מוּזֵאוֹן	פִּתְרוֹן	עִיתוֹן	מִילוֹן	מָלוֹן	חַלוֹן
	museum	solution	newspaper	dictionary	hotel	window

Be careful! The following nouns ending in וֹ- are feminine:

feminine:	אָתוֹן	לָשוֹן
	she-donkey	language, tongue

Did you know?
Nouns with a final root letter תׄ'
Although nouns that end in תׄ' are usually feminine, there are some whose root happens to end in תׄ' and are masculine. For example:

שֵׁירוּת	צוֹמֶת	צֶוֶות	מָוֶת	זַיִת	בַּיִת
service	intersection	staff	death	olive	house

For more examples and details, see "Be careful!" above (p. 22).

3. *Nouns that end in* -ַיִם *and do* **not** *denote body parts*

Contrary to what is often thought, the ending -ַיִם is found **not only** on feminine nouns. In fact, when a noun ends in -ַיִם and does **not** denote a part of the body, it is **almost always** masculine.[23]

The following masculine nouns denote objects containing **two parts** and are usually used only in the plural:

masculine:	אוֹפַנַּיִם	מִסְפָּרַיִם	מִשְׁקָפַיִם	מִכְנָסַיִם
	bicycle	scissors	eyeglasses	pants

---

23 See footnote 14 above for paired parts of the body whose nouns end in -ַיִם and are masculine.

Thus, when adjectives are added, the forms are:

אוֹפַנַּיִם גְּדוֹלִים[24]	מִסְפָּרַיִם קְטַנִּים	מִשְׁקָפַיִם חֲדָשִׁים	מִכְנָסַיִם קְצָרִים
a large bicycle	small scissors	new glasses	shorts

Here are some more masculine nouns whose plural is ‑יִים:

masculine:	מַגָּף	גֶּרֶב
	מַגָּפַיִים	גַּרְבַּיִים
	boots	socks

Be careful! As we mentioned above in the section on feminine nouns, נַעַל / נַעֲלַיִים is one of the only **manufactured items** denoted by a noun whose plural form ends in ‑יִים and is feminine.

In addition to the nouns for manufactured items mentioned thus far, here are two additional nouns that are masculine and always plural:

masculine:	שָׁמַיִם	מַיִם
	sky, heaven	water

Thus, we say: **מַיִם קָרִים** (cold water) and **שָׁמַיִם כְּחוּלִים** (blue sky / skies). Notice that these two words are written with only **one** י even though their ending is pronounced *A-yeem*: *MA-yeem, sha-MA-yeem.*

Did you know?

The word חַיִּים (*cha-YEEM* life) is also always masculine and plural in Hebrew. For example, we say:

masculine:	חַיִּים אֲרוּכִּים	חַיִּים טוֹבִים
	a long life	a good life

Unlike in the case of מַיִם and שָׁמַיִם, here the **regular** plural ending יִם‑ (*-EEM*) is added to the base חַי to create a word with a double י: חַיִּים.

---

24 Many Hebrew speakers mistakenly – and understandably – treat these nouns as if they were feminine.

Let's review

◆ Almost all words that do not have a feminine ending and were not mentioned in the section on feminine nouns are masculine.[25]

◆ The following endings can help you identify a noun as masculine (see above for examples):

- Final ‎-ֶה and final ‎-ֵה, as in: אַרְיֵה, שָׂדֶה, מוֹרֶה.
- Final ‎-וֹן, as in: פִּתְרוֹן, עִיתוֹן.
- Most words that end in ‎-ַיים and denote a **manufactured** item, such as: מִסְפָּרַיים, מִכְנָסַיים.

Want to see if you've understood the chapter?

Circle the noun whose gender is different from the other two.

10. ארץ, גבול, רחוב	1. מקום, חצר, גדר
11. כוס, בית, ארון	2. מפה, שבוע, משפחה
12. ישראל, פריז, קיבוץ	3. לילה, תיק, נערה
13. שָׂדֶה, מִבְנֶה, גִיטָרָה	4. שנה, צבא, צבע
14. אצבע, אף, בטן	5. יד, ספר, ברך
15. שולחן, חנות, מכונית	6. ידיים, אופניים, ציפורניים
16. מחברת, סבלנות, שירות	7. מכנסיים, שיניים, מספריים
17. משטרה, רעיון, זיכרון	8. נעליים, מכנסיים, אופניים
18. לשון, ארון, חלון	9. דרך, כיסא, עיר

Answers:

1. מקום (m.)   2. שבוע (m.)   3. נערה (f.)   4. שנה (f.)   5. ספר (m.)   6. אופניים (m.)   7. שיניים (f.)
8. נעליים (f.)   9. כיסא (m.)   10. ארץ (f.)   11. כוס (f.)   12. קיבוץ (m.)   13. גיטרה (f.)   14. אף (m.)
15. שולחן (m.)   16. שירות (m.)   17. משטרה (f.)   18. לשון (f.)

---

25 We are referring here to words usually learned by students at the intermediate level of Hebrew language study.

2. How Are Nouns Made Plural?

Preview

- *The plural endings* -ים *and* -וֹת
- *Adding* -ים/וֹת: *What happens to the end of the singular form?*
- *The ending* -ַיִים *(the "dual" ending)*
- *Changes in the base form of the noun*
- *Special cases: nouns that have only one form (singular or plural)*

• *The plural endings* -ים *or* -וֹת

Most Hebrew nouns have **both** a singular and a plural form. The plural form usually ends in either -ים or in -וֹת. Many students of Hebrew tend to regard the ending -ים as masculine and -וֹת as feminine. This is indeed the case with both **adjectives** and **present tense verbs**. When an adjective or a present tense verb refers to a masculine noun like תלמידים, they always end in -ים:

      verb   *adj.*   *noun*

◄ התלמידים עייפים. הם לומדים שמונה שעות ביום.

       The students (*m.*) are tired. They study eight hours a day.

Likewise, when an adjective or a present tense verb refers to a feminine noun like תלמידות, they always end in -וֹת:

      verb   *adj.*   *noun*

◄ התלמידות עייפות. הן לומדות שמונה שעות ביום.

       The students (*f.*) are tired. They study eight hours a day.

Q: What is the plural ending on the masculine noun תלמידים in the first sentence?

A: The ending is -ים. It is the **same ending** found on the adjective and verb that match it. However, unlike adjectives and present tense verbs, there are masculine plural **nouns** that take an -וֹת rather than an -ים ending. The following, for example, are masculine nouns with their matching masculine adjectives:

שמות יפים   רחובות ארוכים   שולחנות גדולים ◄

  pretty names   long streets   big tables

Q: What is the plural ending on the feminine noun תלמידות in the second sentence above?

A: The ending is ‎-וֹת, the same ending that appears on the adjective and verb that match it. However, feminine plural **nouns** do not always end in ‎-וֹת. Here, for example, are some with the ending ‎-ִים coupled with their matching adjectives:

אבנים גדולות   דרכים חדשות   שנים קשות

    big stones   new ways   difficult years

In short, when the endings ‎-ִים and ‎-וֹת are added to nouns, they simply indicate that the noun is **plural**. It is the **noun itself** that is masculine or feminine, not its ending.

What are the implications of this fact for learning the plural forms of Hebrew nouns? While ‎-ִים and ‎-וֹת may **both** be found on masculine **and** feminine plural nouns, **most** feminine plural nouns end in ‎-וֹת, and those that end in ‎-ִים must be memorized. In the case of masculine plural nouns, the use of ‎-וֹת is actually **quite common**. You will find lists of these plurals in Appendix II "Plural Forms of Nouns" (pp. 1012-1013, 1015) at the end of this book.

Let's review

- When added to **nouns**, the endings ‎-ִים and ‎-וֹת indicate that the noun is **plural** but **do not** tell us whether it is masculine or feminine.

- Many **masculine** plural nouns end in ‎-ִים, but many others end in ‎-וֹת, for example:

מילון ⇐ מילונים   ספר ⇐ ספרים   ילד ⇐ ילדים

אב ⇐ אבות   כיסא ⇐ כיסאות   מקום ⇐ מקומות

- Most **feminine** plural nouns end in ‎-וֹת, but some end in ‎-ִים, for example:

ילדה ⇐ ילדות   מכונית ⇐ מכוניות   ארץ ⇐ ארצות

אישה ⇐ נשים   שנה ⇐ שנים   דרך ⇐ דרכים

- See lists in the appendix for masculine plurals that end in ‎-וֹת and feminine plurals that end in ‎-ִים.

• *Adding* וֹת-/ים-: *What happens to the end of the singular form?*

We will now examine what happens to the form of singular nouns when plural endings are added.[1] Some nouns, particularly feminine nouns, already have an ending on their singular form, and this ending is often affected by the addition of plural endings.

Feminine singular nouns with endings

1. *Nouns ending in* ה- *and* ת-

Compare the singular and plural forms of the following nouns:

	ת-/ת-		ה-	
singular:	מִקְלַחַת	כְּתוֹבֶת[2]	שָׁנָה	חוּלְצָה
	⇓	⇓	⇓	⇓
plural:	מִקְלָחוֹת	כְּתוֹבוֹת	שָׁנִים	חוּלְצוֹת
	shower	address	year	shirt

Q: What happens to the singular endings ה- and ת- when the plural endings are added?

A: The singular endings (including their vowels) drop off. The process looks like this:

feminine ending ה-:   חוּלְצוֹת ⇐ חולצת ⇐ חוּלְצָה

      שָׁנִים ⇐ שנת ⇐ שָׁנָה

feminine endings ת- / ת-:   כְּתוֹבוֹת ⇐ כתובת ⇐ כְּתוֹבֶת

2. *Nouns ending in* יָיה- *and* ית-

Now let's see what happens when the singular endings are יָיה- and ית-:

	ית-		יָיה-	
singular:	כַּפִּית	מְכוֹנִית	סִפְרִיָּיה	עַגְבָנִיָּיה
	⇓	⇓	⇓	⇓
plural:	כַּפִּיוֹת	מְכוֹנִיּוֹת	סִפְרִיּוֹת	עַגְבָנִיּוֹת
	teaspoon	car	library	tomato

---

1   For changes in the base form to which the plural endings are added (for example: דָּבָר ⇐ דְּבָרִים) see below, pp. 46-47.

2   On words like מחברת see below, p. 48.

Q: Does the **entire** singular ending drop off before the plural ending is added?

A: No. A י (preceded by an *ee* vowel) remains when the plural ending is added:

$$עֲגְבָנִיּוֹת \Leftarrow עֲגְבָנִיּת \Leftarrow עֲגְבָנִיָּיה$$
$$מְכוֹנִיּוֹת \Leftarrow מְכוֹנִית \Leftarrow מְכוֹנִית$$

Note that nouns ending in either יָּיה- or ית- have the **same** plural ending: יּוֹת- (always written with only **one** י). Thus, when a plural noun ends in יּוֹת- (*-ee-YOT*), you cannot know whether its singular ending is יָּיה- or ית- without looking in the dictionary or asking a reliable speaker of Hebrew.[3]

Be careful! Several nouns ending in ית- **retain** their singular feminine ending when the plural ending is added. The most common of these are:

$$בְּרִיתוֹת \Leftarrow בְּרִית \qquad טַלִּיתוֹת \Leftarrow טַלִּית$$
alliance; circumcision   prayer shawl

3. *Nouns ending in* ות-

Here is the way nouns ending in ות- form their plurals:

singular:	תַּרְבּוּת	שְׁטוּת	חֲנוּת
	⇓	⇓	⇓
plural:	תַּרְבּוּיוֹת	שְׁטוּיוֹת	חֲנוּיוֹת
	culture	nonsense	store

Q: Does the **entire** singular ending ות- drop off before the plural ending is added?

A: No. Only the ת drops off. The "ו" remains. Before the ות- ending is added, a י is inserted, so that the end of the plural is pronounced *oo-YOT*:

$$חֲנוּיוֹת \Leftarrow ות + י + חנו \Leftarrow חֲנוּת \Leftarrow חֲנוּת$$

---

3   a. An additional source of plural nouns ending in יּוֹת – is *verbal nouns* such as:
$$עֲלִיּוֹת \Leftarrow עֲלִיָּיה \qquad קְנִיּוֹת \Leftarrow קְנִיָּיה \qquad פְּנִיּוֹת \Leftarrow פְּנִיָּיה$$
raise (e.g., in prices)   shopping   turn

   b. In texts without vowel signs, you may encounter plurals ending in יות- that are pronounced *a-YOT* and are the plural forms of words like בְּעָיָה (problem) (plural: בְּעָיוֹת) or of irregular nouns like אָחוֹת (sister; nurse) (plural: אֲחָיוֹת) or אַרְיֵה (lions) (plural: אֲרָיוֹת).

4. *Singular nouns ending in* ‑וֹת

The most common singular noun with the ending ‑וֹת is אָחוֹת (sister; nurse).[4] Its plural is אֲחָיוֹת ('a-cha-YOT). This form includes a י preceded by an *ah* vowel before the plural ‑וֹת ending:

$$\text{אֲחָיוֹת} \Leftarrow \text{וֹת } + \text{ָי } + \text{ אח} \Leftarrow \text{אחֹוֹת} \Leftarrow \text{אָחוֹת} \quad \blacktriangleleft$$

5. *Nouns originally ending in* ‑אָ *(now written* ‑ה)*

A number of foreign nouns entered Hebrew with the ending ‑אָ.[5] This ending was regarded as equivalent to the Hebrew feminine ending ‑ה, but continued for some time to be written ‑אָ. When the plural ending was added to these nouns, many of them retained the ‑אָ both in their pronunciation and in writing, as in:

$$\text{דֻּגְמָאוֹת} \Leftarrow \text{דֻּגְמָא} \quad \blacktriangleleft$$
doog-ma-'OT   doog-MA
example

Today most of these singular nouns have been "converted" into Hebrew and are written with ‑ה (this is the spelling recommended by the Hebrew Language Academy). Although the preferred plural form is **without** an א, many speakers still use the plural forms with א. Thus:

כֻּרְסָה	קֻפְסָה	טַבְלָה	פִּסְקָה	דֻּגְמָה ◄
⇓	⇓	⇓	⇓	⇓
(כֻּרְסָאוֹת)/כֻּרְסוֹת	(קֻפְסָאוֹת)/קֻפְסוֹת	(טַבְלָאוֹת)/טַבְלוֹת	(פִּסְקָאוֹת)/פִּסְקוֹת	(דֻּגְמָאוֹת)/דֻּגְמוֹת
easy chair	box	chart	paragraph	example

The plural form of אוּנִיבֶרְסִיטָה usually has an א:

$$\text{אוּנִיבֶרְסִיטָה} \Leftarrow \text{אוּנִיבֶרְסִיטָאוֹת}^{6} \quad \blacktriangleleft$$

Nouns whose final root letter is ת' *(feminine or masculine)*

The ת' at the end of the following singular nouns is part of the *root*[7] and is **not** a feminine ending. The majority of nouns ending in ת' happen to be feminine. (You can **assume** they are feminine and commit only the exceptions – i.e., the masculine nouns ending in ת' – to memory). Here are some examples of feminine nouns:

---

4   The word חָמוֹת (mother-in-law) is similar. Its plural form is חֲמָיוֹת.
5   See the internet site of the Academy of the Hebrew Language for more details:
    http://hebrew-academy.huji.ac.il/decision3.html
    Note: What is written above does not refer to the following words whose endings are **not** feminine: אִימָא (*f.*), אַבָּא (*m.*), סַבָּא (*m.*) and סָבְתָא (*f.*).
6   The form אוּנִיבֶרְסִיטוֹת is also used. For other words that have an א in the plural, but **not** in the singular, see Appendix II "Plural Forms of Nouns," pp. 1011, 1013-1014.
7   See the chapter "Root," pp. 3-4. We have included the word דָת here even though it comes from Persian and, therefore, doesn't actually have a root.

◄

אוֹת	קֶשֶׁת	רֶשֶׁת	דֶּלֶת⁸	מַחֲבַת	שַׁבָּת	כַּת	דָּת
⇓	⇓	⇓	⇓	⇓	⇓	⇓	⇓
אוֹתִיּוֹת⁹	קְשָׁתוֹת	רְשָׁתוֹת	דְּלָתוֹת	מַחֲבָתוֹת	שַׁבָּתוֹת	כִּתּוֹת	דָּתוֹת
letter	rainbow;	net;	door	pan	sabbath	sect	religion
of the alphabet	arch	network					

The following are masculine and should be memorized:

◄

אוֹת	שֵׁירוּת	צֹמֶת	צֶוֶת	זַיִת	בַּיִת
⇓	⇓	⇓	⇓	⇓	⇓
אוֹתוֹת	שֵׁירוּתִים	צְמָתִים	צְוָותִים	זֵיתִים	בָּתִּים
signal,	service;	intersection	crew	olive	house
sign	bathroom (*pl.* only)				

Q: What happens to the ת׳ when it is part of the root?

A: In all cases – both feminine and masculine – the ת׳ **remains** in the plural form.

Let's review

♦ The main changes that take place when plural endings are added to feminine nouns with feminine endings are:

- The feminine ending drops off before the plural ending is added:

◄ חוּלְצָה ⇐ חוּלצַת ⇐ חוּלצוֹת

מְקַלַחַת ⇐ מקלחַת ⇐ מקלָחוֹת

כְּתוֹבֶת ⇐ כתובַת ⇐ כְּתוּבוֹת

- **Part** of the ending drops off before the plural ending is added:

◄ כַּפִּית ⇐ כפִיַת ⇐ כַּפִּיוֹת, חֲנוּת ⇐ חנוַת ⇐ חֲנוּיוֹת,

סְפְרִיָּיה ⇐ ספרִיַת ⇐ סְפְרִיּוֹת

♦ Cases of words with א׳ in the plural are discussed above, for example:

◄ אוּנִיבֶרְסִיטָה ⇐ אוּנִיבֶרְסִיטָאוֹת

---

8 Whether the ת׳ on דלת is part of the root or is a feminine ending that remains in the plural is not certain.

9 Note that the feminine word אות (a letter of the alphabet), whose plural has an added י׳ (אותיות), has a different plural form from the masculine אות (sign, signal) (plural: אותות).

♦ When ת is part of the **root** (i.e., it is not an ending), it **remains** in the plural, as in:

שַׁבָּת ⇐ שַׁבָּתוֹת,   שֵׁירוּת ⇐ שֵׁירוּתִים ≺

Want to see if you've understood?

A. Write the plural form of the missing nouns.

1. אנחנו אוהבים ללמוד על _____ עתיקות.
(תרבות)

2. באילו _____ בעיר מוכרים _____ לתינוקות?
(חנות)   (חולצה)

3. לפני הארוחה אל תשכחו לשים _____ , _____ ו_____ על השולחן!
(מפית)   (כפית)   (צלחת)

4. ה_____ הקטנות של רן אוכלות רק _____ , _____ ו_____ .
(אחות)   (בננה)   (עגבנייה)   (עוגייה)

Answers:

1. תַּרְבּוּיוֹת   2. חֲנוּיוֹת, חוּלְצוֹת   3. מַפִּיּוֹת, כַּפִּיּוֹת, צַלָחוֹת   4. אֲחָיוֹת, בְּנָנוֹת, עַגְבָנִיּוֹת, עוּגִיּוֹת

B. Write the plural form of the missing nouns. Remember: if ת is part of the root, it remains in the plural form. If not, it drops off before the plural ending is added.

1. ירושלים קדושה לשלוש ה_____ המונותאיסטיות.
(דת)

2. התלמידים החדשים כבר למדו את כל ה_____ .
(אות)

3. ב_____ בירושלים אפשר לראות גברים עם _____ הולכים לבית הכנסת.
(שבת)   (טלית)

4. לפני החתונה קנו בני הזוג _____ זה לזה.
(טבעת)

Answers:

1. דָתוֹת   2. אוֹתִיּוֹת   3. שַׁבָּתוֹת, טַלִּיתוֹת   4. טַבָּעוֹת

Masculine singular nouns

1. Nouns ending in הֶ־

Let's look at what happens to nouns whose singular form ends in the masculine ending הֶ־:[10]

singular:	שָׂדֶה	מַחֲנֶה	מִקְרֶה	מִבְנֶה	מוֹרֶה ◄
	⇓	⇓	⇓	⇓	⇓
plural:	שָׂדוֹת	מַחֲנוֹת	מִקְרִים	מִבְנִים	מוֹרִים
	field	camp	case	structure	teacher (*m.*)

As was the case with the feminine ending הָ־, the masculine הֶ־ also drops off before the plural ending is added:

teacher (*m.*)	מוֹרֶה ⇐ מורֶֿה ⇐ מוֹרִים ◄
camp	מַחֲנֶה ⇐ מחנֶֿה ⇐ מַחֲנוֹת

Did you know?
Only when a final ה׳ is part of the root (i.e., it represents a consonant), as in a word like גוֹבַהּ (height), does it **remain** in the plural form: גְבָהִים.

2. Nouns ending in י׳

Almost all nouns that end in י׳ are masculine.[11] In nouns such as the following (whose pattern is like דִיבּוּר), the י׳ is part of the root of the noun. When the plural ending (in this case ים־) is added, the plural form has **two** י׳ ("יי"):

נִיסוּי	בִּילוּי	שִׁינוּי ◄
⇓	⇓	⇓
נִיסוּיִים	בִּילוּיִים	שִׁינוּיִים
experiment	recreation	change

---

10 The plural of מַשְׁקֶה (drink) has an added א׳: מַשְׁקָאוֹת.
11 The feminine noun לְחִי (cheek) is an exception.

Now look at more nouns ending in ־י (some end in ־אי):

II		I	
סִינִי	יִשְׂרְאֵלִי	חַקְלַאי[12]	בַּנְקַאי ◄
⇓	⇓	⇓	⇓
סִינִים	יִשְׂרְאֵלִים	חַקְלָאִים	בַּנְקָאִים
a Chinese person	an Israeli	farmer	banker

Q: How many ־י are in these plural forms?

A: Only **one**. It is hard to know whether this is the ־י of the singular form or of the plural ending. In any event, when we form these plurals, we actually need to add only ־ם. Notice that these nouns, as opposed to the ones above, denote **people**. When nouns that denote people end in ־י, there is only one ־י in their plural forms.

> **Be careful!** The above forms with one ־י in the plural are nouns. In contrast, adjective forms related to some of these words have **two** ־י (־יי). For example: כלים חקלאיים (agricultural tools) (compare nouns in Column I above) and סרטים ישראליים (Israeli films) (compare ethnic nouns in Column II).[13]

Some other nouns that end in ־י have only one ־י in their plural form, for example:

כְּלִי	תְּנַאי ◄
⇓	⇓
כֵּלִים	תְּנָאִים
tool, instrument	condition

Note: the plural of פְּרִי is special and has no ־י at all: פֵּרוֹת.

> ## Let's review
>
> ♦ The masculine ending ־ֶה drops off before the plural ending is added:
>
> מוֹרָה ⇐ מוֹר̸ֶ֮ה ⇐ מוֹרִים ◄
> מַחֲנֶה ⇐ מחנ̸ֶ֮ה ⇐ מַחֲנוֹת

---

12 Note that these are the proper forms of these nouns. Many Israelis mistakenly say בַּנְקָאִי and חַקְלָאִי which are actually adjectives as in: צ׳ק בַּנְקָאִי (bank check), כלי חַקְלָאִי (agricultural tool).

13 For more details, see the chapter "How Are Adjectives Formed?" pp. 155-156.

◆ Nouns ending in י ("י") may have either **two** י ("יי") in the plural or **one** (י):

- most **inanimate** nouns have two י ("יי"): שִׁנוּי ⇐ שִׁנּוּיִים, נִסּוּי ⇐ נִסּוּיִים
  but not all, for example: כְּלִי ⇐ כֵּלִים
- most **animate** nouns have one (י): יִשְׂרְאֵלִי ⇐ יִשְׂרְאֵלִים, עִתּוֹנַאי ⇐ עִיתוֹנָאִים

Want to see if you've understood?
Write the plural form of the missing nouns.

1. שמענו על ה_____ בתוכנית.
(שינוי)

2. ה_____ שמחו על הניצחון שלהם במשחק.
(ספורטאי)

3. בסוף הארוחה המלצר הוריד את ה_____ מן השולחן.
(כלי)

4. ב_____ רבים אין קשר בין כותרת המאמר לבין התוכן שלו.
(מִקְרֶה)

5. בסוף החורף כדאי לטייל ב_____ בצפון הארץ.
(שָׂדֶה)

Answers:

1. שִׁנּוּיִים 2. סְפּוֹרְטָאִים 3. כֵּלִים 4. מִקְרִים 5. שָׂדוֹת

• *The ending* ־ַיִים *(the "dual" ending)*

Read the following passage:

בחופשת הקיץ ביליתי יומיים נפלאים אך מעייפים אצל בן הדוד שלי בקיבוץ בצפון. רכבתי בשדות על האופניים החדשים שלו וטיילתי ברגל בהרים שליד הקיבוץ עד שכאבו לי הרגליים.

Over summer vacation I spent two wonderful but tiring days at my cousin's on a kibbutz up north. I rode his new bicycle through the fields and hiked in the mountains next to the kibbutz until my legs hurt.

In the passage above, we have highlighted still another plural ending: ‏ַיִים‎- (*-A-yeem*). This ending appears on the words ‏יומיים‎ (two days), ‏אופניים‎ (bicycle) and ‏רגליים‎ (legs). This is the same ending that appears on the words ‏שתיים‎ / ‏שניים‎ (two *f./m.*), and is called the *dual ending*.

When ‏ַיִים‎- appears on **numbers** or **units of time**, it means *two*:

‏מֵאָה‎	‏אֶלֶף‎	‏יוֹם‎	‏שָׁבוּעַ‎	‏חוֹדֶשׁ‎	‏שָׁנָה‎	‏פַּעַם‎
⇓	⇓	⇓	⇓	⇓	⇓	⇓
‏מָאתַיִים‎	‏אַלְפַּיִים‎	‏יוֹמַיִים‎	‏שְׁבוּעַיִים‎	‏חוֹדְשַׁיִים‎	‏שְׁנָתַיִים‎	‏פַּעֲמַיִים‎
two hundred	two thousand	two days	two weeks	two months	two years	two times, twice

There is no need to add the number ‏שני/שתי‎ before the above words. When we talk about **more than two**, we use the **regular** plural form of these words:

‏מֵאוֹת‎	‏אֲלָפִים‎	‏יָמִים‎	‏שָׁבוּעוֹת‎	‏חוֹדָשִׁים‎	‏שָׁנִים‎	‏פְּעָמִים‎
hundreds	thousands	days	weeks	months	years	times

The ending ‏ַיִים‎- is also used for **parts of the body** and other things that usually come in **pairs** or in **two sets**. Here, unlike above, the ending is **not** used instead of the number *two*, but rather functions as a plural ending. Here are a few of the many examples:

‏רֶגֶל‎	‏יָד‎	‏נַעַל‎	‏שֵׁן‎	‏צִיפּוֹרֶן‎
⇓	⇓	⇓	⇓	⇓
‏רַגְלַיִים‎	‏יָדַיִים‎	‏נַעֲלַיִים‎	‏שִׁינַיִים‎	‏צִיפּוֹרְנַיִים‎
legs	hands	shoes	teeth	fingernails, toenails

Now look again at the words in the passage that end in ‏ַיִים‎- (‏אופניים, רגליים, יומיים‎).

Q: Do they all refer to **more than one** item?

A: No. The words ‏יומיים‎ (two days) and ‏רגליים‎ (legs) **do**, but the word ‏אופניים‎ refers to **one** bicycle. As is the case with other such words (e.g., ‏משקפיים‎ eyeglasses, ‏מכנסיים‎ pants, ‏מספריים‎ scissors), the dual ending is used here when referring to a single object that is made up of two identical parts. All of these **words** are considered plural in Hebrew, as we can see from the adjective or verb that match them:

‏אופניים חדשים‎	‏משקפיים גדולים‎	‏מכנסיים ארוכים‎	‏מספריים חדים‎
a new bicycle	big glasses	long pants	sharp scissors

If this is the case, how do we say **more than one** bicycle / pair of pants / glasses / scissors? We use the word זוגות (pairs). For example:

ארבעה זוגות מספריים	שלושה זוגות משקפיים,	שני זוגות מכנסיים,	שני זוגות אופניים,[14] ◀
four pairs of scissors	three pairs of glasses	two pairs of pants	two bicycles

The ending ־יִים can be added to either masculine or feminine nouns. It is the **noun itself** (יום, שנה...) – and not the ending – that determines the gender.[15] Thus, we say:

m. ⇔ *m.*

◀ ביליתי יומיים נפלאים בקיבוץ בצפון.   I spent two wonderful days at a kibbutz up north.

f. ⇔ *f.*

הייתי שם שלוש פעמים בשנתיים האחרונות.   I have been there three times in the last two years.

Be careful! The words צָהֳרַיִים (noon), מַיִם (water) and שָׁמַיִם (sky, heaven) all take the -*A-yeem* ending and they, too, are always plural:

◀ מים קרים   cold water
שמים כחולים   blue sky

Notice that when written without vowel signs, the endings on the nouns מים and שמים are spelled with only **one** י even though they are pronounced **as if** they have two.

Let's review

- ◆ The dual ending ־יִים (-*A-yeem*) is added onto words denoting:

  - **Numbers** or **units of time** (here the ending means *two*):

    ◀ חוֹדְשַׁיִים יוֹמַיִים

  - **Parts of the body** and other things that usually come in **pairs** or **two sets** (here the ending does not mean two, but rather is simply plural):

    ◀ יָדַיִים רַגְלַיִים שִׁינַיִים

  - Single objects that consist of **two identical parts**:

    ◀ אוֹפַנַיִים מִשְׁקָפַיִים

---

14 Since the noun זוג (plural: זוגות) is masculine, the number that precedes (and matches it) is masculine.

15 See the chapter "The Gender of Nouns," pp. 18-33.

◆ All nouns ending in -*A-yeem*[16] are considered plural, including the words מִים, צָהֳרַיִם and שָׁמַיִם:

➤ רַגְלַיִם אֲרוּכּוֹת   אוֹפַנַּיִם חֲדָשִׁים   מַיִם קָרִים

• *Changes in the base form of the noun*

Until now we have examined the possible changes at the **end** of the singular form when the plural endings are added. Now we will examine other changes that may take place.

When the plural ending is added, sometimes the *base form* to which it is added is exactly the **same** as the singular form, for example:

singular:	וִילוֹן	עוֹלָם	סִיפּוּר	בִּנְיָין	➤ שִׁיר
	⇓	⇓	⇓	⇓	⇓
plural:	וִילוֹנוֹת	עוֹלָמוֹת	סִיפּוּרִים	בִּנְיָינִים	שִׁירִים
	curtain	world	story	building	song, poem

Many times, however, there are changes – especially in the vowels of the base form – and sometimes in the consonants as well (as in אִישׁ ⇐ אֲנָשִׁים).[17]

1. *Change of one vowel to* shva[18]

Look at the singular and plural forms of the following nouns:

(*tsa-VA*) צָבָא	(*ma-KOM*) מָקוֹם	(*na-VEE*) נָבִיא	(*da-VAR*) דָּבָר	➤
⇓	⇓	⇓	⇓	
(*tsva-'OT*) צְבָאוֹת	(*me-ko-MOT*) מְקוֹמוֹת	(*ne-vee-'EEM*) נְבִיאִים	(*dva-REEM*) דְּבָרִים	
army	place	prophet	thing	

Q: What has changed in the base to which the plural ending is added?

A: The *ah* vowel of the first syllable (written ◌ָ) has changed: In the plural forms it is either pronounced *eh* – as in נְבִיאִים – or not pronounced at all – as in דְּבָרִים). This vowel sign is called *shva*.

---

16 This is true except for names of cities and countries like יְרוּשָׁלַיִם (Jerusalem), מִצְרַיִם (Egypt), גִּבְעָתַיִם (Givatayim, a city near Tel Aviv), which are feminine singular.

17 See Appendix II "Plural Forms of Nouns," pp. 1011-1016 for more examples. The changes in the base form are highlighted in red.

18 Often called *shewa* in grammar books.

This phenomenon is called *vowel reduction* or *shortening* (חִיטוּף) and is a result of the shift of the *stress* to the ending.[19]

This shortening can occur in other syllables and with other vowels, too, as in:

(zee-ka-RON) זִיכָּרוֹן	(tee-PESH) טִיפֵּשׁ	◄ שׁוֹטֵר (sho-TER)
⇓	⇓	⇓
זִיכְרוֹנוֹת (zeech-ro-NOT)	טִיפְּשִׁים (teep-SHEEM)	שׁוֹטְרִים (shot-REEM)
memory	stupid person	policeman

It is not always easy for learners of Hebrew to **predict** when a reduction will take place, but being aware that such a reduction does **sometimes** take place and noting some of the word *patterns* in which this change takes place (for example, nouns with patterns like שׁוֹטֵר, נָבִיא, דָבָר and so on) can help you learn to pronounce Hebrew words correctly.[20]

2. Segolate nouns

Singular nouns, such as יֶלֶד, whose **first** syllable is stressed (called *segolate* nouns), form their plural in the following way:[21]

(NE-fesh) נֶפֶשׁ	(BO-ker) בּוֹקֶר	(SE-fer) סֵפֶר	(YE-led) יֶלֶד ◄
⇓	⇓	⇓	⇓
נְפָשׁוֹת (ne-fa-SHOT)	בְּקָרִים (bka-REEM)	סְפָרִים (sfa-REEM)	יְלָדִים (ye-la-DEEM)
soul	morning	book	child

In all cases, the plural form is □ְָ□ָ□ים – just like דְּבָרִים – or □ְָ□ָ□וֹת.[22] When *segolate* nouns take the ending ים-ַ, the plural base form never begins with *shva*, for example:

('O-zen) אוֹזֶן	(BE-rech) בֶּרֶךְ	(RE-gel) רֶגֶל ◄
⇓	⇓	⇓
אוֹזְנַיִים ('oz-NA-yeem)	בִּרְכַּיִים (beer-KA-yeem)	רַגְלַיִים (rag-LA-yeem)
ear	knee	leg

3. Feminine nouns like יַלְדָה / שִׂמְלָה

The following feminine nouns, all of which have a **vowel** (not a *shva*) after the first consonant

---

19 See more on vowel reduction in the chapter "Reduction of Vowels and the *Shva*," pp. 640-645.
20 On patterns, see the chapter "Pattern," pp. 9-16.
21 See the chapter "Segolate Nouns," pp. 93-95 for a more in-depth discussion of segolates and their plural forms.
22 Segolates that begin with *gutturals* are slightly different: אֲבָנִים ⇐ אֶבֶן (stones), עֲצָמוֹת ⇐ עֶצֶם (bone). See more in the chapter "Segolate Nouns," p. 94.

and **no vowel** (marked by a *shva*) after the second, have the same plural base form as the *segolates* (compare: יְלָדִים):[23]

(seem-LA) שִׂמְלָה	(yal-DA) יַלְדָּה ◄
⇓	⇓
(sma-LOT) שְׂמָלוֹת	(ye-la-DOT) יְלָדוֹת
dress	girl

Quite a few other plural feminine nouns also end in *-a-_OT,* for example:

(ma-GE-vet) מַגֶּבֶת	(mach-BE-ret) מַחְבֶּרֶת ◄
⇓	⇓
(ma-ga-VOT) מַגָּבוֹת	(mach-ba-ROT) מַחְבָּרוֹת
towel	notebook

As you can see, the singular form of these nouns ends in ת ֶ- (*-E-et*). Other examples include מִסְגְּרוֹת ⇐ מִסְגֶּרֶת (frame), מַדְפֵּסֶת ⇐ מַדְפְּסוֹת (printer).

Let's review

Sometimes the vowels of the base form of nouns change when the plural ending is added.

♦ Often one vowel changes to *shva* as in:

דָּבָר ⇐ דְּבָרִים, שׁוֹטֵר ⇐ שׁוֹטְרִים ◄

♦ Most segolate nouns have a similar plural form (ְֶ ָֹ ים, ְֶ ָֹ וֹת):

יֶלֶד ⇐ יְלָדִים, בּוֹקֶר ⇐ בְּקָרִים, נֶפֶשׁ ⇐ נְפָשׁוֹת ◄

♦ The plural form of words like שִׂמְלָה and יַלְדָּה has the same pattern as the segolates:

יַלְדָּה ⇐ יְלָדוֹת, שִׂמְלָה ⇐ שְׂמָלוֹת ◄

♦ The base form of segolate nouns that take the ַ-יִם ending begins with a **vowel** (not with a *shva*), as in:

רֶגֶל ⇐ רַגְלַיִם, בֶּרֶךְ ⇐ בִּרְכַּיִם, אוֹזֶן ⇐ אוֹזְנַיִים ◄

---

23 In fact, these singular forms are feminine forms of segolate nouns. Their first vowel is the same as the vowel in forms like יַלְדִּי (my child), סִפְרִי (my book) and נֶכְדִּי (my grandchild).

• *Nouns that have only one form* (singular or plural)

Some nouns have **only** a singular form, for example:

חוֹשֶׁךְ	חוֹם	אֲוֵויר ➤
darkness	heat	air

The word נֶשֶׁק also doesn't have a plural form, for example:

sing. ⇔ sing. ⇔ sing.

Nuclear weapons threaten the world.   הנשק הגרעיני מאיים על העולם. ➤

Here נֶשֶׁק is considered singular even though it actually denotes a **collection** of objects. The English equivalent of nouns like this (here: *weapons*) is not always singular.[24]

Another example is the word נוֹעַר, as in:

sing. ⇔ sing.

Young people spend many hours at the computer.   הנוער מבלה שעות רבות מול המחשב. ➤

Here the verb (מבלה) is singular because the noun (נוער) is considered singular in Hebrew. [25]

In contrast, as mentioned above, some Hebrew words have only a **plural** (or **dual**) **form**, and are considered plural nouns regardless of whether what they denote is plural, for example:

אוֹפַנַּיים גדולים[27]	שָׁמַיים כחולים	פָּנים מעניינים/מעניינות[26]	חַיים טובים ➤
a big bicycle	a blue sky	an interesting face	a good life

A number of words that have only a plural form often appear with the Aramaic plural ending ין- and are almost always considered plural. In many cases, the Hebrew ים- ending is also used – as an alternative form with the same meaning:

פִּיטוּרִין צפויים/	גירושין מכוערים/	נישואין טובים/ ➤
פִּיטוּרים צפויים	גירושים מכוערים	נישואים טובים
an expected dismissal (firing)	an ugly divorce	a good marriage

---

24 We also use the word נֶשֶׁק to mean *a weapon* (short for כְּלִי נֶשֶׁק). In this case, its plural is כְּלֵי נֶשֶׁק, as in השוטרים
 מצאו מאות כְּלֵי נֶשֶׁק במרתף הבית. (The policemen found hundreds of weapons in the cellar of the house). The form
 נְשָׁקים (not approved by the Hebrew Language Academy) is also used by many Hebrew speakers.
25 When we refer to the individuals in the group called נוֹעַר, we use the form נְעָרים / נְעָרות or בְּנֵי נוֹעַר (youths).
26 a. פָּנים is both masculine and feminine.
   b. The singular פַּן has a different meaning: *aspect*.
27 The singular אוֹפַן (wheel) does exist in literary Hebrew, but it is not the singular of אוֹפַנַּיים.

Be careful! The word מוֹדִיעִין (intelligence – e.g., in the army – or information service – e.g., on the telephone) only takes the ending ין- and is regarded as **singular**, for example:

sing. ⇔ *sing.*

◄ הצבא קיבל מוֹדִיעִין טוב על מה שקורה באזור.

The army received good intelligence on what is going on in the area.

Let's review

◆ There are words in Hebrew that have only a singular form (e.g., אוויר air). Some nouns with only a singular form (such as נשק in נשק גרעיני nuclear weapons) may even denote a **collection** of objects.

◆ Other nouns have only a plural form (e.g., פנים face). Some of these nouns take the plural ending ין-, as in נישואין (marriage).

Want to see if you've understood this chapter?

This exercise contains nouns that appear in the chapter above and in Appendix II at the end of this book.

Write the plural form of the missing nouns.

1. בטיול שלנו בצרפת ראינו _____ מיוחדים ו_____ היסטוריים מעניינים,
    (בית)   (מבנה)

    ביניהם _____ ו_____ עתיקים.
    (ארמון)   (כנסייה)

2. יש לנו _____ נעימים מן ה_____ הראשונות שלנו באוניברסיטה.
    (זיכרון)   (שנה)

3. הפסיכולוגית חיפשה _____ חדשות לפתור את ה_____ הרבות של הילדים.
    (דרך)   (בעיה)

    אולי בעתיד היא תמצא _____ מוצלחים.
    (פתרון)

4. הצעירים הישראלים נוסעים ל_____ אקזוטיים כמו הודו ותאילנד ופוגשים שם _____
    (מקום)   (איש)

    מכל העולם.

5.   מתי פותחים את ה_____ במרכז העיר?
                            (חנות)

6.   היום יש הרבה _____, במיוחד ב_____ ה_____ הגדולות,
                  (מכונית)   (כביש)   (עיר)

      ולכן יש הרבה _____ דרכים.
                      (תאונה)

7.   אפשר לשאול ספרים מה_____ של ה_____ הגדולות בארץ גם דרך האינטרנט.
                      (ספרייה)   (אוניברסיטה)

8.   ה_____ עוזרות לתלמידים לענות על ה_____.
          (דוגמה)   (שאלה)

9.   ה_____ החדשות הודיעו לסטודנטים על _____ רבים בתוכנית ה_____.
          (מורה)   (שינוי)   (לימוד)

10.   אני מכיר שתי _____ שלמדו באוניברסיטה יחד עם ה_____ שלהן.
                      (אישה)   (בת)

11.   בקיץ ה_____ ארוכים וה_____ קצרים.
              (יום)   (לילה)

Answers:

1. בָּתִּים, מִבְנִים, כְּנֵסִיּוֹת, אַרְמוֹנוֹת   2. זִכְרוֹנוֹת, שָׁנִים   3. דְּרָכִים, בְּעָיוֹת, פִּתְרוֹנוֹת   4. מְקוֹמוֹת, אֲנָשִׁים
5. חֲנֻיּוֹת   6. מְכוֹנִיּוֹת, כְּבִישִׁים, עָרִים, תְּאוּנוֹת   7. סִפְרִיּוֹת, אוּנִיבֶּרְסִיטָאוֹת (or: אוּנִיבֶּרְסִיטוֹת)
8. דֻּגְמוֹת / דֻּגְמָאוֹת, שְׁאֵלוֹת   9. מוֹרוֹת, שִׁינּוּיִים, לִימּוּדִים   10. נָשִׁים, בָּנוֹת   11. יָמִים, לֵילוֹת

3. Definite and Indefinite Nouns

Preview

- *The definite article* -ה *(the)* ה׳ הַיִּדוּעַ, ה׳ הַיְדִיעָה
- *When do we use* -ה *before a noun?*
- *Definite nouns without* -ה
- *Why is it important to identify nouns?*

• *The definite article* -ה *(the)* ה׳ הַיִּדוּעַ, ה׳ הַיְדִיעָה

Read the following passage:

◄ אימא של יעל קנתה לה תיק אדום ויפה. התיק הוא מתנה ליום ההולדת ה-16 של יעל.

Yael's mother bought her a pretty red purse. The purse is a gift for Yael's sixteenth birthday.

Notice the following words from the passage:

a purse	תיק	1. ◄
the purse	התיק	2.

Q: What difference do you see between these Hebrew words?

A: The first word has **no** -ה added to the front of it (תיק). The word **without** the -ה is called an *indefinite* noun and corresponds to the English *a purse*. Notice that, in this case, English uses the little word *a* to show that תיק is indefinite. Hebrew **does not**, since Hebrew has **no indefinite article** (the equivalent of *a* and *an*).

The second word (התיק) appears with the *definite article* -ה (the) and is called a *definite* noun. The definite article -ה is usually pronounced *ha*.[1] When the letters ב׳, כ׳ or פ׳ follow the -ה, they are pronounced with a hard pronunciation – *b, k* and *p* (written ב׳, כ׳, פ׳ in *standard spelling* with vowel signs),[2] for example:

◄ הַבַּיִת הַכּוֹס הַפְּגִישָׁה

---

[1] In **informal** Hebrew it is always pronounced *ha*. In **formal** Hebrew, the -ה is pronounced according to the rules of classical Hebrew grammar, according to which the usual pronunciation of -ה is *ha* (as in: הַבַּיִת, הָאִישׁ, הָרוּחַ), but before certain letters (ה׳, ח׳, ע׳) under certain conditions, it is pronounced *heh* (הֶ), for example: הֶעָבָר, הֶהָרִים, הֶחָבֵר, הֶחֲדָשִׁים (=הֶחוֹדָשִׁים). For more details, see J. Weingreen, 1959, pp. 23-25.

[2] This is a *strong dagesh* (דָּגֵשׁ חָזָק), also called *dagesh forte*. -ה is always followed by a *dagesh* except when the following letter is א׳, ה׳, ח׳, ע׳ or ר׳. See the chapter "The Pronunciation of ב׳, כ׳, פ׳ and the *Dagesh*," p. 634.

Because **single-letter** Hebrew words never stand alone in writing, ‎ה- is always **attached** to the front of the noun that follows it.

Be careful! Not always is the definite article ‎ה- visible in Hebrew. When the prepositions ‎'ב, ‎'כ or ‎'ל come before ‎ה-, they combine with it:

(ba-da-VAR)	בַּדָּבָר	⇐	בְּ + הַדָּבָר
(la-da-VAR)	לַדָּבָר	⇐	לְ + הַדָּבָר
(ka-da-VAR)	כַּדָּבָר	⇐	כְּ + הַדָּבָר

When a text is written **without** vowel signs, we **can't** tell just by looking whether words like ‎בדבר, ‎לדבר and ‎כדבר are indefinite (*be-da-VAR, le-da-VAR, ke-da-VAR*) or definite (*ba-da-VAR, la-da-VAR, ka-da-VAR*). Only our understanding of the context tells us how to pronounce and understand these words.

In addition, when a noun takes the form of *smeechoot*,[3] ‎ה- is attached only to the **last** noun in the *smeechoot phrase*, but it makes the **entire phrase** definite.

Do you know the school in your neighborhood?   ?אתם מכירים את בית הספר בשכונה שלכם

Did you know?

אימא, אבא, סבא, סבתא

The words אימא (Mom), אבא (Dad), סבא (Grandpa) and סבתא (Grandma) all end in אָ-, which is the Aramaic definite article (the equivalent of the Hebrew ‎ה-). For this reason, they are definite and there is no need to add ‎ה- to them, for example:

 אנחנו לא מכירים את אימא של אורי.
We don't know Uri's mother (lit.: the mother of Uri).

עדי אוהבת את סבתא שלה.
Adi loves her grandmother (lit.: the grandmother of her).

Nonetheless, many Hebrew speakers today **do** add ‎ה- and say "‎...האימא של", "‎...האבא של" and so on.

---

3   On *smeechoot,* see the chapter "*Smeechoot,*" pp. 183-184, 186.

• *When do we use -ה before a noun?*

The use of -ה in Hebrew is quite similar to the use of *the* in English. For example, in the passage above, the first occurrence of the word תיק (a purse) is indefinite in both languages and the next occurrence, in which that תיק is referred to, is definite (התיק – the purse).

There are, however, quite a few cases in which the use of -ה in Hebrew and the use of *the* in English are **not parallel**. You need to be aware of these differences since these are cases in which you **cannot** translate literally from one language to the other. Here are some examples:

1. *Possessives using של*

היומן שלי	המשקפיים שלנו,	הארנק של יעל,	⊰
my calendar (diary)	our glasses	Yael's wallet	
literally: the calendar of mine	the glasses of ours	the wallet of Yael	

The English expressions "my calendar, our glasses…" do **not** contain the word *the*, while in the equivalent Hebrew expressions, -ה almost always precedes the noun before של (e.g., היומן שלי). This -ה is omitted if we wish to say the Hebrew equivalent of "**an** article of mine," for example:

⊰ מאמר שלי התפרסם בעיתון.   **An** article **of mine** appeared in the newspaper.

Today, many Hebrew speakers tend to omit the -ה when they refer to friends or family members:[4]

⊰ חברה שלי   (*colloquial*) my friend
or: a friend of mine

אח שלי   (*colloquial*) my brother
or: a brother of mine

2. *Shortened possessives*

In examples like the following, שלי and שלו are **omitted**. Nevertheless, -ה still comes before the noun in Hebrew. In contrast, the English equivalents do **not** contain the word *the*:

⊰ כואב לי הראש.   My head hurts.
lit.: The head (short for "my head") hurts me.

קובי בַּבַּית עכשיו.   Kobi is (at) home now.
lit.: … at the home (short for "his home")

---

4   In spoken Hebrew, when addressing someone close, expressions such as the following are often used: מוֹתֶק שלי (my sweetheart), יַלְדָה שלי (my child), נְשָׁמָה שלי (lit.: my "soul"), אָהוּב שלי (lit.: my "loved one"). We thank Sarah Israeli for pointing this out.

3. *Pointing to something* (ההוא, הזה *and the like*)[5]

In Hebrew, we place ה- before the noun when a pointing expression (e.g., הזה) is added. The English equivalent does not contain the word *the*:

This house is a mess.	הבית הזה מבולגן! ◄
This apartment is clean.	הדירה הזאת נקייה.
I don't know that man.	אני לא מכירה את האיש ההוא.

4. *Concepts, religions…*

ה- is **frequently**, though **not always**, used before nouns that denote concepts, religions and the like in Hebrew sentences like the following. We do not use *the* in the English equivalents:

Happiness is hard to achieve. lit.: The happiness…	האושר קשה להשגה. ◄
Judaism is an ancient religion. lit.: The Judaism…	היהדות היא דת עתיקה.
Life in Israel is interesting. lit.: The life…	החיים בישראל מעניינים.

5. *Miscellaneous*

ה- is used in Hebrew expressions such as the following, while the word *the* does not usually appear in the English:[6]

We went into town (or: to the city).	נסענו לָעיר. ◄
We came back from town (or: from the city).	חזרנו מהעיר.
My sister is in college. lit.: … studies at the university.	אחותי לומדת בָּאוניברסיטה.
I walked (went on foot) to my uncle's house. lit.: walked on the foot	הלכתי לבית של הדוד שלי בָּרֶגל.
Classes at the university start at 8:30 a.m. lit.: The classes…	השיעורים באוניברסיטה מתחילים ב-8:30.

---

5   See the chapters "How Do Adjectives Behave?" pp. 132-134 and "Pronouns and Pointing Words," pp. 208-209 on the use of ה- before adjectives (הבית הגדול the big house) and words like זה הזה (הבית הזה this house). In **formal** Hebrew, the latter phrases also can appear without ה-, as in: בית זה הוא בית עתיק (This house is an ancient house). This is also discussed in the chapter "Pronouns and Pointing Words," pp. 208-209.

6   See the chapter "*When* Expressions," p. 310 for time expressions using ה- before a noun, as in היום (today).

Be careful! In all of the examples above, Hebrew uses -ה, while English **does not**. In the following, the reverse is the case:

1. *Playing musical instruments*

◄ יצחק מנגן בְּגִיטרה.   מרים מנגנת בְּכִינור.

                (*be-gee-TA-ra*)   (*be-chee-NOR*)

          Yitzchak plays **the** guitar.   Miriam plays **the** violin.

               lit.:   a guitar   lit.:   a violin

2. *Set expressions*

◄ מִצַד אחד אתה לא אוהב לצאת למסעדות. מִצַד אחר אתה לא עוזר להכין ארוחות בבית.[7]

On **the** one hand, you don't like to go to restaurants. On **the** other hand, you don't help prepare meals at home.

lit.: From one side… From another side…

Want to see if you've understood?

A. Translate.

1. Our neighbor (*m.*) went to China. (Use של.) _____

2. Tami went into town by bus. _____

3. Yonatan's office is in this building. _____

4. Class was interesting today. _____

Answers:

1. השכן שלנו נסע לסין.   2. תמי נסעה לָעיר (העירה) באוטובוס.
3. המשרד של יונתן הוא (או: נמצא) בַּבְּניין הזה.   4. השיעור היה מעניין היום.

---

7   The expression ״מצד אחד... מצד אחר״ is considered preferable to the more commonly used expression ״מצד אחד... מצד שני״.

B. Translate.

_____ .התלמידים למדו היום על האיסלאם .1

_____ .הילדים של אורי ושלומית הולכים לבית הספר גם ביום שישי .2

_____ ?האם הפסיכולוגיה היא מדע .3

_____ .החיים קשים .4

Answers:

1. The students learned today about Islam.   2. Uri and Shlomit's children go to school on Friday, too.

3. Is psychology a science?   4. Life is difficult (hard).

• *Definite nouns without* ה-

Thus far we have looked at nouns that are made definite by adding ה-. There are, however, several other situations in which a noun is considered **definite** even though it does **not** have a definite article, for example:

1. *A noun with an added possessive ending*[8]

his book	סִפְרוֹ = הַסֵּפֶר שלו ◄
our students	תַלְמִידֵינוּ = הַתַלְמִידִים שלנו.

2. *Proper nouns – names of people, cities and countries*

Jerusalem	ירושלים ◄
Daniel	דניאל

The following are like proper nouns:

days of the week:	Friday	יום שישי ◄
names of months:	September / Tishrei	(חודש) ספטמבר / תשרי
names of holidays:	Purim	(חג) פורים

3. *Nouns with numbers*

	Room 5	חדר 5 ◄
	Floor 6	קומה 6
	Bus 7	קו 7
	Channel 8	ערוץ 8

_____

8   On possessive endings, see the chapter "Nouns with Possessive Endings," pp. 60-77.

• *Why is it important to identify definite nouns?*

The fact that a noun is definite (in any of the ways mentioned above) has implications for the way we build a correct Hebrew sentence. Definiteness influences the structure of a sentence in two situations:

1. *When we join an adjective to the noun*

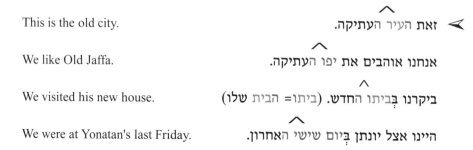

This is the old city.	זאת העיר העתיקה.
We like Old Jaffa.	אנחנו אוהבים את יפו העתיקה.
We visited his new house.	ביקרנו בְּביתו החדש. (ביתו= הבית שלו)
We were at Yonatan's last Friday.	היינו אצל יונתן בְּיום שישי האחרון.

When a noun is **definite**, its adjective is **definite,** too, i.e., it is preceded by the definite article ה-. You can read more about this in the chapter "How Do Adjectives Behave?" (pp. 132-134).

2. *When we add a direct object*

Definiteness affects whether or not we use אֶת in a sentence with a direct object:

B *with* את	A *without* את
יעל חיפשה את התיק שלה. Yael looked for her purse.	יעל חיפשה תיק חדש. Yael looked for a new purse.
פגשנו את אחותך. (=האחות שלך) We met your sister.	בטיול פגשנו אנשים מעניינים. We met interesting people on the trip.
אנחנו רואים את מצרים במפה. We see Egypt on the map.	אנחנו רואים בניינים עתיקים. We see ancient buildings.
הוא אוהב את ערוץ 8. He likes Channel 8.	הוא אוהב מוזיקה קלסית. He likes classical music.

In Column B, the direct object in each sentence (התיק, אחותך, מצרים, ערוץ 8) is definite; therefore, the word אֶת appears in front of them. In Column A, the direct object is not definite, thus there is no אֶת. You can read about the direct object and when אֶת is used in the chapter "The Direct Object and the Use of את" (pp. 697-704).

Chapter summary

- The *definite article* in Hebrew is ה-. It is attached to the front of a word: הבית, הילדים.

- In *smeechoot* it is added to the front of the last word of the phrase and makes the entire phrase definite: בית הספר, ספרי הלימוד.

- The following nouns are considered definite even though they have **no** definite article:

  - a noun with a *possessive ending*: ספרי, אחותו, אחיך, דעתכם
  - a *proper noun* (a name of a person, a city, a country and the like): דויד, ירושלים, צרפת
  - nouns with numbers: ערוץ 8

To see if you've understood, do exercises on pp. 134-135 (on adjectives) and pp. 699, 703, 704 (on את).

4. Nouns with Possessive Endings

Preview

- *Singular nouns with possessive endings* (אֲחוֹתִי, בְּנָךְ)
- *Plural nouns with possessive endings* (דּוֹדָיו, דּוֹדוֹתֶיהָ)

Introduction

Read the following two passages. The first is in **informal** Hebrew; the second is in **formal** Hebrew:

> ⤝ אתמול הלכתי לבית קפה עם הַחֲבֵרוֹת שֶׁלִי – מיכל, דליה ותמר. שתינו קפה ומיכל סיפרה סיפורים מצחיקים על הַבֵּן שֶׁלָּה. דליה רצתה לשמוע את הַדֵעָה שֶׁלָנוּ על הַדִּירָה שֶׁלָּהּ, ותמר סיפרה על הַלִּימוּדִים שֶׁלָּהּ.

> ⤝ אתמול הלכתי לבית קפה עם חֲבֵרוֹתַיי[1] – מיכל, דליה ותמר. שתינו קפה ומיכל סיפרה סיפורים מצחיקים על בְּנָהּ. דליה רצתה לשמוע את דַּעְתֵנוּ על דִּירָתָהּ, ותמר סיפרה על לִימוּדֶיהָ.

Yesterday I went to a café with my friends – Michal, Dalia and Tamar. We had coffee and Michal told funny stories about her son. Dalia wanted to hear our opinion about her apartment, and Tamar told about her studies.

Q: What is the most striking difference between the highlighted words in the two Hebrew passages?

A: While in the first Hebrew passage possession is expressed by adding a **separate word** to the noun (החברות שלי, הבן שלה), in the second passage it is expressed by adding an **ending** to the noun. Thus, what appears in the first passage – and in English as well – as **two** words, appears as **one** word in the second Hebrew passage.

The usual way of expressing possession in spoken (informal) Hebrew is to add a separate word (שלי, שלך...) to a *definite noun* (...הילדים שלי, הדירה שלך), as in the first passage. In **formal** Hebrew, however, possession is often expressed by adding a *possessive ending* to a noun, for example:

	formal		*informal*	
my (girl) friends	חֲבֵרוֹתַיי	=	הַחֲבֵרוֹת שלי	⤝
her son	בְּנָהּ	=	הַבֵּן שלה	

---

1 The pronunciation חֲבֵרוֹתַיי (*cha-ve-ro-TAI*) is found in grammar books. The pronunciation *chav-ro-TAI* (חַבְרוֹתַיי) is more commonly used in today's Hebrew.

Although this division into informal and formal possessive forms is generally true, there are some nouns that take a possessive ending **even** in informal Hebrew. This is especially true in words that denote family relations, as in:

בעלי	אשתי	אחותי	אחי	◄
my husband	my wife	my sister	my brother	

For a list of additional expressions that contain nouns with possessive endings and are used in **informal** as well as formal Hebrew, see below "When do we use possessive endings?" (p. 75).[2]

Note: Generally speaking, we do not add possessive endings onto foreign words. Instead, we use שלי, שלך..., for example:

הגיטרה שלך	האוניברסיטה שלכן	הפסיכולוג שלי	◄
your (*m.*) guitar	your (*f.pl.*) university	my psychologist	

• *Singular nouns with possessive endings* (אֲחוֹתִי, בִּנְךָ)

Read the following sentence:

◄ מיקי אמר לי שדודו גר קרוב לאחותי.   Mickey told me that his uncle lives near my sister.

The words highlighted in the sentence above are both **singular** nouns: דוד (uncle) and אחות (sister).

Let's see what the word דוד looks like when possessive endings are added:

my (*m./f.*) uncle	*do-DEE*	דוֹדִי =	הדוד שֶׁלִי ◄
your (*m.s.*) uncle	*dod-CHA*	דוֹדְךָ =	שֶׁלְךָ
your (*f.s.*) uncle	*do-DECH*	דוֹדֵךְ =	שֶׁלָךְ
his uncle	*do-DO*	דוֹדוֹ =	שֶׁלוֹ
her uncle	*do-DA*[3]	דוֹדָהּ =	שֶׁלָהּ
our (*m./f.*) uncle	*do-DE-noo*	דוֹדֵנוּ =	שֶׁלָנוּ
your (*m.pl.*) uncle	*dod-CHEM*	דוֹדְכֶם =	שֶׁלָכֶם
your (*f.pl.*) uncle	*dod-CHEN*	דוֹדְכֶן =	שֶׁלָכֶן
their (*m.*) uncle	*do-DAM*	דוֹדָם =	שֶׁלָהֶם
their (*f.*) uncle	*do-DAN*	דוֹדָן =	שֶׁלָהֶן

---

2 Nouns with possessive endings are also found – often in formal Hebrew and sometimes in informal Hebrew – as part of a double-possessive structure (called סְמִיכוּת כְּפוּלָה), as in: אשתו של דניאל. See the chapter "Double Possessives," pp. 200-203.

3 The dot (מַפִּיק *mapeek*) in the final ה' indicates that the ה' is to be pronounced as *h*, but speakers of Modern Hebrew do not pronounce it (i.e., the ה' is silent).

Do these endings look familiar to you? The endings on דוד are exactly the same as those on the preposition בשביל. You can use your knowledge of the forms of בשביל in order to remember the forms of דוד:

◄ בשבילִי – דוֹדִי,   בשבילְךָ – דוֹדְךָ,   בשבילֵךְ – דוֹדֵךְ,   בשבילוֹ – דוֹדוֹ,   בשבילָהּ – דוֹדָהּ,
בשבילֵנוּ – דוֹדֵנוּ,   בשבילְכֶם – דוֹדְכֶם,   בשבילְכֶן – דוֹדְכֶן,   בשבילָם – דוֹדָם,   בשבילָן – דוֹדָן

Be careful! While the possessive endings are the **same** as those on בשביל, they are somewhat **different** from the endings on של. Among the differences are the pronunciation of דוֹדֵךְ (do-DECH) and דוֹדֵנוּ (do-DE-noo) – as opposed to שלָךְ (she-LACH) and שלָנו (she-LA-noo), and the short endings on דוֹדָם (do-DAM) and דוֹדָן (do-DAN) – as opposed to שלָהֶם (she-la-HEM) and שלָהֶן (she-la-HEN).

The endings seen above on דוד can be attached to most singular nouns, **masculine or feminine**, as long as the feminine noun **does not** end in ה- (-ah) (see the next section for the forms of these nouns), for example:

masculine singular:	(my turn, your turn…)	◄ התוֹר שלי/שלך = תוֹרִי, תוֹרְךָ ...
	(my friend, your friend…)	החָבֵר שלי/שלך = חֲבֵרִי, חֲבֵרְךָ ...
feminine singular:	(my sister, your sister…)	האָחוֹת שלי/שלך = אֲחוֹתִי, אֲחוֹתְךָ ...
	(my childhood, your childhood…)	היַלדוּת שלי/שלך = יַלדוּתִי, יַלדוּתְךָ ...

Feminine nouns ending in ה-

Read the following sentence:

◄ שמואל אמר שדודתו כבר לא גרה בדירתה.

Shmuel said that his aunt no longer lives in her apartment.

The highlighted words in this sentence are a combination of the following:

◄ דוֹדָתוֹ = **הדוֹדָה** שלו
דִירָתָהּ = **הדִירָה** שלה

Q: What changes in the words דוֹדָה and דִירָה when the possessive endings (ו- and ה-) are added?

A: Instead of the feminine ending ה- (-ah), we get ת- (-at). The possessive ending is then added onto the 'ת:

◄ דוֹדָה ⟸ דוֹדָת- + וֹ ⟸ דוֹדָתוֹ
do-da-TO

Where else does this change from a final הָ- (*-ah*) to תַ- (*-at*) take place in Hebrew? We encounter it also in *smeechoot*, when the feminine ending הָ- becomes תַ- (*-at*), as in:

⯇ עוּגָה + שׁוֹקוֹלָד ⟸ עוּגַת שׁוֹקוֹלָד[4]

In order to add either a noun (as in *smeechoot*) or a possessive ending onto a word that ends in הָ-, the 'ה must become 'ת.

Here is an example of the possessive endings added to a noun that ends in the feminine הָ-. Note that sometimes the 'ת (*t*) is pronounced together with the ending and sometimes it is part of the preceding syllable:

my (*m./f.*) aunt	*do-da-TEE*	דּוֹדָתִי =	⯇ הַדּוֹדָה שֶׁלִּי
your (*m.s.*) aunt	*do-dat-CHA*	דּוֹדָתְךָ =	שֶׁלְּךָ
your (*f.s.*) aunt	*do-da-TECH*	דּוֹדָתֵךְ =	שֶׁלָּךְ
his aunt	*do-da-TO*	דּוֹדָתוֹ =	שֶׁלּוֹ
her aunt	*do-da-TA*	דּוֹדָתָהּ =	שֶׁלָּהּ
our (*m./f.*) aunt	*do-da-TE-noo*	דּוֹדָתֵנוּ =	שֶׁלָּנוּ
your (*m.pl.*) aunt	*do-dat-CHEM*	דּוֹדַתְכֶם =	שֶׁלָּכֶם
your (*f.pl.*) aunt	*do-dat-CHEN*	דּוֹדַתְכֶן =	שֶׁלָּכֶן
their (*m.*) aunt	*do-da-TAM*	דּוֹדָתָם =	שֶׁלָּהֶם
their (*f.*) aunt	*do-da-TAN*	דּוֹדָתָן =	שֶׁלָּהֶן

Want to see if you've understood?
Write the noun with an ending and pronounce the word.

7. הַיָּד שֶׁלִּי _____   4. הַסּוֹד שֶׁלָּהּ _____   1. הַקּוֹל שֶׁלּוֹ _____

8. הַדִּירָה שֶׁלָּהֶן _____   5. הַהַסְכָּמָה שֶׁלָּכֶן _____   2. הָאָחוֹת שֶׁלָּכֶם _____

9. הָרֹאשׁ שֶׁלָּךְ _____   6. הַכִּיתָה שֶׁלָּנוּ _____   3. הַהַרְגָּשָׁה שֶׁלָּךְ _____

Answers:

1. קוֹלוֹ (*ko-LO*)   2. אֲחוֹתְכֶם (*'a-chot-CHEM*)   3. הַרְגָּשָׁתְךָ (*har-ga-shat-CHA*)   4. סוֹדָהּ (*so-DA*)
5. הַסְכָּמַתְכֶן (*has-ka-mat-CHEN*)   6. כִּיתָתֵנוּ (*kee-ta-TE-noo*)   7. יָדִי (*ya-DEE*)   8. דִּירָתָן (*dee-ra-TAN*)
9. רֹאשֵׁךְ (*ro-SHECH*)

---

4   See the chapter "*Smeechoot*," p. 176 and also the chapter "The Gender of Nouns," p. 22, note 7. The הָ- ending on feminine words like עוּגָה is actually a later development in the history of Hebrew. At an earlier stage of the language, the feminine ending was תַ- (*-at*). Thus, the change to -ת in *smeechoot* and with possessive endings is actually a **return** to the **original** form.

Changes in the base form of the noun

Sometimes the form of the noun changes when possessive endings are added.[5] Being **aware** of these changes (without actually memorizing them all) will make it easier for you to learn how to pronounce nouns with possessive endings. Here are some of the major changes (explanations follow):

1. *Changes in* one *vowel only*

		example 2			*example 1*	
	changed	*regular*		*changed*	*regular*	
.1	מְקוֹמִי ⇐	מָקוֹם		שְׁכֵנִי ⇐	שָׁכֵן	
		place			neighbor	
	me-ko-MEE	ma-KOM		shche-NEE	sha-CHEN	
.2	נִסְיוֹנִי ⇐	נִסָּיוֹן		זִכְרוֹנִי[6] ⇐	זִכָּרוֹן	
		experience			memory	
	nees-yo-NEE	nee-sa-YON		zeech-ro-NEE	zee-ka-RON	
.3	חֲבֶרְתִּי ⇐	חֲבֵרָה		אִשְׁתִּי ⇐	אִשָּׁה	
		friend (*f.*)			wife	
	cha-ver-TEE	cha-ve-RA		'eesh-TEE	'ee-SHA	
.4	שְׂעָרִי ⇐	שֵׂעָר		בְּנִי[7] ⇐	בֵּן	
		hair			son	
	se-'a-REE	se-'AR		BNEE	BEN	
.5	לִבִּי ⇐	לֵב		אִמִּי[8] ⇐	אֵם	
		heart			mother	
	lee-BEE	LEV		'ee-MEE	'EM	
.6	צִדִּי ⇐	צַד		בִּתִּי ⇐	בַּת	
		side			daughter	
	tsee-DEE	TSAD		bee-TEE	BAT	

---

5 In some cases, such as יֶלֶד ⇐ יַלְדִּי, יַלְדְּךָ..., a totally different form is used (here: יַלְד) as the base onto which the endings are added. See the chapter "Segolate Nouns," pp. 97-101.

6 In this and other words with this pattern, there is a *dagesh* in the regular form (here: זִכָּרוֹן *zee-ka-RON*). It is lost in the form with the endings (here: זִכְרוֹנִי *zeech-ro-NEE*).

7 Not every form of this word has a *shva*. Here are all the forms:

> בְּנִי, בִּנְךָ, בְּנֵךְ, בְּנוֹ, בְּנָהּ, בְּנֵנוּ, בִּנְכֶם, בִּנְכֶן, בְּנָם, בְּנָן

8 According to the spelling guidelines of the Hebrew Language Academy, because there is no י in the form of these nouns when they have **no endings**, they are to be written **without** a י when they take endings even though they have an *ee* vowel.

The words in lines 1 and 2 have an *ah* sound two syllables before the end of the word: שָׁכֵן, מָקוֹם, זִיכָּרוֹן, נִיסָיוֹן.

Q: What happens to the *ah* vowel when endings are added to these words?

A: It changes (reduces) to a *shva*:[9] שְׁכֵנִי, מְקוֹמִי, זִיכְרוֹנִי, נִיסְיוֹנִי. This is a **very** common change. As you can see, in today's Hebrew sometimes the *shva* is pronounced *eh*, as in מְקוֹמִי (me-ko-MEE), and sometimes it has no sound, as in the other words.

In line 3 we see another case of vowel reduction. As you may recall, we learned above that when we add possessive endings to feminine singular nouns ending in ה-ָ, the *ah* sound is **usually** preserved when ת׳ and an ending are added: דוֹדָתִי (do-da-TEE), דִירָתִי (dee-ra-TEE), יַלְדָתִי (yal-da-TEE). However, there are cases when the *ah* vowel reduces to *shva*, as in the words in line 3: אִשְׁתִי ⇐ אִישָׁה and חֲבֶרְתִי ⇐ חֲבֵרָה.

In most cases in Hebrew, as in lines 1-3, it is an *ah* vowel that changes to *shva*. In line 4, however, we see examples of an *eh* vowel that changes.

Now look at lines 5 and 6.

Q: What is the **new** vowel in the forms with possessive endings?

A: In all cases, the new vowel is *ee*: אִמִי ('ee-MEE), לִבִּי (lee-BEE), בִּתִי (bee-TEE) and צִדִי (tsee-DEE).

2. *Changes in more than one vowel (segolate nouns)*

In the following examples the *base form* to which possessive endings are added is **very different** from the regular form of the noun:

	example 2			example 1		
	changed		*regular*	*changed*		*regular*	
	אַרְצִי	⇐	אֶרֶץ	דַרְכִּי	⇐	דֶרֶך	.1
			land			way	
	'ar-TSEE		'E-rets	dar-KEE		DE-rech	
	עִסְקִי	⇐	עֵסֶק	סִפְרִי	⇐	סֵפֶר	.2
			business			book	
	'ees-KEE		'E-sek	seef-REE		SE-fer	

---

9   See the chapter "Reduction of Vowels and the *Shva*," pp. 640-644.

example 2		example 1		
changed	*regular*	*changed*	*regular*	.3
עֵינִי ⇐	עַיִן	בֵּיתִי ⇐	בַּיִת	
	eye		house	
'ei-NEE	*'A-yeen*	*bei-TEE*	*BA-yeet*	

These nouns belong to a special group of nouns called *segolates*. As you can see, the **regular** form of each of these words has **three letters** and **two syllables**, the **first** of which is always stressed. The forms that these and other segolate nouns take when possessive endings are added are presented and fully explained in the chapter "Segolate Nouns" (pp. 97-101).

Did you know?
The word דֵּעָה *with endings*

When endings are added to the word דֵּעָה (opinion), the form דַּעַת (*DA-'at*) is used as the *base form*. Thus, we say:

What is your opinion?	מה דַּעְתְּךָ? מה דַּעְתֵּךְ? ◄
In my opinion...	לְדַעְתִּי... / לְפִי דַעְתִּי...

3. Singular nouns with י (ee) before the ending

Here are the forms of the words אָח (brother) and אָב (father) when possessive endings are added:

<table>
<tr><td colspan="3">אב</td><td colspan="3">אח</td></tr>
<tr><td>my (m./f.) father</td><td>'a-VEE</td><td>אָבִי</td><td>my (m./f.) brother</td><td>'a-CHEE</td><td>אָחִי</td></tr>
<tr><td>your (m.s.) father</td><td>'a-VEE-cha</td><td>אָבִיךָ</td><td>your (m.s.) brother</td><td>'a-CHEE-cha</td><td>אָחִיךָ</td></tr>
<tr><td>your (f.s.) father</td><td>'a-VEECH</td><td>אָבִיךְ</td><td>your (f.s.) brother</td><td>'a-CHEECH</td><td>אָחִיךְ</td></tr>
<tr><td>his father</td><td>'a-VEEV</td><td>אָבִיו</td><td>his brother</td><td>'a-CHEEV</td><td>אָחִיו</td></tr>
<tr><td>her father</td><td>'a-VEE-ha</td><td>אָבִיהָ</td><td>her brother</td><td>'a-CHEE-ha</td><td>אָחִיהָ</td></tr>
<tr><td>our (m./f.) father</td><td>'a-VEE-noo</td><td>אָבִינוּ</td><td>our (m./f.) brother</td><td>'a-CHEE-noo</td><td>אָחִינוּ</td></tr>
<tr><td>your (m.pl.) father</td><td>'a-vee-CHEM</td><td>אֲבִיכֶם</td><td>your (m.pl.) brother</td><td>'a-chee-CHEM[10]</td><td>אֲחִיכֶם</td></tr>
<tr><td>your (f.pl.) father</td><td>'a- vee-CHEN</td><td>אֲבִיכֶן</td><td>your (f.pl.) brother</td><td>'a- chee-CHEN</td><td>אֲחִיכֶן</td></tr>
<tr><td>their (m.) father</td><td>'a-vee-HEM</td><td>אֲבִיהֶם</td><td>their (m.) brother</td><td>'a-chee-HEM</td><td>אֲחִיהֶם</td></tr>
<tr><td>their (f.) father</td><td>'a-vee-HEN</td><td>אֲבִיהֶן</td><td>their (f.) brother</td><td>'a-chee-HEN</td><td>אֲחִיהֶן</td></tr>
</table>

---

10 In the chart above, we have indicated the pronunciation found in grammar books and used by many speakers. Many other speakers pronounce these words *'a-CHEE-chem*, *'a-CHEE-chen*, *'a-CHEE-hem*, *'a-CHEE-hen*, with the stress on the next to the last syllable.

Notice that a יִ (*ee*) appears in all these forms.[11]

Q: What ending is added to these words in the third person plural ("their") forms?

A: The two-letter ending הֶם-/הֶן-. This is **different** from the one-letter endings ־ם/ן- normally added to singular nouns (דּוֹדָם / דּוֹדָן, דּוֹדָתָם / דּוֹדָתָן).

The word פֶּה (mouth) also has a יִ in the form onto which possessive endings are added:

◄ פֶּה ⇐ פִּי, פִּיךָ, פִּיךְ...[12]

Want to see if you've understood?
Write the noun with an ending and pronounce the word.

.4 הָאָח שֶׁלָכֶם = _____   .1 הַבַּת שֶׁלוֹ = _____

.5 הַפֶּה שֶׁלְךָ = _____   .2 אִימָא (הָאֵם) שֶׁלָהּ = _____

.3 אַבָּא (הָאָב) שֶׁלָנוּ = _____

Answers:

.1 בִּתוֹ (*bee-TO*)   .2 אִמָּהּ (*ee-MA*)   .3 אָבִינוּ (*'a-VEE-noo*)
.4 אֲחִיכֶם (*'a-chee-CHEM* or colloquial: *'a-CHEE-chem*)   .5 פִּיךָ (*PEE-cha*)

For exercises on segolate nouns with possessive endings, see the chapter "Segolate Nouns" (p. 102).

• *Plural nouns with possessive endings* (דּוֹדַיו, דּוֹדוֹתֶיהָ)

In the section above, we saw how possessive endings are added to **singular** nouns. Now let's see what happens when the noun to which the ending is added is **plural**.

---

11 This is actually the form used when these words are in *smeechoot*: אֲבִי יוֹסֵף (the father of Yosef), אֲחִי יוֹסֵף (the brother of Yosef). Note: Sometimes these words – particularly the word אב – appear in *smeechoot* without the יִ: אַב-הַבַּיִת (head custodian), אַב-טִיפּוּס (archetype).

12 The form פִּי is used in *smeechoot*: פִּי הבאר (the mouth of the well). The words לְפִי and עַל פִּי (both of which mean "according to") contain this word. When endings are added to these words, the forms are the same as those listed above, for example: לְפִיו (according to him), לְפִיהֶם (according to them) and so on.

Plural nouns ending in ‎־ים

Read the following sentence:

‎< המורה ביקש מתלמידיו לקרוא את סיפוריהם בקול.

The teacher asked his students to read their stories out loud.

These are the words that appear here with possessive endings:

‎< תַּלְמִידָיו = הַתַּלְמִידִים שלו

‎סִיפּוּרֵיהֶם = הַסִיפּוּרִים שלהם

Q: What happens to the words ‎תַּלְמִידִים and ‎סִיפּוּרִים when the possessive ending is added?

A: The final ‎ם- (of the plural ending) drops off and the possessive endings are added.

tal-mee-DAV	תַּלְמִידָיו	⇐	תלמידי + ו	⇐	תלמידם	‎<
see-poo-rei-HEM [13]	סִיפּוּרֵיהֶם	⇐	סיפורי + הם	⇐	סיפורם	

As you can see, the plural ‎ י **remains** in all these forms. This is the sign that the noun is **plural**.

Here are all the forms of the plural ‎דוֹדִים with possessive endings:[14]

my (*m./f.*) uncles	*do-DAI*	דוֹדַי	=	‎< הדוֹדים שֶׁלִי
your (*m.*) uncles	*do-DE-cha*	דוֹדֶיךָ	=	שֶׁלְךָ
your (*f.*) uncles	*do-DA-yeech*	דוֹדַיִךְ	=	שֶׁלָךְ
his uncles	*do-DAV*	דוֹדָיו	=	שֶׁלוֹ
her uncles	*do-DE-ha*	דוֹדֶיהָ	=	שֶׁלָה
our (*m./f.*) uncles	*do-DEI-noo* [15]	דוֹדֵינוּ	=	שֶׁלָנוּ
your (*m.pl.*) uncles	*do-dei-CHEM* [16]	דוֹדֵיכֶם	=	שֶׁלָכֶם
your (*f.pl.*) uncles	*do-dei-CHEN*	דוֹדֵיכֶן	=	שֶׁלָכֶן
their (*m.*) uncles	*do-dei-HEM*	דוֹדֵיהֶם	=	שֶׁלָהֶם
their (*f.*) uncles	*do-dei-HEN*	דוֹדֵיהֶן	=	שֶׁלָהֶן

---

13 Some speakers pronounce the vowel ‎ֵם as *eh* and not *ei*, thus: *see-poo-re-HEM*.

14 The spelling of the forms in the chart above is the recommended spelling of these forms when vowel signs are **not** used. We have added vowel signs to make the pronunciation clear.

15 Some speakers pronounce the plural ‎דוֹדֵינוּ and the singular ‎דוֹדֵנוּ the same: *do-DE-noo*.

16 See note 13.

Do these endings sound familiar to you? They are exactly the same as the endings on the preposition עַל (and others like it):[17]

➤ עָלַי – דוֹדַי,   עָלֶיךָ – דוֹדֶיךָ,   עָלַיִךְ – דוֹדַיִךְ,   עָלָיו – דוֹדָיו,   עָלֶיהָ – דוֹדֶיהָ,

עָלֵינוּ – דוֹדֵינוּ,   עֲלֵיכֶם – דוֹדֵיכֶם,   עֲלֵיכֶן – דוֹדֵיכֶן,   עֲלֵיהֶם – דוֹדֵיהֶם,   עֲלֵיהֶן – דוֹדֵיהֶן

These endings are added to **almost** all nouns ending in יִם-, whether they are **masculine or feminine**.[18] Here are examples of possessive endings on feminine nouns that end in יִם-:

➤ אֲבָנִים (f.) – אֲבָנֶיהָ   her / its stones

דְּרָכִים (f.) – דְּרָכֵינוּ   our ways

Now let's compare singular nouns with endings to plural nouns with endings:

plural (uncles דוֹדִים)		*singular* (uncle דוֹד)			
do-DAI	דוֹדַי	*do-DEE*	דוֹדִי	=	שֶׁלִּי ___ ה ➤
do-DE-cha	דוֹדֶיךָ	*dod-CHA*	דוֹדְךָ	=	שֶׁלְּךָ
do-DA-yeech	דוֹדַיִךְ	*do-DECH*	דוֹדֵךְ	=	שֶׁלָּךְ
do-DAV	דוֹדָיו	*do-DO*	דוֹדוֹ	=	שֶׁלּוֹ
do-DE-ha	דוֹדֶיהָ	*do-DA*	דוֹדָהּ	=	שֶׁלָּהּ
do-DEI-noo	דוֹדֵינוּ	*do-DE-noo*	דוֹדֵנוּ	=	שֶׁלָּנוּ
do-dei-CHEM	דוֹדֵיכֶם	*dod-CHEM*	דוֹדְכֶם	=	שֶׁלָּכֶם
do-dei-CHEN	דוֹדֵיכֶן	*dod-CHEN*	דוֹדְכֶן	=	שֶׁלָּכֶן
do-dei-HEM	דוֹדֵיהֶם	*do-DAM*	דוֹדָם	=	שֶׁלָּהֶם
do-dei-HEN	דוֹדֵיהֶן	*do-DAN*	דוֹדָן	=	שֶׁלָּהֶן

Q: What is the most striking difference between the two columns?

A: In the plural nouns, a י appears in every form before the ending, whereas the singular nouns have no such י. Most of the forms in the plural column have one more syllable than those in the singular column. The extra syllable is the one that contains the י.

Take special note of the שֶׁלָּנוּ forms in both columns: דוֹדֵנוּ/דוֹדֵינוּ. Both of these forms have three syllables and are even pronounced the same by some speakers. In writing, the only difference between these two forms is that the plural has a י. This is how we know that its equivalent is הדודים שלנו, rather than הדוד שלנו.

---

17 See the chapter "Adding Endings to Prepositions," pp. 244-245.

18 See exceptions such as שָׁנִים and מִילִים below, p. 73.

Q: Besides the י, are there additional differences between how the singular and plural forms are **written**?

A: There are two more differences:

1. The שֶׁלָךְ (*your f.s.*) form in the *plural* column (דּוֹדַיִךְ *do-DA-yeech* – sounds like בַּיִת *BA-yeet*) has an additional י so that we write "יי" in this form. In this way we distinguish it from דּוֹדֶיךָ (*do-DE-cha*) = הדודים שֶׁלָךְ (*your m.s.* uncles).

	plural			*singular*		
your (*m.s.*) uncles	דּוֹדֶיךָ		your (*m.s.*) uncle	דּוֹדְךָ	◄
your (*f.s.*) uncles	דּוֹדַיִךְ		your (*f.s.*) uncle	דּוֹדֵךְ	

2. The שֶׁלָהֶם, שֶׁלָהֶן (*their*) forms in the *plural* column have long endings יהֶם -ֶ (*-ei-HEM*) ֵיהֶן (*-ei-HEN*), while the forms in the *singular* column end with the shorter endings: ם-ָ (*-AM*) and ן-ָ (*-AN*):

	plural			*singular*		
their (*m.pl.*) uncles	דּוֹדֵיהֶם		their (*m.pl.*) uncle	דּוֹדָם	◄
their (*f.pl.*) uncles	דּוֹדֵיהֶן		their (*f.pl.*) uncle	דּוֹדָן	

Be careful! As we saw above, there are several singular words that have a י before their ending. They should not be confused with plural noun forms. In the case of the words אָח/אַחִים: in written Hebrew, only the **context** tells us if the word is singular or plural and, hence, how it is to be pronounced, for example:

◄ א. אלעד ועידן אמרו: "אָחִינוּ **הגדול לומד** באוניברסיטה". (*singular:* '*a-CHEE-noo*)
ב. איילת ועדי אמרו: "אַחֵינוּ **הגדולים נסעו** לדרום אמריקה". (*plural:* '*a-CHEI-noo*) [19]

Plural nouns ending in ־ַיִם *(-A-yeem)*

Nouns ending in ־ַיִם look **the same** as nouns ending in ־ִים when possessive endings are added, for example:

◄ עֵינַיִם/עֵינֵי ⇐ עֵינֵי + ךָ ⇐ עֵינֶיךָ ('*ei-NE-cha*)
eyes   your (*m.s.*) eyes

עֵינֵי + ו ⇐ עֵינָיו ('*ei-NAV*)
his eyes

---

19   The forms of אַחִים are: אַחַי, אַחֶיךָ, אַחַיִיךְ, אָחִיו, אַחֶיהָ, אַחֵינוּ, אֲחֵיכֶם, אֲחֵיהֶם, אֲחֵיכֶן, אֲחֵיהֶן. Since the plural of אָב is אָבוֹת and the plural of פֶּה is פִּיוֹת, their singular and plural forms do not look the same.

Notice that the last **two** letters – יִם- – drop off of עֵינַיִם, leaving only one י. Thus, the end of עֵינֶיךָ looks and sounds like דּוֹדֶיךָ, and עֵינָיו looks and sounds like דּוֹדָיו.

Want to see if you've understood?
Write the noun with an ending and pronounce the word.

Example: אוֹזְנֶיךָ = הָאוֹזְנַיִם שֶׁלְּךָ

1. הַסְּפָרִים שֶׁלָּךְ = _____   4. הַיָּדַיִם שֶׁלָּהּ = _____

2. הַהוֹרִים שֶׁלָּכֶם = _____   5. הַפָּנִים שֶׁלָּנוּ = _____

3. הַבָּנִים שֶׁלּוֹ = _____   6. הַחֲבֵרִים שֶׁלִּי = _____

Answers:

1. סְפָרַיִךְ (sfa-RA-yeech)   2. הוֹרֵיכֶם (ho-rei-CHEM)   3. בָּנָיו (ba-NAV)   4. יָדֶיהָ (ya-DE-ha)
5. פָּנֵינוּ (pa-NEI-noo)   6. חֲבֵרַיי (cha-ve-RAI)

Possessives on plural words ending in תוֹ-

Read the following sentence:

◄ הַמּוֹרָה שָׁאֲלָה אֶת תַּלְמִידוֹתֶיהָ מָהֶן תּוֹכְנִיּוֹתֵיהֶן לְחֻפְשָׁה.

The teacher asked her students what their plans are for vacation.

The words תַּלְמִידוֹתֶיהָ and תּוֹכְנִיּוֹתֵיהֶן are plural nouns with possessive endings:

◄ תַּלְמִידוֹתֶיהָ = הַתַּלְמִידוֹת שֶׁלָּהּ
תּוֹכְנִיּוֹתֵיהֶן = הַתּוֹכְנִיּוֹת שֶׁלָּהֶן

Q: How many plural signs do you see in תלמידותיה and תוכניותיהן?

A: Two! One plural sign is the ending תוֹ- that was in the original word: תּוֹכְנִיּוֹת, תַּלְמִידוֹת. The second plural sign is the י that comes after the תוֹ- – תּוֹכְנִיּוֹתֵיהֶן, תַּלְמִידוֹתֶיהָ – which we saw above in דּוֹדֶיכֶן (=הדודים שֶׁלָּכֶן).

Note: Whenever a plural word ends in תוֹ-, a י is **always added** to it before the possessive ending is added:

◄ _____וֹת + י + י   (דודותַיי, תלמידותַיי...)
_____וֹת + י + ךְ   (דודותֶיךְ, תלמידותֶיךְ...)

Here are all the forms of the word דּוֹדוֹת (aunts):

my (*m./f.*) aunts	*do-do-TAI*	דּוֹדוֹתַיי =	הַדּוֹדוֹת שֶׁלִּי ◄
your (*m.s.*) aunts	*do-do-TE-cha*	דּוֹדוֹתֶיךָ =	שֶׁלְּךָ
your (*f.s.*) aunts	*do-do-TA-yeech*	דּוֹדוֹתַיִךְ =	שֶׁלָּךְ
his aunts	*do-do-TAV*	דּוֹדוֹתָיו =	שֶׁלּוֹ
her aunts	*do-do-TE-ha*	דּוֹדוֹתֶיהָ =	שֶׁלָּהּ
our (*m./f.*) aunts	*do-do-TEI-noo*	דּוֹדוֹתֵינוּ =	שֶׁלָּנוּ
your (*m.pl.*) aunts	*do-do-tei-CHEM*	דּוֹדוֹתֵיכֶם =	שֶׁלָּכֶם
your (*f.pl.*) aunts	*do-do-tei-CHEN*	דּוֹדוֹתֵיכֶן =	שֶׁלָּכֶן
their (*m.*) aunts	*do-do-tei-HEM*	דּוֹדוֹתֵיהֶם =	שֶׁלָּהֶם
their (*f.*) aunts	*do-do-tei-HEN*	דּוֹדוֹתֵיהֶן =	שֶׁלָּהֶן

These are the forms of all plural words ending in **-וֹת**, whether they are **feminine** or **masculine.** Here are examples of some masculine nouns:

זִיכְרוֹנוֹתַיי, זִיכְרוֹנוֹתֶיךָ... ⇐ זִיכְרוֹנוֹת (*m.*) ◄
memories

אֲבוֹתַיי, אֲבוֹתֶיךָ... ⇐ אָבוֹת (*m.*)
fathers, forefathers

Want to see if you've understood?
Write the noun with an ending and pronounce the word.

Example: _____דֵּעוֹתֶיךָ_____ = הַדֵּעוֹת שֶׁלְּךָ

4. הַתּוֹכְנִיּוֹת שֶׁלָּהֶם = _____   1. הַשִּׁיטוֹת שֶׁלּוֹ = _____

5. הַזִּיכְרוֹנוֹת שֶׁלּוֹ = _____   2. הַנִּיסְיוֹנוֹת שֶׁלִּי = _____

6. הַתְּשׁוּבוֹת שֶׁלָּכֶן = _____   3. הָעֲבוֹדוֹת שֶׁלָּנוּ = _____

Answers:

1. שִׁיטוֹתָיו (*shee-to-TAV*) 2. נִיסְיוֹנוֹתַיי (*nees-yo-no-TAY*) 3. עֲבוֹדוֹתֵינוּ ('*a-vo-do-TEI-noo*)
4. תּוֹכְנִיּוֹתֵיהֶם (*toch-nee-yo-tei-HEM*) 5. זִיכְרוֹנוֹתָיו (*zeech-ro-no-TAV*)
6. תְּשׁוּבוֹתֵיכֶן (*tshoo-vo-tei-CHEN*)

Changes in the base form of plural nouns

As we saw above with singular nouns, sometimes the base form of the noun changes when possessive endings are added (for example: מְקוֹמִי, מְקוֹמְךָ... ⇐ מָקוֹם). Similarly, the base forms of plural nouns sometimes undergo changes when the possessive endings are added. The most common changes take place in the **vowels** of the base forms, for example:

בְּנוֹתֶיךָ...	בְּנוֹתַיי	⇐	בָּנוֹת ‹
bno-TE-cha	bno-TAI		ba-NOT
			daughters, girls
יַלְדוֹתֶיךָ...	יַלְדוֹתַיי	⇐	יְלָדוֹת
yal-do-TE-cha	yal-do-TAI		ye-la-DOT
			girls

These changes are described in more detail in "Did you know?" below.

In a small number of words, a major change in form takes place when possessive endings are added. For example, in the words מילים and שנים, the plural ending itself changes from ים- to ות-:[20]

מִילוֹתַיי, מִילוֹתֶיךָ...	⇐	מִילִים ‹
		words
שְׁנוֹתַיי, שְׁנוֹתֶיךָ...	⇐	שָׁנִים
		years

Did you know?

The following are the most common changes in the vowels of the base form of plural nouns. Simply being **aware** of these changes will make it easier for you to learn how to pronounce nouns with possessive endings.

1. *Change to shva at the beginning of the word*

An initial *kamats* (◌ָ) *ah* or *tsere* (◌ֵ) *eh* often change to *shva*,[21] as in:

בְּנוֹתֶיךָ...	בְּנוֹתַיי,	⇐	בָּנוֹת ‹
bno-TE-cha	bno-TAI		ba-NOT
			daughters, girls
שְׁמוֹתֶיךָ...	שְׁמוֹתַיי,	⇐	שֵׁמוֹת
shmo-TE-cha	shmo-TAI		she-MOT
			names

---

20 These words have the ות- ending in *smeechoot*, too. In addition, the word נָשִׁים has two forms in *smeechoot*: נְשׁוֹת-, נְשֵׁי-. When endings are added, it can be either נְשׁוֹתֵיהֶם or נְשֵׁיהֶם.

21 See the chapter "Reduction of Vowels and the *Shva*," pp. 640-645.

In nouns ending in ‎ות-, this reduction takes place in all forms of the noun. When the ending is ‎-ִים or ‎-ַיִם, the change to a *shva* takes place only in the שְׁלָכֶם, שְׁלָכֶן, שְׁלָהֶן, שְׁלָהֶם forms, as in:

	-כֶם, -כֶן, -הֶם, -הֶן		-יי, -יך...-ינו			*plural form*	
	יְמֵיכֶם, ־יכֶן, ־יהֶם, ־יהֶן ye-mei-HEN/-HEM/-CHEN/-CHEM		יָמֶיךָ ... ya-ME-cha	יָמַיי, ya-MAI	⇐	יָמִים ya-MEEM days	◄
	יְדֵיכֶם, ־יכֶן, ־יהֶם, ־יהֶן ye-dei-HEN/-HEM/-CHEN/-CHEM		יָדֶיךָ ... ya-DE-cha	יָדַיי, ya-DAI	⇐	יָדַיִים ya-DA-yeem hands	◄

2. Change to *shva* in places other than the beginning of the word

The change to *shva* can also occur in places **other than** the beginning of the word, as in:

	אֶצְבְּעוֹתֵיכֶם, ־יכֶן, ־יהֶם, ־יהֶן 'ets-be-'o-tei-CHEM...	אֶצְבְּעוֹתֶיךָ ... 'ets-be-'o-TE-cha	אֶצְבְּעוֹתַיי, 'ets-be-'o-TAI	⇐	אֶצְבָּעוֹת 'ets-ba-'OT fingers	◄

With an ‎ות- ending, this change takes place in all the forms, as in אֶצְבְּעוֹת. In nouns ending in ‎-ִים and ‎-ַיִם, only in the last four forms:

	-כֶם, -כֶן, -הֶם, -הֶן		-יי, -יך...ינו			*plural form*	
	מִכְתְּבֵיכֶם, ־יכֶן, ־יהֶם, ־יהֶן meech-te-vei-CHEM...		מִכְתָּבֶיךָ ... meech-ta-VE-cha	מִכְתָּבַיי, meech-ta-VAI	⇐	מִכְתָּבִים meech-ta-VEEM letters	◄
	מִכְנְסֵיכֶם, ־יכֶן, ־יהֶם, ־יהֶן meech-ne-sei-CHEM...		מִכְנָסֶיךָ ... meech-na-SE-cha	מִכְנָסַיי, meech-na-SAI	⇐	מִכְנָסַיִים meech-na-SA-yeem pants	◄

3. Change of two vowels

Often there is a change in **two** vowels in the base form. This is especially common in nouns of the מְסָמִים and מְסָמוֹת pattern, as in the words דְּבָרִים, דְּרָכִים and יְלָדוֹת, בְּרָכוֹת:

base form + -כֶם, -כֶן, -יהֶם, -יהֶן	base form + -יי, -יךָ...-ינו	plural form

With the וֹת- ending – in all the forms:

יַלְדוּתֵיכֶם, -ֵיכֶן, -ֵיהֶם, -ֵיהֶן	יַלְדוּתַיי, יַלְדוּתֶיךָ...	⇐ יַלְדוּת girls
בִּרְכוֹתֵיכֶם, -ֵיכֶן, -ֵיהֶם, -ֵיהֶן	בִּרְכוֹתַיי, בִּרְכוֹתֶיךָ...	⇐ בְּרָכוֹת blessings

With the ים- ending – only in the last four forms:

דִּבְרֵיכֶם, -ֵיכֶן, -ֵיהֶם, -ֵיהֶן	דְּבָרַיי, דְּבָרֶיךָ...	⇐ דְּבָרִים things
דַּרְכֵיכֶם, -ֵיכֶן, -ֵיהֶם, -ֵיהֶן	דְּרָכַיי, דְּרָכֶיךָ...	⇐ דְּרָכִים ways
סִפְרֵיכֶם, -ֵיכֶן, -ֵיהֶם, -ֵיהֶן	סְפָרַיי, סְפָרֶיךָ...	⇐ סְפָרִים books
עֶרְכֵיכֶם, -ֵיכֶן, -ֵיהֶם, -ֵיהֶן	עֲרָכַיי, עֲרָכֶיךָ...	⇐ עֲרָכִים values

When the noun is a *segolate* (as in the case of עֲרָכִים, דְּרָכִים, סְפָרִים and עֲרָכִים), other forms of the noun can help you know what vowel will appear in the first syllable.[22] In the case of other nouns, you must either look in the dictionary or hear these words pronounced correctly.

When do we use possessive endings?

In addition to words denoting family members mentioned at the beginning of the chapter (אָחִי, ...אֲחוֹתִי, בַּעְלִי, אִשְׁתִּי), possessive endings are used in **informal** (spoken) as well as formal Hebrew in expressions such as the following:

עַכְשָׁיו תּוֹרִי!	זֶה מוֹצֵא חֵן בְּעֵינַיי!	זֶה לֹא עִנְיָינְךָ!	מַה דַּעְתֵּךְ?	⇐ מַה שְׁלוֹמְךָ?
Now it's my turn!	I like this!	This is none of	What is your (f.)	How are you (m.)?
	(lit.: This finds grace /	your (m.s.) business.	opinion?	(lit.: What is
	favor in my eyes.)			your well-being?)

---

22 On segolates, see the chapter "Segolate Nouns," pp. 105-107.

Many expressions with possessive endings used in informal (as well as formal) Hebrew begin with -ל:

לְטִיפּוּלְךָ	לִידִיעָתֵךְ	לְשִׂמְחָתִי	לְצַעֲרִי	לְמַזָּלִי	לְדַעְתִּי ≼
This is	For your (f.)	I'm happy	I'm sorry to	I'm lucky	In my opinion...
for you (m.) to take	information...	to say that...	say that…	that...	
care of.					

Others begin with other prepositions (...ב-, כ-, מ-):

מִצִּדִּי	כִּרְצוֹנְךָ! / כִּרְצוֹנֵךְ!	בְּחַיֶּיךָ! / בְּחַיַּיִךְ!	בְּחַיַּי! ≼
As far as I'm concerned...	As you wish!	It can't be!	I swear!
(lit.: from my side)	(lit.: according to your desire)	(lit.: on your life)	(lit.: on my life)

There is one additional construction in which nouns with possessive endings are used in informal as well as formal Hebrew: **שרה היא אשתו של דניאל.** (Sarah is Daniel's wife). This construction is discussed in detail in the chapter "Double Possessives" (pp. 200-203).

Chapter summary

♦ The following base forms and their endings are discussed in this chapter:

הדודות של...	הדודים של...	הדודה של...	הדוד של...		≼
nouns ending	*nouns ending*	*nouns ending*			
in ‏-וֹת	*in* ‏-ים	*in* ‏-ָה			
דּוֹדוֹתַיי	דּוֹדַיי	דּוֹדָתִי	דּוֹדִי	=	שֶׁלִּי ‏ ___ ה
דּוֹדוֹתֶיךָ	דּוֹדֶיךָ	דּוֹדָתְךָ	דּוֹדְךָ	=	שֶׁלְּךָ
דּוֹדוֹתַיִךְ	דּוֹדַיִךְ	דּוֹדָתֵךְ	דּוֹדֵךְ	=	שֶׁלָּךְ
דּוֹדוֹתָיו	דּוֹדָיו	דּוֹדָתוֹ	דּוֹדוֹ	=	שֶׁלּוֹ
דּוֹדוֹתֶיהָ	דּוֹדֶיהָ	דּוֹדָתָהּ	דּוֹדָהּ	=	שֶׁלָּהּ
דּוֹדוֹתֵינוּ	דּוֹדֵינוּ	דּוֹדָתֵנוּ	דּוֹדֵנוּ	=	שֶׁלָּנוּ
דּוֹדוֹתֵיכֶם	דּוֹדֵיכֶם	דּוֹדַתְכֶם	דּוֹדְכֶם	=	שֶׁלָּכֶם
דּוֹדוֹתֵיכֶן	דּוֹדֵיכֶן	דּוֹדַתְכֶן	דּוֹדְכֶן	=	שֶׁלָּכֶן
דּוֹדוֹתֵיהֶם	דּוֹדֵיהֶם	דּוֹדָתָם	דּוֹדָם	=	שֶׁלָּהֶם
דּוֹדוֹתֵיהֶן	דּוֹדֵיהֶן	דּוֹדָתָן	דּוֹדָן	=	שֶׁלָּהֶן

♦ In addition, we have looked at the changes in various base forms when endings are added.

Want to see if you've understood this chapter?

This exercise includes both singular and plural nouns with possessive endings.
Write the equivalent using the appropriate form of שלי, שלך... :שלי, שלך.

Example: <u>הַשּׁוּלְחָן שֶׁלִי</u>   =   שולחני

8.	זיכרונותיה	= _____	1.	שולחנותיו	= _____
9.	התקדמותךָ	= _____	2.	אביךָ	= _____
10.	דבריו	= _____	3.	אבותינו	= _____
11.	ידה	= _____	4.	עירֵךְ	= _____
12.	ביתם	= _____	5.	דרככם	= _____
13.	הצעותיכן	= _____	6.	עיתונם	= _____
14.	ילדותו	= _____	7.	יומניו	= _____

Answers:

1. השולחנות שלו   2. האב שלךָ   3. האבות שלנו   4. העיר שלָךְ   5. הדרך שלכם
6. העיתון שלהם   7. היומנים שלו   8. הזיכרונות שלה   9. ההתקדמות שלךָ
10. הדברים שלו   11. היד שלה   12. הבית שלהם   13. ההצעות שלכן   14. הַיַלְדוּת שלו

5. How Are Hebrew Nouns Formed?

> ### Preview
>
> • *Combining a root and a pattern* (כ-ת-ב + מְ◻◻ָ◻ ⇐ מִכְתָּב)
>
> • *Nouns formed by adding an ending to a base* (כַּף + ־ִית ⇐ כַּפִּית)
>
> • *Joining two nouns to form a new word* (כַּדוּר + רֶגֶל ⇐ כַּדוּרֶגֶל)

• *Combining a root and a pattern*

Many Hebrew nouns are formed by combining a *root* (שׁוֹרֶשׁ) and a *pattern* (מִשְׁקָל).[1] For example, when we combine the root כ-ת-ב and the pattern מִ◻◻ָ◻, we get the word מִכְתָּב. In the chapter "Pattern" above, we discussed both how Hebrew words (nouns, adjectives, verbs) are formed in this way and why knowing word patterns is important. In this chapter, we will look in more detail at some of the more common noun patterns and their meanings.

Examples of noun patterns

Try this:

Divide the following nouns into three groups according to their pattern.

בִּטָּחוֹן[2]	מִדְרָכָה	זִיכָּרוֹן	מִגְדָּל	מִכְבָּסָה	מִסְגָּד	דִּיכָּאוֹן	מִטְבָּח	מִסְפָּרָה	◄
security, safety	sidewalk	memory	tower	laundry	mosque	depression	kitchen	barber shop	

3		2		1		
depression	דִּיכָּאוֹן	kitchen	מִטְבָּח	barber shop	מִסְפָּרָה	◄

---

1   On roots, see the chapter "Root," pp. 3-8. On patterns, see the chapter "Pattern," pp. 9-16.

2   In order to show that a *strong dagesh* is part of a pattern (as in בִּטָּחוֹן), we have written it here and elsewhere in this chapter even when it is not heard.

Here's the solution:

3		2		1	
depression	דִּיכָּאוֹן	kitchen	מִטְבָּח	barber shop	מִסְפָּרָה
memory	זִיכָּרוֹן	mosque	מִסְגָּד	laundry	מִכְבָּסָה
security, safety	בִּיטָחוֹן	tower	מִגְדָּל	sidewalk	מִדְרָכָה

Q: Do the nouns in each column share a common meaning?

A: The words in Column 1 denote **places**: מִסְפָּרָה is a place where one gets a haircut; מִכְבָּסָה is a place where one launders clothes; מִדְרָכָה is a place upon which one walks. Some more examples are: מִרְפָּאָה (clinic), מִסְעָדָה (restaurant), מִשְׁתָּלָה (plant nursery).

The pattern of the words in Column 2 is also used to denote **places**: מִטְבָּח is a kitchen; מִסְגָּד is a mosque; מִגְדָּל is a tower. To these we can add many more examples, such as: מִדְבָּר (desert), מִשְׂרָד (office) and מִקְלָט (shelter).

Note, however, that there are additional words in each of the above patterns that do **not** denote places, for example: מִשְׁפָּחָה (family) and מִסְפָּר (number).

In Column 3 we see nouns that do **not** share one meaning. Actually, quite a few nouns with the pattern □ִ□ָּ□וֹן – like דִּיכָּאוֹן (depression) above – indicate an **ailment** or **negative situation** of some kind (שִׁיגָּעוֹן madness, כִּישָּׁלוֹן failure), whereas many others have an **abstract** meaning like the other two nouns in Column 3: זִיכָּרוֹן (memory) and בִּיטָחוֹן (security, safety). There are also non-abstract words in this pattern such as עִיפָּרוֹן (pencil).

Some noun patterns – for example the *segolate nouns* (סֵפֶר book, יֶלֶד child and so on)[3] – have **no special meaning** associated with them. When this is the case, identifying their pattern helps know how to pronounce them in their various forms (plural, *smeechoot*, with possessive endings), but does not help us guess their meaning or remember it.

Fortunately patterns **do tend** to contain many words with a **common** meaning, and this can often help us guess the meaning of a word (whose root we recognize) in a given context.

More noun patterns that have specific meanings

Here are some more patterns that tend to have specific meanings.

---

3 See the chapter "Segolate Nouns," pp. 89-107.

Try this:

Divide the following nouns into 3 groups according to their pattern:

◄ מַחְשֵׁב   צָהֶבֶת   סַפָּר   זַמָּר   חַיָּיל   נַזֶּלֶת   מַזְרֵק   אַדֶּמֶת   מַסְרֵק   כַּלֶּבֶת   טַבָּח

computer   hepatitis,   barber   singer   soldier   runny   syringe   rubella   comb   rabies   chef
            jaundice   nose

3	2	1
_____	_____	_____
_____	_____	_____
_____	_____	_____
_____	_____	_____
_____	_____	_____

Here's the solution: (the order of your columns may be different)

3		2		1	
barber	סַפָּר	hepatitis, jaundice	צָהֶבֶת	computer	מַחְשֵׁב
singer	זַמָּר	runny nose	נַזֶּלֶת	syringe	מַזְרֵק
soldier	חַיָּיל	rubella	אַדֶּמֶת	comb	מַסְרֵק
chef	טַבָּח	rabies	כַּלֶּבֶת		

◄

Q: What is the meaning of each pattern?

A: Column 1 – מַ◻◻◻ – מַסְרֵק, מַזְרֵק, מַחְשֵׁב – all denote **tools**.
Column 2 – ◻ַ◻ֶ◻ֶת – כַּלֶּבֶת, אַדֶּמֶת, נַזֶּלֶת, צָהֶבֶת – all denote **illnesses**.[4]
Column 3 – ◻ַ◻ָ◻ – סַפָּר, טַבָּח, חַיָּיל, זַמָּר – all denote **people with professions** or **occupations**.

Sometimes, as in the case of the pattern in Column 2, one pattern may have **more than one** meaning. For example, in addition to **illnesses**, this pattern is used for nouns that denote **groups of objects or people**: טַיֶּסֶת (a squadron of aircraft), רַכֶּבֶת (a train of railway cars), שַׁיֶּטֶת (a flotilla of boats).

The pattern in Column 3 – ◻ַ◻ָ◻ – is particularly common. Other nouns that belong to it are צַיָּיר (painter), נַהָג (driver) and גַּנָּב (thief). Since these nouns denote people, they also have a feminine form. This form can have either the ending ת- (זַמֶּרֶת, חַיֶּלֶת, צַיֶּירֶת, נַהֶגֶת, גַּנֶּבֶת) or the ending ית- (סַפָּרִית, טַבָּחִית). In order to know which form is used, you must check the dictionary or ask a reliable Hebrew speaker.

---

4   Even though a *dagesh* is part of the pattern, there is no *dagesh* in צָהֶבֶת because 'ה does not take a *dagesh*.

More patterns denoting people with professions or occupations

In addition to the □ַ□ָ□ pattern, there are other patterns denoting a person with a **profession** or **occupation**. One of these patterns is □ְ□ָ□ָן. The feminine form of these words ends in ית-:

	קַרְיָן	צַרְכָן	שַׂחְקָן	רַקְדָן	◄
	קַרְיָינִית	צַרְכָנִית	שַׂחְקָנִית	רַקְדָנִית	
	(news) broadcaster	consumer	actor	dancer	

Another pattern for people with professions is □ֹו□. The feminine of this form almost always ends in ת-:

	שׁוֹפֵט	שׁוֹטֵר	סוֹפֵר	שׁוֹמֵר	◄
	שׁוֹפֶטֶת	שׁוֹטֶרֶת	סוֹפֶרֶת	שׁוֹמֶרֶת	
	judge	policeman, policewoman	writer	guard	

As you can see, the □ֹו□ pattern is also the pattern of present tense verbs in *beenyan pa'al* (כותב). The present tense verb patterns of other *beenyaneem* are also frequently used for people with professions, for example:

beenyan heef'eel (like מַרְגִישׁ)			*beenyan pee'el* (like מְדַבֵּר)		
מַזְכִּיר	מַלְחִין	מַדְרִיךְ	מְפַקֵּד	מְנַהֵל	◄
מַזְכִּירָה	מַלְחִינָה	מַדְרִיכָה	מְפַקֶּדֶת	מְנַהֶלֶת	
secretary	composer	guide	commander	director, principal	

Let's review

One way nouns are formed is by combining a *root* (שורש) and a *pattern* (משקל).

- In some cases, many nouns in a given pattern share a specific meaning (for example: □ַ□ָ□ for a person with a profession or occupation, such as זַמָּר, סַפָּר). However, not all nouns in a given pattern necessarily have the same general meaning.

- In some cases, a certain meaning may be conveyed by more than one pattern. For example, not only □ַ□ָ□, but also □ְ□ָ□ָן (רַקְדָן) and □ֹו□ (שׁוֹמֵר) are used to denote people with a profession or occupation.

- In addition, one pattern may have several meanings. For example, □ַ□ֶ□ת is used both for illnesses (אַדֶּמֶת) and groups of objects or people (טַיֶּיסֶת).

- Other patterns mentioned in the chapter above are:
  Places: מְ◻◻◻◻ה (מִסְעָדָה), מִ◻◻◻ (מִטְבָּח)
  Instruments and tools: מַ◻◻◻ (מַחְשֵׁב)
  Ailments or negative situations: ◻ִי◻◻וֹן (דִּיכָּאוֹן)

- Some noun patterns – like *segolate nouns* ◻◻◻ (בֶּגֶד, יֶלֶד) – have no special meaning.

Want to see if you've understood?

Each of the words below has a pattern with a specific meaning.

Match each word in Column A with a word of the same pattern in Column B.

	B			A	
computer	מַחְשֵׁב	א.	temple	מִקְדָּשׁ	1.
singer	זַמָּר	ב.	editor	עוֹרֵךְ	2.
dancer	רַקְדָן	ג.	screwdriver	מַבְרֵג	3.
runny nose	נַזֶּלֶת	ד.	plant nursery	מִשְׁתָּלָה	4.
restaurant	מִסְעָדָה	ה.	measles	חַצֶּבֶת	5.
kitchen	מִטְבָּח	ו.	manufacturer	יַצְרָן	6.
policeman	שׁוֹטֵר	ז.	correspondent	כַּתָּב	7.

Answers:

1. מִקְדָּשׁ – מִטְבָּח   2. עוֹרֵךְ – שׁוֹטֵר   3. מַבְרֵג – מַחְשֵׁב   4. מִשְׁתָּלָה – מִסְעָדָה
5. חַצֶּבֶת – נַזֶּלֶת   6. יַצְרָן – רַקְדָן   7. כַּתָּב – זַמָּר

• Nouns formed by adding an ending to a base

Another very common way nouns are formed in Hebrew is by adding an **ending** to a base.

The ending ית-

Read the following nouns, all of which end in ית-:

◄ מְכוֹנִית רוּסִית כַּפִּית אַנְגְלִית חֲלָלִית מוֹנִית פַּחִית מַשָׂאִית צָרְפָתִית מַפִּית
car   Russian   teaspoon   English   spaceship   taxi   can   truck   French   napkin

Try this:

Divide the above words into three groups according to their meaning.

3		2		1		
teaspoon	כַּפִּית	Russian	רוּסִית	car	מְכוֹנִית	◄

Here's the solution: (the order of your columns may be different)

3		2		1		
teaspoon	כַּפִּית	Russian	רוּסִית	car	מְכוֹנִית	◄
can	פַּחִית	English	אַנְגְלִית	spaceship	חֲלָלִית	
napkin	מַפִּית	French	צָרְפָתִית	taxi	מוֹנִית	
				truck	מַשָׂאִית	

Column 1 – מְכוֹנִית, מוֹנִית, מַשָׂאִית, חֲלָלִית are all words for **vehicles**.
Column 2 – צָרְפָתִית, אַנְגְלִית, רוּסִית are the names of **languages**.

And what is common to מַפִּית, פַּחִית, כַּפִּית in Column 3? In order to figure this out, you need to know the meaning of the words כַּף, פַּח and מַפָּה:
כַּף is a spoon; כַּפִּית is a **teaspoon** (i.e., a small spoon).
פַּח is a big can; פַּחִית is a **small can** (e.g., for a soft drink).
מַפָּה is a tablecloth; מַפִּית is a **napkin** (i.e., a small cloth).

Thus, when added to these words, the ending ־ית conveys the notion of **being small**. However, as we see in the other two columns, this ending is used in other cases to convey other meanings (i.e., vehicles, languages).

Sometimes when ־ית is added to a word, the sound of the base does not change, for example:

צָרְפָתִית ⇐ ־ית + צָרְפַת	חֲלָלִית ⇐ ־ית + חָלָל	פַּחִית ⇐ ־ית + פַּח	◄
French (language) France	spaceship space	small can big can	

In other cases, the base noun undergoes a significant change when the ending is added, as in:

מְכוֹנִית ⇐ ־ית + מְכוֹנָ֘ה	רוּסִית ⇐ ־ית + רוּסְ/יָ֘ה	◄
car machine	Russian Russia	

The ending וֹן-

The ending וֹן-, when added to a noun, can have several different meanings. For example, in the following words it shares one of the possible meanings of ית- **small**.

יַלְדוֹן / יַלְדוֹנֶת[6]	שְׁטִיחוֹן	בַּקְבּוּקוֹן	סִפְרוֹן[5] ◄
small child, "little one"	small carpet	small bottle	booklet

Since it is impossible to predict which of the diminutive endings (ית- or וֹן-) will be added to a given noun – or even if a noun can take a diminutive ending – it is important for learners simply to be aware of their existence and to learn the words that take these endings.

Another meaning of וֹן- – to denote a kind of newspaper or journal – can be seen in the following words:

יוֹם + וֹן- ⇐ יוֹמוֹן	שָׁבוּעַ + וֹן- ⇐ שְׁבוּעוֹן	עֵת + וֹן- ⇐ עִיתוֹן ◄
daily newspaper day	weekly newspaper or magazine week	newspaper time

More endings that have specific meanings

Another commonly used ending is יָּיה- (*ee-YA*). We find books at the סִפְרִייָּה (library), and we buy fresh rolls at the מַאֲפִייָּה (bakery). These words all denote **places**.

Looking for a profession? Add the ending ָן- (and possibly make some changes in the base form) and you could be a כַּלְכְּלָן/כַּלְכְּלָנִית (economist), a פְּסַנְתְּרָן/פְּסַנְתְּרָנִית (pianist), a תַּקְלִיטָן/תַּקְלִיטָנִית (disc jockey) or even a כַּדּוּרְסַלָן/כַּדּוּרְסַלָנִית (basketball player).

Add the ending אי- and you could be an עִיתוֹנַאי/עִיתוֹנָאִית (journalist), a חַשְׁמַלַּאי/חַשְׁמַלָּאִית (electrician), a מוּזִיקַאי/מוּזִיקָאִית (musician) or a מַתֵמָטִיקַאי/מַתֵמָטִיקָאִית (mathematician).

To name **some** of the subjects you might like to study, just add the ending וּת- (with some possible changes to the base):

סַפָּרוּת	חַקְלָאוּת	אַדְרִיכָלוּת ◄
hairdressing	agriculture	architecture

---

5   When an ending is added, sometimes there is a change in the vowels of the base form.

6   Since the word יַלְדוֹן denotes a person, it has a feminine form יַלְדוֹנֶת.

The וּת- ending is used not only for some subjects of study, but also for **abstract nouns** in general, for example: אֲלִימוּת (violence), מַנְהִיגוּת (leadership), יְדִידוּת (friendship).[7]

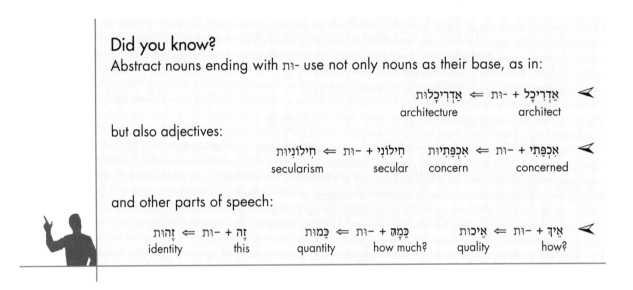

Did you know?
Abstract nouns ending with וּת- use not only nouns as their base, as in:

אַדְרִיכָל + וּת- ⇐ אַדְרִיכָלוּת
architecture   architect

but also adjectives:

אִכְפַּתִי + וּת- ⇐ אִכְפַּתִיוּת   חִילוֹנִי + וּת- ⇐ חִילוֹנִיוּת
concerned   concern   secular   secularism

and other parts of speech:

אֵיךְ + וּת- ⇐ אֵיכוּת   כַּמָה + וּת- ⇐ כַּמוּת   זֶה + וּת- ⇐ זֶהוּת
how?   quality   how much?   quantity   this   identity

Endings of foreign words

Throughout its history, Hebrew has absorbed many words from foreign languages. While some words – such as רַדְיוֹ (radio) and טֶלֶפוֹן (telephone) – have retained their foreign form, others have "assimilated" into Hebrew by fitting into Hebrew noun patterns. For example, אִרְגוּן (organization) is formed according to the pattern of סִיפּוּר, and מְהַפְּנֵט (hypnotist) is formed according to the pattern of מְנַהֵל.

Still another way in which foreign words "assimilate" into Hebrew is by adding a Hebrew ending to a foreign word, as in:

ספוֹרְטַאי   סְטֵקִייָה
athlete   restaurant with meat
                     cooked on a grill

⇕   ⇕
same ending as: עִיתוֹנַאי   סִפְרִייָה

---

7   a. As you can see from the translations, many English abstract nouns also have typical endings, such as: -hood, -ism, -ness, -ity and so on.

     b. There are various patterns that also end in וּת- and denote abstract nouns, for example הִתְמַמְּמוּת, as in:

         הִתְנַגְדוּת   הִתְרַגְּשׁוּת
         opposition   nervousness

What happens when the foreign word itself has an ending?

Some foreign words keep their own **foreign endings** in Hebrew, for example:

פֶּנְסִיוֹנֶר	אֶגוֹאִיסְט	קוֹמוּנִיסְט	פֶמִינִיזְם	סוֹצְיָאלִיזְם ◄
pensioner	egoist	communist	feminism	socialism

In other cases, the ending in Hebrew is somewhat different from the English ending, as in:[8]

אִינְטוֹנַצְיָה	סִיטוּאַצְיָה	בִּיוּרוֹקְרַטְיָה	דֶמוֹקְרַטְיָה	הִיסְטוֹרְיָה ◄
intonation	situation	bureaucracy	democracy	history

הִיפְּנוֹזָה	דִיאַגְנוֹזָה	סְטָטִיסְטִיקָה	מָתֶמָטִיקָה	בִּיוֹלוֹגְיָה	פְּסִיכוֹלוֹגְיָה
hypnosis	diagnosis	statistics	mathematics	biology	psychology

For English speakers it is important to note the correspondence between the endings of these Hebrew words and their English equivalents.

Did you know?

As we have seen, some foreign words denoting people of various types end in יסט-, as in קומוניסט and אגואיסט. But when the noun they come from ends in לוגיה-, they may be formed in the following way:

פְּסִיכוֹלוֹג	⇐	פְּסִיכוֹלוֹגְיָה ◄
psychologist		

בִּיוֹלוֹג	⇐	בִּיוֹלוֹגְיָה
biologist		

סוֹצְיוֹלוֹג	⇐	סוֹצְיוֹלוֹגְיָה
sociologist		

Here the equivalent of "-ist" does not appear in the Hebrew.

---

8   The end of these Hebrew words may correspond to endings in Latin or Greek or another language.

Let's review

Many Hebrew nouns are formed by adding an **ending** to a **base form**.

◆ Some endings have no special meaning, while others may have one or more specific meanings. Here are some examples discussed above:

‏ית‏- may denote *being small* (‏מַפִּית‏), or a *language* (‏צָרְפָתִית‏) or a *vehicle* (‏מְכוֹנִית‏).

‏וֹן‏- may denote *being small* (‏סִפְרוֹן‏).

‏ִיָּה‏- may denote a *place* (‏סִפְרִיָּה‏).

‏ָן‏- and ‏אַי‏- may denote a person with a *profession* or *occupation* (‏תַּקְלִיטָן‏, ‏מָתֶמָטִיקַאי‏).

‏ וּת‏- denotes an *abstract noun* (‏חַקְלָאוּת‏, ‏אֶפְשָׁרוּת‏).

◆ When foreign words enter Hebrew, they sometimes take Hebrew endings (‏סְפּוֹרְטַאי‏). In other cases they retain their foreign endings, which may correspond to English either exactly (‏סוֹצְיָאלִיזְם‏) or to some extent (‏אִינְפוֹרְמַצְיָה‏).

Want to see if you've understood?

Using your knowledge of the meaning of endings, guess the meaning of the following words. (The word in parentheses provides a hint as to the **ending's** meaning).

1. ‏סַנְדְּלָרִיָּה‏ = _____ (‏סְטָקִיָּה‏)

2. ‏כּוֹסִית‏ = _____ (‏כַּפִּית‏)

3. ‏מַחְשְׁבוֹן‏ = _____ (‏סִפְרוֹן‏)

4. ‏מְקוֹמוֹן‏ = _____ (‏שְׁבוּעוֹן‏)

5. ‏מְדִינַאי‏ = _____ (‏מָתֶמָטִיקַאי‏)

6. ‏תַּיָּירוּת‏ = _____ (‏חַקְלָאוּת‏)

Answers:

1. shoemaker's shop (a place where shoes are fixed or made)   2. a shot glass (a little glass)   3. a calculator

4. a local newspaper   5. a diplomat, statesman   6. tourism

• *Joining two nouns to form a new word*

Some Hebrew nouns were created by **joining** two words together. The word קוֹלְנוֹעַ (movie theater) is a combination of two words: קוֹל (voice) and נוֹעַ (moving). The words חַי (living) and דַק (slender) were joined together to form the word חַיְידָק (bacterium).

Sometimes when two words join together, one or more of the original letters drop out, especially when there are letters that appear in both words, for example:

$$\text{כַּדּוּר} + \text{רֶגֶל} \Leftarrow \text{כדור} + \text{רגל} \Leftarrow \text{כַּדּוּרֶגֶל}$$

ball	foot			football

Here are some more examples of words formed in this way:[9]

$$\text{מִדְרָכָה} + \text{רְחוֹב} \Leftarrow \text{מִדְרְחוֹב}$$
sidewalk   street   pedestrian mall

$$\text{רֶמֶז} + \text{אוֹר} \Leftarrow \text{רַמְזוֹר}$$
hint; sign   light   traffic light

$$\text{רַכֶּבֶת} + \text{כֶּבֶל} \Leftarrow \text{רַכֶּבֶל}$$
train   cable   cable car

Let's review

♦ A third way of forming nouns is by joining two nouns together:

$$\text{קוֹל} + \text{נוֹעַ} \Leftarrow \text{קוֹלְנוֹעַ}$$

In the new noun we sometimes find the original words in their entirety (as in קוֹלְנוֹעַ); at other times one or more letters may drop out when the words are combined, as in: כַּדּוּר + רֶגֶל ⇐ כַּדּוּרֶגֶל.

---

9   These words are called *compound nouns*. In Hebrew, a word like קוֹלְנוֹעַ is called a הֶרְכֵּב, and a word like כַּדּוּרֶגֶל (in which part of one of the original words is missing) is called a הֶלְחֵם.

6. Segolate Nouns (יֶלֶד, סֵפֶר, בּוֹקֶר)

Preview
- *Singular and plural forms of segolate nouns*
- *Segolate nouns with possessive endings and in* smeechoot

• *Singular and plural forms of segolate nouns*

What is a segolate noun?

Read the following words out loud:

חֵלֶק	אֶרֶץ	יֶלֶד	סֵפֶר	דֶּרֶךְ	◄
CHE-lek	'E-retz	YE-led	SE-fer	DE-rech	
part	country	boy	book	way	

Q: What do all these words have in common?

A: They all contain **three letters** and are divided into **two syllables**. Unlike nouns like שולחן (shool-CHAN), כיסא (kee-SE) and דבר (da-VAR), whose **last** syllable is stressed, here the **first** of the two syllables is stressed:

$$◄ \quad דֶּ-רֶךְ \ DE\text{-}rech, \quad סֵ-פֶר \ SE\text{-}fer...^1$$

These nouns also share one more common trait: they all contain the **vowel sign** ◌ֶ (three dots called סֶגוֹל *se-GOL*) – pronounced *eh* – in their second syllable. This is true of **most** nouns that belong to this group, and for this reason they are called *segolate nouns* – or *segolates* (in Hebrew: שֵמוֹת סְגוֹלִיִים or שֵמוֹת מִלְעֵילִיִים).[2] The exceptions (segolates without a *segol* in the second syllable) will be discussed below.

As we will see, segolates behave in special, fairly consistent ways when they are made plural, when they take possessive endings and when they appear in *smeechoot*. Thus, identifying a noun as a segolate provides us with a key to the correct pronunciation of the different forms of that noun.

---

1   We are referring to the stressed syllable here as the *first* syllable. In grammar books, this syllable is usually referred to as the *next to last* syllable.

2   מִלְעֵיל in Aramaic means that the stress is on the syllable before last.

Did you know?

The segolate noun אֶרֶץ ('E-rets land, country) behaves in a unique way: its pronunciation changes to 'A-rets when it is preceded by the *definite article* –הָ (the):

the land (also used to refer to Israel) ha-'A-rets הָאָרֶץ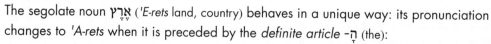

Problems in identifying segolate nouns

Here are some more segolate nouns:

אוזן	שבט	חודש	עבד	בוקר	שמן	מלך	כלב
'O-zen	SHE-vet	CHO-desh	'E-ved	BO-ker	SHE-men	ME-lech	KE-lev
ear	tribe	month	slave	morning	oil	king	dog

Q: Do all these nouns have only **three letters**?

A: Yes, except for the words חודש, בוקר and אוזן, which are written here with **four letters.** This is the way they are written in *full spelling* (i.e., in texts **without** vowel signs and with an added ו to indicate the sound *oh*). However, when written **without** the added ו, these words – like all other segolate nouns – have only **three** letters:

בֹּקֶר חֹדֶשׁ אֹזֶן

All of the words in the list above also have the other tell-tale signs of segolates: a *segol* (◌ֶ) in the second syllable and – most importantly – the **stress** on their **first syllable**.

Thus, singular segolate nouns can be divided into two basic groups according to the vowel sound in their **first** syllable:

	with oh (וֹ◌ / ◌ֹ) *in the first syllable*			*with eh (either ◌ֵ or ◌ֶ)* *in the first syllable*	
אֹזֶן	חֹדֶשׁ	בֹּקֶר	סֵפֶר	יֶלֶד	אֶרֶץ
(אוזן)	(חודש)	(בוקר)			
'O-zen	CHO-desh	BO-ker	SE-fer	YE-led	'E-rets

 Be careful! Two other groups of nouns can easily be confused with segolates when they appear in texts **without** vowel signs. If you have never heard these nouns pronounced or seen them written **with** vowel signs, you may easily confuse them with segolates.

However, they are all stressed on their **last syllable**.[3] The first group is composed of three-letter nouns, such as:

זָקֵן	כְּאֵב	כְּפָר	סַפָּר	מָרָק	דָּבָר	◄
za-KEN	ke-'EV	KFAR	sa-PAR	ma-RAK	da-VAR	
elderly man	pain	village	barber	soup	thing	

The second group is composed of four-letter nouns whose second letter is ו and may be confused with the בוקר, חודש group, such as:

מוֹשָׁב	כּוֹכָב	שׁוֹטֵר	שׁוֹמֵר	רוֹפֵא	◄
mo-SHAV	ko-CHAV	sho-TER	sho-MER	ro-FE	
moshav	star	policeman	guard	doctor	

Let's review

♦ Segolate nouns have **three letters** and **two syllables**, the **first** of which is always stressed. In the segolates we have seen up to this point, the **vowel** ◌ (*segol*) appears in the **second** syllable.

♦ There are two basic groups of segolates:
   - Forms with *eh* in the first syllable (either ◌ or ◌): סֵפֶר (*SE-fer*), יֶלֶד (*YE-led*)
   - Forms with *oh* (ו) in the first syllable: בוקר / בֹּקֶר (*BO-ker*)

Want to see if you've understood?

The following list contains miscellaneous nouns including segolates. We have included only segolate nouns that have a *segol* in their second syllable. When you see a *segol* in the second syllable, you should stress the **first syllable**. Otherwise, stress the **last syllable**.

Read the following nouns out loud and circle the segolates:

סוֹפֵר	שֶׁמֶשׁ	חָלָב	אוֹכֶל	מַדָּע	זָהָב	סֶרֶט	שׁוֹרֶשׁ	נָהָר	שֶׁלֶג	בֶּגֶד	◄
writer	sun	milk	food	science	gold	movie	root	river	snow	article of clothing	

Answers:

שֶׁמֶשׁ	אוֹכֶל	סֶרֶט	שׁוֹרֶשׁ	שֶׁלֶג	בֶּגֶד
SHE-mesh	'O-chel	SE-ret	SHO-resh	SHE-leg	BE-ged

---

3   In words like כְּפָר, the stress is on the only syllable.

Special changes in vowels of segolate nouns

Although the special group we are examining here is called **segolate** nouns, under certain conditions the *segol* in the second syllable disappears and only two characteristic signs remain: **three letters** (divided into two syllables) and the **stress** on the **first syllable**.

Changes resulting from the presence of ע', ח', ה', א' (gutturals)

One instance in which the *segol* does not appear in the second syllable is when the **third letter** of the root is ע' or ח' (and sometimes ה'), for example:

גּוֹבַהּ	נוֹסַח	רוֹבַע	פֶּרַח	רֶגַע	◄
GO-vah	NO-sach	RO-va	PE-rach	RE-ga	
height	version	quarter (of city)	flower	moment	

In addition, the *segol* does not appear in the middle of segolates whose middle letter is א', ה', ח', ע' (the *guttural* consonants). In segolates with a middle guttural and *oh* (וֹ) in the first syllable, the vowels are:

דּוֹאַר	נוֹהַג[4]	בּוֹחַן	פּוֹעַל	◄
DO-'ar	NO-hag	BO-chan	PO-'al	
mail	custom	quiz	verb	

In other segolates with a middle guttural, both vowels are *ah*:

סַהַר	פַּחַד	נַעַל	◄
SA-har	PA-chad	NA-'al	
crescent	fear	shoe	

Note that in all of these forms, the first syllable is always stressed.

Changes resulting from the presence of י'

When the **middle** letter of a segolate is י', the following vowel change takes place:

קַיִץ	זַיִת	בַּיִת	◄
KA-yeets	ZA-yeet	BA-yeet	
summer	olive	house	

---

4   Some exceptions where no vowel change takes place are: אוֹהֶל ('O-hel tent), בּוֹהֶן (BO-hen thumb, big toe).

When the **final** letter is ', we get forms such as:

אוֹפִי	קוֹשִׁי	יוֹפִי	לְחִי	בְּכִי	◄
'O-fee	KO-shee	YO-fee	LE-chee	BE-chee	
character	difficulty	beauty	cheek	crying	

Words like מָוֶת

The word מָוֶת and several other words with "וו" in the middle have a special form:

מָוֶת	◄
MA-vet	
death	

Let's review

♦ When the second or third root letter in segolates is a *guttural* (א', ה', ח', ע'), the vowel *ah* appears in the second syllable instead of *eh* and other vowel changes may take place, for example:

רוֹחַב	נַחַל	נַעַר	רוֹבַע	מֶלַח	פֶּצַע	◄
RO-chav	NA-chal	NA-'ar	RO-va	ME-lach	PE-tsa	

♦ The presence of ' or "וו" in the **middle** or **end** of a segolate also affects the vowels, for example:

מָוֶת	קוֹשִׁי	בְּכִי	בַּיִת	◄
MA-vet	KO-shee	BE-chee	BA-yeet	

Plural forms of segolate nouns

One of the most important benefits of identifying segolate nouns is that once we have done so, it is fairly easy to know their plural form.

The plural form of **most** segolate nouns is סְֶ◌ָ◌ִים. These forms are stressed on the end (יְלָדִים *ye-la-DEEM*). Here are examples of plural segolates:

קוֹשִׁי	רוֹבַע	בּוֹחַן	פּוֹעַל	בּוֹקֶר	פַּחַד		שַׁעַר	פֶּרַח	צֶבַע	סֵפֶר	יֶלֶד	◄
⇓	⇓	⇓	⇓	⇓	⇓		⇓	⇓	⇓	⇓	⇓	
קְשָׁיִים	רְבָעִים	בְּחָנִים	פְּעָלִים	בְּקָרִים	פְּחָדִים		שְׁעָרִים	פְּרָחִים	צְבָעִים	סְפָרִים	יְלָדִים	
difficulties	quarters	quizzes	verbs	mornings	fears		gates	flowers	colors	books	children	

93

Notice that even when there is a ו' in the singular form, the plural form has **no** ו' (בּוֹקֶר ⇐ בְּקָרִים, פּוֹעֵל ⇐ פְּעָלִים).

Now look at the plural forms of nouns whose first letter is א', ע', ח' or ה' and can't take a *shva* (◌ְ):

	חוֹדֶשׁ[5]	עוֹנֶשׁ	אוֹהֶל		חֶדֶר	עֶרֶב	אֶבֶן	◄
	⇓	⇓	⇓		⇓	⇓	⇓	
standard spelling:	(חֳדָשִׁים)	(עֳנָשִׁים)	(אֳהָלִים)		חֲדָרִים	עֲרָבִים	אֲבָנִים	
full spelling:	חוֹדָשִׁים	עוֹנָשִׁים	אוֹהָלִים					
	months	punishments	tents		rooms	evenings	stones	

Q: What is the first vowel in these words?

A: It is usually *ah* (אֲבָנִים); however, when the singular form has a ו' (חוֹדֶשׁ), the plural keeps the *oh* sound (חֳדָשִׁים / חודשים[6] *cho-da-SHEEM*).

Sometimes an ות- ending is used instead of ים-ַ. Since there are many fewer segolates whose plural form ends in ות-, these forms should be memorized. Here are some examples (most, but not all, are feminine).

feminine:	חֶרֶב	עֶצֶם	אֶרֶץ	קֶשֶׁת	רֶשֶׁת	דֶּלֶת	נֶפֶשׁ	◄
	⇓	⇓	⇓	⇓	⇓	⇓	⇓	
	חֲרָבוֹת	עֲצָמוֹת[7]	אֲרָצוֹת	קְשָׁתוֹת	רְשָׁתוֹת	דְּלָתוֹת	נְפָשׁוֹת	
	swords	bones	countries	rainbows; archways	nets; networks	doors	souls	

masculine:						יַעַר	רֶגֶשׁ[8]	◄
						⇓	⇓	
						יְעָרוֹת	רְגָשׁוֹת	
						forests	emotions	

---

5   The plural forms of שוֹרֶשׁ (root) and קוֹדֶשׁ (holiness) keep the *oh* in their first syllable:

◄ שוֹרָשִׁים (שָׁרָשִׁים) *sho-ra-SHEEM*,   קוֹדָשִׁים (קֳדָשִׁים) *ko-da-SHEEM*

These words act **as if** they begin with a guttural (like חודש ⇐ חודשים).

6   The vowel sign ◌ֳ (called *hataf kamatz*) is pronounced *oh*.

7   The word עֶצֶם also means *thing* (as in שֵׁם עֶצֶם = noun, lit.: name of a thing). When it has this meaning, it is **masculine** and the plural form is עֲצָמִים.

8   The plural of the masculine noun קֶבֶר (grave) is קְבָרִים. However, a form with ות- appears in the word for *cemetery*: בֵּית קְבָרוֹת.

Nouns with י in the middle constitute a special group, and their plural forms usually have ◌ַ (ei / eh)[9] in the first syllable:

זַיִת	קַיִץ	יַיִן
⇓	⇓	⇓
זֵיתִים	קֵיצִים[10]	יֵינוֹת
olives	summers	wines

The word בַּיִת has an **irregular** form in the plural: בַּיִת

⇓

בָּתִּים

houses

Some segolate nouns form their plural by adding the ◌ַיִם- (*A-yeem*) ending. The base of these forms is **not** the same as the plurals above, which have a *shva* in the first syllable (יְלָדִים, נְפָשׁוֹת). Rather, these forms have a vowel after the first letter and each has to be learned.[11] Most of these happen to be feminine:

אֹזֶן	בֶּרֶךְ	נַעַל	רֶגֶל
⇓	⇓	⇓	⇓
אוֹזְנַיִים	בִּרְכַּיִים	נַעֲלַיִים	רַגְלַיִים
ears	knees	shoes	legs

masculine:

גֶּרֶב

⇓

גַּרְבַּיִים

socks

Let's review

◆ The basic plural form of segolate nouns is ◌ְ◌ָ◌ִים (יְלָדִים, סְפָרִים, בְּקָרִים) and sometimes ◌ְ◌ָ◌וֹת (רְגָשׁוֹת, נְפָשׁוֹת).

◆ When א׳, ה׳, ח׳ or ע׳ (the gutturals) appear at the **beginning** of the plural form and are expected to take a *shva*, they take an *ah* vowel (אֲבָנִים, עֲבָדִים, חֲרָבוֹת), except when they have וֹ in the singular form (עֹנֶשׁ, חֹדֶשׁ), in which case they keep the *oh* sound (וֹ) (עוֹנָשִׁים, חוֹדָשִׁים)

---

9 Some speakers pronounce ◌ִים (as in זֵיתִים) *zei-TEEM*; others say *ze-TEEM*.
10 The form קֵיצִים also exists but is used less than קַיצִים.
11 As you will see below, pp. 105-107, this vowel is the same vowel that appears in forms like רַגְלוֹ (his leg) and בִּרְכּוֹ (his knee), i.e., singular segolate nouns with possessive endings.

♦ The plural form of segolates with י in the middle is different: זֵיתִים and יֵינוֹת. The word בַּיִת has an irregular plural: בָּתִּים.

♦ Some segolate plurals take the ending יִם-ַ. Their base is unlike regular segolate plurals in that it does not begin with *shva*, for example: רַגְלַיִים, בִּרְכַּיִים and אוֹזְנַיִים.

Want to see if you've understood?

A. Change from singular to plural or from plural to singular and say the word out loud.

	plural		singular	
	_____	⇔	מֶלֶךְ	.1
	אֲבָנִים	⇔	_____	.2
	_____	⇔	עֵרֶךְ	.3
	_____	⇔	בּוֹקֶר	.4
	_____	⇔	סֵפֶל	.5
	פְּרָחִים	⇔	_____	.6
	_____	⇔	פַּחַד	.7
	נְעָרִים	⇔	_____	.8
	_____	⇔	פּוֹעֵל	.9

Answers:

1. מְלָכִים (me-la-CHEEM)   2. אֶבֶן ('E-ven)   3. עֲרָכִים ('a-ra-CHEEM)   4. בְּקָרִים (bka-REEM)
5. סְפָלִים (sfa-LEEM)   6. פֶּרַח (PE-rach)   7. פְּחָדִים (pcha-DEEM)   8. נַעַר (NA-'ar)
9. פְּעָלִים (pe-'a-LEEM)

B. Change from singular to plural or from plural to singular.

	plural		singular	
	_____	⇔	אוֹזֶן	.1
	זֵיתִים	⇔	_____	.2
	רַגְלַיִים	⇔	_____	.3

4. בַּיִת ⇔ _____

5. גֶּרֶב ⇔ _____

Answers:

1. אוֹזְנַיִים (*oz–NA-yeem*) 2. זַיִת (*ZA–yeet*) 3. רֶגֶל (*RE-gel*) 4. בָּתִּים (*ba-TEEM*) 5. גַּרְבַּיִים (*gar-BA-yeem*)

• *Segolate nouns with possessive endings and in smeechoot*

Adding possessive endings to singular segolate nouns

The highlighted words in the following passage are segolate nouns with possessive endings added to them:[12]

> פרופ' לוין סיים לחבר את התרגיל האחרון בסִפְרוֹ החדש לאלגברה. הוא שם את העיפרון מאחורי אוֹזְנוֹ, התמתח מְלוֹא אוֹרְכּוֹ, קם ויצא מֵחַדְרוֹ. הוא חזר לרגע, לקח את סִפְלוֹ, סגר את הדלת והלך לדַרְכּוֹ.

Prof. Levine finished making up the last exercise in his new algebra book. He put his pencil behind his ear, stretched out to his full height (lit.: length), got up and left his room. He went back for a moment, took his mug, closed the door and went on his way.

Try this:

Divide the segolate nouns in the passage above into three groups according to the vowel in their first syllable.

oh	*ee*	*ah*
_____	_____	_____
_____	_____	_____
_____		

Here's the solution:

There are three types of segolates with possessive endings.

the *oh* group	the *ee* group	the *ah* group
אוֹזְנוֹ	סִפְרוֹ	חַדְרוֹ
אוֹרְכּוֹ	סִפְלוֹ	דַּרְכּוֹ

---

12 See the chapter "Nouns with Possessive Endings," pp. 60-67 for a full explanation of possessive endings. The present chapter will deal only with changes in the base of the noun to which the endings are added.

There are three striking differences between the regular singular form of segolate nouns (חֶדֶר, סֵפֶר, אֹזֶן) and the forms with endings:

- The vowel of the first syllable
- The place of the stress
- The pronunciation of 'ב, 'כ or פ' when they appear at the end of the regular form, as in דרך and כלב.

The vowel of the first syllable and the stress

Let's take a closer look at the forms with the endings as compared to their regular forms. (We have added some more examples to each group):

the *ah* group

	with ending			regular form		
his room	chad-RO	חַדְרוֹ	⇐	CHE-der	חֶדֶר	◄
his way	dar-KO	דַּרְכּוֹ	⇐	DE-rech	דֶּרֶךְ	
his dog	kal-BO	כַּלְבּוֹ	⇐	KE-lev	כֶּלֶב	
his money	kas-PO	כַּסְפּוֹ	⇐	KE-sef	כֶּסֶף	
his child	yal-DO	יַלְדוֹ	⇐	YE-led	יֶלֶד	

As you can see, in all the nouns we have listed, there is an *eh* vowel in each syllable of the regular form (חֶדֶר *CHE-der*, דֶּרֶךְ *DE-rech*), whereas the form with the possessive ending has an *ah* vowel at the **beginning** and **no vowel** sound after the second letter (חַדְרוֹ *chad-RO*, דַּרְכּוֹ *dar-KO*, כַּלְבּוֹ *kal-BO*). In addition, the stress has moved to the final syllable.

the *ee* group

	with ending			regular form		
his book	seef-RO	סִפְרוֹ	⇐	SE-fer	סֵפֶר	◄
his mug	seef-LO	סִפְלוֹ	⇐	SE-fel	סֵפֶל	
his flag	deeg-LO	דִּגְלוֹ	⇐	DE-gel	דֶּגֶל	
his garment	beeg-DO	בִּגְדוֹ	⇐	BE-ged	בֶּגֶד	

In this group, too, there is an *eh* vowel in each syllable of the regular form (סֵפֶר *SE-fer*, סֵפֶל *SE-fel*), but this time the form with the possessive ending has an *ee* vowel in the first syllable. Here, too, there is no vowel sound after the second letter (סִפְרוֹ *seef-RO*, סִפְלוֹ *seef-LO*), and the stress has moved to the final syllable.

the *oh* group

	with ending			regular form		
his ear	'oz-NO	אָזְנוֹ	⇐	'O-zen	אֹזֶן	◄
his (its) length	'or-KO	אָרְכּוֹ	⇐	'O-rech	אֹרֶךְ	
his punishment	'on-SHO	עוֹנְשׁוֹ	⇐	'O-nesh	עוֹנֶשׁ	

In this group, as opposed to the others, the same vowel (*oh*) appears in the first syllable of both the regular form and the form with the possessive ending. As was the case in the other groups, here, too, the possessive form has no vowel sound after the second letter (אוֹזְנוֹ *'oz-NO*) and the stress is on the final syllable.

The pronunciation of final ב', כ', פ'

Now look at the nouns whose final letter is ב', כ' or פ' (e.g., דרך, כסף, כלב and אורך).

Q: What happens to them when an ending is added?

A: They are pronounced with a hard pronunciation (with a *dagesh kal*): דַּרְכּוֹ (*dar-KO*), כַּסְפּוֹ (*kas-PO*), כַּלְבּוֹ (*kal-BO*) and אוֹרְכּוֹ (*'or-KO*), whereas without a possessive ending they are pronounced with the soft pronunciation (*ch, f, v*).

Did you know?
Why do the changes in the pronunciation of final ב', כ', פ' take place?

The change in the pronunciation of ב', כ', פ' takes place because of the change in the syllable structure. In the regular form, ב', כ', פ' come after a **vowel** and have a soft pronunciation (כָּלֶב *KE-lev*, דֶּרֶךְ *DE-rech*, כֶּסֶף *KE-sef*). However, when possessive endings are added, ב', כ' and פ' come after a **consonant**: כּלְ-בּוֹ *kal-BO*, דּרְ-כּוֹ *dar-KO*, כּסְ-פּוֹ *kas-PO*.[13] When ב', כ' and פ' follow a **consonant**, they are pronounced as hard sounds: *b, k, p*.

How can we know what the initial vowel will be in forms with endings?

When the regular form of a segolate has a ו', as in אוזן, אורך and עונש, it almost always retains the *oh* sound when endings are added:

◄ אוֹזְנוֹ, אוֹרְכּוֹ, עוֹנְשׁוֹ[14]

All other segolate forms – i.e., those **without** a ו' – will have either an *ah* (דַּרְכִּי, אַרְצִי) or an *ee* (סִפְרִי, בִּגְדִי) in their first syllable (see below for several exceptions). In order to know which of these vowels will appear, you have to either look in the dictionary or hear the word pronounced by a reliable Hebrew speaker.

---

13 For more on the pronunciation of ב', כ' and פ' after a consonant (= after a closed syllable), see the chapter "The Pronunciation of ב', כ', פ' and the *Dagesh*," p. 627.

14 These words are written here in full spelling. When written in standard spelling, we write: אָזְנוֹ, אָרְכּוֹ, עָנְשׁוֹ.

A helpful hint: All segolate nouns like בַּעַל, שַׁעַר, פַּחַד, whose vowels are *A-a*, always keep their first *Ah* vowel when endings are added:

יַחְסָן	טַעְמוֹ	פַּחְדָם	שַׁעֲרֵנוּ	בַּעְלָהּ ◄
their (*f.*) relation	his taste	their (*m.*) fear	our gate	her husband

---

Did you know?
Where do the initial vowels of segolates come from?

One widely-accepted explanation is that segolate nouns started out as words with only **one syllable** and **one vowel**: יַלְד (*YALD*) and סִפְר (*SEEFR*). It is this original vowel that we find in the form with possessive endings: יַלְדוֹ (*yal-DO*) and סִפְרוֹ (*seef-RO*). Nouns in the *oh* group (אֹזֶן) apparently came from אֻזְן (*'OOZN*), which became *'OZN*. This *oh* remains in the forms with possessive endings: אׇזְנוֹ (*'oz-NO*). When these one-syllable nouns appeared **without** endings, a new form appeared. The evolution of this form may have been:

(3)		(2)		(1)
יֶלֶד	⇐	יַלֶד	⇐	יַלְד ◄
YE-led		*YA-led*		*YALD*

(1) The original form at an earlier stage of the language was יַלְד (*YALD*).
(2) The sound *eh* entered between the two final consonants: יַ-לֶד (*YA-led*)
(3) The first vowel matched the second vowel: יֶ-לֶד (*YE-led*)

Through this whole process the stress remained on the **first syllable**, thus explaining why segolate nouns without endings are always stressed on the first syllable.[15]

Several exceptions: words with other vowels in the first syllable

There are two small groups of segolate nouns that have an *eh* or *ei* sound in their first syllable when possessive endings are added.

---

15 Also in the evolution of סִפְר (*SEEFR*) to סֵפֶר (*SE-fer*) and of אֻזְן (*'OOZN*) to אֹזֶן (*'O-zen*) an *eh* entered between the two final consonants. See more on the evolution of these forms in J. Weingreen, 1959, pp. 82-84.

1. A small number of miscellaneous nouns, among them:[16]

his part	*chel-KO*	חֶלְקוֹ	⇐	הַחֵלֶק שלו ◄
his grandson	*nech-DO*	נֶכְדּוֹ	⇐	הַנֶּכֶד שלו
his (its) value	*'er-KO*	עֶרְכּוֹ	⇐	הָעֵרֶךְ שלו

2. Nouns with י in the middle, for example:

his house	*bei-TO*[17]	בֵּיתוֹ	⇐	הַבַּיִת שלו ◄
his eye	*'ei-NO*	עֵינוֹ	⇐	הָעַיִן שלו
his wine	*yei-NO*	יֵינוֹ	⇐	הַיַּיִן שלו

3. Nouns with the same pattern as מָוֶת

When possessive endings are added to the noun מָוֶת (death) and several others like it,[18] the resulting form has "וֹ" (*oh*) in the middle:

his death	*mo-TO*	מוֹתוֹ	⇐	הַמָּוֶת שלו ◄

Let's review

◆ When possessive endings are added to singular segolate nouns, the stress moves to the end of the word and the first syllable usually takes one of the following vowels:

oh	*ee*	*ah*
חוֹדְשׁוֹ = החודש שלו	בִּגְדוֹ = הבגד שלו	דַּרְכּוֹ = הדרך שלו ◄
עוֹנְשׁוֹ = העונש שלו	סִפְרוֹ = הספר שלו	כַּלְבּוֹ = הכלב שלו
שׁוֹרְשׁוֹ = השורש שלו	דִּגְלוֹ = הדגל שלו	כַּסְפּוֹ = הכסף שלו
אוֹרְכּוֹ = האורך שלו	שִׁטְחוֹ = השטח שלו	נַעֲלוֹ = הנעל שלו

All segolate nouns with a וֹ (חודש, שורש) belong to the *oh* group when endings are added. In the case of segolates without וֹ (דרך, בגד), we can't know whether they belong to the *ah* group or to the *ee* group without looking in the dictionary or hearing their forms with endings.

◆ Other special groups are dealt with in the chapter.

---

16 The prepositions נֶגְדִי, נֶגְדְּךָ... and אֶצְלִי, אֶצְלְךָ... take this same form.
17 Some speakers pronounce ◌ֵי *ei*, as in *bei-TO*; others say *be-TO*.
18 For example, תָּוֶךְ (interior) becomes תוֹכוֹ, as in בְּתוֹכוֹ (in it).

Want to see if you've understood?

Read the following sentences. Say the segolate noun out loud.

A. Segolates from the *ah* group:

‏1. התיירים מספרד ראו את **מלכם** בטלוויזיה.

‏2. הילדה שיחקה עם **כלבה**.

‏3. האיש איבד את כל **כספו** בקזינו.

B. Segolates from the *ee* group:

‏1. סטיבן ספילברג דיבר ברדיו על **סרטו** החדש.

‏2. מיכל שכחה את **ספרה** בבית.

‏3. בחרתי בחולצות האלה בגלל **צבען** היפה.

C. Segolates from the *oh* group and with other vowels (*ei*, *eh*):

‏1. קראתי את השיר פעמיים ולא הבנתי את **תוכנו**.

‏2. התלמידה חזרה אל **ביתה** אחרי הצהריים.

‏3. סבא וסבתא לקחו את **נכדם** לחוף הים.

Answers:

A. ‏1. מַלְכָּם (mal-KAM)	‏2. כַּלְבָּה (kal-BA)	‏3. כַּסְפּוֹ (kas-PO)
B. ‏1. סְרְטוֹ (seer-TO)	‏2. סְפְרָה (seef–RA)	‏3. צְבְעָן (tseev-'AN)
C. ‏1. תּוֹכְנוֹ (toch-NO)	‏2. בֵּיתָה (bei-TA / be-TA)	‏3. נֶכְדָם (nech-DAM)

On the forms of plural segolate nouns such as בְּקָרִים and סְפָרִים, יְלָדִים with possessive endings, see below after the next section.

Segolate nouns in smeechoot

As mentioned in the chapter on *smeechoot*, when a noun stands in any but the final position in a *smeechoot* phrase, there is a possibility that its form will change.[19]

Singular nouns

When singular segolate nouns appear in *smeechoot*, their form usually does not change, for example:

קוֹבֶץ סיפורים	סֵפֶר תורה	אֶרֶץ ישראל	מֶלֶךְ ספרד ◄
a collection of stories	a Torah scroll	the Land of Israel	the King of Spain

---

19 See the chapter *"Smeechoot,"* pp. 175-182.

Exception: the word חֶדֶר has two possible forms in *smeechoot*: חֲדַר אוכל or חֶדֶר אוכל (dining room).

Segolates with a י in the middle have a **different** form in *smeechoot*:

⟸ בַּיִת ⟸ בֵּית הכנסת

BEIT or *BET*
synagogue

⟸ עַיִן ⟸ עֵין גדי

'EIN or *'EN*
Ein Gedi

Does this form remind you of something? It is just like the base of בֵּיתוֹ (*bei-TO* or *be-TO*) – the singular form with possessive endings.

Plural nouns

When plural segolate nouns appear in *smeechoot*, their form sounds very different from the regular plural form. Here are some examples:

	singular	plural	plural smeechoot form
⟸ 1.	מֶלֶךְ	מְלָכִים	יש בתנ"ך סיפורים רבים על מַלְכֵי ישראל.
			There are a lot of stories in the Bible about **the kings of Israel.**
2.	סֵפֶר	סְפָרִים	יוסי קנה שלושה סִפְרֵי בישול חדשים בשנה שעברה.
			Yossi bought three new **cookbooks** last year.
3.	חוֹדֶשׁ	חוֹדָשִׁים	בחוֹדְשֵׁי הקיץ בישראל יש מזג אוויר חם.
			In **the summer months** there is hot weather in Israel.

What do the *smeechoot* forms -מַלְכֵי (*mal-CHEI-*),[20] -סִפְרֵי (*seef-REI-*) and -חוֹדְשֵׁי (*chod-SHEI-*) remind you of? They contain the same vowel as do מַלְכִּי (*mal-KEE*), סִפְרִי (*seef-REE*) and חוֹדְשִׁי (*chod-SHEE*) – singular segolates with possessive endings. Here are some more examples:

	sing.	sing. + ending	plural smeechoot
⟸ 1.	דֶרֶךְ	דַּרְכִּי	דַרְכֵי טיפול
		my way	methods (lit.: ways) of treatment

---

20 Some speakers pronounce plural *smeechoot* forms like these without an *i* at the end, and say: *mal-CHE-, dar-CHE-* and so on.

בִּגְדֵי ים	בִּגְדִי	2. בֶּגֶד
bathing suits	my garment	

צוֹרְכֵי הציבור	צוֹרְכִּי	3. צוֹרֶךְ
the public's needs	my need	

חֶלְקֵי הארץ	חֶלְקִי	4. חֵלֶק
parts of the country	my part	

The *smeechoot* form of plural segolates is actually closer in sound to the **singular** form with endings (מַלְכִּי) than it is to the regular **plural** form (מְלָכִים). However, if you read the forms in lines 1 and 3 carefully, you will see that this is not entirely true.

Q: Is the כ׳ pronounced the same in all the forms in lines 1 and 3?

A: No. In nouns that end in ך׳, פ׳ and ב׳ (דרך, כסף and כלב), the singular form with an ending has a **hard sound** (דרכי, כלבי, כספי), while the plural *smeechoot* retains the soft sound of the plural form:[21]

כַּלְבֵי שמירה	אַלְפֵי אנשים[22]	דַּרְכֵי שלום	מַלְכֵי ישראל
kal-VEI	*'al-FEI*	*dar-CHEI*	*mal-CHEI*
guard dogs	thousands of people	paths of peace	kings of Israel

Let's review

- Singular segolate nouns usually remain the same in *smeechoot*, as in:

  דֶּגֶל / דֶּגֶל ישראל

  When there is a י׳ in the middle, the vowels change, as in:

  בַּיִת ⇐ בֵּית ספר

- Plural segolate nouns in *smeechoot* (סְפְרֵי קודש, מַלְכֵי ישראל) sound very different from the regular plural form (סְפָרִים, מְלָכִים). Their first vowel is the same as that of singular segolate nouns with possessive endings (סְפְרוֹ, מַלְכּוֹ).

---

21 As explained above (p. 99), after a **consonant** (= a closed syllable), ב׳, כ׳, פ׳ are pronounced *b, k, p*, as in כַּלְבִּי. In plural *smeechoot* forms (-כַּלְבֵי, -מַלְכֵי etc.), the *shva* that comes before ב׳, כ׳, פ׳ is actually a different kind of *shva* from the one in כַּלְבִּי. After this kind of *shva*, ב׳, כ׳, פ׳ are pronounced *v, ch, f*.

22 The form -כַּסְפֵּי *kas-PEI*, as in כַּסְפֵּי ציבור, is exceptional.

Want to see if you've understood?

Write and pronounce the plural *smeechoot* form. (Use the singular form with the possessive ending as your guide.)

	plural smeechoot	singular with possessive ending	singular	
Example:	הַכִּיתָה _____ יַלְדֵי	יַלְדּוֹ	יֶלֶד	
	ישראל _____	מַלְכּוֹ	מֶלֶךְ	.1
	שינה _____	חַדְרוֹ	חֶדֶר	.2
	ספורט _____	בִּגְדוֹ	בֶּגֶד	.3
	אחיך _____	נֶכְדּוֹ	נֶכֶד	.4
	ילדים _____	סִרְטוֹ	סֶרֶט	.5
	שלום _____	דַּרְכּוֹ	דֶּרֶךְ	.6
	הקיץ _____	חוֹדְשׁוֹ	חוֹדֶשׁ	.7

Answers:

.1 מַלְכֵי ישראל   .2 חַדְרֵי שינה   .3 בִּגְדֵי ספורט   .4 נֶכְדֵי אחיך   .5 סִרְטֵי ילדים   .6 דַּרְכֵי שלום   .7 חוֹדְשֵׁי הקיץ

chod-SHEI   dar-CHEI   seer-TEI   nech-DEI   beeg-DEI   chad-REI   mal-CHEI

Adding possessive endings to plural segolate nouns

The principles involved in adding possessive endings to plural nouns are discussed in detail in the chapter "Plural Nouns with Possessive Endings" (pp. 67-75). In the present chapter, we will examine only the changes that take place in the **base** of plural segolates when endings are added.

Let's look at all the possessive forms of יְלָדִים (whose original vowel in the singular was *ah* - יֶלֶד):

the *ah* group

יַלְדֵיכֶם, יַלְדֵיכֶן, יַלְדֵיהֶם, יַלְדֵיהֶן	יְלָדַיי, יְלָדֶיהָ, יְלָדַייךְ, יְלָדָיו, יְלָדֶיהָ, יְלָדֵינוּ	יְלָדִים:
...*yal-dei-CHEM*[23]	...*ye-la-DE-cha, ye-la-DAI*	*ye-la-DEEM*
		children

Look at the last four forms, whose endings are: ־כֶם, ־כֶן, ־הֶם, ־הֶן.

---

23 Some speakers pronounce the words like this without an *ei* vowel: *yal-de-CHEM*.

Q: To what base are these endings added?

A: To a base that begins with an *ah* vowel. This is exactly the **same base** as appears in יַלְדּוֹ (his child) – the **singular** noun with possessive endings – and in יַלְדֵי הגן (kindergarten children) – the **plural** *smeechoot* form.

In the following examples we see the exact same phenomenon: The base of the last four forms of plural segolate nouns is the same as that of the **singular** noun with possessive endings and of the **plural** *smeechoot* form:

the *ee* group (סֵפֶר book)

◄ סְפָרִים:	(סִפְרוֹ)	(סִפְרֵי תורה)	סְפָרַיי, -יךָ, -ייךְ, -יו, -יה, -ינו	סִפְרֵיכֶם, -כֶן, -הֶם, -הן
sfa-REEM	seef-RO	seef-REI-	...sfa-RE-cha, sfa-RAI	...seef-rei-CHEM

the *oh* group (צוֹרֶךְ need)

◄ צְרָכִים:	(צוֹרְכּוֹ)	(צוֹרְכֵי הילד)	צְרָכַיי, -יךָ, -ייךְ, -יו, -יה, -ינו	צוֹרְכֵיכֶם, -כֶן, -הֶם, -הן
tsra-CHEEM	tsor-KO	tsor-CHEI	...tsra-CHE-cha, tsra-CHAI	...tsor-chei-CHEM

In plurals that end in ־וֹת, we find the same phenomenon. Note that here **all** the base forms with possessive endings contain the changed vowel:

the *ah* group (עֶצֶם bone)

◄ עֲצָמוֹת:	(עַצְמוֹ)	(עַצְמוֹת הגוף)	עַצְמוֹתַיי, -יךָ, -ייךְ, -יו, -יה, -ינו,	עַצְמוֹתֵיכֶם, -כֶן, -הֶם, -הן
'a-tsa-MOT	'ats-MO	'ats-MOT-	...'ats-mo-TAI	

the *ee* group (רֶגֶשׁ emotion)

◄ רְגָשׁוֹת:	(רִגְשׁוֹ)	(רְגָשׁוֹת אשמה)[24]	רְגָשׁוֹתַיי, -יךָ, -ייךְ, -יו, -יה, -ינו,	רְגָשׁוֹתֵיכֶם, -כֶן, -הֶם, -הן
re-ga-SHOT	reeg-SHO	reeg-SHOT-	...reeg-sho-TAI	

In *segolate* plural forms that end in ־יִים, **all** the forms, including the **regular** plural, contain the same vowel as the singular form with the ending (גַּרְבּוֹ, בִּרְכּוֹ):

the *ah* group (גֶּרֶב sock)

◄ גַּרְבַּיִם:	(גַּרְבּוֹ)	(גַּרְבֵּי צמר)	גַּרְבַּיי, -יךָ, -ייךְ, -יו, -יה, -ינו,	גַּרְבֵּיכֶם, -כֶן, -הֶם, -הן
gar-BA-yeem	gar-BO	gar-BEI-	...gar-BAI	

---

24 The form רִגְשֵׁי־ is also used in the plural *smeechoot*: רִגְשֵׁי אשמה.

the *ee* group (בֶּרֶךְ knee)

בִּרְכֵּיכֶם,-כֶן,-הֶם,-הֶן   בִּרְכַּיי, -יךָ,-יִיךְ,-יו,-יהָ,-ינו,   בִּרְכֵּי הילד)   (בִּרְכּוֹ)   בִּרְכַּיִם: ◄
                                    ...*beer-KAI*   *beer-KEI-*   *beer-KO*   *beer-KA-yeem*

In the *oh* group, **all** the forms – including the regular one (אוֹזֶן) – have an *oh* vowel at the beginning:

the *oh* group (אוֹזֶן ear)

אוֹזְנֵיכֶם,-כֶן,-הֶם,-הֶן   אוֹזְנַיי, -יךָ,-יִיךְ,-יו,-יהָ,-ינו,   אוֹזְנֵי המן)   (אוֹזְנוֹ)   אוֹזְנַיִם ◄
                                  ...*'oz-NAI*   *'oz-NEI*   *'oz-NO*   *'oz-NA-yeem*

As you can see from all of the examples above, if you know **one** of the forms that contains the changed vowel – i.e., the **singular** noun with possessive endings (e.g., בִּרְכּוֹ), the **plural** *smeechoot* form (e.g., בִּרְכֵּי) or the changed base of the **plural noun with endings** (e.g., בִּרְכַּיי) – you know them all!

Let's review

◆ When possessive endings are added to plural *segolates* that end in ־ִים, the base changes in the **last four forms** only (־יכֶם, ־יכֶן, ־יהֶם, ־יהן). The vowel in these forms is the same vowel as in the **singular noun with possessive endings** and as in the **plural *smeechoot*** form:

יַלְדֵיכֶם, -יכֶן, -יהֶם, -יהן   יַלְדַיי   יַלְדֵי-השכנים)   (יַלְדוֹ)   יְלָדִים: ◄
          ...*yal-dei-CHEM*   *ye-la-DAI*   *yal-DEI-*   *yal-DO*   *ye-la-DEEM*

◆ When possessive endings are added to plural segolates ending in ־וֹת and ־ַיִים, the base in all forms is the same as that of the singular noun with possessive endings, as in:

עַצְמוֹתֵיכֶם,-כֶן,-הֶם,-הן   עַצְמוֹתַיי   עַצְמוֹת הגוף)   (עַצְמוֹ)   עֲצָמוֹת: ◄
         ...*'ats-mo-TAI*   *'ats-MOT-*   *'ats-MO*   *'a-tsa-MOT*

בִּרְכֵּיכֶם,-כֶן,-הֶם,-הן   בִּרְכַּיי   בִּרְכֵּי הילד)   (בִּרְכּוֹ)   בִּרְכַּיִם: ◄
         ...*beer-KAI*   *beer-KEI-*   *beer-KO*   *beer-KA-yeem*

7. Verbal Nouns שְׁמוֹת פְּעוּלָה

> **Preview**
> • *What is verbal noun?*
> • *Automatic verbal noun forms*
> • *Non-automatic verbal noun forms*

• *What is a verbal noun?*

Read the following sentences:

שמעתי שפתחו את הכביש החדש בטקס חגיגי.

I heard that they opened the new highway with a festive ceremony.

שמעתי על הפְּתִיחָה החגיגית של הכביש החדש.

I heard about the festive opening of the new highway.

In the first sentence, the verb פתחו tells us what action was taken.

Q: What word in the second sentence expresses the **same idea** as the verb פתחו?

A: The noun פְּתִיחָה (opening). We refer to this as a *verbal noun* (שֵׁם פְּעוּלָה),[1] i.e., a noun that expresses the same idea as a verb.[2]

Let's look at some more examples of verbal nouns in Hebrew:

The guard fell asleep after three hours of guarding.	השומר נרדם אחרי שלוש שעות שְׁמִירָה.
(=after he guarded for three hours)	(אחרי ששמר שלוש שעות=)
The students learn driving in school.	התלמידים לומדים נְהִיגָה בבית הספר.
(=how to drive)	(איך נוהגים=)

---

1   In grammar books, verbal nouns are often called *gerunds*. However, the term *gerund* in English is limited to verbal nouns that end in "-ing." Sometimes, the English equivalent of a Hebrew verbal noun does not end in "-ing" and, thus, is not a gerund.

   The Hebrew term שם פעולה (= the noun or name of the **action**) may be misleading since not all verbs and verbal nouns denote actions, for example: לעמוד (to stand), עמידה (standing) denote a state, not an action.

2   See Haiim B. Rosen, 1977, p. 160.

All the Hebrew verbal nouns we have presented so far have the same form: מְםְםִיםָה. This is because they are all related to verbs in the same *beenyan*: *pa'al* (שָׁמַר, פָּתַח, נָהַג). The verbal nouns of other *beenyaneem* have different forms and will be discussed below.[3] But before we look at other verbal noun forms in Hebrew, let's look at several questions that relate to **all** verbal nouns. We will use the form םְםְםִיםָה as our example.

The English equivalents of Hebrew verbal nouns

Q: What are the English equivalents of the verbal nouns mentioned above: שמירה, פתיחה and נהיגה?

A: All three are translated as nouns with an *-ing* ending: opening, guarding and driving. This is often, but **not always**, the case. For example, the word מְכִירָה can be translated as sale, as in:

◄ מְכִירַת סמים אסורה ברוב המדינות.

> The sale (=selling) of drugs is forbidden in most countries.

Thus, when you translate from English to Hebrew, you have to be aware that a variety of forms in English (here, both selling and sale) can be rendered in Hebrew using the form of a Hebrew verbal noun.

Uses of the Hebrew verbal noun form

Now let's take a further look at the uses of the verbal noun form in Hebrew.

Read the following sentence containing the verb סָתַם (to fill a cavity/hole):

◄ רופא השיניים סתם את החור בשן של גלי.

> The dentist filled the cavity in Gali's tooth.

Here is the verbal noun that expresses the same idea as the verb סָתַם:

◄ סתימת החור נמשכה רבע שעה.
(not in *smeechoot*: סתימה)

> Filling the cavity took fifteen minutes.

In a different context, this same verbal noun **form** can have a **different** meaning:

◄ לגלי יש סתימה חדשה.

> Gali has a new filling.

In this last sentence, the verbal noun **form** is used to denote the new "thing" in Gali's mouth. Often, as in this case, this "thing" is the **result** of the action denoted by the verb. In this sentence, the noun סתימה (a filling) has the **form** of a verbal noun, but **not** the **meaning**. In contrast, סתימה in the previous sentence is a **verbal noun** in both **form and meaning**.

---

3 For more on the seven *beenyaneem*, see the chapter "Patterns of Verbs," pp. 361-368.

Note: Words whose **meaning** is that of a verbal noun generally do **not** appear in the plural.[4] When the meaning is that of a regular noun, the word may appear in its singular or plural form (e.g., סתימות fillings).

In some cases, a noun that has the **form** of a verbal noun has the meaning only of a regular noun, for example:

> ◄ התלמידים רשמו את שמם ברשימה.   The students wrote (listed) their names on the list.

Here the noun רשימה (a list) denotes only what **results** from the action (רשמו listed).

Please note: In textbooks, both uses of סתימה, as well as nouns like רשימה, are often referred to as *verbal nouns* (שמות פעולה). When this is the case, it is actually the **form** of the word that is being referred to and **not** necessarily its meaning. The truth is that often it is difficult to determine whether a word is a verbal noun in meaning – i.e., whether it expresses the **same idea** as its verb or whether it expresses the **result** of the verb.

• *Automatic verbal noun forms*

Beenyan pa'al (פָּעַל)

As we mentioned in the introduction above, the words סְתִימָה and נְהִיגָה, שְׁמִירָה, פְּתִיחָה all have the same form (הָ□□י□ָה) because they correspond to verbs from the **same *beenyan*: pa'al**.

Here are the infinitives and past tense הוא forms that correspond to these verbal nouns:

verbal noun שם פעולה		past tense עבר		infinitive שם פועל ◄
□ְ□ִי□ָה	⇐	□ָ□□	⇐	לִ□□ֹ□
פְּתִיחָה		הוא פָּתַח		לִפְתוֹחַ
שְׁמִירָה		הוא שָׁמַר		לִשְׁמוֹר
נְהִיגָה		הוא נָהַג		לִנְהוֹג
סְתִימָה		הוא סָתַם		לִסְתוֹם

---

4 In today's use, sometimes even verbal nouns may have a plural form, as in:

> ◄ במהלך הבדיקות חל שיפור במצבו של החולה.
> In the course of testing, an improvement took place in the patient's condition.
>
> המשטרה עצרה עשרות אנשים במהלך החיפושים אחרי החשוד.
> The police arrested tens of people in the course of searching for the suspect.

The הֶםְםִיּהָ pattern is the **most common** verbal noun pattern for verbs in *beenyan pa'al*. For this reason, it is often called the **"automatic"** verbal noun, i.e., a verbal noun whose pattern is **predictable**. Other verbal noun patterns of *pa'al* will be discussed below, after we look at the "automatic" verbal noun patterns of the other *beenyaneem*.

Note: Since the *passive beenyaneem – poo'al* and *hoof'al* – don't have their own verbal nouns, they use the verbal nouns of their *active* counterparts: *pee'el* and *heef'eel*, respectively.

Beenyan pee'el (פִּיעֵל)

Here are examples of the "automatic" verbal noun of *beenyan pee'el*:

⮜ אסור לְדַבֵּר בטלפון סלולרי בזמן השיעור.
verb:
It is forbidden to speak on a cell phone during class.

verbal noun:
הַדִּיבּוּר בטלפון סלולרי בזמן השיעור אסור.
Speaking on a cell phone during class is forbidden.

⮜ לא בריא לְעַשֵּן סיגריות.
verb: It is not healthy to smoke cigarettes.
verbal noun: Smoking is not healthy.   הָעִישׁוּן אינו בריא.

Thus:

infinitive		past tense		verbal noun
שם פועל		עבר		שם פעולה
לְםַםֵּם	⇐	םִםֵּים	⇐	םִםּוּם
לְדַבֵּר		הוא דִּיבֵּר		דִיבּוּר
לְעַשֵּן		הוא עִישֵּן		עישׁוּן

⮜

Notice that the first syllable of the verbal noun (םִםּוּם) is the same as that of the past tense verb (םִםֵּים).

As we saw above, here and in other *beenyaneem*, too, we have examples of nouns whose **form** is that of a verbal noun, but whose **meaning** is **not**, as in:

⮜ קראתי סיפור מעניין.   I read an interesting story.

The noun סיפור happens to denote the **result** of the actions לְסַפֵּר/סִיפֵּר (to tell).

The verbal noun of *pee'el* serves also as the verbal noun of its passive counterpart: *poo'al*. Thus, תיקון (fixing) expresses the same idea as the following verbs:

active:	The technician fixed the dryer yesterday.	הטכנאי תיקן את מייבש הכביסה אתמול. ◄
passive:	The dryer was fixed yesterday.	מייבש הכביסה תוקן אתמול.
verbal noun of both:		
	We paid a lot for the fixing of the dryer.	שילמנו הרבה על תיקון המייבש.

Beenyan heetpa'el (הִתְפַּעֵל)

Here are examples of the "automatic" verbal noun form of *beenyan heetpa'el*:

verb:	The Knesset member opposed the new law.	חבר הכנסת התנגד לחוק החדש. ◄
verbal noun:		חבר הכנסת הביע הִתְנַגְּדוּת לחוק החדש.
	The Knesset member expressed opposition to the new law.	

verb:	The child is developing nicely.	הילד מתפתח יפה. ◄
verbal noun:		ההורים דיברו עם הרופא על הִתְפַּתְּחוּת הילד.
	The parents spoke with the doctor about the child's development.	

Thus:

verbal noun שם פעולה		past tense עבר		infinitive שם פועל ◄
הִתְ◻◻◻וּת	⇐	הִתְ◻◻◻	⇐	לְהִתְ◻◻◻
הִתְנַגְּדוּת		הוא הִתְנַגֵּד		לְהִתְנַגֵּד
הִתְפַּתְּחוּת		הוא הִתְפַּתֵּחַ		לְהִתְפַּתֵּחַ

Notice that in *heetpa'el* the form of the verbal noun is very similar to its infinitive and past tense forms. We take the **past tense** form and add ות- to the end. When this ending is added, the vowel before it "reduces": it is usually not pronounced (הִתְנַגְּדוּת *heet-nag-DOOT*) and is written as a *shva* (◻).

Beenyan heef'eel (הִפְעִיל)

Here are examples of the "automatic" verbal noun of *beenyan heef'eel*:

verb:	We didn't manage to record the program.	לא הצלחנו להקליט את התוכנית. ◄
verbal noun:		הַקְלָטָה של התוכנית לא הצליחה.
	The recording of the program didn't work out.	

verb:
הבחורה שהדריכה את הקבוצה שלנו בירושלים הייתה מצוינת.

The young woman who guided our group in Jerusalem was excellent.

verbal noun:
הַהַדְרָכָה בטיול בירושלים הייתה מצוינת.

The guiding on the tour in Jerusalem was excellent.

In the case of *beenyan heef'eel*, the "automatic" verbal noun begins with the sound *ha* found in the **infinitive** form. All of its vowels are *ah*, as in הַרְגָשָׁה (*har-ga-SHA* – feeling) and הַזְמָנָה (*haz-ma-NA* – invitation). Its pattern is: הַ◌◌◌ה.

Thus:

verbal noun שם פעולה		past tense עבר		infinitive שם פועל
הַ◌◌◌ה	⇐	הִ◌◌ים	⇐	לְהַ◌◌ים
הַקְלָטָה		הוא הִקְלִיט		לְהַקְלִיט
הַדְרָכָה		הוא הִדְרִיךְ		לְהַדְרִיךְ

The passive *beenyan hoof'al* shares the verbal noun of its active partner, *beenyan heef'eel*. Thus:

active: Moshe recorded his new song yesterday.   משה הקליט את השיר החדש שלו אתמול.
passive: The new song was recorded yesterday.   השיר החדש הוקלט אתמול.
verbal noun of both:
The quality of the recording is excellent.   איכות ההקלטה מצוינת.

Beenyan neef'al (נִפְעַל)

Here is an example of the verbal noun associated with *beenyan neef'al*:

verb: רבים נדבקו בשפעת בשנה שעברה.
Many people got (were infected with) the flu last year.

verbal noun: הרופאים מנסים למנוע את הִידָּבְקוּת האוכלוסייה בשפעת.
The doctors are trying to prevent the population from getting (being infected with) the flu.

This verbal noun form is similar to the infinitive form of *neef'al* (לְהִידָּבֵק). Just remove the לְ- and add ־וּת: הִידָּבְקוּת. Notice that the vowel before the ending "reduces" and usually is not pronounced: הִידָּבְקוּת (*hee-dav-KOOT*).

Thus:

infinitive		past tense		verbal noun
שם פועל		עבר		שם פעולה
לְהִ◌◌◌◌	⇐	נִ◌◌◌	⇐	הִי◌◌◌◌וּת
לְהִדָּבֵק		הוא נִדְבַּק		הִידָּבְקוּת

While the הִי◌◌◌◌וּת form exists for some *neef'al* verbs, many verbs in *neef'al* tend to use the verbal noun of other *beenyaneem*, especially of *pa'al*, for example:

verb: אָסוּר לְהִיכָּנֵס לַמַעְבָּדָה שֶל הַפִיזִיקַאי.
It is forbidden to enter the physicist's laboratory.

verbal noun (like *pa'al*):   Entrance (=entering) is forbidden.   הַכְּנִיסָה אֲסוּרָה.

verb: מָתַי אֶפְשָר לְהֵירָשֵם לַקוּרְס הֶחָדָש?
When is it possible to register for the new course?

verbal noun (like *heef'eel*):   When does registration begin?   מָתַי הַהַרְשָׁמָה מַתְחִילָה?

Did you know?
Variations caused by special roots
The following variations in the forms of verbal nouns are caused by special roots. The changes are highlighted here and are discussed in the chapters on *gutturals* and on verbs with special roots.

heef'eel הפעיל	*heetpa'el* התפעל	*pee'el* פיעל	*pa'al* פעל
הַ◌◌◌◌ה	הִתְ◌◌◌◌וּת	◌ִי◌וּ◌	◌◌ִי◌ָה
model forms:			
לְהַרְגִיש – הַרְגָשָׁה	לְהִתְקַדֵם – הִתְקַדְמוּת	לְדַבֵּר – דִיבּוּר	לִכְתוֹב – כְּתִיבָה
variations:			
initial נ (פ"נ)	*initial* ש,שׂ, ס, צ, ז	*middle* א or ר	*initial guttural*
נ-כ-ר: לְהַכִּיר – הַכָּרָה	ש-ת-פ: לְהִשְׁתַתֵף – הִשְׁתַתְפוּת	ת-א-ר: לְתָאֵר – תֵיאוּר	ע-מ-ד: לַעֲמוֹד – עֲמִידָה
נ-פ-ל: לְהַפִּיל – הַפָּלָה	ס-כ-ל: לְהִסְתַכֵּל – הִסְתַכְּלוּת	פ-ר-ש: לְפָרֵש – פֵּירוּש	א-כ-ל: לֶאֱכוֹל – אֲכִילָה
initial י (פ"י)	*four-letter roots*	*four-letter roots*	*initial* י (פ"י)
י-ר-ד: לְהוֹרִיד – הוֹרָדָה	א-ר-ג-נ: לְהִתְאַרְגֵן – הִתְאַרְגְנוּת	א-ר-ג-נ: לְאַרְגֵן – אִרְגוּן	י-ש-ב: לָשֶבֶת – יְשִׁיבָה
י-ד-ע: לְהוֹדִיעַ – הוֹדָעָה		ש-ח-ר-ר: לְשַחְרֵר – שִחְרוּר	י-ר-ד: לָרֶדֶת – יְרִידָה

הפעיל *heef'eel*	התפעל *heetpa'el*	פיעל *pee'el*	פעל *pa'al*
הַ◌ְ◌ָ◌ָה	הִתְ◌ַ◌ְ◌וּת	◌ִ◌ּ◌וּם	◌ְ◌ִ◌ָה
middle ו or י		**middle י**	**middle ו or י**
(ע״ו, ע״י)		(ע״י)	(ע״ו, ע״י)
כ-ו-נ: לְהָכִין – הֲכָנָה		ט-י-ל: לְטַיֵּיל – טִיּוּל	ט-ו-ס: לָטוּס – טִיסָה
ב-י-נ: לְהָבִין – הֲבָנָה		צ-י-ר: לְצַיֵּיר – צִיּוּר	ש-י-ר: לָשִׁיר – שִׁירָה
		final י or ה	**final י or ה**
		(ל״י (ל״ה))	(ל״י (ל״ה))
		ש-נ-י: לְשַׁנּוֹת – שִׁינּוּי	ב-נ-י: לִבְנוֹת – בְּנִייָה
		ב-ל-י: לְבַלּוֹת – בִּילּוּי	ק-נ-י: לִקְנוֹת – קְנִייָה

Verbal nouns in smeechoot

Like other nouns, verbal nouns can be a part of a *smeechoot* phrase.[5] As is the case with other nouns, when verbal nouns are in the **final position** in the phrase, they do **not** change, as in: שעות פתיחה (opening hours). However, when a verbal noun is in a **non-final** position in a *smeechoot* – e.g., the **first** word in a two-word phrase (פתיחת הבנק the opening of the bank) or one of the **first two** words in a three-word phrase (הופעת מלכת אנגליה the appearance of the Queen of England), the form changes if it ends in ◌ָה (*ah*).

Here are the "automatic" verbal nouns that end in ◌ָה (*ah*) and change in the non-final position of a *smeechoot* phrase:

1. *Beenyan pa'al*: ◌ְ◌ִ◌ָה
   - (the) writing of letters, letter writing ⟸ כְּתִיבַת (ה)מכתבים ⟸ כְּתִיבָה + מכתבים
   - (the) closing of windows ⟸ סְגִירַת (ה)חלונות ⟸ סְגִירָה + חלונות

2. *Beenyan heef'eel*: הַ◌ְ◌ָ◌ָה
   - (the) inviting of guests ⟸ הַזְמָנַת (ה)אורחים ⟸ הַזְמָנָה + אורחים
   - (the) lighting of candles ⟸ הַדְלָקַת (ה)נרות ⟸ הַדְלָקָה + נרות

The form of the other verbal noun *patterns* (מִשְׁקָלִים) mentioned above does **not** change since they do not end in ◌ָה (*ah*): תיקון המכונית (the fixing of the car), הִתְקַדְּמוּת הילדים (the progress of the children), הִידָּבְקוּת האוכלוסייה (the infection of the population).

---

5   On *smeechoot*, see the chapter "*Smeechoot*," pp. 170-188.

Let's review

◆ A *verbal noun* is a noun that expresses the same idea as a verb. The English equivalent often has an *-ing* ending, as in שְׁמִירָה (guarding) and נְהִיגָה (driving), but this is not always the case (e.g., מְכִירָה sale).

◆ In Hebrew the pattern of the verbal noun is usually determined by the *beenyan* to which the corresponding verb belongs. We call the **most common** verbal noun pattern of each *beenyan* its "automatic" verbal noun.

- These are the four most common verbal noun forms:

בניין פָּעַל *pa'al*	בניין פִּיעֵל *pee'el*	בניין הִתְפַּעֵל *heetpa'el*	בניין הִפְעִיל *heef'eel*
◻ְ◻ִי◻ָה	◻ִי◻ו◻	הִתְ◻ַ◻ְ◻ו◻	הַ◻ְ◻ָ◻ָה
לִכְתּוֹב – כְּתִיבָה	לְדַבֵּר – דִיבּוּר	לְהִתְקַדֵּם – הִתְקַדְּמוּת	לְהַרְגִּיש – הַרְגָּשָׁה
לִבְדוֹק – בְּדִיקָה	לַעֲשֵׂן – עִישּׁוּן	לְהִתְפַּתֵּחַ – הִתְפַּתְּחוּת	לְהַקְלִיט – הַקְלָטָה

If a verb is in one of these *beenyaneem*, there's a good chance that its verbal noun will be in the form indicated here.

- The following verbal noun pattern is associated with *beenyan neef'al*:

בניין נפעל *neef'al*
הִי◻ָ◻ְ◻ו◻
לְהִידָבֵק – הִידָבְקוּת

Neef'al verbs often tend to use the verbal noun of **other** *beenyaneem* rather than this form.

- The exclusively passive *beenyaneem* – *poo'al* and *hoof'al* – use the verbal noun of their active partners, *pee'el* and *heef'eel*, respectively.

Want to see if you've understood?

Write the "automatic" verbal noun of the verbs in parentheses.

1. יש _____ רבה בעבודתו של הסטודנט.
(להתקדם)

2. חשוב לקרוא ספרים. ה_____ משפרת את ההבנה.
(לקרוא)

3. בילינו שעות ב_____ המפתחות שלנו.
(לחפש)

4. לבחור הזה יש _____ שלילית על החברים שלו.
(להשפיע)

5. המנהלת ביקשה לדבר עם ההורים של אחד התלמידים בגלל ה _____ הבעייתית שלו.
(להתנהג)

6. שמואל מבזבז שעות על _____ הניירות במשרדו.
(לסדר)

7. קראנו בעיתון על _____ השופט.
(להחליט)

8. אחותי עזרה לי ב _____ העבודה בספרות.
(לכתוב)

Answers:

1. התקדמות 2. קריאה 3. חיפוש 4. השפעה 5. התנהגות 6. סידור 7. החלטת 8. כתיבת

• *Non-automatic verbal noun forms*

In addition to the "automatic" forms discussed in the preceding section, there are other, less common patterns of verbal nouns associated with some of the *beenyaneem*. Since each of these verbs and its verbal noun must be learned individually, we are labeling these as "non-automatic." Here are some examples:

בניין הִפְעִיל *heef'eel*	בניין פִּיעֵל *pee'el*	בניין פָּעַל *pa'al* ◄
☐ְ☐ַ☐ֵ☐ ☐ְ☐ֵ☐	☐ַ☐ָ☐ָה	☐ְ☐ֵ☐ָה
לְהַמְשִׁיךְ – הֶמְשֵׁךְ continuing, – to continue continuation	לְבַקֵּשׁ – בַּקָשָׁה requesting, – to request request	לִשְׂרוֹף – שְׂרֵפָה burning – to burn
לְהַסְבִּיר – הֶסְבֵּר explaining, – to explain explanation	לְקַבֵּל – קַבָּלָה receiving, – to receive receipt	לִגְנוֹב – גְּנֵבָה stealing, – to steal theft
		☐ְ☐ָ☐ָה
		לִדְאוֹג – דְאָגָה worrying, – to worry worry
		לִצְעוֹק – צְעָקָה[6] yelling, – to yell yell

---

6   It can be argued that צעקה (and perhaps also דאגה) are not verbal nouns in meaning. We have included them here since they are presented as such in many grammar books (see, for example, Mazal Cohen-Weidenfeld, 2000, vol. I., p. 84).

Notice that the variations listed under *beenyan pa'al* (שְׂרֵפָה and צְעָקָה) are similar to the "automatic" verbal noun (כְּתִיבָה) in that they all begin with a *shva* and end in ◌ָה.

It is the vowel after the **second** consonant (letter) that differs in each variation:

◅ ◌ְ◌ִ◌ָה: כְּתִיבָה בְּדִיקָה

◅ ◌ְ◌ֵ◌ָה: שְׂרֵפָה גְּנֵבָה

◅ ◌ְ◌ָ◌ָה: דְּאָגָה צְעָקָה

"Borrowing" forms from other **beenyaneem**

Sometimes a verb in one *beenyan* uses the "automatic" verbal noun **pattern** of another *beenyan*. Here's an example:

verb:	I want to learn Italian.	◅ אני רוצה ללמוד איטלקית.
verbal noun:	I bought a book for learning Italian.	קניתי ספר לְלִימוד איטלקית.

The verb ללמוד (to study) belongs to *beenyan pa'al*, yet when we want to talk about the act of studying, we say לימוד. This is the "automatic" verbal noun form of *beenyan pee'el*, like דיבור and עישון.[7] Here are some more such "borrowings" from *pee'el*:

	verbal noun verb
dancing, a dance − to dance	◅ לרקוד – ריקוד
conquering, conquest − to conquer	לכבוש – כיבוש
cutting, a cut − to cut	לחתוך – חיתוך

Beenyan heetpa'el also "likes" to borrow the *pee'el* verbal noun form, for example:

using, use – to use	◅ להשתמש – שימוש
arguing, argument – to argue	להתווכח – ויכוח

On the other hand, we find that *beenyan pee'el* itself may do some borrowing:

playing (a musical instrument) – to play	◅ לנגן – נגינה[8]
laundering, laundry – to launder	לכבס – כביסה

In these examples, *pee'el* has borrowed from *beenyan pa'al*.

---

7   Actually, in the case of this verb, the "automatic" verbal noun למידה does exist, but is used mainly in technical terms connected with psychology and education, such as: בעיות למידה (learning disabilities) and תהליך הלמידה (the learning process).

8   The word ניגון also exists, but not as a verbal noun. ניגון means "a melody" (especially Chassidic).

As mentioned in the previous section, *neef'al* also "likes" to borrow from *pa'al*, but not exclusively, for example:

entering, entrance – to enter	להיכנס – כניסה ◄
registering, registration – to register	להירשם – הרשמה

Here כניסה is borrowed from *pa'al*, while הרשמה is from *heef'eel*.

Since it is impossible to predict if or when a verb will borrow its verbal noun form from another *beenyan*, we have to learn these forms, too, as "non-automatic" verbal nouns.

Other forms of verbal nouns

The verbal noun of some verbs has a form that is different from any of the verbal noun patterns listed above. These are also often referred to as "non-automatic" verbal nouns. Many of these nouns serve also as regular nouns.

Here are some examples:

Pa'al פעל

הסופר עבד חמש שנים על ספרו החדש. ◄
The writer worked for five years on his new book.

הסופר השקיע חמש שנים בַּעֲבוֹדָה על הספר.
The writer invested five years in work on the book.

המשטרה חושדת שהאיש רצח את שכנו.
The police suspects that the man murdered his neighbor.

האיש חשוד בְּרֶצַח שכנו.[9]
The man is suspected of murdering his neighbor.

ההורים שלנו יעברו דירה בקיץ.
Our parents will move in the summer.

מַעֲבַר דירה הוא פרויקט לא קל.
Moving is not an easy undertaking.

הסטודנטים פתרו את כל הבעיות המתמטיות בספר.
The students solved all the math problems in the book.

פִּתְרוֹן בעיות מתמטיות עוזר לפיתוח החשיבה.[10]
Solving math problems helps develop one's thinking.

---

9 The word רציחה also exists, but is less common. It is most frequently used with a possessive ending (e.g., רציחתו) or in its plural form (רציחות).

10 The word פתירה also exists but is less common. Both פתרון and פתירה are used to denote the act of "solving," but only פתרון is used also to denote the result of this act: the solution.

פיעל Pee'el

המורה חילקה את המבחנים לכל התלמידים.

The teacher gave out the exams to all the students.

לאחר חֲלוּקַת המבחנים כל התלמידים התחילו לכתוב.[11]

After the giving out of the exams all the students started writing.

Five actors acted in the performance.

חמישה שחקנים שיחקו בהצגה.

המִשְׂחָק של השחקן הראשי בהצגה היה מצוין.

The acting of the main actor in the play was excellent.

התפעל Heetpa'el

When we exert ourselves, our pulse rate goes up.

When exerting ourselves, our pulse rate goes up.

כשמתאמצים, הדופק עולה.

בשעת מַאֲמָץ הדופק עולה.[12]

Note: Not every verb has a verbal noun. Sometimes verbs that don't have their own verbal noun use the verbal noun of a different verb altogether, for example:

waiting – to wait   לְחַכּוֹת – הַמְתָּנָה

verb: החולים לא תמיד מחכים בסבלנות לתור שלהם אצל הרופא.

The patients don't always wait patiently for their appointment with the doctor.

verbal noun: בזמן ההמתנה לרופא החולים קוראים מגזינים ומדברים עם חולים אחרים.

While waiting for the doctor, the patients read magazines and speak with other patients.

Note: As we have seen above, and as we have noted in the footnotes, some verbs have more than one verbal noun. Sometimes, both verbal nouns have the same meaning or overlapping meanings (התאמצות, מאמץ), but one is used more frequently than the other. In some cases, a verb has more than one meaning and has separate verbal nouns for each meaning (חילוק, חלוקה).[13]

---

11 The word חילוק also exists, but has a different meaning: "division," as in "כֶּפֶל וְחִילוּק" (multiplication and division in arithmetic).

12 The word הִתְאַמְּצוּת also exists, but is less common.

13 See note 11.

Did you know?
Verbal nouns and prepositions

Verbal nouns usually take the same preposition as their verbs. Just as we use
השמירה **על הבניין** in על (to guard the building), so, too, we use לשמור **על הבניין** in על
(guarding the building); just as the preposition of לנסוע is ל- (לנסוע לאילת to travel
to Eilat), it is also the preposition of the verbal noun נסיעה לאילת (traveling
/ the trip to Eilat).

What happens after a verbal noun whose verb is followed by את (e.g., לאכול **את**)?
The verbal noun often joins the following word to form a *smeechoot phrase:*[14]

> ◄ האורחים אכלו את המרק בתיאבון רב.
> The guests ate the soup with a hearty appetite.

> לאחר אכילת המרק אכלו האורחים את המנה העיקרית.
> After eating the soup, the guests ate the main course.

Some verbal nouns take a preposition different from that of their verbs, as in:

> ◄ רון אוהב את מיכל.
> Ron loves Michal.

> האהבה של רון למיכל חזקה מאוד.
> Ron's love for Michal is very strong.

---

14 Here are some cases in which the verbal noun does **not** form a *smeechoot* phrase with the noun that follows it. Rather, prepositions such as את or של may be used.
1. In literary Hebrew, את is sometimes used after a verbal noun, especially if the verbal noun has a possessive ending, as in:

> ◄ בגלל שֶׂנְאָתָם את האויב...   הודות לאַהֲבָתָם את אחיהם...
> Because of their hatred of the enemy...   Thanks to their love for their brothers...

2. Sometimes של is used after the verbal noun. This is especially common when the verbal noun is the second noun in a *smeechoot* phrase, as in:

> ◄ מהי שעת הסגירה של החנות? (לסגור את)   What is the closing time of this/the store?

Also, when there is an adjective after the verbal noun, we often use the word של, as in:

> ◄ אחרי הספירה האחרונה של הקולות ידעו מי זכה בבחירות. (לספור את)
> After the last count of the votes, it will be known/clear who won the elections.

Let's review

In addition to the "automatic" verbal nouns that we have seen in the previous section, some verbs have a "non-automatic" verbal noun.

◆ The following are "non-automatic" verbal nouns that are associated with specific *beenyaneem*:

heef'eel הִפְעִיל	*pee'el* פִּיעֵל	*pa'al* פָּעַל ◄
הֶ◻ְ◻ֵ◻	◻ִ◻ֶ◻ָה	◻ְ◻ֵ◻ָה
לְהַמְשִׁיךְ – הֶמְשֵׁךְ	לְבַקֵּשׁ – בַּקָּשָׁה	לִשְׂרוֹף – שְׂרֵפָה
לְהַסְבִּיר – הֶסְבֵּר	לְקַבֵּל – קַבָּלָה	לִגְנוֹב – גְּנֵבָה

		◻ְ◻ָ◻ָה
		לִדְאוֹג – דְּאָגָה
		לִצְעוֹק – צְעָקָה

◆ The verbal nouns of some verbs are "borrowed" from other *beenyaneem* – and, thus, the connection between the verb and its verbal noun is "non-automatic," for example:

heetpa'el הִתְפַּעֵל	*pee'el* פִּיעֵל	*neef'al* נִפְעַל	*pa'al* פָּעַל ◄
להשתמש – שימוש	לנגן – נגינה	להיכנס – כניסה	לרקוד – ריקוד
להתווכח – ויכוח	לכבס – כביסה	להירשם – הרשמה	לכבוש – כיבוש

◆ Some verbal nouns have none of the patterns listed above. Their **form** is that of a regular noun, but at least one of their **meanings** (and **functions**) is that of a verbal noun, for example:

לחלק – חֲלוּקָה	לעבור – מַעֲבָר	לעבוד – עֲבוֹדָה ◄

Want to see if you've understood?

Write the correct form of the "non-automatic" verbal noun of the verb in parentheses.

1. המורה אמרה לתלמידים שהיא תשמח לעזור להם בשעת ה_____ שלה.
   (לקבל)

2. התלמיד הבין איך לפתור את התרגיל עוד לפני שהמורה סיים את ה_____.
   (להסביר)

3. _____ היא מעשה בלתי חוקי.
(לגנוב)

4. לאחר _____ צרפת על ידי גרמניה במלחמת העולם השנייה, הוקמה בצרפת
(לכבוש)

ממשלת בובות.

5. ה_____ בשקיות ניילון פוגע בסביבה.
(להשתמש)

6. לאחר ה_____ לקורס באוניברסיטה צריך לשלם את התשלום הראשון בבנק.
(להירשם)

7. מי אחראי על _____ העיתונים בצפון ירושלים?
(לחלק)

Answers:

1. קַבָּלָה 2. הֶסְבֵּר 3. גְּנֵבָה 4. כִּיבּוּש 5. שִׁימוּשׁ 6. הַרְשָׁמָה 7. חֲלוּקַת

III. Adjectives שְׁמוֹת תּוֹאַר

In this unit we will discuss the following aspects of adjectives:

1. **How Do Adjectives Behave?: Placement and Matching**
2. **How Are Adjectives Formed?**
3. **Adjectives Resulting from an Action Taken and Completed** (פָּעוּל, מְפוּעָל, מוּפְעָל)

1. How Do Adjectives Behave?: Placement and Matching

Preview

• *Adjectives in noun-adjective phrases* (ילדה קטנה, הילדה הקטנה)

• *Adjectives as the predicate of a sentence* (.הילדה קטנה)

Introduction

Here's a short passage describing the story "Little Red Riding Hood":

> הסיפור מספר על ילדה קטנה שהולכת ביער עם סל גדול. השיער של הילדה ארוך ומתולתל, והיא חובשת כובע אדום מקטיפה. סבתא של הילדה זקנה וחולה, והילדה מביאה לה דברים טובים בסל שלה.

This story is about a little girl who is walking in the forest carrying a big basket. The girl's hair is long and curly, and she is wearing a red hat of velvet. The girl's grandmother is old and ill, and the girl is bringing her good things in her basket.

The highlighted words in the above passage are all adjectives (שְׁמוֹת תּוֹאַר). They all refer to a **noun** and describe it. Adjectives and their nouns can be found in two different kinds of constructions:

a. *Noun-adjective phrases*

Here are examples from the passage above:

adjective + noun ◄

a little girl		ילדה קטנה
a big basket		סל גדול
a red hat		כובע אדום
good things		דברים טובים

These phrases are **not** sentences; rather, they appear in the passage as **parts** of sentences.

b. *Adjectives that are the predicate of a sentence*

The nouns השיער and סבתא are the subjects of the following sentences, while their adjectives are the *predicates*.[1]

◄   .השיער של הילדה ארוך ומתולתל
.סבתא של הילדה זקנה וחולה

The girl's hair is long and curly.
The girl's grandmother is old and ill.

In this chapter, we will deal first with adjectives and their behavior in **noun-adjective phrases** (as in section *a* above). After this, we will examine the behavior of adjectives when they are the **predicate** of the sentence in which they appear (as in section *b* above).

• *Adjectives in noun-adjective phrases*

The adjective comes after its noun

You may recall how surprised Little Red Riding Hood was when she got to her grandmother's house. In her fearful exclamations, she repeated the same adjective over and over:

◄   !אילו **אוזניים** גדולות יש לך
!אילו **עיניים** גדולות יש לך
!איזה **פה** גדול יש לך

Oh, Grandmother, what big **ears** you have!
Oh, Grandmother, what big **eyes** you have!
Oh, Grandmother, what a large (big!) **mouth** you have!

In both the English and Hebrew versions of these sentences, the adjective גדול (big) describes a noun (ears, eyes, mouth) and – with it – forms a phrase. Now let's look at the differences between the English and Hebrew.

---

1   For more on subjects and predicates, see the chapter "Non-Verb Sentences," pp. 705-708.

Q: What major difference do you see in the **placement** of the adjective next to the noun it describes?

A: The answer is, of course, that in English the adjective *big* comes **before** the noun: "a *big* mouth," whereas in Hebrew the adjective גדול comes **after** the noun:

≺   פה גדול

In Hebrew, the wolf has "*ears big, eyes big and a mouth big.*"

We can summarize this simply: In Hebrew, the adjective comes **after** its noun.

A Hebrew adjective has four forms

Little Red Riding Hood brought all kinds of things to her grandmother's house. Among them were:

a big basket	≺ סל גדול

In the basket she carried:

a big cake,	עוגה גדולה,
four big apples	ארבעה תפוחים גדולים
and six big cookies	ושש עוגיות גדולות.

Q: What difference do you see between the **form** of the English adjective *big* and the form of the Hebrew adjectives?

A: In English, the form of the adjective always stays the **same**, whereas in Hebrew, the form **changes**.

Every adjective in Hebrew has not one form, but **four**! The adjective *big* in English may appear in Hebrew, as in the above examples, in one of the following forms:

≺   גָּדוֹל, גְּדוֹלָה, גְּדוֹלִים, גְּדוֹלוֹת

An adjective matches its noun

What determines which of the four forms a Hebrew adjective will take?

The **noun** described by the adjective determines the adjective's form. The adjective in a noun-adjective phrase **matches** its noun in **gender** (*m./f.*), in **number** (*s./pl.*) and in **definiteness**.

1. *Matching in gender: Is the noun masculine (זָכָר) or feminine (נְקֵבָה)?*

In Hebrew, a **masculine** noun is always described by a **masculine** adjective, as in ילד גדול.
A **feminine** noun is always described by a **feminine** adjective, as in ילדה גדולה.[2]

Let's look at a few more examples:

נקבה	זכר
feminine	*masculine*
f. ⇔ f.	m. ⇔ m.
⌃	⌃
אישה נֶחְמָדָה	איש נֶחְמָד
a nice woman	a nice man
תלמידה טוֹבָה	תלמיד טוֹב
a good student (*f.*)	a good student (*m.*)
חולצה אֲדוּמָה	מעיל אָדוֹם
a red shirt	a red coat

Q: What do all the **masculine** adjectives in these examples have in common?

A: They have **no ending**. The masculine singular form is always the most basic form of the adjective and, thus, is the form listed in the dictionary.

Q: And what do the **feminine** adjectives listed above have in common?

A: In all the above examples, the feminine adjective ends in ־ה (*ah*):

נחמָדָה, טובָה, אדומָה ⊲

This is very often the case. There are, however, other adjectives whose feminine singular ending is ת-, as in:

נקבה	זכר
feminine	*masculine*
f. ⇔ f.	m. ⇔ m.
⌃	⌃
תוכנית מְעַנְיֶינֶת	ספר מְעַנְיֵין
an interesting program	an interesting book
ארוחה נֶהְדֶרֶת	סרט נֶהְדָר
a wonderful meal	a wonderful movie

---

2   On gender, see the chapter "The Gender of Nouns," pp. 18-33.

We will deal in the next chapter ("How Are Adjectives Formed?") with the question of **which** ending a given feminine singular adjective will take. The important point to remember is: The feminine singular adjective (unlike the noun) always ends in either ‑ה or ‑ת.[3]

2. *Matching in number: Is the noun singular (יחיד) or plural (רבים)?*

Let's look at the following examples of adjectives added to singular and plural nouns:

		רבים *plural* pl. ⇔ pl.	יחיד *singular* sing. ⇔ sing.	
masculine:	big children	יְלָדִים גְדוֹלִים	יֶלֶד גָדוֹל	☚
	interesting books	סְפָרִים מְעַנְיְינִים	סֵפֶר מְעַנְיֵין	
	red apples	תַפוּחִים אֲדוּמִים	תַפוּחַ אָדוֹם	
feminine:	big girls	יְלָדוֹת גְדוֹלוֹת	יַלְדָה גְדוֹלָה	☚
	blue shirts	חוּלְצוֹת כְחוּלוֹת	חוּלְצָה כְחוּלָה	
	long dresses	שְמָלוֹת אֲרוּכּוֹת	שִׂמְלָה אֲרוּכָּה	

Q: In the plural column, how many different endings do the **adjectives** take?

A: Two: ‑ים and ‑וֹת.

These are the same plural endings that most **nouns** take, but remember: When these endings are added to nouns, they simply indicate that the noun is plural and not whether the noun is masculine or feminine.[4] This is **not so** in the case of **adjectives**: A plural masculine adjective **always** ends in ‑ים, and a plural feminine adjective **always** ends in ‑וֹת.

If you examine the following examples you will understand why we are emphasizing this point:

		רבים *plural* pl. ⇔ pl.	יחיד *singular* sing. ⇔ sing.	
masculine:	big tables	שולחנות גדולים	שולחן גדול	☚
	new windows	חלונות חדשים	חלון חדש	
	old chairs	כיסאות ישנים	כיסא ישן	

---

3 For variations of these endings ‑יָה‑, ‑ית (אישה דָתִיָה, בחורה ישראלית), see the chapter "How Are Adjectives Formed?" pp. 153-155.

4 For more on plural forms of nouns, see the chapter "How Are Nouns Made Plural?" pp. 34-35.

This may look strange, but it is correct: The plural forms of שׁוּלחן, חלון, כיסא happen to be שׁולחנות, חלונות, כיסאות; however, since שׁולחן, חלון, כיסא are all **masculine**, the plural adjective that describes them ends in ־ים:

גְּדוֹלִים, חֲדָשִׁים, יְשָׁנִים ◄

Let's examine another set of nouns with "irregular" plurals:[5]

feminine:	big stones	אבנים גדולות	אבן גדולה ◄
	good years	שנים טובות	שנה טובה
	new words	מילים חדשות	מילה חדשה

Q: Why does the ending of the plural **adjectives** ־ות not match the ending of these plural **nouns**, which is ־ים?

A: Because the nouns themselves are **feminine**. Their plural form happens to end in ־ים, but it is the **gender** of the nouns and **not** their endings that determines the form of the adjectives that describe them. Since the above nouns are **feminine**, their adjectives take the feminine ending ־ות.

A handy way to check matching

Here is a handy way to check if you are using the proper form of the adjective with a plural noun.[6] First, add an adjective to the **singular** form of the noun. To do this, you must know (or check in the dictionary) whether the noun is masculine or feminine. For example, let's take the words ילד and ילדה and add adjectives to them:

feminine	*masculine*	
ילדה נֶחְמָדָה	ילד נֶחְמָד	◄

Now that we have determined the **singular** form of the adjective, we automatically know its **plural** form, even without knowing the plural form of the noun, since all masculine adjectives end in ־ים and all feminine adjectives end in ־ות. Thus:

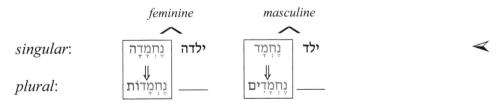

	feminine		*masculine*	
singular:	נֶחְמָדָה ילדה		נֶחְמָד ילד	◄
plural:	נֶחְמָדוֹת	_____	נֶחְמָדִים	_____

---

5   The plural endings of all nouns are unpredictable. For the sake of convenience, we will call masculine nouns that end in ־ות and feminine nouns that end in ־ים *irregular*.

6   A variation of this method of isolating adjectives was originally suggested by Dr. Rivka (Rikki) Bliboim.

Within the box, we can automatically change from singular to plural. Now we must add the plural noun form, whose ending is **not** predictable – it can be either ים- or ות- (in the case of the words ילד and ילדה, the form is "regular").

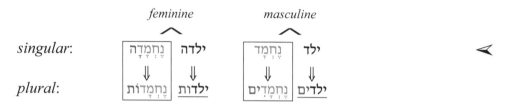

Now let's take a word with an "irregular" plural. Add the singular adjective, and then add the ending to the plural adjective:

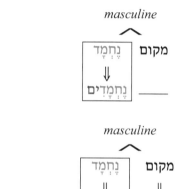

Next, add the noun, and *voila!*:

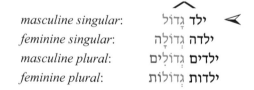

Let's review

♦ An adjective in a noun-adjective phrase comes **after** the noun it describes:

a big boy   ילד גדול   ≪

♦ Hebrew adjectives have **four** forms. The form used is determined by the noun they describe (we call this "matching"):

masculine singular: ילד גָּדוֹל   ≪
feminine singular: ילדה גְּדוֹלָה
masculine plural: ילדים גְּדוֹלִים
feminine plural: ילדות גְּדוֹלוֹת

- *Feminine singular* adjectives may end in ה-ָ or ת-:

טוֹבָה   יָפָה,   גְּדוֹלָה,   ≪
אַחֶרֶת   נֶהְדֶּרֶת,   רְצִינִית,

- *Masculine plural* adjectives **always** end in ים-, even when the noun ends in ות-:

ספרים מעניינים ◄

and also:

שולחנות גדולים

- *Feminine plural* adjectives (the adjective of a feminine plural noun) **always** end in ות-, even when the noun ends in ים-:

כיתות גדולות ◄

and also:

אבנים גדולות

 ◆ In order to use the correct plural form of the adjective, make sure the ending of the plural adjective corresponds to the **gender** (and not necessarily to the ending) of the noun.

 ## Want to see if you've understood?

Write the correct form of the missing adjective.

Examples: קניתי שתי מחברות *חדשות.* ⇐ קניתי מחברת <u>חדשה</u>.

קניתי שתי מחברות <u>חדשות</u>. ⇒ קניתי מחברת *חדשה.*

1. זה מקום <u>חשוב</u>. ⇐ אלה מקומות _____.

2. זאת חנות _____. ⇒ אלה חנויות <u>יקרות</u>.

3. זה בית _____. ⇒ אלה בתים <u>עתיקים</u>.

4. קראתי סיפור <u>מעניין</u>. ⇐ קראתי סיפורים _____.

5. אכלנו פרי _____. ⇒ אכלנו פירות <u>טעימים</u>.

6. קנינו ארון <u>חדש</u>. ⇐ קנינו ארונות _____.

7. שתיתי יין _____. ⇒ שתיתי יינות <u>טובים</u>.

8. זאת הייתה שנה <u>טובה</u>. ⇐ אלה היו שנים _____.

9. טיילנו ברחוב <u>שקט</u>. ⇐ טיילנו ברחובות _____.

Answers:

1. חשובים   2. יקרה   3. עתיק   4. מעניינים   5. טעים   6. חדשים   7. טוב   8. טובות   9. שקטים

3. *Matching in definiteness: Is the noun indefinite or definite?*

An adjective in a noun-adjective phrase matches its noun not only in **gender** and **number**, as we saw above, but also in **definiteness**. Let's look at some examples of this in the end of the story of Little Red Riding Hood, when the hunter arrives:

⤶ הַצַּיָּיד הָאַמִּיץ נכנס לבית של סבתא. הוא לבש מעיל אָרוֹךְ ועל הכתף שלו היה רובה גָדוֹל. הוא הרג
את הזאב הַשָּׁמֵן ופתח את הבטן הַגְּדוֹלָה שלו בסכין חַדָּה. והנה, סבתא יצאה משם בריאה ושלמה.

The brave hunter went into Grandmother's house. He wore a long coat, and on his shoulder was a big rifle. He killed the fat wolf and opened up its big belly with a sharp knife, and lo and behold: Grandmother came out unscathed!

The above passage contains many noun-adjective phrases. Some of the adjectives have a definite article -ה attached and others do not:

⤶ הָאַמִּיץ, אָרוֹךְ, גָדוֹל, הַשָּׁמֵן, הַגְּדוֹלָה, חַדָּה

Q: What determines whether or not the adjective has a -ה?

A: When the noun in the noun-adjective **phrase** is definite (specific), so too is the adjective:

⤶ הצייד הָאַמִּיץ,   הזאב הַשָּׁמֵן,   הבטן הַגְּדוֹלָה שלו
the brave hunter   the fat wolf   his big belly

Notice that in the English versions of these phrases, the word *the* occurs only **once**, before the whole phrase (for example: the brave hunter), whereas in Hebrew we say -ה **twice**: before the noun **and** before the adjective.

When the noun is **not** definite, the adjective isn't definite either:

⤶ מעיל אָרוֹךְ,   סכין חַדָּה
a long coat   a sharp knife

Let's examine a few more examples:

⤶ א. ביקרתי בעיר החדשה.   I visited the new city.
     נכנסנו למוזאון המפורסם.   We went into the famous museum.

⤶ ב. בתמונה רואים את בית הספר הישן.   In the picture we see the old school.
     אתמול הלכנו לחנות הבגדים החדשה.   Yesterday we went to the new clothing store.

Q: Why is the adjective **definite** in these sentences?

A: Because, in each case, the preceding noun is **definite**. Let's look more closely at each group.

In group א׳, the nouns are preceded by a preposition: בָּעיר, למוזאון. Because these sentences are written without vowel signs, you cannot see that in this case these prepositions contain the definite article -ה:[7]

> בְּ + הָ ⇐ בָּעיר
> לְ + הַ ⇐ לַמוזאון

We actually know that these prepositions contain -ה because the adjective that follows the noun has a -ה! The adjective is definite because the preceding noun is definite.

In group ב׳ the adjective is also preceded by a definite noun (in this case, a definite *smeechoot* phrase that is regarded as one word for these purposes). Since a *smeechoot* phrase never has a -ה on its first noun, but rather **only** on its last noun, we see that the entire phrase is definite by looking at the words הספר and הבגדים.[8] The adjective matches the *smeechoot* in definiteness:

> בית הספר הישן
> חנות הבגדים החדשה

Here are two more sentences containing noun-adjective phrases:

We studied about ancient Greece.	למדנו על יוון העתיקה.
I bought your new book.	קניתי את סִפְרְךָ החדש.

Q: Why do the adjectives here take the definite article -ה?

A: Even though the nouns יוון and סִפְרְךָ, which precede the adjectives, do **not** have a definite article, they are considered definite. In the first sentence, the noun יוון is the name of a country. Names of countries, cities and people are always definite, and therefore the adjective that is attached to them is definite, too:

ancient Greece	יוון העתיקה
East Jerusalem	ירושלים המזרחית

The noun in the second sentence – סִפְרְךָ – is made up of two words:

your book	הספר שלך ⇐ סִפְרְךָ

Notice that when the possessive endings are attached to this noun, the definite article -ה is no longer needed, since the ending itself makes the noun definite. Since ספרך is definite, so too is the adjective that follows it.

---

7   See the chapter "How Do Prepositions Behave When No Ending Is Attached?" p. 226.

8   See the chapter "*Smeechoot*," pp. 183-186.

your new book	⌢ ספרך החדש ◄
his cute brother	⌢ אחיו החמוד

Let's review

♦ An adjective that is attached to a noun in a phrase matches its noun in three ways:

   1. In **gender** – masculine or feminine:

a big boy (*m.*)	⌢ יֶלֶד גָדוֹל ◄
a big girl (*f.*)	יַלְדָה גְדוֹלָה

   2. In **number** – singular or plural:

a big boy (*s.*)	⌢ יֶלֶד גָדוֹל ◄
big boys (children) (*pl.*)	יְלָדִים גְדוֹלִים
important places (*pl.*)	מְקוֹמוֹת חֲשׁוּבִים

   3. In **definiteness** – indefinite or definite:

a big boy (*indef.*)	⌢ יֶלֶד גָדוֹל ◄
the big boy (*def.*)	הַיֶלֶד הַגָדוֹל
ancient Greece (*def.*)	יוון הָעַתִיקָה
my new book (*def.*)	סְפָרִי הֶחָדָש

Want to see if you've understood?
Translate.

1. a green cupboard _____

2. pretty dresses _____

3. the difficult problem _____

4. his new house ("his house" – one word: ביתו) _____

5. ancient Egypt _____

6. the new kindergarten _____

7. your (*m.pl.*) interesting opinion ("your opinion" – one word: דעתכם)

_____

8. an important decision _____

9. the white flowers _____

Answers:

1. ארון ירוק   2. שמלות יפות   3. הבעיה הקשה   4. ביתו החדש   5. מצרים העתיקה   6. גן הילדים החדש
7. דעתכם המעניינת   8. החלטה חשובה   9. הפרחים הלבנים

Did you know?
Adjectives that become nouns

Sometimes instead of a noun-adjective phrase, just the adjective is used instead of the phrase. This happens mainly with adjectives that refer to people. Here are some examples:

The young people said...	הצעירים אמרו...	1.
	(= האנשים הצעירים)	
Two old women live in this building.	שתי זקנות גרות בבניין הזה.	2.
	(= שתי נשים זקנות)	
Israelis like (love) to travel.	ישראלים אוהבים לטייל.	3.
	(= "אנשים ישראלים")[9]	

• *Adjectives as the predicate of a sentence*

In the sections above, we examined how adjectives behave when they are part of a **noun-adjective phrase**. Now let's look at the behavior of adjectives when their noun is the subject of a sentence and they appear as the **predicate**.

The student is new.	1. התלמיד חדש.
The beginning is always difficult.	2. ההתחלה תמיד קָשָׁה.
The lessons were interesting.	3. השיעורים היו מעניינים.
The breaks between lessons will be short today.	4. ההפסקות בין השיעורים יהיו קצרות היום.

---

9   The phrase "אנשים ישראלים" is usually not used. We say either "ישראלים" or "אנשים מישראל".

Q: Does the adjective in each of these sentences match its noun (the subject) in gender (*m./f.*), number (*s./pl.*) and definiteness?

A: Yes and no. Each adjective **does** match its noun in *gender* and in *number*:

m.s. ⇔ *m.s.*

1. **התלמיד** חדש.

f.s. ⇔ *f.s.*

2. **ההתחלה** תמיד קָשָׁה.

m.pl. ⇔ *m.pl.*

3. **השיעורים** היו מעניינים.

f.pl. ⇔ *f.pl.*

4. **ההפסקות** בין השיעורים יהיו קצרות.

However, unlike adjectives in phrases, these adjectives do **not** match their nouns in definiteness. Thus, while התלמיד החדש is a **phrase** meaning "the new student," חדש התלמיד – with -ה on the noun only – is a **sentence** meaning "The student is new." In most cases, when an adjective is the predicate of a sentence, it usually is **not** definite, while its subject usually is.[10] Here are some examples:

The students are nice.	התלמידים נחמדים.
Dina and Rina are talented.	דינה ורינה מוכשרות.
Our son was tired and hungry.	בננו היה עייף ורעב.
His school is beautiful and modern.	בית הספר שלו יפה ומודרני.

Let's review

- Adjectives in both phrases and sentences match their noun in **gender** and **number**.

- An adjective in a **phrase** (Column I below) matches its noun in **definiteness**, too: If the noun is indefinite, so is its adjective; if the noun is definite, so is its adjective.

---

10 There are some exceptions to this statement, in which the subjects and predicates are either **both** indefinite or **both** definite, such as:

Earthquakes are dangerous.	רעידות אדמה הן מסוכנות.
The tall dancer is the best in the troupe.	הרקדן הגבוה הוא הטוב ביותר בלהקה.

However, when a noun is **definite** and its adjective is **indefinite,** i.e., there is no matching in definiteness, the result is a **sentence**, not a phrase (Column II).

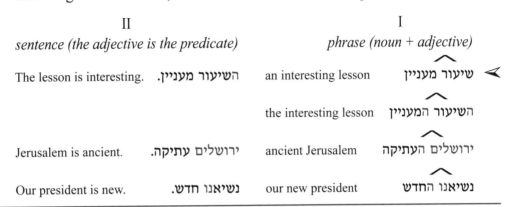

II		I	
sentence (the adjective is the predicate)		*phrase (noun + adjective)*	
The lesson is interesting.	השיעור מעניין.	an interesting lesson	שיעור מעניין
		the interesting lesson	השיעור המעניין
Jerusalem is ancient.	ירושלים עתיקה.	ancient Jerusalem	ירושלים העתיקה
Our president is new.	נשיאנו חדש.	our new president	נשיאנו החדש

Want to see if you've understood?

A. Choose the correct translation.

1. הסרט משעמם = _____

   (The movie is boring. / the boring movie)

2. חברינו נחמדים = _____

   (Our friends are nice. / our nice friends)

3. יונתן הקטן = _____

   (Jonathan is little. / little Jonathan)

4. העט הכחול = _____

   (The pen is blue. / the blue pen)

5. סלט הפסטה טעים = _____

   (The pasta salad tastes good. / the tasty pasta salad)

Answers:

   1. The movie is boring.   2. Our friends are nice.   3. little Jonathan   4. the blue pen   5. The pasta salad tastes good.

B. Translate.

1. I put the black briefcase (תיק) on the small table. _____

2. The sky is blue and the sand is white. _____

3. Your (*m.pl.*) school is new and beautiful. _____

Answers:

1. שמתי את התיק השחור על השולחן הקטן.   2. השמים כחולים והחול לבן.
3. בית הספר שלכם חדש ויפה. or בית ספרכם חדש ויפה.

2. How Are Adjectives Formed?

Preview

- *Combining a root and a pattern* (ג-ד-ל + חָםָ‌ם ⇐ גָדוֹל)
- *Adding an ending (suffix) to a base* (טֶבַע + ‏י- ⇐ טִבְעִי)

Introduction

As we saw in the previous chapter, all adjectives have **four forms** and **match** the nouns they describe in gender (masculine or feminine) and number (singular or plural):

f. pl.   m. pl.   f.s.   m.s.

בירושלים יש קניון מוֹדֶרְנִי וגם חומה עַתִיקָה, מוזאונים מְעַנְייְנִים וגם שכונות מְיוּחָדוֹת.

In Jerusalem there are a modern mall and an ancient wall, interesting museums and distinctive (lit.: special) neighborhoods.

In the next two sections we will concentrate on **how** these and other adjectives are formed. Being familiar with common forms of adjectives can help you **identify** a word as an adjective. This, in turn, helps you form noun-adjective phrases correctly and also provides the key to knowing how to make them **definite** and **plural**.[1]

• Combining a root and a pattern

Some common patterns of adjectives

Here is part of the story of Snow White. The highlighted words are all adjectives (they appear both in noun-adjective phrases and as predicates of sentences):

אחרי ששלגייה ברחה מהצייד של המלכה, היא הלכה ברגל במשך יום שָׁלֵם והגיעה ליער רָחוֹק. ביער היא ראתה בית קָטָן עם גג אָדוֹם. הבית לא היה נָעוּל, ושלגייה נכנסה. הבית היה שָׁקֵט מאוד. באחד החדרים היא ראתה שולחן רָחָב ונָמוּךְ ושבעה כיסאות. מאוחר יותר הגיעו בני הבית. המראה שלהם לא היה רָגִיל: כולם היו גמדים (האיש הכי גָבוֹהַּ מביניהם היה נמוך יותר ממנה). בני הבית הסכימו

---

1 For more on the importance of identifying adjectives, see the chapter "*Smeechoot,*" pp. 193-199.

ששלגייה תישאר לגור איתם. מאותו יום, כשהם חזרו מיום עבודה אָרוֹךְ, חיכה להם בבית אוכל טָעִים ששלגייה בישלה בשבילם.

After Snow White fled from the hunter employed by the queen, she walked for a whole day and came to a distant forest. In the forest she saw a small house with a red roof. The house was not locked, so Snow White went in. The house was very quiet. In one of the rooms Snow White saw a wide, low table and seven chairs. Later on, the occupants of the house arrived. Their appearance was quite unusual: They were all short in stature (the tallest of them was shorter than she). The seven men agreed that Snow White could stay and live with them. From that day on, when they returned from a long day at work, tasty food – prepared for them by Snow White – was waiting for them at home.

All the adjectives in this story can be grouped according to their *patterns*.[2]

Try this:

List the adjectives from the story in the correct place in the chart below. The empty squares in each pattern show the place of the *root* letters.

5. □ָ□וֹ□	4. □ָ□ִי□	3. □ָ□וֹ□	2. □ֵ□□	1. □ָ□□
___	___	___	___	___
___	___	___	___	___
___				
___				

Here's the solution:

5. □ָ□וֹ□	4. □ָ□ִי□	3. □ָ□וֹ□	2. □ֵ□□	1. □ָ□□
A. רָחוֹק	רָגִיל	נָעוּל	שָׁלֵם	קָטָן
גָּבוֹהַ	טָעִים	נָמוּךְ	שָׁקֵט	רָחָב
B. אָדֹם				
אָרֹךְ				

Let's look more closely at the last group. Here are the four forms of the adjectives of this group:

◄ A. רָחוֹק, רְחוֹקָה, רְחוֹקִים, רְחוֹקוֹת
גָּבוֹהַּ, גְּבוֹהָה, גְּבוֹהִים, גְּבוֹהוֹת

◄ B. אָדֹם, אֲדֻמָּה, אֲדֻמִּים, אֲדֻמּוֹת
אָרֹךְ, אֲרֻכָּה, אֲרֻכִּים, אֲרֻכּוֹת

---

2   On patterns, see the chapter "Pattern," pp. 9-16.

Look at the ו in the all the forms of both groups.

Q: In what way does the pronunciation of the ו in Group A differ from its pronunciation in Group B?

A: In Group A the vowel *oh* is present in all the forms (רָחוֹק, רְחוֹקָה, רְחוֹקִים, רְחוֹקוֹת), whereas in Group B only the masculine singular form has *oh* (אָדוֹם); in the rest of the forms the *oh* changes to *oo* אֲדוּמָה, אֲדוּמִים, אֲדוּמוֹת. In addition, the feminine and plural forms of אָדוֹם and אָרוֹךְ have a *dagesh* in the letter before their endings. Thus, instead of the *ch* sound of אָרוֹךְ ('a-ROCH), we say *k*: אֲרוּכָּה, אֲרוּכִּים, אֲרוּכּוֹת ('a-roo-KA, 'a-roo-KEEM, 'a-roo-KOT).[3] Hence, Group 5 is actually not one group, but **two**.

Here are some more adjectives that belong to each of the six patterns presented above:

	חָלָק smooth	לָבָן white	יָשָׁן old	חָדָשׁ new	(קָטָן, רָחָב): wide small	◻ָ◻ָ◻ .1 ◄
רָעֵב hungry	כָּבֵד heavy	שָׂמֵחַ happy	עָיֵיף tired	זָקֵן old	שָׁמֵן fat	(שָׁלֵם, שָׁקֵט): quiet whole ◻ָ◻ֵ◻ .2
אָסוּר forbidden	שָׁמוּר reserved	שָׁבוּר broken	פָּתוּחַ open	סָגוּר closed	(נָעוּל, נָמוּךְ): short locked ◻ָ◻וּ◻ .3
אָכִיל edible	שָׁבִיר breakable	מָהִיר fast	עָדִין delicate	עָשִׁיר rich	נָעִים pleasant	צָעִיר young	(רָגִיל, טָעִים): tasty regular ◻ָ◻ִי◻ .4
		קָדוֹשׁ holy	גָּדוֹל big	(רָחוֹק, גָּבוֹהַּ): tall distant	◻ָ◻וֹ◻ .5
סָגוֹל purple	כָּתוֹם orange	כָּחוֹל blue	צָהוֹב yellow	יָרוֹק green	(אָדוֹם) ◻ְ◻וּ◻ָה / ◻ָ◻וֹ◻: red ◻ָ◻וֹ◻ .6

As you see, the names of many colors are formed according to this last pattern. Thus, it is often referred to as "the pattern of colors."[4] There are, however, other very common adjectives, like אָרוֹךְ, that are formed according to this pattern but do not denote colors:

עָמוֹק deep	עָגוֹל round	מָתוֹק sweet	(אָרוֹךְ): long ◄

---

3 The *dagesh* in the *f.s.* and both plural forms of אדום does not affect their pronunciation.

4 שָׁחוֹר and אָפוֹר also belong to this pattern, but for phonetic reasons they retain the *oh* sound in all forms. Their forms are similar to those of גדול. See the chapter "The Pronunciation of ב, כ, פ and the *Dagesh*," pp. 637-638.

Not all of the six patterns mentioned here are used exclusively for adjectives. You may encounter other words with these patterns that are **not** adjectives, such as דָּבָר (thing) or גָּדֵל (he is growing), for example. In addition, these six patterns are only some of the adjective patterns that exist. More will be dealt with below.

Feminine singular forms of these adjectives: adding ה- (-ah)

Now let's look at the feminine singular forms of all of the above patterns:

◄	1. (...קָטָן):	קְטַנָּה[5] רְחָבָה
	2. (...שָׁלֵם):	שְׁלֵמָה שְׁקֵטָה
	3. (...נָעוּל):	נְעוּלָה נְמוּכָה
	4. (...רָגִיל):	רְגִילָה טְעִימָה
	5. (...רָחוֹק):	רְחוֹקָה גְּבוֹהָה
	6. (...אָדוֹם):	אֲדוּמָה אֲרוּכָּה

Q: What ending do all the forms take?

A: All feminine singular forms in these patterns end in ה-ָ:

◄ קְטַנָּה שְׁלֵמָה נְעוּלָה רְגִילָה רְחוֹקָה אֲדוּמָה

Changes in the first syllable (f.s., m.pl., f.pl.)

So far we have looked at the feminine singular forms of the above adjectives. Now let's look at all **four** forms. We have chosen an example from each of the above groups:

	f.pl.	m.pl	f.s.	m.s.
◄ 1.	קְטַנּוֹת	קְטַנִּים,	קְטַנָּה,	קָטָן,
2.	שְׁקֵטוֹת	שְׁקֵטִים,	שְׁקֵטָה,	שָׁקֵט,
3.	סְגוּרוֹת	סְגוּרִים,	סְגוּרָה,	סָגוּר,
4.	גְּדוֹלוֹת	גְּדוֹלִים,	גְּדוֹלָה,	גָּדוֹל,
5.	צְעִירוֹת	צְעִירִים,	צְעִירָה,	צָעִיר,
6.	צְהוּבּוֹת[6]	צְהוּבִּים,	צְהוּבָּה,	צָהוֹב,

---

5   קְטַנָּה is slightly different from רְחָבָה and other adjectives in this group. Since it sounds the same as the others, we are including it here.

6   The second vowel in all of the adjectives remains the same, **except for** in the pattern of colors in line 6 (צָהוֹב, צְהוּבָּה, צְהוּבִּים, צְהוּבּוֹת). Thus, for example, adjectives like שָׁקֵט in line 2 retain the *eh* sound in the middle of the word:

◄ שָׁקֵט, שְׁקֵטָה, שְׁקֵטִים, שְׁקֵטוֹת
   sha-KET   shke-TA   shke-TEEM   shke-TOT

Q: Aside from their endings, in what way do the **feminine singular** and both **plural** forms differ from the **masculine singular** form?

A: The masculine adjective in the above forms has an *ah* sound in the first syllable – *ka-TAN, sha-KET, sa-GOOR...* – whereas all other forms do **not** have this *ah* sound (the vowel "reduces").[7] When we write the vowel signs, we indicate this reduction with a *shva* (as in קְטַנָה). In today's pronunciation of the feminine singular and both plural forms, sometimes there is **no vowel sound** after the first consonant – *kta-NA, shke-TA, sgoo-RA, gdo-LA, kchoo-LA* – and in some words, such as צְעִירָה, רְגִילָה and יְרוּקָה, there is an *eh* sound: *tse-'ee-RA, re-gee-LA* and *ye-roo-KA*.

Exceptions to first syllable changes

Read aloud the four forms of the following words:

f.pl.	m.pl.	f.s.	m.s
חֲדָשׁוֹת	חֲדָשִׁים,	חֲדָשָׁה,	חָדָשׁ,
cha-da-SHOT	cha-da-SHEEM	cha-da-SHA	cha-DASH
אֲדוּמוֹת	אֲדוּמִים,	אֲדוּמָה,	אָדֹם,
'a-doo-MOT	'a-doo-MEEM	'a-doo-MA	'a-DOM

Whenever a word begins with א, ה, ח, ע (the guttural consonants), the *ah* vowel remains in the first syllable (e.g., *cha-da-SHA, 'a-doo-MA*).[8]

Let's review

- Thus far we have seen various common adjective *patterns*, such as:

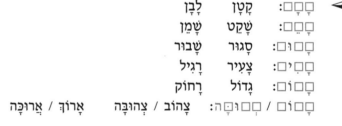

קָטָן	לָבָן	◌ָ◌ָ◌:
שָׁקֵט	שָׁמֵן	◌ָ◌ֵ◌:
סָגוּר	שָׁבוּר	◌ָ◌וּ◌:
צָעִיר	רָגִיל	◌ָ◌ִי◌:
גָּדוֹל	רָחוֹק	◌ָ◌וֹ◌:

צָהֹב / צְהֻבָּה   אָרֹךְ / אֲרוּכָּה   ◌ָ◌וֹ◌ / ◌ְ◌ֻ◌ָה:

---

7   Notice that all of the forms except for the masculine singular have an added **ending**, which is **stressed** when it is pronounced. The movement of the stress to these endings triggers the dropping of the *ah* vowel in the first syllable. This is called *vowel reduction*. For more on vowel reduction, see the chapter "Reduction of Vowels and the *Shva*," pp. 640-653.

8   See more on the gutturals in the chapter "Guttural Consonants: *Beenyan Pa'al*," pp. 450-453.

◆ The adjectives in the above patterns take the *feminine singular* ending ה‍ָ-:

➤ צְהוּבָּה גְדוֹלָה צְעִירָה סְגוּרָה שְׁקֵטָה קְטַנָה

◆ The first syllable loses its *ah* sound when endings are added:

➤ גָדוֹל גְדוֹלָה גְדוֹלִים גְדוֹלוֹת

When these adjectives begin with א', ה', ח', ע', the first syllable keeps its *ah* sound, for example:

➤ חָדָש חֲדָשָׁה חֲדָשִׁים חֲדָשׁוֹת

Want to see if you've understood?

Write the correct form of the adjectives.

1. סבתא קיבלה פרחים _____ מהנכדים ה‍_____ שלה.
                              (מתוק)   (אדום)

2. הַצַלַחַת ה‍_____ כבר _____ !
                            (שבור)   (כחול)

3. אתם גרים בשכונה _____ ו‍_____ .
                            (נעים)   (שקט)

4. החנות ה‍_____ ברחוב יפו _____ היום.
                         (סגור)   (חדש)

5. את _____ מאוד מפה, והדרך אלייך _____ מאוד.
                    (ארוך)   (רחוק)

6. הבת ה‍_____ שלך _____ מאוד.
                    (גבוה)   (צעיר)

7. הדירה ה‍_____ של דני ודבורה הייתה _____ יותר מהדירות ה‍_____
     (חדש)   (קטן)   (ישן)
   שהבנים שלהם קנו.

Answers:

1. אֲדוּמִים, מְתוּקִים 2. כְּחוּלָה, שְׁבוּרָה 3. שְׁקֵטָה, נְעִימָה 4. חֲדָשָׁה, סְגוּרָה 5. רְחוֹקָה, אֲרוּכָּה
6. צְעִירָה, גְבוֹהָה 7. יְשָׁנָה, קְטַנָה, חֲדָשׁוֹת

Patterns shared by adjectives and present tense verbs

Adjectives formed according to other common patterns are highlighted here, in the continuation of the Snow White story:

בני הבית לא היו כל כך מְסוּדָּרִים, אבל הם היו מַקְסִימִים והיו מאוד נֶחְמָדִים לשלגייה. הם אמרו לה ◄
שלפני שהיא הגיעה, הם היו בּוֹדְדִים והיה להם כבר קצת מְשַׁעֲמֵם, אבל עכשיו החיים שלהם יותר
מְעַנְיְינִים. החברים החדשים של שלגייה דאגו לה. הם אמרו לה לא לפתוח את הדלת, כי זה יכול להיות
מְסוּכָּן. הכול היה נֶהְדָּר, כמעט מוּשְׁלָם, עד שיום אחד הגיעה אישה זקנה ולא בדיוק מוֹשֶׁכֶת. היא נתנה
לשלגייה תפוח מוּרְעָל, ואז קרה דבר מַפְחִיד...

The occupants of the house were not very orderly, but they were wonderful and were very kind to Snow White. They told her that before she had arrived, they had been lonely and their lives had been rather boring. Now, however, their lives were interesting! Snow White's new friends looked out for her well-being. They told her not to open the door, since this could be dangerous. Everything was splendid, almost perfect, until one day an old – and not very attractive – woman came to call. She gave Snow White a poisoned apple, and then something scary happened…

Let's look more closely at the patterns of these adjectives.

Try this:

List each adjective in the table below according to its pattern. (Change the form of the adjectives that are not masculine singular to masculine singular).

6. מוּ◻ְ◻ָ◻	5. מַ◻ְ◻ִי◻	4. מְ◻וּ◻ָ◻	3. מְ◻ַ◻ֵ◻ / מְ◻ַ◻ְ◻ֵ◻	2. נִ◻ְ◻ָ◻	1. ◻וֹ◻ֵ◻
_____	_____	_____	_____	_____	_____
_____	_____	_____	_____	_____	_____
		_____	_____		

Here's the solution:

6. מוּ◻ְ◻ָ◻	5. מַ◻ְ◻ִי◻	4. מְ◻וּ◻ָ◻	3. מְ◻ַ◻ֵ◻ / מְ◻ַ◻ְ◻ֵ◻	2. נִ◻ְ◻ָ◻	1. ◻וֹ◻ֵ◻
מוּשְׁלָם	מַקְסִים	מְסוּדָּר	מְעַנְיְין⁹	נֶחְמָד	בּוֹדֵד
מוּרְעָל	מַפְחִיד	מְסוּכָּן	מְשַׁעֲמֵם	נֶהְדָּר	מוֹשֵׁךְ

---

9   מעניין and משעמם are examples of adjectives with **four-letter** *roots*. Four-letter roots are quite common in this pattern, which is the present tense form of *beenyan pee'el*. When three-letter roots appear in this pattern, there is a strong *dagesh* in the middle root letter, as in: מְמַכֵּר (addictive).

All of the adjective patterns listed in the table above are also patterns of present tense verbs. In the table below, we have added one more adjective pattern (מִתְ□□□□) and have presented examples of present tense **verbs**, too. At the top of each column, the name of the *beenyan* to which the verbs and adjectives belong is listed.[10]

Beenyan:	הוּפְעַל	הִפְעִיל	הִתְפַּעֵל	פֻּעַל	פִּעֵל	נִפְעַל	פָּעַל[11]
	hoof'al	*heef'eel*	*heetpa'el*	*poo'al*	*pee'el*	*neef'al*	*pa'al*
Present tense verb:	מוּזְמָן	מַרְגִּישׁ	מִתְלַבֵּשׁ	מְצוּלָם	מְדַבֵּר	נִכְנָס	כּוֹתֵב
Adjective pattern:	מוּ□□□	מַ□□ִ□ים	מִתְ□□□□	מ□וּ□□□ / מ□וּ□□□	מ□□□□ / מ□□□□	נ□□□□	□וֹ□□□
Adjectives:	מוּשְׁלָם	מַקְסִים	מִתְקַדֵּם	מְסוּדָּר	מְעַנְיֵין	נִפְלָא	בּוֹדֵד
	מוּרְעָל	מַפְחִיד	מִתְחַשֵּׁב	מְסוּכָּן	מְשַׁעֲמֵם	נֶחְמָד	מוֹשֵׁךְ
	מוּכְשָׁר	מַצְחִיק		מְצוּיָּן	מְמַכֵּר	נֶהְדָּר	
	מוּכָן			מְפוּנָּק			
				מְיוּחָד			
				מְבוּלְבָּל[12]			
	perfect	fantastic	advanced	orderly	interesting	wonderful	lonely
	poisoned	scary	considerate	dangerous	boring	nice	attractive
	talented	funny		excellent	addictive	fantastic	
	ready			special			
				confused			

Some *beenyaneem* supply us with many more of these adjectives than others (for example, *poo'al* and *hoof'al*). For an in-depth treatment of adjectives from these *beenyaneem*, see the chapter "Adjectives Resulting from an Action Taken and Completed" (pp. 159-169).

Feminine singular forms

Let's look at the feminine singular form of the present tense **verbs** listed above:

הופעל	הפעיל	התפעל	פועל	פיעל	נפעל	פעל
hoof'al	*heef'eel*	*heetpa'el*	*poo'al*	*pee'el*	*neef'al*	*pa'al*
מוּזְמֶנֶת	מַזְמִינָה	מִתְלַבֶּשֶׁת	מְצוּלֶמֶת	מְדַבֶּרֶת	נִכְנֶסֶת	כּוֹתֶבֶת ◄

---

10 The patterns are named according to the **past tense** הוא form of the verb. For example, the present tense verb כּוֹתֵב belongs to the pattern called פָּעַל (*pa'al*) – corresponding to the form כָּתַב.

11 Adjectives such as שָׂמֵחַ, זָקֵן, רָעֵב, which we saw earlier, also belong to *beenyan pa'al*. Their pattern is the same as the present tense verbs יָשֵׁן (sleeps) and גָּדֵל (grows). See the chapter "*Beenyan Pa'al*," pp. 393-395.

12 מבולבל is another example of an adjective with a **four-letter** root, this time in *beenyan poo'al*. Four-letter roots are quite common both in *pee'el* (מעניין and משעמם) and in *poo'al*. Here are more examples: משועמם (bored), מפורסם (advertised – the result of the action פרסם; also means *famous*), מקולקל (spoiled, as in *spoiled milk*).

Q: Which of the above feminine verb forms ends in תׁ?

A: All but מזמינה.

➤ כּוֹתֶבֶת   נִכְנֶסֶת   מְדַבֶּרֶת   מְצוֻלֶמֶת   מִתְלַבֶּשֶׁת   מַזְמִינָה   מוּזְמֶנֶת

Now let's compare the corresponding adjective forms:

מוּכְשֶׁרֶת	מַצְחִיקָה	מִתְקַדֶּמֶת	מְצוּיֶנֶת	מְעַנְיֶינֶת	נֶהְדֶרֶת	מוֹשֶׁכֶת
talented	funny	advanced	excellent	interesting	fantastic	attractive

In almost all cases, feminine adjectives that take the form of present tense verbs have the **same** feminine endings as verbs.

The following are some common exceptions. Their feminine singular ending is **not** the same as the corresponding verb or as other adjectives in the same group. These exceptions simply must be learned.

beenyan:	הופעל	נפעל	פעל
	hoof'al	*neef'al*	*pa'al*
exceptions:	מוּכָן / מוּכָנָה	נֶחְמָד / נֶחְמָדָה	בּוֹדֵד / בּוֹדְדָה[13]
	ready	nice	lonely
	מוּזָר / מוּזָרָה	נִפְלָא / נִפְלָאָה	
	strange	wonderful	

Compare these to the regular adjective forms:

מוּכְשָׁר / מוּכְשֶׁרֶת	נֶהְדָר / נֶהְדֶרֶת	מוֹשֵׁך / מוֹשֶׁכֶת
talented	fantastic	attractive
מוּבָן / מוּבֶנֶת		
understood		

Let's review

♦ In the second part of this section we have looked at adjective patterns whose form is the same as that of present tense verbs:

מוּ◻◻◻	מַ◻◻ִי◻	מִתְ◻◻ֵ◻	מְ◻וּ◻ָ◻ / מְ◻ַ◻ֵ◻	נ◻ְ◻ָ◻	◻וֹ◻ֵ◻
מוּכְשָׁר	מַצְחִיק	מִתְקַדֵּם	מְשׁוּגָע מְעַנְיֵין	נֶהְדָר	מוֹשֵׁך

---

13 When the adjective בּוֹדֵד means *lonely*, its feminine singular form is בּוֹדְדָה. When it means *single* or *individual*, the feminine singular form is בּוֹדֶדֶת, as in "תמונה בּוֹדֶדֶת" (an individual picture).

- As opposed to the adjectives that we examined in the first part of the chapter (גָדוֹל/ה, חָדָש/ה), adjectives that take the form of present tense verbs usually take the ending -ת in their feminine singular form.

	פָּעַל	נִפְעַל	פִּיעֵל	פּוּעַל	הִתְפַּעֵל	הוּפְעַל	beenyan:
	מוֹשֵׁךְ	נֶהְדָּר	מְעַנְיֵין	מְסוּדָּר	מִתְקַדֵּם	מוּכְשָׁר	m.s.:
	מוֹשֶׁכֶת	נֶהְדֶּרֶת	מְעַנְיֶינֶת	מְסוּדֶּרֶת	מִתְקַדֶּמֶת	מוּכְשֶׁרֶת	f.s.:

- Only one beenyan – heef'eel – acts differently. Almost **all** adjectives from this beenyan take the ending -ה in their feminine singular form, like most other adjectives: מַצְחִיק / מַצְחִיקָה.

For some exceptions, see above.[14]

Want to see if you've understood?

A. Write the correct form of the adjective. (All are adjectives that take the form of a present tense verb.)

1. קראנו בעיתון על הצגה _____ ו_____, אבל לדעתי היא הייתה
   (מצחיק)   (מצוין)

   _____.
   (משעמם)

2. רונית היא בחורה _____: היא _____, _____,
   (נהדר)   (מסודר)   (מוכשר)

   ו_____ מאוד.
   (מעניין)

3. ההתנהגות של שלומית קצת _____ בזמן האחרון, והיא נראית _____.
   (מוזר)   (מבולבל)

Answers:

1. מְצוּיֶינֶת, מַצְחִיקָה, מְשַׁעֲמֶמֶת   2. נֶהְדֶּרֶת, מְסוּדֶּרֶת, מוּכְשֶׁרֶת, מְעַנְיֶינֶת   3. מוּזָרָה, מְבוּלְבֶּלֶת

---

14 There are some adjectives in beenyan heef'eel whose feminine singular form takes 'ת, for example: "זְכוּכִית מַגְדֶּלֶת" (a magnifying glass).

B. Write the correct form of the adjective. (This exercise includes material from the entire section "Combining a root and a pattern.")

1. רוני גר בבית _____ עם דלת _____.
   (גדול)   (אדום)

2. כל יום הוא לובש חולצה _____ וז'קט _____.
   (לבן)   (שחור)

3. ליד הדירה ה_____ שלי יש גינה _____ ו _____.
   (חדש)   (קטן)   (מיוחד)

4. השחייה באזור הזה _____.
   (מסוכן)

5. החתולה הזאת _____ אבל _____.
   (מתוק)   (מפונק)

6. בקופסה ה_____ יש צלחת _____.
   (סגור)   (שביר)

7. הדעה שלכם _____ אבל קצת _____.
   (מעניין)   (מוזר)

Answers:

1. גָּדוֹל, אֲדוּמָה   2. לְבָנָה, שָׁחוֹר   3. חֲדָשָׁה, קְטַנָּה, מְיוּחֶדֶת   4. מְסוּכֶּנֶת   5. מְתוּקָה, מְפוּנֶּקֶת
6. סְגוּרָה, שְׁבִירָה   7. מְעַנְיֶינֶת, מוּזָרָה

• Adding an ending (suffix) to a base

In the preceding section we saw that many common adjectives are formed by combining a root and a pattern. In this section we will examine yet another way in which many common adjectives are formed: by adding an *ending* to a *base*. Here is an example:

adjective = *ending* + *base* ◄
דָתִי = ־ִי + דָת
religious   religion

Masculine singular forms ending in ־ִי

The ending ־ִי

Read the following:

◄ הסיפור על שלגייה אינו סיפור אֲמִיתִי או הִיסְטוֹרִי, אבל זה לא ממש בְּעָיָיתִי. זהו סיפור רוֹמַנְטִי מן הפולקלור הגֶרְמָנִי. אולפני וולט דיסני עשו ממנו סרט מִשְׁפַּחְתִּי מאוד יפה וְאֶסְתֵטִי. כדאי לראות אותו!

The tale of Snow White is neither a true nor a historical story, but this is not really problematic. It is a romantic tale from German folklore. Disney Studios made it into a lovely, aesthetic movie for the whole family (literally: familial movie). It's worth seeing!

Q: What do all the adjectives highlighted above have in common?

A: They all end in ‏י-‏. Usually the final ‏י-‏ is stressed, as in ‏אֲמִיתִי‏ (*'a-mee-TEE*) and ‏בְּעָיָיתִי‏ (*be-'a-ya-TEE*). Sometimes adjectives of foreign origin have an unstressed ‏י-‏, as in ‏הִיסְטוֹרִי‏ (*hees-TO-ree*), ‏רוֹמַנְטִי‏ (*ro-MAN-tee*) and ‏אֶסְתֶטִי‏ (*'es-TE-tee*).

Many adjectives that end in ‏י-‏ are formed from nouns. Sometimes ‏י-‏ is simply added to the end of a noun to create an adjective, as in:

‏יַלְדוּתִי‏	‏צִיבּוּרִי‏	‏דָתִי‏	◄
yal-doo-TEE	*tsee-boo-REE*	*da-TEE*	
childish	public	religious	

This is also so in the case of some adjectives denoting nationality, such as:

‏יַפָּנִי‏	‏סִינִי‏	‏סְפָרַדִי‏	‏צָרְפָתִי‏	◄
ya-PA-nee	*SEE-nee*	*sfa-ra-DEE*	*tsar-fa-TEE*	
Japanese	Chinese	Spanish	French	

Now let's look at the adjective ‏אֲמִיתִי‏ (true) from the passage above.

Q: What happened when ‏י-‏ was added to the noun ‏אֱמֶת‏ (truth) to form this adjective?

A: The vowels of ‏אֱמֶת‏ changed. The same is true of many other words, for example: ‏צְבָאִי‏ (military) from ‏צָבָא‏ (army), ‏טִבְעִי‏ (natural) from ‏טֶבַע‏ (nature) and ‏יְוָנִי‏ (Greek) from ‏יָוָן‏ (Greece).

Other adjectives ending in ‏י-‏, such as ‏הִיסְטוֹרִי‏ (historical) and ‏גֶרְמָנִי‏ (German) from the passage above, are formed in a slightly different way. In order to turn the nouns from which they come into adjectives, the final ‏יָה-‏ is removed and ‏י-‏ is added:[15]

‏גֶרְמָנִי‏	⇐	‏גֶרְמַנְיָה‏	‏הִיסְטוֹרִי‏,	⇐	‏הִיסְטוֹרְיָה‏	◄
ger-ma-NEE			*hees-TO-ree*			
German			historical			

Here are some more examples of academic subjects and nouns denoting nationality formed in this way:

---

15 We present here one possible explanation of how various adjectives are formed. There may be others.

➤ בִּיוֹלוֹגְיָה ⇐ בִּיוֹלוֹגִי,   סוֹצְיוֹלוֹגְיָה ⇐ סוֹצְיוֹלוֹגִי
            bee-yo-LO-gee   *sots-yo-LO-gee*
             biological   sociological

➤ רוּסְיָה ⇐ רוּסִי,   אַנְגְלִיָה ⇐ אַנְגְלִי,   רוֹמַנְיָה ⇐ רוֹמָנִי
    roo-SEE   *'an-GLEE*   *ro-ma-NEE*
    Russian   English   Romanian

An exception is the word for *Italian*: אִיטַלְקִי (from אִיטַלְיָה). In this adjective, the letter 'ק is added before the ending ִי-.

Other adjectives ending in ִי- are formed from nouns with an ָה- ending. Here, too, the ending drops off and ִי- is added:

➤ יְהוּדָה ⇐ יְהוּדִי,   כַּלְכָּלָה ⇐ כַּלְכָּלִי,   רְפוּאָה ⇐ רְפוּאִי,   מְדִינָה ⇐ מְדִינִי
   Judah   Jew/Jewish   economy   economic   medicine   medical   state   diplomatic

Sometimes the ָה- ending of a noun does not simply drop off when its adjective is formed. Rather, as in the cases of בְּעָיָיתִי and מִשְׁפַּחְתִּי in the passage above, 'ת **replaces** the final ה- and then the ending ִי- is added (sometimes accompanied by vowel changes):

➤ בְּעָיָה ⇐ בְּעָיָיתִי,   מִשְׁפָּחָה ⇐ מִשְׁפַּחְתִּי
   problem   problematic   family   familial

Here are some more adjectives ending in תִי-:

➤ חֶבְרָתִי   שִׁיטָתִי   שְׁנָתִי   אוֹפְנָתִי
   social   systematic   annual   fashionable, stylish

 Be careful! Since it is impossible to predict how a specific adjective will be formed, when you try creating adjectives from nouns, be sure to check the dictionary to see if the form exists.

Adding נִי- (-a-NEE) *and* וֹנִי- (-o-NEE)

Here are examples of two more endings on adjectives:

➤ הבחור הגיע לפגישה לבוש בבגד צִבְעוֹנִי ובידו פרח רֵיחָנִי.
The young man came to the meeting dressed in a colorful outfit with a fragrant flower in his hand.

In the case of רֵיחָנִי, the ending נִי- (-a-NEE) is added to the end of a noun:

◄ רֵיחַ ⇐ רֵיחָנִי
smell,   fragrant
fragrance

Here are some more adjectives with the ending נִי-:

◄ סוֹפָנִי   קוֹלָנִי   גוּפָנִי   רוּחָנִי   כּוֹחָנִי
terminal   loud   physical spiritual aggressive,
power-oriented

In צִבְעוֹנִי, the ending וֹנִי- (-o-NEE) is added (and some vowel changes also take place).

◄ צֶבַע ⇐ צִבְעוֹנִי
color   colorful

Here are some more adjectives that end in וֹנִי-:

◄ עִירוֹנִי   צִמְחוֹנִי   פִּרְחוֹנִי[16]
municipal vegetarian flowered, floral

Adjectives ending in אִי- (-a-'EE)

Look at the following sentences:

◄ דוד מבלה עם חבריו במקום לעבוד. הוא בחור עַצְמָאִי אבל מאוד לא אַחֲרָאִי.

David spends time with his friends instead of working. He is an independent young man, but very irresponsible.

The adjectives עצמאי and אחראי in the second sentence end in אִי- (-a-'EE):

◄ עַצְמָאִי   אַחֲרָאִי

Often the א' in these words exists also in the noun to which they are related, as in עַצְמָאוּת (independence), but this is not always the case, as we see in אַחֲרָיוּת (responsibility). Here are some more adjectives that end in אִי-:

◄ בַּנְקָאִי (צ'ק בַּנְקָאִי)   חַקְלָאִי (אזור חַקְלָאִי)   אוּנִיבֶרְסִיטָאִי (תואר אוּנִיבֶרְסִיטָאִי)[17]
bank check   agricultural area   university degree

---

16 For more examples and exercises, see Meira Rom and Rina Rafaeli, 2008, pp. 127-128, 137-138, 146.

17 The Hebrew phrases listed in parentheses are all *noun + adjective* phrases in which the form of each adjective is clearly adjectival. In the English translations, however, only in the phrase *agricultural area* does the adjective (*agricultural*) have a form different from the related noun (*agriculture*).

Be careful! When no vowel signs are used, adjectives and nouns that end in אי- look, but – according to rules of grammar – do not **sound** the same, for example:

This is an agricultural tool.	(adjective)	(chak-la-'EE)	.זה כלי חַקְלָאִי ◄
He works as a farmer.	(noun)	(chak-LAI)	הוא עובד כחַקְלַאי

I received a bank check.	(adjective)	(ban-ka-'EE)	.קיבלתי צ'ק בַּנְקָאִי
	(noun)	(ban-KAI)	מר כהן הוא בַּנְקַאי בכיר בבנק לאומי.
Mr. Cohen is a senior banker at Bank Leumi.			

Many speakers do not distinguish between the two, and pronounce both אָי- (a-'EE).

Did you know?

The adjective *American* can be either אָמֶרִיקָנִי or אָמֶרִיקָאִי (the latter form is probably influenced by the English ending -an). Similarly, we may say אַפְרִיקָאִי or אַפְרִיקָנִי (African), מֶקְסִיקָאִי or מֶקְסִיקָנִי (Mexican) (Moroccan), מָרוֹקָנִי or מָרוֹקָאִי (מֶקְסִיקָנִי is the form favored in today's Hebrew). For *Brazilian* we usually use only the form בְּרָזִילָאִי.

Let's review

Thus far we have seen that many adjectives are built from a *base* form to which an *ending* is added.

◆ Many masculine adjectives end in י-: צִיבּוּרִי, מְדִינִי, בְּעָיָיתִי. This ending is very common in adjectives denoting national origin (יִשְׂרְאֵלִי, צָרְפָתִי, גֶרְמָנִי) and in adjectives of foreign origin (בִּיוֹלוֹגִי, אוֹפְּטִימִי, רוֹמַנְטִי).

Usually the י- ending is stressed (דָתִי da-TEE), but – especially in foreign words – sometimes it isn't (רוֹמַנְטִי ro-MAN-tee). Sometimes the base remains the same (מְדִינִי, בְּעָיָיתִי) and sometimes it changes when the ending is added (דָתִי).

◆ Some adjectives are formed by adding the ending נִי- (-a-NEE) or וֹנִי- (-o-NEE) to the base: רוּחָנִי, עִירוֹנִי.

◆ Some adjectives end in אָי- (-a-'EE): עַצְמָאִי, אַחְרָאִי.

The feminine singular form of adjectives ending in יִ-

The following passage contains **feminine singular** forms of adjectives whose masculine singular form ends in יִ-.

◄ במסעדה ישבו סביב שולחן גדול צעירות מארצות שונות. המקום היה נעים והאווירה הייתה מאוד מִשְׁפַּחְתִּית. הבחורה הָאִיטַלְקִייָה לבשה שמלה אוֹפְנָתִית והזמינה עוגה דִיאֶטִית. הבחורה הַצָּרְפָתִייָה לבשה חולצה צִבְעוֹנִית ואכלה, כמובן, גבינה צָרְפָתִית. הבחורה הָאֲמֶרִיקָאִית אמרה שהיא צִמְחוֹנִית והזמינה נקניקייה צִמְחוֹנִית, והבחורה הַיִשְׂרְאֵלִית הייתה עסוקה בשיחת טלפון פְּרָטִית.

Young women from different countries sat around a table in a restaurant. The place was pleasant, and there was a "family" atmosphere (lit.: the atmosphere was familial). The young Italian woman wore a stylish dress and ordered a dietetic cake. The young French woman wore a colorful blouse and (obviously) ate French cheese. The young American woman said that she was vegetarian and ordered a vegetarian hotdog. The young Israeli woman was occupied with a private phone call.

Q: What is the ending of the feminine singular forms included in this paragraph?

A: Most end in ית- and some end in יָּיה, i.e., the endings ת- and יָּה- are added on to the masculine singular ending יִ-.

The feminine adjectives in the passage above that describe an **inanimate** noun all end in ית-, whether the adjective is non-ethnic (מִשְׁפַּחְתִּית, צָרְפָתִית, צִבְעוֹנִית) or ethnic (יִשְׂרְאֵלִית, צָרְפָתִית). (We are using the term "ethnic" for adjectives that denote nationality, religion or ethnic group.)

◄
אווירה מִשְׁפַּחְתִּית
שמלה אוֹפְנָתִית
עוגה דִיאֶטִית
חולצה צִבְעוֹנִית
גבינה צָרְפָתִית
נקניקייה צִמְחוֹנִית
שיחת טלפון פְּרָטִית

What happens when we describe a **person**?
Non-ethnic adjectives used to describe a **person** almost always take the ending ית-, as in the following examples from the passage above:

◄
a vegetarian young woman	בחורה צִמְחוֹנִית
a practical woman	אישה פְּרָקְטִית
a hyperactive girl	ילדה הִיפֶּרְאַקְטִיבִית
a passive student (*f.*)	תלמידה פָּסִיבִית

153

It is when **ethnic** adjectives are used to describe **people** that confusion sets in. In the above passage, some ethnic adjectives take ‎יָּיה- when referring to a woman, and others take ‎ית-:

ending in ‎יָּיה-:	בחורה איטלקָיָּיה, בחורה צרפתָיָּיה ⤙
ending in ‎ית-:	בחורה אמריקאִית, בחורה ישראלִית

‎יָּיה- or ‎ית-?

There is no fool-proof way for knowing whether a specific ethnic adjective that refers to a woman will take ‎יָּיה- or ‎ית-. However, the following rule-of-thumb helps us know in the majority of cases:[18]

When the stress in the **masculine adjective** is on the **last** syllable, the feminine ending is usually ‎יָּיה- (*-ee-YA*) (the stress moves to the end), as in:

יְהוּדִיָּיה	⇐	יְהוּדִי		רוּסִיָּיה,	⇐	רוּסִי	⤙
ye-hoo-dee-YA		*ye-hoo-DEE*		*roo-see-YA*		*roo-SEE*	
		Jewish				Russian	

Here are some more examples:

עֲרָבִיָּיה	נוֹצְרִיָּיה	אַשְׁכְּנַזִיָּיה	סְפָרַדִיָּיה	גֶּרְמָנִיָּיה	אַנְגְּלִיָּיה	צָרְפָתִיָּיה	אִיטַלְקִיָּיה ⤙
Arab	Christian	Ashkenazic	Sephardic, Spanish	German	English	French	Italian

When the stress in the **masculine adjective** is on the syllable **before the last**, the feminine ending is usually ‎ית- (and the placement of the stress remains the same), as in:

הוֹלַנְדִית	⇐	הוֹלַנְדִי		יַרְדֵּנִית,	⇐	יַרְדֵּנִי	⤙
ho-LAN-deet		*ho-LAN-dee*		*yar-DE-neet*		*yar-DE-nee*	
		Dutch				Jordanian	

Here are some more examples:

בּוּדְהִיסְטִית	דְּרוּזִית	שְׁוֵייצָרִית ⤙
bood-HEES-teet	*DROO-zeet*	*shve-TSA-reet*
Buddhist	Druze	Swiss

Here are some noteworthy exceptions (their feminine form takes ‎ית- even though the **last** syllable of the **masculine singular** adjective is stressed):

מוּסְלְמִית	⇐	מוּסְלְמִי		יִשְׂרְאֵלִית,	⇐	יִשְׂרְאֵלִי	⤙
moos-le-MEET		*moos-le-MEE*		*yees-re-'e-LEET*		*yees-re-'e-LEE*	
		Muslim				Israeli	

---

18 According to Rivka Bliboim, 1995, p. 28, who acknowledges Esther Goldenberg as her source.

The feminine singular form of the adjective דָתִי (religious) when referring to a woman is either דָתִית or דָתִיָּיה.

The plural forms of adjectives ending in -ִי

Masculine plural

The following passage contains **masculine plural** forms of adjectives whose masculine singular form ends in -ִי. Read the passage:

◄ בשולחן אחר במסעדה ישבו כמה בחורים. היו שם בחורים צָרְפָתִים ששתו יינות צָרְפָתִיִּים, בחורים איטלקים בבגדים צִבְעוֹנִיִּים שדיברו על עניינים פּוֹלִיטִיִּים וכמה בחורים מֶקְסִיקָנִים רְצִינִיִּים עם כובעים מֶקְסִיקָנִיִּים רחבים שדיברו על נושאים חֶבְרָתִיִּים.

At a different table in the restaurant sat several young men. There were young French men drinking French wines, young Italian men in colorful clothes, who were speaking about political matters and several young Mexican men in wide Mexican hats, who were speaking about social issues.

Q: What are the endings of the masculine plural adjectives highlighted above?

A: Some end in -ִים (צָרְפָתִים, מֶקְסִיקָנִים) and some end in -ִיִּים (צָרְפָתִיִּים, פּוֹלִיטִיִּים).

What determines whether the masculine plural adjective ending has two י or one?
If an adjective describes an **inanimate** noun, it (the adjective) always ends in two י (-ִיִּים), whether it is a regular adjective (פּוֹלִיטִיִּים, צִבְעוֹנִיִּים) or an ethnic adjective (מֶקְסִיקָנִיִּים, צָרְפָתִיִּים):

◄ בגדים צִבְעוֹנִיִּים, עניינים פּוֹלִיטִיִּים, נושאים חֶבְרָתִיִּים, יינות צָרְפָתִיִּים, כובעים מֶקְסִיקָנִיִּים

This is so because the ending -ִים is added on to the singular base form, which ends in -ִי:

◄ ישראלי |
◄ ישראלי | ים

And what if the adjective describes a **person**?

If the adjective is **regular** (non-ethnic), it usually ends in **two** י (-ִיִּים):

בחורים רְצִינִיִּים	אנשים פְּרַקְטִיִּים	סטודנטים דָתִיִּים
serious young men	practical people	religious students

If the adjective is **ethnic**, it usually ends in **one** י (-ִים), as in:

בחורים צָרְפָתִים	בחורים איטלקים	בחורים מֶקְסִיקָנִים

The above guidelines state the norm. In reality, however, Hebrew speakers do not always abide by them. For example, we might find people described as either:[19]

		not according to the norm:	the norm:
a regular adj.:	vegetarians (lit.: vegetarian people)	אנשים צִמְחוֹנִיִּים or	אנשים צִמְחוֹנִים ◅
an ethnic adj.:	Israeli soldiers	חיילים יִשְׂרְאֵלִים or	חיילים יִשְׂרְאֵלִיִּים[20]

Feminine plural

Read the continuation of our story:

אחרי כמה זמן הגיעו למסעדה עוד בחורות צָרְפָתִיּוֹת לבושות בחולצות צִבְעוֹנִיּוֹת. הן התחילו לדבר ◅
עם הבחורים הצרפתים. הגיעו גם עוד בחורות אִיטַלְקִיּוֹת לבושות בשמלות אוֹפְנָתִיּוֹת והן דיברו עם
הבחורים האיטלקים. כמה בחורות יִשְׂרְאֵלִיּוֹת וַאֲמֶרִיקָאִיּוֹת שהתיישבו בשולחן דיברו עם הבחורים
המקסיקנים בעברית ובאנגלית.

After a while more French women wearing colorful blouses arrived at the restaurant. They began speaking with the French men. More Italian women wearing stylish dresses arrived, too, and they spoke with the Italian men. Several Israeli and American women who sat down at the table spoke with the Mexican men in Hebrew and English.

The highlighted words are feminine plural forms of adjectives whose masculine singular form ends in ־ִי.

Q: What ending do they all have?

A: The ending is ־ִיּוֹת in all instances (for describing both inanimate nouns and people, with regular and ethnic adjectives):

חולצות צִבְעוֹנִיּוֹת, שמלות אוֹפְנָתִיּוֹת, בחורות צָרְפָתִיּוֹת, בחורות אִיטַלְקִיּוֹת, בחורות יִשְׂרְאֵלִיּוֹת ◅

---

19 The norms mentioned above regarding the forms of ethnic adjectives also apply to certain animals. For example, there is a tendency to say פילים הוֹדִיִּים (Indian elephants), but we also hear פילים הוֹדִים.
20 Forms denoting nationality, religion and ethnic group are also used as **nouns**, as in הצרפתים (the French), הישראלים (the Israelis). When this is the case, only one י is used.

Let's review

These are the endings of feminine singular adjectives and of plural adjectives whose singular forms end in ‏יַ- :

	inanimate	animate (people)	
	ethnic and non-ethnic adjs.	*non-ethnic adjs.*	*ethnic adjs.*
◆ *fem. sing.:*	always ‏ית-: שמלה מוֹדֶרְנִית גבינה צָרְפָתִית	usually ‏ית-: בחורה צִמְחוֹנִית exception: בחורה דָתִיָּיה / דָתִית	sometimes ‏ית-: בחורה אָמֶרִיקָאִית sometimes ‏ייה-: בחורה אִיטַלְקִיָּיה (detailed list in chapter)
◆ *masc. pl.:*	always two *yodeem* ‏יים-: בגדים צִבְעוֹנִיִּים ספרים צָרְפָתִיִּים	usually two *yodeem* ‏יים-: בחורים רְצִינִיִּים	usually one *yod* ‏ים-: בחורים צָרְפָתִים but also ‏יים-: בחורים צָרְפָתִיִּים
◆ *fem. pl.:*	always ‏יות-: חולצות צִבְעוֹנִיּוֹת	always ‏יות-: בחורות צִמְחוֹנִיּוֹת	always ‏יות-: בחורות אִיטַלְקִיּוֹת

Want to see if you've understood?
Write the correct form of the adjective.

1. במוזאון יש ציורים _____ וגם צילומים _____ .
   (קלסי)   (מודרני)

2. העובדים ה_____ יצאו לחופשה _____ ארוכה.
   (אמריקאי)   (שנתי)

3. הסיטואציות בסרט הזה לא _____ .
   (אמיתי)

4. הזמרת ה_____ שרה שירים _____ .
   (איטלקי)   (רומנטי)

5. כדאי לכם להביא לחברים ה_____ שלכם יינות _____ במתנה.
   (ישראלי)   (צרפתי)

6. בטלוויזיה ה_____ יש גם תוכניות _____ וגם קומדיות.
   (ישראלי)   (רציני)

7. התיירים ה_____ אוהבים לבקר באילת.
   (שוודי)

8. כדאי לשתות מיצים _____ .
   (טבעי)

Answers:

1. קְלַסִיִּים, מוֹדֶרְנִיִּים   2. אֲמֶרִיקָאִים, שְׁנָתִית   3. אֲמִיתִיוֹת   4. אִיטַלְקִיָּה, רוֹמַנְטִיִּים   5. יִשְׂרְאֵלִים, צָרְפָתִיִּים
6. יִשְׂרְאֵלִית, רְצִינִיוֹת   7. שְׁוֵדִים   8. טִבְעִיִּים

158

3. Adjectives Resulting from an Action Taken and Completed: פָּעוּל, מְפוּעָל, מוּפְעָל

Preview

* *Identifying "adjectives of completed action"*
* *The forms of "adjectives of completed action"*
* *The function of "adjectives of completed action" in a sentence*
* *The adjective-verb connection*

Introduction

Yossi and Sarah are throwing a party. Here's part of their conversation:

Yossi: Who (lit.: Whom) shall we invite to the party?	יוסי: אֶת מי נזמין למסיבה?
Sarah: David, because he is nice,	שרה: אֶת דוד כי הוא נֶחְמָד,
Dafna, because she is funny,	אֶת דפנה כי היא מַצְחִיקָה,
Ruti, because she is sociable,	אֶת רותי כי היא חַבְרוּתִית,
Mickey, because he is sweet,	אֶת מיקי כי הוא מָתוֹק,
And Orna, because she is interesting.	וְאֶת אורנה כי היא מְעַנְיֶינֶת.

In the list of guests above, we also see a list of their characteristics, which are expressed as adjectives (נֶחְמָד, מַצְחִיקָה...). As you can see, these adjectives take a variety of different forms.

A few minutes before the guests arrive, Sarah breathes a sigh of relief. She and Yossi have worked hard for hours, and now she can say to Yossi:

> יוסי, האורחים עוד מעט מגיעים, וסוף סוף הבית מְאוּרְגָן, האוכל מְבוּשָׁל, הפונץ' מְחוּמָם, הרצפה
> שְׁטוּפָה, העוגות מוּכָנוֹת והשולחן עָרוּךְ! אז למה אתה מוּדְאָג?

> Yossi, the guests will be arriving any minute, and finally the house is in order (lit.: organized), the food is cooked, the punch is heated, the floor is washed, the cakes are ready (lit.: prepared), and the table is set! So why are you worried?

Do you feel a difference in meaning between the **first** group of adjectives and the **second**?

The adjectives in the **second** group are all the **result of an action**: The house is מְאוּרְגָן (in order / organized) because someone put it in order or "organized" it (אִרְגֵן אותו); the food is מְבוּשָׁל (cooked) because someone cooked it (בִּישֵׁל אותו); the punch is מְחוּמָם (heated) because someone heated it (חִימֵם אותו); the floor is שְׁטוּפָה (washed) because someone washed it

(שָׁטַף אותה), the cakes are מוּכָנוֹת (ready, prepared) because someone prepared them (הֵכִין אותן), the table is עָרוּךְ (set) because someone set it (עָרַךְ אותו) and Yossi is מוּדְאָג (worried) because something is worrying him (מַדְאִיג אותו).[1]

As opposed to the adjectives in this second set of adjectives, those in the first set (נֶחְמָד, מַצְחִיק, חֲבְרוּתִי, מָתוֹק, מְעַנְיֵין) are **not** necessarily the result of an action taken.

• *Identifying "adjectives of completed action"*

Here are the "adjectives of completed action" from the story above in their masculine singular form. Try saying them out loud:

מְאוּרְגָן   מְבוּשָׁל   מְחוּמָם   שָׁטוּף   מוּכָן   עָרוּךְ   מוּדְאָג ◄

These adjectives can be divided into three groups according to their form: פָּעוּל (pa-'OOL), מְפוּעָל (me-foo-'AL) and מוּפְעָל (moof-'AL).

Try this:

List these adjectives in the correct place in the chart below. The empty squares in each pattern show the place of the *root* letters.[2]

מוּפְעָל	מְפוּעָל	פָּעוּל
מוּ◻◻ָ◻	מְ◻וּ◻ָ◻	◻ָ◻וּ◻
____	____	____
____	____	____
____	____	____

Here's the solution:

מוּפְעָל	מְפוּעָל	פָּעוּל
מוּכָן[4]	מְאוּרְגָן[3]	שָׁטוּף
מוּדְאָג	מְבוּשָׁל	עָרוּךְ
	מְחוּמָם	

---

1 With verbs like לְהַדְאִיג, which denote a state more than an actual action, we can see the adjective מוּדְאָג as the result of a verb in the present: משהו מדאיג אותו.

2 On roots, see the chapter "Root," pp. 3-8.

3 מְאוּרְגָן is an example of an adjective with a **four-letter** root (א-ר-ג-נ). As we pointed out in the chapter "How Are Adjectives Formed?" p. 145, note 12, four-letter roots are quite common in this form. Here are more examples: מְפוּרְסָם (advertised – the result of the action פִּרְסֵם; also means *famous*), מְקוּלְקָל (spoiled, as in spoiled milk).

4 מוּכָן looks somewhat different because the ו in the middle of its root (כ-ו-נ) has dropped out. Since מוּכָן begins with מוּ, we know that it belongs to the מוּפְעָל pattern. מוּבָן (understood) is similar in structure. (Here the root is ב-י-נ, and the י has dropped out.)

These three forms denote the result of a completed action.[5] The two adjective forms that begin with מ- – מְפוּעָל and מוּפְעָל – may look familiar to you, since they are the same forms as the present tense verbs of the passive *beenyaneem* פּוּעַל (*poo'al*) and הוּפְעַל (*hoof'al*). Below we will deal with the connection between the patterns of these adjectives and the *beenyaneem*.

Q: What **sound** do all of these adjectives have in common?

A: They all contain the sounds *oo* and *ah*, but it is the *oo* sound that makes them **different** from other adjectives. In each of the forms, the 'ו (the *oo* vowel) is in a different place:

מוּפְעָל		מְפוּעָל		פָּעוּל	
moo-CHAN	מוּכָן	*me-'oor-GAN*	מְאוּרְגָּן	*sha-TOOF*	שָׁטוּף
mood-'AG	מוּדְאָג	*me-voo-SHAL*	מְבוּשָׁל	*'a-ROOCH*	עָרוּךְ
		me-choo-MAM	מְחוּמָּם		

Here are some more examples:

1. Examples of פָּעוּל (*pa-'OOL*) (here the "ו" is in the last syllable):

This is a stolen car.	זה אוטו גָּנוּב. ◄
I sat next to the open window.	ישבתי ליד החלון הפָּתוּחַ.[6]
His heart is broken.	הלב שלו שָׁבוּר.
The bank is closed now.	הבנק סָגוּר עכשיו.

2. Examples of מְפוּעָל (*me-foo-'AL*) (here the "ו" is in the middle):

Rina likes cooked carrots.	רינה אוהבת גזר מְבוּשָׁל. ◄
Your computer is already fixed / repaired.	המחשב שלכם כבר מְתוּקָן.
The telephone line is disconnected.	קו הטלפון מְנוּתָּק.

3. Examples of מוּפְעָל (*moof-'AL*) (here the "ו" is at the beginning):

I found a typed letter.	מצאתי מכתב מוּדְפָּס. ◄
I'm sending you an enlarged photo.	אני שולחת לך צילום מוּגְדָּל.
Why are you worried?	למה אתה מוּדְאָג?
You look surprised.	אתה נראה מוּפְתָּע.

---

5 These forms may **also** be used for adjectives that do not denote a completed action, as you can read below.

6 In words that end in ח or ע, such as פָּתוּחַ (open) and יָדוּעַ (known), an extra *ah* vowel is added before the final ח' or ע', creating an extra syllable: *pa-TOO-ach, ya-DOO-a'* (compare: סָגוּר *sa-GOOR*, which has only **two** syllables).

Let's review

Three forms are used for "adjectives of completed action":[7]

◆ **פָּעוּל**	(*pa-'OOL*):	סָגוּר	שָׁבוּר	פָּתוּחַ
		closed	broken	open
◆ **מְפוּעָל** ◆	(*me-foo-'AL*):	מְנוּתָק	מְתוּקָן	מְבוּשָּׁל
		disconnected	fixed	cooked
◆ **מוּפְעָל** ◆	(*moof-'AL*):	מוּפְתָע	מוּדְאָג	מוּגְדָל
		surprised	worried	enlarged

Want to see if you've understood?

Choose the adjectives that belong to the categories פָּעוּל, מְפוּעָל, מוּפְעָל. Write them in the appropriate column in the chart underneath them:

אָכוּל, אָדוֹם, מְשׁוּפָּר, יָפֶה, גָּדוֹל, מְעַנְיֵין, מוּרְחָב, מַצְחִיק, מְחוּבָּר,
מוּסְבָּר, רָחוֹק, קָטָן, נָעוּל, שָׁלֵם, קָשֶׁה, מְקוּשָּׁט, זָקֵן, מוּשְׂכָּר

מוּפְעָל	מְפוּעָל	פָּעוּל
_____	_____	_____
_____	_____	_____
_____	_____	_____

Answers:

מוּפְעָל		מְפוּעָל		פָּעוּל	
widened	מוּרְחָב	improved	מְשׁוּפָּר	eaten	אָכוּל
explained	מוּסְבָּר	attached	מְחוּבָּר	open	פָּתוּחַ
rented	מוּשְׂכָּר	decorated	מְקוּשָּׁט	locked	נָעוּל

---

7   At more advanced levels of Hebrew, you will sometimes encounter adjectives denoting the result of an action whose form follows the pattern of נֶחְמָד and נֶהְדָּר. This is the case even though this form does not contain an *oo* sound. Examples include נִבְחָר (chosen) and נִרְדָּף (persecuted). At the beginning and intermediate levels, however, almost all adjectives that take this form (like נֶחְמָד and נֶהְדָּר) are "regular" in meaning.

• *The forms of "adjectives of completed action"*

Like all adjectives, those that fall into the three categories פָּעוּל, מְפוּעָל, מוּפְעָל all have **four** forms:

	מוּפְעָל	מְפוּעָל	פָּעוּל
m.s.:	מוּדְפָּס	מְבוּשָּׁל	סָגוּר
f.s.:	מוּדְפֶּסֶת	מְבוּשֶּׁלֶת	סְגוּרָה
m.pl.:	מוּדְפָּסִים	מְבוּשָּׁלִים	סְגוּרִים
f.pl.:	מוּדְפָּסוֹת	מְבוּשָּׁלוֹת	סְגוּרוֹת

See the chapter "How Are Adjectives Formed?" pp. 141-142, 144-146 for more details concerning these forms.

Did you know?

A special group of פָּעוּל adjectives ends in י (in the *m.s.* form). Here are two examples:

	f.pl.	m.pl.	f.s.	m.s.
built	בְּנוּיוֹת	בְּנוּיִים	בְּנוּיָה	בָּנוּי
bought	קְנוּיוֹת	קְנוּיִים	קְנוּיָה	קָנוּי

Most פָּעוּל adjectives with a final י are related to verbs that end in ה: בָּנָה (he built), קָנָה (he bought). In fact, י and not ה is actually the third root letter of these verbs. (Their roots are ב-נ-י and ק-נ-י). In the verb forms, the י in the original בני and קני dropped off, and the letter ה was added. The original י is seen in the adjectives קָנוּי and בָּנוּי. Notice that בְּנוּיִים has a **double** י: בְּנוּיִים ⇐ יִם + בנוי.

An interesting case is the root נ-שׂ-א, often used to speak about marriage. These are the פָּעוּל forms of this root:

married	נְשׂוּאוֹת	נְשׂוּאִים	נְשׂוּאָה	נָשׂוּי

Notice that all but the masculine singular form are **regular** (they contain the root נ-שׂ-א). Only in the masculine singular form נָשׂוּי does a י take the place of the original א.

• *The function of "adjectives of completed action" in a sentence*

Adjectives that denote the result of a completed action function in a sentence like any other adjective, for example:

1. They form noun-adjective **phrases**:

Tom ate cooked carrots.	תום אכל גזר מְבוּשָׁל.
He is sitting next to the open window.	הוא יושב ליד החלון הַפָּתוּחַ.

2. They can be the **predicate** of a *non-verb* sentence:

Our house is locked.	הבית שלנו נָעוּל.
This paper is typed (printed) nicely.	העבודה הזאת מוּדְפֶּסֶת יפה.

When such sentences are in the past or future tenses, the appropriate form of the verb להיות (to be) is added, in the same way that it is added to sentences with "regular" adjectives:

future tense		past tense		present tense	
regular adjective:					
הוא יהיה עָשִׁיר.	⇐	הוא היה עָשִׁיר.	⇐	השכן שלי עָשִׁיר.	
He will be rich.		He was rich.		My neighbor is rich.	
adjectives of completed action:					
היא תהיה לבוּשָׁה יפה.	⇐	היא הייתה לבוּשָׁה יפה.	⇐	האישה לבוּשָׁה יפה.	
She will be dressed nicely.		She was dressed nicely.		The woman is dressed nicely.	
השיעור יהיה מְאוּרְגָן.	⇐	השיעור היה מְאוּרְגָן.	⇐	השיעור מְאוּרְגָן.	
The lesson will be organized.		The lesson was organized.		The lesson is organized.	
האוכל יהיה מוּכָן עוד מעט.	⇐	האוכל היה מוּכָן לפני שעה.	⇐	האוכל מוּכָן.	
The food will be ready in a little while.		The food was ready an hour ago.		The food is ready. (prepared)	

• *The adjective-verb connection*

We have seen above that many adjectives whose patterns are פָּעוּל, מְפוּעָל, מוּפְעָל denote the **result of an action**. Now we will look at the connections between each of these three adjective patterns and certain *beenyaneem* (verb patterns).

פָּעוּל *pa-'OOL*

action		*result*
מישהו כָּתַב אותו.	–	המכתב כָּתוּב. ◄
Someone wrote it.		The letter is written.
מישהו בָּדַק אותו.	–	המבחן בָּדוּק.
Someone checked it.		The exam is checked.
מישהו שָׁבַר את הבקבוק.	–	אני רואה את הבקבוק השָׁבוּר.
Someone broke the bottle.		I see the broken bottle.

Q: What do the verbs כָּתַב, בָּדַק and שָׁבַר have in common?

A: They all belong to *beenyan* פָּעַל (*pa'al*).[8] When the adjective looks and sounds like כָּתוּב (ka-TOOV), בָּדוּק (ba-DOOK) and שָׁבוּר (sha-VOOR) (i.e., פָּעוּל *pa-'OOL*), its past tense verb usually takes the same form as כָּתַב (ka-TAV), בָּדַק (ba-DAK) and שָׁבַר (sha-VAR).

The reverse is also true. If we begin with a verb in *beenyan* פָּעַל (*pa'al*), we can usually (but not always) predict that the adjective describing the result of the action will be in the פָּעוּל form:

action		*result*
עכשיו המלפפון שָׁטוּף.	⇐	יוני שָׁטַף את המלפפון. ◄
Now the cucumber is rinsed.		Yoni rinsed the cucumber.
עכשיו המלפפון חָתוּךְ.	⇐	הוא חָתַךְ את המלפפון.
Now the cucumber is cut up.		He cut up the cucumber.
עכשיו המעיל תָּלוּי בארון.	⇐	הוא תָּלָה את המעיל בארון.
Now the coat is hanging in the closet.		He hung up the coat in the closet.

---

8   See the chapter "Patterns of Verbs," pp. 361-364.

Did you know?

In addition to פָּעוּל (*pa'ool*) forms, *beenyan* נִפְעַל (*neef'al*) forms, too, can denote the result of an action that is expressed with a verb in *beenyan pa'al*. Thus:

neef'al		*pa'al* (action)
החלון נפתח עכשיו.	⇐	1. פותחים את החלון עכשיו.
The window is opening (or: is being opened) now.		Someone is opening the window.

pa'ool		*pa'al* (action)
עכשיו החלון פתוח.	⇐	2. פתחו את החלון.
The window is open.		Someone opened the window.

Neef'al forms (e.g., sent. 1) are used mainly as verbs (less as adjectives). They usually denote an action in progress, whereas *pa'ool* forms (e.g., sent. 2) are adjectives that denote a completed action.

מְפוּעָל *me-foo-'AL*

Now let's look at the second group:

action		result
מישהו בִּישֵׁל אותו.	—	האוכל מבושָׁל. ◄
Someone cooked it.		The food is cooked.
מישהו תִיקֵן אותו.	—	האוטו מתוקָּן.
Someone fixed it.		The car is fixed.
מישהו פִּינֵק אותו.	—	זה ילד מפונָּק.
Someone spoiled him.		This is a spoiled child.

Q: What do the verbs בִּישֵׁל, תִיקֵן and פִּינֵק have in common?

A: They all belong to *beenyan* פִּיעֵל (***pee'el***). If an adjective sounds and looks like מבושָׁל (*me-voo-SHAL*), מתוקָּן (*me-too-KAN*) and מפונָּק (*me-foo-NAK*) (i.e., מְפוּעָל *me-foo-'AL*), then the active verb in the past tense will usually be like בִּישֵׁל (*bee-SHEL*), תִיקֵן (*tee-KEN*) and פִּינֵק (*pee-NEK*) – and vice versa:

result		action
עַכְשָׁיו הַחֶדֶר מְסֻדָּר.	⇐	יוֹסֵף סִידֵּר אֶת הַחֶדֶר. ◄
Now the room is tidy (in order).		Yosef tidied up the room.

מוּפְעָל *moof-'AL*

Here's the third group. Notice that these adjectives **begin** with the sound *moo*:

action		result
מִישֶׁהוּ הִדְפִּיס אוֹתוֹ.	—	הַמִּכְתָּב כְּבָר מֻדְפָּס. ◄
Someone typed it.		The letter is already typed
מִישֶׁהוּ הֵכִין אוֹתוֹ.	—	הַמָּרָק מוּכָן.
Someone prepared it.		The soup is ready (prepared).
מִישֶׁהוּ הִמְלִיץ עַל הַסֶּרֶט.	—	רָאִינוּ אֶת הַסֶּרֶט הַמּוּמְלָץ.
Someone recommended the movie.		We saw the recommended movie.

Q: What do the verbs הִדְפִּיס, הֵכִין and הִמְלִיץ have in common?

A: They all belong to *beenyan* הִפְעִיל (***heef'eel***). Adjectives that sound and look like מֻדְפָּס (*mood-PAS*) and מוּמְלָץ (*moom-LATS*) (i.e., מוּפְעָל *moof-'AL*) are usually the result of actions denoted by verbs whose form is like הִדְפִּיס (*heed-PEES*) and הִמְלִיץ (*heem-LEETS*). מוּכָן (*moo-CHAN*) and its active verb הֵכִין (*he-CHEEN*) also belong to this group, but are slightly different because they contain only two of their three root letters (the ו in their root כ-ו-נ has dropped out).

As with the other two groups, here, too, we can usually predict the adjective form on the basis of the verb, for example:

result		action
הַמִּשְׁפָּט מוּבָן.	⇐	הַתַּלְמִיד הֵבִין (אוֹ: מֵבִין) אֶת הַמִּשְׁפָּט. ◄
The sentence is understood.		The student understood (or: understands) the sentence.

Did you know?
מוּפְעָל *and* מְפוֹעָל, פָּעוּל *are also used as* "regular" *adjectives*

It is important to note that each of the forms פָּעוּל, מְפוֹעָל *and* מוּפְעָל may also be used as regular adjectives that are not the direct result of an action.

Here are examples of both regular adjectives and adjectives of completed action that have the same form:

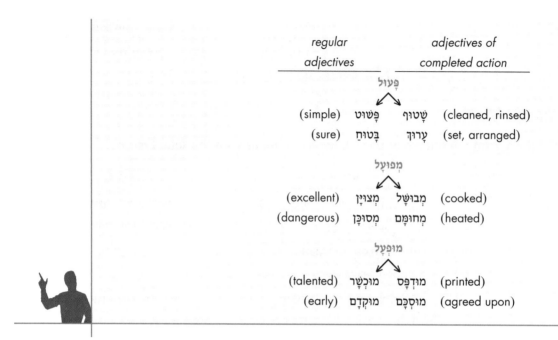

	regular adjectives		adjectives of completed action	
		פָּעוּל		
(simple)	פָּשׁוּט		שָׁטוּף	(cleaned, rinsed)
(sure)	בָּטוּחַ		עָרוּךְ	(set, arranged)
		מְפוֹעָל		
(excellent)	מְצוּיָן	מְבוּשָׁל		(cooked)
(dangerous)	מְסוּכָּן	מְחוּמָם		(heated)
		מוּפְעָל		
(talented)	מוּכְשָׁר	מוּדְפָּס		(printed)
(early)	מוּקְדָּם	מוּסְכָּם		(agreed upon)

The connections between these three adjective patterns and the *beenyaneem* are not always automatic, and there are exceptions to be learned, but it is important and very useful to learn these connections.

Let's review

- ◆ Each of the three forms used for "adjectives of completed action" is usually connected to a specific active *beenyan*:

  - **פָּעוּל** forms such as בָּדוּק and שָׁבוּר are connected to the verbs בָּדַק and שָׁבַר of *beenyan* **פָּעַל** (pa'al).

  - **מְפוֹעָל** forms such as מְסוּדָּר and מְפוּנָּק are connected to the verbs סִידֵּר and פִּינֵּק of *beenyan* **פִּיעֵל** (pee'el).

  - **מוּפְעָל** forms such as מוּבָן and מוּמְלָץ are connected to the verbs הֵבִין and הִמְלִיץ of *beenyan* **הִפְעִיל** (heef'eel).

- ◆ These same forms are used also as "regular" adjectives, for example: פָּשׁוּט (simple), מְצוּיָן (excellent) and מוּכְשָׁר (talented).

168

Want to see if you've understood?

A. Fill in the correct form of the verb that corresponds to the underlined adjective.

Example: הגזר <u>חתוך</u> (cut). מי **חתך** _____ אותו?

1. ראינו את החלון <u>השבור</u> (broken). מי _____ את החלון?

2. הארון <u>פתוח</u> (open). מי _____ אותו?

3. הטלפון <u>מנותק</u> (disconnected). מי _____ אותו?

4. קראתי את המכתב <u>המודפס</u> (typed). מי _____ אותו?

5. ניסינו לפתוח את החדרים <u>הנעולים</u> (locked). מי _____ את החדרים?

6. ההצגה <u>מבוטלת</u> (cancelled). מי _____ אותה?

7. הקפה <u>מוכן</u> (prepared). מי _____ אותו?

8. העובד <u>המפוטר</u> (fired) מחפש עבודה. מי _____ אותו?

9. אתם <u>מופתעים</u> (surprised)? מה _____ אתכם?

Answers:

1. שָׁבַר 2. פָּתַח 3. נִיתֵק 4. הִדְפִּיס 5. נָעַל 6. בִּיטֵל 7. הֵכִין 8. פִּיטֵר 9. הִפְתִּיע / מַפְתִּיע

B. Fill in the correct form of the adjective that corresponds to the underlined verb.

Example: <u>כתבתי</u> את המכתב. הוא כבר **כתוב** _____ .

1. יוסי <u>שבר</u> (broke) את הכוס, ואני זרקתי את הכוס ה_____ לפח.

2. ההורים שלך <u>פינקו</u> (spoiled) אותך יותר מדיי, ולכן אתה ילד _____ !

3. מישהו <u>סגר</u> (closed) את הדלת, ועכשיו היא _____ .

4. דני <u>הדביק</u> (glued, stuck) את הבול על המעטפה. הבול _____ במקום הלא נכון.

5. אנחנו לא <u>מבינים</u> (understand) את השאלה הראשונה. גם השאלה השנייה לא _____ .

6. דנה <u>ערכה</u> (set) את השולחן. השולחן _____ בצורה אלגנטית.

7. אימא <u>בישלה</u> (cooked) ירקות, אבל מיכל לא אוהבת ירקות _____ .

Answers:

1. שְׁבוּרָה 2. מְפוּנָק 3. סְגוּרָה 4. מוּדְבָּק 5. מוּבֶנֶת 6. עָרוּךְ 7. מְבוּשָׁלִים

IV. *Smeechoot*: Noun-Noun Phrases
סְמִיכוּת

> ### *Preview*
>
> • *What is* smeechoot*?*
>
> • *The semantic connection between nouns in* smeechoot
>
> • *Changes in the first noun(s) in a* smeechoot *phrase*
>
> • *Making* smeechoot *phrases definite (specific)*
>
> • Smeechoot *phrases with more than two nouns*
>
> • *Making* smeechoot *phrases plural*
>
> • *Adding an adjective to a* smeechoot *phrase*
>
> • Smeechoot *phrases vs. noun-adjective phrases*

In the previous unit we examined phrases in which a noun was followed by an adjective that described it (ספר מעניין an interesting book). In this chapter we will examine a different kind of phrase in which information is added to a noun (called a *smeechoot phrase*).[1]

• *What is* smeechoot*?*

Here's a short account of Mrs. Levy's visit to the mall before her daughter's wedding:

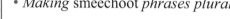

> גברת לוי הלכה לחנות בגדים כדי לקנות שמלה. אחר כך היא הלכה לחנות נעליים כדי לחפש נעליים
> מתאימות. בסוף היא הלכה לחנות כובעים. שם היא מצאה כובע יפה, שבדיוק התאים לשמלה שלה.

Mrs. Levy went to a clothing store to buy a dress. Afterwards she went to a shoe store to look for matching shoes. In the end she went to a hat store. There she found a pretty hat that matched her dress exactly.

Mrs. Levy entered three different stores. In each case a word is added to the noun חנות (store) in order to tell us what **kind** of store she went to.

---

1   In grammar books these are often called *construct phrases*.

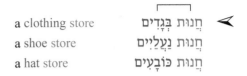

a clothing store	חֲנוּת בְּגָדִים
a shoe store	חֲנוּת נַעֲלַיִים
a hat store	חֲנוּת כּוֹבָעִים

Q: What kind of word is the **added** word? Is it a noun, an adjective or a verb?

A: Both in English and in Hebrew a noun is added to the word חֲנוּת. This added noun describes (or modifies) the noun חֲנוּת.

These "noun-noun" phrases are called סְמִיכוּת (*smee-CHOOT*) in Hebrew.[2]

Let's concentrate now on one of the *smeechoot* phrases mentioned above: חֲנוּת בְּגָדִים.

Q: In this noun-noun phrase, which is the **base** noun – the one being described?

A: The **first** noun – חֲנוּת – is the base noun. The second noun describes (or modifies) it in some way. All of the following nouns tell us something about the חנות:

2		1
בְּגָדִים		
נַעֲלַיִים	>	חֲנוּת
כּוֹבָעִים		

Note that in English the **base** noun *store* comes **last** rather than first:

1	2
a clothing	
a shoe	store
a hat	

Let's look at some more examples:

סָלַט יְרָקוֹת	סָלַט פֵּירוֹת	סָלַט חַסָּה	סָלַט טוּנָה
vegetable salad	fruit salad	lettuce salad	tuna salad

---

2 There are also other types of *smeechoot* phrases, such as "*number + noun*" phrases (שְׁלוֹשֶׁת הבנים = the three sons) and "*adjective + noun*" phrases (אֲרוֹךְ רגליים = long legged). In this chapter we will deal only with the most common type of *smeechoot*: noun-noun phrases.

As you may have noticed, sometimes the second noun (the describing noun) in these *smeechoot* phrases is **singular** (as in טוּנָה, חַסָה) and sometimes it is **plural** (פֵּירוֹת, יְרָקוֹת). This is not necessarily the case in the English equivalent. Thus, you cannot necessarily translate noun-noun phrases directly from English to Hebrew. You have to learn that *fruit* salad is סָלָט פֵּירוֹת and *vegetable* salad is סָלָט יְרָקוֹת. Likewise, we saw above that *a shoe* store is חֲנוּת נַעֲלַיִים and *a hat* store is חֲנוּת כּוֹבָעִים.

Up until now, we have only mentioned *smeechoot* phrases that contain **two** nouns. Not infrequently, however, a *smeechoot* phrase may contain **more** than two nouns, as in:

  סָלָט ירקות שׁוֹרֶשׁ   a root vegetable salad

We will deal with such *smeechoot* phrases below. In the meantime, we will discuss only two-word *smeechoot* phrases.

 Be careful! English and Hebrew may use different kinds of constructions to express the same thing. For example, in Hebrew we usually use a **noun-noun** phrase – דֶּגֶל יִשְׂרָאֵל – when we refer to the *Israeli flag*. English uses the **adjective** *Israeli*, and **not** the noun *Israel,* to describe the noun *flag*. Similarly, while in English we say either *a wooden table* or *a wood table*, in Hebrew we use only a **noun-noun** phrase שׁוּלְחַן עֵץ.

Did you know?
Are words like lemon nouns or adjectives?

In English, many words are labeled in the dictionary as being both a noun and an adjective, depending on their usage. For example, *lemon* is labeled as a noun **and** an adjective (in the sentence "I bought a *lemon*" it is a noun, whereas in "The *lemon* tree is pretty," it is an adjective). In contrast, in Hebrew, the word לימון is labeled **only** as a noun because it has only **two** forms (לימון / לימונים), rather than the four forms that every Hebrew adjective has (e.g., גדול, גדולה, גדולים, גדולות). Even when לימון **describes** a noun, as in עץ לימון (a *lemon* tree), it is still regarded as a **noun**. See below, pp. 193-195, for more on this subject.

• *The semantic connection between nouns in smeechoot*

The second noun in a *smeechoot* phrase may relate to the first (base) noun in a variety of ways. Let's look at some of the more common ones.

Q: How does the second noun in the following phrases relate to the base noun?

חֲדַר שֵׁינָה	חֲדַר אוֹכֶל	חֲדַר עֲבוֹדָה	שׁוּלְחַן כְּתִיבָה	שׁוּלְחַן אוֹכֶל
bedroom	dining room	work room, study	desk	dining table
(lit.: sleeping room)	(lit.: food room)		(lit.: writing table)	(lit.: food table)

A: In all of these phrases, the second noun tells **what the base noun is used for**.

Now look at the following phrases:

שִׂמְלַת מֶשִׁי	שִׂמְלַת צֶמֶר	שִׂמְלַת כּוּתְנָה	שׁוּלְחַן פְּלַסְטִיק	שׁוּלְחַן עֵץ
silk dress	wool dress	cotton dress	plastic table	wooden table

Q: How does the second noun in them relate to the base noun?

A: Here the second noun tells **what the base noun is made of.**

Sometimes *smeechoot* phrases are used to indicate **possession**. Here are some examples:

בֵּית הַשְׁכֵנִים	אַרְמוֹן הַמֶּלֶךְ
the neighbors' house	the king's palace

In Modern Hebrew, however, we usually prefer to use the word של – and not *smeechoot* – to indicate possession. Thus, while certain fixed possessive phrases like the above are used in everyday speech, in today's Hebrew we do not freely create and use **possessive** *smeechoot* phrases. For example, we say הַסֵּפֶר שֶׁל הַשָׁכֵן (the neighbor's book) or הַמַחְבֶּרֶת שֶׁל הַיַלְדָה (the girl's notebook) rather than making these into *smeechoot* phrases.[3] There are no fixed rules for when we do or do not use *smeechoot* for expressing possession. The more you are exposed to Hebrew, the more of a feel you will get for correct usage.

---

3   In more formal Hebrew we may say or write ספרו של השכן or מחברתה של הילדה.

Many *smeechoot* phrases correspond to the English *of*, but do not indicate actual possession:

דִּבְרֵי הַמְנַהֵל
the words **of** the principal,
the principal's words

רֹאשׁ מֶמְשָׁלָה
Prime Minister
(lit.: head **of** government)

חֲבֵר כְּנֶסֶת
Knesset member
member **of** the Knesset
(Israel's parliament)

Other common uses of *smeechoot* in Modern Hebrew include naming families and stating years, as in:

שְׁנַת 1948
the year 1948

מִשְׁפַּחַת סִימְפְּסוֹן
the Simpson family

Creating new concepts with smeechoot

Sometimes the object or concept indicated by *smeechoot* phrases really **is** the combination of the two elements combined in the phrase. This is the case in such phrases as סָלַט פֵּרוֹת (fruit salad) and בַּת הַשְּׁכֵנִים (the neighbors' daughter). In other cases, however, the words of a *smeechoot* combine to form a totally **new concept** that transcends the meaning of the two words in the phrase. This is the case with a phrase such as בֵּית סֵפֶר. Literally, this means *a house of a book*, but we use it to mean *a school*. In fact, בֵּית סֵפֶר is used for any kind of school, even those with neither a building (a "house") nor books. The fact that בֵּית סֵפֶר is translated by **one word** in other languages such as English emphasizes the fact that it represents a concept different from the sum total of its elements. Here are some other examples:

synagogue	(lit.: house of gathering)	בֵּית כְּנֶסֶת
potato	(lit.: apple of the earth, like the French *pomme de terre*)	תַּפּוּחַ אֲדָמָה
praying mantis	(lit.: camel of Shlomo)	גְּמַל שְׁלֹמֹה

Did you know?
Two adjacent nouns do not always form a smeechoot *phrase*
Usually, when two or more nouns stand next to each other, they form a *smeechoot* phrase. However, this is not always the case. For example, when a noun-noun phrase contains a title and a name, such as דויד המלך / המלך דויד (King David) or המורה רינה (the teacher Rina), it is not *smeechoot*.[4]

---

4   The second noun in these phrases is called a תְּמוּרָה (appositive).

Let's review

◆ "Noun-noun" phrases such as חֲנוּת כּוֹבָעִים (a hat store) and חֲבֵר קִיבּוּץ (a kibbutz member) are called סְמִיכוּת in Hebrew.

◆ The first noun is the ***base* noun** of the *smeechoot* phrase. The second noun describes (or modifies) the base noun in some way. For example, the second noun may tell what the base noun is used for (שׁוּלְחַן אוֹכֶל) or what it is made of (שׁוּלְחַן עֵץ). Alternatively, it may indicate possession (אַרְמוֹן הַמֶּלֶךְ), or it may correspond to other meanings of the English *of* (חֲבֵר כְּנֶסֶת).

◆ Sometimes the words of a *smeechoot* combine to form a totally new **concept**, as in: בית ספר (school).

Why is it important to identify smeechoot?

You may have noticed that Hebrew teachers and grammar books place a lot of emphasis on *smeechoot*. Why do phrases like בֵּית סֵפֶר, תַחֲנַת אוֹטוֹבּוּס and עוּגַת גְבִינָה get so much attention?

The answer to this question does not lie in the meaning of these phrases. Rather, it has to do with their grammatical **behavior** – with the behavior of the nouns that form the phrase and with the behavior of the phrase as a whole.

Let's now have a look at some of the special features of *smeechoot*.

• *Changes in the first noun(s) in a* smeechoot *phrase*

If you look back at some of the examples above, you will see that the **first** noun (or nouns) in a *smeechoot* phrase **sometimes** looks or sounds different from the form of the same word when it is **not** in *smeechoot* (for example: בֵּית ספר ⇐ בַּיִת). However, not all nouns change when they are in the first position(s) in a *smeechoot* phrase (for example, the word גַן does not change in the phrase גַן יְלָדִים). Nouns that are in the **last** position in a *smeechoot* phrase **don't change**.

Changes that always occur in the first noun(s)

It is not always easy to know if a noun form will change when it loses its independence and becomes part of a *smeechoot* phrase. There are, however, certain changes that **always** take place:

1. *The feminine ending* הָ- *(-ah) becomes* ת- *(-at)*

Here is a list of nouns and their *smeechoot* forms.

	in smeechoot	*regular form*	
	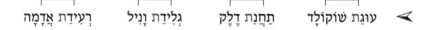		
chocolate cake	עוּגַת שׁוֹקוֹלָד	עוּגָה	◄
gas station	תַחֲנַת דֶלֶק	תַחֲנָה	
vanilla ice cream	גְלִידַת וָנִיל	גְלִידָה	
earthquake	רְעִידַת אֲדָמָה	רְעִידָה	

Q: What is the difference between the **form** of the above nouns when they stand alone and when they are the first word in a *smeechoot?*

A: When these nouns stand alone, they all end in ה-ָ, whereas when they are the first word in a *smeechoot*, they end in ת-:

רְעִידַת אֲדָמָה   גְלִידַת וָנִיל   תַחֲנַת דֶלֶק   עוּגַת שׁוֹקוֹלָד   ◄

 Be careful! We are **not** speaking here of words that end in ה-ֶ (-*eh*) such as מוֹרֶה and שָׂדֶה! These words retain their ה' in *smeechoot*:

the teacher (m.) of the class	מוֹרֶה הַכִּיתָה	מוֹרֶה	◄
airport	שְׂדֵה תְעוּפָה	שָׂדֶה	

Note, too, that the ה-ָ (-*ah*) ending that changes to ת- (-*at*) is **stressed** (as in תַ-חֲ-נָה *ta-cha-NA*), thus the word לַיְלָה (*LAI-la*) (which, in any event, is masculine) is not included in this group.[5]

2. *The endings* ים- *(-eem) and* יִים-ַ *(-A-yeem) become* י-ֵ

Here is another list of nouns and their *smeechoot* forms:

	in smeechoot	*regular form*	
	תַלְמִידֵי יְשִׁיבָה		
yeshiva students	תַלְמִידֵי יְשִׁיבָה	תַלְמִידִים	◄
math lessons	שִׁיעוּרֵי מָתֶמָטִיקָה	שִׁיעוּרִים	
sneakers, running shoes	נַעֲלֵי סְפּוֹרְט	נַעֲלַיִים	

---

5   The ה' in לַיְלָה is **not** a feminine ending like the ending on עוּגָה. The word לַיְלָה becomes לֵיל- in *smeechoot*, as in לֵיל מְנוּחָה (Sleep well!, lit.: a night of rest) or לֵיל שַׁבָּת (Sabbath eve).

Q: What is the difference between the **form** of the above nouns when they stand alone and when they are the first word in a *smeechoot*?

A: When these nouns stand alone, they end in either ‑ים and ‑יִים. When they stand as the first word(s) in a *smeechoot* phrase, they lose their ‑ם (נעליים loses its ‑ים). As a result, a י is left dangling on the end:

נַעֲלֵי סְפּוֹרְט שִׁיעוּרֵי מָתֵמָטִיקָה תַּלְמִידֵי יְשִׁיבָה

Some Hebrew speakers pronounce the י and say *tal-mee-DEI-,* while others do not pronounce the י at all, and say *tal-mee-DE-.*[6] Both pronunciations are acceptable.

> **Be careful!** The final ‑ם drops off in the *smeechoot* form of **all** words ending in ‑ים / ‑יִים, be they masculine (תַּלְמִידֵי יְשִׁיבָה) or feminine (נַעֲלֵי סְפּוֹרְט, אַבְנֵי הַכּוֹתֶל). It is the **form** that counts, **not the gender**.

Remember: When we look up a plural noun in the dictionary, we look up the regular form of the singular. Thus, when looking up בָּתֵי סֵפֶר, we would look under בַּיִת.

Additional changes that frequently occur in the first noun(s)

The two changes mentioned above (the change of ‑ה to ‑ת and the change of ‑ים/‑יִים to ‑י) are predictable changes in the **ending** of the first noun(s) in a *smeechoot* phrase. Other endings, notably the plural ‑וֹת, do **not** change in *smeechoot*.

תַּחֲנוֹת אוֹטוֹבּוּס	תַּחֲנוֹת
עוּגוֹת שׁוֹקוֹלָד	עוּגוֹת

bus stops
chocolate cakes

However, other predictable changes in the *smeechoot* form may also take place, either **in addition** to the changes in the word's ending mentioned above or when there is no change in the ending.[7]

---

6 According to traditional rules of grammar, the main stress in a *smeechoot* phrase is on the last word in the phrase. Today, however, we tend also to stress one of the syllables in the first word. This is the pronunciation we have indicated in our transcription.

7 We are dealing here only with vowel changes that can be heard. There are additional changes in vowel signs that do not affect the way the word sounds.

1. *Changes of the vowel (of the regular form) to shva*

Look at the following words, whose first syllable ends with a *vowel*:[8]

	in smeechoot	regular form	
place of birth	מְקוֹם לֵידָה *me-KOM-*	מָקוֹם *ma-KOM*	1.
passenger plane	מְטוֹס נוֹסְעִים *me-TOS-*	מָטוֹס *ma-TOS*	2.
domestic harmony	שְׁלוֹם בַּיִת *shlom-*	שָׁלוֹם *sha-LOM*	3.
a talk on a text from the Torah	דְּבַר תּוֹרָה *dvar-*	דָּבָר *da-VAR*	4.

Q: In what way does the regular form of these words differ from their *smeechoot* form?

A: When we pronounce these words, we hear that the *ah* at the beginning of the regular forms either becomes *eh* (as in 1 and 2 above) or disappears entirely (as in 3 and 4). When we write the vowel signs, we can see that the *kamats* (ָ) in the first syllable of the regular forms changes to a *shva* (ְ).

We see this same change in the following words, whose ending also changes:

year of birth	שְׁנַת לֵידָה *shnat-*	שָׁנָה *sha-NA*
rest hour	שְׁעַת מְנוּחָה *sh'at-*	שָׁעָה *sha-'A*

It also occurs when the first vowel is *tsere* (ֵ *eh*), as in:

hibernation (lit.: winter sleep)	שְׁנַת חוֹרֶף *shnat-*	שֵׁינָה *shei-NA/she-NA*

---

8 This is an *open syllable* (see the chapter "Basic Concepts: Sounds and Syllables," pp. 621-623 for more details). We are not speaking here of nouns like תלמיד, whose first syllable – *tal* – is *closed* (it ends in a consonant).

The change of the first vowel to *shva* (called *vowel reduction*) may take place in plural words, too:

the children of Israel	בְּנֵי יִשְׂרָאֵל bnei-	⌐¬ בָּנִים ba-NEEM ◄
the daughters of Jacob	בְּנוֹת יַעֲקֹב bnot-	בָּנוֹת ba-NOT
surnames, last names	שְׁמוֹת מִשְׁפָּחָה shmot-	שֵׁמוֹת she-MOT

The reduction to *shva* can take place not only at the beginning of the word, but also in the middle, as in:

(*eh* or no sound) ☐   ⇐   `   (*ah*) ☐

letters of recommendation	מִכְתְּבֵי הַמְלָצָה meech-te-VEI-	מִכְתָּבִים meech-ta-VEEM ◄
time sentences (in grammar)	מִשְׁפְּטֵי זְמַן meesh-pe-TEI-	מִשְׁפָּטִים meesh-pa-TEEM
holy ground	אַדְמַת קוֹדֶשׁ 'ad-MAT-	אֲדָמָה 'ada-MA

(*eh* or no sound) ☐   ⇐   (*eh*) ☐

kibbutz members	חַבְרֵי קִיבּוּץ chav-REI-	חֲבֵרִים cha-ve-REEM ◄

Although the reduction of the *ah* vowel is very widespread, there are also many words in which *ah* at the beginning of the *smeechoot* form does **not** change, for example:

yeshiva student	בַּחוּר יְשִׁיבָה	בַּחוּר ◄
the cities of Israel	עָרֵי יִשְׂרָאֵל	עָרִים
schools	בָּתֵּי סֵפֶר	בָּתִּים
kindergartens	גַּנֵּי יְלָדִים	גַּנִּים

Since it is difficult to predict when the reduction will **not** take place, you should simply be aware when learning the *smeechoot* form of nouns that there are some irregularities.

Note: When we write without vowel signs, we do not **see** the changes in vowels that do take place.

2. *Changes in plurals like* יְלָדִים

Look at the following plural nouns and their *smeechoot* forms:

		in *smeechoot*	regular form	
kindergarten children	yal-DEI-	יַלְדֵי גַן	יְלָדִים	א.
the kings of Israel	mal-CHEI-	מַלְכֵי יִשְׂרָאֵל	מְלָכִים	
paths of peace, peaceful ways	dar-CHEI-	דַרְכֵי שָׁלוֹם	דְרָכִים	
watch dogs	kal-VEI-	כַּלְבֵי שְׁמִירָה	כְּלָבִים	
discourses on the Bible	deev-REI-	דִבְרֵי תוֹרָה	דְבָרִים	ב.
holy books	seef-REI-	סִפְרֵי קוֹדֶשׁ	סְפָרִים	
wild flowers	peer-CHEI-	פִּרְחֵי בָר	פְּרָחִים	
oil colors	tseev-'EI-	צִבְעֵי שֶׁמֶן	צְבָעִים	

Q: What do all the regular forms have in common?

A: They all have the same vowel pattern: ‌ְ‌ָ‌ִים.

As is to be expected, the ending of the *smeechoot* form has changed from ‌ים- to ‌ֵי- (*ei* or *eh*), however the vowels at the beginning of the form are unexpectedly different from those in the regular form.

Now let's look more closely at the *smeechoot* forms in the two groups: The *smeechoot* forms all have a vowel in their first syllable. The words in group 'א above have the vowel *ah*, while the words in group 'ב have the vowel *ee*.[9] It is hard to predict which of these vowels a word with the pattern ‌ְ‌ָ‌ִים will take in *smeechoot*. We note them here so that you will be aware of this kind of change when you learn these words.[10]

---

9   Many of these words are *segolate* nouns. See the chapter "Segolate Nouns," pp. 89-107 for a more in-depth discussion of them.

10   Another possible, but less common, *smeechoot* form of words with this plural pattern is found in the following:

		in *smeechoot*	regular plural		
adverbs	to-'o-rei-	תוֹאֲרֵי פוֹעַל	תְאָרִים	(.sing: תוֹאַר)	
verbs of motion	po-'o-lei-	פוֹעֲלֵי תְנוּעָה	פְּעָלִים	(.sing: פּוֹעַל)	
work procedures	no-ho-lei-	נוֹהֲלֵי עֲבוֹדָה	נְהָלִים	(.sing: נוֹהַל)	
the walls of the house	kot-lei-	כּוֹתְלֵי הַבַּיִת	כְּתָלִים	(.sing: כּוֹתֶל)	

Special changes you should remember

The following common words or word groups change when they are the first noun(s) in *smeechoot*. They are worth committing to memory:

1. *Miscellaneous words*[11]

		in *smeechoot*	regular form
school	*beit-*[12]	בֵּית סֵפֶר	בַּיִת
Air Force	*cheil-*	חֵיל אֲוִויר	חַיִל
dining room	*cha-DAR-*	חֲדַר אוֹכֶל[13]	חֶדֶר

2. *Words with the pattern* מִםְםָםָה

In the *smeechoot* forms of words with the pattern מִםְםָםָה, the vowels and ending change from *ah-ah* to *eh-et* and the stress is on the **second** syllable rather than on the third:

		in *smeechoot*	regular form
fish restaurant	*mees-'E-det-*	מִסְעֶדֶת דָּגִים	מִסְעָדָה
world war	*meel-CHE-met-*	מִלְחֶמֶת עוֹלָם	מִלְחָמָה
traffic police	*meesh-TE-ret-*	מִשְטֶרֶת תְּנוּעָה	מִשְׁטָרָה

The vowels in the *smeechoot* form of the following word remain *ah-ah* because of the ח׳. Here, too, the stress is on the second syllable of the *smeechoot* form.

		in *smeechoot*	regular form
the Simpson family	*meesh-PA-chat -*	מִשְׁפַּחַת סִימְפְּסוֹן	מִשְׁפָּחָה

3. *Changing from* ־ים *to* ־וֹת

In the following words the ending of the plural *smeechoot* form changes completely:

		in *smeechoot*	regular form
the Fifties	*shnot-*	שְׁנוֹת הַחֲמִישִׁים	שָׁנִים
prepositions	*mee-LOT-*	מִילּוֹת יַחַס	מִילִּים

 Be careful! When we look up a noun in the dictionary, we look up its regular, singular, non-*smeechoot* form. For example, we look up the word שִׂמְלַת, which is the first word in the *smeechoot* phrase שִׂמְלַת כַּלָּה, under שִׂמְלָה. Many dictionaries give the *smeechoot* form in parentheses (שִׂמְלַת-) under the entry of the non-*smeechoot* form, especially when the *smeechoot* form is different from the regular form.

---

11 See the chapter "Segolate Nouns," pp. 92, 103.

12 Some speakers pronounce these words *bet-*, *chel-*, with an *e* rather than *ei*.

13 The alternative form חֶדֶר אוֹכֶל is considered correct and is commonly used.

Let's review

◆ The **first** noun (or nouns) in a *smeechoot* phrase **sometimes** looks or sounds different from the form of the same word when it is **not** in *smeechoot*. Some changes cannot be predicted and must simply be learned. Others are quite predictable.

Here are some examples:

- The ending ‎הָ- (-*ah*) becomes ‎תַ- (-*at*):

תַחֲנָה ⇐ תַחֲנַת דלק ◄

- The endings ‎ים- (-*eem*) and ‎יִים-ַ (-*A-yeem*) become ‎יֵ- (-*ei* or -*eh*):

שִׁיעוּרִים ⇐ שִׁיעוּרֵי מתמטיקה ◄

נַעֲלַיִים ⇐ נַעֲלֵי ספורט

- The vowels at the beginning of words like ‎מָקוֹם and ‎שֵׁמוֹת reduce to *shva*:

מָקוֹם ⇐ מְקוֹם לידה, שֵׁמוֹת ⇐ שְׁמוֹת משפחה ◄

This also occurs in the middle of words:

מִכְתָּבִים ⇐ מִכְתְּבֵי אהבה, חֲבֵרִים ⇐ חַבְרֵי כנסת ◄

- Plural nouns whose pattern is ‎□ָ□ָ□ים often take one of the following *smeechoot* forms:

יְלָדִים ⇐ יַלְדֵי רחוב ◄

סְפָרִים ⇐ סִפְרֵי קודש

See the chapter for additional forms.

Want to see if you've understood?

Join the two nouns together to form a *smeechoot* phrase.

Example:    ⇐ עוּגָה + שׁוֹקוֹלָד

1. ‎_____ ⇐ בַּיִת + חוֹלִים

2. ‎_____ ⇐ מְסִיבָּה + כִּיתָה

3. ‎_____ ⇐ שִׁיטוֹת + לִימוּד

4. מִשְׁטָרָה + יְרוּשָׁלַיִם ⇐ _____

5. חֲדָרִים + שֵׁינָה ⇐ _____

6. פֵּירוֹת + קַיִץ ⇐ _____

7. שָׁנִים + אוֹר ⇐ _____

8. סְפָרִים + תּוֹרָה ⇐ _____

9. מְלָכִים + יִשְׂרָאֵל ⇐ _____

Answers:

1. בֵּית חוֹלִים   2. מְסִיבַּת כִּיתָה   3. שִׁיטוֹת לִימוּד   4. מִשְׁטֶרֶת יְרוּשָׁלַיִם   5. חַדְרֵי שֵׁינָה   6. פֵּירוֹת קַיִץ
7. שְׁנוֹת אוֹר   8. סִפְרֵי תּוֹרָה   9. מַלְכֵי יִשְׂרָאֵל

• *Making* smeechoot *phrases definite (specific)*

Read the following passage about Tali Levy, who is about to be married:

שבוע לפני החתונה של טלי היא הזמינה חברות למסיבה. היא הלכה לקונדיטוריה וראתה שם שלוש
עוגות: עוגת תפוחים, עוגת גזר ועוגת שוקולד. עוגת התפוחים נראתה טעימה, אבל היא הייתה יקרה
מאוד. עוגת הגזר לא נראתה טעימה, ולכן טלי לא קנתה אותה. עוגת השוקולד נראתה טעימה וגם
לא הייתה יקרה. טלי קנתה אותה והלכה הביתה. בערב המסיבה אכלו החברות שלה את העוגה כולה,
ולא השאירו אפילו פירור.

A week before Tali's wedding, she invited friends to a party. She went to a bakery and saw three cakes there: an apple cake, a carrot cake and a chocolate cake. The apple cake looked good, but it was very expensive. The carrot cake didn't look good, so Tali didn't buy it. The chocolate cake looked good and wasn't expensive. Tali bought it and went home. The night of the party her friends ate the whole cake and didn't leave even a crumb.

The following indefinite *smeechoot* phrases appear in the passage above:

עוגת תפוחים
an apple cake

עוגת גזר
a carrot cake

עוגת שוקולד
a chocolate cake

Q: How are these phrases made definite (specific) in the passage above (i.e., **the** apple cake…)?

A: Rather than adding ה- to the beginning of the whole phrase, as we do in English, we add ה- to the **last** (here, the **second**) word of the phrase:

עוגת התפוחים

עוגת הגזר

עוגת השוקולד

This -ה makes the **entire** *smeechoot* phrase **definite**.

Remember: A definite *smeechoot* **never begins** with the definite article -ה (the). If you want to know if a *smeechoot* phrase is definite, always look at the **last** word of the *smeechoot*. If it is definite, the **whole phrase** – which is considered **one unit** – is definite.

Smeechoot *phrases without* **'ה** *that are definite*

A *smeechoot* phrase may be definite even if there is no 'ה on the last word. The following phrases are definite in Hebrew:

קבר דויד	מגדל אייפל	אוניברסיטת חיפה	1.
David's tomb	the Eiffel Tower	Haifa University	
יום הולדתה	כף ידו	בת אחותי	2.
her birthday	his palm	my niece	
	(lit.: the palm of his hand)	(lit.: the daughter of my sister)	

We do not add a definite article to the second word in these phrases since the second word is already definite.

In the first set of phrases, the second word is a **name** – either of a place or a person. Names (*proper nouns*) are considered **definite**, so we don't have to add -ה to make them definite. The same is true of the second group of phrases, which have a possessive ending (see the chapter "Nouns With Possessive Endings," pp. 60-77). The ending on אחותי, ידו, הולדתה makes these nouns **definite**, thus a -ה (the) is never added onto the front of them. Since the **last noun** in all of the above phrases is definite, all of the phrases are definite.

Be careful! Since definite *smeechoot* phrases never have -ה attached to the **front**, when the prepositions -כ, -ל, -ב precede definite *smeechoot* phrases, they (the prepositions) will never contain -ה:

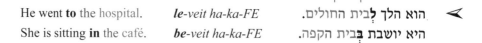

He went **to** the hospital.	*le-veit ha-ka-FE*	הוא הלך **ל**בית החולים.
She is sitting **in** the café.	*be-veit ha-ka-FE*	היא יושבת **ב**בית הקפה.

Similarly, when the preposition **את** appears before a definite *smeechoot* phrase, there is no -ה after this את:

They see the roof of the building.	הם רואים **את** גג הבניין.
She knows (is familiar with) the port of Haifa.	היא מכירה **את** נמל חיפה.
We like (love) your niece (the daughter of your sister).	אנחנו אוהבים **את** בת אחותך.

• Smeechoot *phrases with more than two nouns*

Until now we have examined phrases with only two nouns. However, as mentioned above, a *smeechoot* phrase can be comprised of more than two nouns. Here is an example:

the school principal's daughter   בַּת מְנַהֵל בֵּית הַסֵּפֶר   ◄

This phrase is actually composed of a number of *smeechoot* phrases: The word מנהל is added to the beginning of the phrase בית הספר to form מנהל בית הספר, and the word בת is added to the beginning of this phrase to form בת מנהל בית הספר.

Each of the words added to the beginning of a *smeechoot* phrase will take its *smeechoot* form. It so happens that in the phrase בַּת מְנַהֵל בֵּית הַסֵּפֶר only the word בֵּית has a *smeechoot* form different from its normal form (בַּיִת). Here is an example of a *smeechoot* in which you can clearly see the *smeechoot* forms of all but the final word:

the university presidents' words   דִּבְרֵי נְשִׂיאֵי הָאוּנִיבֶרְסִיטָאוֹת   ◄
(lit.: the words of the presidents of the universities)

Here the word נְשִׂיאִים changed to נְשִׂיאֵי and the word דְּבָרִים changed to דִּבְרֵי:

דִּבְרֵי
נְשִׂיאֵי הָאוּנִיברסיטאות

Remember: It is only the very **first** word in a long *smeechoot* that is the **base** noun. That is, when we say דברי נשיאי האוניברסיטאות, we are speaking about דברים (words). The job of the nouns that follow the base noun is to describe (or modify) it. This means that if this long *smeechoot* is the subject of a sentence, for example, the verb will match the **first** word, as in:

The school principal's daughter plays the guitar.   בת מנהל בית הספר מנגנת בגיטרה.   ◄

The verb מנגנת matches the first word of the *smeechoot*: בת.

In a *non-verb* sentence, the connector or adjective in the predicate will also match the first word of the *smeechoot*:

The school principal's daughter is my best friend.   בת מנהל בית הספר היא החברה הכי טובה שלי.   ◄
The school principal's daughter is nice.   בת מנהל בית הספר נחמדה.

Here the connector היא and the adjective נחמדה match the first word of the *smeechoot*: בת.

Making a long smeechoot *definite*

Now let's take a closer look at the two phrases mentioned above:

◄ בת מנהל בית הספר

דברי נשיאי האוניברסיטאות

These phrases are both **definite**.

Q: Where is the definite article -ה added in each?

A: -ה is added only to the **last** noun in the phrase, and it makes the **entire** phrase definite:

◄ בת מנהל בית הספר

דברי נשיאי האוניברסיטאות

Thus, with a verb that takes את, we would say:

◄ שמענו את דברי נשיאי האוניברסיטאות.   We heard the words of the university presidents.

Let's review

◆ A *smeechoot* phrase is made definite by adding -ה to the **last** word of the phrase no matter how many words there are in the *smeechoot*:

◄ עוגת התפוחים, בת מנהל בית הספר

◆ In the following cases, a *smeechoot* phrase is considered definite **without** having a -ה at all:

- When the last word in the *smeechoot* phrase is a **name** – either of a place or a person:

◄ אוניברסיטת חיפה, קבר דויד

- When the last word in the *smeechoot* phrase has a possessive ending:

◄ בת אחותי, יום הולדתוֹ
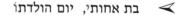

Want to see if you've understood?

a. Circle the *smeechoot* phrases that are definite.
b. Add -ה to make the remaining indefinite *smeechoot* phrases definite.

Example: חולצת הכותנה   ⇐   חולצת כותנה

5. רחובות ירושלים _____	1. כיתת לימוד _____
6. חנות בגדי ילדים _____	2. כוס תה _____
7. בית הוריך _____	3. משפחת כהן _____
8. יום הולדת _____	4. תיקי תלמידי כיתתו _____

Answers:

a. The following are already definite and should be circled: 3, 4, 5, 7.
b. The following are made definite by adding -ה:

1. כיתת הלימוד   2. כוס התה   6. חנות בגדי הילדים   8. יום ההולדת

• *Making* smeechoot *phrases plural*

Smeechoot phrases are special not only in the way they are made **definite,** but also in the way a singular *smeechoot* phrase is made **plural.** (A reminder: When we speak of a singular *smeechoot* **phrase**, we are referring to the fact that the **first word** of the phrase is singular, as in עוגת תפוחים an apple cake.)

Read the following passage about Tali and Yair:

◄ יומיים לפני החתונה שלהם הלכו טלי ויאיר לבית קפה. שניהם אוהבים מאוד לשבת בבתי קפה. טלי רצתה עוגת תפוחים וכוס קפה, ויאיר החליט להזמין אותו הדבר. כשהמלצר בא לשולחן, טלי הזמינה שתי עוגות תפוחים ושתי כוסות קפה. היא ביקשה גם עיתון בוקר. המלצר הביא להם את העוגות, את הקפה וגם שני עיתוני בוקר.

Two days before their wedding, Tali and Yair went to a café. They both like sitting in cafés. Tali wanted apple cake and a cup of coffee, and Yair decided to order the same thing. When the waiter came to their table, Tali ordered two pieces of apple cake (lit.: apple cakes) and two cups of coffee. She also asked for the (lit.: a) morning paper. The waiter brought them the cake, the coffee and two morning papers.

In the passage above there are four *smeechoot* phrases, in **singular** and in **plural**:

	רבים	יחיד
	plural	*singular*
coffee shop(s), café(s)	בתי קפה	בית קפה ◄
morning newspaper(s)	עיתוני בוקר	עיתון בוקר
apple cake(s)	עוגות תפוחים	עוגת תפוחים
cup(s) of coffee	כוסות קפה	כוס קפה

Q: Do **both** of the nouns in each of these *smeechoot* phrases change?

A: No! Only the **first** (base) noun changes to plural; the second noun stays as it was.

The same is true when there are more than two words in a *smeechoot* phrase: Only the first word changes:

	plural	*singular*
the proposal(s) of the school principal	הצעות מנהל בית הספר	הצעת מנהל בית הספר ◄

Want to see if you've understood?
A. Make the following *smeechoot* phrases plural.

	plural		*singular*
Example:	עיתוני בוקר	⇐	עיתון בוקר
	_____	⇐	תחנת אוטובוס .1
	_____	⇐	בית חולים .2
	_____	⇐	שולחן עץ .3
	_____	⇐	חולצת כותנה .4
	_____	⇐	חבר כנסת .5
	_____	⇐	כוס פלסטיק .6
	_____	⇐	תוכנית טלוויזיה .7
	_____	⇐	ספר לימוד .8
	_____	⇐	עוגת תות שדה .9

Answers:

1. תחנות אוטובוס   2. בתי חולים   3. שולחנות עץ   4. חולצות כותנה   5. חברי כנסת   6. כוסות פלסטיק
7. תוכניות טלוויזיה   8. ספרי לימוד   9. עוגות תות שדה

B. Make the following *smeechoot* phrases singular.

	plural		singular
Example:	עיתוני בוקר	⇒	*עיתון בוקר*
	תיקי עור	⇒	_____ .1
	נעלי ספורט	⇒	_____ .2
	ארונות קיר	⇒	_____ .3
	סלטי פירות	⇒	_____ .4
	עוגות שוקולד	⇒	_____ .5
	שמלות ערב	⇒	_____ .6
	כוסות יין	⇒	_____ .7
	ספרי תורה	⇒	_____ .8
	בתי עץ	⇒	_____ .9
	גני ילדים	⇒	_____ .10

Answers:

1. תיק עור   2. נעל ספורט   3. ארון קיר   4. סלט פירות   5. עוגת שוקולד   6. שמלת ערב   7. כוס יין
8. ספר תורה   9. בית עץ   10. גן ילדים

• *Adding an adjective to a* smeechoot *phrase*

Here is an example of a *smeechoot* phrase with an **adjective**:

There is a **big** shoe store in the mall.   יש בקניון חנות נעליים **גדולה.**   ⩻

Q: What is "big" (גדולה) here? The חנות or the נעליים?

A: Since the adjective גדולה is **feminine** and **singular**, we know that it refers to חנות, which is also feminine and singular.

חנות נעליים **גדולה**

Let's look now at another *smeechoot* with an adjective:

I bought a book for learning **spoken** Arabic.   קניתי ספר ללימוד ערבית **מדוברת.**   ⩻

This example is different from the previous one: Here the adjective מדוברת (spoken), which is **feminine** and **singular**, refers to the word preceding it: ערבית (Arabic), which is the **second** word of the *smeechoot*.

We could look at it as a combination of these two components:

These two examples show that the adjective can match either the first or the second noun in the *smeechoot* phrase.

Adding an adjective to a definite smeechoot *phrase*

Until now, we have looked at **indefinite** *smeechoot* phrases. Now let's look at some **definite** phrases.

> I like to buy shoes in the **big** shoe store.   .אני אוהבת לקנות נעליים בחנות הנעליים **הגדולה** .1 ◄

> Who is taking care of inviting the **important** guests?   ?מי מטפל בהזמנת האורחים **החשובים** .2

Q: What happens to the adjective when we add it to a **definite** *smeechoot*?

A: When the *smeechoot* phrase is **definite** (indicated by the fact that the **last word** of the phrase is definite), the adjective must **also** be made definite (with a ה-). This is true both when the adjective matches the **base noun**, as in sentence 1, and when it matches the **second noun**, as in sentence 2.

Now look at the following phrases:

> The **famous** King of England got married eight times.   .מלך אנגליה **המפורסם** התחתן שמונה פעמים ◄

> My **big** sister's son lives in Tel Aviv.   .בן אחותי **הגדולה** גר בתל אביב

Q: Why is -ה added to the adjectives המפורסם and הגדולה?

A: As we saw earlier, a *smeechoot* phrase is definite in two more cases: when the last word of the *smeechoot* is a **name** of a place or a person (as in the first sentence above) and when the last word of the *smeechoot* has a **possessive ending** (as in the second sentence). Since these *smeechoot* phrases are **definite**, so, too, is the adjective added to them (no matter which word the adjective describes):

Adding an adjective can be problematic

As we saw above, an adjective can relate to either the first or the second noun in a *smeechoot*. For this reason, if we wish to translate a phrase like בית המלך החדש, we encounter a problem, since this phrase could mean one of two things: *the king's new house* or *the new king's house*. In this specific expression it is hard to know whether the adjective חדש refers to בית or to מלך, since both words are **masculine** and **singular** and since both can be "new."

You can see the two options graphically here:

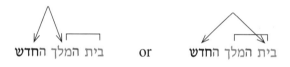

In order to avoid ambiguity here, it is advisable to break up this phrase and say either הבית של המלך החדש or הבית החדש של המלך.

Let's review

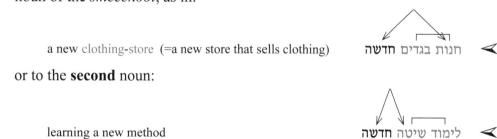

♦ An **adjective** that is added to a *smeechoot* phrase may refer either to the **first** noun of the *smeechoot*, as in:

    a new clothing-store (=a new store that sells clothing)   חנות בגדים חדשה

or to the **second** noun:

    learning a new method   לימוד שיטה חדשה

◆ When the *smeechoot* is definite, so is its adjective (no matter which word of the *smeechoot* it describes):

חנות הבגדים **החדשה**

לימוד השיטה **החדשה**

מלכת הולנד **הנחמדה**

בן אחותי **הגדולה**

Want to see if you've understood?
Choose the correct form.

1.   אחרי שאכלתי עוגיית שוקולד _____ , הרגשתי לא טוב.
      (גדול / הגדול / גדולה / הגדולה)

2.   ראש הממשלה _____ ביקר בעשר מדינות בחודשיים האחרונים.
      (צעיר / הצעיר / צעירה / הצעירה)

3.   הבן שלי עוזר לי בשטיפת הכלים _____ .
      (מלוכלכת / המלוכלכת / מלוכלכים / המלוכלכים)

4.   שכחתי בבית את מתנת אחי _____ .
      (צעיר / הצעיר / צעירה/ הצעירה)

5.   קראתי ספרים רבים על מלחמת העולם _____ .
      (שני / השני / שנייה / השנייה)

6.   נסענו במכונית הספורט _____ .
      (אדום / האדום / אדומה / האדומה)

7.   מי מטפל בהזמנת האורחים _____ ?
      (מפורסמת / המפורסמת / מפורסמים / המפורסמים)

8.   למסיבה אתמול לבשת את מכנסי הג'ינס _____ . (מכנסיים *m.*)
      (ארוכות / הארוכות / ארוכים / הארוכים)

‎9.‏ החדר הזה קטן מדיי לכיתה שלנו. המורה דואג למציאת חדר _____.

(אחר / האחר / אחרת / האחרת)

‎10.‏ אימא עוזרת לי בבחירת בגדים _____.

(חדשה/ החדשה/ חדשים/ החדשים)

‎11.‏ נשיא צרפת _____ יבקר בישראל בעוד חודש.

(חדש / החדש / חדשה / החדשה)

Answers:

‎1.‏ גדולה ‎2.‏ הצעיר ‎3.‏ המלוכלכים ‎4.‏ הצעיר ‎5.‏ השנייה ‎6.‏ האדומה ‎7.‏ המפורסמים ‎8.‏ הארוכים
‎9.‏ אחר ‎10.‏ חדשים ‎11.‏ החדש

• Smeechoot *phrases vs. noun-adjective phrases*

Here are some examples of Hebrew **phrases**. Some are *smeechoot* (**noun-noun**) phrases and others are **noun-adjective** phrases:

עיר מיוחדת	סלט ירקות	שיר אהבה
קורס מחשבים		עיר בירה
כוס יין	סלט טעים	
שיר ישראלי	כוס קטנה	קורס מעניין

In the chapters on adjectives ("How Do Adjectives Behave?" pp. 124-137) and in the section on *smeechoot* phrases above, we saw that each of these two kinds of phrases behaves in a unique way – especially when it is made **definite** or **plural**. In order for us to know how to make a phrase definite or plural, we must first **identify** it as either a *smeechoot* (noun-noun) phrase or as a noun-adjective phrase.

Try this:

Put each of the above phrases in its proper place in the chart below.

noun + adjective phrase שם עצם + שם תואר	smeechoot *(noun + noun) phrase* שם עצם + שם עצם
שיר ישראלי	שיר אהבה
_____	_____
_____	_____
_____	_____
_____	_____

Here's the solution:

שיר ישראלי	שיר אהבה
סלט טעים	סלט ירקות
עיר מיוחדת	עיר בירה
כוס קטנה	כוס יין
קורס מעניין	קורס מחשבים

Q: What is the key to deciding if a phrase is a *smeechoot* or a noun-adjective phrase?

A: In all of the above phrases, the **second (last)** word of the phrase is the key. If it is a **noun**, as in the following, the phrase is *smeechoot*:

◄ קורס מחשבים   כוס יין   עיר בירה   סלט ירקות   שיר אהבה

If the second (last) word is an **adjective**, the phrase is a noun-adjective phrase:

◄ קורס מעניין   כוס קטנה   עיר מיוחדת   סלט טעים   שיר ישראלי

How do we know if the last word is a **noun** *or an* **adjective**?

It is not always easy to know if the last word in a phrase is a noun or an adjective. If you are writing or speaking, and thus using words with which you are familiar, you can ask yourself the following questions:

1. Does the word have **four forms**, as does גדול: גָּדוֹל / גְּדוֹלָה / גְּדוֹלִים / גְּדוֹלוֹת? If so, it is an adjective (unless it is an animate noun like רוֹפֵא / רוֹפְאָה / רוֹפְאִים / רוֹפְאוֹת).

2. Can you make the word **possessive**, as in האהבה שלי (**my** love) or הירקות שלי (**my** vegetables)? If so, the word is usually a noun.

If you encounter a word with which you are not familiar, it is not always possible to know whether it is a noun or an adjective.

In the chapters on the forms of nouns ("How Are Hebrew Nouns Formed?" pp. 78-87) and of adjectives ("How are Adjectives Formed?" pp. 138-158), we saw that certain patterns and forms are typical of nouns or of adjectives (for example, if a word ends in י, it is **usually** an adjective). However, we can't **depend** on form as the means of identifying a word as a noun or an adjective, since some forms are used for both. For example: שׁוֹמֵר (a guard) is a noun, while מוֹשֵׁךְ (attractive) is an adjective.

Why is it helpful to differentiate between a **smeechoot** and a noun-adjective phrase?

Knowing whether a noun phrase is a *smeechoot* or a noun-adjective phrase is helpful to you both as a speaker of Hebrew and as a reader. Here are some areas in which it is important:

1. Pronunciation and forming words

Let's say, for example, that you encounter the word בית in a text or wish to use it in speech. Oddly, in order to read the word out loud or to pronounce it properly when you speak, you must first check what comes **after** it! If you see that an adjective follows it, as in בית מודרני, then you will know to pronounce it בַּיִת. If you see that a noun follows it, as in בית ספר, you will know to say בֵּית (i.e., the *smeechoot* from).

This kind of differentiation also affects how you form words. For example, it helps you to know whether to say עוגה or עוגת- and, when forming the plural of a word like בַּיִת, whether to say בָּתֵי- or בָּתִּים.

2. Adding the definite article ה- and changing a phrase from singular to plural (and vice versa)

When you form phrases, you must, of course, assess whether you are using a *smeechoot* or a noun-adjective phrase in order to know where to place the definite article ה- (הבית הגדול or בית הספר) and how to make a singular phrase plural (בתי ספר or בתים גדולים) and vice versa.

3. *Using the dictionary*

When reading a text, differentiating between a *smeechoot* and a noun-adjective phrase also helps you know how to look up a word in the dictionary. For example, if you meet the phrase ילדות מאושרת and recognize that the second word is an adjective (and is feminine singular), you should realize that the word ילדות is **not** the plural of ילדה (girl), but rather is the feminine singular form יַלְדוּת. If you don't know that this means *childhood*, hopefully you would know to look up the singular form ילדות and not ילדה.

Let's review

The following chart summarizes the differences between these two types of phrases.

	noun + adjective	**smeechoot (*noun + noun*)**
◆ **Last word:**	Last word is an **adjective**:	Last word is a **noun**:
	adj. + noun	*noun + noun*
	a new song שיר חדש	a love song שיר אהבה
	a fresh salad סלט טרי	a vegetable salad סלט ירקות
		With more than two nouns:
		a root vegetable salad סלט ירקות שורש
◆ **First word:**	**No** changes in first word:	Changes in **first** word(s):
		Main changes:
		1. Final תָ (-*ah*) becomes תַ (-*at*):
	a big cake עוגה גדולה	an apple cake עוגת תפוחים
	a new class חוּלצה חדשה	a cotton shirt חולצת כותנה
		2. Plural ים- and ַיים- become יֵ-:
	good friends חברים טובים	Knesset members חברי כנסת
	comfortable shoes נעלַיים נוחות	bedroom slippers נעלי בית
		school principals מנהלי בתי ספר

	noun + adjective	smeechoot (*noun + noun*)
◆ *Matching*:	Matching in **gender** and **number**:	**No** matching:

noun + adjective column:

m.s. ⇔ *m.s.*
שיר חדש

f.s. ⇔ *f.s.*
עוגה גדולה

m.pl. ⇔ *m.pl.*
חברים טובים

f.pl. ⇔ *f.pl.*
נעליים נוחות

smeechoot column:

f.s. m.s.
שיר אהבה

m.pl. f.s.
עוגת תפוחים

◆ *Definiteness*:

noun + adjective: ה- on both words:

ה_____ ה_____
הסלט הטרי   the fresh salad

When the first word is already definite:

ירושלים העתיקה   ancient Jerusalem

בנו הגדול   his big son

smeechoot: ה- on the **last** word only:

סלט הירקות   the vegetable salad

מנהל בית הספר   the school principal

When the last word is already definite:

מלכת אנגליה   the Queen of England

בית ספרנו   our school

ראש ממשלת קנדה
the Prime Minister of Canada

◆ *Making plural*:

noun + adjective: **Both** words are made plural:

plural	singular
סלטים טריים ⇐	סלט טרי
fresh salads	
שְׂמָלוֹת חדשות ⇐	שִׂמְלָה חדשה
new dresses	
דְּרָכִים נוחות ⇐	דֶּרֶךְ נוחה
convenient ways / roads	
שולחנות שחורים ⇐	שולחן שחור
black tables	

smeechoot: Only the **first** word changes:

plural	singular
סלטי ירקות ⇐	סלט ירקות
vegetable salads	
שְׂמָלוֹת כלה ⇐	שִׂמְלַת כלה
wedding dresses	
דַּרְכֵי לימוד ⇐	דֶּרֶךְ לימוד
study methods	
שולחנות עץ ⇐	שולחן עץ
wooden tables	

Want to see if you've understood?

A. Change from singular to plural.

	plural		*singular*
Examples:	מכתבים חשובים	⇐	מכתב חשוב
	מכתבי אהבה	⇐	מכתב אהבה
	ـــــــــــــــــــــــــــــ	⇐	1. בית חולים
	ـــــــــــــــــــــــــــــ	⇐	2. בית חדש
	ـــــــــــــــــــــــــــــ	⇐	3. ספר מעניין
	ـــــــــــــــــــــــــــــ	⇐	4. ספר לימוד
	ـــــــــــــــــــــــــــــ	⇐	5. עוגה חמה
	ـــــــــــــــــــــــــــــ	⇐	6. עוגת יום הולדת

Answers:

1. בתי חולים   2. בתים חדשים   3. ספרים מעניינים   4. ספרי לימוד   5. עוגות חמות   6. עוגות יום הולדת

B. Change from plural to singular.

	plural		*singular*
Examples:	מכתבים חשובים	⇒	מכתב חשוב
	מכתבי אהבה	⇒	מכתב אהבה
	כוסות יין	⇒	ـــــــــــــــــــــــــــــ .1
	כוסות גבוהות	⇒	ـــــــــــــــــــــــــــــ .2
	שולחנות כתיבה	⇒	ـــــــــــــــــــــــــــــ .3
	שולחנות שחורים	⇒	ـــــــــــــــــــــــــــــ .4
	תלמידים אינטליגנטיים	⇒	ـــــــــــــــــــــــــــــ .5
	תלמידי בית ספר	⇒	ـــــــــــــــــــــــــــــ .6
	חברות טובות	⇒	ـــــــــــــــــــــــــــــ .7
	חברות כנסת	⇒	ـــــــــــــــــــــــــــــ .8

Answers:

‏5. תלמיד אינטליגנטי   4. שולחן שחור   3. שולחן כתיבה   2. כוס גבוהה   1. כוס יין

‏8. חברת כנסת   7. חברה טובה   6. תלמיד בית ספר

C. Circle the phrases that are already definite. Make all the rest of the phrases definite
   by adding a ה-.

	definite		indefinite
Examples:	החנות החדשה	⇐	חנות חדשה
	חנות הבגדים	⇐	חנות בגדים
1.	_____	⇐	בחור גבוה
2.	_____	⇐	בחור ישיבה
3.	_____	⇐	ארון בגדים
4.	_____	⇐	ארון כחול
5.	_____	⇐	חברת כנסת
6.	_____	⇐	חברה ותיקה
7.	_____	⇐	נשיא פקיסטאן
8.	_____	⇐	נשיא צעיר
9.	_____	⇐	בית הורינו
10.	_____	⇐	בית כנסת
11.	_____	⇐	בית מיוחד
12.	_____	⇐	ירושלים העתיקה

Answers:

Circled (already definite):   ‏12. ירושלים העתיקה   9. בית הורינו   7. נשיא פקיסטן

The rest made definite: ‏4. הארון הכחול   3. ארון הבגדים   2. בחור הישיבה   1. הבחור הגבוה

‏11. הבית המיוחד   10. בית הכנסת   8. הנשיא הצעיר   6. החברה הוותיקה   5. חברת הכנסת

V. Double Possessives (בְּנוֹ שֶׁל שְׁמוּאֵל)
סְמִיכוּת כְּפוּלָה

Preview
- *What is a double possessive?*
- *When do we use double possessives?*
- *Creating double possessive phrases*

• *What is a double possessive?*

Read the following two sentences:

1. המטרה של הפגישה עם המורה הייתה לדבר על הבעיות של הילד.
   The aim of the meeting with the teacher was to speak about the child's problems.

2. מטרתה של הפגישה עם המורה הייתה לדבר על בעיותיו של הילד.
   The aim of the meeting with the teacher was to speak about the child's problems.

Note that the highlighted phrases in both of these sentences have **the same** translation in English even though their structure in Hebrew is different.

Q: What does each of the highlighted phrases in sentence 1 have **in common** with the corresponding phrase in sentence 2?

A: They both contain a smaller phrase that begins with של:

של הילד,   של הפגישה,

Q: In what way are the highlighted phrases different from each other?

A: The difference is found in what comes **before** של.
In sentence 1, the noun before של is preceded by -ה:

הבעיות של הילד,   המטרה של הפגישה,

In contrast, in sentence 2 the noun has a possessive ending:

בעיותיו של הילד,   מטרתה של הפגישה,

In sentence 2, possession is actually expressed **twice** (a *double possessive*): once with an ending added onto the noun and again with the של phrase:[1]

In grammar books, this construction is often called סמיכות כפולה ("double *smeechoot*") even though there is no real *smeechoot*, as we know it, here.[2]

To what does the possessive ending refer?

Usually, in **other** uses of a "noun + possessive ending," the possessive ending refers **back** to someone or something that was already mentioned before, for example:

David met **his son** in the center of town.   דוד פגש את **בנו** במרכז העיר.

In this sentence, the ending on בנו (his son) refers **back** to דוד. In contrast, in the double possessive (״סמיכות כפולה״) construction the ending on the noun refers **forward** to the noun that **follows** של and **matches** it:

When we first encounter the noun with the possessive ending in these phrases, we do not know to whom or to what the ending refers until we read the של phrase.

• *When do we use double possessives?*

The use of double possessive phrases is simply a matter of style. Some phrases like these are used in informal speech – especially phrases that refer to family members: אִשתו של דויד (David's wife), בעלה של מירי (Miri's husband), אחותו של משה (Moshe's sister). However, usually the use of double possessives makes the style of a passage **more formal**.

---

1   We are referring to the relationship between the **two nouns joined by של** as possession even though this relationship is sometimes not exactly one of possession (as in המטרה של הישיבה).

2   On *smeechoot* phrases, see the chapter "*Smeechoot*," pp. 170-174.

• *Creating double possessive phrases*

When you create double possessive phrases on your own, you first have to convert the של phrase into a possessive ending and add this ending onto the first noun. Then, after this, you repeat the של phrase as it originally appeared. This is how it is done:

המטרה של הישיבה (1)

המטרה שלה (2)

מטרתה של הישיבה (3)

The possessor in these phrases is always in the ***third person*** (שלו his/its, שלה hers/its, שלהם their *m.*, שלהן their *f.*). Therefore, the endings on the first noun are always one of the following:

plural noun ending (הצעות) -ות *in*	plural noun ending *in* (דברים) -ִים	singular noun ending *in* ָ-ה (תגובה)	singular noun that doesn't end in ָ-ה (רצון)	possessor
דעותיו של האיש the man's opinions	דבריו של האיש the man's words	תגובתו של האיש the man's reaction	רצונו של האיש the man's wish	שלו
דעותיה של האישה the woman's opinions	דבריה של האישה the woman's words	תגובתה של האישה the woman's reaction	רצונה של האישה the woman's wish	שלה
דעותיהם של השרים the ministers' opinions	דבריהם של השרים the ministers' words	תגובתם של השרים the ministers' reaction	רצונם של השרים the ministers' (*m.*) wish	שלהם
דעותיהן של המורות the teachers' opinions	דבריהן של המורות the teachers' words	תגובתן של המורות the teachers' reaction	רצונן של המורות the teachers' (*f.*) wish	שלהן

Be careful! Not **all** nouns that are joined together by של can automatically be expressed with a double possessive. Usually, when their relationship is one of **possession**, we can use this structure, as in בעיותיו של הילד (the boy's problems). When two nouns joined by של do **not** have a relationship of possession, there is no clear-cut rule as to whether the double possessive structure **can** be used (e.g., מטרתה של הישיבה the aim of the meeting) or **cannot** be used.

Chapter summary

♦ Double possessive phrases begin with a "noun + possessive ending" followed by a phrase that begins with של:

≺ מטרתה של הישיבה,   בנו של משה,   ילדיהם של השכנים

The possessive ending on the first noun **matches** the noun that comes after של.

♦ Double possessives have the **same meaning** (and translation) as possessive phrases like the following, but are usually more **formal**:

≺ המטרה של הישיבה,   הבן של משה,   הילדים של השכנים

Want to see if you've understood?

Write the following phrases as double possessives. (For help with the forms, see the chart above or the chapter "Nouns with Possessive Endings," pp. 60-77).

Example:	____שירה של רחל____	⇐ ≺ השיר של רחל
1.	_____	⇐ המכונית של השכנים
2.	_____	⇐ הספרים של הסופרת
3.	_____	⇐ הדעה של המנהלת
4.	_____	⇐ הדעה של המנהלים
5.	_____	⇐ העוזרים של החוקרים
6.	_____	⇐ העוזרים של החוקרת
7.	_____	⇐ המכנסיים של הילדה
8.	_____	⇐ החולצה של הילד
9.	_____	⇐ הציפורניים של החתול
10.	_____	⇐ התיק של הנערה
11.	_____	⇐ הבקשות של העובדים
12.	_____	⇐ הבקשה של הבנות

Answers:

1. מכוניתם של השכנים   2. ספריה של הסופרת   3. דעתה של המנהלת   4. דעתם של המנהלים
5. עוזריהם של החוקרים   6. עוזריה של החוקרת   7. מכנסיה של הילדה   8. חולצתו של הילד
9. ציפורניו של החתול   10. תיקה של הנערה   11. בקשותיהם של העובדים   12. בקשתן של הבנות

VI. Pronouns and Pointing Words

Preview

• *Personal pronouns* (אֲנִי, אַתָה...)

• *Pointing words (demonstratives)* (זֶה..., הַהוּא...)

• *Each other* (זֶה אֶת זֶה, אֶחָד אֶת הַשֵּׁנִי...)

• *Personal pronouns* (אני, אתה...)

Read the following passage:

> הסופרת דיברה עם סטודנטים באוניברסיטה. היא הראתה להם את הספר החדש שלה ושאלה אותם
> אם הם קראו אותו.
>
> The author spoke with students at the university. She showed them her new book and asked them if
> they had read it.

The words highlighted in this passage are all *pronouns*.

Q: Which of the Hebrew pronouns above appear as **separate words** (not as an ending)?

A: Only היא and הם. The other pronouns appear as endings and are discussed elsewhere in this book.[1] היא and הם are examples of personal pronouns that can serve as the subject of a sentence. Here are others:[2]

plural		singular		person
אֲנַחְנוּ		אֲנִי		I
we (*m./f.*)		I (*m./f.*)		
אַתֶּן	אַתֶּם	אַתְּ	אַתָּה	II
you (*f.pl.*)	you (*m.pl.*)	you (*f.s.*)	you (*m.s.*)	
הֵן	הֵם	הִיא	הוּא	III
they (*f.*)	they (*m.*)	she / it (*f.*)	he / it (*m.*)	

---

1   See the chapter "Adding Endings to Prepositions," pp. 229-252. On numbers with pronoun endings, see the chapter "Numbers," pp. 283-285. On nouns with pronoun endings, see the chapter "Nouns with Possessive Endings," pp. 60-77.

2   For other pronouns that can serve as the subject (and in other capacities), see the following: On זה and the like, see the continuation of this chapter. On מי, מה and other question words, see the chapter "Asking Questions," pp. 808-819. On ש- מי, מה ש-, see the chapter "Sentences with ש- מה (כל), מי ש- (כל)," pp. 877-881.

The Hebrew equivalents of *I* and *we* (the *first person* pronouns) both begin with אֲנ-: אֲנִי (I) and אֲנַחְנוּ (we). Each is used for **both** masculine and feminine.

The English *you* (the *second person* pronoun for *m.s., f.s., m.pl., f.pl.*) is expressed by four **different** Hebrew pronouns, all of which begin with אַת-. Notice that in the singular, the **masculine** form (אַתָה) is **longer** than the feminine form (אַתְ). In the plural, the masculine form ends in ם- (אַתֶם) and the feminine in ן- (אַתֶן).

The Hebrew equivalents of *he, she, it* and *they* (the *third person* pronouns) all begin with ה': הוא, היא, הם, הן. Since Hebrew has no neuter (*it*), it has only two singular forms: masculine (הוא) and feminine (היא), both of which end in a silent א'. The masculine הוא corresponds to the English *he* and *it* (when what it refers to is masculine in Hebrew), for example:

➤ עוד לא ראיתי את הסרט "החיים יפים". שמעתי שהוא מצוין.
(הסרט=)

I haven't yet seen the film "Life is Beautiful." I've heard that it (=the film) is excellent.

The feminine היא corresponds to the English *she* and *it* (when what it refers to is feminine), for example:

Have you tasted the pizza? It is very good.
(= the pizza)

➤ טעמת את הפיצה? היא טעימה מאוד.
(הפיצה=)

The endings of the plural forms (הם they *m.* and הן they *f.*) are the same as אתם and אתן.

• *Pointing words (demonstratives)*

זה, זאת, אלה *and the like*

Read the following sentences:

The author said: This is my new book.
This book came out a month ago.

➤ 1. הסופרת אמרה: זה הספר החדש שלי.
2. הספר הזה יצא לאור לפני חודש.

Q: In which of these sentences does the word זה come after a noun, as **part of** a noun phrase?

A: In sentence 2. In this sentence, זה is part of the noun phrase הספר הזה (this book). In sentence 1, on the other hand, זה is not part of a noun phrase, but rather stands alone.

We will first discuss the use of זה and other pointing words when they stand **alone**, and then we will look at these words when they are part of a noun phrase.

זה, זאת, אלה *when they stand alone*

In the following sentences, the speaker points at an object close by and says something about it:

	plural		*singular*		
masculine:	These are books.	אֵלֶה ספרים.	This is a book.	זֶה ספר.	◄
feminine:	These are notebooks.	אֵלֶה מחברות.	This is a notebook.	זֹאת מחברת.	

The words highlighted in these sentences are the most common words used to point at something (or someone): זה is used for masculine singular (ספר), זאת for feminine singular (מחברת) and אלה both for masculine and feminine plural (מחברות, ספרים).

In more formal Hebrew, two more pointing words are sometimes used: זוֹ, which means the same as זאת, and אֵלוּ, which means the same as אלה.[3] The following sentences have the same meaning as those above:

זוֹ מחברת.   אֵלוּ ספרים / מחברות.   ◄

Pointing words are very versatile: They can function **not only** as the subject of a sentence (as in the sentences above), but also in other capacities. For example, we could point to something like a pen or a notebook and ask:

Are you using this now?	את משתמשת בזה עכשיו?	1.	◄
Where did you buy this?	איפה קנית את זה?	2.	

In these sentences, זה functions **not** as the subject, but rather as the object.[4] Note that when it is a *direct object* (as in sentence 2), we use the word את before it because it is considered *definite* (specific) even though it has **no** -ה on the front.[5] Notice, too, that in these sentences the name of the object that is pointed at is not mentioned. זה here refers in a general way to the "thing" to which we are pointing, without regard for whether the **word** for this object is masculine or feminine. This is the case also when we point to something and ask "?מה זה" (not knowing whether it is masculine or feminine).

---

3   זאת and אלה are characteristic of Biblical Hebrew, while זו and אלו are characteristic of Mishnaic Hebrew. Modern Hebrew has inherited all of these forms.

4   In the first Hebrew sentence, it is an *indirect object* and in the second it is a *direct object*. (On *direct objects* see the chapter "The Direct Object and the Use of את," pp. 697-704.)

5   For more on this, see the chapter "The Direct Object and the Use of את," pp. 698-702.

Did you know?

1. The word זה is also used to refer to a whole sentence or a whole idea, as in:

◄ .1 החיים קשים. רק עכשיו הבנתי את זה.   Life is difficult. Only now do I understand this.

.2 זה מעניין.   This / That is interesting.

= The things that we have seen, for example.

.3 ראינו סרט ואחרי זה הלכנו לבית קפה.

We saw a movie, and after that (= after we saw the movie), we went to a café.

In literary Hebrew, the word זאת is used in the same way as זה in sentence 1, but usually **without** את:

◄ החיים קשים. רק עכשיו הבנתי זאת.   Life is difficult. Only now do I understand this.

2. זה, זאת and אלה can also be used to refer back to a specific noun in a sentence like the following:

◄ קראתי את הספר האחרון של הפרופסור שלי. לדעתי, זה הספר הטוב ביותר שלו.

I read my professor's latest book. In my opinion, it (lit.: this) is his best book.

Note that, unlike in English, we usually use זה (and not הוא) in Hebrew when the *predicate*[6] of the second sentence is a noun.[7]

◄ קראתי את הספר האחרון של הפרופסור שלי. לדעתי, זה הספר הטוב ביותר שלו.

...it (lit.: this) is his best book.

When the predicate is **not** a noun, we say הוא (it) (as in English):

adjective

◄ את מכירה את הספר הזה? הוא מצוין.   Do you know this book?   It is excellent.

verb

– איפה הספר? – הוא נפל.   "Where is the book?"   "It fell."

---

6   For a clarification of the term *predicate*, see p. 705.

7   We always use זה, זאת, אלה (rather than הוא, היא, הם, הן) when the noun that follows is **definite**, and also many times when the noun is indefinite.

זה, זאת, אלה *as part of a noun phrase*

The pointing words אלה, זאת, זה and the like can also come after a noun in a phrase, in the same way that a regular adjective does, for example:

Have you read this book?	1. קראת את הספר הזה? (*m.s.*)
This student does not speak Hebrew.	2. הסטודנטית הזאת לא מדברת עברית. (*f.s.*)
Maya bought these flowers.	3. מאיה קנתה את הפרחים האלה. (*m.pl.*)
Who put wine in these small glasses?	4. מי שם יין בכוסות הקטנות האלה? (*f.pl.*)

In the above sentences, the pointing words match their nouns in **gender** (*masc.* ⇔ *masc.*, *fem.* ⇔ *fem.*) and in **number** (*sing.* ⇔ *sing.*, *pl.* ⇔ *pl.*). In addition, all of the above nouns are **definite**, and the pointing words are all preceded by -ה (הספר הזה). In this way, the pointing word behaves like a regular adjective, as in: הספר המעניין.

In more formal, written Hebrew, we sometimes find phrases such as the following:

This book was published a year ago.	1. ספר זה פורסם לפני שנה.
This young woman has many talents.	2. לבחורה זו יש כישרונות רבים.
We heard these things in the lecture last week.	3. שמענו דברים אלו בהרצאה בשבוע שעבר.

In these phrases, there is no -ה on **either** the noun **or** the pointing word, but they **mean** exactly the same as those with -ה (הספר הזה = ספר זה = this book). Nevertheless, unlike phrases with -ה, there is no את before them when they are the *direct object* (as in sentence 3).

Did you know?

The use of -ה before pointing words and the noun before them (e.g., האיש הזה) is typical of Biblical Hebrew, where the pronoun forms זֶה, זֹאת and אֵלֶּה are used. The absence of -ה in such phrases (e.g., איש זה) is typical of later (Mishnaic) Hebrew, where the forms זֶה, זוֹ and אֵלּוּ are used. Therefore, when we use -ה, the forms in Column I (below) are preferred, and when we omit -ה, the forms in Column II are preferred:

	II		I	
	ספר זה	or	הספר הזה	◄
	בחורה זו	or	הבחורה הזאת	
	דברים אלו	or	הדברים האלה	
	כוסות אלו	or	הכוסות האלה	

Today, we often find a mixing of these forms (for example: הבחורה הזו, which uses the Biblical structure ה....ה... with the Mishnaic form זו).

ההוא, ההיא, ההם, ההן (that, those)

Sometimes זה, זאת and the like are the equivalent of the English *that* and *those*, as you can see in some of the translations above. This is especially the case when these pointing words stand alone (**not** as part of a noun phrase). For example, if we point to a house in the distance, we might say:

◄ זה הבית שאנחנו רוצים לקנות.   That is the house we want to buy.

However, when pointing words are part of a noun phrase, we have two options when pointing to a house (or something / someone else) in the distance (i.e., "over there"):

◄ 1. אתם רואים את הבית הזה?   Do you see that house?
(lit.: this)

2. אתם רואים את הבית ההוא?   Do you see that house?

Note that the expressions ההוא (*m.s.*), ההיא (*f.s.*), ההם (*m.pl.*) and ההן (*f.pl.*) may be added **only** to a definite noun with ‑ה on the front.[8] They always match the noun that they follow in gender, number and definiteness, for example:

◄ את רואה את הבית ההוא? (*m.s.*)   Can you see that house?

השיטה ההיא טובה יותר מהשיטה הזאת. (*f.s.*)   That method is better than this method.

הבתים ההם ישנים. (*m.pl.*)   Those houses are old.

אתם מעדיפים את העוגות האלה או את העוגות ההן? (*f.pl.*)
Do you prefer these cakes or those cakes?

---

8   In spoken language, we sometimes hear these expressions used without a noun in front of them, as in:
◄ ההוא אמר שאי אפשר לתקן את זה.   That guy (over there) said that it's impossible to fix this.

These expressions can also refer to something distant **in time**, as in:

In those days   בימים ההם ◄

Let's review

◆ זה, זו/זאת, אלו/אלה are used for pointing at something.

- They can stand **alone** (i.e., **not** as part of a noun phrase):

f.pl.	*m.pl.*	*f.s.*	*m.s.*
אלה / אלו מחברות.	אלה / אלו ספרים.	זאת / זו מחברת.	זה ספר. ◄
These are notebooks.	These are books.	This is a notebook.	This is a book.

In these examples, they are the subject of the sentence and match the word denoting the object being pointed at. They can also have other functions in the sentence. For example, here they are an object:

◄ את משתמשת בזה?   את צריכה את זה?

Do you need this?   Are you using this?

- They can appear **after** a noun as part of a noun phrase:

המחברת הזאת קטנה.   הספר הזה מעניין. ◄

המחברות האלה קטנות.   הספרים האלה מעניינים.

In these examples, they match their noun in the same way that a regular adjective does. However, unlike a regular noun-adjective phrase (e.g., הספר המעניין), if ה- is dropped from the phrase (e.g., הספר הזה ⇐ ספר זה), the **meaning** does not change, but the style is more formal.

◆ The pointing words ההוא, ההיא, ההם, ההן (that / those) are used after a definite noun that has ה- on the front:

המחברת ההיא קטנה.   הספר ההוא מעניין. ◄

המחברות ההן קטנות.   כבר קראתי את הספרים ההם.

Want to see if you've understood?

A. Write one of the following forms – אלה/האלה or זאת/הזאת, זה/הזה – in the blank.

4. השולחנות _____ חדשים.   1. _____ בית גדול.

5. _____ שאלה טובה.   2. _____ ילדות נחמדות.

6. המפתחות _____ של מיכל.   3. המרק _____ טעים.

Answers:

1. זה   2. אלה   3. הזה   4. האלה   5. זאת   6. האלה

B. Translate.

1. This is an interesting question. _____

2. This question is interesting. _____

3. These are old newspapers. _____

4. These books are old. _____

5. This table is new. _____

6. Those are my books. _____

7. Those shoes are pretty. _____

8. We (*m.pl.*) know that man. _____

Answers:

1. זאת שאלה מעניינת. or זו שאלה מעניינת.   2. השאלה הזאת מעניינת. or שאלה זו מעניינת.
3. אלה עיתונים ישנים. or אלו עיתונים ישנים.   4. הספרים האלה ישנים. or ספרים אלו ישנים.
5. השולחן הזה חדש. or שולחן זה חדש.   6. אלה הספרים שלי. or אלו הספרים שלי.
7. הנעליים ההן יפות. or הנעליים האלה יפות. / נעליים אלו יפות.
8. אנחנו מכירים את האיש ההוא. or אנחנו מכירים את האיש הזה.

• *Each other* (זֶה אֶת זֶה, אֶחָד אֶת הַשֵּׁנִי...)

Read the following sentences:

1. דויד ויונתן לא ראו זה את זה הרבה זמן. ◄

David and Yonatan hadn't seen each other in a long time.

Yossi's brothers are angry at each other.

2. האחים של יוסי כועסים זה על זה.

3. אמיר ויובל רבו. הם לא מדברים זה עם זה כבר חודשיים.

Amir and Yuval had a fight. They haven't spoken with each other for two months.

David and Ruthie sat next to each other on the bus.

4. דויד ורותי ישבו זה ליד זה באוטובוס.

Q: What expressions are used in the above Hebrew sentences to say *each other*?

A: ‏זה ליד זה‎ and ‏זה עם זה‎, ‏זה על זה‎, ‏זה את זה‎.

Q: What do all these expressions have in common?

A: In each of them, the word ‏זה‎ appears **twice** with a preposition **in between**. The preposition used depends on the verb that precedes the expression (‏לדבר עם‎, ‏לכעוס על‎, ‏לראות את‎, ‏לשבת ליד‎).[9]

Let's take a closer look at how these work. Read the following two sentences:

Amir and Yuval are angry at their sister.	‏אמיר ויובל כועסים על אחותם.‎
Amir and Yuval are angry at each other.	‏אמיר ויובל כועסים זה על זה.‎

In the first sentence, the preposition ‏על‎ comes **right after** the verb ‏כועסים‎. The same is true of its English equivalent *angry at*.

Q: In the second sentence, does the preposition ‏על‎ also come **right after** the verb ‏כועסים‎?

A: No. When we use the expression ‏זה...זה‎, the preposition comes **in the middle**, unlike the English equivalent *at each other*.

Here is another example:

David and Amir don't know Avi.	‏דויד ואמיר לא מכירים את אבי.‎
David and Amir don't know each other.	‏דויד ואמיר לא מכירים זה את זה.‎

In the first sentence, ‏את‎ comes right after the verb ‏מכירים‎, whereas in the second sentence, the first ‏זה‎ comes right after ‏מכירים‎ and the preposition ‏את‎ comes **in the middle** of ‏זה...זה‎. In this case, the English has no word parallel to the Hebrew ‏את‎.

When do we use ‏זה...זה‎ to say *each other*?

If you look at the original four sentences, you will see examples of the kinds of words to which ‏זה...זה‎ can refer: two masculine nouns (‏דויד‎ and ‏יונתן‎ – sentence 1), a masculine plural noun (‏האחים‎ – sentence 2), a masculine plural pronoun (‏הם‎ – sentence 3) and a masculine noun and a feminine noun (‏דויד‎ and ‏רותי‎ – sentence 4). According to the rules of grammar, when we refer to two nouns, even if only one is masculine, we use ‏זה...זה‎.

---

9 See Appendix IV: "Verbs and their Prepositions," pp. 1019-1029.

Here are some more examples of this structure, this time with the feminine זו:

◄ **רותי ותמר ראו זו את זו מרחוק.**
Ruthie and Tamar saw each other from afar.

הן קראו זו לָזו.[10]
They called out to each other.

We use זו...זו when we refer to **two** feminine nouns or their equivalent (e.g., החברות or הן, as in the second sentence). Note that only the pronoun זו (and never זאת) can be used in this structure.

The above expressions are used mainly in formal Hebrew. In daily speech, the following equivalents are usually used:

- Instead of זה...זה, the masculine forms אחד...השני:[11]

◄ **דויד ויונתן לא ראו אחד את השני הרבה זמן.**
David and Yonatan hadn't seen each other / one another in a long time.

הם לא מתווכחים אחד עם השני.
They don't argue with each other.

- Instead of זו...זו, the feminine forms אחת...השנייה:

◄ **רותי ותמר ראו אחת את השנייה.**
Ruthie and Tamar saw each other.

הן קראו אחת לשנייה.
They called out to each other.

Sometimes the expression אלה...אלה (or אֵלוּ...אֵלוּ) – with a preposition in the middle – is used when referring to the relations between two groups, as in either of the following:

◄ **השחקנים דיברו אלה עם אלה לאחר המשחק.**
The players spoke with each other after the game.

אלו עם אלו

Let's review

◆ Expressions like זה את זה and זו את זו denote mutuality ("each other"). In informal Hebrew, we often use אחד...השני and אחת...השנייה instead. The verb that precedes these expressions determines what preposition is used in the middle, for example:

◄ **הם ראו זה את זה ודיברו זה עם זה.**

---

10 When the one-letter prepositions -ל and -ב appear before זה and זו, they have an *ah* vowel: זו בָּזו, זה לָזה. Nonetheless, many speakers who use this construction often pronounce it with an *eh* vowel: זה לְזה.

11 These are widely used even though they are not considered correct by the Hebrew Language Academy. This is primarily because, when understood literally, the expression אחד את השני sounds as if the two sides do not relate to each other equally; rather, only one side relates to the other.

◆ The following variations are discussed above:

- זה...זה and אחד...השני for two masculine nouns or a masculine noun and a feminine noun or their equivalent (הילדים, הם...):

◄ הילדים אוהבים זה את זה. הם משחקים זה עם זה.
דני ושרית אוהבים אחד את השני. הם מדברים אחד עם השני כל יום.

- זו...זו and אחת...השנייה for two feminine nouns or their equivalent (הילדות, הן...).

- אלה...אלה or אלו...אלו are sometimes used when referring to relations between two groups.

Want to see if you've understood

A. Complete the sentences using one of the following expressions with the appropriate preposition in the middle: זה...זה / אחד...השני // זו...זו / אחת...השנייה

1. דויד ועידו רבים עם כולם. הם גם רבים _____.

2. אתה עוזר לי ואני עוזרת לך. אנחנו עוזרים _____.

3. הוא מבין אותה והיא מבינה אותו. הם מבינים _____.

4. מיכל מדברת על רונית, ורונית מדברת על מיכל. הן מדברות _____.

5. כשהייתי ילד, הרבה פעמים השכנים שלנו עזרו לנו ואנחנו עזרנו להם. עזרנו _____.

Answers:

3. זה את זה / אחד את השני   2. זה לזה / אחד לשני   1. זה עם זה / אחד עם השני

5. זה לזה / אחד לשני   4. זו על זו / אחת על השנייה

B. Translate.

1. Gadi and Shira spoke with each other yesterday.

   _____

2. The girls sat next to each other at the party.

   _____

3. Ron and David, why are you (m.pl.) yelling at each other?

   _____

Answers:

2. הילדות ישבו זו ליד זו / אחת ליד השנייה במסיבה.   1. גדי ושירה דיברו זה עם זה / אחד עם השני אתמול.
3. רון ודויד, למה אתם צועקים זה על זה / אחד על השני?

VII. Prepositions מִילוֹת יַחַס

Introduction

Read the following passage:

עמדתי בתחנת האוטובוס ודיברתי עם דויד. גם הוא חיכה לאוטובוס. שנינו רצינו לנסוע מירושלים לקיבוץ ליד תל אביב.

I stood at the bus stop and spoke with David. He too was waiting for the bus. Both of us wanted to go from Jerusalem to a kibbutz next to Tel Aviv.

The highlighted words ב-, ל-, מ-, עם, ליד are *prepositions*.

In the following chapters we will look at:

1. **Prepositions and Their Meanings**
2. **How Do Prepositions Behave When No Ending Is Attached?: Writing and Pronunciation**
3. **Adding Endings to Prepositions**

1. Prepositions and Their Meanings

Preview

• *Do prepositions have meaning?*

• *Uses of prepositions in Hebrew and English: Are they the same?*

• *A helpful way to learn verbs and their prepositions*

• *Do prepositions have meaning?*

Some prepositions have fixed meanings, and some don't.

Prepositions with fixed meanings

Consider the preposition בִּגְלַל. No matter where it appears, it will always mean *because of*.

Here are some more prepositions with fixed meanings:

behind	מֵאֲחוֹרֵי	◄
next to	עַל יַד	
because	בִּגְלַל	

Some prepositions may have a limited number of **different** meanings. For example, the preposition לִפְנֵי has two:

a. before:	We ate lunch before class.	אכלנו ארוחת צהריים לפני השיעור.
b. in front of:	I am standing in front of Dan.	אני עומד לפני דן.

The preposition אצל

The preposition אֵצֶל deserves special attention. It has a fairly fixed meaning, but has no exact equivalent in English. It is similar to the French preposition *chez* in an expression like *chez vous* (at your place) or to the Yiddishism *How's by you?*, which means: *How are things with you?*, *at your place?*, *in your life?*.

Here are some examples of how we use אצל:

Dalit lives at her parents' (house).	דלית גרה אצל ההורים. ◄
I was at Michal's yesterday.	הייתי אצל מיכל אתמול.
(or: I visited Michal at home yesterday.)	

In these first two examples, when we speak of **physically** being with someone – living with someone, visiting someone – the **assumption** is that all of this takes place at their **home**.

When we speak about being with someone at a place **other than** his or her home, we must state this **explicitly** (for example, by adding בעבודה at work):

I visited Michal at work.	ביקרתי אצל מיכל בעבודה. ◄

The use of אצל is very common in advertisements, as in the following ad for a restaurant:

Our food is the best! (lit.: At our place it is tastiest)	אצלנו הכי טעים! ◄

Here the "speaker" is the owner of the restaurant; hence, when he says אצלנו, he is referring to his restaurant.

The following example is different:

How is Yossi?	?מה נשמע אצל יוסי – ◄
Everything's fine with Yossi ("by" Yossi).	.אצל יוסי הכול בסדר –

Here אצל refers to a person's life and surroundings: his or her work, family, etc.

Note that אצל never comes after verbs of **motion**. These always require -ל or אל, even when the English does not use the preposition *to*:

We went to our parents' (house).	(or אל ההורים.)	נסענו להורים. ◄
We arrived at our parents' (house).	(or אל ההורים.)	הגענו להורים. ◄

Prepositions without a fixed meaning

Now let's look at the preposition -ב:

a. -ב is often used to express the English words *in* (a place) or *at* (a place or a time) or sometimes *on* (a day):

He lives in Nigeria.	הוא גר בניגריה. ◄
He works at home.	הוא עובד בבית.
She arrived at 10:00.	היא הגיעה ב-10.
They called on Sunday.	הם צלצלו ביום ראשון.

b. -ב can also mean *with* in the sense of *with the help of* or *by means of*:

She is writing in pencil (= with a pencil).	היא כותבת בעיפרון. ◄
They are playing with the ball.	הם משחקים בכדור.

c. -ב also has other uses in Hebrew. Here's an example:

He is using a dictionary.	הוא משתמש במילון. ◄

Q: What does -ב mean in this sentence?

A: -ב has a **function** here – it is a connecting word – but it has no **meaning** of its own. The -ב in this sentence is **part of the verb** -להשתמש ב.[1]

In English, too, we have prepositions that are part of the verb. Take the sentence: "I depend on my friends." The verb in this sentence is (*to*) *depend on* and not *to depend*.

Students of English obviously must learn verbs like *to depend on* **with their prepositions**. Similarly, students of Hebrew must learn each verb together with its required preposition, if it has one, for example:

לצְפּות ב-	לטפל ב-	לכעוס על	לדאוג ל- ◄
to watch	to take care of	to be angry with, to be mad at	to worry about

---

1 In Hebrew such a preposition is called מִילַת יַחַס מוּצְרֶכֶת.

Do such verbs always use their prepositions?

Some verbs, like -ב להשתמש and -ב לטפל, **always** use their prepositions. Others may appear **without** a preposition, as in:

אנחנו כועסים.   ◄   We are angry.

However, when we note **with whom** or **at what** we are angry, we **must** use the preposition:

אנחנו כועסים על משה.   ◄   We are angry *with* Moshe.

• *Uses of prepositions in Hebrew and English: Are they the same?*

In quite a few cases, the uses of prepositions in Hebrew and English are the same. In such cases, learning the preposition that goes with a given verb requires no special effort. Here are examples of such "freebies":

1. Verbs that require the **"same"** preposition in both languages:

◄ -להאמין ב	to believe *in*
-לִפְנוֹת ל	to turn *to*
-להקשיב ל	to listen *to*
לחלום על	to dream *about*

When you learn these and other verbs like them, you need only make a mental note that their prepositions are the "same" as in English.

2. Verbs that require **no** preposition before their *object,*[2] as in:

אני רואה רכבת.   ◄   I see a train.

For English speakers, a verb like לראות is a "freebie." However, this is so only when the object (here, רכבת a train) is **indefinite** (= **not** specific). When the object is **definite** (specific), we add את, as in:

אני רואה את הרכבת.[3]   ◄   I see **the** train.

For this reason, it is worth learning the verb לראות and other verbs like it as: (את) לראות.

---

2   For an explanation of what an *object* is, see the chapter "The Direct Object and the Use of אֶת," pp. 687-698.

3   For more on אֶת, see the chapter "The Direct Object and the Use of אֶת," pp. 698-702.

There are, of course, many Hebrew verbs that are **not** "freebies." The following verbs, for example, require special attention because their corresponding English verb takes either **no** preposition (1 and 2) or takes a **different** one (3-6):

The boy is watching a movie.	‫1. הילד צופה בסרט.‬
He is using a VCR.	‫2. הוא משתמש בווידאו.‬
We worry about our children.	‫3. אנחנו דואגים לילדים שלנו.‬
The child is dependent on his mother.	‫4. הילד תלוי באימא שלו.‬
Dalit is looking for a new apartment.	‫5. דלית מחפשת דירה חדשה.‬
Miri is looking for her keys.	‫6. מירי מחפשת את המפתחות שלה.‬

Be careful! A certain verb in Hebrew may have several translations:

to fear, **to be afraid of	‫לפחד מ-‬
to enjoy, **to derive enjoyment from	‫ליהנות מ-‬
**to request (something), to ask for (something)	‫לבקש את‬

It is often easier to remember the translation that is **closer** to the Hebrew (noted above with **), if there is one. For example, if you learn that ‫לבקש את‬ is *to request*, you may be less likely to use ‫-ל‬ (by mistake) after ‫לבקש‬. In a case like this, you would need to make a mental note that *to ask for* is the same as *to request*: ‫לבקש את‬.

• *A helpful way to learn verbs and their prepositions*

Aside from noting when the English and Hebrew prepositions are **different** and concentrating on learning the differences, we can make learning verbs and their required prepositions easier by grouping together all of the verbs requiring the **same** preposition.

In addition, if we list together all of the verbs that require the same preposition (for example, ‫-מ‬), we may even be able to find some common meaning that will help us remember that these verbs belong to the same group.

Here's an example: the following words indicate fear and take ‫-מ‬. In each case, whatever triggered the fear will come after ‫-מ‬:

to fear, be afraid of	-מ לפחוד / -מ לפחד	◄
to fear, be anxious about	-מ לחשוש	
to be frightened of (suddenly)	-מ להיבהל	

Other verbs of emotion can be added to this group. Here, too, whatever triggered the emotion will come after -מ:

to be excited by	-מ להתרגש	◄
to enjoy (derive enjoyment from)	-מ ליהנות	
to be disappointed by/with	-מ להתאכזב	
to be satisfied with	-מ להיות מרוצה	

At the back of this book, we have included a chart grouping verbs together in a way that is intended to help you remember their prepositions. (See Appendix IV, pp. 1019-1029.)

Remember: You need make a special effort only to learn those verbs whose prepositions are **different** from the ones used in English.

Want to see if you've understood?

Some of the sentences below do not need a preposition added in Hebrew, while others do.

a. Add the appropriate preposition where necessary. (You may refer to Appendix IV for help.)

b. Put an asterisk (*) next to each sentence in which the Hebrew preposition is different from the English.

1. בכל שבוע אנחנו מבקרים _____ מוזיאון ישראל.
   Every week we visit the Israel Museum.

2. אנחנו רואים שם _____ ציורים מעניינים.
   We see interesting pictures there.

3. אנחנו לא נוגעים _____ תמונות.
   We don't touch the pictures.

4. אחר כך אנחנו תמיד הולכים _____ מסעדה.
   Afterwards, we always go to a restaurant.

5. אנחנו נכנסים _____ (ה)מסעדה.
   We go into (enter) the restaurant.

6. אנחנו מסתכלים _____ תפריט ומדברים _____ המלצר.
   We look at the menu and speak with the waiter.

7. אנחנו מזמינים _____ קפה ועוגה. We order coffee and cake.

8. אנחנו שותים _____ הקפה ואוכלים _____ העוגה.

We drink the coffee and eat the cake.

9. אנחנו משלמים _____ החשבון. We pay the bill.

10. אנחנו יוצאים _____ המסעדה. We go out of (leave) the restaurant.

Answers:

*1. כל שבוע אנחנו מבקרים במוזיאון ישראל. (different from English *to visit*)

2. אנחנו רואים שם ציורים מעניינים.

*3. אנחנו לא נוגעים בתמונות. (different from English *to touch*)

4. אחר כך אנחנו הולכים למסעדה.

5.(*) אנחנו נכנסים לַמסעדה or אל המסעדה. (same as *to go into*, different from *to enter*)

*6. אנחנו מסתכלים בתפריט ומדברים עם המלצר. (different from *to look at*)

7. אנחנו מזמינים קפה ועוגה.

8.(*) אנחנו שותים את **הקפה** ואוכלים את **העוגה**. (The verbs require את before *the*.)

9.(*) אנחנו משלמים את **החשבון**. (The verb requires את before *the*.)

10. אנחנו יוצאים מהמסעדה. (different from *to go out of*, different from *to leave*)

2. How Do Prepositions Behave When No Ending Is Attached?: Writing and Pronunciation

Preview

- *Which prepositions are written as separate words and which are not?*
- *The pronunciation of* -מ ,-כ ,-ל ,-ב
- *The effect of* -כ ,-ל ,-ב *and* -מ *on the pronunciation of the following word*
- *What happens to prepositions before the definite article* -ה *(the)?*
- *Some prepositions are (sometimes) interchangeable (*ל/-אל ,-מ/מן*)*

• *Which prepositions are written as separate words and which are not?*

-מ ,-כ ,-ל ,-ב

The prepositions -מ ,-כ ,-ל ,-ב are one-letter words. As is the case with all one-letter words in Hebrew, these prepositions never stand alone: they are always connected to the beginning of the next word, for example:[1]

on Sunday	בְּיום ראשון
from Tel Aviv	מִתל אביב

עַל, אל, עם, עד, מן, ליד, לפני, אחרי, בגלל *and similar words*

In contrast, prepositions of **two letters or more** stand as independent words:

I spoke with David.	דיברתי עם דויד.
We stood next to the house.	עמדנו ליד הבית.

---

1   Other examples of one-letter words that are always attached to the word that follows them are -ה (the) and -ש (that, which, who…).

• *The pronunciation of* -כ, -ל, -ב *and* -מ

-כ, -ל, -ב

The prepositions -כ, -ל, -ב are pronounced: *beh*, *leh* and *keh*, as in:

כְּאנגליה	לְאנגליה	בְּאנגליה	◄
ke-'AN-glee-ya	le-'AN-glee-ya	be-'AN-glee-ya	

According to traditional rules of grammar, the pronunciation of these prepositions changes in certain cases (see "Did you know?" below). Most speakers today, especially when speaking informally, do not follow these rules, but rather simply maintain the *beh*, *leh*, *keh* pronunciation.

Did you know?

In formal Hebrew the pronunciation of -כ, -ל, -ב changes in the following cases:

1a. Before a *shva* (בְּ)
When -כ, -ל, -ב come before a consonant with a *shva*, the pronunciation changes from *eh* to *ee*:[2]

כִּטבריה	לִטבריה	בִּטבריה	טְבֶרְיה	◄
kee-TVER-ya	lee-TVER-ya	bee-TVER-ya	TVER-ya	

1b. Before a י with a *shva* (יְ)
If the word begins with "יְ", the pronunciation of -כ, -ל, -ב changes to *ee* and, in addition, the י loses its *shva*:

כִּירושלים	לִירושלים	בִּירושלים	יְרושלים	◄
kee-roo-sha-LA-yeem	lee-roo-sha-LA-yeem	bee-roo-sha-LA-yeem	ye-roo-sha-LA-yeem	

2. Before a *half-vowel* (חֲ חֱ חֳ)
The *half-vowels* take the place of *shva* after guttural consonants (א', ה', ח', ע'). When the prepositions -כ, -ל, -ב are attached to the beginning of the word, their vowel matches the sound of the *half-vowel*. (Note: The following words are not definite.)

כַּחֲלום	לַחֲלום	בַּחֲלום	חֲלום	:A ◄
ka-cha-LOM	la-cha-LOM	ba-cha-LOM	cha-LOM	

כֶּאֱמת[3]	לֶאֱמת	בֶּאֱמת	אֱמת	:E
ke-'e-MET	le-'e-MET	be-'e-MET	'e-MET	

---

2   For more on this change, see J. Weingreen, 1959, pp. 10, 27.

3   Here the pronunciation sounds like the pronunciation of -כְּ, -לְ, -בְּ *beh*, *leh*, *keh*.

כָּאֳנִייה	לָאֳנִייה	בָּאֳנִייה	אֳנִייה :O
ko-'o-nee-YA	lo-'o-nee-YA	bo-'o-nee-YA	'o-nee-YA

3. Sometimes before a one-syllable word or before a word whose first syllable is stressed, the pronunciation changes to *ah*, as in:

איפה מוצאים ספרים כָּאֵלֶה?	אנחנו לא נחיה לָנֶצַח.	הם הסתכלו זה בָּזֶה.
ka-'E-le	la-NE-tsach	ba-ZE
Where can one find books like these?	We won't live forever.	They looked at each other.

-מ

The preposition -מ is pronounced *mee*, as in:

מניו יורק	מברזיל
mee-nyoo-YORK	mee-bra-ZEEL

The pronunciation -מִ (*mee*) changes to -מֵ (*meh*) before א', ה', ח', ע', ר' (including before the definite article -ה *the*), for example:[4]

me-'ar-gen-TEE-na	הם באים מֵארגנטינה,
me-HO-land	מֵהולנד,
me-chei-FA	מֵחיפה,
me-'ee-RAK	מֵעיראק,
me-ROOS-ya	מֵרוסיה,
me-ha-BA-yeet	מֵהַבַּיִת,
me-ha-mees-RAD	מֵהַמִשְׂרָד.

One of the few cases in which this change does **not** occur is before the word חוץ (outside), for example:

סטודנטים רבים באים לישראל מֵחוץ לארץ כדי ללמוד עברית.
mee-CHOOTS
Many students come to Israel from abroad in order to study Hebrew.

---

4 In texts that are written with vowel signs, a *strong dagesh* is – as a rule – written after the preposition -מ when it is pronounced *mee* (-מִ). This *dagesh* traditionally denotes a "doubling" of the consonant – a phenomenon that occurred at one time, but does not occur in today's pronunciation. In the letters א', ה', ח', ע', ר', a *dagesh* almost never appears because, apparently, the consonants denoted by these letters were rarely doubled. Traditional grammar books often explain that, as a result – and to "compensate" for the fact that no doubling of א', ה', ח', ע', ר' took place and no *dagesh* was written in them – the vowel of -מִ (*mee*) changed to what was then called a "longer" vowel -מֵ (*meh*). In traditional grammar books, this is often called *compensatory lengthening* (תַשְׁלוּם דָגֵשׁ). See more on this subject on p. 637 ("Did you know?").

• *The effect of -ב, -ל, -כ and -מ on the pronunciation of the following word*

-ב, -ל, -כ

There **may** be a change in a word to which -ב, -ל, -כ are attached only when the word begins with 'פ or 'ב or 'כ, as in: פֶּתַח תִּקְוָה (Petach Tikva), בֵּית לֶחֶם (Bethlehem), כַּרְמִיאֵל (Carmiel).

Most speakers of Hebrew continue to pronounce words like these with a **hard** pronunciation – *p, b, k* – even after they add the prepositions to the front of them, for example:

informal:	כּכרמיאל	לבית לחם	בּפתח תקווה ◄
	ke-kar-mee-'EL	*le-bet-LE-chem*	*be-pe-tach-TEEK-va*

According to formal rules of pronunciation, we would have a **soft** sound *f* (פ), *v* (ב), *ch* (כ) after the prepositions -ב, -ל, -כ.

formal:	כּכרמיאל	לבית לחם	בּפתח תקווה ◄
	ke-char-mee-'EL	*le-vet-LE-chem*	*be-fe-tach-teek-VA*[5]

Note: This rule does not apply to **foreign** place names. Therefore, a name such as פריז (Paris) keeps its hard *p* even when -בְּ, -לְ, -כְּ are added to the front: בְּפריז (*be-pa-REEZ*).

-מ

When the preposition -מ comes before 'ב, 'כ, 'פ, they keep their **hard** pronunciation – *p, b, k* – (both in formal and informal Hebrew), as in:[6]

mee-pe-tach-TEEK-va	הוא בא מפתח תקווה. ◄
mee-bet-LE-chem	מבית לחם
mee-kar-mee-'EL	מכרמיאל

5　This is the proper pronunciation of this name. Most Israelis say *TEEK-va*.

6　As mentioned in footnote 4 above, this is a strong *dagesh*. For an explanation, see the chapter "The Pronunciation of ב, 'כ, 'פ and the *Dagesh*," pp. 634-636.

• *What happens to prepositions before the definite article -ה (the)?*

ב-, ל-, כ-

When the one-letter prepositions -כְּ, -לְ, -בְּ come before -ה (the), they not only attach themselves to the next word, but also **fuse** with the -ה. Thus:

be + ha ⇒ *ba*	בַּבַּיִת ⇐ בְּ + הַבַּיִת	◄
le + ha ⇒ *la*	לַבַּיִת ⇐ לְ + הַבַּיִת	
ke + ha ⇒ *ka*	כַּבַּיִת ⇐ כְּ + הַבַּיִת	

For example: She went to the kibbutz. **הִיא נסעה לַקיבוץ.**

מ-

Unlike the other one-letter prepositions, -מִ does ***not*** fuse with -ה. However, as noted above, the vowel after -מִ always changes from *ee* (מִ) to *eh* (מֶ) before -ה:

mee + ha ⇒ *meh + ha*	מֵהַ- ⇐ מִ + הַ- ◄

For example: He went out of (lit: from) the house. **הוא יצא מֵהַבַּיִת.**

עם, אל, על, מן *and others*

All other prepositions remain unchanged when they precede -ה, for example:

He sat on the chair. **הוא ישב על הכיסא.** ◄

• *Some prepositions are (sometimes) interchangeable*

מן / מ-

מן and -מ are actually two forms of the same preposition (-מ is a shortened form of מן). מן is used much less than -מ in Modern Hebrew. One reason for this is that the long form can only be used under particular circumstances: i.e., when the word that follows it begins with the definite article -ה (the), as in:

He went out of (lit: from) the house. **הוא יצא מן הבית.** ◄

The use of the short form is not limited in this way.

Generally speaking, the long form – הוא בא מן הבית – sounds more formal than the short form – הוא בא מהבית.

There are certain fixed expressions in Hebrew that require one form and cannot take the other. For example, only the long form is used in the following:

≼	יוצא מן הכלל	exceptional
	טובים השניים מן האחד.	Two are better than one.

אֶל / לְ-

The prepositions -ל and אל without an ending are only sometimes interchangeable. אל without an ending is more formal than -ל, and its meaning is much more limited: אל almost always means *to* and indicates direction, whereas -ל means not only *to* (in more than the directional sense), but also *for*. Thus, when אל appears without an ending, it may always be replaced by the less formal -ל, as in:

≼	הוא חזר אֶל העיר.	/	הוא חזר לָעיר.	He returned to the city.
	(more formal)		*(less formal)*	

However, if we wish to make our style more formal by replacing -ל with אל, we may do so only after certain verbs (and some other parts of speech) and almost only when -ל means *to* in a directional sense. Words after which אל and -ל are interchangeable are listed in Appendix IV under ל-/אל.

Is there any way of predicting which verbs will be in the ל-/אל list?

There are some guidelines that can help you remember which verbs appear in the ל-/אל list. For example, many of them are **verbs of motion and direction**, as in:

≼	ללכת ל-/אל	to go to
	להגיע ל-/אל	to get to, to arrive at
	לחזור ל-/אל	to return to
	לִפנות ל-/אל	to turn to (someone)
		(with a question / request)

Others are verbs that involve **turning *to*** someone **via telephone**:

≼	להתקשר ל-/אל, לצלצל ל-/אל, לטלפן ל-/אל	to call, to phone

When you look at the rest of the ל-/אל list in the appendix, you can try to come up with several other categories that will help you remember them all.

Adding endings: ...אליך, אליי / ...לך, לי

Learning the verbs in the ל-/אל list is particularly important for the following reason: When these verbs take a preposition **with** an ending (e.g., ...אֵלֶיךָ, אֵלַיי to me, to you...), we **almost always** use אל (and **not** ל-) as the base onto which the endings are added.[7]

Thus, when there is **no ending** on the preposition, we can say **either** of the following (the version with ל- is less formal and more commonly used):

Rami turned to the principal.   רמי פנה אל המנהל. / רמי פנה למנהל.   ≺

However, when an ending is added, we can say **only**:

Rami turned to him.   רמי פנה אליו.   ≺

The forms of prepositions with endings are discussed in the next chapter.

---

7   In the case of several verbs, both לו and אליו are used, for example:

I sent him a letter.   שלחתי אליו מכתב. or   שלחתי לו מכתב.   ≺

3. Adding Endings to Prepositions

Preview

- *Adding endings without an additional* י׳
- *Adding endings with an additional* י׳

Introduction

What follows a preposition?

Let's return to the short passage we read in the Introduction to Prepositions:

עמדתי בתחנת האוטובוס ודיברתי עם דויד. גם הוא חיכה לאוטובוס. שנינו רצינו לנסוע מירושלים לקיבוץ ליד חיפה.

I stood at the bus stop and spoke with David. He too was waiting for the bus. Both of us wanted to go from Jerusalem to a kibbutz next to Haifa.

Q: What kind of word comes after each preposition (ב-, עם...).

A: In all of the sentences a **noun** follows the preposition (e.g., תחנת האוטובוס bus stop, דויד David, אוטובוס bus, etc.). The noun may sometimes be preceded by the words *a* or *the* in English.

Often, however, instead of a noun, a **pronoun** (e.g., him, her, it, me) comes after a preposition, for example:

I waited for Rina. I waited for her all morning.   חיכיתי לרינה. חיכיתי לה כל הבוקר.

Notice that in English, the preposition *for* and the pronoun *her* are **separate** words, whereas in Hebrew this is not the case. In Hebrew the pronoun *her* is written as an ending on the preposition: לה.

This means that learners of Hebrew need to learn the forms of each preposition with the *endings* added (called the *declension*). Luckily, this is easier than it sounds at first because there are groups of prepositions that take the same endings.

The two main declension groups

There are two basic kinds of endings added to prepositions. Let's have a look at them:

II	I
על	-ל
עליי	לי
עליך	לך
עלייך	לך
עליו	לו
עליה	לה

Q: Can you see the most basic difference between the two kinds of endings?

A: In Group I ("The -ל Group"), there is **no** י **between** the preposition and the ending. The ending is added straight onto the preposition.

In contrast, in Group II ("The על Group"), there is always **at least one** י before the ending.

For a concise list of the forms of the prepositions presented in this chapter, see Appendix III, pp. 1017-1018.

• *Adding endings without an additional* י

In the introduction above, we have called Group I "The -ל Group." This group contains all the prepositions whose endings do **not** contain an additional י. Not all of the prepositions in Group I, however, behave exactly like -ל. We have divided Group I into the following subcategories: Group Ia, Group Ib and special cases.

Group Ia (-ל)

In addition to -ל, the prepositions -ב and של also belong to this group (Group Ia).[1]
Here are the forms of these prepositions:

	של	-ב		-ל
my / me[2]	שֶׁלִי	בִּי	*-EE*	לִי
your / you (*m.s.*)	שֶׁלְךָ	בְּךָ	*-CHA*	לְךָ
your / you (*f.s.*)	שֶׁלָךְ	בָּךְ	*-ACH*	לָךְ
his / him	שֶׁלוֹ	בּוֹ	*-O*	לוֹ
her / her	שֶׁלָה	בָּהּ	*-A*	לָהּ

---

1   של takes the same endings as -ל since it is actually a combination of "שֶׁ + לְ ◁".

2   *My* is the translation of שלי, and *me* is added onto the translation of each of the other prepositions, for example *to me, for me, at me.*

של	ב-		ל-	
our / us	שֶׁלָּנוּ	בָּנוּ	-A-noo	לָנוּ
your / you (m.pl.)	שֶׁלָּכֶם	בָּכֶם	-a-CHEM	לָכֶם
your / you (f.pl.)	שֶׁלָּכֶן	בָּכֶן	-a-CHEN	לָכֶן
their / them (m.pl.)	שֶׁלָּהֶם	בָּהֶם	-a-HEM	לָהֶם
their / them (f.pl.)	שֶׁלָּהֶם	בָּהֶם	-a-HEN	לָהֶן

Notice that this group likes the *ah* sound a lot. All but two of the forms contain an *ah*:

לָהּ, לֵהּ, לָנוּ, לָכֶם, לָכֶן, לָהֶם, לָהֶן

Want to see if you've understood?

Write the missing preposition with its ending and read the sentences aloud.

1. – רינה, איפה הספר _____ ? – הספר שלי בבית.
   your (f.s.) (של)

2. – רינה ואלעד, איפה הבית שלכם? – הבית _____ ברחוב בן-יהודה.
   our (של)

3. – משה, יש _____ זמן לצאת למסעדה? – כן, יש לי זמן עכשיו!
   you (m.s.) (-ל)

4. – בנות, בואו, מיכל רוצה לתת _____ מתנות.
   you (f.pl.) (-ל)

5. הספרים של דן ושל יעל בתיק. גם המחברות _____ בתיק.
   their (של)

6. – ניר, אתה זוכר את שושנה? היא טיפלה בך ובמיכאל. היא טיפלה _____ כשהייתם בני שנתיים.
   you (m.pl.) (-ב)

Answers:

1. שֶׁלָּךְ   2. שֶׁלָּנוּ   3. לְךָ   4. לָכֶן   5. שֶׁלָּהֶם   6. בָּכֶם

Group Ib (בִּשְׁבִיל)

In the following chart you can see the forms of בשביל (Group Ib) alongside the forms of -ל:

		Ib בשביל		Ia -ל
me	-EE	בִּשְׁבִילִי	-EE	לִי
you (*m.s.*)	-CHA	בִּשְׁבִילְךָ	-CHA	לְךָ
you (*f.s.*)	-ECH	בִּשְׁבִילֵךְ	-ACH	לָךְ
him	-O	בִּשְׁבִילוֹ	-O	לוֹ
her	-A	בִּשְׁבִילָהּ	-A	לָהּ
us	-E-noo	בִּשְׁבִילֵנוּ	-A-noo	לָנוּ
you (*m.pl.*)	-CHEM	בִּשְׁבִילְכֶם	-a-CHEM	לָכֶם
you (*f.pl.*)	-CHEN	בִּשְׁבִילְכֶן	-a-CHEN	לָכֶן
them (*m.*)	-AM	בִּשְׁבִילָם	-a-HEM	לָהֶם
them (*f.*)	-AN	בִּשְׁבִילָן	-a-HEN	לָהֶן

Q: How are the forms of בשביל different from those of -ל (the representative of Group Ia)?

A: There are two basic differences.

1. בשביל doesn't like the *ah* sound as much as -ל. Look at the differences between the following forms:

	Ib	Ia	
	בִּשְׁבִילֵךְ	לָךְ	◄
	בִּשְׁבִילֵנוּ	שֶׁלָּנוּ	

and also:

	Ib	Ia
	בִּשְׁבִילְכֶם	שֶׁלָּכֶם
	בִּשְׁבִילְכֶן	שֶׁלָּכֶן

2. In the last two plural forms, בשביל makes do with a short, one-letter ending: -ם, -ן, whereas -ל has a full two-letter ending: -הם, -הן. This probably happens because -ל is so short. Thus:

	Ib	Ia	
	בִּשְׁבִילָם	לָהֶם	◄
	בִּשְׁבִילָן	לָהֶן	

Examples of other prepositions that belong to Group Ib are:

אֵצֶל ◄	– אֶצְלִי, אֶצְלְךָ, אֶצְלֵךְ... אֶצְלֵנוּ, אֶצְלְכֶם... אֶצְלָם	(at the home / place of)
לְיַד	– לְיָדִי, לְיָדְךָ, לְיָדֵךְ, לְיָדָהּ... לְיָדֵנוּ, לְיַדְכֶם[3]... לְיָדָם	(next to)

---

3 Most speakers pronounce this form לְיַדְכֶם (*le-yad-CHEM*). The form found in grammar books is לְיֶדְכֶם.

(because of)	בִּגְלַל, בִּגְלָלִי, בִּגְלָלְךָ, בִּגְלָלֵךְ... בִּגְלָלֵנוּ, בִּגְלַלְכֶם... בִּגְלָלָם	בִּגְלַל –
(thanks to)	בִּזְכוּתִי, בִּזְכוּתְךָ, בִּזְכוּתֵךְ... בִּזְכוּתֵנוּ, בִּזְכוּתְכֶם... בִּזְכוּתָם	בִּזְכוּת –
(instead of)	בִּמְקוֹמִי, בִּמְקוֹמְךָ, בִּמְקוֹמֵךְ... בִּמְקוֹמֵנוּ, בִּמְקוֹמְכֶם... בִּמְקוֹמָם	בִּמְקוֹם –

Want to see if you've understood?

Write the missing preposition with its ending and read the sentences aloud.

א. יש לנו כרטיסים לקונצרט, ואנחנו לא יכולים ללכת. אתם רוצים ללכת _____?
1. (במקום) instead of us

גם תמר ומיכל יהיו שם. אתם תֵּשְׁבוּ ממש _____.
2. (ליד) next to them (f.pl.)

ב. אסתי, אני _____ לא הייתי מסכימה לשלם כל כך הרבה.
3. (במקום) lit.: in your place (f.s.)
(=if I were you)

ג. רונית: דבורה, את עוזבת מוקדם _____ או בגלל רון ודויד?
4. (בגלל) because of me

דבורה: האמת היא שאני עוזבת גם _____ וגם _____.
5. (בגלל) because of you (f.s.)
6. (בגלל) because of them (m.pl.)

Be careful! In the following we mix Groups Ia (ל-) and Ib (בשביל):

ד. שרית, קניתי את המתנה הזאת _____. אֶתֵּן _____ אותה מחר.
7. (בשביל) for you (f.s.)
8. (ל-) to you (f.s.)

ה. הדודים שלנו גרים בצפון. כשביקרנו _____, ראינו את הבית החדש _____.
9. (אצל) at their place
10. (של) their

ו. שמעון גר _____. הוא בא לבית _____ כל יום ונותן _____
11. (ליד) next to us
12. (של) our
13. (ל-) us

פרחים מהגינה _____. הוא יושב _____ חצי שעה, שותה קפה וחוזר הביתה.
14. (של) his
15. (אצל) at our place

Answers:

1. בִּמְקוֹמֵנוּ 2. לְיָדָן 3. בִּמְקוֹמֵךְ 4. בִּגְלָלִי 5. בִּגְלָלֵךְ 6. בִּגְלָלָם 7. בִּשְׁבִילֵךְ 8. לָךְ 9. אֶצְלָם 10. שֶׁלָהֶם
11. לְיָדֵנוּ 12. שֶׁלָנוּ 13. לָנוּ 14. שֶׁלוֹ 15. אֶצְלֵנוּ

Special cases in Group I

Usually, the prepositions in **Group I** do not change when they take an ending. In five cases, however, the **base** to which we add the endings changes significantly.

‏1. אֶת‏

Let's look at אֶת in the following sentence:

‏◄ אני רואה את המלצר.‏ I see the waiter.

(Notice that את is not translated into English when it has no ending.)

What happens when we want to say: "I see **him**"?

We expect an ending to be added to את. But, surprisingly, when the ending is added, the form of אֶת changes to ‏אוֹת-‏:

‏◄ אני רואה את המלצר.‏ ⇐ ‏אני רואה אותו.‏

I see the waiter. I see him.

Here are all the forms of את with endings. For the sake of comparison, we have listed the forms of ‏ל-‏ next to them.

		אֶת		‏ל-‏
me		אוֹתִי		לִי
you (*m.s.*)		אוֹתְךָ		לְךָ
you (*f.s.*)		אוֹתָךְ		לָךְ
him		אוֹתוֹ		לוֹ
her		אוֹתָהּ		לָהּ
us		אוֹתָנוּ		לָנוּ
you (*m.pl.*)	-CHEM	אֶתְכֶם	-*a*-CHEM	לָכֶם
you (*f.pl.*)	-CHEN	אֶתְכֶן	-*a*-CHEN	לָכֶן
them (*m.*)	-AM	אוֹתָם	-*a*-HEM	לָהֶם
them (*f.*)	-AN	אוֹתָן	-*a*-HEN	לָהֶן

Q: In which forms does the base **not** change to ‏אוֹת-‏?

A: Only in the *you plural* forms: ‏אֶתְכֶם, אֶתְכֶן‏. However, many Hebrew speakers use the ‏אוֹת-‏ base (‏אוֹתְכֶם, אוֹתְכֶן‏) for these forms as well, especially in informal Hebrew.[4]

---

4 The forms אותכם and אותכן are not recognized as "correct" by the Hebrew Language Academy.

Q: Where do the **endings** of את differ from those of ל-?

A: The major difference is in the *them* forms (אוֹתָם, אוֹתָן). Here the **short** endings -*AM* and -*AN* are added to אות- (as in בִּשְׁבִילָם, בִּשְׁבִילָן). There is also a slight difference in the *you plural* forms (אֶתְכֶם, אֶתְכֶן), where there is no *ah* between את and the endings. (This is similar to בִּשְׁבִילְכֶם / בִּשְׁבִילְכֶן and different from לָכֶם / לָכֶן *la-CHEM / la-CHEN*.)

Want to see if you've understood?

Write the missing preposition with its ending and read the sentences aloud.

א. דויד ורינה הם חברים טובים: היא אוהבת _____ והוא אוהב _____.
   1. (את) him   2. (את) her

ב. – חברֹ'ה, לא ראינו _____ הרבה זמן. איפה הייתם?
   3. (את) you (*m.pl.*)

   – נסענו לצרפת לטיול, לכן לא ראיתם _____.
   4. (את) us

Be careful! In the following we mix Groups Ia (-ל), Ib (בשביל) and את:

ג. – אתם מכירים אותנו? – כן, אנחנו מכירים _____ וגם את ההורים _____.
   5. (את) you (*m.pl.*)   6. (של) your (*m.pl.*)

   – ואתם מכירים גם את החברים שלנו? – כן, אנחנו מכירים _____ וגם את ההורים _____.
   7. (את) them   8. (של) their

ד. משה ואני קיבלנו שתי חבילות בדואר. לקחנו _____ אתמול מבית הדואר.
   9. (את) them (*f.pl.*)

   היו _____ ספרים. הפקיד אמר _____: יש פה שתי חבילות _____.
   10. (ב-) in them   11. (ל-) to us   12. (בשביל) for you

   כשהדוור הביא _____ לבית _____, לא הייתם שם.
   13. (את) them (*f.pl.*)   14. (של) your (*m.pl.*)

ה. אורית, החברה שלי, רותי, אומרת שהיא מכירה _____ ואת השותפות הקודמות _____.
   15. (את) you (*f.s.*)   16. (של) your

   היא אומרת ש_____ השותפות עזבו את הדירה.
   17. (בגלל) because of you (*f.s.*)

Answers:

1. אוֹתוֹ   2. אוֹתָהּ   3. אֶתְכֶם   4. אוֹתָנוּ   5. אֶתְכֶם   6. שֶׁלָּכֶם   7. אוֹתָם   8. שֶׁלָּהֶם   9. אוֹתָן   10. בָּהֶן
11. לָנוּ   12. בִּשְׁבִילְכֶם   13. אוֹתָן   14. שֶׁלָּכֶם   15. אוֹתָךְ   16. שֶׁלָּךְ   17. בִּגְלָלֵךְ

2. עִם (*with*)[5]

Look at the following:

דיברתי איתו.[6]	⇐	◄ דיברתי עם יונתן.
I spoke with him.		I spoke with Yonatan.
הוא רקד איתָה.	⇐	יונתן רקד עם שרה.
He danced with her.		Yonatan danced with Sarah.

Q: What change takes place in the preposition when we want to say: *with me, with you, with him*, etc.?

A: When endings are added, the *base* is not עם, but rather אֶת- (-אית). This change takes place in everyday speech and in most writing.[7] The endings are exactly the same as those added to אות-.

		עם
with me		אִיתִי
with you (*m.s.*)		אִיתְךָ
with you (*f.s.*)		אִיתָךְ
with him		אִיתוֹ
with her		אִיתָהּ
with us		אִיתָנוּ
with you (*m.pl.*)	-CHEM	אִיתְכֶם
with you (*f.pl.*)	-CHEN	אִיתְכֶן
with them (*m.*)	-AM	אִיתָם
with them (*f.*)	-AN	אִיתָן

In literary style only, endings may be added to the preposition עם:

דיברתי עימו (עמו).[8]	⇐	◄ דיברתי עם משה.
I spoke with him.		I spoke with Moshe.

---

5   We offer just one or two of the possible translations of each preposition.

6   Although these forms should be written **without** a י according to the Hebrew Language Academy, the י is often written for the sake of clarity.

7   In Biblical Hebrew, there are two words that look and sound the same: אֶת used before the definite direct object ("בראשית ברא אלהים את השמים") "In the beginning God created the heavens" Gen. 1:1) and אֶת that means *with* ("את האלהים התהלך נח") "Noah walked with God." Gen. 6:9). The only remnant of this usage in **Modern** Hebrew – i.e., in which את (=with) has no endings – is in names of businesses or firms: "גרינפלד את לוי" "Greenfeld and (=with) Levy." Oddly, it is this את that is the base to which endings are added in informal Modern Hebrew. Its vowel changes to *ee*: אִיתָי, אִיתְךָ... (...אִיתִי, אִיתוֹ).

8   The declension of עם is as follows. (The vowels of the *you plural* forms are slightly different from those of אֶת-):

◄ עִמִי עִמְּךָ, עִמּוֹ, עִמָהּ, עִמָנוּ, עִמְכֶם, עִמְכֶן, עִמָם (עִמָהֶם), עִמָן (עִמָהֶן)

Want to see if you've understood?

Write the missing preposition with its ending and read the sentences aloud.

א. הילדים ביקשו ממני לשחק _____ . אמרתי להם: "די, כבר שיחקתי
     1. (עם) with them (m.pl.)

_____ שלוש שעות". אבל נועה כל כך רצתה שאמשיך לשחק _____
2. (עם) with you (m.pl.)   3. (עם) with her

שנשארתי שם עוד קצת.

Be careful! In the following we mix Groups Ia (ל-) and Ib (בשביל), את and עם:

ב. הזמנתי _____ לבוא עם ירון ו_____ לראות את הסרט. את לא רוצה
     4. (את) you (f.s.)   5. (עם) with me

לבוא _____?
6. (עם) with us

ג. שרה, אני מצטער שרבתי _____ כשהייתי _____.
                        7. (עם) with you (f.s.)   8. (אצל) at your (f.s.) place

ד. כדאי לכם לבוא _____ למשחק הכדורגל. תוכלו לשבת _____
                   9. (עם) with us   10. (ליד) next to us

ויהיה _____ כיף ביחד.
         11. (ל-) lit.: to us
         (=we will have)

Answers:

1. אִיתָּם 2. אִיתְּכֶם 3. אִיתָּהּ 4. אוֹתָךְ 5. אִיתִּי 6. אִיתָּנוּ 7. אִיתָּךְ 8. אֶצְלֵךְ 9. אִיתָּנוּ 10. לְיָדֵנוּ 11. לָנוּ

3. כְּמוֹ (like, as)

Another preposition whose forms change when endings are added is כְּמוֹ. Here are its forms:

			כְּמוֹ
like me	ka-MO-**nee**		כָּמוֹנִי
like you (m.s.)	ka-MO-cha		כָּמוֹךָ
like you (f.s.)	ka-MOCH		כָּמוֹךְ
like him	ka-MO-**hoo**	(kmo-TO | כְּמוֹתוֹ[9])	כָּמוֹהוּ
like her	ka-MO-**ha**	(kmo-TA | כְּמוֹתָה)	כָּמוֹהָ

---

9 Forms based on כמות- (כמותי, כמותך...) also exist in Modern Hebrew. We have listed the most commonly used ones in parentheses. Often these forms sound more formal. The forms whose base is כמו- are found in Biblical Hebrew; those whose base is כמות- come from Mishnaic Hebrew.

			כְּמוֹ
like us	*ka-MO-noo*		כָּמוֹנוּ
like you (*m.pl.*)	*kmo-CHEM*		כְּמוֹכֶם
like you (*f.pl.*)	*kmo-CHEN*		כְּמוֹכֶן
like them (*m.*)	*kmo-HEM*	(*kmo-TAM* כְּמוֹתָם)	כְּמוֹהֶם
like them (*f.*)	*kmo-HEN*	(*kmo-TAN* כְּמוֹתָן)	כְּמוֹהֶן

Note that the pronunciation of כמו in the upper part of the table is כָּ-מוֹ (*ka-MO*). The stress is on *MO* in these forms. In contrast, in the lower part of the table (כְּמוֹהֶם, כְּמוֹכֶם, כְּמוֹכֶן, כְּמוֹהֶן), the **ending** is stressed, and the beginning of the word sounds just like the word כְּמוֹ when it has no endings (*kmo-CHEM*, *kmo-CHEN*, etc.). This is true especially in formal Hebrew. In informal, spoken Hebrew, however, many speakers do not stress the endings -כם, -כן, -הם, -הן, but rather continue saying *ka-MO* in all of the forms:

informal:[10]	*ka-MO-chem*	כְּמוֹכֶם
	ka-MO-chen	כְּמוֹכֶן
	ka-MO-hem	כְּמוֹהֶם
	ka-MO-hen	כְּמוֹהֶן

Q: How do the endings of כמו compare with the prepositions we have seen so far?

A: Two of the endings are unlike any we have seen thus far. They are noted above in bold: the **נִי**- (*-nee*) ending on *like me* and the **הו**- (*-hoo*) ending on *like him*. All the rest of the endings are the same.

Want to see if you've understood?
Write the missing form of כמו with its ending and read the sentences aloud.

א. יוסי, תודה רבה. אתה נהדר! אין _____ !
  1. (כמו) like you (*m.s.*)

ב. שמעתם איך יורם מדבר? הבן שלו מדבר בדיוק _____ .
  2. (כמו) like him

ג. תמר בגובה של מאיה. היא גם רזה _____.[11]
  3. (כמו) like her

---

10 This pronunciation is not recognized as "correct" by the Hebrew Language Academy.
11 Note the English: She is also as thin as she (is). – Literally: She is also thin like her.

ד. הבנים האלה חזקים מאוד. חבל שאנחנו לא חזקים _____.[12]
4. (כמו) like them

ה. הילדות האלה מתלבשות בדיוק _____ ומסתרקות בדיוק _____ .
5. (כמו) like us   6. (כמו) like you (f.pl.)

ו. האחות שלנו דומה לנו. היא שותה חמש כוסות קפה ביום _____ , ומגדלת בבית הרבה
7. (כמו) like me

בעלי חיים _____ .
8. (כמו) like you (f.s.)

Answers:

1. כָּמוֹךָ   2. כָּמוֹהוּ   3. כָּמוֹהָ   4. כְּמוֹהֶם   5. כָּמוֹנוּ (או: כְּמוֹתָם)   6. כְּמוֹכֶן   7. כָּמוֹנִי   8. כָּמוֹךְ

4. *The erratic* מ- *(from, than)*

The preposition מ- is like no other preposition and acts in an erratic manner when endings are added to it. Let's have a look:

◄   קיבלנו מכתב מדויד.   ⇐   קיבלנו מִמֶנוּ מכתב.[13]

(*mee*)   (*mee-ME-noo*)

We got a letter from David.   We got a letter from him.

קיבלנו מכתב מדניאל ונדב.   ⇐   קיבלנו מֵהֶם מכתב.

(*mee*)   (*me-HEM*)

We got a letter from Daniel and Nadav.   We got a letter from them.

Q: To what *base* are the endings added?

A: Sometimes the base is מִמ-, and sometimes it is מ-. Let's have a closer look at all the different variations:

---

12 Note the English: It is a shame that we are not as strong as they (are). – Literally: not strong like them.
13 Often, as in this sentence, when the preposition takes an ending, it comes immediately after the verb.

	C single -מ		B single -מ		A double -ממ
from me					me-ME-nee מִמֶּנִּי
from you (*m.s.*)					meem-CHA מִמְּךָ
from you (*f.s.*)					me-MECH מִמֵּךְ
from him					me-ME-noo מִמֶּנּוּ
from her					me-ME-na מִמֶּנָּה
from us			me-'ee-TA-noo מֵאִיתָנוּ (מִמֶּנּוּ)[14]		
from you (*m.pl.*)	mee-KEM מִכֶּם				
from you (*f.pl.*)	mee-KEN מִכֶּן				
from them (*m.*)	me-HEM מֵהֶם				
from them (*f.*)	me-HEN מֵהֶן				

Column A

Q: What is the base in Column A?

A: A double מ' (-ממ).

Let's take a closer look.

Q: Which of the endings on the מִמֶּ- begin with a נ'?

A: Three endings:

from me	mee-ME-nee	מִמֶּנִּי	◄
from him	mee-ME-noo	מִמֶּנּוּ	
from her	mee-ME-na	מִמֶּנָּה	

Note that the stress in these forms is on *ME* (pronounced *meh*).

The other two forms in this column have no נ' and their endings are just like the endings on בשביל (בִּשְׁבִילְךָ, בִּשְׁבִילֵךְ):

from you (*m.s.*)	meem-CHA	מִמְּךָ	◄
from you (*f.s.*)	mee-MECH	מִמֵּךְ	

---

14 The form מִמֶּנּוּ also exists. See explanation of "Column B" below.

Want to see if you've understood?

Write the missing form of -מ with its ending and read the sentences aloud.

א. מרים כל כך נחמדה! קיבלתי _____ מכתב בשבוע שעבר.
from her (-מ) .1

אולי בשבוע הבא אקבל מכתב גם _____ .
from you (f.s.) (-מ) .2

ב. נדב גבוה יותר _____ , אבל הוא נמוך יותר _____ .
than me (-מ) .4   than you (m.s.) (-מ) .3

ג. איפה הכלב שלך? הבת שלי פוחדת _____ . אתה יכול להוציא אותו החוצה, בבקשה?
of him (-מ) .5

Answers:

1. מִמֶּנָּה   2. מִמֵּךְ   3. מִמְּךָ   4. מִמֶּנִּי   5. מִמֶּנּוּ

Column C

Now let's skip over to Column C.

Q: What is the base of מֵכֶם, מִכֶּן, מֵהֶם, מֵהֶן?

A: Here the endings are added to the single letter -מ.

Q: Where is the stress placed in these words?

A: It is always on the **end**.

Note that the endings כֶם- and כֶן- begin with the hard sound *k* (*-KEM, -KEN*).[15]

Before the endings הֶן- ,הֶם-, the pronunciation of the -מ is *me* (pronounced *meh*).[16]

Column B

Here's a little riddle: If *from me* is מִמֶּנִּי (*mee-ME-nee*), what would you expect *from us* to be?

Perhaps you guessed מִמֶּנּוּ (*mee-ME-noo*)? This form indeed exists. However, since it also means *from **him***, we use a different form in Modern Hebrew to say *from **us***: מֵאִיתָנוּ (*me-'ee-TA-noo*).

---

15 This happens because the נ- of the preposition מן has "dropped out" (assimilated). On the presence of a strong *dagesh* in the letter after a נ "drops out," see the chapter "The Pronunciation of ב', כ', פ' and the *Dagesh*," pp. 635-636.

16 This is always the case when -מ is followed by a guttural consonant (here: ה'). For more details, see the preceding chapter "How Do Prepositions Behave When No Ending Is Attached?", p. 224, note 4.

Q: Can you see the two words from which this form is built?

A: It is built from -מ added to the word meaning *with us*: אִיתָנוּ. Before א', -מ is pronounced -מֵ (*meh*), thus: מֵאִיתָנוּ.

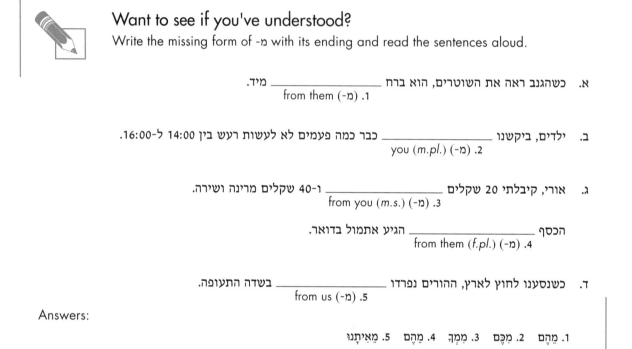

Want to see if you've understood?

Write the missing form of -מ with its ending and read the sentences aloud.

א. כשהגנב ראה את השוטרים, הוא ברח _____ מיד.
.1 from them (-מ)

ב. ילדים, ביקשנו _____ כבר כמה פעמים לא לעשות רעש בין 14:00 ל-16:00.
.2 you (m.pl.) (-מ)

ג. אורי, קיבלתי 20 שקלים _____ ו-40 שקלים מרינה ושירה.
.3 from you (m.s.) (-מ)

    הכסף _____ הגיע אתמול בדואר.
.4 from them (f.pl.) (-מ)

ד. כשנסענו לחוץ לארץ, ההורים נפרדו _____ בשדה התעופה.
.5 from us (-מ)

Answers:

.1 מֵהֶם .2 מִכֶּם .3 מִמְּךָ .4 מֵהֶם .5 מֵאִיתָנוּ

5. -ל *(to)*

As we mentioned at the end of the previous chapter, after certain verbs the preposition -ל changes to אֶל when endings are added. For example, when -ל is followed by a **noun**, we say:

◄ התקשרתי לדליה אתמול.   I called Dalia yesterday.

However, when we say *I called her*, substituting a **pronoun** (her) for the noun (Dalia), we must use אל as the base form to which the ending is added:

◄ התקשרתי אֵלֶיהָ אתמול.   I called her yesterday.

The verbs after which this switch from -ל to אל occurs when endings are added are listed in Appendix IV under ל-/אל.[17] For the forms of אל with endings, see below, p. 1025.

---

17 See the previous chapter "How Do Prepositions Behave When No Ending Is Attached?", pp. 227-228 for more on the switching of -ל and אל when **no** endings are added.

Let's review

◆ This chart summarizes the prepositions in Group I.

מן	כמו	בשביל, אצל...	את	עם	ל-, ב-, של
special cases		Ib		Ia	
מִמֶּנִּי	כָּמוֹנִי	בִּשְׁבִילִי	אוֹתִי	אִיתִי	לִי
מִמְּךָ	כָּמוֹךָ	בִּשְׁבִילְךָ	אוֹתְךָ	אִיתְךָ	לְךָ
מִמֵּךְ	כָּמוֹךְ	בִּשְׁבִילֵךְ	אוֹתָךְ	אִיתָךְ	לָךְ
מִמֶּנּוּ	כָּמוֹהוּ	בִּשְׁבִילוֹ	אוֹתוֹ	אִיתוֹ	לוֹ
מִמֶּנָּה	כָּמוֹהָ	בִּשְׁבִילָהּ	אוֹתָהּ	אִיתָהּ	לָהּ
מֵאִיתָּנוּ	כָּמוֹנוּ	בִּשְׁבִילֵנוּ	אוֹתָנוּ	אִיתָנוּ	לָנוּ
מִכֶּם	כְּמוֹכֶם	בִּשְׁבִילְכֶם	אֶתְכֶם	אִיתְכֶם	לָכֶם
מִכֶּן	כְּמוֹכֶן	בִּשְׁבִילְכֶן	אֶתְכֶן	אִיתְכֶן	לָכֶן
מֵהֶם	כְּמוֹהֶם	בִּשְׁבִילָם	אוֹתָם	אִיתָם	לָהֶם
מֵהֶן	כְּמוֹהֶן	בִּשְׁבִילָן	אוֹתָן	אִיתָן	לָהֶן

Want to see if you've understood?

In the following exercise, you can practice all of the prepositions learned in this section.
Write the missing preposition with its ending and read the sentences aloud.

א. ענת, סיפרנו ___ 1. (ל-) you (f.s.) ___ שאתמול פגשנו את דורית ומיכל? פגשנו ___ 2. (את) them (f.pl.) ___ ברחוב,

___ 3. (עם) with them (f.pl.) ___ והלכנו ___ למסעדה. הן אמרו שהן לא ראו ___ 4. (את) you (f.s.) ___ המון זמן וביקשו

___ 5. (מ-) us ___ את מספר הטלפון ___ 6. (של) your (f.s.) ___ , אז נתנו ___ 7. (ל-) them (f.pl.) ___

___ 8. (את) it (m.s.) ___ .

ב. יוסי ורמי, איפה המטריות שביקשנו ___ 9. (מ-) you (m.pl.) ___ להביא ___ 10. (ל-) us ___ ?

ג. יש ___ 11. (ל-) lit.: to you (m.pl.) (=you have) ___ מכונית, או שגם אתם באתם ברגל ___ 12. (כמו) like us ___ ?

ד. מירי, שלום!

בונים ‎_____ next to us (ליד) .13 ‎_____ בניין חדש, והרעש מאוד מפריע ‎_____ us (-ל) .14 ‎. אולי אנחנו יכולים

להיות ‎_____ at your (f.s.) place (אצל) .15 ‎_____ כמה ימים? אני מחכה לתשובה ‎_____ from you (f.s.) (מן) .16 ‎.

ה. דויד פוחד מכלבים. אמרתי ‎_____ to him (-ל) .17 ‎: "אל תפחד ‎_____ of them (-מ) .18 ‎, תשחק

‎_____ with them (עם) .19 ‎_____ like me (כמו) .20 ‎. הם לא יעשו ‎_____ to you (m.s.) (-ל) .21 ‎ שום דבר".

ו. – יונתן, מה אתה מוכן לעשות בשביל הילדים ‎_____ your (m.s.) (של) .22 ‎?
(willing)

– אני מוכן לעשות ‎_____ for them (m.) (בשביל) .23 ‎ הכול. אני אתֵּן ‎_____ them (-ל) .24 ‎ את כל מה שהם רוצים.

גם אם הם יבקשו ‎_____ me (-מ) .25 ‎_____ (moon) הַיָּרֵחַ, אני אנסה להוריד להם ‎_____ it (m.s.) (את) .26 ‎.

Answers:

א. 1. לְךָ 2 אוֹתָן 3 אִיתָן 4. אוֹתְךָ 5. מֵאִיתָנוּ 6. שֶׁלְךָ 7. לָהֶן 8. אוֹתוֹ
ב. 9. מִכֶּם 10. לָנוּ ג. 11. לָכֶם 12. כָּמוֹנוּ ד. 13. לְיָדֵנוּ 14. לָנוּ 15. אֶצְלֵךְ 16. מִמֵּךְ
ה. 17. לוֹ 18. מֵהֶם 19. אִיתָם 20. כָּמוֹנִי 21. לְךָ 22. שֶׁלְךָ ו. 23. בִּשְׁבִילָם 24. לָהֶם 25. מִמֶּנִּי
26. אוֹתוֹ

• *Adding endings with an additional ‎י‎*

In the section above, we looked at Group I ("The ‎ל‎- Group"), which has endings **without** a ‎י‎. Now we will concentrate on Group II ("The ‎על‎ Group") – the group that requires a ‎י‎ before the ending.

Group II

Here are examples of three prepositions in this group with their endings:

	לְפָנֵי	אֶל	על	
me	לְפָנַיי	אֵלַיי	-Al	עָלַיי
you (m.s.)	לְפָנֶיךָ	אֵלֶיךָ	-E-cha	עָלֶיךָ
you (f.s.)	לְפָנַיִיךְ	אֵלַיִיךְ	-A-yeech	עָלַיִיךְ
him	לְפָנָיו	אֵלָיו	-AV	עָלָיו
her	לְפָנֶיהָ	אֵלֶיהָ	-E-ha	עָלֶיהָ

	לִפְנֵי	אֶל	עַל	
us	לְפָנֵינוּ	אֵלֵינוּ	-EI-noo	עָלֵינוּ
you (m.pl.)	לִפְנֵיכֶם	אֲלֵיכֶם[18]	-ei-CHEM	עֲלֵיכֶם
you (f.pl.)	לִפְנֵיכֶן	אֲלֵיכֶן	-ei-CHEN	עֲלֵיכֶן
them (m.)	לִפְנֵיהֶם	אֲלֵיהֶם	-ei-HEM	עֲלֵיהֶם
them (f.)	לִפְנֵיהֶן	אֲלֵיהֶן	-ei-HEN	עֲלֵיהֶן

Notice that in the first form in each column – עָלַיי, אֵלַיי, לְפָנַיי – the syllable containing -AI is stressed, as in: עָ-לַיי ('a-LAI). This is the second syllable of the word.

Q: In which of the other forms of על is the stress **not** on the second syllable of the word?

A: In the four forms at the bottom of the chart. In these forms – and in all of the parallel forms in the other columns – the stress is on כֶם-, כֶן-, הֶם-, הֶן-. For this reason, the vowels at the beginning of these words sometimes change. We do not hear this vowel change in the forms of על, but we do hear it in **לִפְנֵיכֶם, לִפְנֵיכֶן, לִפְנֵיהֶם, לִפְנֵיהֶן** (leef-nei-CHEM...).[19] We also hear the change in the forms of אֶל listed in the chart: ...אֲלֵיכֶם ('a-lei-CHEM...). These are the grammatically correct forms. However, many speakers of Hebrew do not say אֲלֵיכֶם, but rather keep the same first vowel as in the rest of the forms and say ...אֵלֵיכֶם, אֵלֵיכֶן ('e-lei-CHEM), so as to differentiate between אליכם (to you) and עֲלֵיכֶם (on you, about you).

The following prepositions also belong to this group:

after	אַחֲרַיי, אַחֲרֶיךָ...	אַחֲרֵי
without	בִּלְעָדַיי, בִּלְעָדֶיךָ...	בְּלִי / בִּלְעֲדֵי
behind	מֵאֲחוֹרַיי, מֵאֲחוֹרֶיךָ...	מֵאֲחוֹרֵי
above	מֵעָלַיי, מֵעָלֶיךָ...	מֵעַל
under	מִתַּחְתַּיי, מִתַּחְתֶּיךָ...	מִתַּחַת

Want to see if you've understood?
Write the missing preposition with its ending and read the sentences aloud.

א. אבישי ואבנר, התקשרנו _____ כל הבוקר ולא עניתם לנו.
1. (אל) (m.pl.) you

---

18 The formal pronunciation is with an *ah* after the א', but most Hebrew speakers pronounce an *eh* sound instead, just as in the top part of the chart: אֵלֵיכֶם, אֵלֵיכֶן, אֵלֵיהֶם, אֵלֵיהֶן.

19 Actually, the preposition לפני originates from the form לְפָנִים (le-fa-NEEM). When the stress moves to the end (as in the lower part of the chart), the base changes to לִפְנֵי (leef-).

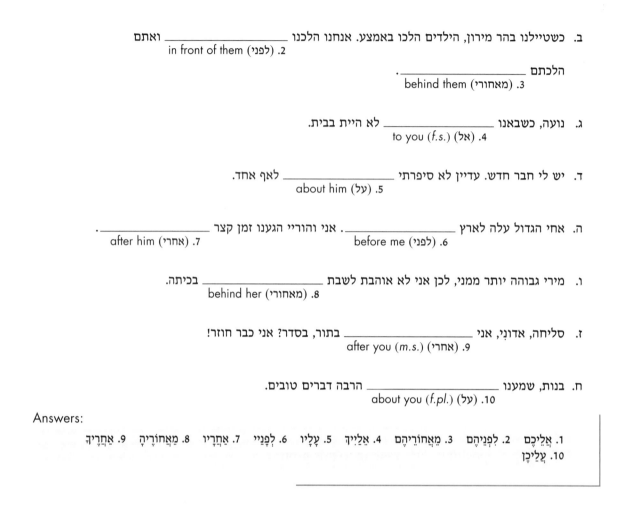

ב. כשטיילנו בהר מירון, הילדים הלכו באמצע. אנחנו הלכנו _____ ואתם
2. (לפני) in front of them

_____ הלכתם
3. (מאחורי) behind them

ג. נועה, כשבאנו _____ לא היית בבית.
4. (אל) to you (f.s.)

ד. יש לי חבר חדש. עדיין לא סיפרתי _____ לאף אחד.
5. (על) about him

ה. אחי הגדול עלה לארץ _____. אני והוריי הגענו זמן קצר _____.
6. (לפני) before me   7. (אחרי) after him

ו. מירי גבוהה יותר ממני, לכן אני לא אוהבת לשבת _____ בכיתה.
8. (מאחורי) behind her

ז. סליחה, אדוני, אני _____ בתור, בסדר? אני כבר חוזר!
9. (אחרי) after you (m.s.)

ח. בנות, שמענו _____ הרבה דברים טובים.
10. (על) about you (f.pl.)

Answers:

1. אֲלֵיכֶם   2. לִפְנֵיהֶם   3. מֵאֲחוֹרֵיהֶם   4. אֵלַיִךְ   5. עָלָיו   6. לְפָנַיי   7. אַחֲרָיו   8. מֵאֲחוֹרֶיהָ   9. אַחֲרֶיךָ
10. עֲלֵיכֶן

Special cases in Group II (the על Group)

1. אֶל *(to – usually expressing direction)*

In Chapter 2 on prepositions, we mentioned that in formal Hebrew אל may be used instead of
-ל after certain verbs.[20] For example:

◄   הוא בא למקום. / הוא בא אל המקום.

The use of אל **with** endings is much more common than the use of אל **without** endings. The
reason for this is that all of the verbs listed as taking ל-/אל will **almost always** use the forms
אליי, אליך... (and **not** ...לי, לך) when endings are added. This is true in both formal and informal
Hebrew.

◄   התקשרתי אליה.   ⇐   התקשרתי לשרה.
     I called her.   I called Sarah.

---

20 See above "How Do Prepositions Behave When No Ending Is Attached?" p. 227. Verbs that can take אל are
    listed in Appendix IV, p. 1025.

◄ היא קשורה אליה. ⇐ הילדה קשורה לאמא שלה.
She is attached to her The girl is attached to her mother.

Be careful! When the name of a **place** comes after ל- (for example: נסענו לירושלים),
we don't use a form of אל, but rather לְשָׁם.

◄ נסענו לְשָׁם. ⇐ נסענו לירושלים.
We went there. We went to Jerusalem.

Want to see if you've understood?
A. Write the correct form of אל.

1. אתמול נסענו <u>לסבתא</u>. נסענו _____ בשעות הבוקר. (לנסוע ל-/אל)

2. אנחנו בדרך כלל מתקשרים <u>להורים שלנו</u> לפחות פעם בשבוע, אבל החודש עדיין לא

   התקשרנו _____ . (להתקשר ל-/אל)

3. בנות, <u>אתן</u> יודעות למה ההורים שלכן התקשרו כל יום כשהם היו בחו"ל? כי הם התגעגעו

   _____ מאוד ורצו לדבר איתכן. (להתגעגע ל-/אל)

Answers:

1. אֵלֶיהָ 2. אֲלֵיהֶם 3. אֲלֵיכֶן

B. Write the missing form of ל- or אל as required by the verb (or adjective).

1. לא אמרתם <u>לשכנים</u> שתהיה אצלכם מסיבה היום? מדוע לא אמרתם _____ ? (לומר ל-)

2. פנינו <u>למנהלת</u> כדי לבקש לעבור לכיתה אחרת. היא אמרה שפנינו _____ מאוחר מדיי, ושכבר
   אי אפשר לעבור לכיתה אחרת. (לפנות ל-/אל)

3. התקרבנו <u>אל השלט</u> כדי לראות מה כתוב בו. רק כשעמדנו מאוד קרוב _____ , ראינו שלא
   היה כתוב בו כלום. (קרוב ל-/אל)

4. הודיעו <u>לתלמידים</u> לבוא מחר בחולצות לבנות, אבל שכחו להודיע _____ שמתחילים
   מאוחר. (להודיע ל-)

5. ‏הרעש של הטרקטור מפריע <u>ליצחק</u> ללמוד למבחן. האמת היא שכל רעש קטן מפריע

‏_____. (להפריע ל-)

6. ‏רותי, <u>את</u> כועסת עליי? לא באתי _____ אתמול, כי שכחתי שאמרת _____

‏לבוא. אני מצטערת! (לבוא ל-/אל, לומר ל-)

Answers:

‏1. לָהֶם   2. אֵלֶיהָ   3. אֵלָיו   4. לָהֶם   5. לוֹ   6. אֵלַיִךְ, לִי

2. ‏בְּלִי (without)

The preposition ‏בְּלִי cannot take endings. How, then, do we say *without him*, *without her*, etc.? Since the word ‏בִּלְעֲדֵי is sometimes used in formal language instead of ‏בְּלִי, it serves in both formal and informal Hebrew as the base onto which endings are added. Note that there is always a ‏'י before the endings.

◄   ‏אנחנו לא הולכים לסרט בְּלִי רינה.   ⇐   ‏אנחנו לא הולכים בִּלְעָדֶיהָ.
We are not going to the movie without Rina.   We are not going without her.

Want to see if you've understood?
Write the missing form.

1. ‏בטיול הכיתתי לגליל חיכינו שעה לשני תלמידים, ובסוף יצאנו לטיול _____.
without them (m.) (‏בלי)

‏אחר כך הם צלצלו אלינו בפלאפון וצעקו: "למה יצאתם לטיול _____?"
without us (‏בלי)

2. ‏שלמה אמר לגלי: "אל תעזבי אותי! אני לא יכול לחיות _____!"
without you (f.s.) (‏בלי)

3. ‏יוני ואלעד, _____ לא היינו מצליחים להגיע למקום הראשון.
without you (m.pl.) (‏בלי)

Answers:

‏1. בִּלְעֲדֵיהֶם, בִּלְעָדֵינוּ   2. בִּלְעָדַיִךְ   3. בִּלְעֲדֵיכֶם

3. עַל יְדֵי *(by)*

Read the following:

◄ המכתב נשלח על ידי משה. ⇐ המכתב נשלח על ידו.[21]

The letter was sent by Moshe.   The letter was sent by him.

When the doer of the action is known (משה in this sentence), Hebrew usually prefers using an **active** verb, as in משה שלח את המכתב, rather than a passive verb followed by על ידי. However, since passive sentences with על ידי (followed by the doer of the action) **do** exist in current Hebrew, we have presented the above sentences here. The forms of על ידי belong to Group II.

A split personality: the declension of בֵּין *(between, among)*

In the following two sentences, the preposition בֵּין is used:

◄ התאומים דומים מאוד. כמעט אין הבדל ביניהם.

The twins are very similar. There is almost no difference between them.

אני מדברת עם אחותי כל יום. הקשר בינינו חשוב לי מאוד.

I speak with my sister every day. My relationship with her (lit.: the connection between us)
is very important to me.

Here are the forms of בין:

בֵּין	
-EE	בֵּינִי
-CHA	בֵּינְךָ
-ECH	בֵּינֵךְ
-O	בֵּינוֹ
-A	בֵּינָהּ
-EI-noo	בֵּינֵינוּ
-ei-CHEM	בֵּינֵיכֶם
-ei-CHEN	בֵּינֵיכֶן
-ei-HEM	בֵּינֵיהֶם[22]
-ei-HEN	בֵּינֵיהֶן

---

21 According to the Hebrew Language Academy, when a passive verb is used, it is preferable not to mention by whom the action was performed. In cases where the doer **is** mentioned, it is preferable to use בידי rather than על ידי when the action was performed by a person.

    In today's Hebrew, when על יְדֵי **is** used and is declined, speakers often use על יד as the base of the declined forms (e.g. על ידו instead of על ידיו). In such cases, the context tells us whether to translate על ידו as *next to him* or *by him* (as in: "It was sent *by him*").

22 The forms בֵּינָם and בֵּינָן also exist and are sometimes used. See "Did you know?" below for an explanation.

Q: Does it belong to Group I (without an additional י) or to Group II (with a י)?

A: The first half of the declension of בין is exactly like that of בשביל (Group Ib). There is **no** י before the ending. The second half of this declension is like that of על: in all these forms there is a י between the preposition and the ending.

בֵּין... לְבֵין... / בֵּין... וּבֵין... / בֵּין... לְ-...

Unlike the English *between*, the preposition בֵּין often appears **twice** in the same sentence, as in the following:

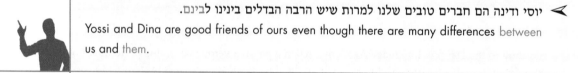

אני יושב בֵּין יורם לְבֵין נעמי.   I am sitting between Yoram and Naomi.

or: אני יושב בֵּין יורם וּבֵין נעמי.

Here are examples with pronouns after בין:

אני יושב בֵּינוֹ לבֵינָהּ.   I am sitting between **him** and **her**.

or: אני יושב בֵּינוֹ וּבֵינָהּ.

The first two sentences (with a noun at the end) can also be expressed using the shorter "בֵּין...לְ...", as in:

אני יושב בֵּין יורם לנעמי.[23]

This sounds **less formal** than the first two alternatives.

Did you know?
When do we use בֵּינָם *and* בֵּינָן *instead of* בֵּיניהם *and* בֵּיניהן?

When בין appears only **once** and we wish to say *between them*, the forms ביניהם and ביניהן are used, as in the second sentence here:

נועה יושבת בין דני לבין יוסי.   ⇐   היא יושבת ביניהם.
Noa is sitting between Danny and Yossi.   She is sitting between them.

However, when the two-part structure "בין ... ובין..." or "בין ... לבין.." is used, we tend to use בינן or בינם instead of ביניהן or ביניהם, as in the following sentence:

יוסי ודינה הם חברים טובים שלנו למרות שיש הרבה הבדלים בינינו לבינם.
Yossi and Dina are good friends of ours even though there are many differences between us and them.

---

23 The combination "בין... ו-..." is used by many speakers when a noun – and not a pronoun – follows ו-, as in: אני יושבת בין יונתן ודניאל (I am sitting between Yonatan and Daniel). The other combinations mentioned above are often viewed as preferable, especially in writing.

Want to see if you've understood?

Write the correct form of בֵּין with its endings.

1. אני אשב פה, יוסי ישב שם, ואתה תשב _____.
   between us (בֵּין)

2. יש הרבה הבדלים _____ ל _____.
   between me (בֵּין)   you (m.s.) (בֵּין)

3. בשיחה שהייתה _____ ל _____ דיברתם על כל הבעיות שלכם.
   between you (m.pl.) (בֵּין)   her (בֵּין)

Answers:

1. בֵּינֵינוּ   2. בֵּינִי, בֵּינְךָ   3. בֵּינֵיכֶם, בֵּינָהּ

Let's review

◆ This chart summarizes the prepositions in Group II.

special case בֵּין		לִפְנֵי	אֶל	עַל, אַחֲרֵי, בִּלְעָדַי...	
-EE	בֵּינִי	לְפָנַיי	אֵלַיי	-AI	עָלַיי
-CHA	בֵּינְךָ	לְפָנֶיךָ	אֵלֶיךָ	-E-cha	עָלֶיךָ
-ECH	בֵּינֵךְ	לְפָנַייִךְ	אֵלַייִךְ	-A-yeech	עָלַייִךְ
-O	בֵּינוֹ	לְפָנָיו	אֵלָיו	-AV	עָלָיו
-A	בֵּינָהּ	לְפָנֶיהָ	אֵלֶיהָ	-E-ha	עָלֶיהָ
	בֵּינֵינוּ	לְפָנֵינוּ	אֵלֵינוּ	-EI-noo	עָלֵינוּ
	בֵּינֵיכֶם	לִפְנֵיכֶם	אֲלֵיכֶם	-ei-CHEM	עֲלֵיכֶם
	בֵּינֵיכֶן	לִפְנֵיכֶן	אֲלֵיכֶן	-ei-CHEN	עֲלֵיכֶן
	בֵּינֵיהֶם	לִפְנֵיהֶם	אֲלֵיהֶם	-ei-HEM	עֲלֵיהֶם
	בֵּינֵיהֶן	לִפְנֵיהֶן	אֲלֵיהֶן	-ei-HEN	עֲלֵיהֶן

251

Want to see if you've understood this chapter?

In the following exercise, you can practice all the prepositions learned in this chapter.
Write the missing preposition with its ending.

א. נוח ואבנר, לא ראינו _____ הרבה זמן, התגעגענו _____ ! אנחנו
1. (את) you (m.pl.)   2. (אל) you (m.pl.)

רוצים שתבואו _____ כדי לצאת _____ למסעדה טובה.
3. (אל) to us, to our place   4. (עם) with us

ב. אילנה, דיברנו _____ ובדיוק הגעת לצלצל _____ או להיפגש
5. (על) about you (f.s.)   6. (אל) you (f.s.)

_____ ולספר _____ על דינה ועל החבר _____.
7. (עם) with you (f.s.)   8. (ל-) you (f.s.)   9. (של) her

אומרים שעבר _____ חתול שחור (= They are not on good terms.). ידעת?
10. (בין) between them

ג. כשביקרנו _____ בשנה שעברה, ביקשתם _____ שבפעם
11. (אצל) at your (m.pl.) place   12. (מ-) us

הבאה נביא _____ גם את הילדים _____. אז הנה, הפעם הבאנו
13. (עם) with us   14. (של) our

גם _____.
15. (את) them (m.)

ד. חבר'ה, אנחנו רוצים לצלם _____. יעל, תעמדי פה. רחל, את תעמדי
16. (את) you (m.pl.)

_____, משה אתה תעמוד _____, ויונתן אתה תעמוד
17. (מאחורי) behind her   18. (על יד) next to her

_____.
19. (לפני) in front of them

ה. אני רוצה שנשמור את הסוד _____. לא נספר _____ לאף אחד.
20. (בין) between us   21. (את) it

ו. גם אם אתה לא חושב _____, אתה לא צריך לכעוס _____.
22. (כמו) like me   23. (על) at me, with me

אם תבקש _____, אני אסביר _____ את דעתי.
24. (מן) me   25. (ל-) to you

ז. חבל ששמעון לא בא למסיבה. לא היה כֵּיף _____.
26. (בלי) without him

Answers:

1. אֶתְכֶם 2. אֲלֵיכֶם 3. אֵלֵינוּ 4. אִיתָנוּ 5. עָלַיִיךְ 6. אֵלַיִיךְ 7. אִיתָךְ 8. לָךְ 9. שֶׁלָּה 10. בֵּינֵיהֶם
11. אֶצְלְכֶם 12. מֵאִיתָנוּ 13. אִיתָנוּ 14. שֶׁלָּנוּ 15. אוֹתָם 16. אֶתְכֶם 17. מֵאֲחוֹרֶיהָ 18. עַל יָדָהּ
19. לִפְנֵיהֶם 20. בֵּינֵינוּ 21. אוֹתוֹ 22. כָּמוֹנִי 23. עָלַיי 24. מִמֶּנִּי 25. לְךָ 26. בִּלְעָדָיו

252

VIII. Numbers and Quantifiers

Numbers[1] and quantifiers – like כָּל (all) and חֵלֶק (part) – will be discussed in the following chapters:

1. Numbers (...8:30 אחד..., ראשון..., א'=1..., שְׁנֵינוּ..., השעה)
2. All, Part of...: Quantifiers (...כָּל הַ-, חֵלֶק מֵהַ-..., כּוּלָם..., רוּבָּם)

1. Numbers

Preview

- *Numbers[2] from 1 to 10*
- *Numbers 11 and up*
- *Ordinal numbers* (...רִאשׁוֹן, שֵׁנִי)
- *Hebrew letters as numbers*
- *Numbers with endings:* ...שְׁנֵינוּ, שְׁלוֹשְׁתֵּנוּ (*both of us, the three of us*)
- *Telling the time*

• Numbers from 1 to 10

Counting from 1 to 10 (masculine and feminine)

Imagine a line of between one to ten girls waiting to buy tickets. If we ask how many girls are standing in the line, the answer may be any one of the following:

---

1 Technically, the words that **refer to** numbers are called *numerals*. We have chosen to use the less technical term *number* to refer to both the number and the word that refers to the number.

2 In English grammar books, the numbers presented in the first two sections of this chapter are called *cardinal numerals* or *cardinal numbers* (מִסְפָּרִים מוֹנִים).

10	9	8	7	6	5	4	3	2	1	◄
עֶשֶׂר	תֵּשַׁע	שְׁמוֹנֶה	שֶׁבַע	שֵׁשׁ	חָמֵשׁ	אַרְבַּע	שָׁלוֹשׁ	שְׁתַּיִם	אַחַת	
'E-ser	TE-sha	shmo-NE SHMO-ne	SHE-va	SHESH	cha-MESH	'ar-BA[3] 'AR-ba	sha-LOSH	SHTA-yeem	'a-CHAT	

Now imagine a similar line of boys and the possible answers to the same question:

10	9	8	7	6	5	4	3	2	1	◄
עֲשָׂרָה	תִּשְׁעָה	שְׁמוֹנָה	שִׁבְעָה	שִׁשָּׁה	חֲמִשָּׁה	אַרְבָּעָה	שְׁלוֹשָׁה	שְׁנַיִם	אֶחָד	
'a-sa-RA	teesh-'A	shmo-NA	sheev-'A	shee-SHA	cha-mee-SHA	'ar-ba-'A	shlo-SHA	SHNA-yeem	'e-CHAD	

Q: Are the two sets of numbers exactly the same?

A: No! There is a difference between the numbers used for **girls** and other feminine nouns and those used for **boys** and other masculine nouns. We will call the first set "the feminine numbers," and the second set – "the masculine numbers."

There are several basic differences between the two sets:

Numbers 1 and 2
Compare:

	זכר	נקבה	
	masculine	*feminine*	
1 –	אֶחָד	אַחַת	
2 –	שְׁנַיִם	שְׁתַּיִם	

The **feminine** numbers for *one* and *two* have a 'ת: אחת, שתיים. ת is often a sign of the feminine, as in the ending of words such as מחברת, עברית, כותבת.

The **masculine** number for *one* (אֶחָד *'e-CHAD*) ends in 'ד, and its vowels are slightly different from the feminine form (אַחַת *'a-CHAT*).

---

3   The officially "correct" pronunciation is *'ar-BA* and *shmo-NE*, but most speakers say *'AR-ba* and *SHMO-ne*.

Both words for *two* have a *dual ending* (*-A-yeem*): שְׁתַּיִם (*f.*) and שְׁנַיִם (*m.*).[4] These are the forms used when **no noun** follows the number. (See below for the forms that come before nouns.)

Numbers 3-10

In other parts of speech with feminine and masculine forms, the feminine is almost always **longer** than the masculine: in nouns (יֶלֶד / יַלְדָה), in adjectives (גָדוֹל / גְדוֹלָה) and in verbs (קָם / קָמָה). Now let's see if this is the case with numbers, too.

Look again at the feminine and masculine numbers:

זכר *masculine*	נקבה *feminine*	
שְׁלוֹשָׁה	שָׁלוֹשׁ	3 –
אַרְבָּעָה	אַרְבַּע	4 –
חֲמִישָׁה	חָמֵשׁ	5 –
שִׁישָׁה	שֵׁשׁ	6 –
שִׁבְעָה	שֶׁבַע	7 –
שְׁמוֹנָה	שְׁמוֹנֶה	8 –
תִּשְׁעָה	תֵּשַׁע	9 –
עֲשָׂרָה	עֶשֶׂר	10 –

Q: Which forms are longer?

A: Surprisingly, the **masculine** numbers are the longer ones: they all end in ה- (which is usually a feminine ending!). Note also that the vowels of the masculine forms are often different from those of the shorter feminine form (e.g., שִׁבְעָה *sheev-'A* / שֶׁבַע *SHE-va*).

When we refer to a feminine noun – מחברות, for example – we use the shorter, feminine forms of the number, and when we refer to a masculine noun – ספרים, for example – we use the longer, masculine forms, as in:

How many notebooks are there here?	⊰ – כמה **מחברות** יש פה?
Seven.	– שֶׁבַע. (*f.*)
How many books do you have?	– כמה **ספרים** יש לך?
Seven.	– שִׁבְעָה (*m.*)

In the answers to the above questions, the nouns (ספרים, מחברות) are not stated, but they are **assumed**, and we match the number to them.

---

4   See the chapter "How Are Nouns Made Plural?" pp. 43-45 for more on the *dual ending* (e.g., on יוֹמַיִם *two days*, שְׁבוּעַיִם *two weeks*).

Note: Although we have called the feminine numbers **shorter** and the masculine numbers **longer** – and this is generally true, especially in the numbers 3-10 – the words for 1, 2 and 8 are really the same length:

How many candies are here?	?כמה **סוכריות** יש פה – ⫷
One. / Two. / Eight.	(.f) אחת. / – שתיים. / – שמונָה –
How many apples are here?	?כמה **תפוחים** יש פה –
One. / Two. / Eight.	(.m) אחד. / – שניים. / – שמונָה –

Additional uses of feminine (short) numbers

It is the shorter, feminine numbers that are used when we do simple counting or reading of numbers without a noun attached, as in math problems or telephone numbers, for example:

➢   1 + 5 = 6   We say:

אחת ועוד חמש הם שש. ⫷

or: אחת ועוד חמש שָׁוֶוה שש.

➢   02-671345 (a phone number) We say:

אפס שתיים שש שבע אחת שלוש ארבע חמש ⫷

Feminine numbers are also used when we speak of a year, as in the last number of 1942:

אלף ארבע מאות תשעים ושתיים ⫷

When we speak of buses, addresses or room numbers, we use these short forms:

I take bus 9 every day.	.אני נוסעת בקו 9 (תשע) כל יום ⫷
He lives at 7 King David Street.	.(הוא גר ברחוב המלך דויד 7 (שבע
We are studying in room 207.	.(אנחנו לומדים בחדר 207 (מאתיים ושבע

Likewise, when we state someone's age, we use feminine numbers (but unlike in English, we do not add the word שנים years):[5]

Amit is seven years old and his friends are six.	.עמית בֶּן שבע והחברים שלו בְּנֵי שש ⫷

---

5   However, for a one year-old we say בן/בת שנה and for a two year-old we say: בן/בת שנתיים.

Did you know?
Stating hours and years: בשעה *and* בשנת
Read the following sentences:

The lesson begins at 8:00.	השיעור מתחיל בְּשָׁעָה 8:00 (שמונֶה).
Herzl died in 1904.	הרצל נפטר בִּשְׁנַת 1904 (אלף תשע מאות וארבע).

Note that both words בְּשָׁעָה and בִּשְׁנַת appear before a number; however, only in the case of שָׁנָה do we use the *smeechoot* form שְׁנַת.

Additional uses of masculine (long) numbers

The longer, masculine forms are used without a noun attached in the following cases:

- Dates (days of the month):[6]

the ninth of Av (a Hebrew month)	תשעה באב
the fourth of July	ארבעה ביולי

- "Two / three… times as…" (...פי שניים, פי שלושה):

מחיר התפוחים בסופרמרקט גדול פִּי שלושה[7] מהמחיר שלהם בשוק.

The price of apples in the supermarket is three times their price in the *shuk* (open air market).

Let's review

Thus far we have examined how numbers behave when they are **not** followed by a noun. The feminine and masculine numbers have different forms.

♦ The feminine numbers for 1 and 2 have a ת':

feminine:	שתיים. /	– אחת.	– כמה מחברות יש פה?
masculine:	שניים. /	– אחד.	– כמה ספרים יש פה?

---

6 For dates, many speakers do not follow the guidelines for proper usage and use **ordinal** numbers. For example, for the fourth of July (written 4.7 – with the day before the month), they say: הרביעי לשביעי (lit., the fourth of the seventh). See below for ordinal numbers.

7 Many speakers use the shorter feminine number after פי (here: שלוש) even though according to the rules of grammar a masculine number should be used, as in the example above.

◆ The feminine numbers between 3 and 10 are generally **shorter** than the masculine numbers. It is the masculine numbers that end in ‏ָה‏:

feminine:	– ארבע. / – שלוש.	– כמה סוכריות יש פה?
masculine:	– ארבעָה. / – שלושָה.	– כמה תפוחים יש פה?

Various uses of these forms are discussed above.

Want to see if you've understood?

Write the proper form of the number (without adding the noun), as in the following example:

Example: כמה אחים יש לרינה?
‏**שניים**‏
(2)

1. כמה פרחים קניתם? _____
   (3)

2. כמה ילדות יש בחדר? _____
   (2)

3. כמה חברים נמצאים בבית של יונתן עכשיו? _____
   (1)

4. כמה שקלים יש לך? _____
   (10)

5. _____ ועוד _____ הם/שווה _____ (6 + 3 = 9)
   (6)   (3)   (9)

6. קו _____ מגיע לתחנה המרכזית בתל אביב.
   (5)

7. יונתן היה בן _____ כשמשפחתו נסעה ללונדון.
   (8)

Answers:

1. שלושה   2. שתיים   3. אחד   4. עשרה   5. שש, שלוש, תשע   6. חמש   7. שמונֶה

Adding a number to a noun

Read the following passage:

> ◄ ביום שישי בבוקר נועה ואיילת הלכו לסופרמרקט. נועה קנתה ארבע קלמנטינות, שלוש אשכוליות, שתי בננות ופומלה אחת. איילת קנתה ארבעה תפוחים, שלושה תפוזים, שני אגסים ומֶלון אחד. בערב הן הכינו ביחד סלט פירות.

On Friday morning Noa and Ayelet went to the supermarket. Noa bought four tangerines, three grapefruits, two bananas and one pomelo. Ayelet bought four apples, three oranges, two pears and one melon. In the evening they made a fruit salad together.

Q: Are any of the forms of the numbers in this passage different from those we saw above without an added noun?

A: Yes. The forms of the words for *two* are different. As we saw above, its forms are שניים (*m.*) and שתיים (*f.*) when no noun follows them. But when a noun is added, the -ים drops off, as in the *smeechoot* form of words like נעליים (נעלֵי-),[8] and the resulting forms are:

feminine:	שְׁתֵּי בננות ◄
masculine:	שְׁנֵי אגסים

In all other numbers the form remains the same.

Q: Is the order of the noun and the number the same in all the examples above?

A: No! The words אחת and אחד (1) appear **after** the noun.

feminine:	one pomelo	פומלה אחת ◄
masculine:	one melon	מֶלון אחד

In all other cases, the number appears **before** the noun (as in English), as in:

> ◄ שתי בננות, שלוש אשכוליות, ארבע קלמנטינות
> שני אגסים, שלושה תפוזים, ארבעה תפוחים

Here is a list of numbers 1-10 with a noun added to them:

	נקבה *feminine*	זכר *masculine*
1 –	תלמידה אַחַת	תלמיד אֶחָד
2 –	שְׁתֵּי תלמידות	שְׁנֵי תלמידים
3 –	שָׁלוֹשׁ תלמידות	שְׁלוֹשָׁה תלמידים

---

8   See the chapter *"Smeechoot,"* pp. 176-177.

זכר	נקבה	
masculine	*feminine*	
אַרְבָּעָה תלמידים	אַרְבַּע תלמידות	– 4
חֲמִשָּׁה תלמידים	חָמֵשׁ תלמידות	– 5
שִׁישָׁה תלמידים	שֵׁשׁ תלמידות	– 6
שִׁבְעָה תלמידים	שֶׁבַע תלמידות	– 7
שְׁמוֹנָה תלמידים	שְׁמוֹנֶה תלמידות	– 8
תִּשְׁעָה תלמידים	תֵּשַׁע תלמידות	– 9
עֲשָׂרָה תלמידים	עֶשֶׂר תלמידות	– 10

Let's review

In this section we have seen how numbers behave when they appear with nouns.

♦ The number 1 comes **after** the noun:

≺ יֶלֶד אחד,   ילדה אחת

♦ All other numbers come **before** the counted noun:

≺ שלושה ספרים,   שלוש בנות

♦ Forms of the number 2 lose their ם- ending before the noun. Their final vowel changes, too:

≺ שְׁנֵי בנים,   שְׁתֵּי בנות

Want to see if you've understood?

Answer the following questions in two ways: a. without a noun   b. with a noun

Example: כמה אנשים גרים פה?   *חמישה.* / *חמישה אנשים.*
(5)

1. כמה סטודנטיות לומדות בקורס? ____ . / ____ ____ .
(2)

2. כמה חדרים יש בדירה שלכם? ____ . / ____ ____ .
(4)

3. כמה עמודים כבר קראת? ____ . / ____ ____ .
(1)

4. כמה הצגות ראית השנה? ____ . / ____ ____ .
(2)

Answers:

1. שתיים / שתי סטודנטיות   2. ארבעה / ארבעה חדרים   3. אחד / עמוד אחד   4. שתיים / שתי הצגות

Adding a number to a definite noun

Read the following passage:

➤ בשבוע שעבר דני יצא לאכול במסעדה יחד עם שלושה חברים. הם הזמינו שלושה סלטים וארבעה סטיקים. אחרי עשרים דקות המלצר הביא לשולחן את שלושת הסלטים, את ארבעת הסטיקים וגם חמוצים ופיתות.

Last week Danny went out to eat at a restaurant with three friends. They ordered three salads and four steaks. Twenty minutes later the waiter brought to the table the three salads, the four steaks and also olives, pickles and *pitot*.

The words סלטים and סטיקים appear **twice** in this passage. Let's look more closely at the phrases in which they appear each time they are mentioned:

2nd mention		1st mention		
the three salads	שְׁלוֹשֶׁת הסלטים	three salads	שְׁלוֹשָׁה סלטים	➤
the four steaks	אַרְבַּעַת הסטיקים	four steaks	אַרְבָּעָה סטיקים	

As you can see, these phrases are made **definite** the second time they are mentioned.

Q: To which word is ה- added to make them definite?

A: Unlike the English equivalents in which *the* is added before the number to make the **whole phrase** definite (the three salads, the four steaks), Hebrew adds ה- before the **noun** (הסלטים, הסטיקים), which here is the last word in the phrase. When there is **more than one** noun, the ה- is on the **last** one, as in:

➤ ארבע עוגות השוקולד   the four chocolate cakes

This is typical of *smeechoot* phrases.[9]

Now look again at the two mentions of the phrases with numbers.

Q: Does the form of the numbers change when they are attached to **definite** nouns?

A: Yes. The number שְׁלוֹשָׁה (*shlo-SHA*) changes to שְׁלוֹשֶׁת (*SHLO-shet*); the number אַרְבָּעָה (*'ar-ba-'A*) changes to אַרְבַּעַת (*'ar-BA-'at*).

When **masculine** numbers from 3 to 10 are added to a **definite** noun, the ה- at the end of the number changes to ת'. This is **similar** to *smeechoot* forms (e.g., קְבוּצָה becomes קְבוּצַת הכדורגל), but there are some **differences**: In masculine numbers, the vowel before the ת' is sometimes *eh*

---

9   See the chapter "Smeechoot," pp. 183-184, 186.

(שְׁלוֹשֶׁת) and sometimes *ah* (אַרְבַּעַת), and sometimes the stress in these words moves back one syllable, as in *SHLO-shet* and *'ar-BA-'at*. There are some additional changes in the vowels as well, as you can see in the following list:

	definite		indefinite		
the three pages	שְׁלוֹשֶׁת העמודים *SHLO-shet*	⇐	שְׁלוֹשָׁה עמודים *shlo-SHA*	–	3
the four books	אַרְבַּעַת הספרים *'ar-BA-'at*	⇐	אַרְבָּעָה ספרים *'ar-ba-'A*	–	4
the five children	חֲמֵשֶׁת הילדים *cha-ME-shet*	⇐	חֲמִישָׁה ילדים *cha-mee-SHA*	–	5
the six days	שֵׁשֶׁת הימים *SHE-shet*	⇐	שִׁישָׁה ימים *shee-SHA*	–	6
the seven weeks	שִׁבְעַת השבועות *sheev-'AT*	⇐	שִׁבְעָה שבועות *sheev-'A*	–	7
the eight chairs	שְׁמוֹנַת הכיסאות *shmo-NAT*	⇐	שְׁמוֹנָה כיסאות *shmo-NA*	–	8
the nine months	תִּשְׁעַת החודשים *teesh-'AT*	⇐	תִּשְׁעָה חודשים *teesh-'A*	–	9
the ten tribes	עֲשֶׂרֶת השבטים *'a-SE-ret*	⇐	עֲשָׂרָה שבטים *'a-sa-RA*	–	10

So far we've seen numbers with definite **masculine** nouns. The change is less noticeable in the **feminine** numbers 3-10. Only in number 3 can you **hear** a difference:[10]

שְׁלוֹשׁ הבנות *shlosh*	⇐	שָׁלוֹשׁ בנות *sha-LOSH*

In the feminine numbers 4-10, there is no change in pronunciation, for example:

the five daughters / girls	חֲמֵשׁ הבנות	⇐	חֲמֵשׁ בנות
the nine countries	תֵּשַׁע הארצות	⇐	תֵּשַׁע ארצות

The numbers 1 and 2 with definite nouns

As we saw above, the words for the number *two* take a *smeechoot* form before **any** noun – both feminine and masculine – even when it is **indefinite**. Thus, the form remains the same before a **definite** noun:

the two daughters / girls	שְׁתֵּי הבנות	⇐	שְׁתֵּי בנות
the two sons / boys	שְׁנֵי הבנים	⇐	שְׁנֵי בנים

---

10 The change is similar to the change in מָקוֹם ⇐ מְקוֹם לידה. See *"Smeechoot,"* pp. 178-179 for details.

Did you know?

When we place אחד / אחת **in front of** a definite noun, it means *one of (the)...*,
as in:

◄ אַחַת הַתלמידות בכיתה קיבלה חבילה מֵאַחַד החברים שלה.

One of the students (*f.*) in the class got a package from one of her friends (*m.*).

In this construction, the pronunciation of the masculine אֶחָד (*'e-CHAD*) changes
to אַחַד (*'a-CHAD*). The feminine אַחַת stays the same.

Note: A noun may be **definite** not only when it has the *definite article* -ה. Words like ילדיו (his
children) and בנותינו (our daughters) – with a *possessive ending* – are definite, too. Therefore, when
we add numbers to them, the same changes take place in the form of the number:

◄ שְׁלוֹשֶׁת ילדיו   his three children
  שְׁלוֹש בנותינו   her three daughters

Let's review

◆ When the noun after the number is **definite** (either with –ה or with a possessive
ending), the following changes take place:

- The ending on masculine numbers from 3-10 changes from ה- to ת-, as in:

◄ יש לרינה שלושָׁה ילדים. שלושֶׁת הילדים שלה עדיין לומדים בבית הספר.

- In feminine numbers, there is a change in pronunciation only in the word
for 3:

◄ לדויד יש שָׁלוש בנות. שְׁלוש הבנות כבר נשואות.

◆ There is no change in the words for 2 before a definite noun:

◄ שתי הבנות, שני הבנים

Want to see if you've understood?
Write the correct form of the number.

1. התיקים החדשים שלך יפים בעיניי. _____
(2)

2. למיכל יש _____ ילדים. כל _____ ילדיה עדיין לומדים בבית ספר. הבן
(4)   (4)

הגדול שלה לומד בבית ספר תיכון ו_____ הילדים הקטנים לומדים בבית ספר יסודי.
(3)

3. קניתי _____ ספרים חדשים וקיבלתי _____ ספרים במתנה.
(2)   (3)

קראתי את כל _____ הספרים תוך חודש.
(5)

4. _____ ההרצאות ששמעתי היום היו מצוינות. אחרי הצוהריים אשמע עוד
(2)

_____ הרצאות.
(3)

5. מלחמת _____ הימים הייתה ב־1967.
(6)

6. מירי הרגישה מצוין בכל _____ חודשי ההיריון שלה.
(9)

7. נסענו לצרפת ל_____ ימים. ב_____ הימים הראשונים ירד גשם כל הזמן,
(7)   (10)

ורק ב_____ הימים האחרונים יצאה השמש.
(3)

8. רונית הגיעה לפגישה עם גלי באיחור של _____ דקות.
(10)

Answers:

1. שני 2. ארבעה / ארבעת / שלושת 3. שלושה / שני / חמשת 4. שתי / שלוש 5. שֵשֶת 6. תֵשְעַת
7. עשרה / שִבְעַת / שלושת 8. עשר

• *Numbers 11 and up*

Numbers 11-19 (masculine and feminine)

These are the Hebrew numbers from 11 to 19:

masculine זכר		*feminine* נקבה	
'a-CHAD 'a-sar	11 – אֶחָד עָשָׂר	'a-CHAT 'es-re[12]	11 – אַחַת עֶשְׂרֵה
SHNEM 'a-sar	12 – שְׁנֵים עָשָׂר	SHTEM 'es-re	12 – שְׁתֵּים עֶשְׂרֵה
shlo-SHA 'a-sar	13 – שְׁלוֹשָׁה עָשָׂר	SHLOSH 'es-re	13 – שְׁלוֹשׁ עֶשְׂרֵה
'ar-ba-'A 'a-sar	14 – אַרְבָּעָה עָשָׂר	'ar-BA 'es-re	14 – אַרְבַּע עֶשְׂרֵה
cha-mee-SHA 'a-sar	15 – חֲמִישָׁה עָשָׂר	cha-MESH 'es-re	15 – חֲמֵשׁ עֶשְׂרֵה
shee-SHA 'a-sar	16 – שִׁישָׁה עָשָׂר	SHESH 'es-re	16 – שֵׁשׁ עֶשְׂרֵה
sheev-'A 'a-sar	17 – שִׁבְעָה עָשָׂר	SHVA 'es-re	17 – שְׁבַע עֶשְׂרֵה
shmo-NA 'a-sar	18 – שְׁמוֹנָה עָשָׂר	SHMO-ne 'es-re	18 – שְׁמוֹנֶה עֶשְׂרֵה
teesh-'A 'a-sar	19 – תִּשְׁעָה עָשָׂר	TSHA 'es-re	19 – תְּשַׁע עֶשְׂרֵה

First let's look at numbers 13-19.

Numbers 13-19

Read the following sentence:

בקבוצה שלנו יש חֲמֵשׁ עֶשְׂרֵה בנות וחֲמִישָׁה עָשָׂר בנים. ◄

In our group there are fifteen girls and fifteen boys.

Q: What is the difference between the two numbers above?

A: In the feminine number (חמש עשרה), the first part of the number (חמש) is **short** – as in the feminine number 5 (חמש) – but the second part is **long** (עֶשְׂרֵה) – compensating, as it were, for the short part. In the masculine number, the reverse is true: the **first** word is long (חמישה), while the **second** is short (עָשָׂר).

This happens in all numbers from 11-19. Here are some more examples:

		19	17	13
feminine numbers:	(בנות)	שְׁלוֹשׁ עֶשְׂרֵה / שְׁבַע עֶשְׂרֵה / תְּשַׁע עֶשְׂרֵה			◄
masculine numbers:	(בנים)	שְׁלוֹשָׁה עָשָׂר / שִׁבְעָה עָשָׂר / תִּשְׁעָה עָשָׂר		

Now look more closely at the feminine numbers 13, 17 and 19.

---

12 We have transcribed the most common pronunciation. According to the rules of grammar, the pronunciation is: *'a-chat 'es-RE, shtem 'es-RE*, etc. When 18 is used before feminine nouns, the form שמונה עשרה – combining the masculine form שְׁמוֹנָה (*shmo-NA*) with the feminine עֶשְׂרֵה (*'esre*) – is very often used.

Q: Is the first part of these numbers exactly the same as 3 (שָׁלוֹשׁ), 7 (שֶׁבַע) and 9 (תֵּשַׁע)?

A: No. In each of these forms, the first vowel is shortened to *shva*.[13] Of the feminine numbers from 13 to 19, this change is heard **only** in these three:

SHLOSH-'es-re	שְׁלוֹשׁ עֶשְׂרֵה – 13	⇐	sha-LOSH	שָׁלוֹשׁ – 3	⪻
SHVA-'es-re	שְׁבַע עֶשְׂרֵה – 17	⇐	SHE-va	שֶׁבַע – 7	
TSHA-'es-re[14]	תְּשַׁע עֶשְׂרֵה – 19	⇐	TE-sha	תֵּשַׁע – 9	

Be careful! In the preceding section, we saw that before a **definite** feminine noun, שָׁלוֹשׁ changes to שְׁלוֹשׁ (שְׁלוֹשׁ הבנות), as it does in שְׁלוֹשׁ עשרה. However, the forms שֶׁבַע and תֵּשַׁע undergo this change only in שְׁבַע עשרה and תְּשַׁע עשרה and **not** before a definite noun (תֵּשַׁע הבנות, שֶׁבַע הבנות).

Number 12

Read the following sentence:

⪻ בשנה יש שְׁנֵים עָשָׂר חודשים, וביום יש שְׁתֵּים עֶשְׂרֵה שעות.
In a year there are twelve months, and in a day there are twelve hours.

Q: In what way is the first word in שְׁתֵּים עֶשְׂרֵה and שְׁנֵים עָשָׂר different from the words for *two* (שְׁנַיִם / שְׁנֵי- and שְׁתַּיִם / שְׁתֵּי-)?

A: The vowels are the same as in שְׁתֵּי ילדות and שְׁנֵי ילדים, but there is a ם- on the end.

feminine:	(שעות) שְׁתֵּים עֶשְׂרֵה – 12	⇐	-שְׁתֵּי / שְׁתַּיִם – 2	⪻
masculine:	(ימים) שְׁנֵים עָשָׂר – 12	⇐	-שְׁנֵי / שְׁנַיִם – 2	

Notice that there is only **one** י in שתים עשרה and שנים עשר.

Number 11

Now let's see how the words for *eleven* are formed:

⪻ אַחַת עֶשְׂרֵה דקות לפני ההרצאה היו באולם רק אַחַד עָשָׂר סטודנטים.
Eleven minutes before the lecture there were only eleven students in the lecture hall.

---

13 Originally the stress was on the second word: 'es-RE. The change from שָׁלוֹשׁ (sha-LOSH) to שְׁלוֹשׁ (SHLOSH) in שְׁלוֹשׁ עֶשְׂרֵה is therefore similar to the change from מָקוֹם to מְקוֹם in the *smeechoot* phrase מְקוֹם לֵידָה. See the chapter "Reduction of Vowels and the *Shva*," p. 645. The forms שְׁבַע and תְּשַׁע seem to imitate the reduction in שְׁלוֹשׁ.

14 *Tsha* sounds like the first word in the name of the dance "the Cha-cha."

In the feminine number (אַחַת עֶשְׂרֵה), the first word is the same as the word for *one*:

feminine: 1 – אַחַת   ⇐   11 – אַחַת עֶשְׂרֵה   ◄

Only in the masculine number (אַחַד עָשָׂר) is there a change in the pronunciation of the first word (its vowels are like those of אַחַת).

masculine: 1 – אֶחָד   ⇐   11 – אַחַד עָשָׂר   ◄
        'e-CHAD   'a-CHAD 'a-sar

Numbers 11 and up before a definite noun

Unlike many numbers from 1 to 10 (e.g., שְׁלוֹשֶׁת הבנים, שְׁלוֹשׁ הבנות), numbers from 11 and up **do not** change before a definite noun:

	definite noun	*indefinite noun*
feminine:	שְׁבַע עֶשְׂרֵה **החברות**	שְׁבַע עֶשְׂרֵה חברות
masculine:	שְׁלוֹשָׁה עָשָׂר **העצים**	שְׁלוֹשָׁה עָשָׂר עצים

◄

Nouns like איש and שנה with numbers 11 and up

Read the following sentence:

◄ למסיבה הגיעו שְׁלוֹשָׁה עָשָׂר אִישׁ.   Thirteen people came to (lit.: arrived at) the party.

It looks like there is a mistake in this sentence: thirteen people came to the party, but the noun איש is **singular**! The truth is that with certain nouns, when the numbers 11 and up are added, it is possible to use either a **singular** noun (שלושה עשר איש) or a **plural** noun (שלושה עשר אנשים). Here are some of the nouns that can be used in this way: איש, יום, שנה, שקל, קילו, מטר, אחוז. Many of these nouns are measures of amounts, weights and distance.[15]

Let's review

♦ In feminine numbers 13-19, the first part of the number is **short** and the second is **long**, e.g.: שְׁלוֹשׁ עֶשְׂרֵה (בנות). In masculine numbers 13-19, the first part of the number is **long** and the second is **short**, e.g.: שְׁלוֹשָׁה עָשָׂר (בנים).

♦ The feminine number 11 is אַחַת עֶשְׂרֵה with a ת'. The masculine number 11 is אַחַד עָשָׂר with a ד'.

---

15 We have listed just some of the currencies, weights, etc. that may appear in the singular after 10.

◆ The feminine number 12 is שְׁתֵּים עֶשְׂרֵה with a ת'. The masculine number 12 is שְׁנֵים עָשָׂר with a נ'. Note that in both cases, the vowel in the first word is *eh* (*SHTEM-, SHNEM-*).

◆ In numbers 11-19, the **same form** of the number is used before an **indefinite** and a **definite** noun, for example:

definite noun	indefinite noun	
שְׁבַע עֶשְׂרֵה **הַחברות**	שְׁבַע עֶשְׂרֵה חברות	◄
שְׁלוֹשָׁה עָשָׂר **הַעצים**	שְׁלוֹשָׁה עָשָׂר עצים	

◆ Some nouns following numbers 11 and up can appear in the plural **or** the singular, for example:

חמש עשרה **שנים** / **שנה** ◄

חמישה עשר **אנשים** / **איש**

Want to see if you've understood?
Write the correct form of the number.

3. _____ (16) ימים (*m.*)   1. _____ (12) מחברות (*f.*)

4. _____ (13) שורות (*f.*)   2. _____ (18) מחשבים (*m.*)

Answers:

1. שְׁתֵּים עֶשְׂרֵה מחברות   2. שְׁמוֹנָה עָשָׂר מחשבים   3. שִׁשָּׁה עָשָׂר ימים   4. שָׁלוֹשׁ עֶשְׂרֵה שורות

Multiples of ten

Read the following:

למסיבת סוף השנה קנינו חמישים פיתות, חמישים מלפפונים חמוצים, עשרים עגבניות ועשרים מלפפונים. ◄

For the end-of-the-year party we bought fifty *pitot*, fifty pickles, twenty tomatoes and twenty cucumbers.

Two numbers appear in the passage above:

masculine	*feminine*	
חמישים מלפפונים	חמישים פיתות	50 –
עשרים מלפפונים	עשרים עגבניות	20 –

Q: Is there a difference between the forms of the numbers added to feminine and masculine nouns here?

A: No. For multiples of ten there is only **one form**. Here are the words for these numbers:

90	80	70	60	50	40	30	20
תִּשְׁעִים	שְׁמוֹנִים	שִׁבְעִים	שִׁישִׁים	חֲמִישִׁים	אַרְבָּעִים	שְׁלוֹשִׁים	עֶשְׂרִים

All of these forms end in ים- (the plural ending). This ending never drops off, even before a definite noun, as in עשרים הסטודנטים (the twenty students). The **beginning** of most of these forms is pronounced (and spelled) just like the masculine numbers from 3 to 9. Compare:

תִּשְׁעָה	שְׁמוֹנָה	שִׁבְעָה	שִׁישָׁה	חֲמִישָׁה	אַרְבָּעָה	שְׁלוֹשָׁה
תִּשְׁעִים	שְׁמוֹנִים	שִׁבְעִים	שִׁישִׁים	חֲמִישִׁים	אַרְבָּעִים	שְׁלוֹשִׁים

These forms are used in referring to decades, as in:

הסרטים הישראליים של שְׁנות התשעים היו מעניינים מאוד.

Israeli films of the nineties were very interesting.

השכנים שלנו הגיעו לארץ בשְׁנות השישים של המאה העשרים.

Our neighbors came to Israel in the sixties (lit.: in the sixties of the twentieth century).

Numbers between multiples of ten (21, 22...99)

Now let's look at the numbers **between** the multiples of ten (21, 22...).

לטיול השנתי של כיתה ד' יצאו שלושים וַחֲמישה בנים וארבעים וְחָמש בנות. לטיול השנתי של כיתה ג' יצאו ארבעים וּשְׁניים בנים ושלושים וּשְׁתיים בנות.

Thirty-five boys and forty-five girls went on the class trip of the fourth grade. Forty-two boys and thirty-two girls went on the class trip of the third grade.

Numbers between multiples of ten are comprised of three parts:

1. a multiple of ten (שלושים, ארבעים) – this form never changes.

2. a -ו (and) – this is pronounced either -וְ (*veh*), -וַ/-וְ (*va*) or -וּ (*oo*) – depending on what number follows it.[16]

3. a number between 1 and 9 – if a noun follows this form, the form of the number will match it (either masculine or feminine). Thus, in the sentences above:

masculine	*feminine*
35 – שלושים וחמישה בנים	45 – ארבעים וחמש בנות
42 – ארבעים ושניים בנים	32 – שלושים ושתיים בנות

Notice that whenever these numbers end in 2 (as in 32, 42...), the **full form** שניים / שתים is used.

And what happens when the noun that follows these numbers is **definite**? Here's an example:

בספר יש עשרים ושמונה ציורים. כל עשרים ושמונה הציורים הם בשחור-לבן.
There are twenty-eight drawings in the book. All twenty-eight drawings are black and white.

The form **does not** change (i.e., שמונה does not change to שמונת- as it does in שמונת הציורים).

Here are the Hebrew numbers from 21 to 29. For numbers up to 99, we simply substitute other multiples of ten for עשרים.

masculine זכר		*feminine* נקבה	
(בנים / הבנים)	עשרים וְאֶחָד	(בנות / הבנות)	21 – עשרים וְאַחַת
	עשרים וּשְׁנַיִים		22 – עשרים וּשְׁתַיִים
	עשרים וּשְׁלוֹשָׁה		23 – עשרים וְשָׁלוֹשׁ
	עשרים וְאַרְבָּעָה		24 – עשרים וְאַרְבַּע
	עשרים וַחֲמִישָׁה		25 – עשרים וְחָמֵשׁ
	עשרים וְשִׁישָׁה		26 – עשרים וָשֵׁשׁ[17]
	עשרים וְשִׁבְעָה		27 – עשרים וָשֶׁבַע
	עשרים וּשְׁמוֹנָה		28 – עשרים וּשְׁמוֹנָה
	עשרים וְתִשְׁעָה		29 – עשרים וָתֵשַׁע

---

16 On the pronunciation of -ו, see the chapter "Sentences with And, Or, But and the Like," pp. 836-837. Most Hebrew speakers today do not follow all the rules for the proper pronunciation of -ו and tend to pronounce it -וְ (*veh*) in all cases.

17 Before the numbers שש, שבע and תשע the -ו can be pronounced *vah*, as indicated above, or *veh* (-וְ). *Vah* is the officially "correct" pronunciation and is used in formal Hebrew. In informal spoken Hebrew, *veh* is much more common.

Telling the time requires the use of all the numbers mentioned above. See below, pp. 286-290 for details on how to say what time it is.

Want to see if you've understood?

Write the correct form of the number.

3. ‎(m.) ימים _____
(51)

1. ‎(f.) חולצות _____
(28)

4. ‎(f.) כוסות _____
(36)

2. ‎(m.) ילדים _____
(86)

Answers:

‏1. עשרים ושמונה חולצות   2. שמונים ושישה ילדים   3. חמישים ואחד ימים   4. שלושים ושש כוסות

Multiples of one hundred (100-900)

Here are the hundreds:

(בנים / הבנים / בנות / הבנות)	100 – מֵאָה ◀
	200 – מָאתַיִם
	300 – שְׁלוֹשׁ מֵאוֹת
	400 – אַרְבַּע מֵאוֹת
	500 – חֲמֵשׁ מֵאוֹת
	600 – שֵׁשׁ מֵאוֹת
	700 – שְׁבַע מֵאוֹת
	800 – שְׁמוֹנֶה מֵאוֹת
	900 – תְּשַׁע מֵאוֹת

These forms never change. They are used whether a noun follows them or not. They are used before masculine and feminine nouns, both indefinite and definite.

200 (מָאתַיִם ma-TA-yeem) is actually a *dual form* of מאה. It is never preceded by a form of שתיים: its *dual ending* makes this superfluous.

Now look at the words for 300-900.

Q: Is the number before the word מאות feminine or masculine?

A: It is feminine (ארבע, חמש, שש...). This number matches the word מאות (which is feminine) – thus, this first word is always feminine, even when a masculine noun follows מאות:

masculine	feminine
שְׁלוֹשׁ מֵאוֹת בנים	שְׁלוֹשׁ מֵאוֹת בנות

Notice that the words שלוש, שבע and תשע in 300 (שְׁלוֹשׁ מאות), 700 (שְׁבַע מאות) and 900 (תְּשַׁע מאות) have a *shva* (ְ) in the first syllable, just as do the forms שְׁלוֹשׁ עשרה (13), שְׁבַע עשרה (17) and תְּשַׁע עשרה (19).

For numbers above 100 that are not multiples of 100 (i.e., 120, 568), see below.

Multiples of one thousand (1,000-900,000)

These are the thousands in Hebrew:

(בנים / הבנים / בנות / הבנות)	אֶלֶף –	1,000
	אַלְפַּיִים –	2,000
	שְׁלוֹשֶׁת אֲלָפִים –	3,000
	אַרְבַּעַת אֲלָפִים –	4,000
	חֲמֵשֶׁת אֲלָפִים –	5,000
	שֵׁשֶׁת אֲלָפִים –	6,000
	שִׁבְעַת אֲלָפִים –	7,000
	שְׁמוֹנַת אֲלָפִים –	8,000
	תִּשְׁעַת אֲלָפִים –	9,000
	עֲשֶׂרֶת אֲלָפִים –	10,000

As is the case with the hundreds, there is only one form of each number. This form is used before all nouns, be they masculine or feminine, indefinite or definite. The form אַלְפַּיִים (2000) has a **dual ending** (as does מאתיים) and, therefore, we do not place a form of שניים before it.

Now look at the words for 3,000 and up.

Q: Is the number before the word אֲלָפִים masculine or feminine?

A: It is masculine. אלף is masculine, thus the number telling **how many** thousands is masculine. Notice that this number takes the *smeechoot* form (as we saw in שְׁלוֹשֶׁת הבנים), even though there is **no** ה- before the word אלפים.

Now let's see how we say thousands **above** 10,000:

◄	11,000	–	אַחַד עָשָׂר אֶלֶף	(בנים / הבנים / בנות / הבנות)
	12,000	–	שְׁנֵים עָשָׂר אלף
	13,000	–	שְׁלוֹשָׁה עָשָׂר אלף...
	20,000	–	עֶשְׂרִים אלף...
	100,000	–	מֵאָה אלף...
	900,000	–	תְּשַׁע מֵאוֹת אלף...

As you can see, when we count from 11,000 and up, we use the singular form אלף and before it a **masculine** number. Remember: in numbers ending in 0 like 20 (עשרים), 100 (מאה), 900 (תשע מאות), there is only **one form**, and it serves as both masculine and feminine.

For numbers like 5,621 (that are not rounded off), see below.

One million and up

When the numbers *one million* and up appear without a noun after them, they are usually stated as follows:

◄	1,000,000	–	מִילְיוֹן	one million
	2,000,000	–	שני מיליון	two million
	6,000,000	–	שישה מיליון	six million
	10,000,000	–	עשרה מיליון	ten million
	100,000,000	–	מאה מיליון	one hundred million
	1,000,000,000	–	מִילְיַארְד	one billion[18]

It is also possible to use the form מיליונים instead of מיליון (e.g., שני מיליונים).
Note that – unlike אלפיים and מאתיים – the word for *two million* does **not** have a dual ending. We say: שני מיליון or שני מיליונים. The same is true for שני מיליארד or שני מיליארדים (two billion).

מיליון is **masculine**, thus the number before the word מיליון is masculine.

◄	3,000,000	–	שלושה מיליון

Notice that the **regular** form שלושה (and not שלושת) is used here with the singular מיליון. The form for *three billion* is similar: שלושה מיליארד.

___

18 In today's Hebrew you may hear the word ביליון used, but its meaning is, as in British and German usage, a million million (and not a thousand million as in American usage).

When we add a noun, the following options are possible:

	definite	*indefinite*
◄	שלושה **מיליון** הספרים	שלושה **מיליון** ספרים
	שלושת **מיליוני** הספרים	שלושה **מיליוני** ספרים[19]

Did you know?
Tens of..., hundreds of..., thousands of..., millions of..., billions of...

The following plural forms of round numbers are sometimes used without nouns:

מִילְיַארְדִים	מִילְיוֹנִים	אֲלָפִים	מֵאוֹת	עֲשָׂרוֹת	◄
meel-YAR-deem	meel-YO-neem	'a-la-FEEM	me-'OT	'a-sa-ROT	
billions	millions	thousands	hundreds	tens	

For example:

◄ בהפגנה לא היו אלף אנשים, אלא רק כמה מֵאוֹת.

There weren't a thousand people at the demonstration, but rather only several hundred.

Usually, however, these numbers appear before nouns and are in the *smeechoot* form (before **both** indefinite and definite nouns):

◄ עֲשָׂרוֹת אנשים חיכו בתור כדי לקבל ויזה.

Tens of people waited in line in order to get a visa. *'es-ROT-*

עֲשָׂרוֹת **האנשים** שחיכו בתור היו עצבניים.[20]

The tens of people who waited in line were irritable.

◄ מֵאוֹת אזרחים קיבלו מכתב ממשרד הפנים.

Hundreds of citizens received a letter from the Ministry of the Interior. *me-'OT-*

מֵאוֹת **האזרחים** שקיבלו את המכתב באו למשרד הפנים ביום ראשון.

The hundreds of citizens who received the letter came to the Ministry of the Interior on Sunday.

◄ אַלְפֵי אנשים באו לאולימפיאדה

Thousands of people came to the Olympics. *'al-FE-/ 'al-FEI-*

אַלְפֵי **האנשים** שבאו לאולימפיאדה קנו כרטיסים חודשים לפני כן.

The thousands of people who came to the Olympics bought tickets months ahead of time.

---

19 According to the Hebrew Language Academy, שלושה מיליונים ספרים is also acceptable.
20 According to the Hebrew Language Academy, there are two pronunciations of this *smeechoot* form: -עֲשֹרוֹת and -עֲשָׂרוֹת.

More on large numbers

1100: Eleven hundred or a thousand one hundred?

Read the following:

◄ לחתונה של דויד ומיכל הגיעו 1,100 (אלף ומאה or אלף מאה) אורחים.

Eleven hundred guests came to David and Michal's wedding.

or: A thousand one hundred guests…

בשנת 1900 (אלף תשע מאות) דויד בן-גוריון היה בן 14.

In nineteen hundred (lit.: a thousand nine hundred) David Ben-Gurion was fourteen years old.

Notice the difference between the Hebrew and the English in these sentences. In Hebrew, we always begin reading numbers between 1,000 (אלף) and 9,999 (תשעת אלפים תשעים ותשע) with a form of אלף and not with multiples of one hundred like *eleven hundred* or *ninety-nine hundred*.

Using 'ו in large numbers

When large numbers end in 0, we can say them with or without 'ו. For example, we can read the numbers in 120 + 130 = 250 in two ways:

◄ מאה ועשרים **ועוד** מאה ושלושים **שווה** / **הם** מאתיים וחמישים.

or: מאה עשרים **ועוד** מאה שלושים **שווה** / **הם** מאתיים חמישים.

Here is an example containing larger numbers: 1,100 + 3,700 = 4,900. Here, too, we can read this in two ways in Hebrew:

◄ אלף ומאה **ועוד** שלושת אלפים ושבע מאות **שווה**/**הם** ארבעת אלפים ותשע מאות.

or: אלף מאה **ועוד** שלושת אלפים שבע מאות **שווה**/**הם** ארבעת אלפים תשע מאות.

Now let's see what happens when a large number does not end in 0, as in: 345 + 729 = 1074. We can read these numbers in only one way:

◄ שלוש מאות ארבעים וחמש **ועוד** שבע מאות עשרים ותשע **שווה** / **הם** אלף שבעים וארבע.

Q: Where is the ו- placed?

A: Before the last digit.

Here is another example:

◄ דויד בן גוריון נולד בשנת 1886 (אלף שמונה מאות שמונים ושש).

David Ben-Gurion was born in eighteen eighty-six (lit.: a thousand eight hundred eighty and six).

When there is a noun after the number, the last part of the number matches the noun in gender, as in:

➤ אלף מאתיים ארבעים ושש תמונות *feminine:*

1,246 pictures

אלף מאתיים ארבעים ושישה עמודים *masculine:*

1,246 pages

Let's review

◆ The following numbers ending in 0 have **one form**, which is used both when the numbers are followed by a masculine or a feminine noun and when they stand alone:

➤ עֶשְׂרִים / שְׁלוֹשִׁים (בנים, הבנים, בנות, הבנות)   20, 30… (up to 90)

מֵאָה / מָאתַיִם / שְׁלוֹשׁ מֵאוֹת   100, 200, 300… (up to 900)

אֶלֶף / אַלְפַּיִם / שְׁלוֹשֶׁת אֲלָפִים   1,000, 2,000, 3,000… (up to 10,000)

אֶחָד עָשָׂר אֶלֶף / שְׁנֵים עָשָׂר אֶלֶף / שלושה עָשָׂר אֶלֶף…

11,000, 12,000, 13,000 (up to 99,000)

מִילְיוֹן / שני מיליון / שלושה מיליון

one million, two million, three million…

מִילְיַאְרְד / שני מיליארד / שלושה מיליארד

one billion, two billion, three billion…

Variations of the millions are mentioned in the chapter (e.g.: שישה מִילְיוֹן אנשים).

◆ When the numbers 1-19 appear on the end of a larger number, they **match** the noun that follows them (**masculine** or **feminine**), but always remain in the regular (non-*smeechoot*) form:

➤ עשרים ושָׁלוֹש (ה)בנות / מאתיים שבעים וחמש (ה)בנות

עשרים ושלושה (ה)בנים / מאתיים שבעים וחמישה (ה)בנים

◆ In these and larger numbers, usually -ו appears before the **last** number.

➤ אלף מאתיים ארבעים ושתיים (1,242)

Want to see if you've understood?

Write the following numbers in words.

1. 736 בנות — _____

2. 549 בקבוקים — _____

3. שנת 1847 — _____

4. שנת 1789 — _____

5. שנת 2010 — _____

Answers:

1. שבע מאות שלושים ושש   2. חמש מאות ארבעים ותשעה   3. אלף שמונה מאות ארבעים ושבע
4. אלף שבע מאות שמונים ותשע   5. אלפיים ועשר

• Ordinal numbers (...שֵׁנִי ,רִאשׁוֹן)[21]

Read the following passage:

> בקיץ שעבר נסענו ללונדון. ביום השלישי שלנו שם, הלכנו להצגה בתאטרון. ישבנו בשורה השלישית ויכולנו לראות את הכול. היה נפלא!

Last summer we went to London. On our third day there, we went to a show (lit.: in the theater). We sat in the third row, and we could see everything. It was wonderful!

Q: What is the English translation of Hebrew words שלישי and שלישית?[22]

A: **Both** of these words are translated as *third*. While English has only **one** set of ordinal numbers (*first, second, third...*), Hebrew has **two** sets, one masculine and one feminine. These forms are added to nouns in the same way that adjectives are: each comes **after** its noun and **matches** it (*masc.* ⇔ *masc., fem.* ⇔ *fem., definite* ⇔ *definite*), for example:

feminine	*masculine*
⌒	⌒
השורה השלישית	היום השלישי

---

21 In Hebrew: מִסְפָּרִים סוֹדְרִים. The proper grammatical term is *ordinal numerals*.

22 Until this section, blue has been used for masculine numbers and red for feminine. From this point on, we have used colors for other purposes.

Let's look at the forms of the ordinal numbers from 1 to 10:

	feminine	*masculine*	
first	רִאשׁוֹנָה	רִאשׁוֹן	◄
second	שְׁנִיָּיה	שֵׁנִי	
third	שְׁלִישִׁית	שְׁלִישִׁי	
fourth	רְבִיעִית	רְבִיעִי	
fifth	חֲמִישִׁית	חֲמִישִׁי	
sixth	שִׁישִׁית	שִׁישִׁי	
seventh	שְׁבִיעִית	שְׁבִיעִי	
eighth	שְׁמִינִית	שְׁמִינִי	
ninth	תְּשִׁיעִית	תְּשִׁיעִי	
tenth	עֲשִׂירִית	עֲשִׂירִי	

Q: Do all the masculine forms end in 'י?

A: All but the first do. The word רִאשׁוֹן is different, both in its form and in the fact that it is not related to the cardinal number אחד.

Q: In which of the masculine forms are the last two vowel sounds "*ee...ee*'(ימִי)?

A: In all but the first two (רִאשׁוֹן, שֵׁנִי). The forms from שְׁלִישִׁי to עֲשִׂירִי are similar to each other in this respect. In addition, their feminine forms are all created simply by adding ת- to the end: שְׁלִישִׁית, רְבִיעִית and so on.

The numbers רִאשׁוֹן and שֵׁנִי are **different**. Their feminine forms end in ָה-, as do many feminine adjectives (e.g., גדולה). Note that when we write without vowels, the word שנייה (*shnee-YA*) is spelled with "יי".[23]

Ordinal numbers above *tenth* take the **same form** as cardinal (counting) numbers and match their noun, for example:

---

23 The form שֵׁנִית exists, but is used in today's Hebrew to mean either *again*, as in:

The teacher went over the exercise again.   המורה חזר על התרגיל שֵׁנִית.   ◄

or *second(ly)* in enumeration, as in:

בחרנו לנסוע ללונדון משלוש סיבות. רֵאשִׁית, רצינו לבקר חברים שגרים שם. שֵׁנִית, רצינו ללכת להצגה באנגלית, וּשְׁלִישִׁית,   ◄
אף פעם לא היינו שם ורצינו לראות את העיר.

We chose to go to London for three reasons. First(ly), we wanted to visit friends who live there. Second(ly), we wanted to see a show in English, and third(ly), we've never been there and we wanted to see the city.

feminine	*masculine*
המאה האַחַת עֶשְׂרֵה	השבוע האַחַד עָשָׂר
the eleventh century	the eleventh week
השורה העֶשְׂרִים וָשֵׁשׁ	החודש העֶשְׂרִים וְשִׁישָׁה
the twenty-sixth row	the twenty-sixth month

Note that, unlike the English *twenty-sixth*, Hebrew ordinals above *tenth* do **not** end with an ordinal form.

Ordinals with and without -ה

The addition of ordinals to definite nouns, as in the examples above and in the following sentences, is very common:[24]

‫1.זאת הפעם הראשונה שהחברים שלנו באו לביתנו החדש.‬

This is the first time that our friends came to our new house.

‫2. הנרי השמיני היה מלך אנגליה בַּמאה השש עשרה.‬

Henry the Eighth was the King of England in the sixteenth century.

‫3. יובל הוא בעלה השני של טלי.‬

Yuval is Tali's second husband (lit.: the second husband of Tali).

As we see above, ordinals that follow definite nouns are made definite with a -ה on the front, just like regular adjectives. Ordinals may also follow indefinite nouns – and match them (*indef.* ⇔ *indef.*), as in the following:

‫לפי המחקר, כל ילדה שנייה חולמת להיות שחקנית.‬

According to the study, every second girl dreams about being an actress.

‫למרצה יש תואר ראשון בביולוגיה ותואר שני בכימיה.‬

The lecturer has a B.A. (lit.: a first degree) in biology and an M.A. (lit.: a second degree) in chemistry.

---

24 For more on definiteness, see the chapter "Definite and Indefinite Nouns," pp. 52-59.

Did you know?

The names of the days of the week – except for שבת (Saturday) – end in ordinal numbers:

יום שישי	יום חמישי	יום רביעי	יום שלישי	יום שני	יום ראשון
Friday	Thursday	Wednesday	Tuesday	Monday	Sunday

These words are regarded as **names** (*proper nouns*), like *Sarah* and *Tel Aviv*, and are definite even though they have no ה-. Thus, we say:

I like Friday.	1. אני אוהבת את יום שישי.
Last Wednesday we went to Eilat.	2. בְּיום רביעי האחרון נסענו לאילת.

The plural forms of these expressions are not as we might expect:

בימי שישי אנחנו אוהבים לאכול ארוחת בוקר בבית קפה.

On Fridays we like to eat breakfast at a café.

The form יְמֵי (instead of יָמִים) shows that the ordinal number (שישי) behaves here as if it were a **noun** (and not an adjective), as in: ימי הולדת (birthdays).

Plural forms of ordinal numbers

The ordinal number ראשון often appears in the plural, as in:

During the first days of the strike…	בימים הראשונים של השביתה...
In the first years of the twentieth century…	בשנים הראשונות של המאה העשרים...

The use of the other numbers in the plural is rare:

אלו הנישואים השניים של משה והנישואים השלישיים של שושנה.

This is Moshe's second marriage and Shoshana's third marriage.

Ordinal numbers larger than *tenth* do not have a plural form.

Ordinal numbers without a noun

Read the following:

➤ אתמול במסיבה שמעתי שלוש בדיחות חדשות. הראשונה הייתה מצחיקה מאוד, השנייה הייתה
טיפשית, ואת השלישית לא הבנתי.

Yesterday at the party I heard three new jokes. The first (one) was really funny, the second (one) was
stupid and the third (one) I didn't understand.

Here הראשונה, השנייה and השלישית appear **without** a noun and, in effect, turn into nouns, just as
regular adjectives can, as in:

➤ יש לנו שני בנים. הגדול הוא בן 14, והצעיר בן 8.

We have two sons. The older one is 14 years old, and the younger one is 8.

Want to see if you've understood?
Write the correct form of the ordinal number.

1. מיכל לומדת לתואר _____ בספרות אנגלית.
   (2)

2. רונית נמצאת בחודש ה_____ להיריון.
   (9)

3. בחנות הספרים בקניון יש השבוע הנחה על כל ספר _____ שקונים.
   (3)

4. מירי ידעה שהיא תתחתן עם גדי כבר אחרי הפגישה ה_____.
   (3)

5. הסופר הרוסי לֶב טוֹלְסְטוֹי חי במאה ה_____.
   (19)

6. בפעם ה_____ שראיתי את הסרט הבנתי אותו טוב יותר.
   (2)

7. דני הוא האמריקאי ה_____ שזכה במרתון.
   (25)

Answers:

1. שני   2. תשיעי   3. שלישי   4. שלישית   5. תשע עשרה   6. שנייה   7. עשרים וחמישה

• *Hebrew letters as numbers*

Each Hebrew letter has a numerical value, and combinations of letters are also used:[25]

...125 = 5 + 20 + 100 = קכ"ה	21 = 1 + 20 = כ"א	11 = 1 + 10 = י"א	1 = א'
200 = ר'	22 = כ"ב	12 = י"ב	2 = ב'
300 = ש'	30 = ל'	13 = י"ג	3 = ג'
400 = ת'	40 = מ'	14 = י"ד	4 = ד'
... 769 = 9 + 60 + 300 + 400 = תשס"ט	50 = נ'	15 = 6 + 9 = ט"ו	5 = ה'
	60 = ס'	16 = 7 + 9 = ט"ז	6 = ו'
	70 = ע'	17 = 7 + 10 = י"ז	7 = ז'
	80 = פ'	18 = י"ח	8 = ח'
	90 = צ'	19 = י"ט	9 = ט'
	100 = ק'	20 = כ'	10 = י'

The numbers ט"ו and ט"ז highlighted above are special in that they do not begin with י like the other teens. This is done in order to avoid writing forms of the divine name in the Bible (both *yod-heh* and *yod-vav* are forms of the divine name in the Bible).[26]

Letters are used instead of numbers in expressions such as the following:

בראשית ז', 21	ט"ו בשבט[27]	תרגיל ג'	שנה א'	רמה ב'	כיתה ו'	יום א'
Genesis 7:21	Tu Bishvat (15th of Shvat)	exercise 3	first year (of university study)	level two	sixth grade	Sunday

Years are often written using letters, for example: תרפ"ט. The numerical value of these numbers is 400 + 200 + 80 + 9 = 689. To arrive at the Hebrew year, add 5000: 5689. To convert 689 to the Gregorian year, add 1240 (= 1929).[28]

---

25 This system of assigning a numerical value to each letter is called *gematria* (גִּימַטְרִיָה).

26 See, for example, Psalms 115:18 and the first syllable of names like יואל and יונתן.

27 Usually the names of the letters are pronounced, as in כיתה י"ב *kee-TA yood-BET*, but in rare cases the letters are pronounced as if they were a word, as in ט"ו בשבט (*TOO beesh-VAT)* the 15th day of the Hebrew month Shvat.

28 Subtract 1 from the result (1929) to arrive at the Gregorian year in which the Hebrew year began. Thus, תרפ"ט is 1928-1929.

• *Numbers with endings: ...*שְׁנֵינוּ, שְׁלוֹשְׁתֵנוּ
(both of us, the three of us...)

שְׁתֵּינוּ, שְׁנֵינוּ *and the like*

Read the following passage written by a young girl:

> אנחנו ארבעה ילדים במשפחה: שתי בנות ושני בנים. אחותי ואני דומות זו לזו. שתינו רזות ונמוכות, ◄
> לשתינו יש שֵׂעָר שחור ארוך ושתינו אוהבות לצחוק. גם שני האחים שלנו דומים זה לזה. שניהם
> בלונדינים ושניהם שקטים ורציניים.
>
> We are four children in our family: two girls and two boys. My sister and I resemble each other. Both of us are thin and short, we both have long, black hair and we both like to laugh. Our brothers also resemble each other. Both of them are blond and both of them are quiet and serious.

Q: To whom do the highlighted words שְׁתֵּינוּ and שְׁנֵיהֶם in the above passage refer?

A: שתינו refers to אחותי ואני (my sister and I), which could also be expressed with the pronoun אנחנו. We can regard שתינו as a combination of שתי and אנחנו.

שניהם refers to שני האחים שלי, which could also be expressed with the pronoun הם. Here, too, we can regard שניהם as a combination of שני and הם.

Let's look again at the first form: שתינו, whose base form is שתי.

Q: Why do we use the feminine number שתי?

A: Because both אחותי and אני refer to females. If the reference had been to two males or to a female and a male, the form שנינו would have been used. The ending נו- (like אנחנו) is **both** masculine and feminine.

Now let's look at the other form in the passage above: שניהם, whose base form is שני.

Q: Is **only** this part of the word masculine?

A: No, **both** the base form שני and the ending הם- are masculine. We use the masculine forms to refer to two males (as is the case here) or to a male and a female. In the form used to refer to two females, **both** elements are feminine:

◄ שתי + הן ⇦ שְׁתֵּיהֶן

The same principles that apply to the forms שניהם / שתיהן (both of them), apply also when we turn to two people (אתם or אתן) and address them. Here are examples of their use:

<table>
<tr><td>masculine:</td><td>?מַרְסֶל וְריקַרְדוֹ, שניכם מברזיל</td></tr>
</table>

Marcel and Ricardo, are both of you from Brazil?

<table>
<tr><td>feminine:</td><td>?מרים וּבּרִיזִ'יט, שתיכן מדברות צרפתית</td></tr>
</table>

Miriam and Brigitte, do both of you speak French?

The forms שְׁנֵיכֶם and שְׁתֵּיכֶן have **two** parts, both of which are either masculine or feminine. Notice that the ending here is **not** like that of אתם and אתן, but rather is the same ending as that on עֲלֵיכֶן / עֲלֵיכֶם and דוֹדֵיכֶן / דוֹדֵיכֶם.

Here are all the possible forms of שני / שתי with endings:

	feminine	masculine	
	(שְׁתֵּי-)	(שְׁנֵי-)	
both of us	שְׁתֵּינוּ	שְׁנֵינוּ	I
both of you (*pl.*)	שְׁתֵּיכֶן	שְׁנֵיכֶם	II
both of them	שְׁתֵּיהֶן	שְׁנֵיהֶם	III

אַרְבַּעְתֵּנוּ ,שְׁלוֹשְׁתֵּנוּ *and the like*

The numbers 3 and 4 and sometimes even 5 and 6 can also appear with endings. However, the forms of all of these numbers are **simpler** than those of 2, since the base form of 3, 4, 5 and 6 (and so on) **never changes**. Thus:

	feminine	masculine	
the three of us	שְׁלוֹשְׁתֵּנוּ		I
the three of you (*pl.*)	שְׁלוֹשְׁתְּכֶן	שְׁלוֹשְׁתְּכֶם	II
the three of them	שְׁלוֹשְׁתָּן	שְׁלוֹשְׁתָּם	III

Q: What is the base form of all these forms?

A: The masculine *smeechoot* form שְׁלוֹשֶׁת-, used in phrases such as שְׁלוֹשֶׁת הדוּבִּים (the three bears).[29] Strangely enough, this masculine form is used with both masculine and feminine endings (e.g., שְׁלוֹשְׁתָּן / שְׁלוֹשְׁתָּם).

---

29 See above, pp. 261-262.

Q: Are the endings the same as those on שנינו and שניהם?

A: They are similar, but **not the same**. Because the base forms שני / שתי are actually **plural** *smeechoot* forms (they end in י and are based on שניים / שתיים), their endings are the same as those on עליהם and דודיהם.[30] In the case of שלושת-, the endings are the same as those on דודם / דודתם and בשבילם.[31]

The same is true of other numbers. Here, for example, is the number 4, whose base is the **masculine** *smeechoot* form אַרְבַּעַת-:[32]

	feminine	*masculine*	
the four of us	אַרְבַּעְתֵּנוּ		I
the four of you (*pl.*)	אַרְבַּעְתְּכֶן	אַרְבַּעְתְּכֶם	II
the four of them	אַרְבַּעְתָּן	אַרְבַּעְתָּם	III

Let's review

The words for *two*, *three*, *four* and sometimes *five* and *six* commonly appear with endings and mean *both of us / you / them, the three of us / you / them* and so on.

♦ The number *two* has two base forms: שְׁנֵי (*m.*) and שְׁתֵּי (*f.*). To these, the appropriate endings are added:

f.	*m.*	*f.*	*m.*	*f.*	*m.*
שְׁנֵינוּ / שְׁתֵּינוּ,		שְׁנֵיכֶם / שְׁתֵּיכֶן,		שְׁנֵיהֶם / שְׁתֵּיהֶן	
both of us		both of you (*pl.*)		both of them	

To refer to two males or to a male and a female, we use **masculine** forms. For two females, we use **feminine** forms.

♦ The numbers *three* and above have only **one** base form (the **masculine** *smeechoot* form שלושת-, ארבעת-...). To this **all** the endings are added, for example:

...-נ, ם-, כן-, כם-, אַרְבַּעְתֵּנוּ; שְׁלוֹשְׁתָן / שְׁלוֹשְׁתָם, שְׁלוֹשְׁתְּכֶן / שְׁלוֹשְׁתְּכֶם / שְׁלוֹשְׁתֵּנוּ

| the four of us... | the three of them | the three of you (*pl.*) | the three of us |

---

30 See the chapter "Nouns with Possessive Endings," pp. 67-71.

31 See the chapter "Nouns with Possessive Endings," pp. 61-63.

32 The numbers 5 and 6 also have endings, for example: *The five of us...* is חֲמִשְׁתֵּנוּ (note that the vowels are different from חֲמֵשֶׁת-); *the six of us* is שִׁשְׁתֵּנוּ, based on שֵׁשֶׁת-. (Most speakers today say שִׁשְׁתֵּנוּ).

Want to see if you've understood?
Write the correct form of the number.

1.   יוסי ואורי, למה אתם מתווכחים? לדעתי, _____ צודקים.
        (2)

2.   רונית אמרה: "תמר ואני ניסינו לענות על השאלות בהיסטוריה, אבל _____
        (2)
     לא הבנו את השאלה האחרונה".

3.   דויד, מיכל ורון נסעו ביחד להודו. _____ רוצים להישאר שם עד סוף השנה.
        (3)

4.   יש לרותי שתי בנות. _____ מנגנות בגיטרה.
        (2)

5.   שני האחים שלי, אחותי ואני גרים ליד הורינו. _____ קשורים אליהם מאוד.
        (4)

6.   מי היו דויד ושלמה? _____ היו מלכי ישראל.
        (2)

Answers:

שניכם   2. שתינו   3. שלושתם   4. שתיהן   5. ארבעתנו   6. שניהם .1

• *Telling the time*

Full hours and fifteen minute intervals

What time is it?   מה השעה? ◄

Six o'clock   6:00 – (השעה) שש.³³

Six fifteen (lit.: six and a quarter).   שש וחמש עשרה דקות.   or   6:15 – (השעה) שש וָרֶבַע.

Six thirty (lit.: six and a half).   שש ושלושים.   or   6:30 – (השעה) שש וָחֵצִי.

---

33 Since "השעה שש" and sentences like it that begin with השעה are *non-verb* sentences, we can also use the
    connector היא and say: "השעה היא שש".

A quarter to/of seven. // Six forty-five.   ‏6:45 – (השעה) רֶבַע לְשֶבַע. or שש ארבעים וְחמש.‏

One o'clock.   ‏13:00 – (השעה) אחת.‏
(= 1:00 p.m.)

In Hebrew, hours are stated with **feminine** (short) numbers: שש, שבע and so on. For hours after 12:00 noon, we often **write** numbers above twelve (e.g., 13:00), but when we **say** these numbers, we subtract 12 and say: ‏השעה אחת.‏

For intervals of 15 minutes, the words רֶבַע (quarter) and חֲצִי (half) are usually used. Sometimes the number of minutes is given instead (see alternatives above).

Five and ten minutes after and before the hour

There are two basic options[34] for expressing these times:

‏מה השעה?‏ ◄

more common

שש וַחמישה.   or   ‏6:05 – (השעה) שש וְחמש דקות.‏

שש וַעשרה.   or   ‏6:10 – (השעה) שש וְעשר דקות.‏

עשרה לְשבע.   or   ‏6:50 – (השעה) עשר דקות לְשבע.‏

חמישה לְשבע.   or   ‏6:55 – (השעה) חמש דקות לְשבע.‏

---

34 A third option (e.g., שש וחמישים for 6:50) will be discussed below.

As you can see, when the word דקות (minutes) is used, we use **feminine** numbers (חמש, עשר). Very often, however, the word דקות is not mentioned. When this happens, a **masculine** (longer) number is used (חמישה, עשרה).[35] Note: This happens **only** with these numbers and in one other case (which is discussed in the next section).

25 minutes before *the hour*

Also for 25 minutes **before** the hour (here 6:35), the same two options exist:

6:35 – (השעה) עשרים וחמש דקות לְשבע.   or   עשרים וחמישה לְשבע.

In addition, there is a third way to state this time: שש שלושים וחמש. See the next section for an explanation.

25 minutes after *the hour and other times ending in 0 and 5*

The way we say 25 minutes **after** the hour (here 6:25) is exceptional in that there is only **one** option – the short one:

6:25 – (השעה) שש עשרים וְחמש.

Here only the **feminine** חמש is used. This is the way we can state all of the times ending with 0 or 5, beginning with 20 minutes after the hour:

lit.: six and twenty   6:20 – (השעה) שש וְעשרים.

lit.: six twenty and five   6:25 – (השעה) שש עשרים וְחמש.

---

35 Perhaps this is because at one time the masculine רגעים (moments) was used instead of דקות.

lit.: six and thirty	6:30 – (השעה) שש ושלושים.[36]
lit.: six thirty and five	6:35 – (השעה) שש שלושים וְחמש.
lit.: six (and) forty	6:40 – (השעה) שש (וְ)ארבעים.
lit.: six forty and five	6:45 – (השעה) שש ארבעים וְחמש.
lit.: six (and) fifty	6:50 – (השעה) שש (וְ)חמישים.
lit.: six fifty and five	6:55 – (השעה) שש חמישים וְחמש.

Times that are not 5-minute intervals

For all other times up to 20 minutes we use **feminine** numbers only and add the word דקות:

6:07 – (השעה) שש ושבע דקות.
6:18 – (השעה) שש וּשְמוֹנֶה עֶשְׂרֵה דקות.

For times above 20 minutes after the hour, most people say:

6:26 – (השעה) שש עשרים ושש.
6:37 – (השעה) שש שלושים ושבע.

---

36 As mentioned above, we have noted the pronunciation of the וּ according to rules of grammar. Speakers of Hebrew today tend to pronounce it וְ (*veh*).

Some speakers add the word דקות and say: שש ועשרים ושש דקות and the like.

When we use -ל (to, of) with these times, we **always** use the word דקות:

6:42 – (השעה) שמונה עשרה דקות לְשבע. ◄

6:53 – (השעה) שבע דקות לְשבע.

Want to see if you've understood?
Write the time in words. Choose one of the possible options noted above.

_____ –	5:47 .1
_____ –	8:30 .2
_____ –	10:05 .3
_____ –	10:55 .4
_____ –	12:25 .5
_____ –	8:15 .6
_____ –	9:10 .7
_____ –	11:50 .8
_____ –	11:28 .9
_____ –	13:45 .10

Answers:

1. (השעה) חמש ארבעים ושבע. / שלוש עשרה דקות לשש.
2. (השעה) שמונה וחצי. / שמונה ושלושים.
3. (השעה) עשר וחמש דקות. / עשר וחמישה.
4. (השעה) עשר חמישים וחמש./ חמישה לאחת עשרה./ חמש דקות לאחת עשרה.
5. (השעה) שתים עשרה עשרים וחמש. / (השעה שתים עשרה ועשרים וחמש דקות).
6. (השעה) שמונה ורבע. השעה שמונה וחמש עשרה דקות.
7. (השעה) תשע ועשרה. / תשע ועשר דקות.
8. (השעה) אחת עשרה (ו)חמישים. / עשר דקות לשתים עשרה. / עשרה לשתים עשרה.
9. (השעה) אחת עשרה עשרים ושמונה./ (השעה אחת עשרה ועשרים ושמונה דקות).
10. (השעה) אחת ארבעים וחמש. השעה רבע לשתיים.

2. All, Part of...: Quantifiers

Preview

- ‎כָּל הַ-, חֵלֶק מֵהַ- *and the like*
- *Adding endings to quantifiers* (‎...כּוּלָם, רוּבָּם)

• ‎כָּל הַ-, חֵלֶק מֵהַ- *and the like*

Read the following passage:

> ‎רינה ויוסי הזמינו את כָּל החברים שלהם למסיבה. חֵלֶק מהחברים שהגיעו למדו איתם עוד בתיכון, אבל רוֹב החברים שבאו היו איתם בצבא. כולם נהנו מאוד במסיבה. חֲצִי מהזמן הם שרו ורקדו, וּשְׁאָר הזמן הם אכלו ודיברו.

Rina and Yossi invited all (of) their friends to a party. Some of the friends who came had studied with them in high school, but most of the friends who came had been with them in the army. Everybody enjoyed the party very much. Half of the time they sang and danced, and the rest of the time they ate and talked.

All of the highlighted words in the passage above denote quantities in relation to a whole: ‎כָּל (all), חֵלֶק (some, part), רוֹב (most), חֲצִי (half), שְׁאָר (the rest).

Q: What follows these quantifiers in Hebrew?

A: Some are followed by a **definite** noun (here made definite with ‎-ה): ‎כל ה-, רוב ה-, שאר ה-.[1] These quantifiers actually form *smeechoot* phrases with the noun that follows them.[2] Other quantifiers require ‎-מ before the **definite** noun: ‎חלק מהחברים, חצי מהזמן.

Here is a list of common Hebrew quantifiers that are **not** followed by ‎-מ (or ‎מן) and ones that are. (We are including here only one of the possible translations of these words. Others will be presented below.)

---

1   On definiteness, see "Definite and Indefinite Nouns," pp. 52-59.
2   For more on *smeechoot*, see the chapter "*Smeechoot*," pp. 170-172, 183-184.

with מ-/מן in _Hebrew_[3]			_no_ מ-/מן in _Hebrew_	
part of the...	חלק מה-		all (of) the...	כל ה-
half / a quarter / a third of the...	חצי / רבע / שליש מה-		most of the...	רוב ה-
50% / 20%...of the...	50% / 20%... מה-		the rest of the...	שְׁאָר ה-
	חמישים / עשרים... אחוז(ים) מה-			
two / three... of the...	שניים / שלושה... מה-			

 Be careful! כל, רוב and שאר are **never** followed by מ-/מן in Hebrew, whereas their English equivalents **do** often contain the word _of_.

The following are some examples of how these quantifiers are used. Note the variety of ways they can be rendered in English. The English translations are often influenced by whether a **singular** or **plural** noun follows the quantifier.

The boy opened all (of) **the presents** that he received	הילד פתח את כל **המתנות** שהוא קיבל.
Not all **people** like avocado.	לא כל **האנשים** אוהבים אבוקדו.
The whole **class** came to the exam.	כל **הכיתה** הגיעה למבחן.
Most of **the secretaries** in our office do not smoke.	רוב **המזכירות** במשרד שלנו לא מעשנות.
Most **people** like chocolate.	רוב **האנשים** אוהבים שוקולד.
The guests ate only part of **the cake**.	האורחים אכלו רק חלק **מהעוגה**.
Some of **the students** didn't come to class.	חלק **מהסטודנטים** לא הגיעו לשיעור.[4]
	שליש **מהילדים** בכיתה משחקים במחשב כל יום.

A third of **the children** in the class play on the computer every day.

 Be careful! The word or phrase that follows the Hebrew quantifiers in both groups is **always** definite.[5] This is **not** always the case in English (e.g., all people = כל האנשים, most people = רוב האנשים).

---

3 Other expressions with מ- used in formal Hebrew include רבים מה- (many of the) and אחדים מה- (a few of the../ some of the...). In spoken Hebrew we also hear הרבה מה- (many of the...) and כמה מה- (several / a few / some of the...).

4 It is also possible to say: חלק מן הסטודנטים לא הגיע לשיעור. For more on this topic, see below.

5 We have indicated definiteness in the list above by writing ה-; however, the noun may have a possessive ending **instead** (which makes it definite): כל **חבריו** של משה באו למסיבה (All of Moshe's friends came to the party).

Did you know?

1. The word כל is also used to express other meanings, such as *each*, *every* or *any*. When this is the case, the word following כל is **not** definite. Here are examples:

   a. Using כל to mean *each / every*:

   כל **סטודנט** בכיתה קנה מילון. ◄

   Each / every **student** in the class bought a dictionary.

   לכל **ספר** בספרייה יש מספר משלו.

   Each / every **book** in the library has its own number.

   When used in this sense, כל refers to each **individual** object denoted by the word that follows it (as opposed to כל הסטודנטים, which refers to **all the** students together, or כל הכיתה, which also refers to the **whole** group).

   b. Using כל to mean *any*:

   אתם יכולים לבוא לבקר אותנו בכל **שעה** שתרצו. ◄

   You can come visit us any **time** you wish.

2. Words like רֶבַע / שְׁלִישׁ / חֲצִי... are often used as measurements. When this is the case, they are usually followed by an **indefinite** noun, for example:

   בעוגה הזאת יש חצי **כוס** שמן ורבע **כוס** חלב.

   In this cake there are half **a cup** of oil and a quarter **cup** of milk.

Which word does the predicate match: the quantifier or its noun?[6]

כל ה-

Read the following sentences:

	m.pl. ⇔ *m.pl.*	
All the students laughed.	כל התלמידים צחקו.	◄
	f.s. ⇔ *f.s.*	
The whole class laughed.	כל הכיתה צחקה.	

When the quantifier כל is used in the subject of a sentence, the predicate (here, the verb) always matches the **noun** that follows כל.

---

6   For an explanation of *predicate*, see the introduction to "Non-Verb Sentences," p. 705.

-חצי מה- ,חלק מה- // שאר ה- ,רוב ה- *and the like*

When one of the quantifiers other than כל (e.g., רוב, שאר, חצי, חלק) is used in the subject of the sentence, the predicate **usually** matches the noun (especially in informal Hebrew), but can sometimes match the quantifier itself.

m.pl. ⟺ *m.pl.*

➤ חלק מהמשתתפים בדיון הציעו לקיים דיון נוסף.

Some of the participants in the discussion suggested holding an additional discussion.

m.s. ⟺ *m.s.*

חלק מהמשתתפים בדיון הציע לקיים דיון נוסף.

Some of the participants in the discussion suggested holding an additional discussion.

It is hard to come up with any hard and fast rules regarding what form of the predicate should be used in a given sentence. Sometimes there are two options, but sometimes only one sounds acceptable. Suffice it to say that, more often than not, the predicate matches the noun.[7]

• *Adding endings to quantifiers* (כּוּלָם, רוּבָּם...)

Read the following passage:

➤ המסיבה הייתה נהדרת. כל האורחים נהנו. רובם עזבו אחרי 1:00. חלק מהם נשארו עוד קצת כדי לעזור לנקות ולסדר. כולנו הסכמנו שצריך להיפגש לעתים קרובות יותר.

The party was wonderful. All the guests enjoyed themselves. Most of them left after 1 a.m. Some of them stayed a little longer in order to help clean up and put things in order. We all agreed that we should get together more often.

כל *and* רוב *with endings*

As you can see in the passage above, when we wish to use a **pronoun** (us, them…) after the words כל (as in: all of us, all of them…) and רוב (as in: most of us, most of them…), we do this by adding **endings** to these words. Here are the most commonly used forms of each of these words with some additional possible translations:

---

7   In the Hebrew Language Academy's website (www.hebrew-academy.huji.ac.il, February, 2010), it is noted that at times there may even be **three** acceptable forms of the predicate, for example:

➤ חלק מן האוכלוסייה לא יוכל / תוכל / יוכלו להצביע.   Part of the population won't be able to vote.

רוב		כל	
		all of me // I'm all…	כּוּלִי
		all of you (*m.s.*) // you are all…	כּוּלְךָ
		all of you (*f.s.*) // you are all…	כּוּלֵךְ
most of him/it	רוּבּוֹ	all of him/it // he/it is all…	כּוּלוֹ
most of her/it	רוּבָּה	all of her/it // she/it is all…	כּוּלָה
most of us	רוּבֵּנוּ	all of us // we all // we are all…	כּוּלָנוּ
most of you (*m.pl.*)	רוּבְּכֶם	all of you (*m.pl.*) // you all // you are all…	כּוּלְכֶם
most of you (*f.pl.*)	רוּבְּכֶן	all of you (*f.pl.*) // you all // you are all…	כּוּלְכֶן
most of them (*m.*)	רוּבָּם	all of them (*m.*) // they all // they are all…	כּוּלָם
most of them (*f.*)	רוּבָּן	all of them (*f.*) // they all // they are all…	כּוּלָן

Q: What are the **base forms** to which the endings are added?

A: In the case of both כל and רוב, the *oh* vowel in כָּל ה- (*kol ha-*) and in רוֹב ה- (*rov ha-*) turns into an *oo* vowel in the base form: -כּוּל (*kool-*) and -רוּב (*roob-*) (note the *b* in the latter form).

The endings on **almost** all of these forms are the same as those added to בשביל (and אצל).[8]

Q: Which ending above (on כל and רוב) is **not** the same as the endings added to בשביל?

A: The ending on כּוּלָנוּ. Here there is an *ah* vowel in the middle, in contrast to בשבילֵנוּ (and also רוּבֵּנוּ).

Here are some more examples of how the forms of כל and רוב are used:

Tell me what happened. I'm "all ears."	תְּסַפְּרִי לִי מה קרה. כּוּלִי אוזן.
(lit.: all of me is an ear)	
Here, take a towel! You're shaking all over.	הִנֵּה, קְחִי מגבת! את כּוּלֵךְ רועדת.
(lit.: all of you is shaking)	
We ate the whole cake. (lit.: the cake all of it)	אכלנו את העוגה כּוּלָה.
All of us know that…	כּוּלָנוּ יודעים ש...
Most of us think that…	רוּבֵּנוּ חושבים ש...

Notice that when a form of כל or רוב is the subject of the sentence, the predicate usually matches the **ending**:

$$f.s. \Leftrightarrow f.s.$$

You are shaking all over. (lit.: All of you is shaking.)	כּוּלֵךְ רועדת.

---

8   See the chapter "Adding Endings to Prepositions," pp. 232-233.

m.pl. ⇔ *m.pl.*

◄ ...רוּבֵּנוּ חוֹשְׁבִים ש

Most of us think that...

m.pl. ⇔ *m.pl.*   *m.pl.* ⇔ *m.pl.*

◄ ...כּוּלָּנוּ חֲכָמִים, וְלָכֵן כּוּלָּנוּ יוֹדְעִים ש

All of us are wise and, therefore, we all know that...

f.pl. ⇔ *f.pl.*

הַמּוֹרָה אָמְרָה לַתַּלְמִידוֹת: "כּוּלְּכֶן שַׂחְקָנִיּוֹת מְצוּיָּנוֹת".

The teacher said to the students (*f.*): "All of you are excellent actresses."

or: "You are all..."

"וַאֲפִילוּ כּוּלָּנוּ חֲכָמִים, כּוּלָּנוּ נְבוֹנִים, כּוּלָּנוּ זְקֵנִים, כּוּלָּנוּ יוֹדְעִים אֶת הַתּוֹרָה,
מִצְוָה עָלֵינוּ לְסַפֵּר בִּיצִיאַת מִצְרַיִם". (הַהַגָּדָה שֶׁל פֶּסַח)

"So, even if all of us were wise, all of us full of understanding, all of us elders, all of us knowledgeable
in the Torah – we would still be obligated to tell the story of the exodus from Egypt."

(The Passover Haggadah)

Did you know?
The words כולם and כולן mean *all of them*, as in:

◄ יש עשרה בנים בכיתה. כולם מתל אביב.

There are ten boys in the class. All of them are from Tel Aviv.

יש תשע בנות בכיתה. אנחנו מכירים את כולן.

There are nine girls in the class. We know all of them.

Most speakers also use these words, especially in informal Hebrew, to mean
everyone or *everybody*, as in:

◄ נכנסתי לכיתה וראיתי שכולם יושבים בשקט ועובדים.

I went into the classroom and saw that everyone was sitting quietly and working.

 אימא נכנסה לחדר של הבנות ושאלה: "כולן בסדר? אולי אתן רעבות?" (*colloquial*) [9]

Mom went into the girls' room and asked: "Is everybody okay? Are you hungry?"

---

9   According to formal rules of grammar, the expression כל התלמידים (all the students) would be used in the first
     sentence, and כולכן (all of you) would be used in the second sentence.

חלק מ-, חצי מ-...

Now look again at the following passage:

◄ המסיבה הייתה נהדרת. כל האורחים נהנו. רובם עזבו אחרי 1:00. חלק מהם נשארו עוד קצת כדי לעזור
לנקות ולסדר. כולנו הסכמנו שצריך להיפגש לעתים קרובות יותר.

While in this passage the quantifiers רובם and כולנו have **endings**, the word חלק does not. In fact, when we add pronouns (us, them…) to quantifiers that are followed by -מ, we add the ending to -מ and say:

◄ חלק מהם, חצי מהם, רבע מהם, 50% מהם, שניים מהם...

In more formal Hebrew, we can add endings to the word חלק and say:[10]

◄ חֶלְקָם נשארו לעזור.   Some of them stayed to help.

The most commonly used forms of חלק with an ending are:

◄ חֶלְקוֹ, חֶלְקָהּ, חֶלְקֵנוּ, חֶלְקְכֶם, חֶלְקְכֶן, חֶלְקָם, חֶלְקָן

Here's another example:

◄ ראש הממשלה אמר לאנשים בקהל: "חלקכם בוודאי מכירים (or: מכיר) את דעותיי".
(חלק מכם=)

The Prime Minister said to the people in the audience: "Some of you are certainly familiar with my views."

Chapter summary

♦ All Hebrew quantifiers that denote all or part of a whole are followed by a **definite** noun. Some **never** take מ/-מן before the definite noun and some require that מ/-מן be used:

with מ/-מן *in Hebrew*	*no* מ/-מן *in Hebrew* ◄
חלק מה-	כל ה-
חצי / רבע / שליש מה-	רוב ה-
50% / 20%... מה-	שְׁאָר ה-
שניים / שלושה... מה-	

---

10 In formal Hebrew, additional words may also take endings, for example:

◄ לא כל התלמידים בכיתה גרים בירושלים. חֶצְיָים גרים בירושלים וחֶצְיָים גרים מחוץ לירושלים.
Not all the students in the class live in Jerusalem. Half of them live in Jerusalem and half of them live outside of Jerusalem.

◆ When a predicate matches a subject containing a quantifier, it usually matches the **noun** that comes after the quantifier (sent. 1). In some cases, it matches the quantifier itself (sent. 2):

m.pl.⇔ *m.pl.*

Some of the people think that…   ...חלק מהאנשים חושבים ש .1 ◄

m.s ⇔ *m.s.*

Some of the people think that…   ...חלק מהאנשים חושב ש .2

◆ Some quantifiers can take an ending, for example:

...כּוּלָנוּ / רוּבֵּנוּ / חֶלְקֵנוּ יודעים ש ◄

When these serve as the subject, a matching predicate usually matches the **endings**.

Want to see if you've understood?

A. Write מ- where it is needed and X where it is not needed. When the blank is long, write the quantifier with the appropriate ending.

1. איפה כל _____התלמידים? איפה _____?
(כל)

2. חלק _____האנשים שלא אוהבים את השם שלהם מחליטים להחליף אותו בגיל 18, ו_____
(חלק)
ממשיכים לחיות עם שם שהם לא אוהבים.

3. רוב _____הספרים שרחל קונה הם של סופרים ישראלים.

4. כבר תלינו חלק _____התמונות שהיו לנו בדירה הקודמת. את שאר _____התמונות נתלה מחר.

5. הלכתי לקולנוע עם שתי חברות. סוף הסרט היה עצוב מאוד, ו_____ בכינו.
(כל)

6. 30% _____הסטודנטים נכשלו בבחינה. _____ רוצים להיבחן שוב.
(רוב)

Answers:

1. X, כולם   2. מ, חלקם   3. X   4. מ, X   5. כולנו   6. מ, רובם

B. Translate.

1. Most Israelis like to travel. _____

2. Some (חלק) of the students in our class didn't do the homework, but most of them finished everything.

    _____

    _____

3. All children like to play. _____

4. The tourists told the waiter: "Most of us know Hebrew, but some (חלק) of us know only French."

    _____

    _____

Answers:

1. רוב הישראלים אוהבים לטייל.
2. חלק מהתלמידים בכיתה שלנו לא עשו את שיעורי הבית, אבל רובם סיימו/גמרו (את) הכול.
3. כל הילדים אוהבים לשחק.
4. התיירים אמרו למלצר: "רובנו יודעים עברית, אבל חלק מאיתנו יודעים (יודע) רק צרפתית".

IX. Adverbials

Introduction

Compare the Hebrew sentences in Columns A and B:

B		A	
Yossi stood at the bus stop.	יוסי עמד בתחנת האוטובוס. .1	Yossi stood.	יוסי עמד. .1
He waited there.	הוא חיכה שם.	He waited.	הוא חיכה.
	האוטובוס הגיע מִיָד. .2		האוטובוס הגיע. .2
The bus arrived immediately.		The bus arrived.	
	האוטובוס נסע אחרי דקה.		האוטובוס נסע.
The bus departed a minute later.		The bus departed.	
Yossi sat alone.	יוסי ישב לבד. .3	Yossi sat.	יוסי ישב. .3
He read quietly.	הוא קרא בשקט.	He read.	הוא קרא.

Q: What is the difference between the two columns?

A: In Column A, we have sentences with **only** a subject and a verb, whereas in Column B, information is added to the verb.

Q: What kind of information is added in Column B in each of the groups of sentences (1, 2 and 3)?

A: In Group 1, we are told **where** Yossi stood and waited.
In Group 2, we are told **when** the bus arrived and departed.
In Group 3, we are told **how** Yossi sat and read.

Notice that the additions in Column B include **single words** called *adverbs*[1] (שם, מיד, לבד) and **prepositional phrases** (בתחנת האוטובוס, אחרי דקה, בשקט).

We have only given you a **taste** here of these additions, which are called *adverbials* (תֵיאוּרִים). In this unit, we will deal with the following adverbials:

---

1   In Hebrew these are called תּוֹאֲרֵי פּוֹעַל.

1. *Where* Expressions
2. *When* Expressions
3. *How Long* Expressions and *How Often* Expressions (לְשָׁבוּעַ, שָׁבוּעַ, כָּל הַבּוֹקֶר, כָּל בּוֹקֶר)
4. *How* Expressions (מַהֵר, בִּמְהִירוּת...)

Further treatment of adverbials can be found in Part Five "Telling When, Why and the Like in Sentences of Three Types" (chapters on Time Sentences, Reason Sentences, etc.), pp. 903-1003.

1. *Where* Expressions (כָּאן, לַמִּשְׂרָד, הַבַּיְתָה...)

Preview

• *Adverbials of place and direction*

• *The directional ending*   ה' הַמְּגַמָּה

• *Adverbials of place and direction*

Read the following passage:

> יובל ורחל גרים פה בירושלים, אבל יובל עובד חלק מהשבוע בחיפה. כל יום ראשון הוא יוצא מירושלים
> ב-5:00 בבוקר כדי להגיע בזמן למשרד. אם הוא מגיע לשם לפני 7:30, הוא נכנס לבית קפה וקורא שם
> את עיתון הבוקר עד 8:00. יובל עובד בחיפה שלושה ימים וישן שם אצל אחותו. הוא חוזר לביתו ביום
> שלישי בערב.

Yuval and Rachel live here in Jerusalem, but Yuval works part of the week in Haifa. Every Sunday he leaves Jerusalem at 5:00 a.m. in order to get to his office on time. If he gets there before 7:30, he goes into a café and reads the morning paper there until 8:00. Yuval works three days in Haifa and sleeps there at his sister's house. He returns home (lit.: to his home) on Tuesday evening.

The words and phrases highlighted in the passage above are *adverbials of place and direction*.[2] *Adverbials of place* answer the question איפה? (Where?), while *adverbials of direction* answer the questions מאין? / מאיפה? (From where?) and לאן? (Where? = (to) where).[3]

---

2 Many grammar books include *adverbials of direction* under the rubric of *adverbials of place*. We have chosen to differentiate between them in our discussion: We use *adverbials of place* for those with a static quality, while *adverbials of direction* indicate the direction of movement.

3 On question words referring to place, see the chapter "Asking Questions," pp. 821-824.

Try this:

List the adverbials highlighted in the passage above in the appropriate column:

adverbials of direction (?מאין? לאן)	*adverbials of place* (?איפה)
_____	_____
_____	_____
_____	_____
_____	_____
_____	_____
_____	_____

Here's the solution:

adverbials of direction (?מאין? לאן)	*adverbials of place* (?איפה)
מירושלים	פה
למשרד	בירושלים
לשם	בחיפה
לבית קפה	שם
לביתו	בחיפה
	שם
	אצל אחותו

Q: In which of the two columns above is there a **preposition** in each expression?

A: The adverbials of **direction** (in the left-hand column) all have a preposition in Hebrew – either מ- or ל-. In contrast, adverbials of **place** (in the right-hand column) can appear either with a preposition (such as ב-, אצל and the like) added to a noun (ירושלים, אחותו...) or **without** a preposition (in the case of one-word *adverbs*): שם and פה.

Adverbials of **place** are used with "static" (non-motion) verbs, such as גר (live), עובד (work), קורא (read) and ישן (sleep), as we see in the passage above. They can also appear in *non-verb* sentences such as: אני פה. יוסי בבית. (I am here. Yossi is at home.).

Let's concentrate now on the adverbials of **direction** in the above passage (מירושלים, למשרד...).

Q: Which verbs come before these adverbials?

A: Verbs of motion, all of which require ‎מ- (or ‎מן) and/or ‎ל- (or ‎אל) when the direction of the motion is indicated:[4]

(he) leaves Jerusalem	מירושלים	**יוצא**
to get to the office	למשרד	**להגיע**
(he) gets there	לשם	**מגיע**
(he) goes into a café	לבית קפה	**נכנס**
(he) returns home	לביתו	**חוזר**

> ***Be careful!*** As you can see in the sentences above, the corresponding English verbs of motion do **not** always require the use of the preposition *to* (e.g., he gets / arrives there, he returns home).

The *verbal nouns* of verbs that require ‎מ- / מן and ‎ל- / אל take the same prepositions as their verbs when adverbials of direction follow them:

‎בחג הפסח אנחנו קוראים בהגדה על **היציאה** ממצרים.

On Passover we read in the *haggadah* about the **Exodus** from Egypt.

‎**הנסיעה** לאילת הייתה מעייפת.

The **trip** to Eilat was tiring.

• *The directional ending* ‎ה' הַמְּגַמָּה

Read the following passage:

‎לפני חודשיים טיילנו ארבעה ימים בצפון. בדרך הביתה עברנו ליד כרמיאל, ושם פנינו ימינה במקום שמאלה. רק כעבור עשר דקות הבנו שטעינו.

Two months ago we traveled around the north for four days. On the way home, we took the road next to Carmiel, where we turned right instead of left. Only after ten minutes did we realize that we had made a mistake.

Unlike the sentences in the previous section, here the two *verbs of motion* (‎חזרנו and ‎פנינו) are not followed in the Hebrew by the preposition ‎ל-, but rather by the words ‎הביתה, ימינה and ‎שמאלה, which are adverbials of direction.

---

4   For another option, see the discussion on the directional ending ‎ה- below. It should also be noted that the preposition ‎מ- can be used also in *non-verb* sentences, as in: ‎בוריס מרוסיה (Boris is from Russia).

Q: What do these adverbials have in common?

A: They all end in an unstressed הָ-: הַבַּיְתָה (*ha-BAI-ta*), יָמִינָה (*ya-MEE-na*), שְׂמֹאלָה (*SMO-la*). This is often called the *directional heh*[5] (ה' הַמְּגַמָּה) and usually has the same meaning as אל/-ל (to) or לְכִיוּון (in the direction of):

◄ הביתה = אל הבית (שלי, שלך, שלו...)[6]   (to) home
     ימינה = לכיוון ימין   (to the) right
     שמאלה = לכיוון שמאל   (to the) left

The *directional ending* הָ- may be added only to a **limited number** of words. Here are some more examples:

◄ 1. זוז הַצִּדָּה, בבקשה, כדי שגם אנחנו נוכל לראות.   Move to the side, please, so that we, too, can see.

2. העולים הגיעו אַרְצָה בשנת 2000.   The immigrants arrived in (= got to) Israel in 2000.

3. כדי להגיע מירושלים לטבריה נוסעים מַעֲרָבָה עד שמגיעים לכביש 6. משם נוסעים צָפוֹנָה. אפשר גם לנסוע מִזְרָחָה לים המלח ושם לפנות צָפוֹנָה.
In order to get from Jerusalem to Tiberias, you go west until you reach the Route 6 exit.
From there, you go north. You can also go east to the Dead Sea and turn north there.

4. אורי, בוא הֵנָה![7] אני רוצה לדבר איתך!   Uri, come here! I want to talk to you!

5. סע קצת קָדִימָה, זהו, ועכשיו קצת אָחוֹרָה. זהו, מצוין!
Go a little forward. That's it! Now – back a little. That's it – great!

Some words with a directional ending are used also with verbs that are not strictly verbs of motion, such as להתקשר / לצלצל / לטלפן (the phone) – or להסתכל (to look – in a certain direction), as in:

◄ יובל התקשר הביתה.   Yuval called home.

הילדים הסתכלו שמאלה וימינה לפני שהם חצו את הכביש.
The children looked left and right (= to the left and to the right) before they crossed the street.

---

5   Alternative terms include the *directive heh* and the *locative ending*.

6   הביתה means *home*, as in "We went home." It is different from most of the other expressions with a directional ending in that it is **not** equivalent to לבית ("to **the** house"). When we say "We went home," we mean: "We went to **our** house / home." הביתה always refers to the home of the doer of the action.

7   The word הֵנָה, as in "בוא הֵנָה" (Come here!), means לכאן. There is no word הן that means *here*. In addition, the word קדימה, as in "סע קדימה!" (Go forward!) in sentence 5, is based on the word קדים, which is not used today to mean *front*.

Did you know?

In informal (spoken) Hebrew, we often hear a sentence like the following:

> ◄ החברות נפגשו בבית קפה. הן ישבו שמה שעתיים.
>
> The friends met at a café. They sat there for two hours.

The final 'ה on שמה (there) is actually the *directional ending* (the equivalent of לשם), but here שמה is used as an *adverb of place*, as an alternative to שם.[8] Interestingly, speakers today do not use שמה at all to mean לשם.

Here is a list of the words with a directional הֶ- that are most commonly used today:

פְּנִימָה	הַחוּצָה //	הַצִדָּה	אֲחוֹרָה	קָדִימָה //	שְׂמֹאלָה //	יָמִינָה ◄
in, inward(s)	out	to the side	backward(s)	forward	(to the) left	(to the) right

אַרְצָה //	מַעֲרָבָה	מִזְרָחָה	דָרוֹמָה	צָפוֹנָה
to Israel	(to the) west, westward	(to the) east, eastward	(to the) south, southward	(to the) north, northward

הֵנָה	הָעִירָה //	הַבַּיְתָה
here	to the city, into town	home

Q: In what way do the words הביתה, הצדה, החוצה and העירה differ from the rest of the words with a directional ending?

A: The words החוצה, הצדה, הביתה and העירה always have the *definite article* -ה in front of them **in addition** to the directional הֶ-. The other words do **not**.

> **Be careful!** The Hebrew and English use of the definite article -ה with these directional words is not always parallel, for example:

If you go outside you'll see the sunset.	אם תצאו החוצה, תראו את שקיעת השמש. ◄
Look to the left to see if cars are coming.	תסתכלי שמאלה כדי לראות אם מכוניות באות.

---

8   Already in Biblical Hebrew שמה is used to mean not only לשם, but also שם (33 times!). For two other examples in which the directional ending has lost its directional meaning, see the discussion of למעלה and למטה below.

לְמַעְלָה / לְמַטָּה *(up / down)*

Read the following two sentences:

We went up / upstairs.	עלינו לְמַעְלָה. ◄
We went down / downstairs.	ירדנו לְמַטָּה.

Q: In what way are the words למעלה and למטה different from the other words with a directional ending that we have seen so far?

A: These words have **both** a ־ל of direction in front of them **and** a directional ending:

◄ למעלה   למטה

This is not the only way in which these words are peculiar. Look at the following sentences:

We sat upstairs.	ישבנו למעלה. ◄
We played downstairs.	שיחקנו למטה.

Q: Do the words למעלה and למטה in these sentences mean *to* or *in the direction of*?

A: No. Here they follow the verbs ישבנו and שיחקנו, which **do not** require adverbials of **direction**. Even though למעלה and למטה have **two** signs of direction (ל־ and ה־ָ), in these sentences they are adverbials of **place**, like שם or בית.

The verb that accompanies למעלה and למטה determines their meaning. If it is a verb of **motion**, they indicate direction (*to, towards, up / upstairs* or *down / downstairs*). If the verb is **not** a verb of motion, they indicate a place (*upstairs* or *downstairs*).

Did you know?

In Biblical Hebrew the directional ending was much more common than it is today. For example, the following expressions appear in the Bible but are not used in Modern Hebrew:

קֵדְמָה	נֶגְבָּה	יָמָּה ◄
to the east	to the south	to the west
	(lit.: to the Negev)	(lit.: to the sea)

In the Bible, the directional ending is often used at the end of place names, as in:

לְבָנוֹנָה	בָּבֶלָה	מִצְרַיְמָה ◄
to Lebanon	to Babylon	to Egypt

We still encounter remnants of this usage in literary or pseudo-literary Hebrew today, as in:

בבוקר נסענו ירושלימה, ובערב חזרנו תל אביבה.

In the morning we went to Jerusalem, and in the evening we returned to Tel Aviv.

Note: Today, we add ‎הָ‎ only to **certain** place names.

"וּפָרַצְתָּ יָמָּה וָקֵדְמָה וְצָפֹנָה וָנֶגְבָּה" (בראשית כ"ח, 14)

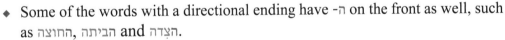

"...you shall spread out to the west and to the east,
to the north and to the south" (Genesis 28:14, JPS translation)

Let's review

- The *directional ending* (an unstressed ‎הָ‎) is added onto a limited number of words in Modern Hebrew. This ending is equivalent in meaning to ‎ל- / אל / לכיוון‎ (to, toward, in a direction).

The driver turned right (= to the right). ‎הנהג פנה ימינה.‎
We went out / outside. ‎יצאנו החוצה.‎

- Some of the words with a directional ending have ‎ה-‎ on the front as well, such as ‎הצדה‎ and ‎הביתה, החוצה.‎

- The directional ending is used on words after verbs of **motion** such as ‎הלך, הגיע,‎ ‎נסע‎ or after verbs which involve direction, such as ‎צלצל‎ and ‎הסתכל.‎

Want to see if you've understood?

A. Choose the correct form.

1. הילדים סיפרו: עמדנו ליד _____ והסתכלנו _____. ראינו מכונית פונה
   א. (הבית / הביתה) ב. (ימין / ימינה)

   _____ ואחר כך עוצרת _____ הכביש. הנהג יצא _____
   ג. (שמאל / שמאלה) ד. (בצד / הצדה) ה. (בחוץ / החוצה)

   וצעק לנו להיכנס _____. הוא אמר שאנחנו עומדים במקום מסוכן.
   ו. (בפנים / פנימה)

2. בשבוע הבא ניסע _____ ונטייל בגליל. לא היינו _____ כבר חצי שנה.
   (צפון / צפונה) (בצפון / צפונה)

3. לא היינו _____ הרבה זמן ולא התקשרנו _____ כבר שבוע.
   (בבית / הביתה) (בית / הביתה)

Answers:

1. א. הבית ב. ימינה ג. שמאלה ד. בצד ה. החוצה ו. פנימה   2. צפונה, בצפון   3. בבית, הביתה

B. Translate into Hebrew using a form with the directional הָ.

1. When you (*m.s.*) go **backward**s (i.e., in reverse), you need to check that no one is behind the car.

   _____

   _____

2. The guard asked the people who were standing next to the gate to move **to the side**.

   _____

Answers:

1. כשאתה נוסע **אחורה**, אתה צריך לבדוק שאין אף אחד מאחורי המכונית.
2. השומר ביקש מהאנשים שעמדו ליד השער לזוז **הצדה**.

2. *When* Expressions

Preview

- *Expressing* when *from the present moment*
  (הַיּוֹם, בְּיוֹם שְׁלִישִׁי, בְּעוֹד שָׁבוּעַ, בַּשָּׁבוּעַ הַבָּא...)

- *Expressing* when: *Telling a story that begins at a different point in time*
  (לְמָחֳרָת, יוֹם קוֹדֶם לָכֵן...)

- *The expressions* עֲדַיִן, כְּבָר *and the like*

• *Expressing* when *from the present moment*
(הַיּוֹם, בְּיוֹם שְׁלִישִׁי, בְּעוֹד שָׁבוּעַ, בַּשָּׁבוּעַ הַבָּא...)

Let's look at a few lines that Miri wrote in her diary when she was a child:

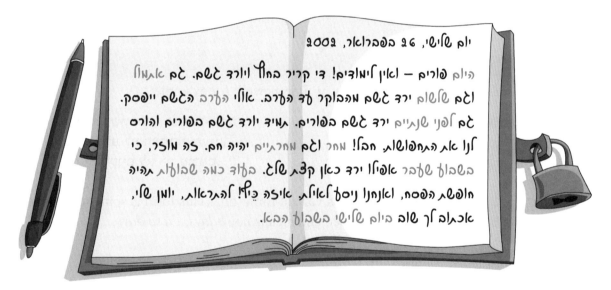

Tuesday, February 26, 2002

Today is Purim[1] and there's no school! It's quite cool outside and it's raining. Both yesterday and the day before yesterday it rained from morning till evening. Two years ago it also rained on Purim. Maybe tonight the rain will stop. It always rains on Purim, and our costumes get ruined. What a shame! Tomorrow and the day after tomorrow it'll be warm. That's strange, since last week it even snowed here a little. In a few weeks it'll be Passover vacation, and we'll be going to Eilat. I can't wait! So long, dear diary, I'll write to you again next Tuesday (lit.: on Tuesday next week).

---

1   *Purim* is a Jewish holiday.

All of the *when* expressions highlighted in the passage above relate to time from the perspective of the **present moment**. They are examples of the expressions that will be discussed in this section.[2]

When *expressions with* ‎-ה‎: ‎היום, הבוקר...‎ *(today, this morning…)*

Miri uses many time expressions in her diary, including ‎הַיּוֹם‎ and ‎הָעֶרֶב‎.

Q: What do these expressions have in common?

A: They both begin with ‎-ה‎. Here are some similar expressions:

this morning	הַבּוֹקֶר
this evening	הָעֶרֶב
this week	הַשָּׁבוּעַ
this year	הַשָּׁנָה

In these expressions, ‎-ה‎ is equivalent to the English *this*. The expressions ‎היום‎ and ‎הלילה‎ happen to have a different translation:

today	הַיּוֹם
tonight	הַלַּיְלָה

We use this same ‎-ה‎ (= this) with other units of time as well, for example:

I barely used the computer this semester.	כמעט לא השתמשתי במחשב הסמסטר.
Our team didn't succeed this season.	הקבוצה שלנו לא הצליחה העונה.
This time the players weren't prepared.	הפעם השחקנים לא היו מוכנים.

Of all the expressions above, only ‎הַיּוֹם‎ has a variant form: ‎כַּיּוֹם‎. This form is sometimes used in formal Hebrew, especially in the newspaper, and means *nowadays, these days*.

Special single-word when *expressions:* ‎מָחֳרָתַיִים‎ *and* ‎שִׁלְשׁוֹם‎

In her diary Miri wrote:

Both yesterday and the day before yesterday it rained.	גם אֶתמוֹל וגם שִׁלְשׁוֹם ירד גשם.

---

2 For more time expressions, see the next chapter and also the chapter "When?: Time Sentences," pp. 917-943.

When we count days backwards, starting from today, we go back one day to אתמול, and if we go back another day, we reach שלשום:

הַיּוֹם	⇒	אתמול	⇒	שִׁלְשׁוֹם
today		yesterday		the day before yesterday

The word שִׁלְשׁוֹם is a bit confusing in that it is based on the number שלוש (three), i.e., three days before today **including** today. It may be easier to disregard this connection. The meaning of שִׁלְשׁוֹם is similar to לפני יומיים (two days ago). There is no one-word equivalent of שלשום in English.

Miri also wrote:

◄   מחר וגם מחרתיים יהיה חם יותר.

Tomorrow and also the day after tomorrow it will be warmer.

The word מָחֳרָתַיִם (*mo-cho-ra-TA-yeem*),[3] too, doesn't have a one-word equivalent in English.

When we count the days that come after today, the next day is מחר and the one following it is מחרתיים:

מָחֳרָתַיִם	⇐	מחר	⇐	היום
the day after tomorrow		tomorrow		today

The meaning of מחרתיים is similar to בעוד יומיים (in two days). The form מחרתיים has a *dual ending* ־ַיִם (*-A-yeem*), often used to indicate the number two. In this case: in **two** days.[4]

Let's review

◆ So far we have seen the following time expressions relating to the present moment:

מָחֳרָתַיִם	⇐	מחר	⇐	היום	⇒	אתמול	⇒	שִׁלְשׁוֹם
the day after tomorrow		tomorrow		today		yesterday		the day before yesterday

---

3   The first two syllables of the pronunciation *mo-cho-ra-TA-yeem* are usually combined, and the word is pronounced *moch-ro-TA-yeem* by most native speakers today. The incorrect pronunciation *mach-ra-TA-yeem* is also commonly heard.

4   See "Did you know?" below on time words with the dual ending ־ַיִם.

When *expressions with* -בְּ

When we ask ?מתי (When?), our answer often begins with -בְּ, as in Miri's final lines:

אכתוב לך שוב בְּיוֹם שלישי.

I'll write to you again on Tuesday.

Notice that the English equivalent of -בְּ when we speak of days of the week is *on*. In other time expressions, the English equivalent may be *at* or *in*, for example:

נִיפּגש בְּ-6:00 / בְּ-8:00 / בְּשעה 10:00.

We'll meet at 6:00 / at 8:00 / at 10 o'clock.

נדבר בַּצהריים.

We'll speak at noon (lit.: at the noon).

לא נקום מוקדם בַּבּוֹקר.

We won't get up early in the morning.

נצא לאכול בָּעֶרֶב.

We'll go out to eat in the evening.

 Be careful! Despite the frequent use of -בְּ in time expressions, the Hebrew equivalent of *in the afternoon* has **no** -בְּ. Rather, it begins with אַחַר or אַחֲרֵי:

עשינו את שיעורי הבית שלנו אחר הצהריים / אחרי הצהריים.

We did our homework in the afternoon.

Want to see if you've understood?

Translate the following sentences.

1. The day before yesterday we wrote a composition.

   _____

2. On Tuesday the doctor arrived at the hospital.

   _____

3. In the morning Dalit runs one kilometer. In the afternoon she goes to the pool.

   _____

4. Avi buys the newspaper in the morning, but he reads it at night.

   _____

5. The day after tomorrow we'll be in Italy.

   _____

6. There's an important meeting tonight.

   _____

Answers:

1. שלשום כתבנו חיבור.   2. ביום שלישי הגיע הרופא לבית החולים.
3. בבוקר דלית רצה קילומטר. אחרי הצהריים היא הולכת לברכה.
4. אני קונה עיתון בבוקר אבל קורא אותו בלילה.   5. מחרתיים נהיה באיטליה.
6. יש פגישה / ישיבה חשובה הערב.

More expressions with -ב: ...בַּשָּׁנָה שֶׁעָבְרָה / בַּשָּׁבוּעַ שֶׁעָבַר *(last week / last year...)*
...בַּשָּׁנָה הַבָּאָה / בַּשָּׁבוּעַ הַבָּא   *(next week / next year...)*

In her diary, Miri used other time expressions that begin with -ב:

1. בַּשָּׁבוּעַ שֶׁעָבַר אפילו ירד כאן קצת שלג.   Last week it even snowed here a little.
2. אכתוב לך שוב בַּשָּׁבוּעַ הַבָּא.   I'll write to you again next week.

Until now, we have seen that -ב in Hebrew time expressions can be translated *on*, *at* and *in*. Here, on the other hand, -ב has no equivalent preposition in English.

ב-...שעבר

Let's take a closer look at expressions similar to בַּשָּׁבוּעַ שֶׁעָבַר.

1. בַּשָּׁנָה שֶׁעָבְרָה מירי מצאה את היומן הישן שלה.   Last year Miri found her old diary.
2. בַּחוֹדֶשׁ שֶׁעָבַר היא קראה אותו שוב.   Last month she read it again.

Notice that the **past tense** verb עבר changes according to the time word used. In the first sentence, the word שנה is feminine, therefore the verb עברה is feminine. In the next sentence, חודש is masculine, thus the verb עבר is masculine. ב-...שעבר/שעברה may be used with other words, too, such as:

בָּעוֹנָה שעברה	בַּסֶמֶסְטֶר שעבר	בַּפַּעַם שעברה	בַּשיעור שעבר[5]
last season	last semester	last time	at the last lesson / class

 Be careful! In the following two sentences, two **different** Hebrew expressions have the same English equivalent – *last week*:

1. הַשבוע שעבר היה שבוע קשה.   Last week was a difficult week.
2. בַּשבוע שעבר טסנו ליוון.   Last week we flew to Greece.

---

5 This usage is limited to certain words, such as those mentioned here. With words such as פגישה we tend to say: בַּפגישה הקודמת (at the previous / last meeting). We also say, as an alternative to the above: בַּשיעור הקודם, בַּפעם הקודמת, בַּסמסטר הקודם.

In the first sentence, השבוע שעבר doesn't describe **when** (it is not an *adverbial*), but rather it is the **subject** of the sentence. In the second sentence, the opening phrase – בשבוע שעבר – answers the question *When?* and thus has a -ב.

ב-...הבא

When we talk about the **future** from the perspective of the present moment, we can use phrases that correspond to *next week, next month, next year* (lit.: *in the week that comes* or *in the coming week*).

Next week Miri will be in Haifa.	1. בַּשָּׁבוּעַ הַבָּא מירי תהיה בחיפה.
Next month she'll fly to England.	2. בַּחוֹדֶשׁ הַבָּא היא תטוס לאנגליה.
Next year she'll visit the United States.	3. בַּשָּׁנָה הַבָּאָה היא תבקר בארה"ב.

Here the **present tense** verb בא changes according to the time word used. In sentences 1 and 2, the words שבוע and חודש are masculine, thus the verb בא is masculine. In sentence 3, we use the feminine form באה because the word שנה is feminine. Notice that in these expressions we use -ה instead of -ש.[6]

Here are more examples:

בְּיוֹם שְׁלִישִׁי הַבָּא	בַּפַּעַם הַבָּאָה	בַּסֶמֶסְטֶר הַבָּא
next Tuesday	next time	next semester

Want to see if you've understood?
Translate the following sentences.

1. Last month we saw an interesting movie.

   _____

2. Next month we'll go to the theater.

   _____

3. You (*m.pl.*) were in Eilat last year.

   _____

4. Next Tuesday we'll go to the supermarket.

   _____

5. Last Shabbat we went to the synagogue.

   _____

---

6   On the use of -ה instead of -ש, see the chapter "Clauses the Add Information to Nouns," pp. 873-875.

6. Last semester I took a course on the history of Spain.

    _____

7. I want to go up north next week.

    _____

Answers:

1. בַּחֹדֶשׁ שֶׁעָבַר רָאִינוּ סֶרֶט מְעַנְיֵין.   2. בַּחֹדֶשׁ הַבָּא נֵלֵךְ לַתֵּיאַטְרוֹן.   3. הֱיִיתֶם בְּאֵילַת בַּשָּׁנָה שֶׁעָבְרָה.
4. בַּיּוֹם שְׁלִישִׁי הַבָּא נֵלֵךְ לַסּוּפֶּרְמַרְקֶט.   5. בְּשַׁבָּת שֶׁעָבְרָה (בַּשַּׁבָּת שֶׁעָבְרָה) הָלַכְנוּ לְבֵית הַכְּנֶסֶת.
6. בַּסֶּמֶסְטֶר שֶׁעָבַר לָמַדְתִּי (לָקַחְתִּי) קוּרְס עַל הַהִיסְטוֹרְיָה שֶׁל סְפָרַד.   7. אֲנִי רוֹצָה לִנְסֹעַ לַצָּפוֹן בַּשָּׁבוּעַ הַבָּא.

לִפְנֵי *and* בְּעוֹד *before units of time*

Two more expressions that we use to talk about the past and future from the perspective of the present moment begin with the prepositions לִפְנֵי and בְּעוֹד.

לפני שבוע, חודש... *(a week ago, a month ago...)*

If we wish to speak about Miri's **past**, including her immediate past, we can use the preposition לִפְנֵי and add a unit of time (for example: דקה, יומיים, שבוע, חודש, שנה),[7] as in:

◄   לפני חמש שנים מירי עברה מחיפה לירושלים.
Five years ago Miri moved from Haifa to Jerusalem.

In Hebrew, *five years ago* is, literally, *before five years*.

Here are some more examples:

A year ago she began to work at the university.   לפני שנה היא התחילה לעבוד באוניברסיטה.   ◄
A minute ago the president of the university called her.   לפני דקה נשיא האוניברסיטה התקשר אליה.

בעוד שבוע, חודש... *(in a week, in a month...)*

If we wish to speak about the future, we can use the word בְּעוֹד (lit.: in another) followed by a unit of time:

In a second Yaron will call Miri.   בעוד שנייה ירון יצלצל אל מירי.   ◄
She will finish her research in a month.   היא תסיים את המחקר בעוד חודש.

Notice that the compound form בְּעוֹד – and not just the preposition -בְּ – corresponds to the English *in* in these expressions.

---

7   As in English, we do not add the word יום to לפני, but rather we use the single word אתמול (yesterday).

Did you know?
Time words with the dual ending ‎ַיִים-

The ending ‎ַיִים- (*-A-yeem*), found on the words שְׁנַיִים / שְׁתַּיִים (two), is added to the following time words to mean *two*:

פַּעֲמַיִים	שְׁנָתַיִים	חוֹדְשַׁיִים	שְׁבוּעַיִים	יוֹמַיִים	שְׁעָתַיִים
two times, twice	two years	two months	two weeks	two days	two hours

In the above forms, the dual ending is added to the **singular** form:

פַּעַם ⇐ פַּעֲמַיִים   חוֹדֶשׁ ⇐ חוֹדְשַׁיִים   יוֹם ⇐ יוֹמַיִים

When the singular form begins with ‎ַ (*ah*), the vowel changes to *shva*.[8]

she-'a-TA-yeem   שָׁעָה ⇐ שְׁעָתַיִים   *shvoo-'A-yeem*   שָׁבוּעַ ⇐ שְׁבוּעַיִים

shna-TA-yeem   שָׁנָה ⇐ שְׁנָתַיִים

In the forms of שעה and שנה, a ת' takes the place of the final ה': שְׁעָתַיִים, שְׁנָתַיִים.[9] We also get a ת' in other time words that have a dual ending: מָחֳרָתַיִים (the day after tomorrow, i.e., two days from today) and בֵּינָתַיִים (in the meantime), which seems to mean: *between* **two** times.[10]

The word צָהֳרַיִים (noon) (*tso-ho-RA-yeem*) appears to have a dual ending, which may reflect the fact that it comes in between two time periods: morning and afternoon.[11]

Want to see if you've understood?
Translate the following sentences.

1. We're going home in ten days.

---

8   See the chapter "Reduction of Vowels and the *Shva*," pp. 640-644.
9   This is the same phenomenon as when the ה- (*-ah*) ending changes to ת- (*-at*) in phrases like שִׂמְלָה⇐שִׂמְלַת כַּלָּה and when possessive endings are added: שִׂמְלָתִי. See the chapter "Nouns with Possessive Endings," pp. 62-63.
10 See the chapter, "When?: Time Sentences," p. 940, for the way בינתיים is used.
11 There is also a possibility that this is not really a dual ending. See Paul Joüon and T. Muraoka, 1996, vol. I, p. 275.

2. We were there a month ago.

   _____

3. Tamar flew to Europe a week ago.

   _____

4. She'll come back in another two weeks.

   _____

5. I was in Italy two years ago.

   _____

6. ‏ראינו את עופר לפני שלושה ימים.‏

   _____

7. ‏נראה את טלי בעוד שבוע.‏

   _____

Answers:

‏1. אנחנו נוסעים (או: ניסע) הביתה בעוד עשרה ימים.   2. היינו שם לפני חודש.‏
‏3. תמר טסה לאירופה לפני שבוע.   4. היא תחזור בעוד שבועיים.   5. הייתי באיטליה לפני שנתיים.‏
6. We saw Ofer three days ago.   7. We'll see Tali in a week / in another week.

Let's review

♦ In Hebrew, the definite article ‏-ה‏ is used to express *this* in time words, as in:

‏הבוקר‏	‏הערב‏	‏השבוע‏	‏השנה‏
this morning	this evening	this week	this year

The following two words have a different translation:

‏היום‏	‏הלילה‏
today	tonight

♦ Hebrew has special single-word time indicators that English doesn't have:

‏שִׁלְשׁוֹם‏	‏מָחֳרָתַיִים‏
the day before yesterday	the day after tomorrow

◆ Often the preposition -בְּ is used to indicate a point in time:

בְּיוֹם שְׁלִישִׁי	בַּבּוֹקֶר	בַּצָּהֳרַיִם	בַּשָּׁבוּעַ שֶׁעָבַר	בַּשָּׁנָה הַבָּאָה
on Tuesday	in the morning	at noon	last week	next year

◆ The last word in the following expressions matches the noun that precedes it:

	masculine:	בשבוע הבא	בשבוע שעבר
	feminine:	בשנה הבאה	בשנה שעברה

◆ We use לִפְנֵי and בְּעוֹד in the following expressions:

a week ago	לפני שבוע
in a week	בעוד שבוע

Want to see if you've understood?
Translate the following sentences.[12]

1. The day before yesterday I spoke to Yonatan about our philosophy course.

   _____

2. The day after tomorrow we have an exam on Plato (אַפְּלָטוֹן).

   _____

3. We met twice to speak about Hegel's philosophy.

   _____

4. On Monday we'll meet at noon.

   _____

5. Today, at 4:00 o'clock in the afternoon, we'll speak on the phone.

   _____

6. Tonight I'll take (lit.: make) a break from studying and go to a movie.

   _____

---

12 Afternoon and evening hours in Hebrew are usually written as 13:00 (=1:00 p.m.), 20:00 (=8:00 p.m.). We have written hours like this (by adding 12 to afternoon and evening hours) in the answers.

7. This week I'm going to go to the pool every morning at 6:30.

_____

Answers:

1 שָׁלְשׁוֹם דִּבַּרְתִּי עִם יוֹנָתָן עַל הַקּוֹרְס שֶׁלָּנוּ בְּפִילוֹסוֹפְיָה. 2. מָחֳרָתַיִם יֵשׁ לָנוּ מִבְחָן עַל אַפְּלָטוֹן.
3. נִפְגַּשְׁנוּ פַּעֲמַיִם כְּדֵי לְדַבֵּר עַל הַפִּילוֹסוֹפְיָה שֶׁל הֶגֶל. 4. בְּיוֹם שֵׁנִי נִיפָּגֵשׁ בַּצָּהֳרַיִם.
5. הַיּוֹם בְּשָׁעָה 16:00 אַחֲרֵי הַצָּהֳרַיִם נְדַבֵּר בַּטֶּלֶפוֹן. 6. הַלַּיְלָה אֶעֱשֶׂה הַפְסָקָה בַּלִּימּוּדִים וְאֵלֵךְ לְסֶרֶט.
7. הַשָּׁבוּעַ אֵלֵךְ לַבְּרֵכָה כָּל בּוֹקֶר בְּ-6:30.

• *Expressing* when: *Telling a story that begins at a different point in time* (...לְמָחֳרָת, יוֹם קוֹדֶם לָכֵן)

Starting from a point in the past

Let's look again at a few lines from Miri's diary when she was a child:

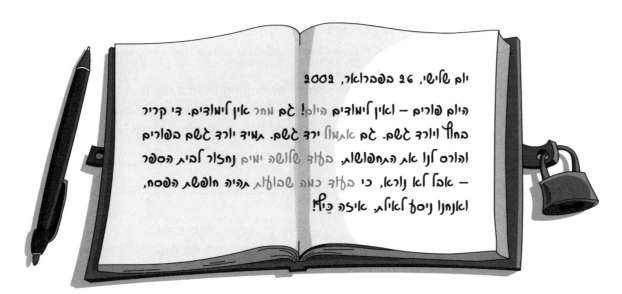

Tuesday, Februrary 26, 2002

It's Purim and there's no school today! Also tomorrow there's no school. It's quite cool outside and it's raining. Yesterday it also rained. It always rains on Purim and our costumes get ruined. In three days we go back to school – but it's not so bad since in a few weeks it'll be Passover vacation, and we'll go to Eilat. I can't wait!

319

Some years have passed since Miri wrote in her diary on February 26, 2002. Today Miri finds her diary, reads the entry and recalls what happened. She begins with the events that took place on February 26, 2002 and continues on from there:

היום	יום חמישי	יום רביעי		יום שלישי		יום שני
today	Thurs.	Wed.	←	Tues.	→	Mon.
Miri reads	March 28	Feb. 27		Feb. 26		Feb. 25
her old diary	2002	2002		2002		2002
	Passover	no school		Purim		rainy day
				(no school)		
				date of diary		

Now let's see what *when* expressions she will use when she recalls what happened.

בְּאוֹתוֹ יוֹם, בַּיּוֹם הַהוּא... *(on that day...)*

When Miri begins recalling what happened, she thinks:

> יום שלישי, 26 בפברואר, 2002 היה פורים ולא היו לימודים בְּאוֹתוֹ יוֹם.
> Tuesday, February 26, 2002 was Purim, and there was no school (on) that day.

Notice that when Miri thinks about what happened beginning from a point in time **other than now**, she can't use the same time expressions she had used at the time the events took place. Instead of היום (today) she uses בְּאוֹתוֹ יוֹם (on that day).[13] In more formal style, she could say בַּיּוֹם הַהוּא.

When we have a situation like this, we use expressions like בְּאוֹתוֹ יוֹם / בַּיּוֹם הַהוּא. For describing longer periods of time, we use:

	בְּאוֹתָן שָׁנִים	בְּאוֹתָהּ שָׁנָה	בְּאוֹתוֹ שָׁבוּעַ
or:	בַּשָּׁנִים הָהֵן	בַּשָּׁנָה הַהִיא	בַּשָּׁבוּעַ הַהוּא

These expressions may be translated in various ways depending on the context: *in that year (month, week...)*, *that same year (month, week...)* and the like.

---

13 For a more in-depth discussion of expressions using אותו, אותה..., see the chapter "Making Comparisons," pp. 350-351.

לְמָחֳרָת (the next day)

When Miri continues to recall what happened, she thinks:

Also the next day there was no school.   .גם לְמָחֳרָת לא היו לימודים ◄

Now Miri is thinking about the day after Purim in 2002. She cannot use מָחָר (tomorrow) any more. Here she uses the formal word לְמָחֳרָת (le-mo-cho-RAT)[14] to refer to the **next day**.

אַחֲרֵי יומַיים..., כַּעֲבוֹר יומַיים... (two days / a week...later)

When we speak of two or more days later, there are a variety of expressions that may be used. Here are some of them:

Two days / a week / a year later...   (informal) אַחֲרֵי יומיים / שבוע / שנה _____ . ◄
(sentence)

Two days / a week / a year later...   (formal) לְאַחַר יומיים / שבוע / שנה _____ .

Two days / a week / a year later...   (formal) כַּעֲבוֹר יומיים / שבוע / שנה _____ .

These expressions are always preceded by a sentence (i.e., they never appear at the beginning of a story). Here are some examples, all of which have the same meaning:

(informal) .מירי כתבה ביומן בפורים. אחרי כמה שבועות היא נסעה לאילת ◄

(formal) .מירי כתבה ביומן בפורים. לאחר כמה שבועות היא נסעה לאילת

(formal) .מירי כתבה ביומן בפורים. כעבור כמה שבועות היא נסעה לאילת

Miri wrote in her diary on Purim. Several weeks later she went to Eilat.

Please note: The word כַּעֲבוֹר when referring to time may **only** be followed by a **unit of time** כעבור שבוע, כעבור חודש... or by a phrase with the word זמן, as in: כעבור זמן קצר (a short time later).[15] The words אחרי and לאחר are similar to כעבור in that – as you can see above – they, too, may be followed by a unit of time when they mean "later," as in: *a week later, a month later*. The words אחרי and לאחר are, however, more versatile than כעבור since they can be followed by nouns that are **not** units of time (...אחרי ההצגה, לאחר השיעור).

---

14 This expression may also be pronounced לַמָחֳרָת (la-mo-cho-RAT), which is a more formal pronunciation.

15 There are also uses where כעבור is followed by a measure of distance, for example:

.נסענו מירושלים לאילת. כעבור מאה קילומטרים עצרנו להפסקה ◄

We traveled from Jerusalem to Eilat. After (going) a hundred kilometers, we stopped and took a break.

יוֹם אַחַר כָּךְ, יוֹם לְאַחַר מִכֵּן... *(a day later, the day after that...)*

Instead of לְמָחֳרָת and אַחֲרֵי/כַּעֲבוֹר יוֹמַיִם/שָׁבוּעַ, we can also use expressions that **begin** with the time unit (...יוֹם, יוֹמַיִם, שָׁבוּעַ), for example:

a day later, a day after that	יוֹם אַחַר כָּךְ ◄
(formal)	יוֹם לְאַחַר מִכֵּן
(formal)[16]	יוֹם אַחֲרֵי כֵן
two days later	יוֹמַיִם אַחַר כָּךְ ◄
a week later	שָׁבוּעַ אַחַר כָּךְ

Like the other expressions which are used for telling a story from a different point of time, these, too, never begin a story, but rather appear at some point **after** the opening sentence. For example, Miri might recall:

◄ בְּיוֹם שני בערב חגגנו את פורים. כַּמָּה שָׁבוּעוֹת לְאַחַר מִכֵּן הייתה חופשת הפסח ונסענו לאילת. באמת היה כיף!

On Monday evening we celebrated Purim. A few weeks later was Passover vacation, and we went down to Eilat. It was really a lot of fun!

יוֹם קוֹדֶם לָכֵן, יוֹם לִפְנֵי כֵן... *(on the day before, a day before that...)*

Once Miri referred back to the date on which she wrote her diary entry, she could either refer to what happened **after** that date, as we saw above (למחרת, אחרי / כעבור שבוע, כמה שבועות אחר כך), or she could recall what happened **before** that date, as in the following:

◄ בפורים היה די קריר בחוץ וירד גשם. גם יוֹם קוֹדֶם לָכֵן ירד גשם.

On Purim it was quite cool outside and it rained. Also the day before that it rained.

When Miri refers to something that happened on **the day** before, she can use one of the following expressions (in this case she used the first one):

the day before (that)	*(formal)*	יוֹם קוֹדֶם לָכֵן ◄
	(formal)[17]	יוֹם לִפְנֵי כֵן
	(less formal)	יוֹם קוֹדֶם
	(informal)	יוֹם לִפְנֵי זֶה

---

16 In formal Hebrew, we also use expressions like: בַּיּוֹם שֶׁלְּאַחַר מִכֵּן – on the day after that.

17 We can also use expressions similar to: בַּיּוֹם שֶׁלִּפְנֵי כֵן – on the day before (that).

Let's review

Comparing Miri's diary and her recollection of what happened

Here is a comparison of Miri's diary entry and her recollection of what happened. Note the changes in the time expressions. See the next "Let's review" for a list of these time expressions.

◆ Miri's present day recollection of what happened:	◆ The diary (written on Tuesday, Feb. 26, 2002):

1. יום שלישי 26.2.02 היה פורים, ולא היו לימודים בְּאוֹתוֹ יום.

   Tuesday, February 26, was Purim, and there was no school (on) that day.

1. היום פורים – ואין לימודים היום!

   It's Purim and there's no school today!

2. גם למחרת לא היו לימודים.

   Also the next day there was no school.

2. גם מחר אין לימודים.

   Also tomorrow there's no school.

3. היה די קריר בחוץ וירד גשם. גם יום קוֹדֶם לָכֵן ירד גשם.

   It was quite cool outside and it rained. The day before that it also rained.

3. די קריר בחוץ ויורד גשם. גם אתמול ירד גשם.

   It's quite cool outside and it is raining. Yesterday it also rained.

4. כעבור שלושה ימים חזרנו לבית הספר, אבל...

   Three weeks later we went back to school, but...

4. בעוד שלושה ימים נחזור לבית הספר – אבל לא נורא, כי...

   In three days we go back to school – but it's not so bad since…

5. כַּמָה שָבוּעוֹת לְאַחַר מִכֵּן הייתה חופשת הפסח ונסענו לאילת. באמת היה כיף!

   A few weeks later was Passover vacation, and we went down to Eilat. It was really a lot of fun!

5. בעוד כמה שבועות תהיה חופשת פסח, ואנחנו ניסע לאילת. איזה כיף!

   In a few weeks it will be Passover vacation, and we'll go to Eilat. I can't wait!

Starting a story from a point in the future

Let's say today is Friday, February 22, 2002 – the Friday **before** Miri wrote the diary entry on Purim.

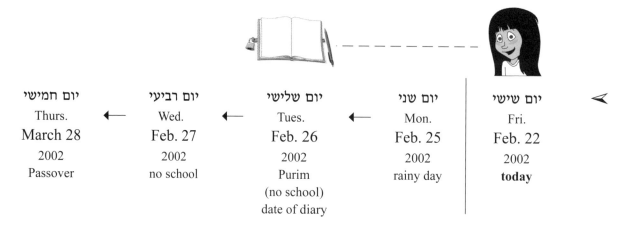

יום חמישי		יום רביעי		יום שלישי		יום שני		יום שישי
Thurs.	←	Wed.	←	Tues.	←	Mon.		Fri.
March 28		Feb. 27		Feb. 26		Feb. 25		Feb. 22
2002		2002		2002		2002		2002
Passover		no school		Purim		rainy day		**today**
				(no school)				
				date of diary				

If Miri had **predicted** on that day – Friday, February 22, 2002 – what would happen the next week on Purim, she could have written the following:

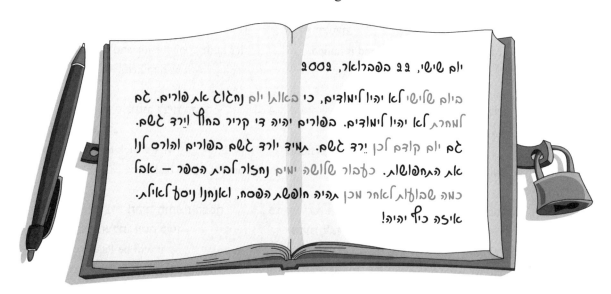

Friday, February 22, 2002

On Tuesday there won't be school because we'll celebrate Purim (on) that day. Also the next day there won't be school. On Purim it'll be quite cool outside and it'll rain. Also the day before that it'll rain. It always rains on Purim and ruins our costumes. Three days later we'll go back to school, but a few weeks later it'll be Passover vacation, and we'll go down to Eilat. It's really going to be fun!

Compare the expressions used here to those used above, when Miri recalled what had happened ten years before (באותו יום, למחרת, יום קודם לכן, כעבור שלושה ימים, כמה שבועות לאחר מכן).

Q: Are the time expressions here **different** from those she used above when **recalling** the events after they had occurred?

A: No. These are the **same** time expressions.

Whenever we start a story from a moment **other than** the present, we first note the beginning point of the story (here: ביום שלישי) and then use the expressions we saw above: באותו יום, למחרת, אחרי שבוע, שבוע אחר כך and the like. This is true when we begin a story in the **past**, as Miri did above, or when we begin in the **future**.

Let's review

The choice of time expressions in a story depends on the starting point:

◆ *Starting the story from a point other than the present – looking to the future*

באותו יום / ביום ההוא
(on) that day, the same day

למחרת / יום אחר כך,
the next day, a day later
(יום אחרי כן, יום לאחר מכן)

יומיים / שבוע אחר כך
two days (a week...) later

אחרי יומיים / שבוע...
two days (a week...) later
לאחר יומיים / שבוע...
כַּעֲבוֹר יומיים / שבוע...

◆ *Starting the story from the present – looking to the future*

היום today

מחר tomorrow

בעוד יומיים / שבוע...
in two days (in a week...)

◆ *Starting from a point other than the present – looking to the past*

יום קודם לכן the day before (that)
יום לפני כן
יום קודם
informal: יום לפני זה

יומיים / שבוע... קודם לכן two days (a week...) before that
לפני כן
קודם
informal: לפני זה

◆ *Starting from the present – looking to the past*

אתמול yesterday

לפני יומיים / שבוע...
two days (a week...) ago

Want to see if you've understood?

You are responsible for the Italian Prime Minister's upcoming visit to Israel. Here is his tentative schedule:

Sunday, Nov. 13		**13.11 ,יום ראשון**
8:30 a.m.	Arrival in Israel	הגעה לישראל 8:30
10 a.m.	Yad Vashem	יד ושם 10:00
2 p.m.	Rabin's grave, Mt. Herzl	קבר רבין בהר הרצל 14:00
Monday, Nov. 14		**14.11 ,יום שני**
		ארוחת בוקר עם ראש הממשלה 8:00
8 a.m.	Breakfast with the Prime Minister	
4 p.m.	Speech at the Knesset	נאום בכנסת 16:00
		מופע של להקת המחול "בת שבע" 20:00
8 p.m.	Performance by Bat Sheva dance troupe	
Tuesday, Nov. 15		**15.11 ,יום שלישי**
8 a.m.	Breakfast with the President	ארוחת בוקר עם הנשיא 8:00
12 noon	Return flight to Italy	טיסה חזרה לאיטליה 12:00

It is now a month **before** the visit and the Israeli president's secretary calls to ask about the Prime Minister's schedule. Start by telling when the Prime Minister will meet with the Israeli president. Use the following expressions to fill in the blanks.

> כמה שעות לאחר מכן / באותו בוקר / יומיים לפני כן / שעתיים אחר כך / למחרת (2x)

ביום שלישי (15.11) ב-8:00 בבוקר ראש הממשלה יאכל ארוחת בוקר עם הנשיא. הוא יגיע לישראל

‏_____ (13.11-ב) ב-8:30 בבוקר. _____ , בשעה 10:00, הוא
(1)   (2)

יבקר ב"יד ושם". _____ הוא יבקר בקבר רבין ב"הר הרצל". _____
(3)   (4)

‏(14.11), ב-8:00 בבוקר, הוא יאכל עם ראש הממשלה הישראלי. בשעה 16:00 הוא יְנָאֵם בכנסת.

הוא יעזוב את הכנסת בשעה 18:00. _____ , בשעה 20:00, הוא יראה מופע של
(5)

להקת המחול "בת שבע". _____ (15.11), בשעה 12:00 בצהריים, הוא יטוס חזרה לאיטליה.
(6)

Answers:

‏1. יומיים לפני כן   2. באותו בוקר   3. כמה שעות לאחר מכן   4. למחרת   5. שעתיים אחר כך   6. למחרת

• *The expressions* כְּבָר ,עֲדַיִין *and the like*

עֲדַיִין # כְּבָר לֹא *(still # not...anymore / no longer)*

Hanna meets Rebecca, a friend she hasn't seen in twenty years. Here's the dialogue between the two:

H: Do you still live in Tel Aviv?

חנה: את עדיין גרה בתל אביב?

R: Yes, I still live in Tel Aviv.
And you? Do you still live in Eilat?

רבקה: כן, (אני עדיין גרה בתל אביב),
ואת? את עדיין גרה באילת?

H: No, unfortunately I don't live there anymore.
I found a job in Beer Sheva
and moved there a year ago.

חנה: לא, לצערי, אני כבר לא גרה באילת.
מצאתי עבודה בבאר שבע, ועברתי לשם לפני שנה.

R: Are you still with Moshe?

רבקה: את עדיין עם משה?

H: No, we're not together anymore.
Are you still with Tsvika?

חנה: לא, אנחנו כבר לא ביחד.
ואת עדיין עם צביקה?

R: Yes, we're still together, and our son is already in the army.

רבקה: כן, אנחנו עדיין ביחד, והבן שלנו כבר בצבא.

H: Wow, that's hard to believe! And do you still draw?

חנה: קשה להאמין! ואת עדיין מציירת?

R: No, I don't draw anymore (I no longer draw), but in the last few years I started writing poetry...

רבקה: לא, אני כבר לא מציירת, אבל בשנים האחרונות התחלתי לכתוב שירה...

Q: When the question in the dialogue above includes עדיין (still), as in:
"?את עדיין גרה בתל אביב / באילת", what expression is used in the answer?

A: When the answer is **positive** (כן), the word עדיין (still) is repeated:

⤶ כן, אני עדיין גרה בתל אביב.

But when the answer is **negative** (לא), the expression כבר לא (not...anymore, no longer) is used:

⤶ לא, אני כבר לא גרה באילת.

Note: Instead of the word עדיין in the dialogue above, we can use the word עוד:

⤶ אני עוד גרה עם ההורים שלי. I still live with my parents.

כְּבָר # עֲדַיִין לא (*already # not yet*)

Two friends, Yael and Tamar, are planning a trip to Greece together. Here is part of their conversation:

Y: Have you bought a map yet? (or: Have you already bought a map?)   יעל: כבר קנית מפה?

T: Yes, don't worry, I've already bought a map.   תמר: כן, אל תדאגי, כבר קניתי מפה.

יעל: כבר סימנת על המפה את המקומות שנרצה לבקר בהם.
Y: Have you circled the places we want to visit yet? (or: Have you already circled...?)

T: No, I haven't circled them yet. There's still time for that!   תמר: לא, עדיין לא סימנתי, יש זמן!

יעל: כבר לקחת את הכרטיסים מסוכנת הנסיעות?
Y: Have you picked up the tickets from the travel agent yet?

תמר: לא, עדיין לא לקחתי. אסע אליה מחר. את קצת לחוצה, לא? את בטח כבר ארזת...
T: No, I haven't picked them up yet. I'll go there tomorrow. You seem a little uptight. I'll bet you've already packed!

יעל: כן, ודאי שכבר ארזתי. את עדיין לא?
Y: Yes, of course I've already packed. Haven't you (packed yet)?

תמר: לא, אני עדיין לא ארזתי. יש עוד שבוע שלם!
T: No, I haven't packed yet. We do have another whole week!

Q: When the question in the above dialogue includes the word כבר (yet or already) (e.g., כבר קנית מפה?), what expression is used in the answer?

A: When the answer is **positive** (כן), כבר (already) is used.

◄   כן, כבר קניתי מפה.

When the answer is **negative** (לא), the expression עדיין לא (not yet) is used.

◄   לא, עדיין לא סימנתי את המקומות...

Instead of עדיין לא we can use עוד לא:

◄   לא, עוד לא סימנתי את המקומות...

Both expressions – עדיין לא and עוד לא – indicate that the change that has not yet taken place is still **expected**. They are translated in the above sentences as *not yet*. An alternative translation is *still not*:

➤ עדיין לא סימנתי את המקומות.

I haven't circled the places yet.

or: I still haven't circled the places.

עוד לא / עדיין לא are usually followed by past tense verbs, as in the dialogue above. However, they can be found with all tenses:

➤ אני עדיין לא **מכירה** את העיר.

I still don't know the city. Or: I don't know the city yet.

אולי גם בעוד שנה עדיין לא **תהיה** לי עבודה.

Perhaps in a year from now I still won't have work.

Let's review

◆ The words עדיין and עוד both mean *still*. Their opposite is כבר לא (anymore, no longer):

את עדיין / עוד גרה שם?

Do you still live there?

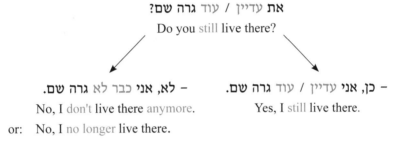

– לא, אני כבר לא גרה שם.

No, I don't live there anymore.

or: No, I no longer live there.

– כן, אני עדיין / עוד גרה שם.

Yes, I still live there.

◆ The expressions עדיין לא / עוד לא and כבר are opposites, too:

כבר קנית מפה?

Have you bought a map yet? (or: already...?)

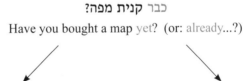

– לא, עדיין לא / עוד לא קניתי מפה.

No, I haven't bought a map yet.

or: I still haven't bought a map.

– כן, כבר קניתי מפה.

Yes, I've already bought a map.

In short, it is handy to keep the following pairs of opposites in mind:

עדיין # כבר לא

(עוד)

כבר # עדיין לא

(עוד לא)

Want to see if you've understood?
Write one of the following in the appropriate blanks.

עדיין / כבר לא / כבר / עדיין לא

השכן שלנו כבר בן שמונים, אבל הוא _____ מרגיש צעיר. הוא עדיין עושה ספורט, הוא
(1)

_____ יוצא לטיולים במדבר יהודה, והוא _____ מטייל בעולם. יש לו חמישה ילדים,
(3)   (2)

ו_____ יש לו 20 נכדים. הוא יוצא הרבה לתאטרון ולקולנוע, אבל הוא _____ הולך
(5)   (4)

למסיבות ריקודים. הוא _____ מבלה עד שלוש לפנות בוקר, כי הוא אוהב ללכת לישון לפני
(6)

אחת עשרה. לשכן שלנו יש עוד הרבה תוכניות: יש ארצות שהוא _____ ביקר בהן,
(7)

והוא רוצה לראות אותן, ויש עוד הרבה דברים שהוא _____ עשה.
(8)

Answers:

1. עדיין   2. עדיין   3. עדיין   4. כבר   5. כבר לא   6. כבר לא   7. עדיין לא   8. עדיין לא

3. *How Long* Expressions and *How Often* Expressions

Preview

- How long *expressions* (...לְשָׁבוּעַ, בְּמֶשֶׁךְ שָׁבוּעַ, כָּל הַבּוֹקֶר)
- How often *expressions* (...כָּל בּוֹקֶר..., מְדֵי יוֹם..., יוֹם יוֹם..., פַּעַם בַּחוֹדֶשׁ)

• How long *expressions*

לשבוע *versus* שבוע: *when do we use* -ל?

Read the following sentences about Yaron:

Yaron went to Tel Aviv for three days.	1. ירון נסע לתל אביב לשלושה ימים.
He stayed there a week.	2. הוא נשאר שם שבוע.
or: He stayed there for a week.	

In the first Hebrew sentence above, we **must** use -ל before the time expression שלושה ימים: לשלושה ימים. This is also the case in the English: He went to Tel Aviv for three days. In contrast, in the second Hebrew sentence, we **do not** use -ל.

Q: Does the English translation of sentence 2 correspond exactly to the Hebrew?

A: The first translation corresponds exactly, whereas the alternative translation (He stayed there for a week) does not, since it contains the word *for*.

Now let's look more closely at the two **Hebrew** sentences above in order to see more clearly when we **must** or **must not** use -ל in Hebrew.

Q: Which of the above sentences tells us about Yaron's **plans**?

A: Only sentence 1. The time phrase לשלושה ימים tells us **not** how long it took Yaron to get to Tel Aviv, but rather how long Yaron **intended** to **stay** in Tel Aviv once he got there.

We can sketch this sentence like this:

		intention	
Yaron went to Tel Aviv for three days.		לשלושה ימים	ירון נסע לתל אביב.	1.

Q: Which word tells us that this was his **intention**?

A: The same word in both Hebrew and English: ‎-ל‎ (for). This word is **required** in both languages.

Now let's look closely at sentence 2, which does **not** contain ‎-ל‎:

He stayed there a week.	הוא נשאר שם שבוע.	2.
or: He stayed there for a week.		

We can sketch this sentence like this:

He stayed there a week.	הוא נשאר שם	2.
or: He stayed there for a week.	שבוע	

Q: Is there any indication of Yaron's **intentions** in this sentence?

A: No. Sentence 2 tells us only **what happened** (הוא נשאר בתל אביב) and **how long** he stayed (שבוע).

 Be careful! In sentences like sentence 2, in which **no intention** is expressed and the word *for* is **optional** in English, we **do not** use ‎-ל‎ in Hebrew.

Here's another example:

שלחו את אביגיל לסבא ולסבתא שלה לשבוע, אך בסופו של דבר היא הייתה שם עשרה ימים.
Avigail was sent to her grandparents for a week, but in the end she was there (for) ten days.

Here the **intention** was that Avigail go to her grandparents for a week (לשבוע). But this is not what really happened. The real duration of the stay was ten days.

		intention	
She was sent to her grandparents for a week.		לשבוע.	שלחו אותה לסבא ולסבתא	

She was there ten days.	היא הייתה שם	
or: She was there for ten days.	עשרה ימים	

Note that the verb in a time sentence that does **not** contain -ל typically does **not** involve motion, but rather has a **static** quality. Verbs such as להיות (to be), להישאר (to stay), לבקר (to visit), ללמוד (to study), לגור (to live) typically appear in such sentences.

בְּמֶשֶׁךְ *(for)*

In time sentences that **do not** use -ל (i.e., where we speak of **actual duration** and not of intention), we sometimes use the preposition בְּמֶשֶׁךְ (for, over the course of) in Hebrew, but this is **optional**:

> They studied (for) ten hours.   הם למדו עשר שעות.
>
> or: הם למדו במשך עשר שעות.

Let's review

- In Hebrew we use -ל with units of time only when we speak of an **intended plan**:

> נסענו ללונדון לשבוע (אבל נשארנו שם רק יומיים).
>
> We went to London for a week (but we stayed there only two days).

- We do **not** use the preposition -ל (in Hebrew) to express the **duration** of an action or a state of being. For this we use either **nothing** or במשך.

> We worked (for) three hours.   עבדנו שלוש שעות.
>
> or: עבדנו במשך שלוש שעות.

Want to see if you've understood?

Write the preposition -ל only where it is required in Hebrew. (The English translation is provided for your convenience).

They went to Eilat for a month.	1. הם נסעו לאילת _____ חודש.
We'll come to your house for two days.	2. אנחנו נבוא לבית שלך _____ יומיים.
Uri was in Haifa for three days.	3. אורי היה בחיפה _____ שלושה ימים.
We traveled for six hours to get to London.	4. נסענו _____ שש שעות כדי להגיע ללונדון.
We were at the museum for three hours.	5. היינו במוזאון _____ שלוש שעות.

6. רונית באה למוזאון _____ שעתיים, אבל היא נשארה שם _____ ארבע שעות.

Ronit came to the museum for two hours, but she stayed there for four hours.

Answers:

In sentences 1, 2, 6a we must use -ל.   In sentences 3, 4, 5 and 6b we do not use -ל.

כָּל הַ- (בּוֹקֶר, יוֹם...) *(all morning, the whole morning...)*

Read the following passage about Noa, an art history student. Here's what she did on the day before a big exam:

נועה נסעה למוזאון והייתה שם כל הבוקר. ב-12:00 היא נסעה הביתה לאכול, וב-13:00 היא הלכה לספרייה. היא הייתה בספרייה כל אחר הצהריים. ב-17:00 היא חזרה הביתה וישבה ולמדה כל הערב.

Noa went to the museum and was there the whole morning. At 12:00 she went home to eat, and at 1:00 she went to the library. She was at the library all afternoon. At 5:00 she returned home and sat and studied all evening.

Q: What comes after כל in all the highlighted expressions in the above passage?

A: -ה followed by a unit of time: כל הבוקר, כל הערב. These expressions are actually in *smeechoot*.[1] For this reason, the -ה appears only before the **last word** of the expression, but makes the **entire phrase** definite. (The English equivalent – *the whole morning* – shows this clearly.) Note that when -ה כל is added to אחר הצהריים (afternoon), which is itself a *smeechoot phrase*, the -ה comes only before the last word:

כל אחר הצהריים

In addition to translating these as *the whole morning, afternoon...–* which is closer to the Hebrew – we can also translate these expressions as *all morning, afternoon....* They tell us **how long** something was done.[2]

Want to see if you've understood?
Translate the following sentences.

1. Yael slept all morning.

   _____

2. Ron worked all night.

   _____

3. I haven't gone to the pool all year.

   _____

---

1   See the chapter "*Smeechoot*," pp. 183-184.
2   On כל with definite nouns other than time units (כל הכיתה, כל התלמידים), see the chapter "All, Part of...: Quantifiers," pp. 291-292.

4. Your phone was busy the whole afternoon (=all afternoon)!

_____

Answers:

1. יעל ישנה כל הבוקר.   2. רון עבד כל הלילה.   3. לא הלכתי לבֶּרֶכה כל השנה.
4. הטלפון שלך היה תפוס כל אחר הצהריים.

• How often *expressions*

כָּל (בּוֹקֶר...) *(every morning...)*

Here is another passage about Noa, the art history student. This time we hear about her daily schedule:

כל בוקר נועה נוסעת לאוניברסיטה. היא נמצאת שם כל יום עד 16:00. אחרי הלימודים היא נוסעת לעבודה. היא עובדת במסעדה כל ערב עד 20:00. ב-20:15 היא נוסעת הביתה ונפגשת עם חברים עד 23:00. מ-23:00 עד 2:00 בבוקר היא יושבת ולומדת. היא לומדת כל לילה עד השעות הקטנות של הבוקר.

Every morning Noa goes to the university. She is there every day until 4:00 p.m. After her classes she goes to work. She works in a restaurant every evening until 8:00. At 8:15 she goes home and meets with friends until 11:00. From 11:00 to 2:00 in the morning she sits and studies. She studies every night until the wee hours of the morning.

The expressions כל בוקר, כל יום, כל ערב, כל לילה tell us that something happens **consistently**: **every** morning, **every** day and so on. Notice that there is **no** -ה after the word כל when it means *every*.[3]

Sometimes -בְּ is used before these expressions:

Every morning she leaves the house at 7:00.   בְּכל בוקר היא יוצאת מהבית ב-7:00.
Every week new members join the group.   בְּכל שבוע חברים חדשים מצטרפים לקבוצה.

This is the same -בְּ that appears in time expressions like בְּיום שני (on Monday).

_____

3   On כל used with indefinite nouns that are not units of time (כל תלמידה...), see the chapter "All, Part of...: Quantifiers," p. 293.

IX. Adverbials / 3. *How Long* Expressions and *How Often* Expressions

...מדי יום *(every day…)*

Another way to say that something happens **consistently** is by using the expression מְדֵי (*mee-DEI*) before a unit of time, as in:

◄ מְדֵי יום יוצאות מספר טיסות מישראל לטורקיה.

    A number of flights leave Israel for Turkey every day (daily).

    Michal takes the dog for a walk every morning.   מיכל לוקחת את הכלב לטיול מְדֵי בוקר.

The expression מְדֵי פעם is also commonly used, as in:

    We all make mistakes (every) once in a while.   ◄ כולנו טועים מְדֵי פעם.

Double words: לילה לילה ,יום יום

Here is still another way to say that something happens **consistently**:

    Noa goes to the university every day (daily).   ◄ נועה נוסעת לאוניברסיטה יום יום.

    She works at the restaurant every night (nightly).   לילה לילה היא עובדת במסעדה.

Only certain time units can be doubled in this way. These expressions are used less frequently than (...יום ,בוקר) כל. Doubling is also used for non-time expressions.[4]

...פַּעֲמַיים בְּ- / ...פַּעַם בְּ- *(once a week, twice a month…)*

Here's some more information about Noa:

◄ נועה מטלפנת להורים שלה פעם בְּשבוע ונוסעת אליהם פעמיים בְּחודש. היא מתקשרת לסבא ולסבתא
שלה פעם בְּשְׁלושה ימים.

    Noa calls her parents once a week and goes to see them twice a month. She calls her grandparents once every three days.

פַּעַם בְּ- and its variations are another way to tell **how often** something happens.

---

4   See the chapter "*How* Expressions," p. 346.

Let's review

◆ For expressing the **entire length** of time (*all...*, *the whole...*) we use כָּל הַ-
followed by a noun:

➤ כל הבוקר, כל היום   all morning, all day long (the whole day)

◆ For expressing **frequency** (*every...*, *once in a...*):

- We can use כל followed by a noun that is **not** definite:

➤ כל בוקר, כל יום   every morning, every day
or: בְּכל בוקר, בְּכל יום

- We can use מְדֵי followed by a noun:

➤ מְדֵי בוקר, מְדֵי שבוע   every morning, every week

- We can double the time unit, as in:

➤ יום יום, בוקר בוקר   every day / daily, every morning

- We can use variations of -פעם בְּ:

➤ הם אוכלים בשר פעם בְּשבוע.   They eat meat once a week.
הם נפגשים שלוש פעמים בְּחודש.   They meet three times a month.

Want to see if you've understood?

Choose the correct Hebrew translation.

1. הם נפגשים _____.
(כל השבוע / שבוע שבוע)

    They meet weekly.

2. אנחנו נוסעים לטורקיה _____.
(כל השנה / כל שנה)

    We travel to Turkey every year.

3. בישלתי _____.
(כל הבוקר / כל בוקר)

    I cooked all morning.

4. הם נוסעים לאילת _____.
(פעם בשנה / כל השנה)

    They go to Eilat once a year.

5. חשבתי עלייך _____.
(קיץ קיץ / כל הקיץ)

    I thought about you all summer.

6. היא צופה בחדשות בטלוויזיה _____.
(כל הערב / ערב ערב)

    She watches the news on television every night.

7. הספורטאי מתאמן _____.   The athlete trains twice a day.
(פעמיים ביום / כל היום)

8. הוא הסתכל בשעון שלו _____.   He looked at his watch every hour.
(כל שעה / כל השעה)

9. לא ישנתי _____.   I didn't sleep the whole night.
(כל לילה / כל הלילה)

10. יוני נוסע לעבודה באוטובוס _____.   Yoni goes to work by bus every morning.
(מדי בוקר / כל הבוקר)

Answers:

1. שבוע שבוע   2. כל שנה   3. כל הבוקר   4. פעם בשנה   5. כל הקיץ   6. ערב ערב   7. פעמיים ביום
8. כל שעה   9. כל הלילה   10. מדי בוקר

4. *How* Expressions

Preview

- *Single-word* how *expressions* (מהר, קשה)
- *Phrases expressing* how (במהירות, בצורה ישירה, בלי לחכות)
- *Double words* (...אחד אחד, ילד ילד)
- *How? In what state?*

Introduction

Read the following passage about Ron, a sixteen-year-old who decided to drop out of school. Ron had already made his decision, but he wasn't sure **how** he should break the news to his parents.

רון לא ידע איך לספר להוריו על החלטתו. האם לספר להם לאט לאט, או אולי פשוט להודיע להם מהר ולצאת מיד מהחדר – בלי לחכות לתגובה. הוא לא ידע אם הם יגיבו בכעס או בהבנה. לבסוף הוא החליט לספר להם בצורה ישירה בתקווה שהם יגיבו בדרך הגיונית.

Ron didn't know how to tell his parents about his decision. Should he tell them slowly and gradually – or should he simply tell them quickly and then leave the room immediately, without waiting for their reaction. He wasn't sure if they would react angrily or with understanding. In the end he decided to tell them straight-out (in a direct, straightforward way), in the hope that they would react in a reasonable way.

All the highlighted words in this passage describe **how** the actions are done. They answer the question ?איך (How?), or in more formal Hebrew: ?כֵּיצַד.

As you can see, many of these *how* expressions in English end in *-ly*, but this is not the only form that they take in English. In Hebrew, too, *how* expressions are constructed in a variety of ways.

• *Single-word* how *expressions*

Adverbs

Some *how* expressions are single words (*adverbs*):[1]

◄   מַהֵר   פִּתְאוֹם   הֵיטֵב
     quickly   suddenly   well

Some of the Hebrew expressions are perceived by us as single words, but they are actually made up of two parts:

◄   מִיָּד   לְאַט   לְבַד   לְגַמְרֵי   לְפֶתַע
     immediately   slowly   alone   totally, completely   suddenly

Here are some examples of how they are used:

They speak well.	הם מדברים הֵיטֵב. ◄
He always sits alone.	הוא תמיד יושב לְבַד.
Suddenly he started crying.	פִּתְאוֹם הוא התחיל לבכות.

Adjectives used as how *expressions*

Here are some more *how* expressions that are single words:

He is working hard.	הוא עובד קשה. ◄
They draw nicely.	הם מציירים יפה.
They are sleeping soundly.	הם ישנים עמוק.
She is progressing wonderfully.	היא מתקדמת נפלא.

Q: What is common to the words עמוק, יפה, קשה and נפלא?

A: They are all **adjectives**, but here they describe **not** a noun, but a **verb**. Like the **adverbs** מהר (quickly) and פתאום (suddenly), they tell **how**: how he works, how they draw, how they sleep, how she is progressing.

Q: Do these adjective *how* expressions match the verb? (For example: if the verb is plural, are they plural?)

A: No, when adjectives are used as *how* expressions they are always used in the **masculine singular** (הוא) form even with verbs that are **not** masculine singular.

---

1   These are called *adverbs of manner*.

Here are some more examples:

You (*m.pl.*) sing well.	אתם שרים טוב. ◄
They write beautifully (excellently).	הן כותבות מצוין.

Want to see if you've understood?
Choose the correct form.

1. השירים האלה ממש _____ , ואתם שרים כל כך _____ .
   (מקסים / מקסימים)   (מקסים / מקסימים)

2. המכונית הזאת _____ , ואת נוהגת _____ .
   (נהדר / נהדרת)   (נהדר / נהדרת)

3. התרגילים _____ . התלמידים עובדים _____ כדי לפתור אותם.
   (קָשֶׁה / קשים)   (קָשֶׁה / קשים)

4. תדברי _____ . חשוב לדבר עברית _____ .
   (נכון / נכונה)   (נכון / נכונה)

Answers:

‏1. מקסימים, מקסים   2. נהדרת, נהדר   3. קשים, קָשֶׁה   4. נכון, נכונה

• *Phrases expressing* how

The preposition -ב followed by a noun

In the passage above, we saw that Ron didn't know whether his parents would react בְּכַעַס (angrily) or בַּהֲבָנָה (with understanding).

Q: What do the expressions בכעס and בהבנה have in common?

A: They are both made up of -ב followed by a noun: ב+הבנה, ב+כעס.[2] Usually they are translated with the English *-ly* ending. Sometimes the English parallel contains *with*: *with* understanding (בהבנה), *with* pleasure (ברצון).

---

2   The pronunciation of -ב is often affected by the first vowel of the word that follows it. Thus, according to the rules of grammar, the vowel of -בְּ changes in expressions like בַּהֲבָנָה and בִּרְצִינוּת (seriously). In a word like בַּהֲבָנָה, today's Hebrew speakers often pronounce the initial -ב as *beh*, without regard for the rules of grammar.

Here are some more *how* expressions with the same structure:

He did it gladly.	◄ הוא עשה זאת בְּשִׂמְחָה.
Why are you talking quietly?	למה את מדברת בְּשֶׁקֶט?
I didn't do it on purpose.	לא עשיתי את זה בְּכַוָּנָה.

Many nouns that are added to -בְּ to create *how* expressions have the abstract ending ות-:

She spoke excitedly.	◄ היא דיברה בְּהִתְרַגְּשׁוּת.
They are working very seriously.	הם עובדים בִּרְצִינוּת רבה.

Though, in theory, a great many nouns can be added to -בְּ to make a *how* expression, in practice only **certain** nouns are used. Knowing which ones are used is a matter of exposure: once you encounter one of these expressions in use, you can begin to use it yourself.

בְּאוֹפֶן, בְּדֶרֶךְ, בְּצוּרָה *followed by an adjective*

There are still other ways to say *how*. In the passage at the beginning of this chapter, we read the following:

Ron decided to tell them straight-out (in a direct, straightforward way).	◄ רון החליט לספר להם בצורה ישירה.

בְּצוּרָה (lit.: in a ... form) is always followed by an **adjective**. Here it is followed by ישירה (direct), creating a *how* expression that means *in a direct manner*.

Q: Why is the feminine form ישירה used?

A: Because the word צורה, which it describes, is feminine.

Here are some more examples:

	f. ⇔ *f.*
He spoke in a clear manner (clearly).	◄ הוא דיבר בצורה ברורה.
	f. ⇔ *f.*
Think logically!	תחשוב בצורה הגיונית!
	f. ⇔ *f.*
You presented this in an interesting way.	הצגתם את זה בצורה מעניינת.

Instead of בְּצוּרָה sometimes the words בְּדֶרֶךְ (lit.: in a ... way) and בְּאוֹפֶן (lit.: in a ... manner) are used, also followed by an adjective, as in:

The interviewer asked difficult questions pleasantly.	◄ 1. המראיינת שאלה שאלות קשות בדרך נעימה.
The newscaster spoke clearly (lit.: in a clear manner).	2. הקריינית דיברה באופן ברור.

Notice that דרך, like צורה, is **feminine**, so the adjective after it is feminine, too (in sentence 1: בדרך נעימה). In contrast, אופן is **masculine**, therefore the adjective that follows it is in the masculine form (in sentence 2: באופן ברור).

 Be careful! You can't use just **any** adjective with any one of these (בצורה, בדרך, באופן). Again it is a matter of what sounds right to the native speaker – there are no rules here.

בְּלִי *followed by an infinitive*

In the passage at the beginning of this chapter, we read that Ron was thinking of leaving the room בלי לחכות לתגובה של ההורים (without waiting for his parent's response). בלי means *without*.

Q: What comes after בלי in this example?

A: The infinitive לחכות. Note the English translation is *without **waiting***, whereas the Hebrew is, literally, *without **to wait***.

It is very common to find an infinitive after בלי. Here are some more examples:

We did this without thinking.	◄ עשינו את זה בלי לחשוב.
You succeeded on the exam without studying.	◄ הצלחת במבחן בלי ללמוד.

Let's review

◆ Hebrew has a limited number of single-word *how* expressions that are **adverbs**, as in:

◄ הוא מדבר היטב.   He speaks well.

◆ Sometimes the masculine singular form of an **adjective** is used as a *how* expression, as in:

◄ עבדנו קשה.   We worked hard.

◆ Often the **preposition** -ב is combined with a **noun** to form a *how* expression:

◄ עשית זאת ברצון.   You did it willingly.

◆ Many *how* expressions are formed with the words בצורה, בדרך, באופן followed by an **adjective**, as in:

≺ הוא מתלבש בצורה מיוחדת.   הוא מדבר בדרך מיוחדת.   הוא הגיע לפה באופן מיוחד.

He came here specially.   He speaks in a special way.   He dresses in a special way.

♦ Another kind of *how* expression is formed by using בלי followed by an **infinitive**:

She answered without thinking.   היא ענתה בלי לחשוב. ≺

Want to see if you've understood?

Translate the following sentences using *how* expressions as indicated.

A. Use one of the following adverbs: מהר, לאט, מיד, לבד, היטב.

1. They write well.

    _____

2. We asked that they (*m.pl.*) leave immediately.

    _____

B. Use one of the following adjectives: מהיר, איטי, יפה, טוב.

3. She speaks nicely.

    _____

4. They write well.

    _____

C. Use -ב followed by a noun, as in: בכעס, בהבנה.

5. She learns languages easily.

    _____

6. I will do it (lit.: this) willingly.

    _____

7. She went (traveled) there quickly.

    _____

8. Stop (*m.pl.*) speaking cynically!

    _____

D. Use דרך בדרך followed by an adjective, as in: בדרך מיוחדת.

    9.   You (*m.pl.*) solved the problem elegantly.

_____

    10.   Miri celebrated her birthday in an original way.

_____

E. Use באופן followed by an adjective, as in: באופן מיוחד.

    11.   We asked that they (*m.pl.*) leave immediately.

_____

    12.   It is possible to solve the matter discreetly (adj. דיסקרטי).

_____

F. Use בצורה followed by an adjective, as in: בצורה ברורה.

    13.   The child doesn't know how to speak in a different way.

_____

G. Use בלי followed by an infinitive, as in: בלי לחכות.

    14.   One can't (lit.: It is impossible to) succeed without trying.

_____

    15.   It's hard to build the plane without reading the instructions (הוראות).

_____

Answers:

1. הם כותבים היטב. 2. ביקשנו שהם יעזבו מיד. 3. היא מדברת יפה. 4. הם כותבים טוב.
5. היא לומדת שפות בקלות. 6. אני אעשה את זה ברצון. 7.היא נסעה לשם במהירות.
8. תפסיק לדבר בציניות. 9. פתרתם את הבעיה בדרך אלגנטית.
10. מירי חגגה את יום הולדתה בדרך מקורית. 11. ביקשנו שהם יעזבו באופן מיידי.
12. אפשר לפתור את הבעיה באופן דיסקרטי. 13. הילד אינו יודע לדבר בצורה אחרת.
14. אי אפשר להצליח בלי לנסות. 15. קשה לבנות את המטוס בלי לקרוא את ההוראות.

• *Double words*

Here is another way of forming *how* expressions:

הילדים נכנסו אחד אחד. The children entered one by one.

תקראו את הסיפור קטע קטע. Read the story one passage at a time.

Q: What is common to both these *how* expressions?

A: In both of them a word is **repeated**. This kind of construction is commonly used with numbers, groups and time units:

הם נכנסו שניים שניים / שלושה שלושה / זוגות זוגות...

They entered two-by-two (in twos) / three-by-three (in threes) / in pairs...

היא באה אלינו יום יום / שבוע שבוע...

She comes to our house every day (daily) / every week (weekly)...

When numbers are used, they match the noun in **gender**:

masculine: הבנים נכנסו אחד אחד / שניים שניים.

The boys entered one-by-one / two-by-two.

feminine: הבנות נכנסו אחת אחת / שתיים שתיים.

The girls entered one-by-one / two-by-two.

"שְׁנַיִם שְׁנַיִם בָּאוּ אֶל־נֹחַ אֶל־הַתֵּבָה זָכָר וּנְקֵבָה" (בראשית ז׳, 9)

"...two of each, male and female, came to Noah into the ark" (Gen. 7:9, JPS translation)

We also find doubling in expressions such as:

הילד קרא את הסיפור לאט לאט. The boy read the story very slowly.

בשקט בשקט נכנסנו לחדר של התינוק הישן. We went very quietly into the room of the sleeping baby.

The doubling in these expressions adds intensity and can be translated as *very*.

• How? In what state?

In the following sentences we hear about Daniel and Michal, a hard-working couple:

➤ דניאל הגיע הביתה עייף. Daniel arrived home tired.
מיכל הגיעה הביתה עייפה. Michal arrived home tired.

We learn here in what **state** Daniel and Michal came home: they were tired.

Q: In addition to the verb, what else matches the words דניאל and מיכל in **gender** (m./f.) and **number** (s./pl.)?

A: The words עייף and עייפה.

Each of the above sentences is a shortened version of two separate sentences:

➤ א. **דניאל** הגיע הביתה. + ב. הוא היה עייף. ⬅ **דניאל** הגיע הביתה עייף.
Daniel arrived home. He was tired. Daniel arrived home tired.

➤ א. **מיכל** הגיעה הביתה. + ב. היא הייתה עייפה. ⬅ **מיכל** הגיעה הביתה עייפה.
Michal arrived home. She was tired. Michal arrived home tired.

Here are some more examples:

➤ **ענת** ישבה בצד עצובה. Anat sat on the side in a sad state (lit.: Anat sat on the side sad).

מצאנו את **הכוסות** שבורות. We found the glasses broken.

Each of these examples contains an **adjective** (עייף, עייפה, עצובה, שבורות) that describes the condition or state of the "noun" (i.e., of the person or thing indicated by the noun). Such sentences can, instead, use a **verb** to indicate the condition or state of the noun. Here are some examples:

1. **יוני** חזר הביתה בוכה. Yoni returned home crying.

2. **הילדה** תעמוד שם מחייכת. The girl will stand there smiling.

3. ראינו את **הילדים** משחקים.

We saw the children playing.

4. אני שומע את **הבנות** מדברות עם הוריהן.

I hear the girls speaking with their parents.

Q: In the Hebrew sentences, what is the **tense** of the verb that indicates the state of the person / people?

A: In all cases it is in the **present tense**, no matter what tense the first verb in the sentence is in. It also matches its noun in both **gender** (*m./f.*) and **number** (*s./pl.*):

f.pl. ⇔ f.pl.	m.pl.⇔ m.pl.	f.s.⇔ f.s.	m.s.⇔ m.s.	
הבנות מדברות.	**הילדים** משחקים.	**הילדה** מחייכת.	**יוני** בוכֶה.	◄

Let's review

♦ We have seen that certain *how* expressions are formed by doubling the word, as in:

◄ הם נכנסו אחד אחד.

They entered one by one / one at a time.

♦ We have also seen that in order to express the condition or state of someone or something, we can use an adjective or a present tense verb in the following way:

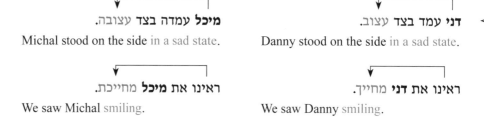

◄ **דני** עמד בצד עצוב.

Danny stood on the side in a sad state.

מיכל עמדה בצד עצובה.

Michal stood on the side in a sad state.

ראינו את **דני** מחייך.

We saw Danny smiling.

ראינו את **מיכל** מחייכת.

We saw Michal smiling.

Want to see if you've understood?

Translate the following sentences.

1. I photographed you (*m.s.*) swimming in the Dead Sea.

   _____

2. Yael watched us (*m.pl.*) playing on the computer.

   _____

3. The teacher (*f.s.*) entered the room in an angry state.

   _____

4. The children heard their mother talking about them.

   _____

5. Sarah found the books thrown on the floor. (thrown = זרוק)

   _____

6. The patients went into the doctor one at a time (one-by-one).

   _____

Answers:

1. צילמתי אותך שוחה בים המלח.   2. יעל הסתכלה בנו משחקים במחשב.
3. המורה נכנסה לכיתה/לחדר כועסת.   4. הילדים שמעו את אמם (אימא שלהם) מדברת עליהם.
5. שרה מצאה את הספרים זרוקים על הרצפה.   6. החולים נכנסו לרופא אחד אחד.

X. Making Comparisons: Comparatives, Superlatives and the Like

Preview

- אותו... / אותה... / אותם... / אותן... *(the same...)*[1]
- *Comparatives:* יותר מ-, פָּחוֹת מ- and the like
- *Superlatives:* ...הֲכִי-ה, ...ה-ה-...ביותר

• אותו... / אותה... / אותם... / אותן... *(the same...)*[2] •

Read the following passage about twin brothers, David and Jonathan:

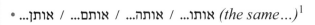

דויד ויונתן דומים מאוד. יש להם אותו קול, אותן עיניים ואותו חיוך נעים. יש להם גם

אותה תספורת, ולפעמים הם גם לובשים אותם בגדים.[3] אנשים כל הזמן מתבלבלים ביניהם.

> David and Jonathan are very similar. They have the same voice, the same eyes and the same pleasant smile. They have the same haircut and sometimes they also wear the same clothes. People confuse them all the time.

Q: How do we say *the same* in Hebrew?

A: We use אותו, אותה, אותם, אותן. The form matches the noun that comes after it:

When the noun is *masculine singular*, we use אותו: אותו קול, אותו חיוך;

---

1   For more on expressions of comparison, see the chapter "Similarity and Difference: Sentences of Comparison," pp. 970-990.

2   Forms of אותו followed by a noun may also mean *that* or *those*, for example:

> קראתי על שנות ה-50 בארץ. אותם ימים היו ימים קשים לישראל.
> I read about the fifties in Israel. Those days were difficult ones for Israel.

3   When forms of אותו (=the same) are used with the direct object, as in this sentence, it is possible to add את before them, as in: הם לובשים **את** אותם בגדים.

When the noun is *feminine singular*, we use אותה :אותה צורה;

When the noun is *masculine plural*, we use אותם :אותם בגדים;

When the noun is *feminine plural*, we use אותן :אותן עיניים.

We can say the above phrases either with or without -ה before the noun **without** changing the meaning:

➤ אותו חיוך or אותו **ה**חיוך
אותם בגדים or אותם **ה**בגדים

In Hebrew, as in English, this construction has two different meanings:

1. It can refer to **two** different items that are similar, as in:

➤ היי, אנחנו לובשים אותה חולצה היום! Hey, we're wearing the same shirt today.
שרון קוראת אותו ספר כמו רותי. Sharon is reading the same book as Ruthie.

2. It can refer to only **one** item:

כל יום ראשון ירון לובש אותה חולצה. Yaron wears the same shirt every Sunday.

In this case, Yaron wears the same one shirt over and over again.

A very common expression using אותו is אותו הדבר or אותו דבר, meaning *the same thing,* as in:

➤ מלצר: מה תשתו? Waiter: What would you like to drink?
מיכאל: אני רוצה קפה שחור. Michael: I'd like Turkish coffee.
מלצר: ואת? Waiter: And you?
שירה: אותו דבר. Shira: The same thing.

Want to see if you've understood?

Write the correct answer: אותן or אותם, אותה, אותו.

1. דן ורן אוהבים (את) _____ הספרים.   (ספרים *m.pl.*)

2. יש לי _____ בעיה כמו לשרה.   (בעיה *f.s.*)

3. אנחנו פוחדים מ_____ דברים.   (דברים *m.pl.*)

4. התכתבתן עם _____ בחור.   (בחור *m.s.*)

5. הוא תמיד רוקד עם _____ הבנות.   (בנות *f.pl.*)

Answers:

1. אותם   2. אותה   3. אותם   4. אותו   5. אותן

• Comparatives: -יותר מ-, פחות מ   *and the like*

יותר מ-/מאשר   *(more than...)*

Which country is **larger**: the U.S. or France? Which continent is **smaller**: America or Europe? Which cities in Israel are **more famous** than Haifa? The answers to these questions in Hebrew are:

1. ארה"ב **גדולה** יותר מְצרפת.
The U.S. is **larg**er than France.

2. יבשת אוסטרליה **קטנה** יותר מִיבשת אסיה.
The continent of Australia is **small**er than the continent of Asia.

3. ירושלים ותל אביב **מפורסמות** יותר מֵחיפה.
Jerusalem and Tel Aviv are more **famous** than Haifa.

Notice that an **adjective** followed by -יותר מ corresponds to English words like *larger* and *smaller than* and also to expressions like *more famous than*.[4]

יותר is placed in the above sentences **after** the adjective, but in **informal** Hebrew it often comes **before** the adjective:

1. ארה"ב יותר **גדולה** מצרפת.
2. יבשת אוסטרליה יותר **קטנה** מיבשת אמריקה.
3. ירושלים ותל אביב יותר **מפורסמות** מחיפה.

In many cases the word יותר is omitted in sentences like these. For example, we sometimes find:

יבשת אוסטרליה **קטנה** מיבשת אמריקה.
The continent of Australia is **small**er than the continent of America.

---

4   מן can be used instead of -מ before nouns with the definite article (-ה), as in:
The new proposal is better than the previous one.   ההצעה החדשה טובה יותר מן ההצעה הקודמת.

מ- *instead of* מאשר

Often, especially before a preposition, many speakers of Hebrew use מאשר instead of מ-.[5]

‎◄ הימים בקיץ **ארוכים** יותר מאשר **בחורף.** Days in the summer are **long**er than days in the winter.

‎המכנסיים האלה **מתאימים** לחולצה הירוקה יותר מאשר **לחולצה הסגולה.**

These pants **match** the green shirt better than they match the purple shirt.

In formal Hebrew, the use of מ- in such cases is considered preferable, as in:

‎◄ בתל אביב חם יותר **מירושלים.**

(*less than / fewer than...*) פחות מ- / מאשר

The opposite of יותר מ- is פחות מ-.

‎◄ אופנוע **יקר** פחות ממכונית. A motorcycle is less **expensive** than a car.

‎or: אופנוע פחות **יקר** ממכונית.

As you can see, the placement of פחות is the same as that of יותר.

The word מאשר is also sometimes used after פחות instead of מ-, for example:

‎◄ פחות **נוח** לנסוע באוטובוס מאשר **ברכבת.** It is less **comfortable** to travel by bus than by train.

Did you know?

יותר מ- / פחות מ- (*more than / fewer, less than*) with nouns[6]

When the יותר and פחות are used with **nouns** (e.g., books, students), their placement is the same as in English – **before** the noun, for example:

‎◄ מרים קנתה יותר **ספרים** מדניאל. Miriam bought more **books** than Daniel.

‎השנה נרשמו לאוניברסיטה פחות **סטודנטים** מאשר בשנה שעברה.

This year fewer **students** registered for the university than last year.

---

5   Many Hebrew speakers today use מאשר not only before a preposition or a sentence, but also before a noun, as in: ארה"ב גדולה יותר מאשר צרפת. This usage is not found in ancient sources; thus, in sentences like this, the wording ארה"ב גדולה יותר מצרפת is considered preferable.

6   Just as in English, יותר (more) and פחות (less) are used not only with adjectives and nouns. Here is an example with an adverb:

‎◄ הרכבת נוסעת **מהר** יותר מהאוטובוס. The train travels faster than the bus.

‎or: יותר **מהר**

When a **number** precedes the noun, the word order is **different** (as in English):

◄ בכיתה א' יש **חמישה סטודנטים** פחות מאשר בכיתה ב'.

In the Alef class there are **five students** fewer than in the Bet class.

Want to see if you've understood?
Translate.

1. The green shirt suits (מתאימה) you better than the red shirt.

   _____

2. There are fewer students in my class than in your (m.s.) class.

   _____

3. Dan is shorter than Gali.

   _____

4. Your recipe (מַתְכּוֹן) is easier than mine.

   _____

5. The second book is less frightening than the first one.

   _____

6. Are clothes more expensive in England than in Israel?

   _____

7. We sold more computer games this week than last week.

   _____

Answers:

1. החולצה הירוקה מתאימה לך יותר / יותר מתאימה לך מ(החולצה) האדומה.
2. יש פחות סטודנטים בכיתה שלי מ-/ מאשר בכיתה שלך.
3. דן נמוך יותר /יותר נמוך מגלי.
4. המתכון שלך קל יותר / יותר קל מ(המתכון) שלי.
5. הספר השני מפחיד פחות / פחות מפחיד מ(הספר) הראשון.
6. (האם) הבגדים יקרים יותר / יותר יקרים באנגליה מ-/ מאשר בישראל?
7. מכרנו יותר משחקי מחשב השבוע מ/מאשר בשבוע שעבר.

• *Superlatives:* ‫ה-...הֲכִי...‪,‬ ה-...ה-...בְּיוֹתֵר‬

When we compare three or more people or objects in informal Hebrew, we often say:

Shai is the **tall**est **student** in the class.   ‫1. שי הוא התלמיד הֲכִי גבוה בכיתה.‬

The Dead Sea is the **low**est **place** on earth.   ‫2. ים המלח הוא המקום הֲכִי נמוך בעולם.‬

Here is the construction we use:

		‫ה- + שם עצם + הֲכִי + שם תואר‬		
		adjective + ‫הֲכִי‬	‫ה- + noun‬	
m.s.:	‫בכיתה.‬	‫גבוה‬	‫הכי‬	‫התלמיד‬	‫שי הוא‬
f.s.:	‫בכיתה.‬	‫גבוהה‬	‫הכי‬	‫התלמידה‬	‫שרית היא‬
m.pl.:	‫בכיתה.‬	‫גבוהים‬	‫הכי‬	‫התלמידים‬	‫שי ורון הם‬
f.pl.:	‫בכיתה.‬	‫גבוהות‬	‫הכי‬	‫התלמידות‬	‫שרית ותמר הן‬

In more formal Hebrew, and sometimes also in informal Hebrew, we use an alternative construction to express the same thing:[7]

Shai is the **tall**est **student** in the class.   ‫1. שי הוא התלמיד הגבוה ביותר בכיתה.‬

The Dead Sea is the **low**est **place** on earth.   ‫2. ים המלח הוא המקום הנמוך ביותר בעולם.‬

In this construction, ‫ה-‬ is repeated twice, and then the word ‫ביותר‬ is added:

		‫בְּיוֹתֵר‬ ‫ה- + שם עצם + ה- + שם תואר‬			
		‫בְּיוֹתֵר‬	adjective + ‫ה-‬	‫ה- + noun‬	
m.s.:	‫בכיתה.‬	‫ביותר‬	‫הגבוה‬	‫התלמיד‬	‫שי הוא‬
f.s.:	‫בכיתה.‬	‫ביותר‬	‫הגבוהה‬	‫התלמידה‬	‫שרית היא‬
m.pl.:	‫בכיתה.‬	‫ביותר‬	‫הגבוהים‬	‫התלמידים‬	‫שי ורון הם‬
f.pl.:	‫בכיתה‬	‫ביותר‬	‫הגבוהות‬	‫התלמידות‬	‫שרית ותמר הן‬

Want to see if you've understood?

A. Translate using ‫הכי‬:

1. What is the longest river (‫נהר‬) in the world?

_____

2. This is the most boring movie (that) I have ever (‫אֵי פַעַם‬) seen.

_____

---

7   Other, more literary ways of expressing superlatives exist, but they are beyond the scope of this book.

3. You are the nicest person I've met at the university.

   _____

4. This is the funniest joke (בדיחה) I (m.) know.

   _____

5. Who are the most successful actors in Israel?

   _____

B. Translate the sentences above using ביותר...-ה...-ה.

   _____ 1.

   _____ 2.

   _____ 3.

   _____ 4.

   _____ 5.

Answers:

B	A
מה (מהו / מה הוא) הנהר הארוך ביותר בעולם?	1. מה (מהו / מה הוא) הנהר הכי ארוך בעולם?
זה (זהו) הסרט המשעמם ביותר שראיתי אֵי פעם.	2. זה (זהו) הסרט הכי משעמם שראיתי אֵי פעם.
אתה האדם הנחמד ביותר שפגשתי באוניברסיטה.	3. אתה האדם הכי נחמד שפגשתי באוניברסיטה.
זאת (זוהי / זו) הבדיחה המצחיקה ביותר שאני מכיר.	4. זאת (זוהי / זו) הבדיחה הכי מצחיקה שאני מכיר.
מי (הם) השחקנים המצליחים ביותר בישראל?	5. מי (הם) השחקנים הכי מצליחים בישראל?

Did you know?

Here are two other common uses of the words הכי and ביותר:

1. הכי *with a verb*

In informal Hebrew, speakers use הכי also with **verbs**, as in:

◄ מה אתה הכי **אוהב**?   What do you **like** the most?

מה שהכי **כואב** לה זה שבעלה לשעבר כבר לא מתקשר לילדים.

What **hurts** her the most is that her ex-husband doesn't call the children anymore.

מה שגיל הכי **רוצה** זה להיות עיתונאי.   What Gil wants the most is to be a journalist.

This usage is common especially with verbs that express emotions.

To express the opposite, we use הכי פחות:

◄ איזה מאכל אתה הכי פחות **אוהב**?   Which food do you **like** the least?

2. ביותר *without* ...ה-...ה-

ביותר is also used without ה-...ה-... to mean *very*, as in:

◄ זה **טעים** ביותר.   This is most (= very) **tasty**.

זה היה יום **מרגש** ביותר.   This has been a most (= very) **exciting** day.

Chapter summary

◆ When comparing things that are the same, we use forms of the word אותו (the same) followed by a noun:

◄ *noun* + אותו / אותה / אותם / אותן

אותו (ה)ספר   (*m.s.*)   the same book

אותה (ה)בחורה   (*f.s.*)   the same girl

אותם (ה)שירים   (*m.pl.*)   the same songs

אותן (ה)כוסות   (*f.pl.*)   the same glasses

◆ Hebrew uses יותר מ-/מאשר to say *more than* and פחות מ-/מאשר to say *less than* or *fewer than*.

◄ הספר שלי **מעניין** יותר מהספר שלך.   My book is more **interesting** than yours.

ארה"ב יותר **גדולה** מצרפת.   The U.S. is **larg**er than France.

השיעור היום פחות **מעניין** מהשיעור אתמול.

Today's lesson is less **interesting** than yesterday's.

◄ פחות **נוח** לנסוע באוטובוס מאשר ברכבת.

It is less **comfortable** to travel by bus than by train.

◆ We have examined the two most common ways of expressing *the most*:

- The informal ...הכי-...ה:

◄ שלומי הוא **הילד** הכי **גבוה** בכיתה.   Shlomi is the **tall**est **boy** in class.

- The more formal ביותר ...ה-...ה:

◄ שלומי הוא **הילד** **הגבוה** ביותר בכיתה.   Shlomi is the **tall**est **boy** in class.

Want to see if you've understood the chapter?
Translate.

1. Shlomi is taller than Oren. _____

2. This exercise is less difficult than the first exercise.

   _____

3. Your family's history is more interesting than my family's.

   _____

4. We (f.) are wearing the same dress. _____

5. What is the size (גודל) of the largest pizza in the world?

   _____

6. I keep on (כל הזמן) getting the same announcement (הודעה).

   _____

7. You are the smartest students (f.) in class.

   _____

Answers:

1. שלומי יותר גבוה (גבוה יותר) מאורן.
2. התרגיל הזה פחות קשה (קשה פחות) מהתרגיל הראשון.
3. ההיסטוריה של המשפחה שלך מעניינת יותר (יותר מעניינת) מההיסטוריה של המשפחה שלי.
4. אנחנו לובשות אותה שמלה.
5. מה (מהו / מה הוא) הגודל של הפיצה הכי גדולה בעולם? / מה (מהו / מה הוא) הגודל של הפיצה הגדולה ביותר בעולם?
6. אני כל הזמן מקבל/ת (את) אותה (ה)הודעה.
7. אתן התלמידות הכי חכמות בכיתה. / אתן התלמידות החכמות ביותר בכיתה.

PART TWO: VERBS

I. Patterns of Verbs:
The Seven *Beenyaneem* הַבִּנְיָינִים

Preview

- *Five* beenyaneem: pa'al,[1] neef'al, pee'el, heetpa'el, heef'eel
- *Two* beenyaneem *with* oo-ah *vowels:* poo'al, hoof'al

Introduction

In this chapter we will present an overview of the seven *beenyaneem*. We'll use the following passage as the basis of our discussion:

במשך חמש שנים – מגיל 10 עד גיל 15 – התכתב ילד ישראלי בשם דן עם ג'וש, ילד מארה"ב שדן מעולם לא פגש. דן כתב לג'וש על הלימודים בבית הספר, על החברים ועל המשפחה שלו. הוא סיפר לו סודות אישיים ולפעמים גם הסביר לו קצת על הפוליטיקה בישראל. כשדן היה בן 15, ג'וש הזמין אותו לבקר אצלו בארה"ב. דן התרגש מאוד לקראת הביקור. אחרי שדן נפגש עם ג'וש בביתו בארה"ב, הוא ביקש מג'וש לבוא לבקר אצלו בישראל. כשג'וש נפרד מדן, הוא הבטיח שהוא יבוא יום אחד לבקר אותו בארץ. וג'וש באמת הגיע – אבל רק 15 שנים אחר כך, כשהוא כבר נשוי ואב לשלושה ילדים.

For five years – from age ten to age fifteen – an Israeli boy named Dan corresponded with Josh, a boy from the U.S. whom Dan had never met. Dan wrote to Josh about his studies, about his friends and about his family. He told him personal secrets and sometimes also explained to him a bit about politics in Israel. When Dan was fifteen years old, Josh invited him to come visit him in the U.S. Dan was very excited about the upcoming visit. After Dan met with Josh at his home in the U.S., he asked Josh to come visit him in Israel. When Josh said goodbye to Dan, he promised that he would come one day to visit him in Israel. And – fifteen years later – Josh did come for a visit to Israel, as a married man and the father of three children.

The subject of each of the ten verbs highlighted above is either Dan or Josh, both of whom are males. For this reason, all ten verbs are **masculine** and **singular** (...הוא התכתב, הוא פגש). They

---

1   *Beenyan pa'al is often referred to as* beenyan kal *(קל).*

are also all in the **past tense**. We can group these ten verbs into five different groups – two in each group – according to their *pattern*.[2]

Try this:

Each column in the chart below is devoted to a different verb pattern. In each column we have listed a verb from the passage above.

Place the five remaining verbs from the passage in the appropriate columns below.

הִפְעִיל	הִתְפַּעֵל	פִּיעֵל	נִפְעַל	פָּעַל
הֻסְֻֻים	הִתֻֻֻ	ֻֻיֻ	נִֻֻֻ	ֻֻֻ
הִסְבִּיר	הִתְכַּתֵּב	סִיפֵּר	נִפְגַּשׁ	פָּגַשׁ
_____	_____	_____	_____	_____

Here's the solution:

הזמין	התרגש	ביקש	נפרד	כתב

Now let's substitute the letters פ-ע-ל for the *root* letters[3] of the past tense הוא forms listed in the chart above.

	הִפְעִיל	הִתְפַּעֵל	פִּיעֵל	נִפְעַל	פָּעַל
pronunciation:	heef-'EEL	heet-pa-'EL	pee-'EL	neef-'AL	pa-'AL
name:	*heef'eel*	*heetpa'el*	*pee'el*	*neef'al*	*pa'al*

The result is the **name** that we give to each verb group – called in Hebrew a **beenyan** (been-YAN, literally: *a building*). We have listed here the names of five of the seven *beenyaneem* in Hebrew.

The **past tense** הוא form (for example, כָּתַב), which we call the *past tense base form*, actually **represents** the full conjugation of the verb (in all tenses and forms).

---

2   See the chapter "Pattern," pp. 9-16.
3   On roots, see the chapter "Root," pp. 3-8.

Did you know?
The beenyan *as a collection of patterns*

The *past tense base form*, for example כָּתַב, represents not only all the past tense forms of this verb – כָּתַבְתָּ, כָּתַבְתִּי and so on, but also כּוֹתֵב and other present tense forms, יִכְתּוֹב and other future tense forms, לִכְתּוֹב – the infinitive – and כְּתוֹב – the imperative (command form). When we say that a verb like סָגַר is also in *beenyan pa'al* (פָּעַל), this means not only that סָגַר shares the same past tense base form as כָּתַב, but also that the forms of סָגַר in all the tenses are similar to those of כָּתַב.

Thus, when we speak of a *beenyan*, we are referring to a **collection** of all the patterns (past, present, future and imperative – in all persons – and the infinitive) that make up the full conjugation of a verb.

In this chapter we will examine the past tense base forms of all seven *beenyaneem*. We will limit the examples that we bring here to *regular* verbs (שְׁלֵמִים *shle-MEEM*), i.e., verbs whose root letters are present in all forms of the verb.[4] It should be noted that when we examine the conjugations of *special root groups* in later chapters, the **name** of each *beenyan* remains **fixed,** even if the base form of the verb does not exactly correspond to it (for example, קָם, whose root is ק-ו-מ, belongs to *beenyan pa'al* פָּעַל, even though its past tense base form contains only two letters).

Now let's look more closely at the past tense base form of regular verbs in each *beenyan*.

• *Five beenyaneem: pa'al, neef'al, pee'el, heetpa'el, heef'eel*

Beenyan pa'al פָּעַל

The past tense base form of *beenyan pa'al* (פָּגַשׁ, כָּתַב) has only **three** letters. No other letters are added to the root letters. The vowels of this form are ⇒ *a-A* (pronounced *ah-AH).*

---

4   Although we regard verbs with root letters that are *gutturals* – ע, 'ח ,ה, 'א – as a **subcategory of regular verbs** (שְׁלֵמִים), we will not deal with them in this chapter. On the forms of verbs with gutturals, see the unit "Verbs with Guttural Consonants," pp. 448-487.

Here are some more verbs that belong to *beenyan pa'al* (פָּעַל):

בדק	שמר	זכר	סגר
check[5]	guard / keep	remember	(to) close

Beenyan neef'al נִפְעַל

The past tense base form of *beenyan neef'al* always has the *prefix* -נ at the beginning: נִפְגַשׁ, נִפְרַד. The vowels of this form are *ee-A* (pronounced *ee-AH*).

Here are some more verbs that belong to *beenyan neef'al* (נִפְעַל):

נפגש	נפרד	נזכר	נכשל	נשאר
meet (with)	part (from)	recall	fail	(to) remain

Beenyan pee'el פִּיעֵל

The vowels of the past tense base form of *beenyan pee'el* are *ee-E* (pronounced *ee-EH*). In *standard spelling*, with vowel signs,[6] we write דִּבֵּר, סִפֵּר; in *full spelling* without vowel signs, we write these forms with an added י after the first root letter: דיבר, סיפר.[7]

Pee'el forms written with vowel signs always have a *dagesh* (dot) in the **middle** root letter.[8] This means that when the letters ב, כ, פ' appear in the middle of the root, they are pronounced *b* (ב), *k* (כ), *p* (פ). When this *dagesh* appears in other letters, it has no affect on their pronunciation in today's Hebrew.

Here are some more verbs that belong to *beenyan pee'el* (פִּיעֵל):

לימד	ביקר	קיבל	ביקש	חיפש	שיחק
teach	visit	receive/get	ask for/request	look for	(to) play (a game…)

Beenyan heetpa'el הִתְפַּעֵל

The past tense base form of *beenyan heetpa'el* begins with הת- (*heet-*): הִתְכַּתֵּב, הִתְרַגֵּשׁ. The vowels after the initial *heet-* are *a-E* (pronounced *ah-EH*). As in *beenyan pee'el*, here, too, the

---

5   We have given the translation of the infinitive form, since the past tense base forms given here **represent** all forms of the verb.

6   We are using the term *vowel signs* to denote all vowel signs and diacritical marks such as *dagesh*.

7   For rules of full spelling, see the chapter "Hebrew Spelling," pp. 654-669.

8   Except when the middle letter is א, ה, ח, ע, ר'. For more on this, see the chapter "Guttural Consonants and ר': *Beenyaneem Pee'el, Poo'al* and *Neef'al*," pp. 474-487.

middle root letter has a *dagesh* (dot) in texts written with vowel signs, so that when the letters ב, כ, פ appear in the middle of the root, they are pronounced *b* (ב), *k* (כ), *p* (פ).[9]

Here are some more verbs that belong to *beenyan heetpa'el* (הִתְפַּעֵל):

	התלבש	התרחץ	התפלל	התנדב	התקדם
≺	get dressed	get washed	pray	volunteer	(to) progress

Beenyan heef'eel הִפְעִיל

The past base form of *beenyan heef'eel* begins with הִ- (*hee*) that is attached to the first letter of the root. Here you can see the division of this form into its two syllables:

	הִזְ־מִין	הִסְ־בִּיר	
	heez-MEEN	*hees-BEER*	≺
	(to) invite, order	explain	

Notice that even though **no** י is written in the first syllable, the vowel sound is *ee*. This same vowel sound repeats in the second syllable, where a י **does** appear.[10]

Here are more verbs that belong to *beenyan heef'eel* (הִפְעִיל):

	הקשיב	הסכים	הפסיק	המשיך	הדליק	הרגיש
≺	(to) listen	agree	stop	continue	light	feel

Two beenyaneem *with* oo-A *vowels:* poo'al, hoof'al

There are two more *beenyaneem*, both of which have the vowels *oo-A* (pronounced *oo-AH*).

In the following collection, past tense base forms of verbs from both of these *beenyaneem* are mixed together.

---

9 There are a few cases in which there is no *dagesh*, e.g., לְהִתְחַבֵּר (*le-heet-cha-VER*) =*to become friends with*, as opposed to לְהִתְחַבֵּר (*le-heet-cha-BER*) =*to join*. The first verb keeps the sound *v* as in the noun חָבֵר (=friend).

10 See the chapter "Hebrew Spelling," pp. 657-660, 664 for an explanation of when a י is and is not added to indicate the *ee* vowel sound.

Try this:

List each of the above verbs under the name of its *beenyan*. Remember: the name of the *beenyan* looks and sounds like the past base form of the verbs in that *beenyan*.

<table>
<tr><td align="center">*hoof'al* הוּפְעַל</td><td align="center">*poo'al* פּוּעַל</td></tr>
<tr><td>_____</td><td>_____</td></tr>
<tr><td>_____</td><td>_____</td></tr>
<tr><td>_____</td><td>_____</td></tr>
</table>

Here's the solution:

The two groups are:

hoof'al הוּפְעַל		*poo'al* פּוּעַל	
was felt	הורגש	was told	סופר
was made earlier	הוקדם	was broadcast	שודר
was invited, ordered	הוזמן	was treated	טופל

These two *beenyaneem* – *poo'al* and *hoof'al* – are usually learned after the first five *beenyaneem*.

Beenyan poo'al פּוּעַל

The past tense base form of *beenyan poo'al* begins with its **first root letter**: סוּפַר, שוּדַּר, טוּפַּל. In full spelling, as shown here, this first root letter is immediately followed by a 'ו, which indicates the first of its vowels: *oo-AH* (in standard spelling with vowel signs there is no 'ו: סֻפַּר, שֻׁדַּר, טֻפַּל). As in *pee'el* and *heetpa'el*, here, too, the middle root letter has a *dagesh* (dot) in standard spelling with vowel signs, so that when the letters ב, כ', פ' appear in the middle of the root, they are pronounced *b* (ב), *k* (כ), *p* (פ).

Here are some more verbs that belong to *beenyan poo'al* (פּוּעַל):

צוייר	פוטר	◄
(to be) drawn	fired	
	(from work)	

Beenyan hoof'al הוּפְעַל

The past tense base form of *beenyan hoof'al* also contains the vowels *oo-AH*:

הוּזְמַן	הוּקְדַם	הוּרְגַש ◄
hooz-MAN	*hook-DAM*	*hoor-GASH*

Q: How does this form differ from the past tense base form of *beenyan poo'al:* שוּדַּר, סוּפַּר, טוּפַּל?

A: The *hoof'al* forms begin – in full spelling – with הו (in standard spelling: הֻרְגַש, הֻקְדַם, הֻזְמַן). The -הו prefix comes **before** the first root letter. Note the two syllables in each of the forms:

הוּז-מַן	הוּק-דַם	הוּר-גַש ◄
hooz-MAN	*hook-DAM*	*hoor-GASH*

In contrast, there is **no prefix** added to the *poo'al* forms. They begin with their first root letter:

טו-פַּל¹¹	שו-דַּר	סו-פַּר ◄
too-PAL	*shoo-DAR*	*soo-PAR*

Here are some more verbs that belong to *beenyan hoof'al* (הוּפְעַל):

הוסכם	הולבש	הופסק ◄
(to be) agreed	dressed (by someone)	stopped

Let's review

♦ There are seven *beenyaneem* (בְּנְיָינִים) in Hebrew. Each *beenyan* is actually a **collection** of the *patterns* (past, present, future and imperative – in all persons – and infinitive) that make up the full conjugation of a verb. The name of each *beenyan* is created by plugging the root פ-ע-ל into its **past tense הוא** pattern.

♦ Here are the names and a model verb from each *beenyan*.

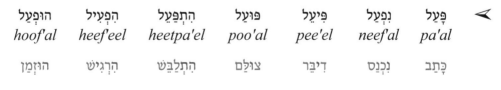

הוּפְעַל	הִפְעִיל	הִתְפַּעֵל	פּוּעַל	פִּיעֵל	נִפְעַל	פָּעַל ◄
hoof'al	*heef'eel*	*heetpa'el*	*poo'al*	*pee'el*	*neef'al*	*pa'al*
הוּזְמַן	הִרְגִיש	הִתְלַבֵּש	צוּלַם	דִיבֵּר	נִכְנַס	כָּתַב

---

11 We have divided the syllables here according to the way in which they are pronounced. The division according to traditional grammar rules is: סוּפ-פַּר, שוּד-דַּר, טוּפ-פַּל (with a doubled middle root letter).

Want to see if you've understood?

Next to each of the following verbs write the name of its *beenyan*.

.9 הוכנס _____		.1 גדל _____	
.10 חובר _____		.2 הסביר _____	
.11 טיפל _____		.3 נכשל _____	
.12 נזכר _____		.4 שיקר _____	
.13 סגר _____		.5 התרגש _____	
.14 התרגל _____		.6 נישק _____	
.15 הדליק _____		.7 נפרד _____	
.16 שולם _____		.8 הולבש _____	

Answers:

1. פעל   2. הפעיל   3. נפעל   4. פיעל   5. התפעל   6. פיעל   7. נפעל   8. הופעל   9. הופעל   10. פועל
11. פיעל   12. נפעל   13. פעל   14. התפעל   15. הפעיל   16. פועל

II. Signs of Tenses and Forms: Past, Present, Future and Infinitive

Preview

- *Signs of the present tense*   הוֹוֶה
- *Signs of the past tense*   עָבָר
- *Signs of the infinitive*   שֵׁם הַפּוֹעַל
- *Signs of the future tense*   עָתִיד

In this chapter we will look at the characteristic signs of the three tenses and of the infinitive in all the *beenyaneem*.

• *Signs of the present tense*   הוֹוֶה

Read the following sentences in the present tense:

I (*m.s.*) get up at 6 a.m.	אני קָם ב-6:00 בבוקר. ◄
You (*m.s.*) get up at 7 a.m.	אתה קָם ב-7:00 בבוקר.
He gets up at 8 a.m.	הוא קָם ב-8:00 בבוקר.

Each of these sentences begins with a different masculine singular pronoun (הוא and אני, אתה).

Q: Do you see a difference between the verb forms used with these pronouns?

A: No. As in the case of adjectives (אני עייף / אתה עייף / הוא עייף, for example), there is only **one** present tense verb form for the masculine singular. Similarly, there is only one form for the feminine singular (אני, את, היא), one for the masculine plural (אנחנו, אתם, הם) and one for the feminine plural (אנחנו, אתן, הן).

In the following chart, you can see all four present tense forms of the verb לקום (to get up). Next to them are the four forms of the verb לכתוב (to write):

לכתוב	לקום				
כּוֹתֵב ko-TEV	קָם KAM	(m.s.)	הוא he	אתה, you	אני, I
כּוֹתֶבֶת ko-TE-vet	קָמָה KA-ma / ka-MA[1]	(f.s.)	היא she	את, you	אני, I
כּוֹתְבִים kot-VEEM	קָמִים ka-MEEM	(m.pl.)	הם they	אתם, you	אנחנו, we
כּוֹתְבוֹת kot-VOT	קָמוֹת ka-MOT	(f.pl.)	הן they	אתן, you	אנחנו, we

Q: In what way do the masculine singular forms in the first row (קם, כותב) differ from all the other forms?

A: They have **no endings** added to them.

We shall call the masculine singular form the ***present tense base form***. The other forms are created by adding an ending (*suffix*) to the base form.

Q: What are the endings on the feminine singular forms?

A: We see the ending ה- (*-AH*) on קָמָה and ת- (*-t*) on כּותבת. These are the two possible endings of feminine singular verbs. As we look at each *beenyan* in the following chapters, we will note which of these two endings is used in the feminine singular form in the present tense of each of them.

The ending of the masculine plural present tense form is always ים- (כותבים, קמים); the ending of the feminine plural is always וֹת- (כותבות, קמות). These endings are always **stressed**.

Once we have established the present tense base form of any regular verb and have learned whether its feminine ending is ה- or ת-, it is relatively simple to learn its entire present tense conjugation. Here are some examples:

The conjugation of the verb whose present tense base form is מְדַבֵּר is:

◄ מְדַבֵּר, מְדַבֶּרֶת, מְדַבְּרִים, מְדַבְּרוֹת

---

1 According to the rules of grammar, the ה- (*-a*) ending in present tense verbs is **stressed**, as in מַרְגִּישָׁה (*mar-gee-SHA* – she feels) and רוֹצָה (*ro-TSA* – she wants). Thus the pronunciation of קָמָה should be *ka-MA*. Most Israeli speakers of Hebrew pronounce this word and other verbs of this group with the stress on the first syllable – *KA-ma* – just like the past tense היא form.

The conjugation of the verb whose present tense base form is מִתְלַבֵּשׁ is:

◄ מִתְלַבֵּשׁ,‏ מִתְלַבֶּשֶׁת,‏ מִתְלַבְּשִׁים,‏ מִתְלַבְּשׁוֹת

The conjugation of the verb whose present tense base form is מַרְגִּישׁ is:

◄ מַרְגִּישׁ,‏ מַרְגִּישָׁה,‏ מַרְגִּישִׁים,‏ מַרְגִּישׁוֹת

Let's review

◆ Each *beenyan* has its own *present tense base form*: the **masculine singular** (הוא) form.

◆ Present tense verbs in all *beenyaneem* are formed by adding one of the following sets of **endings** to the base form:

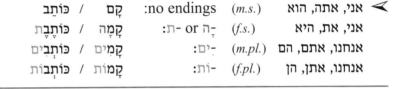

◄ אני, אתה, הוא	(*m.s.*)	:no endings	קָם / כּוֹתֵב
אני, את, היא	(*f.s.*)	‎-ָה or ‎-ת:	קָמָה / כּוֹתֶבֶת
אנחנו, אתם, הם	(*m.pl.*)	‎-ִים:	קָמִים / כּוֹתְבִים
אנחנו, אתן, הן	(*f.pl.*)	‎-וֹת:	קָמוֹת / כּוֹתְבוֹת

For exercises on verb forms in each of the tenses and *beenyaneem*, see the chapters on each *beenyan*.

• *Signs of the past tense* עָבָר

As discussed in the previous chapter, each of the *beenyaneem* has a *past tense base form* (the הוא form), upon which the name of the *beenyan* is based.

The following is the full conjugation of a past tense verb. We have chosen to use the verb לקום in this sample conjugation because its base form (קָם) does not undergo major changes as we move from form to form.[2] (The changes that take place in the past tense base forms of other verbs will be discussed in the following chapters on each *beenyan*.)

---

2   The minor change of the vowel *kamatz* ◻ to *patach* ◻ in this conjugation **does not** cause a change in pronunciation.

		plural				singular	
I	אני:	קָמְתִי	KAM-tee	אנחנו:	קָמְנוּ	KAM-noo	
II	אתה:	קָמְתָ	KAM-ta	אתם:	קָמְתֶם	KAM-tem[3]	
	את:	קָמְתְ	KAMT	אתן:	קָמְתֶן	KAM-ten	
III	הוא	**קָם**	KAM	הם, הן	קָמוּ	KA-moo	
	היא	קָמָה	KA-ma				

As you can see, in the past tense almost every pronoun (אני, אתה...) has its own special form.

Q: In what way is the base form (קָם) different from all the other forms?

A: The other forms all have endings (suffixes).

Let's look more closely now at the endings added above to the base form **קָם**. They are fairly easy to remember because most of them rhyme with or sound like their pronoun's ending. We'll start with the "upper part" (the first and second *persons*)[4] of the conjugation:

		plural רבים			singular יחיד	
I	אני:	תִי-	(-tee)	אנחנו:	נוּ-	(-noo)
II	אתה:	תָ-	(-ta)	אתם:	תֶם-	(-tem)
	את:	תְ-	(-t)	אתן:	תֶן-	(-ten)

Q: Do these endings **begin** with a consonant or a vowel?

A: They all begin with a consonant. Most begin with the consonant *t* (ת), while one (-noo נו-) begins with the consonant *n*.

In modern Israeli pronunciation, none of these endings is stressed. In addition, it should be noted that the ending on the אתה form of the verb is written תָ-, **without** a final 'ה: אתה קמת ('a-TA KAM-ta).

Now let's look at the endings in the "bottom part" (the third person forms) of the conjugation:

		plural רבים			singular יחיד	
III	הוא:	----		הם, הן:	וּ-	(-oo)
	היא:	ָה-	(-a)			

---

3   Traditionally, קָמְתֶם and קָמְתֶן are pronounced with the stress on the end: *kam-TEM / kam-TEN*. Most Israelis, however, place the stress on the first syllable: *KAM-tem / KAM-ten*.

4   For an explanation of the term *persons*, see the chapter "Pronouns and Pointing Words," pp. 204-205.

Q: Do these endings (-ָה and ו-) also begin with a consonant?

A: No, unlike the other endings, these begin with – and consist of – only a vowel. The היא ending is -*a* (indicated by -ָה), and the ending shared by הם and הן is -*oo* (indicated by ו-).

Whether an ending begins with a consonant or vowel has no effect on the pronunciation of forms of the verb לקום; however, in many verbs, this distinction is very significant. Its effect will be discussed in the chapters on the individual *beenyaneem*.

All the endings added to קם above are the **same endings** that we add to any past tense base form, no matter what its *beenyan*. Here are some examples:

	endings beg. with a vowel			endings beginning with a consonant					
	הם, הן	היא	הוא	אתן	אתם	אנחנו	את	אתה	אני
model verb:	קָמוּ	קָמָה,	**קָם,**	קַמְתֶן,	קַמְתֶם,	קַמְנוּ,	קַמְתְ,	קַמְתָ,	קַמְתִי,
beenyan pee'el:	דִיבְּרוּ	דִיבְּרָה,	**דִיבֵּר,**	דִיבַּרְתֶן,	דִיבַּרְתֶם,	דִיבַּרְנוּ,	דִיבַּרְתְ,	דִיבַּרְתָ,	דִיבַּרְתִי,
beenyan pa'al:	כָּתְבוּ	כָּתְבָה,	**כָּתַב,**	כְּתַבְתֶן,	כְּתַבְתֶם,[5]	כָּתַבְנוּ,	כָּתַבְתְ,	כָּתַבְתָ,	כָּתַבְתִי,

---

Did you know?
Habitual action in the past (he used to, he would...) (היה + הווה)

Although past tense verb forms are those usually used to convey something that happened or "was" in the past, we **sometimes** use a different form to emphasize the **habitual** nature of a past action. This form consists of a past tense form of היה followed by a present tense verb form, as in:[6]

היה + הווה
כשהייתי קטנה, הייתי הולכת לבית הספר ברגל.
When I was little, I used to walk to school.

בכל פעם שהילדים היו מבקשים מאימא לקנות משהו, היא היתה אומרת להם: "לא עכשיו".
Every time the children would ask Mother to buy something, she would (used to) say to them: "Not now!"

---

5   In the אתם and אתן forms, we have presented the form that reflects the pronunciation of most speakers today. According to the rules of grammar, the stress in these forms should be on the final syllable. In *regular* verbs in *beenyan pa'al* only, the stress on the final syllable causes a change in the vowel of the first syllable: כְּתַבְתֶם, כְּתַבְתֶן.

6   This construction (היה followed by a present tense verb form) is also used to convey other meanings, such as "I would like..." (הייתי רוצה...), "You would go / would have gone..." (היית הולך...). On its use in certain conditional sentences, see the chapter "What If?: Conditional Sentences," pp. 996-1002.

Let's review

◆ Except for the הוא form (=the *base form*), all verbs in the past tense have endings.

		plural			*singular*			
-noo	קַמְנוּ	אנחנו:		*-tee*	קַמְתִּי	אני:	I	◄
-tem	קַמְתֶּם	אתם:		*-ta*	קַמְתָּ	אתה:	II	
-ten	קַמְתֶּן	אתן:		*-t*	קַמְתְּ	את:		
-oo	קָמוּ	הם, הן		---	**קָם**	הוא	III	
				-a	קָמָה	היא		

All the endings in the "upper part" of the conjugation (the first and second persons) begin with a consonant (*t* or *n*), whereas in the "lower part" (the third person) the endings consist of a vowel alone (*a* and *oo*).

• Signs of the infinitive שֵׁם הַפּוֹעַל

Here are some infinitives of different verbs:

לְהִתְלַבֵּשׁ	לְדַבֵּר	לִכְתּוֹב	לָקוּם	◄
to get dressed	to speak	to write	to get up	

Q: What do all these infinitive forms have in common?

A: They all begin with -לְ.

The vowel sound after the initial -לְ differs from *beenyan* to *beenyan* and sometimes within the same *beenyan*, as you will see in the following chapters.

As we will also see in the following chapters, Hebrew has two *beenyaneem* that are always passive – *beenyan poo'al* and *beenyan hoof'al*. These *beenyaneem* have **no** infinitive form.

• Signs of the future tense עָתִיד

Here are examples of the base form (הוא) of the future tense:

יִתְלַבֵּשׁ	יְדַבֵּר	יִכְתּוֹב	יָקוּם	◄

Q: What do all of these forms have in common?

A: They all **begin** with the letter יְ.

Let's take the first verb – יָקוּם – and compare it to the other forms of this verb that we have learned:

		present	past	infinitive
◄	הוא	קָם	קָם	לָקוּם

Q: Which of these forms does יָקוּם most resemble?

A: יָקוּם looks and sounds most like the infinitive לָקוּם.

Now let's compare יִכְתוֹב to the other forms we have learned:

		present	past	infinitive
◄	הוא	כּוֹתֵב	כָּתַב	לִכְתוֹב

Here, too, the future base form יִכְתוֹב resembles the infinitive לִכְתוֹב.

In all the *beenyaneem* that have infinitive forms (i.e., in all but *poo'al* and *hoof'al*) there is a striking resemblance between the **infinitive** and the **future tense base form**. We will examine this resemblance in more detail in the following chapters on the individual *beenyaneem*.

Prefixes and endings in the future tense

Now let's look at the full conjugation of the future tense.

	plural רבים			*singular* יחיד			
na-KOOM	נָקוּם	אנחנו:	'a-KOOM	אָקוּם	אני:	I	◄
ta-KOO-moo	תָקוּמוּ	אתם, אתן:	ta-KOOM	תָקוּם	אתה:	II	
			ta-KOO-mee	תָקוּמִי	את:		
ya-KOO-moo	יָקוּמוּ	הם, הן	ya-KOOM	יָקוּם	הוא	III	
			ta-KOOM	תָקוּם	היא		

As you can see, all verbs in the future tense have *prefixes* added onto the front of their first root letter, while some forms have **both** prefixes and endings (suffixes). The function of the prefixes and endings in the future tense conjugation is to make every form **different** from every other form.[7]

---

7   Although this is true in principle, it does not work in the case of the היא form (תָקוּם), which is the same as the אתה form (תָקוּם), as we will see below.

First person forms (אני, אנחנו)

In the אני form, we replace the **prefix** of the future tense base form יָקוּם with -אָ to create אָקוּם. The prefix of this form corresponds to the first letter of אני. The אנחנו form נָקוּם uses the -נ of אנחנו as its prefix. There is no need for an ending to be added in order to differentiate between these two forms.

Second person forms (אתה, את, אתם, אתן)

All second person future tense forms have the prefix -ת, a letter that appears in all the second person pronouns: אתה, את, אתם, אתן. In order to differentiate between the masculine and feminine singular forms, -י (-ee) is added to the end of the feminine form.

ta-KOOM	תָקוּם	אתה:	◄
ta-KOO-mee	תָקוּמִי	את:	

The two plural forms, both masculine אתם and feminine אתן, are differentiated from the other forms by adding the ending -ו (-oo):

ta-KOO-moo	תָקוּמוּ	אתם, אתן:[8]	◄

Third person forms (הוא, היא, הם, הן)

As we saw above, the הוא form begins with -י: יָקוּם.

And how is this made plural?

We add the ending -ו (-oo). The result is יָקוּמוּ. This serves as the form of both the masculine הם and the feminine הן in Modern Hebrew.[9]

Now, what about the feminine singular היא form?

Look at the chart above.

---

8   Biblical Hebrew uses the ending -נָה on the end of the אתן form: תָקֹמְנָה. In Modern Hebrew, this form is used mainly in very formal contexts and in literary Hebrew.

9   Biblical Hebrew has a different form for הן: תָקֹמְנָה. This is the same form as that used for אתן. It is used today in very formal contexts and in literary Hebrew.

Q: Do we add the ending ‏‎ִי‎ to make the ‏הוא‎ form feminine?

A: No! Unexpectedly, to create this form we change only the prefix:

הוא   יָקוּם

⇓

היא   תָקוּם

Q: Where have we seen this form before?

A: It is the **same** as the ‏אתה‎ form!: ‏אתה תָקוּם / היא תָקוּם‎.[10]

Learning the future tense forms

The above division into persons affords us the best view of the future prefixes and endings and their connection to their respective pronouns (‏אני, אתה‎...). Now we would like to suggest an alternative way to learn the forms. This time we will arrange them in two groups according to the way they are formed: those with **only** a prefix and those with **both** a prefix and an ending.

prefix and ending	*only prefix*	
	אָקוּם	אני:
	תָקוּם	אתה:
		את:
תָקוּמִי	יָקוּם	הוא:
	תָקוּם	היא:
	נָקוּם	אנחנו:
תָקוּמוּ		אתם, אתן:
יָקוּמוּ		הם, הן:

Here is a comparison between the future tense of ‏לקום‎ and of two verbs with different bases. If you look down the column of each pronoun, you can see that the letter prefixed to each of the bases is the same, though the vowels of the prefixes are different. The endings are always the same.

		prefixes and endings				*only prefixes*				
	הם, הן	אתם, אתן	את	אנחנו	היא	הוא	אתה	אני		
model verb:	יָקוּמוּ	תָקוּמוּ,	תָקוּמִי,	נָקוּם	תָקוּם,	יָקוּם,	תָקוּם,	אָקוּם,	לָקוּם:	
beenyan pee'el:	יְדַבְּרוּ	תְדַבְּרוּ,	תְדַבְּרִי,	נְדַבֵּר	תְדַבֵּר,	יְדַבֵּר,	תְדַבֵּר,	אֲדַבֵּר,	לְדַבֵּר:	
beenyan pa'al:	יִכְתְבוּ	תִכְתְבוּ,	תִכְתְבִי,	נִכְתוֹב	תִכְתוֹב,	יִכְתוֹב,	תִכְתוֹב,	אֶכְתוֹב,	לִכְתוֹב:	

---

10 Perhaps we can think of this ‏ת‎- on the beginning of the ‏היא‎ form as the same sign of the feminine singular that appears on the end of nouns such as ‏מחברת‎ (notebook) and on feminine verb forms like ‏כותבת‎ (writes). If so, the fact that the ‏אתה‎ and ‏היא‎ forms are the same is simply coincidental.

Let's review

♦ The infinitive and future tense base form are usually similar, for example:

שם הפועל		הוא
לָקוּם	⇔	יָקוּם
לִכְתוֹב	⇔	יִכְתוֹב
לְדַבֵּר	⇔	יְדַבֵּר

♦ Some future tense forms have **only** a prefix. Others have a prefix **and** an ending:

	prefix and ending	*only prefix*	
אֲנִי:		_____ א	
אַתָּה:		_____ ת	
אַתְּ:	י _____ ת		
הוּא:		_____ י	
הִיא:		_____ ת	
אֲנַחְנוּ:		_____ נ	
אַתֶּם, אַתֶּן:	וּ_____ ת		
הֵם, הֵן:	וּ_____ י		

Chapter summary

Here are the prefixes and suffixes of all three tenses and the infinitive:

שם הפועל ♦ infinitive	עתיד ♦ future	עבר ♦ past	הווה ♦ present		
לָקוּם	אָקוּם	קַמְתִּי	כּוֹתֵב, כּוֹתֶבֶת /	קָם, קָמָה /	אֲנִי:
	תָּקוּם	קַמְתָּ	כּוֹתֵב	קָם	אַתָּה:
	תָּקוּמִי	קַמְתְּ	כּוֹתֶבֶת	קָמָה	אַתְּ:
	יָקוּם	קָם	כּוֹתֵב	קָם	הוּא:
	תָּקוּם	קָמָה	כּוֹתֶבֶת	קָמָה	הִיא:
נָקוּם	קַמְנוּ	כּוֹתְבִים, כּוֹתְבוֹת /	קָמִים, קָמוֹת /	אֲנַחְנוּ:
	תָּקוּמוּ	קַמְתֶּם	כּוֹתְבִים	קָמִים	אַתֶּם:
	תָּקוּמוּ	קַמְתֶּן	כּוֹתְבוֹת	קָמוֹת	אַתֶּן:
	יָקוּמוּ	קָמוּ	כּוֹתְבִים	קָמִים	הֵם:
	יָקוּמוּ	קָמוּ	כּוֹתְבוֹת	קָמוֹת	הֵן:

You will find exercises on the various tenses in the following chapters.

III. Regular Verbs in the Seven *Beenyaneem* הַשְׁלֵמִים

Introduction

In the next chapters we will take a closer look at each one of the seven *beenyaneem*. We will examine the conjugations of ***regular*** verbs in each *beenyan*: in the present tense, the past tense and the future tense. We will also look at the infinitive form.[1]

As part of our presentation of regular verbs (שְׁלֵמִים – those whose root letters remain present in all forms), we will point out changes in the pronunciation of the consonants 'ב (*b/v*), 'כ (*k/ch*) and 'פ (*p/f*). The effect of the *guttural* consonants – 'א ,ה ,ח ,ע' – on pronunciation will be discussed in a separate unit.[2]

Verbs with four-letter roots (מְרוּבָּעִים), which can appear in three of the *beenyaneem* (*pe'el, poo'al* and *heetpa'el*), are presented at the end of each of the relevant chapters.

In the chapters in this section, we will present the seven *beenyaneem* in the following order:

1. *Beenyan Pee'el*	פִּיעֵל
2. *Beenyan Pa'al* [3]	פָּעַל
3. *Beenyan Heetpa'el*	הִתְפַּעֵל
4. *Beenyan Heef'eel*	הִפְעִיל
5. *Beenyan Neef'al*	נִפְעַל
6. *Beenyan Poo'al*	פּוּעַל
7. *Beenyan Hoof'al*	הוּפְעַל

8. Regular Verbs in All *Beenyaneem*: Summary

---

1   The imperative (command form) will be dealt with separately.
2   See the unit "Verbs with Guttural Consonants," pp. 448-487.
3   *Beenyan pa'al* is often referred to as *beenyan kal* (קל).

1. Beenyan Pee'el פִּיעֵל

Preview

- *Present tense* (מְדַבֵּר)
- *Past tense* (דִּיבֵּר)
- *Infinitive* (לְדַבֵּר)
- *Future tense* (יְדַבֵּר)
- *The pronunciation of* 'ב', כ', פ *when they are the first root letter* (בִּיקֵר, לְבַקֵר)
- *Verbs whose first or second root letter is* 'י (יִיבֵּש, טִייֵל)
- *Roots with four letters* (תִּרְגֵם) מְרוּבָּעִים

The verb דִּיבֵּר / לְדַבֵּר will serve as our model of a *regular* verb in *beenyan pee'el*.

• *Present tense* (מְדַבֵּר)

Here are the present tense forms of the verb דִּיבֵּר:

אני, אתה, הוא	(m.s.):	מְדַבֵּר	me-da-BER[1]
אני, את, היא	(f.s.):	מְדַבֶּרֶת	me-da-BE-ret
אנחנו, אתם, הם	(m.pl.):	מְדַבְּרִים	me-dab-REEM[2]
אנחנו, אתן, הן	(f.pl.):	מְדַבְּרוֹת	me-dab-ROT

Q: What *prefix* appears at the beginning of all present tense *pee'el* forms (before the root ד-ב-ר)?

A: All the forms begin with מְ (*me*) (pronounced *meh*):

מְדַבֵּר,   מְדַבֶּרֶת,   מְדַבְּרִים,   מְדַבְּרוֹת

---

1   We have transcribed and divided the syllables according to the pronunciation of speakers of Modern Hebrew. The traditional syllable division is different: *me/dab-BER*.

2   We have chosen to present the syllable division as noted above. However, another possible syllable division of this specific verb is: *me-da-BREEM*, *me-da-BROT*. In the past and future tenses, as well, we will examine forms that have two possible ways of dividing their syllables, for example: דיברה (*deeb-RA* or *dee-BRA*), ידברו (*ye-dab-ROO* or *ye-da-BROO*).

Another characteristic common to all the forms of מְדַבֵּר is the *hard* pronunciation of the 'ב (pronounced *b*) in the middle of the word (מְדַבֵּר *me-da-BER*). As we mentioned in the chapter "Patterns of Verbs" (p. 364), when we write with vowel signs there is always a *dagesh*[3] (dot) in the **middle** root letter of verbs in this *beenyan*. This *dagesh* is part of the **pattern** of the *beenyan*. Thus, when the letters 'ב, כ', פ appear in the middle of the root, they are pronounced *b* (ב), *k* (כ), *p* (פ), as in:

מְסַפֵּר	מְסַכֵּם	מְדַבֵּר ◄
me-sa-PER	*me-sa-KEM*	*me-da-BER*
he is telling	he is summarizing	he is speaking

Adding endings

The *base form* מְדַבֵּר has three syllables: מְ-דַ-בֵּר (*me-da-BER*). In order to form the feminine singular form, we add the ending תֶ- (*E-et*) to this base form. The result is: מְ-דַ-בֶּ-רֶת (*me-da-BE-ret*).

In the plural forms, the stress moves to the last syllable (and the syllable division changes):

מְ-דַבְּ-רוֹת	מְ-דַבְּ-רִים ◄
me-dab-ROT	*me-dab-REEM*

If we compare the plural forms to the base form מְדַבֵּר (*me-da-BER*), we see that the vowel after the 'ב (□ *eh*) changes and is written as a *shva* (□). In today's Hebrew, this *shva* is usually not pronounced.[4]

Want to see if you've understood?
Write the correct present tense form of the missing verb.

1. אתה <u>מחפש</u> עבודה חדשה?

גם את _____ עבודה?

אם אתם _____ עבודה, הגעתם למקום הנכון!

---

3   This is a *strong dagesh* (דָּגֵשׁ חָזָק) (see the chapter "The Pronunciation of ב', כ', פ' and the *Dagesh*," pp. 630-633). This *dagesh* does not appear in the letters א', ה', ח', ע', ר'. For more on this, see the chapter "Guttural Consonants: *Pee'el, Poo'al* and *Neef'al*," pp. 474-487. Note: In the answers to the exercises, we have written a strong *dagesh* only where it affects the pronunciation (i.e., in ב', כ', פ').

4   This change to *shva* is called *vowel reduction*. See the chapter "Reduction of Vowels and the *Shva*," pp. 640-653. In traditional pronunciation, a *shva* like the one in מְדַבְּרִים is pronounced *eh*, e.g., *me-da-be-REEM*. In today's pronunciation this *shva* is pronounced *eh* only in rare cases, e.g., when the last two letters of the root are identical, for example: מְחַמְּמִים (*me-cha-me-MEEM*), מְבָרְרִים (*me-va-re-REEM*).

2. מירי <u>מסדרת</u> את החדר כל יום.

רון _____ את החדר פעם בשבוע.

מירי ושרה _____ את החדר פעמיים בשבוע.

Answers:[5]

1. אֶת מְחַפֶּשֶׂת, אַתֶם מְחַפְּשִׂים   2. רוֹן מְסַדֵּר, מירי ושרה מְסַדְרוֹת

• *Past tense* (דִּיבֵּר)

Here are the past tense forms of the verb דִּיבֵּר:

	plural			singular		
dee-BAR-noo	דִּיבַּרְנוּ	אנחנו:	dee-BAR-tee	דִּיבַּרְתִּי	אני:	◄
dee-BAR-tem[6]	דִּיבַּרְתֶּם	אתם:	dee-BAR-ta	דִּיבַּרְתָּ	אתה:	
dee-BAR-ten	דִּיבַּרְתֶּן	אתן:	dee-BART	דִּיבַּרְתְּ	את:	
deeb-ROO	דִּיבְּרוּ	הם, הן	dee-BER	**דִּיבֵּר**	הוא	
			deeb-RA	דִּיבְּרָה	היא	

Q: Do these forms have a prefix (an addition **before** the first root letter ד')?

A: No. All past tense forms in *beenyan pee'el* **begin** with the first root letter (ד' in this case).

Q: Which vowel comes after the first root letter?[7]

A: In *beenyan pee'el*, the vowel after the first root letter is *ee* in all past tense forms.[8] When we write in *full spelling* without vowel signs, we write a י' after the **first** root letter: דיבר, דיברתי.... This is the sign that distinguishes *pee'el* past tense verbs from those of other *beenyaneem*.[9]

---

5   It is not necessary for you to write vowel signs in your answers. We have added vowel signs to the answers in the chapters on verbs in order to make clear how the forms are pronounced.

6   This is the pronunciation used by most Hebrew speakers today. In traditional pronunciation, the stress is on the ending of the אתם and אתן forms: *dee-bar-TEM, dee-bar-TEN*.

7   For the sake of simplicity, we are using the term *letter* instead of *consonant*, which is the correct way to refer to a **sound**.

8   As noted in the introduction to this chapter, we are not dealing in this chapter with roots that contain guttural consonants (א', ה', ח', ע'). On the changes in pronunciation that these consonants cause, see the chapter "Guttural Consonants and ר': *Pee'el, Poo'al* and *Neef'al*," pp. 474-487.

9   Past tense verbs with four-letter roots (e.g., תרגם *teer-GEM* – he translated) are **not** written with a י' after the first letter. For an explanation, see below the section on "Roots with four letters," p. 389.

Third person forms (הוא, היא, הם, הן)

Let's begin with the base form (הוא), focusing now on the vowel after the **middle** root letter: דִּבֵּר (*dee-BER*).

Q: What happens to this *eh* vowel in the other third person forms (היא and הם/הן) when the endings are added?

◄	הוא:	דִּבֵּר	*dee-BER*
		⇓	⇓
	היא:	דִּבְּרָה	*deeb-RA*
	הם/הן:	דִּבְּרוּ	*deeb-ROO*

A: The ◻ (*eh*) becomes a *shva* (◻), which is usually not pronounced.

As we saw previously, in the chapter "Signs of Tenses and Forms" (pp. 372-373), the endings on the היא and the הם/הן forms are vowels: *-AH* (in *deeb-RA*) and *-OO* (in *deeb-ROO*). In many *beenyaneem*, including *pee'el*, when the ending is a vowel, the stress moves to the ending and the vowel before it "reduces" (becomes shorter). In texts with vowel signs, a *shva* (◻) is written under the middle root letter. As mentioned above, this *shva* is usually not pronounced in spoken Hebrew.

This is the same vowel reduction that we saw above in the plural present tense forms:

	forms with vowel reduction			base forms	
present tense:	מְדַבְּרוֹת	מְדַבְּרִים	⇐	מְדַבֵּר	◄
past tense:	דִּבְּרוּ	דִּבְּרָה	⇐	דִּבֵּר	

First and second person forms (אני, אתה, את, אנחנו, אתם, אתן)

In the first and second persons, we add endings that begin with a consonant (*-tee, -ta, -t, -noo, -tem, -ten*):

◄	הוא:	דִּבֵּר	*dee-BER*
		⇓	⇓
	אני:	דִּבַּרְתִּי	*dee-BAR-tee*
	אתה:	דִּבַּרְתָ	*dee-BAR-ta*
	את:	דִּבַּרְתְ	*dee-BART*
	אנחנו:	דִּבַּרְנוּ	*dee-BAR-noo*
	אתם:	דִּבַּרְתֶם	*dee-BAR-tem*[10]
	אתן:	דִּבַּרְתֶן	*dee-BAR-ten*

---

10 We have indicated the pronunciation used by most Hebrew speakers today. In traditional pronunciation, the stress is on the last syllable of the אתם and אתן forms: *dee-bar-TEM, dee-bar-TEN*.

Q: What happens to the *eh* vowel of the base form דִּבֵּר in the syllable **before** these endings?

A: There is always an *AH* sound in the syllable before these endings.

Want to see if you've understood?
Write the correct form of the underlined verb.

1. <u>סיפרתם</u> לחברים על הטיול. את _____ אני _____ אנחנו _____.

   דני _____ מיכל_____.

2. המורה <u>לימדה</u> שיר של יהודה עמיחי. אתם _____ המורות _____.

   אתה _____ אתן _____ הם _____.

Answers:

1. סִיפַּרְתָּ, סִיפַּרְתִּי, סִיפַּרְנוּ, סִיפֵּר, סִיפְּרָה   2. לִימַדְתֶּם, לִימְדוּ, לִימַדְתָּ, לִימַדְתֶן, לִימַדְתָּ, לִימְדוּ

• *Infinitive* (לְדַבֵּר)

Here are some *pee'el* infinitives:

לְנַגֵּן	לְסַפֵּר	לְדַבֵּר
to play	to tell	to speak
(an instrument)		

The -לְ of *pee'el* infinitives has an *eh* sound: *le-da-BER, le-sa-PER, le-na-GEN.*

Notice that in *beenyan pee'el* (but **not** in most of the other *beenyaneem*), the whole vowel pattern is the same as the present tense base form:

present:	*me-da-BER*	מְדַבֵּר
infinitive:	*le-da-BER*	לְדַבֵּר

Want to see if you've understood?
Write the infinitive of the underlined verb.

1. המורים באולפן <u>מלמדים</u> עברית. הם אוהבים _____ עברית.

2. לא <u>סיפרת</u> לי מה קרה. את לא רוצה _____ לי מה קרה?

Answers:

1. לְלַמֵּד   2. לְסַפֵּר

• *Future tense* (יְדַבֵּר)

Here are the future tense forms of the verb דִּבֵּר:

	prefixes and endings		*only prefixes*		
			'a-da-BER	אֲדַבֵּר	אני: ◄
			te-da-BER	תְּדַבֵּר	אתה:
te-dab-REE	תְּדַבְּרִי				את:
			ye-da-BER	**יְדַבֵּר**	הוא:
			te-da-BER	תְּדַבֵּר	היא:
			ne-da-BER	נְדַבֵּר	אנחנו:
te-dab-ROO	תְּדַבְּרוּ				אתם/אתן:
ye-dab-ROO	יְדַבְּרוּ				הם/הן:

As we pointed out in the chapter "Signs of Tenses and Forms" (p. 375), the future tense base form of many verbs, including those in *beenyan pee'el*, resembles their infinitive form:

infinitive:	le-da-BER	לְדַבֵּר ◄
future base form:	ye-da-BER	הוא: יְדַבֵּר

To arrive at the future tense base form from the infinitive, we just drop the ל- and add י-.

It so happens that in *beenyan pee'el*, but **not** in most *beenyaneem*, these forms are similar to the present tense base form (מְדַבֵּר) as well.

Now let's look more closely at the right-hand column of verbs in the chart above.

Q: Which prefix contains a vowel **different** from that of the others?

A: The -אֲ in the אני form (אֲדַבֵּר). All future *pee'el* prefixes have an *eh* vowel like their infinitive and present tense forms (e.g., יְדַבֵּר *ye-da-BER*, תְּדַבֵּר *te-da-BER*) except for the אני form, which begins with an *ah* sound: אֲדַבֵּר (*'a-da-BER*).

Let's focus now on the vowel after the **second** root letter (ב') of these forms. The base form (הוא) and all other forms **without** endings (in the right-hand column of verbs in the chart) have an *eh* sound:

ye-da-BER	יְדַבֵּר	הוא: ◄
te-da-BER	תְּדַבֵּר	אתה:

Q: What happens to this ◻ (*eh*) vowel when the vowel endings *-EE* (◌ִי) and *-OO* (◌ֹו) are added and the stress moves to the end of the word to create תְדַבְּרִי (*te-dab-REE*), תְדַבְּרוּ (*te-dab-ROO*) and יְדַבְּרוּ (*ye-dab-ROO*) (in the left-hand column of the chart)?

A: The ◻ (*eh*) becomes a *shva* (◻) and is usually not pronounced.

te-da-BER	תְדַבֵּר	אתה:	◄
⇓	⇓		
te-dab-REE	תְדַבְּרִי	את:	
te-dab-ROO	תְדַבְּרוּ	אתם/אתן:	

ye-da-BER	יְדַבֵּר	הוא:	◄
⇓	⇓		
ye-dab-ROO	יְדַבְּרוּ	הם/הן:	

This is the same change that we saw above when *-AH* (ה◌ָ) and *-OO* (◌ֹו) were added in the past tense: דִיבְּרָה, דִיבְּרוּ and when *-EEM* (◌ִים) and *-OT* (◌ֹות) were added in the present: מְדַבְּרִים, מְדַבְּרוֹת.

Q: Do all these endings (*-EE, -OO, -AH, -EEM, -OT*) **begin** with a consonant or a vowel?

A: They all begin with a **vowel**. When a vowel ending is added, the vowel that **precedes** the ending often "reduces" and is written with a *shva*.

For variations caused by the presence of ע׳, ח׳, ה׳, א׳ (the *guttural consonants*), see the chapter "Reduction of Vowels and the *Shva*," (pp. 651-652) and also the chapter "Guttural Consonants and ר׳: *Pee'el, Poo'al* and *Neef'al*," (pp. 474-487).

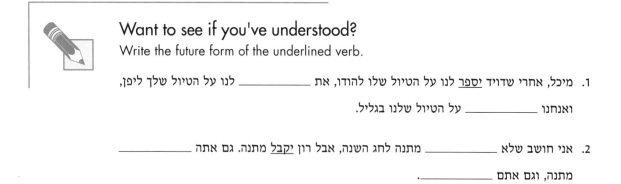

Want to see if you've understood?
Write the future form of the underlined verb.

1. מיכל, אחרי שדויד <u>יספר</u> לנו על הטיול שלו להודו, את _____ לנו על הטיול שלך ליפן,

   ואנחנו _____ על הטיול שלנו בגליל.

2. אני חושב שלא _____ מתנה לחג השנה, אבל רון <u>יקבל</u> מתנה. גם אתה _____

   מתנה, וגם אתם _____.

3. דויד <u>ילמד</u> אותנו היסטוריה בשנה הבאה, ושרה _____ אותנו ספרות.

Answers:

1. תְּסַפְּרִי, נְסַפֵּר   2. אֲקַבֵּל, תְּקַבֵּל, תְּקַבְּלוּ   3. תְּלַמֵּד

• *The pronunciation of 'ב', 'כ', 'פ when they are the first root letter* (בִּיקֵּר, לְבַקֵּר)

We saw above that when we write with vowel signs, verbs in *pee'el* always have a *dagesh*[11] in the **middle** root letter, which causes the letters ב', 'כ', 'פ always to be pronounced *b, k, p* when they are in the middle position. Now let's see what happens in *beenyan pee'el* when the letters ב', 'כ', 'פ are the **first** letter of the root:

	עתיד *future*	שם הפועל *infinitive*	הווה *present*	עבר *past*	שורש *root*	
to ask for, request	יְבַקֵּשׁ *ye-va-KESH*	לְבַקֵּשׁ *le-va-KESH*	מְבַקֵּשׁ *me-va-KESH*	בִּיקֵּשׁ *bee-KESH*	ב-ק-שׁ	◄
to launder	יְכַבֵּס *ye-cha-BES*	לְכַבֵּס *le-cha-BES*	מְכַבֵּס *me-cha-BES*	כִּיבֵּס *kee-BES*	כ-ב-ס	
to fire (someone)	יְפַטֵּר *ye-fa-TER*	לְפַטֵּר *le-fa-TER*	מְפַטֵּר *me-fa-TER*	פִּיטֵּר *pee-TER*	פ-ט-ר	

As you can see, when ב', 'כ', 'פ are the first root letter, their pronunciation is hard (*b, p, k*) only in the **past** tense form. In all the other forms, their pronunciation is *soft*: *v* (ב), *ch* (כ) and *f* (פ').[12]

The *dagesh* that appears in ב', 'כ', 'פ at the beginning of the past tense forms is a *weak dagesh*;[13] it is a different kind of *dagesh* from the one that appears in the middle root letter in *pee'el*.[14] This weak *dagesh* appears in *pee'el* only in the past tense, since in this *beenyan*, it is only in the past tense that the letters ב', 'כ', 'פ are at the **beginning** of the word.

---

11 This is a *strong dagesh* (דָּגֵשׁ חָזָק). It appears in all letters except for א', ה', ח', ע', ר'. See the chapter "The Pronunciation of ב', 'כ', 'פ and the *Dagesh*," pp. 630-633.

12 This is because they **follow a vowel** (*eh*) in these forms. When this is the case, ב', 'כ', 'פ always have a soft pronunciation: *v, ch, f*.

13 In traditional grammar books this is often called *dagesh lene*.

14 The two kinds of *dagesh* – the weak *dagesh* and the strong *dagesh* – have different functions and different reasons for appearing. (See the chapter "The Pronunciation of ב', 'כ', 'פ and the *Dagesh*," pp. 624-639). Today, the presence of both kinds of *dagesh* affects the pronunciation **only** of ב', 'כ', 'פ: They both indicate that ב', 'כ', 'פ are pronounced as hard sounds (*b, k, p*).

Want to see if you've understood?
Write the missing form of the underlined verb, and say both forms out loud.

1. מאיה ורינה לא רצו _____ סליחה מהחברים שלהן, אבל בסוף הן <u>ביקשו</u> סליחה.

2. בן ומירי, מתי תבואו <u>לבקר</u> אותנו? לא _____ אותנו כבר המון זמן.

3. עדיין לא <u>כיבסנו</u> את הבגדים הלבנים. אולי _____ אותם מחר.

Answers:

1. לְבַקֵּשׁ *le-va-KESH* / בִּיקְשׁוּ *beek-SHOO*   2. לְבַקֵּר *le-va-KER* / בִּיקַרְתֶּם *bee-KAR-tem*

3. כִּיבַּסְנוּ *kee-BAS-noo* / נְכַבֵּס *ne-cha-BES*

• *Verbs whose first or second root letter is* י (יִיבֵּשׁ, טִייֵל)

Now let's compare verbs whose **first** root letter is י (י-ב-שׁ) and those whose **second** root letter is י (ט-י-ל) to the model verb דיבר (ד-ב-ר). Pay special attention to the spelling:

	עתיד *future*	הווה *present*	עבר *past*	שם הפועל *infinitive*	שורש *root*	
model verb:	**ידבר, תדבר...**	**מדבר**	**דיבר, דיברתי...**	**לדבר**	**ד-ב-ר**	◄
to dry	יְיֵבֵּשׁ, תְייֵבֵּשׁ...	מְייֵבֵּשׁ	יִיבֵּשׁ, יִיבַּשְׁתִּי...	לְייֵבֵּשׁ	י-ב-שׁ	
to travel (or walk around)	יְטַייֵל, תְטַייֵל...	מְטַייֵל	טִייֵל, טִייַלְתִּי...	לְטַייֵל	ט-י-ל	

When י is the first or second root letter, it is always written as a **double yod** (יי).[15] However, we **never** write more than two י in a row.

Be careful! Students often find it difficult to identify verb forms like טייל and צייר as *pee'el* verbs (they are pronounced *tee-YEL* and *tsee-YER*, just like דיבר *dee-BER*). It should be noted that there are also non-verb forms spelled with the same letters, but pronounced differently. Some examples are: the noun צייר (צַייָר *tsa-YAR* painter) and words like קיים (קַייָם exists), which is not a verb in Hebrew.

---

15 Note that the verbal noun of verbs whose middle root letter is י (לטייל, לצייר) is written with only **one** י (that of the root):

	צִיּוּר *tsee-YOOR* drawing	טִיּוּל *tee-YOOL* trip	◄

These forms are different from the model form דִיבּוּר (speaking) in that here no **additional** י is written between the first and second root letters.

• *Roots with four letters* מְרוּבָּעִים (תִּרְגֵּם)

Some *pee'el* verbs have **four** root letters. Here are the infinitives of some of them:

לְבַלְבֵּל	לְאַרְגֵּן	לְצַלְצֵל	לְתַרְגֵּם
to confuse	to organize	to ring, phone	to translate

The pattern of these infinitives is very much like that of לְדַבֵּר, only with an extra root letter:

ל - דַ - בֵּר
ל - תַּר - גֵּם

The present and future forms of verbs with **four** root letters are also similar to those of regular *pee'el* verbs. Compare:

	future	*present*
	יְ - דַ - בֵּר	מְ - דַ - בֵּר
	יְ - תַּר - גֵּם	מְ - תַּר - גֵּם

There is no strong *dagesh* in verbs with four root letters; however, when the third root letter is ב׳, כ׳, פ׳ (מְבַלְבֵּל), it has a hard pronunciation (*b*, *k*, *p*) and is written with a *dagesh* in texts with vowel signs.[16]

In the past tense, when there are four letters in the root, we do **not** write a י after the first root letter (according to official spelling rules) when we write without vowel signs.[17] Thus, we write: דיבר (*dee-BER*) but תרגם (*teer-GEM*). Compare:

regular three-letter root:	דיברה	דיבר,	דיברת,	דיברתי,
	deeb-RA	*dee-BER*	*dee-BAR-ta*	*dee-BAR-tee*
four-letter root:	תרגמה	תרגם,	תרגמת,	תרגמתי,
	teer-ge-MA	*teer-GEM*	*teer-GAM-ta*	*teer-GAM-tee*

---

16 This is a weak *dagesh*, which comes after a closed syllable. For an explanation, see the chapter "The Pronunciation of ב, כ, פ׳ and the *Dagesh*," pp. 624-629.

17 According to the Hebrew Language Academy, we do not add a י in the middle of a closed syllable whose end is marked by a *shva* (-ְ). See the chapter "Hebrew Spelling," pp. 657-660.

Want to see if you've understood?

Pronounce the following past tense verbs, and change them to the present and future. Remember to pronounce *ee* in the first syllable of the past tense, even though there is no *י* there.

‎1. אתמול רינה <u>צלצלה</u> לאימא שלה. עכשיו רינה _____. מחר רינה _____

לאימא שלה.

‎2. בשבוע שעבר (את) <u>ארגנת</u> מסיבה נהדרת. עכשיו את _____ מחר (את)

_____ מסיבה.

Answers:

‎1. *tseel-tse-LA*, מְצַלְצֶלֶת, תְּצַלְצֵל   ‎2. *eer-GANT*, מְאַרְגֶנֶת, תְּאַרְגְּנִי

Chapter summary

♦ These are the base forms and the infinitive of **regular** *beenyan pee'el* verbs:

	infinitive	future	present	past	
full spelling without vowel signs:	לדבר	ידבר	מדבר	דיבר	◄
standard spelling with vowel signs:	לְדַבֵּר	יְדַבֵּר	מְדַבֵּר	דִּבֵּר	
	le-da-BER	*ye-da-BER*	*me-da-BER*	*dee-BER*	

- When *ב׳, כ׳, פ׳* are the middle root letter, they are always pronounced *b, k, p*.

- Other changes in pronunciation and spelling involving the letters *ב׳, כ׳, פ׳* and also *י׳* are discussed in detail in the chapter above.

♦ Some *pee'el* verbs have **four** root letters. Here is an example of their base forms and infinitive:

	infinitive	future	present	past	
full spelling without vowel signs:	לתרגם	יתרגם	מתרגם	תרגם	◄
standard spelling with vowel signs:	לְתַרְגֵם	יְתַרְגֵם	מְתַרְגֵם	תִּרְגֵם	
	le-tar-GEM	*ye-tar-GEM*	*me-tar-GEM*	*teer-GEM*	

Want to see if you've understood the chapter?

Write the correct form of the underlined verb (past, present, future or infinitive).

1. דינה, איפה המשקפיים שלי? אני <u>מחפשת</u> אותם כבר חצי שעה! עוד מעט ＿＿＿＿＿＿

   (future)

   אותם גם במכונית.

2. אימא לרותי: עוד לא <u>סידרת</u> את החדר שלך? ＿＿＿＿＿＿ אותו מיד, בבקשה. את צריכה

   (future)

   ＿＿＿＿＿＿ את החדר גם בלי שאבקש.

3. מיכל ＿＿＿＿＿＿ אלייך אתמול וביקשה <u>שתצלצלי</u> אליה היום. בזמן האחרון היא

   ＿＿＿＿＿＿ אלייך כל יום, נכון?

   (present)

4. אנחנו אוהבים <u>לטייל</u> בירושלים. בשבוע שעבר ＿＿＿＿＿＿ בעיר העתיקה, ובשבוע הבא

   ＿＿＿＿＿＿ בהר הצופים.

Answers:

1. אֲחַפֵּשׂ   2. תְּסַדְּרִי, לְסַדֵּר   3. צִלְצְלָה, מְצַלְצֶלֶת   4. טִיַּלְנוּ, נְטַיֵּל

2. Beenyan Pa'al פָּעַל

> **Preview**
> - *Present tense* (סוֹגֵר)
> - *Past tense* (סָגַר)
> - *Infinitive* (לִסְגּוֹר)
> - *Future tense* (יִסְגּוֹר, יִלְמַד)
> - *The pronunciation of* ב׳, כ׳, פ׳

The verb סָגַר / לִסְגּוֹר (to close) will serve as our model of a *regular* verb in *beenyan pa'al*.[1]

• *Present tense* (סוֹגֵר)

Here are the present tense forms of the verb סָגַר:

so-GER	סוֹגֵר	(m.s.):	אני, אתה, הוא
so-GE-ret	סוֹגֶרֶת	(f.s.):	אני, את, היא
sog-REEM	סוֹגְרִים	(m.pl.):	אנחנו, אתם, הם
sog-ROT	סוֹגְרוֹת	(f.pl.):	אנחנו, אתן, הן

Compare these forms to the present tense forms in *beenyan pee'el* (מדבר, מדברת...).

Q: Do the verbs in *beenyan pa'al* have a *prefix* before the root letters?

A: No. There is no prefix in present tense *pa'al* verbs.

Q: What characteristic is common to all these forms?

A: They all have "וֹ" (*oh*) after the first root letter:

סוֹגֵר, סוֹגֶרֶת, סוֹגְרִים, סוֹגְרוֹת ◄

---

1 For the changes that occur in verbs with *gutturals* (א׳, ה׳, ח׳, ע׳), such as לִשְׁמוֹעַ, לִשְׁאוֹל, לַעֲבוֹד, see the chapter
"Guttural Consonants: *Beenyan Pa'al*," pp. 450-460.

As in *pee'el*, the feminine present tense forms of *pa'al* end in תֶ-ֶ (*E-et*). Compare:

me-da-BE-ret	מְדַבֶּרֶת ◄
so-GE-ret	סוֹגֶרֶת

Note that – as is the case in *pee'el* (מְדַבְּרים, מְדַבְּרוֹת) – when the plural endings are added to verbs in *pa'al*, the *eh* vowel before them (סוֹגֵר + ים) changes and is written as a *shva* (סְ). In today's Hebrew, this *shva* is usually not pronounced.[2]

סוֹגְרוֹת,	סוֹגְרים, ◄
sog-ROT	*sog-REEM*

Want to see if you've understood?
Write the correct form of the underlined verb.

1. אתה <u>כותב</u> מכתב למשפחה שלך. היא _____ . אנחנו (*m.*) _____ .

2. אנחנו <u>לומדות</u> מהר. את _____ . הוא _____ . הם _____ .

3. למה הם לא <u>סוגרים</u> את הדלת? הוא _____ . הן _____ . את _____ .

Answers:[3]

1. כּוֹתֶבֶת, כּוֹתְבים   2. לוֹמֶדֶת, לוֹמֵד, לוֹמְדים   3. סוֹגֵר, סוֹגְרוֹת, סוֹגֶרֶת

A special present tense pattern: pa'el (פָּעֵל)[4]

There are some verbs in *pa'al* that have a different pattern in the present tense. Here is the הוא form of the most common of these verbs:

קָטֵן	יָשֵׁן	גָּדֵל ◄
(he/it) is getting smaller	is sleeping	is growing (up), getting bigger

---

2   This change to *shva* is called *vowel reduction*. See the chapter "Reduction of Vowels and the *Shva*," pp. 640-641, 648-650. In traditional pronunciation this *shva* is pronounced *eh* (*so-ge-REEM*). In today's pronunciation this is so only in rare cases, e.g., when the last two letters of the root are identical, as in: חוֹגְגים (*cho-ge-GEEM*).

3   It is not necessary for you to write vowel signs in your answers. We have added vowel signs to the answers in the chapters on verbs only in order to make clear how the forms are pronounced.

4   Biblical Hebrew grammars often refer to these as *stative verbs*, i.e., as verbs that denote a **state** or a **change of state**. Note that **not** all verbs that denote a state (for example: יושב sitting and שוכב lying down) take this form. For more on פָּעֵל see Joüon-Muraoka, 1996, p. 127, section 41b. For more on statives, see the chapter "Verbs that Are Neither Active Nor Passive," pp. 606-608.

Q: What vowel do the verbs גָּדֵל and יָשֵׁן have in their **first** syllable instead of the "וֹ" (*oh*) of סוגר?

A: They have the vowel ◌ָ (*ah*):

קָטֵן   יָשֵׁן   גָּדֵל   ◄

ka-TEN   *ya-SHEN*   *ga-DEL*

The **second** syllable of these verbs has the same vowel as סוֹ-גֵר (*so-GER*):

גָּ-דֵל   (*ga-DEL*)

יָ-שֵׁן   (*ya-SHEN*)

Now let's look at all four present tense forms of verbs with this pattern:

ga-DEL	גָּדֵל	:(m.s.)	אני, אתה, הוא ◄
gde-LA	גְּדֵלָה	:(f.s.)	אני, את, היא
gde-LEEM	גְּדֵלִים	:(m.pl.)	אנחנו, אתם, הם
gde-LOT	גְּדֵלוֹת	:(f.pl.)	אנחנו, אתן, הן

Q: Which vowel remains **constant** in all four of these forms?

A: The ◌ֵ (*eh*) vowel in the middle of the word:

גְּדֵלוֹת,   גְּדֵלִים,   גְּדֵלָה,   גָּדֵל,   ◄

gde-LOT   *gde-LEEM*   *gde-LA*   *ga-DEL*

These forms may seem familiar to you. They are the same as the forms of the following adjectives:

fat	שְׁמֵנוֹת	שְׁמֵנִים,	שְׁמֵנָה,	שָׁמֵן, ◄
happy	שְׂמֵחוֹת[5]	שְׂמֵחִים,	שְׂמֵחָה,	שָׂמֵחַ,

Notice that it is the *ah* vowel at the **beginning** of these forms (גָּדֵל *ga-DEL*) that "reduces" when endings are added. The reduced vowel is written as *shva* and is often not pronounced (e.g., גְּדלה, גְּדלים, גְּדלות *gde-LA*, *gde-LEEM*, *gde-LOT*). This is **different** from the regular present tense verb forms – סוֹ-גֵר ⇐ (*סו-גֵ-רים/-רות*) ⇐ סוגְ-רים / סוגְ-רות – in which the reduction to *shva* takes place in the syllable **immediately before** the ending.

---

5   The separation of these words into two different categories – verbs and adjectives – is often blurred. Thus, שמח (happy) may be considered an adjective or a verb that describes a state of being.

Notice that the feminine singular form of the *pa'el* pattern (גָּדְלָה) does **not** end in ת- as do the
regular *pa'al* verbs (for example: סוֹגֶרֶת). Rather, its ending is ‏ָה (-*AH*).

◄

יְשֵׁנָה	גָּדְלָה
ye-she-NA	gde-LA

Want to see if you've understood?
Write the correct form of the underlined verb.

1. כמה זמן אתה <u>ישן</u> כל לילה?   את _____ . אתן _____ . הם _____ .

2. המשכורת שלך <u>גָּדְלָה</u> כל שנה. גם המשכורות שלכם _____ .

Answers:

1. יְשֵׁנָה, יְשֵׁנוֹת, יְשֵׁנִים   2. גָּדְלוֹת

• *Past tense* (סָגַר)

Here are the past tense forms of the verb סָגַר:

	plural				singular	
sa-GAR-noo	סָגַרְנוּ	אנחנו:		sa-GAR-tee	סָגַרְתִּי	אני: ◄
sa-GAR-tem / sgar-TEM	סָגַרְתֶּם / סְגַרְתֶּם [6]	אתם:		sa-GAR-ta	סָגַרְתָּ	אתה:
sa-GAR-ten / sgar-TEN	סָגַרְתֶּן / סְגַרְתֶּן	אתן:		sa-GART	סָגַרְתְּ	את:
sag-ROO	סָגְרוּ	הם, הן		sa-GAR	**סָגַר**	הוא:
				sag-RA	סָגְרָה	היא:

Beenyan pa'al has **no prefix** in the past tense, nor does it have any added letters indicating its
first vowel, as does דיבר in *beenyan pee'el*.

---

6   The pronunciation used by most Hebrew speakers today is סָגַרְתֶּם, סָגַרְתֶּן (*sa-GAR-tem, sa-GAR-ten*). It should
be noted that according to the rules of grammar, the stress is on the **ending** of the אתם and אתן forms, and this
causes the first vowel to "reduce" (it is written as a *shva*): סְגַרְתֶּם, סְגַרְתֶּן (pronounced *sgar-TEM, sgar-TEN* or,
traditionally, *se-gar-TEM, se-gar-TEN*). See the chapter "Reduction of Vowels and the *Shva*," pp. 640-647.

Q: What is the **first vowel** in all the *pa'al* past tense forms?

A: The first vowel is *ah*, as in the base form סָגַר (*sa-GAR*), for example:

סָגַרְתְּ	סָגַרְתָּ,	סָגַרְתִּי,
sa-GART	*sa-GAR-ta*	*sa-GAR-tee*

The **second vowel** in the past tense *base form* (הוא) is also *ah*: סָגַר (*sa-GAR*). In forms that have a vowel ending – היא and הם/הן (at the bottom part of the chart) – we see the same phenomenon that we saw in *pee'el*: the stress moves to the ending and the vowel before it "reduces" (and is usually not pronounced):[7]

beenyan pee'el:

דִּיבְּרוּ	דִּיבְּרָה,
deeb-ROO	*deeb-RA*

beenyan pa'al:

סָגְרוּ	סָגְרָה,
sag-ROO	*sag-RA*

In forms whose endings begin with a **consonant** (ת- or נ-) (in the upper part of the chart), the vowel ◌ַ (*AH*) always appears in the syllable before the ending – just as is the case in *pee'el*.

beenyan pee'el:

דִּיבַּרְתְּ	דִּיבַּרְתָּ,	דִּיבַּרְתִּי,
dee-BART	*dee-BAR-ta*	*dee-BAR-tee*

beenyan pa'al:

סָגַרְתְּ	סָגַרְתָּ,	סָגַרְתִּי,
sa-GART	*sa-GAR-ta*	*sa-GAR-tee*

Want to see if you've understood?
Write the correct form of the underlined verb.

1. <u>שכחתי</u> את השם של המזכירה החדשה. את _____ . אנחנו _____ .

   אורי _____ .

2. <u>כתבנו</u> אי מייל לחברים שלנו. אני _____ . אתם _____ .

   אילנה _____ .

---

7   In rare cases, such as when the last two root letters are the same, the *shva* is always pronounced, for example: היא חָגְגָה (*cha-ge-GA* she celebrated).

‎3. מיכל <u>למדה</u> סינית בשנה שעברה. מיכל ורן ‎_____ . רן ‎_____ .

אתה ‎_____ .

• *Infinitive* ‎(לִסְגּוֹר)

Here are some *pa'al* infinitives:

לִרְקוֹד	◄ לִסְגּוֹר
to dance	to close

These *infinitives* have two syllables:

lees-GOR	◄ לִס-גּוֹר
leer-KOD	◄ לִר-קוֹד

In these *pa'al* forms, the vowel of the ‎ל- is *ee*: ‎לִ- (*lee*). When we add ‎ל- to the front of these verbs, their first root letter joins the first syllable to form: ‎לִס- (*lees-*), ‎לִר- (*leer-*). Notice that even though the vowel here is *ee*, we do **not** insert a ‎י in the middle of the syllable.[8]

Q: What vowel appears in the second syllable of these infinitives?

A: The vowel *oh*, written with a ‎ו.

There is one "official" exception: the infinitive of the verb ‎שָׁכַב is ‎לִשְׁכַּב (to lie down).[9]

Want to see if you've understood?
Write the infinitive of the underlined verb.

‎1. יוסף <u>רקד</u> במסיבה כי הוא אוהב ‎_____ .

‎2. כל יום אני <u>לובשת</u> מכנסיים, אבל היום אני רוצה ‎_____ חצאית.

---

8   This is because *lees-* and *leer-* are *closed* syllables (= they end in a **consonant**). For details on when we add a ‎י and when we don't, see the chapter "Hebrew Spelling," pp. 657-660.

9   The infinitive of one other verb – ‎רוכב / רכב (to ride) – is often pronounced like ‎לִשְׁכַּב, i.e., without a ‎ו: ‎לִרְכַּב (*leer-KAV*) rather than ‎לִרְכּוֹב (the grammatically correct form).

3. יש לי חום ואני <u>שוכבת</u> במיטה כבר שלושה ימים. נמאס לי _____ במיטה.

4. למה אתם <u>סוגרים</u> את הדלת? אין סיבה _____ אותה עכשיו.

Answers:

1. לִרְקוֹד   2. לִלְבּוֹשׁ   3. לִשְׁכַּב   4. לִסְגוֹר

• *Future tense* (יִסְגּוֹר, יִלְמַד)

Most regular verbs in *beenyan pa'al* have the following future tense base form:

ירקוד	יסגור	(הוא)
he will dance	he will close	

As we saw above in *beenyan pee'el*, it is easy to arrive at this form if you know the infinitive:

future		*infinitive*
יִסְגוֹר	⇐	לִסְגוֹר
yees-GOR		*lees-GOR*

We simply drop off the ל-, and add the future prefix -י. The vowel of both prefixes is the same: ☐ (*ee*), however no **extra** י is added to either form.

Here are the future tense forms of the verb לִסְגוֹר / יִסְגוֹר:

prefixes and endings		*only prefixes*		
		'es-GOR	אֶסְגוֹר	אני:
		tees-GOR	תִּסְגוֹר	אתה:
tees-ge-REE	תִּסְגְּרִי			את:
		yees-GOR	**יִסְגוֹר**	הוא:
		tees-GOR	תִּסְגוֹר	היא:
		nees-GOR	נִסְגוֹר	אנחנו:
tees-ge-ROO	תִּסְגְּרוּ			אתם/אתן:
yees-ge-ROO	יִסְגְּרוּ			הם/הן:

Q: Which prefix contains a vowel **different** from the others?

A: -אֶ in אֶסְגוֹר.[10] Except for this אני form, all future tense forms in *pa'al* begin with the sound *ee*:

יִסְגוֹר,	תִּסְגוֹר,	נִסְגוֹר...
yees-GOR	tees-GOR	nees-GOR

The אני form begins with an *eh* sound: אֶסְגוֹר ('es-GOR).

The vowel after the second root letter: 'ef'ol (אֶפְעוֹל)

Q: Which vowel appears between the second and third root letter in the forms **without** an ending: יסגור, תסגור...?

A: The vowel *oh* which is written with a ו when we write without vowel signs:

אֶסְגוֹר,	תִּסְגוֹר,	נִסְגוֹר...
'es-GOR	tees-GOR	nees-GOR

Q: What happens to this *oh* ("ו") when endings are added: תסגרי, תסגרו, יסגרו?

A: When the stress moves to the ending, the *oh* vowel "reduces" and is written as a *shva* (ְ). This *shva* is pronounced *eh*:

תִּסְגְּרִי,	תִּסְגְּרוּ,	יִסְגְּרוּ
tees-ge-REE	tees-ge-ROO	yees-ge-ROO

> ***Be careful!*** When we write **without** vowels, future tense verbs **with endings** look the same in *pa'al* and *pee'el*, for example (note the difference in pronunciation):
>
>
>
> | *beenyan pa'al*: | תסגרי, | תסגרו, | יסגרו |
> |---|---|---|---|
> | | tees-ge-REE | tees-ge-ROO | yees-ge-ROO |
> | *beenyan pee'el*: | תדברי, | תדברו, | ידברו |
> | | te-dab-REE | te-dab-ROO | ye-dab-ROO |
>
>

Only our familiarity with the specific verbs that appear in a given context helps us to know to which *beenyan* they belong and, thus, how to pronounce them.

---

10 א often shows a preference for the sound *eh*. See the chapter "Guttural Consonants: *Beenyan Pa'al*," pp. 453-454.

Want to see if you've understood?

Write the missing form of the underlined verb.

‏1. המטפלת <u>תשמור</u> על הילדים. אתה _____. אנחנו _____. אני _____.

‏2. הרקדן <u>ירקוד</u> עוד ריקוד אחד. הרקדנית _____. אתה _____.

‏את _____. אתם _____. הם _____.

Answers:

‏1. תשמור, נשמור, אשמור   2. תרקוד, תרקוד, תרקדי, תרקדו, ירקדו

A special future tense pattern: 'ef'al (אֶפְעַל)

Some *pa'al* verbs have a somewhat different future tense base form. Here, for example, is the future tense conjugation of the verb לָמַד / לִלְמוֹד:

prefixes and endings		*only prefixes*		
		'el-MAD	אֶלְמַד	אני: ◄
		teel-MAD	תִלְמַד	אתה:
teel-me-DEE	תִלְמְדִי			את:
		yeel-MAD	יִלְמַד	הוא:
		teel-MAD	תִלְמַד	היא:
		neel-MAD	נִלְמַד	אנחנו:
teel-me-DOO	תִלְמְדוּ			אתם/אתן:
yeel-me-DOO	יִלְמְדוּ			הם/הן:

Q: In what way are the future forms of למד / ללמוד different from those of סגר / לסגור?

A: The future base form יִלְמַד and all the other forms with **prefixes only** (in the right-hand column above) have an *AH* sound in their second syllable instead of an *OH* sound. Thus, they have no "ו" and are quite **different** from their infinitive form ללמוד.

The forms **with** endings (in the left-hand column above) look and sound exactly like the forms of לסגור:

יִסְגְרוּ	תִסְגְרוּ,	תִסְגְרִי, ◄
yees-ge-ROO	*tees-ge-ROO*	*tees-ge-REE*
יִלְמְדוּ	תִלְמְדוּ,	תִלְמְדִי,
yeel-me-DOO	*teel-me-DOO*	*teel-me-DEE*

Pa'al verbs with no "ו" in the future are often called אֶפְעַל (*'ef'al*) verbs, according to the pattern of their אני form – אֶלְמַד, אֶלְבַּשׁ, while verbs whose future is like אֶסְגּוֹר and אֶרְקוֹד are referred to as אֶפְעוֹל (*'ef'ol*) verbs.

Here are the base forms of some commonly used אֶפְעַל (*'ef'al*) verbs:

יִקְטַן	יִגְדַּל	יִרְכַּב	יִשְׁכַּב	יִלְבַּשׁ	יִלְמַד	◄
will get smaller	will grow, get larger	will ride	will lie down	will wear	will study, learn	

Note that verbs whose present tense form is like גָּדֵל (of the *pa'el* pattern) are always like יִלְמַד in the future tense, for example:

present tense:	יָשֵׁן	קָטֵן	גָּדֵל	◄
future tense:	יִישַׁן	יִקְטַן	יִגְדַּל	
	he will sleep	it/he will get smaller	it/he will grow, get larger	

The אפעל form is actually very common in future tense forms of *beenyan pa'al* because when the middle or final root letter is ע, א, ה, ח or ע, it is always used (e.g., יִשְׁאַל, יִשְׁמַע...). For more information, see the chapter "Guttural Consonants: *Beenyan Pa'al*" (p. 458).

> ***Be careful!*** When we write **without** vowels, **all** future tense אֶפְעַל (*'ef'al*) verbs are
> written **the same** as verbs in *beenyan pee'el*. Here, too, it is only our familiarity with the
> specific verbs in a given context that helps us know to which *beenyan* they belong and,
> thus, how to pronounce them. Compare the following forms:
>
> | | | | | |
> |---|---|---|---|---|
> | *beenyan pee'el*: | ילמד | יספר | ידבר | ◄ |
> | | ye-la-MED | ye-sa-PER | ye-da-BER | |
> | | he will teach | he will tell | he will speak | |
> | *beenyan pa'al*: | ילמד | ישכב | ילבש | |
> | | yeel-MAD | yeesh-KAV | yeel-BASH | |
> | | he will study, learn | he will lie down | he will wear | |

Want to see if you've understood?
A. Write the missing form of the underlined verb.

1. תמר <u>תלמד</u> באוניברסיטה בשנה הבאה. אתה ــــــــــ. אני ــــــــ ــــــــ.

   אתם ــــــــــ.

2. מחר <u>אשכב</u> לישון מוקדם יותר. אתה ــــــــ. הוא ــــــــ.

   את ــــــــ. הילדים ــــــــ.

3. <u>תלבשי</u> את השמלה הכחולה למסיבה? היא ــــــــ ــــــــ. אני ــــــــ.

Answers:

1. תִּלְמַד, אֶלְמַד, תִּלְמְדוּ   2. תִּשְׁכַּב, יִשְׁכַּב, תִּשְׁכְּבִי, יִשְׁכְּבוּ   3. תִּלְבַּשׁ, אֶלְבַּשׁ

B. Write the future tense form of the underlined verb (it may be אפעל or אפעול).

1. אתה רוצה <u>ללמוד</u> פיזיקה בשנה הבאה? איפה (אתה) ــــــــ?

2. רמי לא אוהב <u>לרקוד</u>, אבל הוא הבטיח שהוא ــــــــ בחתונה של אחותו.

3. אני צריכה <u>לכתוב</u> עבודה סמינריונית. אולי ــــــــ על משפט דרייפוס.

4. הילדה רוצה <u>לשכב</u> על הרצפה ולראות טלוויזיה. ההורים שלה לא רוצים שהיא

   ــــــــ שם כל הערב.

5. הצמח הזה לא יכול <u>לגדול</u> בלי הרבה אור. הוא ــــــــ טוב יותר מחוץ לבית.

Answers:

1. תִּלְמַד   2. יִרְקוֹד   3. אֶכְתּוֹב   4. תִּשְׁכַּב   5. יִגְדַּל

• *The pronunciation of* 'בּ, כּ, פּ (*the weak* dagesh דָּגֵשׁ קַל)

When the first root letter is 'בּ, כּ, פּ

Read the forms of the following verbs whose **first** root letter is 'בּ, כּ, פּ:

הווה present	עבר past	שם הפועל infinitive	עתיד future
בּודק	בּדק	לבדוק	יִבְדוק
כּותב	כּתב	לכתוב	יִכְתּוב
פּוגש	פּגש	לפגוש	יִפְגּוש

When the letters ב, כ, פ are at the beginning of a word, they are pronounced as *hard* sounds – ב (*b*), כ (*k*), פ (*p*) – as in בודק (bo-DEK), כותב (ko-TEV), פוגש (po-GESH). When -ל is added immediately before them to form the infinitive, they have a *soft* pronunciation – ב (*v*), כ (*ch*), פ (*f*) – as in: לב-דוק (leev-DOK), לכ-תוב (leech-TOV) and לפ-גוש (leef-GOSH). This is true also in the future tense: יב-דוק (yeev-DOK), יכ-תוב (yeech-TOV) and יפ-גוש (yeef-GOSH).[11]

Want to see if you've understood?

Write the missing forms of the underlined verbs and read all the forms out loud.

1. כ̲עסתי על החברה שלי. לא היה לי נעים _____ עליה.

2. המורה למתמטיקה פ̲תר את התרגיל הקשה על הלוח. רק תלמיד אחד הצליח

_____ את התרגיל בבית. מחר אנחנו _____ עוד תרגילים ביחד.

3. ב̲דקנו את שיעורי הבית בכיתה. כל יום אנחנו _____ את שיעורי הבית בכיתה
(present)

כי חשוב _____ אותם ביחד. גם מחר _____ את שיעורי הבית בכיתה.

Answers:
1. כָּעַסְתִי (ka-'AS-tee), לִכְעוֹס (leech-'OS)   2. פָּתַר (pa-TAR), לִפְתּוֹר (leef-TOR), נִפְתּוֹר (neef-TOR)
3. בָּדַקְנוּ (ba-DAK-noo), בּוֹדְקִים (bod-KEEM), לִבְדּוֹק (leev-DOK), נִבְדּוֹק (neev-DOK)

When the second root letter is ב, כ, פ

In the following verbs, the **second** root letter is ב, כ or פ. Let's see when these are pronounced as *hard* sounds (*b, k, p*) and when they are pronounced as *soft* sounds (*v, ch, f*).

הווה *present*	עבר *past*	שם הפועל *infinitive*	עתיד *future*
לו-בש ◄	ל-בש	לל-בוש	יל-בש
מו-כר	מ-כר	למ-כור	ימ-כור
סו-פר	ס-פר	לס-פור	יס-פור

---

11 This is because in these forms ב, כ, פ follow a vowel. See the chapter "The Pronunciation of ב, כ, פ and the *Dagesh*," pp. 626-629.

First let's look at the infinitive and the future columns.

Q: How are ב', כ', פ' pronounced in the infinitive and the future forms?

A: They have a hard pronunciation (*b, k, p*) as, for example, in לִלְ-בּוֹשׁ (*leel-BOSH*) and יִלְ-בַּשׁ (*yeel-BASH*).[12]

Now look at the verbs in the first two columns: the present and past tenses. Here we see that ב', כ', פ' are pronounced with a soft pronunciation (*v, ch, f*). This is so whenever ב', כ', פ' are the second root letter in the past and in the present, as in לוֹ-בֵשׁ (*lo-VESH*) and לָ-בַשׁ (*la-VASH*).[13]

Want to see if you've understood?
Pronounce the following verb forms.

1. למה החתן שובר / ישבור / מנסה לשבור / שבר את הכוס?
2. אנחנו שוכבים / רוצים לשכב / נשכב / שכבנו על חוף הים בימי הקיץ החמים.
3. הילדה שפכה / תשפוך / שופכת / לא התכוונה לשפוך מיץ ענבים על הספה.

Answers:

1. שׁוֹבֵר (*sho-VER*), יִשְׁבּוֹר (*yeesh-BOR*), לִשְׁבּוֹר (*leesh-BOR*), שָׁבַר (*sha-VAR*)
2. שׁוֹכְבִים (*shoch-VEEM*), לִשְׁכַּב (*leesh-KAV*), שָׁכַבְנוּ (*sha-CHAV-noo*)
3. שָׁפְכָה (*shaf-CHA*), תִּשְׁפּוֹךְ (*teesh-POCH*), שׁוֹפֶכֶת (*sho-FE-chef*), לִשְׁפּוֹךְ (*leesh-POCH*)

Chapter summary

♦ These are the *base forms* (the past, present and future tense הוא forms) and the infinitive of most regular verbs in *beenyan pa'al*:

infinitive	future	present	past
לִסְגוֹר	יִסְגוֹר	סוֹגֵר	סָגַר

---

12 This is because they follow a ***closed*** syllable. See the chapter "Basic Concepts: Sounds and Syllables," p. 622 and the chapter "The Pronunciation of ב', כ', פ' and the *Dagesh*," p. 627 for an explanation.

13 This is because they follow an ***open*** syllable, i.e., a vowel. See the chapter "Basic Concepts: Sounds and Syllables," p. 622 and the chapter "The Pronunciation of ב', כ', פ' and the *Dagesh*," p. 628 for an explanation.

◆ Some verbs have a פָּעֵל (*pa'el*) pattern in the present tense, for example:

> יָשֵׁן   קָטֵן   גָּדֵל ◀

◆ The most common future tense form of regular *pa'al* verbs has an *OH* ("וֹ") in the second syllable and is called אֶפְעוֹל (*'ef'ol*). An alternative future tense form without a וֹ – called אֶפְעַל (*'ef'al*) – is used for some regular *pa'al* verbs, such as:

> יִרְכַּב   יִשְׁכַּב   יִלְבַּשׁ   יִלְמַד ◀

Verbs whose present tense form is *pa'el* (e.g., גָּדֵל) also take the *'ef'al* form in the future (e.g., יִגְדַּל).

◆ When the letters ב, כ, פ are the first or second root letters, various changes in pronunciation take place. These are discussed in the chapter above.

Want to see if you've understood this chapter?
Write the missing forms of the underlined verb.

1. <u>רקדנו</u> עד מאוחר אתמול. אני מאוד אוהבת _____ . מתי _____ שוב? (אנחנו)

2. <u>בדקת</u> את מצב החשבון בבנק? כדאי _____ את החשבון כל שבוע.

3. אנחנו צריכות <u>לכתוב</u> חיבור בעברית. אני _____ על המשפחה שלי. (future)

   על מה את _____? (future)

4. הילדים כל כך <u>גדלו</u>. הם _____ כל כך מהר! (present)

5. אתה <u>לומד</u> באוניברסיטה העברית? גם אני _____ שם בשנה הבאה.

6. אבי, אתמול _____ את החולצה הלבנה. מחר כדאי <u>שתלבש</u> את החולצה האדומה.

Answers:

1. לִרְקוֹד, נִרְקוֹד   2. לִבְדּוֹק   3. אֶכְתּוֹב, תִּכְתְּבִי   4. גְּדֵלִים   5. אֶלְמַד   6. לָבַשְׁתָּ

3. *Beenyan Heetpa'el* הִתְפַּעֵל

Preview
- *Present tense* (מִתְלַבֵּשׁ)
- *Past tense* (הִתְלַבֵּשׁ)
- *Infinitive* (לְהִתְלַבֵּשׁ)
- *Future tense* (יִתְלַבֵּשׁ)
- *Roots that begin with* שׂ׳, שׁ׳, ס׳, צ׳, ז׳[1]
- *Four-letter roots* (הִתְאַרְגֵּן) מְרוּבָּעִים

The verb הִתְלַבֵּשׁ / לְהִתְלַבֵּשׁ (to get dressed) will serve as our model of a *regular* verb in *beenyan heetpa'el*.

• *Present tense* (מִתְלַבֵּשׁ)

Here are the present tense forms of the verb הִתְלַבֵּשׁ:

◄	אני, אתה, הוא	(m.s.):	מִתְלַבֵּשׁ	*meet-la-BESH*

◄   אני, אתה, הוא   (m.s.):   מִתְלַבֵּשׁ   *meet-la-BESH*
   אני, את, היא   (f.s.):   מִתְלַבֶּשֶׁת   *meet-la-BE-shet*
   אנחנו, אתם, הם   (m.pl.):   מִתְלַבְּשִׁים   *meet-lab-SHEEM*
   אנחנו, אתן, הן   (f.pl.):   מִתְלַבְּשׁוֹת   *meet-lab-SHOT*

Q: What *prefix* appears at the beginning of all present tense *heetpa'el* forms?

A: All the forms begin with מִת- (*meet*):

◄   מִתְלַבֵּשׁ,   מִתְלַבֶּשֶׁת,   מִתְלַבְּשִׁים,   מִתְלַבְּשׁוֹת

Another characteristic common to all these forms is the *hard* pronunciation of the middle root letter ב׳ (pronounced *b*), as in מִתְלַבֵּשׁ. As we pointed out in the chapter "Patterns of Verbs" (pp. 364-365), in texts written with vowel signs, there is always a *dagesh*[2] (dot) in the **middle**

---

1   The group of consonants indicated by the letters שׂ׳, שׁ׳, ס׳, צ׳, ז׳ is called *sibilants* (עִיצוּרִים שׁוֹרְקִים).
2   This is a *strong dagesh* (see the chapter "The Pronunciation of ב׳, כ׳, פ׳ and the *Dagesh*," pp. 630-633). This *dagesh* does not appear in the letters א׳, ה׳, ח׳, ע׳, ר׳.

root letter of verbs in this *beenyan* (just as there is in *beenyan pee'el*). Thus, when the letters ,בּ
כּ, פּ appear in the middle of the root, they are pronounced *b* (בּ), *k* (כּ), *p* (פּ), as in:

מתנפל	מתרכז	מתלבש ⋖
meet-na-PEL	*meet-ra-KEZ*	*meet-la-BESH*
is attacking	is concentrating	is getting dressed

As in *pee'el* and *pa'al*, the feminine present tense forms of *heetpa'el* end in ת ֶ (*E-et*).
Compare:

me-da-BE-ret	מְדַבֶּרֶת ⋖
so-GE-ret	סוֹגֶרֶת
meet-la-BE-shet	מִתְלַבֶּשֶׁת

The plural forms of *heetpa'el* are very similar to those in *pee'el*, for example:

beenyan pee'el:	מְ -דַבְּ-רִים, מְ -דַבְּ-רוֹת ⋖
beenyan heetpa'el:	מִתְ-לַבְּ-שִׁים, מִתְ-לַבְּ-שׁוֹת

In both *beenyaneem*, the vowel after the בּ in the base form (מִתְ-לַ-בֵּשׁ and מְ-דַ-בֵּר) "reduces" and
is written as a *shva* (מִתְ-לַבְּ-שִׁים, מְ-דַבְּ-רִים). In today's Hebrew, the *shva* under the בּ is usually
not pronounced.[3]

Want to see if you've understood?
Write the correct form of the underlined verb.

1. דוד <u>מתכתב</u> עם חבר מצרפת כבר חמש שנים. מיכל _____ עם חברה מאיטליה.

   אתן לא _____ עם אף אחד מחו"ל?

2. את <u>מתנדבת</u> בבית חולים. גם אתה _____? איפה אתם _____?

Answers:[4]

1. מִתְכַּתֶּבֶת, מִתְכַּתְבוֹת   2. מִתְנַדֵּב, מִתְנַדְבִים

---

3   See the chapter "Reduction of Vowels and the *Shva*," pp. 648-650. The *shva* is sometimes pronounced *eh*,
     as – for example – in verbs like מִתְפַּלְלִים (*meet-pa-le-LEEM*), whose second and third root letters are identical
     (פ-ל-ל). This is so also in past and future forms, for example: הִתְפַּלְלוּ (*heet-pa-le-LOO*), יִתְפַּלְלוּ (*yeet-pa-le-LOO*).
4   It is not necessary for you to write vowel signs in your answers. We have added vowel signs to the answers in
     the chapters on verbs only in order to make clear how the forms are pronounced.

• *Past tense* (הִתְלַבֵּשׁ)

Here are the past tense forms of the verb הִתְלַבֵּשׁ:

	plural			*singular*	
heet-la-BASH-noo	הִתְלַבַּשְׁנוּ	אנחנו:	*heet-la-BASH-tee*	הִתְלַבַּשְׁתִּי	אני:
heet-la-BASH-tem[5]	הִתְלַבַּשְׁתֶּם	אתם:	*heet-la-BASH-ta*	הִתְלַבַּשְׁתָּ	אתה:
heet-la-BASH-ten	הִתְלַבַּשְׁתֶּן	אתן:	*heet-la-BASHT*	הִתְלַבַּשְׁתְּ	את:
heet-lab-SHOO	הִתְלַבְּשׁוּ	הם, הן	*heet-la-BESH*	**הִתְלַבֵּשׁ**	הוא
			heet-lab-SHA	הִתְלַבְּשָׁה	היא

Q: What prefix appears in all the past tense forms in *beenyan heetpa'el*?

A: All the forms begin with ‑הִתְ (*heet*‑): הִתְלַבַּשְׁתִּי, הִתְלַבַּשְׁתָּ...

The base form הִתְלַבֵּשׁ has an *EH* sound after the second root letter (ב') – just as דִּבֵּר in *beenyan pee'el* does. When the vowel endings (‑ָה and ‑וּ) – at the bottom of the chart – are added, the preceding *eh* vowel "reduces" and is written as *shva* (◌ְ). This *shva* is usually not pronounced in Modern Hebrew. Compare:

	הם / הן		היא		
beenyan pee'el:	*deeb-ROO*	דִּבְּ-רוּ	*deeb-RA*	דִּבְּ-רָה	◄
beenyan heetpa'el:	*heet-lab-SHOO*	הִתְ-לַבְּ-שׁוּ	*heet-lab-SHA*	הִתְ-לַבְּ-שָׁה	

All other past tense forms – i.e., those with an ending that begins with a consonant (in the upper part of chart) – have an *AH* sound in the syllable **before** the ending, just as in the *beenyaneem* that we have seen thus far, for example:

beenyan pee'el:	דִּבַּרְתְּ	דִּבַּרְתָּ,	דִּבַּרְתִּי, ◄
	dee-BART	*dee-BAR-ta*	*dee-BAR-tee*
beenayn heetpa'el:	הִתְלַבַּשְׁתְּ	הִתְלַבַּשְׁתָּ,	הִתְלַבַּשְׁתִּי,
	heet-la-BASHT	*heet-la-BASH-ta*	*heet-la-BASH-tee*

---

5   In traditional pronunciation, the stress is on the ending of the אתם and אתן forms: *heet-la-bash-TEM, heet-la-bash-TEN*.

Want to see if you've understood?

Write the missing form of the underlined verb.

1. <u>הִתְרַגַשְׁתִּי</u> מאוד בחתונה שלכם. אני בטוח שהחתן והכלה _____ עוד יותר ממני.

   ראיתי שאימא של הכלה מאוד _____ . גם אתה _____?

2. אורי <u>הִתְקַדֵם</u> יפה בלימודי האנגלית. גם אתם _____ !

Answers:

1. הִתְרַגְשׁוּ, הִתְרַגְשָׁה, הִתְרַגַשְׁתָּ   2. הִתְקַדַמְתֶּם

• *Infinitive* (לְהִתְלַבֵּשׁ)

Here is the infinitive form of verbs in *beenyan heetpa'el*:

◄ לְהִתְלַבֵּשׁ   לְהִתְכַּתֵּב   לְהִתְרַגֵּשׁ

to get dressed   to correspond   to get excited

Q: How do all these infinitive*s* begin?

A: The -לְ of the *heetpa'el* infinitive has an *eh* sound (*le*), and is followed by -הִתְ to form -לְהִתְ (*le-heet*):

◄ לְהִתְלַבֵּשׁ   לְהִתְכַּתֵּב

le-heet-la-BESH   *le-heet-ka-TEV*

Notice that the pattern is similar to the past tense base form הִתְלַבֵּשׁ.

Want to see if you've understood?

Write the infinitive of the underlined verb.

1. <u>הִתְנַדַבְתִּי</u> בגן החיות בשנה שעברה. כדאי גם לכם _____ שם, זה כיף.

2. מתי מיכל ודויד <u>מִתְחַתְּנִים</u>? שמעתי שהם רוצים _____ על חוף הים.

Answers:

1. לְהִתְנַדֵב   2. לְהִתְחַתֵּן

• *Future tense* (יִתְלַבֵּשׁ)

Here are the future tense forms of the verb הִתְלַבֵּשׁ:

	prefixes and endings		only prefixes		
			'et-la-BESH	אֶתְלַבֵּשׁ	אני: ◄
			teet-la-BESH	תִתְלַבֵּשׁ	אתה:
	teet-lab-SHEE	תִתְלַבְּשִׁי			את:
			yeet-la-BESH	**יִתְלַבֵּשׁ**	הוא:
			teet-la-BESH	תִתְלַבֵּשׁ	היא:
			neet-la-BESH	נִתְלַבֵּשׁ	אנחנו:
	teet-lab-SHOO	תִתְלַבְּשׁוּ			אתם, אתן:
	yeet-lab-SHOO	יִתְלַבְּשׁוּ			הם, הן:

The base forms of all the tenses in *beenyan heetpa'el* are similar. Only the first letter changes:

present tense:	מִתְלַבֵּשׁ	הוא	◄
past tense:	הִתְלַבֵּשׁ	הוא	
future tense:	יִתְלַבֵּשׁ	הוא	

As we noted in previous chapters, in most *beenyaneem* the **usual** path to the future tense form is via the **infinitive**. In *heetpa'el,* as well, the future base form is similar to the infinitive; however, as in all *beenyaneem* whose infinitive contains a ה׳, the ה׳ drops out when we form the future base form:

$$ \text{יִתְלַבֵּשׁ} \Leftarrow \text{לְהִתְלַבֵּשׁ} \Leftarrow \text{לְהִתְלַבֵּשׁ} \qquad ◄ $$

Now look at all the future tense forms in the chart above.

Q: Which prefix contains a vowel **different** from the others?

A: אֶת- in the אני form: אֶתְלַבֵּשׁ.[6] All other future forms in *heetpa'el* begin with the sound *ee*:

נִתְלַבֵּשׁ...	תִתְלַבֵּשׁ,	יִתְלַבֵּשׁ, ◄
neet-la-BESH	teet-la-BESH	yeet-la-BESH

Now let's look at the **left** column of the chart above. Here, as in other *beenyaneem*, the vowel endings ־ִי and ־וּ are added. The changes that take place as a result are similar to the changes that we saw in *pee'el* and *pa'al*, for example:

---

6   As we saw in *beenyan pa'al* (אֶסְגּוֹר), א׳ often shows a preference for the sound *eh*.

beenyan pee'el:	יְ-דַבְּ-רוּ	תְּ-דַבְּ-רוּ	תְּ-דַבְּ-רִי	⇐	יְ-דַ-בֵּר ◄
	ye-dab-ROO	te-dab-ROO	te-dab-REE		ye-da-BER
beenyan heetpa'el:	יִתְ-לַבְּ-שׁוּ	תִּתְ-לַבְּ-שׁוּ,	תִּתְ-לַבְּ-שִׁי,	⇐	יִתְ-לַ-בֵּשׁ
	yeet-lab-SHOO	teet-lab-SHOO	teet-lab-SHEE		yeet-la-BESH

Want to see if you've understood?
Write the missing form of the underlined verb.

1. אני חושבת שרון יִתְרַגֵּשׁ מאוד בחתונה של אחותו. אימא שלו _____.

    אנחנו _____. אתם _____.

2. רן, אני בטוחה שֶׁתִּתְקַבֵּל לאוניברסיטה. גם מיכל _____, וגם טל ושמעון _____.

Answers:

1. תִּתְרַגֵּשׁ, נִתְרַגֵּשׁ, תִּתְרַגְּשׁוּ   2. תִּתְקַבֵּל, יִתְקַבְּלוּ

• *Roots that begin with* 'שׁ, 'שׂ, 'ס, 'צ, 'ז

If you pronounce the consonants indicated by the letters 'שׁ, 'שׂ, 'ס, 'צ, 'ז – *sh, s, ts, z*[7] – you can hear that they all are close to a hissing sound. As we will see below, when these consonants follow the 'ת of the *heetpa'el* prefixes יִתְ-, הִתְ-, מִתְ- and the like, certain changes in the verb forms take place.

'שׁ, 'שׂ *and* 'ס (*the sounds* sh *and* s)

Read the following past tense הוא forms:

הִסְתַּכֵּל	הִשְׂתַּכֵּר	הִשְׁתַּמֵּשׁ ◄
hees-ta-KEL	hees-ta-KER	heesh-ta-MESH
he looked	he earned (a salary)	he used

These, too, are base forms of *heetpa'el*.

---

7   The consonants indicated by the letters 'שׁ, 'שׂ, 'ס, 'צ, 'ז are called *sibilants* (עִיצוּרִים שׁוֹרְקִים).

Q: What happened to the 'ת of the prefix -הִתְ in these verbs?

A: It switched places with the first root letter:[8]

before the switch:	הִ תְ סַ כֵּ ל*	הִ תְ שַׂ כֵּ ר*	הִ תְ שַׁ מֵ שׁ*[9]
after the switch:	הִ סְ תַ כֵּ ל	הִ שְׂ תַ כֵּ ר	הִ שְׁ תַ מֵ שׁ

This switching takes place for phonetic reasons. It occurs in all tenses and forms of *heetpa'el* whenever the first *root letter* is 'שׂ, 'שׁ or 'ס, as in:

infinitive	future	present	past
לְהִשְׁתַמֵשׁ	יִשְׁתַמֵשׁ	מִשְׁתַמֵשׁ	הִשְׁתַמֵשׁ

'צ and 'ז (*the sounds* ts *and* z)

Now read these past tense הוא forms:

הִזְדַקֵן	הִצְטַעֵר
heez-da-KEN	heets-ta-'ER
he grew old	he was sorry

These, too, belong to *beenyan heetpa'el*. The root of הִצְטַעֵר is צ-ע-ר, and the root of הִזְדַקֵן is ז-ק-נ.

Q: Do you see the 'ת of הִתְפַּעֵל in these verbs?

A: No, it is nowhere to be seen. The process of its disappearance is as follows:

(1) *before the switch:*	הִ תְ זַ קֵ ן*	הִ תְ צַ עֵ ר*
(2) *after the initial switch:*	הִ זְ תַ קֵ ן*	הִ צְ תַ עֵ ר*
(3) *after one more change:*[10]	הִ זְ דַ קֵ ן	הִ צְ טַ עֵ ר

As you can see, these verbs undergo not only a "switch" of the 'ת and the first root letter (stage 2), as did הִשְׁתַמֵשׁ, but in addition the 'ת undergoes a transformation when it passes from stage 2 to stage 3.

---

8   This phenomenon whereby consonants switch places is called *metathesis* (שִׁיכּוּל עִיצוּרִים).

9   The symbol "*" indicates that the form doesn't exist.

10   This change takes place for phonetic reasons. (The *t* of התפעל partially assimilates to the first consonant of the root.) This process is called *partial assimilation* (הִידַמוּת חֶלְקית). For a more detailed explanation, see Coffin and Bolozky, 2005, pp. 99-100.

Q: After 'צ in verbs like הִצְטַעֵר – what does the 'ת of *heetpa'el* (-הת) turn into?

A: It always becomes a 'ט as in:

הצטיין	הצטלם	הצטער ◄
he excelled	he was photographed	he was sorry

Q: And after 'ז in verbs like הִזְדַקֵן – what happens to the 'ת of *heetpa'el* (-הת)?

A: It always turns into a 'ד, as in:

הזדרז	הזדקן ◄
he hurried up	he grew old

These changes take place in all tenses and forms of *heetpa'el* whenever the first root letter is 'צ
or 'ז, as in:

infinitive	*future*	*present*	*past*	
לְהִצְטַעֵר	יִצְטַעֵר	מִצְטַעֵר	הִצְטַעֵר	◄
לְהִזְדַקֵן	יִזְדַקֵן	מִזְדַקֵן	הִזְדַקֵן	

Want to see if you've understood?

Write the missing form of the underlined verb.

1. דויד, _____ כבר? למה אתה לא רוצה <u>להצטלם</u>? אני רוצה שאתה ורונית
(past)

_____ ביחד!
(future)

2. בחלק הראשון של הבחינה <u>השתמשתם</u> במילון, אבל בחלק השני לא תוכלו _____
(infinitive)

במילון.

Answers:

1. הִצְטַלַמְתָ, תִצְטַלְמוּ   2. לְהִשְתַמֵש

• *Four-letter roots*   מְרוּבָּעִים   (הִתְאַרְגֵן)

Like *beenyan pee'el* (e.g., תִּרְגֵם, פִּרְסֵם), *beenyan heetpa'el*, too, contains many verbs with **four-letter roots**,[11] for example:

הִתְקַלְקֵל	הִתְבַּלְבֵּל	הִתְאַרְגֵן ◄
it got spoiled (food); it broke (machine)	he got confused	he got organized

The following are four-letter roots whose first root letter is 'ס, 'שׁ, 'שׂ:

הִסְתַּחְרֵר	הִשְׁתַּחְרֵר	הִשְׁתַּעֲמֵם ◄
he got dizzy	he was released	he got bored

The forms of verbs with four-letter roots in *heetpa'el* are the same as regular *heetpa'el* verbs, for example:

present tense:	הִיא מִתְבַּלְבֶּלֶת	הוּא מִתְבַּלְבֵּל, ◄
past tense:	הִיא הִתְבַּלְבְּלָה	הוּא הִתְבַּלְבֵּל,
future tense:	הִיא תִתְבַּלְבֵּל	הוּא יִתְבַּלְבֵּל,
infinitive:		לְהִתְבַּלְבֵּל

Chapter summary

♦ These are the base forms (the הוּא forms) and the infinitive of regular *beenyan heetpa'el* verbs:

infinitive	*future*	*present*	*past*
לְהִתְלַבֵּשׁ	יִתְלַבֵּשׁ	מִתְלַבֵּשׁ	הִתְלַבֵּשׁ ◄

♦ When the first root letter is 'ס, 'שׂ,'שׁ, the ת of the *heetpa'el* prefixes (-הִתְ, מִתְ- and so on) switches places with them, as in:

הִסְתַּכֵּל	הִשְׁתַּכֵּר,	הִשְׁתַּמֵּשׁ, ◄

♦ When the first root letter is 'צ, besides switching places, the 'ת changes into 'ט:

הִצְטַעֵר ◄

---

11   The middle root letter of regular verbs in *beenyaneem pee'el, poo'al* and *heetpa'el* has a strong *dagesh*, and the consonant is considered "doubled" (see the chapter "The Pronunciation of ב, כ, פ and the *Dagesh*," p. 631). Because this "doubling" is built into the pattern of these three *beenyaneem*, they are all able to accommodate roots with **four** consonants. When four-letter roots appear in these *beenyaneem*, there is no longer a strong *dagesh* in these verb forms, since no consonant is considered to be "doubled."

◆ When the first root letter is 'ז, besides switching places, the 'ת changes into 'ד:

◄ הִזְדַּקֵּן

◆ Some *heetpa'el* verbs have four root letters:

◄ הִתְבַּלְבֵּל, הִתְאַרְגֵּן, הִשְׁתַּחְרֵר

Want to see if you've understood this chapter?

Write the correct form of the underlined verb (past, present, future or infinitive).

1. אין סיבה <u>להתנגד</u> להצעה שלנו. לפני חודשיים (אתם) _____ להצעה.

   אנחנו מקווים שעכשיו אתם כבר לא _____ לה.

2. מירי, <u>השתמשת</u> בעט שלי? כשאת _____ בדברים שלי, את צריכה להגיד לי.

   בפעם הבאה ש _____ בעט שלי, תבקשי, בסדר?

3. מכונת הכביסה <u>התקלקלה</u>. זאת הפעם השנייה השנה שהיא _____ .
   (present)

4. ריקי: <u>הצטערתי</u> שלא הצלחנו להיפגש.

   דליה: אַל _____ , נמצא הזדמנות אחרת.
   (future)

Answers:

1. הִתְנַגַּדְתֶּם, מִתְנַגְּדִים   2. מִשְׁתַּמֶּשֶׁת, תִּשְׁתַּמְּשִׁי   3. מִתְקַלְקֶלֶת   4. תִּצְטַעֲרִי

415

4. *Beenyan Heef'eel* הִפְעִיל

> **Preview**
> * *Present tense* (מַרְגִּישׁ)
> * *Past tense* (הִרְגִּישׁ)
> * *Infinitive* (לְהַרְגִּישׁ)
> * *Future tense* (יַרְגִּישׁ)

The verb הִרְגִּישׁ / לְהַרְגִּישׁ (to feel) will serve as our model of a *regular* verb in *beenyan heef'eel*.

• *Present tense* (מַרְגִּישׁ)

Here are the present tense forms of the verb הִרְגִּישׁ:

mar-GEESH	מַרְגִּישׁ	*(m.s.)*:	אני, אתה, הוא ◄
mar-gee-SHA	מַרְגִּישָׁה	*(f.s.)*:	אני, את, היא
mar-gee-SHEEM	מַרְגִּישִׁים	*(m.pl.)*:	אנחנו, אתם, הם
mar-gee-SHOT	מַרְגִּישׁוֹת	*(f.pl.)*:	אנחנו, אתן, הן

Q: What is the *prefix* in present tense *heef'eel* forms?

A: All forms begin with a מ- followed by an *ah* sound: -מַ (*ma-*).

All present tense forms also have a י in the second syllable between the second and third root letters.

Now let's look more closely at the feminine singular form: מַרְגִּישָׁה.

Unlike the feminine singular form in regular verbs in other *beenyaneem*, the feminine singular form of *heef'eel* ends with a ה-ָ:

mar-gee-SHA   מַרְגִּישָׁה ◄

Also, unlike the feminine singular forms in other *beenyaneem* (e.g., לוֹמֶדֶת *lo-ME-det*, מְדַבֶּרֶת *me-da-BE-ret*), the stress here is on the **last** syllable (*mar-gee-SHA*) and **not** on the next-to-last syllable.

416

In the plural forms, the stress – as in other *beenyaneem* – is on the ending. But notice: in *beenyan heef'eel* the preceding vowel stays the **same** (it does **not** "reduce" as does the vowel in לוֹמְדִים and מְדַבְּרִים), for example:

מַרְ-גִּי-שׁוֹת, מַרְ-גִּי-שִׁים, ◄
mar-gee-SHOT *mar-gee-SHEEM*

Want to see if you've understood?
Write the missing form of the underlined verb.

1. כשאתה <u>מסביר</u> לי, אני מבין. כשרינה _____, אני אף פעם לא מבין.

2. היום אני <u>מתחיל</u> ללמוד בשמונה. מתי אתן _____ ללמוד?

   מתי יוסי ושמעון _____ ללמוד?

Answers:[1]

1. מַסְבִּירָה 2. מַתְחִילוֹת, מַתְחִילִים

• *Past tense* (הִרְגִּישׁ)

Here are the past tense forms of the verb הִרְגִּישׁ:

	plural				*singular*		
heer-GASH-noo	הִרְגַּשְׁנוּ	אנחנו:		*heer-GASH-tee*	הִרְגַּשְׁתִּי	אני:	◄
heer-GASH-tem[2]	הִרְגַּשְׁתֶּם	אתם:		*heer-GASH-ta*	הִרְגַּשְׁתָּ	אתה:	
heer-GASH-ten	הִרְגַּשְׁתֶּן	אתן:		*heer-GASHT*	הִרְגַּשְׁתְּ	את:	
heer-GEE-shoo	הִרְגִּישׁוּ	הם, הן		*heer-GEESH*	הִרְגִּישׁ	הוא	
				heer-GEE-sha	הִרְגִּישָׁה	היא	

Q: What is the prefix shared by all the past tense forms in *beenyan heef'eel*?

A: All forms begin with הֶ- (*hee*), which joins with the first root letter to form a syllable (הִרְ-גִּישׁ). Note that we do **not** write י after the ה-: הִרְגִּישׁ.

---

1 It is not necessary for you to write vowel signs in your answers. We have added vowel signs to the answers in the chapters on verbs in order to make clear how the forms are pronounced.

2 In traditional pronunciation, the stress is on the **ending** of the אתם and אתן forms. Thus, the traditional pronunciation of these forms is: *heer-gash-TEM, heer-gash-TEN.*

Now look at the bottom of the chart above.

Q: What is common to the base form (הוא) and to the הם/הן, היא forms?

A: They all have a י in the second syllable (הִרְגִּישׁ, הִרְגִּישָׁה, הִרְגִּישׁוּ). The stress in these forms **remains** on the syllable with the י:

הִרְ-גִּי-שׁוּ   הִרְ-גִּי-שָׁה,   הִרְ-גִּישׁ, ◄
heer-GEE-shoo   *heer-GEE-sha*   *heer-GEESH*

In this respect these are **different** from the היא and הם/הן forms in all the other *beenyaneem*, where the vowel endings (ה‎ָ and ‎וּ) draw the stress to them, and the preceding vowel "reduces":

	הם/הן	היא	הוא
pa'al:	לָמְ-דוּ	לָמְ-דָה	לָ-מַד ◄
pee'el:	דִּבְּ-רוּ	דִּבְּ-רָה	דִּי-בֶּר
heetpa'el:	הִתְ-לַבְּ-שׁוּ	הִתְ-לַבְּ-שָׁה	הִתְ-לַ-בֵּשׁ

Now look at the top of the *heef'eel* chart.

Q: What vowel is in the syllable **before** the endings?

A: As in all the *beenyaneem*, a stressed *AH* vowel comes before the endings that begin with a consonant (*-tee, -ta…*):

הִרְ-גַּשְׁ-תָ ...   הִרְ-גַּשְׁ-תִּי, ◄
heer-GASH-ta   *heer-GASH-tee*

Thus, in **all** the past tense forms of *beenyan heef'eel* (including the third person), the stress is on the second syllable:

הִרְ-גִּי-שׁוּ   הִרְ-גִּי-שָׁה,   הִרְ-גִּישׁ,   הִרְ-גַּשְׁ-תָ ...   הִרְ-גַּשְׁ-תִּי, ◄

Be careful! The place of the stress in the היא forms in the past and present tenses is different:

past tense: *heer-GEE- sha*   הִרְ-גִּי-שָׁה   היא ◄
present tense: *mar-gee-SHA*   מַרְ-גִּי-שָׁה   היא

Want to see if you've understood?
Write the missing form of the underlined verb.

1.‏ אתמול במסעדה את <u>הזמנת</u> חומוס, מירי ודויד _____ טחינה, ואני _____ סלט.

2.‏ מיכל <u>הסבירה</u> לי את התרגיל, ואני _____ אותו לתמר.

Answers:

1.‏ הִזְמִינוּ, הִזְמַנְתִּי   2.‏ הִסְבַּרְתִּי

• *Infinitive* (לְהַרְגִּיש)

Here is the infinitive form of some *heef'eel* verbs:

לְהַדְרִיךְ	לְהַזְמִין	לְהַרְגִּיש
to guide	to invite/order	to feel

Q: What is common to all these infinitives?

A: They all begin with לְהַ- (*le-ha*) before the first root letter. They join with the root as follows:

לְ-הַזְ-מִין	לְ-הַרְ-גִּיש
le-haz-MEEN	*le-har-GEESH*

These forms also have a י in their final syllable.

Want to see if you've understood?
Write the infinitive of the underlined verb.

1.‏ תמר לא <u>הסבירה</u> לי איך מגיעים לתחנה המרכזית. מישהו יכול _____ לי
איך מגיעים לשם?

2.‏ למה <u>הסכמת</u> עם לירון? לא צריך _____ לכל מה שהוא אומר.

Answers:

1.‏ לְהַסְבִּיר   2.‏ לְהַסְכִּים

• *Future tense* (יַרְגִּישׁ)

Here are the future tense forms of the verb הִרְגִּישׁ:

prefixes and endings		only prefixes			
		'ar-GEESH	אַרְגִּישׁ	אני:	◄
		tar-GEESH	תַּרְגִּישׁ	אתה:	
tar-GEE-shee	תַּרְגִּישִׁי			את:	
		yar-GEESH	יַרְגִּישׁ	הוא:	
		tar-GEESH	תַּרְגִּישׁ	היא:	
		nar-GEESH	נַרְגִּישׁ	אנחנו:	
tar-GEE-shoo	תַּרְגִּישׁוּ			אתם, אתן:	
yar-GEE-shoo	יַרְגִּישׁוּ			הם, הן:	

As in other *beenyaneem*, the infinitive of *heef'eel* easily leads us to the future tense base form. Here, too, as in *beenyan heetpa'el* (הִתְפַּעֵל) and in all *beenyaneem* that have ה׳ in their infinitive, we must remove both the ל׳ and ה׳ before adding the future prefix:

◄ לְהַרְגִּישׁ ⇐ לְהַרְגִּישׁ ⇐ יַרְגִּישׁ

The vowel pattern of the future tense base form in *heef'eel* also resembles the present tense base form:

present:	mar-GEESH	מַרְגִּישׁ ◄
infinitive:	le-har-GEESH	לְהַרְגִּישׁ
future:	yar-GEESH	יַרְגִּישׁ

All these forms have an *ah* sound at or near the beginning. It is only the **past tense** – הִרְגִּישׁ – that has an *ee* in the first syllable and, thus, is different.

Now let's concentrate on the **second** syllable of the future tense forms in the chart above. Notice that the *EE* sound (ִי) remains in the second syllable of **all** the forms, and the stress remains on this same syllable, even when an ending is added (unlike in other *beenyaneem*):

תַּר-גִּי-שִׁי ...	תַּר-גִּישׁ,	אַר-גִּישׁ, ◄
tar-GEE-shee	tar-GEESH	'ar-GEESH

Also, the אני form has the same initial vowel (*ah*) as the other forms.

Want to see if you've understood?

Write the future form of the underlined verb.

1. אנחנו <u>נמשיך</u> לשיר רק אם רותי _____ לנגן בפסנתר.

2. יעל, <u>תסבירי</u> לי בבקשה מה לעשות. אם לא אבין את ההסברים שלך, דני _____ לי.

Answers:

1. תַּמְשִׁיךְ   2. יַסְבִּיר

Chapter summary

◆ These are the base forms (the past, present and future הוא forms) and the infinitive of regular *beenyan heef'eel* verbs. Notice that the past tense form has a different vowel in the first syllable:

infinitive	*future*	*present*	*past*
לְהַרְגִּיש	יַרְגִּיש	מַרְגִּיש	הִרְגִּיש ◄
le-har-GEESH	*yar-GEESH*	*mar-GEESH*	*heer-GEESH*

Want to see if you've understood this chapter?

Write the correct form of the underlined verb (past, present, future or infinitive).

1. מאיה ורון, <u>הזמנתם</u> את דנה למסיבה? כדאי ש_____ אותה. כדאי _____
   (infinitive)   (future)

   גם את מיכל ודן.

2. אם אתה לא _____ טוב, תאכל מרק עוף ואז <u>תרגיש</u> הרבה יותר טוב.
                    (present)

3. אל <u>תפסיקו</u> לשיר. למה (אתם) _____?
                                   (past)

Answers:

1. תַּזְמִינוּ, לְהַזְמִין   2. מַרְגִּיש   3. הִפְסַקְתֶּם

5. *Beenyan Neef'al* נִפְעַל

> **Preview**
> - *Present tense* (נִכְנָס)
> - *Past tense* (נִכְנַס)
> - *Infinitive* (לְהִיכָּנֵס)
> - *Future tense* (יִיכָּנֵס)
> - ב', כ', פ' *as the second root letter in* neef'al *verb forms*

The verb נִכְנַס / לְהִיכָּנֵס (to enter) will serve as our model of a *regular* verb in *beenyan neef'al*.

• *Present tense* (נִכְנָס)

Here are the present tense forms of the verb נִכְנַס:

neech-NAS	נִכְנָס	:(m.s.)	אני, אתה, הוא
neech-NE-set	נִכְנֶסֶת	:(f.s.)	אני, את, היא
neech-na-SEEM	נִכְנָסִים	:(m.pl.)	אנחנו, אתם, הם
neech-na-SOT	נִכְנָסוֹת	:(f.pl.)	אנחנו, אתן, הן

Q: What *prefix* is shared by all present tense *neef'al* forms?

A: They all begin with -נ followed by an *ee* vowel: -נִ (*nee*). Note that we do **not** write י after the -נ.

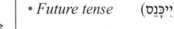 נִכְנָס, נִכְנֶסֶת, נִכְנָסִים, נִכְנָסוֹת

As in *pa'al, pee'el* and *heetpa'el*, here, too, the feminine singular form ends in *E-et*:

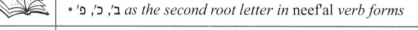 *neech-NE-set* נִכְנֶסֶת

However, unlike the plural forms of *pa'al, pee'el* and *heetpa'el* (סוֹגְרִים, מְדַבְּרִים, מִתְלַבְּשִׁים), where the vowel before the plural ending "reduces" (in texts with vowel signs, it is written ◌ְ), in *neef'al* the vowel before the plural endings remains *ah*:

נִכְ-נָ-סוֹת   נִכְ-נָ-סִים,
neech-na-SOT   *neech-na-SEEM*

As we will see, this is true also of *beenyan poo'al* (מְצוּלָמִים) and *beenyan hoof'al* (מוּזְמָנִים).

![pencil icon] **Want to see if you've understood?**
Write the correct present tense form of the underlined verb.

‏1. היום את נפגשת עם אחותך בבית קפה? אתה _____ איתה?

‏אתם _____ איתה?

‏2. דן לא מבין למה הוא נכשל כל הזמן במתמטיקה. דלית אף פעם לא _____ ,

‏וגם שרה ורונית לא _____ .

Answers:[1]

‏1. נִפְגָּשׁ, נִפְגָּשִׁים   2. נִכְשֶׁלֶת, נִכְשָׁלוֹת

• *Past tense* (נִכְנַס)

Here are the past tense forms of the verb נִכְנַס:

	plural				singular		
neech-NAS-noo	נִכְנַסְנוּ	אנחנו:		neech-NAS-tee	נִכְנַסְתִּי	אני:	◄
neech-NAS-tem[2]	נִכְנַסְתֶּם	אתם:		neech-NAS-ta	נִכְנַסְתָּ	אתה:	
neech-NAS-ten	נִכְנַסְתֶּן	אתן:		neech-NAST	נִכְנַסְתְּ	את:	
neech-ne-SOO	נִכְנְסוּ	הם, הן		neech-NAS	**נִכְנַס**	הוא	
				neech-ne-SA	נִכְנְסָה	היא	

Q: What prefix is shared by all past tense *neef'al* forms?

A: The same prefix as in the present tense: -נִ (*nee-*).[3] Here, too, there is **no** י after the -נ, even when we write without vowels:

‏◄ נכנסתי, נכנסתָ, נכנסתְ ...

---

1 It is not necessary for you to write vowel signs in your answers. We have added vowel signs to the answers in the chapters on verbs only in order to make clear how the forms are pronounced.

2 In traditional pronunciation, the stress is on the ending of the אתם and אתן forms: *neech-nas-TEM, neech-nas-TEN.*

3 Except for roots beginning with a *guttural* (א, ה, ח, ע), e.g., נֶעֱלַם. On gutturals see the chapter "Guttural Consonants and ר: *Beenyaneem Pee'el, Poo'al* and *Neef'al*," pp. 480-482.

Note that the base forms of the present and past tenses sound and are written the same: נכנס (*neech-NAS*).[4]

Now let's look at the bottom part of the chart above.

As in all the *beenyaneem* – except for *heef'eel* – the vowel before the ־ָה and ־וּ endings of the היא and the הם/הן forms "reduces." This vowel is pronounced *eh*. When these forms are written with vowel signs, this reduced vowel is written as *shva* (◌ְ):

◄ נִכְ-נְ-סָה,   נִכְ-נְ-סוּ
      neech-ne-SA   *neech-ne-SOO*

In the forms in the upper part of the chart, the vowel before the ending is a stressed *AH* – as in all other *beenyaneem*. This also happens to be the same vowel as that of the base form נִכְנַס:

◄ נִכְ-נַס-תִּי,   נִכְ-נַס-תָּ,   נִכְ-נַסְתְּ...
   neech-NAS-tee   *neech-NAS-ta*   *neech-NAST*

Want to see if you've understood?
Write the correct past tense form of the underlined verb.

1. _____? מתי האחים שלך _____? מתי אתה _____ נרדמתי אתמול בשעה 22:00.

2. מהם? _____ רוני, מיכל כבר נפרדה מבני הדודים. גם את כבר

Answers:

1. נִרְדַּמְתָּ,   נִרְדְּמוּ   2. נִפְרַדְתְּ

• *Infinitive* (לְהִיכָּנֵס)

Here are some *neef'al* infinitives:

◄ לְהִיכָּנֵס   לְהִיבָּדֵק   לְהִיפָּגֵשׁ
   le-hee-ka-NES   *le-hee-ba-DEK*   *le-hee-pa-GESH*
   to enter   to be checked   to meet with

---

4   When vowel signs are added, the present tense form is נִכְנָס with ◌ָ and the past tense form is נִכְנַס with ◌ַ. The pronunciation of these two forms is the same.

Q: How do all these infinitive*s* begin?

A: They all begin with -לְהִי (*le-hee*):

לְהִיכָּנֵס   לְהִיבָּדֵק   לְהִיפָּגֵשׁ

As you can see, the -נ of *neef'al* (נפעל) does **not** appear in the infinitive. Instead, in *full spelling*[5] – used throughout this book – י is written where the נ would have been (לְהִיכָּנֵס ⇐ להיכנס*).[6] In texts written **with** vowel signs, a *strong dagesh* appears in the letter **after** the י.[7] When this letter happens to be ב, כ or פ, as in the examples above, it is pronounced as a *hard* sound: *b*, *k* or *p*.

Note that in today's pronunciation there are **four** syllables in the infinitive: לְ-הִי-כָּ-נֵס.[8]

ב, כ, פ *as the first root letter in* neef'al *verbs*

Compare the present, past and infinitive forms of the following verbs whose **first** root letter is ב, כ or פ:

שם הפועל		עבר		הווה	
infinitive		*past*		*present*	
le-hee-ka-NES	לְהִיכָּנֵס	neech-NAS	נִכְנַס	neech-NAS	נִכְנָס
le-hee-ba-DEK	לְהִיבָּדֵק	neev-DAK	נִבְדַק	neev-DAK	נִבְדָק
le-hee-pa-GESH	לְהִיפָּגֵשׁ	neef-GASH	נִפְגַשׁ	neef-GASH	נִפְגָשׁ

Q: What is the difference between the pronunciation of ב, כ, פ in the present and past and their pronunciation in the infinitive?

A: In the present and past, when ב, כ, פ are the first root letter, they have a *soft* pronunciation – *v*, *ch*, *f*, whereas in the infinitive they have a hard sound: *b*, *k*, *p*.

---

5   See the chapter "Hebrew Spelling," pp. 657-660.

6   The symbol "*" indicates that the form is only theoretical and does not exist today. Note: In *standard* (not *full*) spelling, the *neef'al* infinitive is written **without** י, as in לְהִכָּנֵס.

7   Grammar books describe the *n* of *neef'al* as *assimilating* to the following consonant. For an explanation of this phenomenon, see the chapter "The Pronunciation of ב, כ, פ and the *Dagesh*," p. 636 ("Did you know?").

8   The division in classical grammar is different: ל/הכ-כ-נס.

Want to see if you've understood?
Write the infinitive of the underlined verb.

1. <u>נִפְגַּשְׁתֶּם</u> לקפה לפני הסרט. אתם אוהבים ــــــــــــ בבתי קפה.

2. רון, אני מבינה שעדיין לא <u>נבחנת</u>. מתי אתה צריך ــــــــــــ?

Answers:

1. לְהִיפָּגֵשׁ   2. לְהִיבָּחֵן

• *Future tense* (יִיכָּנֵס)

Here are the future tense forms of the verb נִכְנַס:

prefixes and endings		only prefixes		
		'e-ka-NES	אֶכָּנֵס	אני:
		tee-ka-NES	תִּיכָּנֵס	אתה:
tee-kan-SEE	תִּיכָּנְסִי			את:
		yee-ka-NES	יִיכָּנֵס	הוא:
		tee-ka-NES	תִּיכָּנֵס	היא:
		nee-ka-NES	נִיכָּנֵס	אנחנו:
tee-kan-SOO	תִּיכָּנְסוּ			אתם, אתן:
yee-kan-SOO	יִיכָּנְסוּ			הם, הן:

Here is how we arrive at the future tense form of *neef'al* from its infinitive:

לְהִיכָּנֵס ⇐ לְהִיכָּנֵס ⇐ יִיכָּנֵס

As in all *beenyaneem* whose infinitive contains a ה' (להרגיש, להתלבש), here, too, the ה' drops off with the -ל when we add the future tense prefixes.

Now look closely at all the prefixes in the chart above.

Q: Which prefix contains a vowel **different** from the others?

A: אֶ- in אֶכָּנֵס (אני).[9] This prefix has an *eh* sound and, therefore, it is not followed by a י. All the other prefixes in *neef'al* contain the vowel *ee* and, when written in full spelling, are followed by a י, as is the case in the infinitive (להיכנס):[10]

תיכנס,	ייכנס ...
tee-ka-NES	*yee-ka-NES*

As is the case in the infinitive form, the נ of *neef'al* is also not present in the future tense forms. Instead, in all but the אני form, a י takes the place of the missing נ and, when the following letter is ב׳, כ׳ or פ׳, it has a hard pronunciation:

ייפָּגֵשׁ	ייבָּדֵק	ייכָּנֵס
yee-pa-GESH	*yee-ba-DEK*	*yee-ka-NES*

In the forms with the endings (on the left side of the chart), we see that – as in all the *beenyaneem* (except for *heef'eel*) – the stress moves to the ending (e.g., תי-כָּנְ-סִי *tee-kan-SEE*) and the vowel before the ending "reduces." In texts written with vowel signs, the reduced vowel is written as a *shva* (◌). In Modern Hebrew, this *shva* is usually not pronounced.

Notice that the future tense base form – יי-כָּ-נֵס (*yee-ka-NES*) – has **three** syllables. In contrast, the present and past tense base forms have only **two** syllables and an initial נ-: נכ-נס.

Want to see if you've understood?
Write the correct future tense form of the underlined verb.

1. אני אֶפָּגֵשׁ עם מנהלת בית הספר מחר, ואתם _____ איתה מחרתיים.

2. לפני הבדיקה אצל הרופא רון אמר לאח שלו: "הילד שיושב לידך יִיבָּדֵק ראשון,

   אתה _____ שני, ואני _____ אחרון."

Answers:

1. תיפָּגְשׁוּ   2. תיבָּדֵק, אֶבָּדֵק

---

9   As in *pa'al* (אֶסגור) and *heetpa'el* (אֶתלבש), א- often shows a preference for the vowel sound *eh*.
10 In *standard spelling*, the future tense prefixes are not followed by a י: יִכָּנֵס, תִכָּנֵס...

• ב׳, כ׳, פ׳ *as the second root letter in* neef'al *verb forms*

Above, in the section on the infinitive, we saw what happens when ב׳, כ׳, פ׳ are the **first** root letter in *neef'al* verbs (נִכְנָס, נִכְנַס // יִיכָּנֵס, לְהִיכָּנֵס). Now let's see what happens when ב׳, כ׳, פ׳ are the **second** root letter:

	עתיד	שם הפועל	עבר	הווה
	future	*infinitive*	*past*	*present*
to break (The glass broke.)	יִישָׁבֵר	לְהִישָׁבֵר	נִשְׁבַּר	נִשְׁבָּר
	yee-sha-VER	*le-hee-sha-VER*	*neesh-BAR*	*neesh-BAR*
to spill (The water spilled.)	יִישָׁפֵךְ	לְהִישָׁפֵךְ	נִשְׁפַּךְ	נִשְׁפָּךְ
	yee-sha-FECH	*le-hee-sha-FECH*	*neesh-PACH*	*neesh-PACH*
to recall	יִיזָכֵר	לְהִיזָכֵר	נִזְכַּר	נִזְכָּר
	yee-za-CHER	*le-hee-za-CHER*	*neez-KAR*	*neez-KAR*

Q: In which forms are ב׳, כ׳, פ׳ pronounced as hard sounds (*b, k, p*) and in which as soft sounds (*v, ch, f*)?

A: In the present and past, they are hard sounds since they appear after a *closed* syllable (e.g., נִשְׁ־בַּר *neesh-BAR*). In the infinitive and future, where they appear after an *open* syllable, they are pronounced as soft sounds (e.g., לְ־הִי־שָׁ־בֵר *le-hee-sha-VER*).[11]

Want to see if you've understood?
Write the missing form of the underlined verb and read all the forms out loud.

١.‏ עדיין לא <u>נזכרתם</u> בשם הסרט שראיתם בשבוע שעבר? כש_____, תגידו לי, בבקשה.

٢.‏ <u>נשפך</u> קצת קפה על השולחן. תיזהרו שהקפה לא _____ גם עליכם, הוא חם!

Answers:

1. נִזְכַּרְתֶּם *neez-KAR-tem*, תִּיזָכְרוּ *tee-zach-ROO*   2. נִשְׁפַּךְ *neesh-PACH*, יִישָׁפֵךְ *yee-sha-FECH*

---

11 See the chapter "The Pronunciation of ב׳, כ׳, פ׳ and the *Dagesh*," pp. 626-629.

Chapter summary

◆ These are the base forms (the past, present and future הוא forms) and the infinitive of regular *beenyan neef'al* verbs:

infinitive	future	present	past
לְהִיכָּנֵס	יִיכָּנֵס	נִכְנָס	נִכְנַס
le-hee-ka-NES	yee-ka-NES	neech-NAS	neech-NAS

◄

Note how different the present and past tense forms are from the future and infinitive: While the present and past forms begin with a נ and have **two** syllables, the future and infinitive have **three** syllables and no נ.

◆ When the letters ב', כ', פ' are the first or second root letters, various changes in pronunciation take place. These are discussed in the chapter above.

Want to see if you've understood this chapter?

Write the correct form of the underlined verb (past, present, future or infinitive).

1. מאיה ואני מזמן לא _____ . מחר _____ סוף סוף.
   (past)

   נחמד לְהִיפָּגֵשׁ שוב אחרי כל כך הרבה זמן.

2. מיכל נסעה לשנה לאוסטרליה. כשהיא _____ מאיתנו, היא אמרה שעצוב לה
   (past)

   לְהִיפָּרֵד מחברים.

3. סוף סוף נִזְכַּרְת איפה הפגישה! לקח לך המון זמן _____ .

Answers:

1. נִפְגַּשְׁנוּ, נִיפָּגֵשׁ   2. נִפְרְדָה   3. לְהִיזָכֵר

429

6. Beenyan Poo'al פּוּעַל

Preview

- *Present tense* (מְצוּלָם)
- *Past tense* (צוּלַם)
- *Future tense* (יְצוּלַם)
- ב׳, כ׳, פ׳ as the first root letter in *poo'al* verbs (בּוּטַל, מְבוּטָל)
- When י is *the first or second root letter* (יוּצָא, צוּיַּר)
- *Four-letter roots* (תוּרְגַם) מְרוּבָּעִים

Introduction

Beenyan poo'al is the **passive** counterpart of *beenyan pee'el*, for example:[1]

passive (poo'al)		active (pee'el)
הסיפור סוּפַּר בּייידיש (על ידי השחקן).	⇔	השחקן סִיפֵּר סיפור בּיידיש. 
The story was told in Yiddish (by the actor).		The actor told a story in Yiddish.
הפרח צוּלַם באביב (על ידי רון).	⇔	רון צִילֵם את הפרח באביב.
The flower was photographed in the spring (by Ron).		Ron photographed the flower in the spring.

In order to arrive at the past tense base form (הוא), we simply change the vowels of צִילֵם (*tsee-LEM*) to *oo-AH*: צוּלַם (*tsoo-LAM*). In *full spelling*, we always write a ו between the first and second root letters: צולם.[2] This is true in all the tenses of *poo'al*, as we will see below.

Beenyan poo'al belongs to the same "family" of *beenyaneem* as *pee'el* and *heetpa'el*. The characteristic shared by all three of these *beenyaneem* is that a dagesh is written in their **middle** root letter in *standard spelling* with vowel signs.[3] Thus, when ב׳, כ׳, פ׳ appear in the middle of *poo'al* verbs, they are pronounced as *hard* sounds:

---

1 For an explanation of the meaning of *active* and *passive* verbs, see the chapter "Active and Passive Verbs," pp. 580-592.

2 These forms in standard (non-full) spelling with vowel signs are: צֻלַּם ⇔ צֻלָּם. In standard spelling, there is no ו in *poo'al* in any of the tenses.

3 This is a *strong dagesh* (דָגֵשׁ חָזָק) (see the chapter "The Pronunciation of ב׳, כ׳, פ׳ and the *Dagesh*," pp. 630-633).

doo-BAR	soo-KAM	soo-PAR
דּוּבַּר ◄	סוּכַּם	סוּפַּר

Here are some more special features that are worth noting:

- *Beenyan poo'al*, like the one other exclusively passive *beenyan* – *hoof'al*, has **no** infinitive or command forms.

- The past tense base form (צוּלַם) also appears as part of the base forms of the other tenses:

past:	צוּלַם ◄
present:	מְצוּלָם
future:	יְצוּלַם

- As you can see, the *prefixes* of the present and future tenses are the **same** as those of *beenyan pee'el*: מְצַלֵם, יְצַלֵם.

• *Present tense* (מְצוּלָם)

Here are the present tense forms of the verb צוּלַם:[4]

me-tsoo-LAM	מְצוּלָם	(*m.s.*):	אני, אתה, הוא ◄
me-tsoo-LE-met	מְצוּלֶמֶת	(*f.s.*):	אני, את, היא
me-tsoo-la-MEEM	מְצוּלָמִים	(*m.pl.*):	אנחנו, אתם, הם
me-tsoo-la-MOT	מְצוּלָמוֹת	(*f.pl.*):	אנחנו, אתן, הן

As in most *beenyaneem* that we have seen, the feminine singular of *poo'al* ends in *E-et*:

me-tsoo-LE-met	מְצוּלֶמֶת ◄

In the plural forms, the stress moves to the ending:

מְ-צוּ-לָ-מוֹת	מְ-צוּ-לָ-מִים ◄
me-tsoo-la-MOT	me-tsoo-la-MEEM

The *ah* vowel of מְצוּלָם does **not** change when the plural endings are added. This is also the case in *beenyan neef'al* (נִכְנָסִים) and in *beenyan hoof'al* (מוּזְמָנִים).

---

4 Many *poo'al* present tense forms serve as adjectives. For more details, see the chapter "Adjectives Resulting from an Action Taken and Completed," pp. 159-169.

Want to see if you've understood?

Write the correct present tense form of the underlined word.

1. הסרט "מישהו לרוץ איתו" <u>מצולם</u> ברחובות ירושלים. בתחילת הסרט _____

   נער וכלב רצים במרכז העיר.

2. הסיפור שקראנו היום בכיתה <u>מסופר</u> בגוף ראשון. הסיפורים האחרים שקראנו _____ בגוף שלישי.

Answers:[5]

1. מְצוּלָמִים   2. מְסוּפָּרִים

• *Past tense* (צוּלַם)

Here are the past tense forms of the verb צוּלַם:

	plural			singular	
tsoo-LAM-noo	צוּלַמְנוּ	אנחנו:	tsoo-LAM-tee	צוּלַמְתִּי	אני:
tsoo-LAM-tem	צוּלַמְתֶּם	אתם:	tsoo-LAM-ta	צוּלַמְתָּ	אתה:
tsoo-LAM-ten	צוּלַמְתֶּן	אתן:	tsoo-LAMT	צוּלַמְתְּ	את:
tsool-MOO	צוּלְמוּ	הם, הן	tsoo-LAM	**צוּלַם**	הוא
			tsool-MA	צוּלְמָה	היא

Let's look at the bottom part of the chart.

When the endings ־ָה and ־וּ are added to the היא and הם/הן forms respectively, they attract the stress, and the vowel that comes before them "reduces," as in all the *beenyaneem* except for *heef'eel*:

צוּלְ-מוּ   צוּלְ-מָה,
tsool-MOO   tsool-MA

---

5   It is not necessary for you to write vowel signs in your answers. We have added vowel signs to the answers in the chapters on verbs only in order to make clear how the forms are pronounced.

The reduced vowel is written with a *shva* (◌ְ) in texts written with vowel signs and is usually not pronounced in Modern Hebrew.[6]

All other forms, i.e., those in the top part of the chart – whose endings begin with a consonant (ת׳ or נ׳) – have a stressed *AH* sound in their second syllable:

➤ צוּ-לַמְ-תְּ ... | צוּ-לַמְ-תָּ, | צוּ-לַמְ-תִּי,
       tsoo-LAMT | *tsoo-LAM-ta* | *tsoo-LAM-tee*

Want to see if you've understood?

Write the correct past tense form of the underlined verb.

1. הילדים <u>טופלו</u> במרפאה של ד"ר לוין. אנחנו _____ . אתם _____ .

2. למזלי, לא <u>פוטרתי</u> מהעבודה. גם אתה לא _____ , וגם מירי לא _____ .

Answers:

1. טוּפַּלְנוּ, טוּפַּלְתֶּם   2. פּוּטַרְתָּ, פּוּטְרָה

• *Future tense* (יְצוּלַּם)

As we noted at the beginning of this chapter, the future tense base form of *poo'al* is יְצוּלַּם, and the prefixes of *poo'al* verbs are the same as those used in *beenyan pee'el* (אֲדַבֵּר, תְּדַבֵּר...):

prefixes and endings		only prefixes		
		'a-tsoo-LAM	אֲצוּלַּם	אני: ➤
		te-tsoo-LAM	תְּצוּלַּם	אתה:
	te-tsool-MEE	תְּצוּלְּמִי		את:
		ye-tsoo-LAM	יְצוּלַּם	הוא:
		te-tsoo-LAM	תְּצוּלַּם	היא:
		ne-tsoo-LAM	נְצוּלַּם	אנחנו:
te-tsool-MOO	תְּצוּלְּמוּ			אתם, אתן:
ye-tsool-MOO	יְצוּלְּמוּ			הם, הן:

---

6   See the chapter "Reduction of Vowels and the *Shva*," pp. 648-650. The *shva* is sometimes pronounced *eh*, as – for example – in verbs like חוּמְּמוּ (*choo-me-MOO*), whose second and third root letters are identical (ח-מ-מ). This is so also in future forms such as יְחוּמְּמוּ (*ye-choo-me-MOO*).

Note that only the אני form begins with an *ah* sound: אֲצוּלַם (*'a-tsoo-LAM*). All the others have *eh* in the first syllable:

יְצוּלַם...	תְּצוּלַם,
ye-tsoo-LAM	*te-tsoo-LAM*

As in all *beenyaneem* except for *heef'eel*, in the forms with an ending (in the left-hand column above), the stress moves to the ending, and the preceding vowel "reduces":

יְ-צוּלְ-מוּ	תְ-צוּלְ-מוּ,	תְ-צוּלְ-מִי,	⇐	יְ-צוּ-לַם
ye-tsool-MOO	*te-tsool-MOO*	*te-tsool-MEE*		*ye-tsoo-LAM*

The reduced vowel is written as a *shva* (◌ְ) in texts with vowel signs. In Modern Hebrew it is usually not pronounced.

Want to see if you've understood?
Write the missing form of the underlined verb.

1. הטכנאי אמר שהטלוויזיה _____ בתוך יומיים ושהמחשב יְתוּקַן בתוך שבוע.

2. התוכנית שאנחנו אוהבים תְשוּדַר שוב מחר. בשבוע הבא _____ פרקים מעונות קודמות.

Answers:

1. תְּתוּקַן   2. יְשוּדְרוּ

• ב׳, כ׳, פ׳ *as the first root letter in* poo'al *verbs* (בּוּטַל, מְבוּטָל)

Now let's see what happens when the **first** *root letter* is ב׳, כ׳ or פ׳:

	עתיד	הווה	עבר
	future	*present*	*past*
to be canceled	יְבוּטַל	מְבוּטָל	בּוּטַל
to be laundered	יְכוּבַּס	מְכוּבָּס	כּוּבַּס
to be fired from work	יְפוּטַר	מְפוּטָר	פּוּטַר

In the past tense, where ב׳, כ׳, פ׳ appear at the **beginning** of the word, they are pronounced with a hard sound: *b, k, p*.[7] In the other tenses, where they do not stand at the beginning of the word, their pronunciation is soft: *v, ch, f*.[8]

Want to see if you've understood?

Write the missing form of the underlined verb. Say all the *poo'al* verbs out loud.

١. בשבוע שעבר <u>בוטלה</u> הפגישה של תלמידי בית הספר עם סופר ישראלי חשוב.

אני מקווה שבשבוע הבא הפגישה לא ـــــــــــــــــــ .

٢. עובדים רבים <u>פוטרו</u> לאחרונה, ובקרוב אולי ـــــــــــــــــــ עובדים נוספים.

Answers:

١. בוּטְלָה *boot-LA*, תְבוּטַל *te-voo-TAL*   ٢. פוּטְרוּ *poot-ROO*, יְפוּטְרוּ *ye-foot-ROO*

• *When* י׳ *is the first or second root letter* (יוּצָא, צוּיַר)

Now let's compare verbs whose **first** root letter is י׳ (י-צ-א) and those whose **second** root letter is י׳ (צ-י-ר) to the model verb צוּלַם (צ-ל-מ). Pay special attention to the spelling:

	עתיד	הווה	עבר	שורש
	future	*present*	*past*	*root*
model verb:	יְצוּלַם	מְצוּלָם	צוּלַם	צ-ל-מ ◄
to be exported	יְיוּצָא	מְיוּצָא	יוּצָא	י-צ-א
to be drawn, sketched	יְצוּיַר	מְצוּיָר	צוּיַר	צ-י-ר

When י׳ is the first or second root letter in a *poo'al* verb, an additional י׳ is never added to it.[9] In contrast, in *pee'el* verbs, we write an additional י׳ in most forms (e.g., לצייר, לייצא).[10]

---

7   The *dagesh* written in these letters in texts with vowel signs is a weak *dagesh*. See the chapter "The Pronunciation of ב׳, כ׳, פ׳ and the *Dagesh*," p. 626.

8   This is because they follow a prefix that ends with a vowel (*eh*). See the chapter "The Pronunciation of ב׳, כ׳, פ׳ and the *Dagesh*," p. 628.

9   According to spelling rules of the Hebrew Language Academy, another י׳ is never added to a י׳ that stands next to a ו׳. For more details see the chapter "Hebrew Spelling," pp. 663-665.

10   See the chapter "*Beenyan Pee'el*," p. 388.

• *Four-letter roots* (מְרוּבָּעִים (תוּרְגַם

Like verbs in *pee'el* and *heetpa'el*, some *poo'al* verbs have **four** root letters. Here are some examples:

שׁוּחְרַר	עוּרְבַּב	פּוּרְסַם	אוּרְגַּן	תוּרְגַם
he was freed	it was mixed	it was published	it was organized	it was translated

The forms of verbs with **four** root letters are similar to those of regular *poo'al* verbs. Compare:

future	*present*	*past*
יְ-צוּ-לַם	מְ-צוּ-לָם	צוּ-לַם
יְ-שׁוּחְ-רַר	מְ-שׁוּחְ-רָר	שׁוּחְ-רַר

As you can see, the extra root letter joins the end of the syllable that contains "וּ", and there is no strong *dagesh* as there is in regular verbs (צוּלַם). When the third root letter is ב׳, כ׳, פ׳, as in עוּרְבַּב, it has a *hard* pronunciation: *b, k, p*.[11] From all other points of view, *poo'al* verbs with **four** root letters are like *poo'al* verbs with **three** root letters.

Want to see if you've understood?
Write the missing form of the underlined verb.

1. המודעה על המכונית שלנו פורסמה אתמול בעיתון, והמודעה על הדירה שלכם _____ מחר.

2. הספר תורגם להרבה שפות. בקרוב הוא _____ גם לעברית.

Answers:

1. תְפוּרְסַם   2. יְתוּרְגַם

---

11 This is a *weak dagesh*, which comes after a closed syllable. See the chapter "The Pronunciation of ב׳, כ׳, פ׳ and the *Dagesh*," pp. 626-630 for more details.

Chapter summary

♦ These are the base forms (past, present and future הוא forms) of regular *beenyan poo'al* verbs:

future	present	past	
יְצוּלָם	מְצוּלָם	צוּלָם	◄
ye-tsoo-LAM	*me-tsoo-LAM*	*tsoo-LAM*	

♦ When 'ב, כ', פ' are the **middle** root letter, they are pronounced *b*, *k*, *p* (e.g., דוּבָּר, סוּכַּם, סוּפַּר).

♦ Other changes in pronunciation and spelling involving 'ב, כ', פ' and also 'י are discussed in detail in the chapter above.

♦ Some *poo'al* verbs have **four** root letters. Here is an example of their base forms:

future	present	past	
יְשׁוּחְרַר	מְשׁוּחְרָר	שׁוּחְרַר	◄

Want to see if you've understood this chapter?

Write the correct form of the underlined verb (past, present, future or infinitive).

1. חשבונות החשמל והטלפון <u>שולמו</u> אתמול, וחשבון המים _____ מחר.
   (future)

   החשבונות האלה תמיד _____ בתחילת החודש.
   (present)

2. הטיול לגליל _____ אתמול בגלל הגשם. הבוקר שמעתי שגם הטיול של היום
   (past)

   _____ . אני מקווה שהטיולים של השבוע הבא לא <u>יבוטלו</u>.
   (present)

3. המסיבה _____ ברגע האחרון, לכן לא הכול <u>מאורגן</u> כמו שצריך.
   (past)

Answers:

7. *Beenyan Hoof'al* הוּפְעַל

Preview

- *Present tense* (מוּזְמָן)
- *Past tense* (הוּזְמַן)
- *Future tense* (יוּזְמַן)

Introduction

Beenyan hoof'al is the **passive** counterpart of *beenyan heef'eel*, for example:[1]

passive (hoof'al)		*active (heef'eel)*
אבי הוּזְמַן למסיבה (על ידי רון).	⇐	רון הִזְמִין את אבי למסיבה.
Avi was invited to the party (by Ron).		Ron invited Avi to the party.

In order to arrive at the past tense base form (הוא), we simply change the vowels of הִזְמִין (*heez-MEEN*) to *oo-AH*: הוּזְמַן (*hooz-MAN*). In *full spelling*, we always write a 'ו **before** the first root letter: הוזמן.[2]

Q: What letter appears at the beginning of both the *heef'eel* and the *hoof'al* forms mentioned above?

A: Both begin with 'ה. This is the characteristic sign of the *heef'eel-hoof'al* "family" of *beenyaneem*.

Here are some more special features that are worth noting:

- *Beenyan hoof'al*, like the one other exclusively passive *beenyan – poo'al,* has **no** infinitive or command forms.

- In each of the three base forms, a *prefix* containing the vowel "ו" (*oo*) appears **before** the first root letter (-הוּ, מוּ, יוּ). Each of the base forms contains the vowels *oo-AH*:

---

1 For an explanation of the meaning of *active* and *passive* verbs, see the chapter "Active and Passive Verbs," pp. 580-592.

2 These forms in standard (non-full) spelling with vowel signs are: הִזְמִין ⇔ הֻזְמַן.

past:	*hooz-MAN*	הוּזְמַן ◄
present:	*mooz-MAN*	מוּזְמָן
future:	*yooz-MAN*	יוּזְמַן

> 🛑 ***Be careful!*** Both *hoof'al* and *poo'al* contain the vowels *oo-AH*. As we see above, the "וּ" (*oo*) in *hoof'al* is always **part of** the prefix and **before** the root. In contrast, in *poo'al* the "וּ" (*oo*) always comes **between** the first and second root letters and is not part of the prefix. Compare the following *poo'al* forms to the *hoof'al* forms above:

past:	*tsoo-LAM*	צוּלַם ◄
present:	*me-tsoo-LAM*	מְצוּלָם
future:	*ye-tsoo-LAM*	יְצוּלַם

• *Present tense* (מוּזְמָן)

Here are the present tense forms of our model verb הוּזְמַן:[3]

mooz-MAN	מוּזְמָן	(m.s.):	אני, אתה, הוא ◄
mooz-ME-net	מוּזְמֶנֶת	(f.s.):	אני, את, היא
mooz-ma-NEEM	מוּזְמָנִים	(m.pl.):	אנחנו, אתם, הם
mooz-ma-NOT	מוּזְמָנוֹת	(f.pl.):	אנחנו, אתן, הן

Q: What **prefix** is shared by all present tense *hoof'al* verbs?

A: They all begin with מוּ- (*moo*), which joins the first root letter to form the first syllable:

מוּז-מָ-נוֹת	מוּז-מָ-נִים,	מוּז-מָ-נֶת,	מוּז-מָן, ◄
mooz-ma-NOT	*mooz-ma-NEEM*	*mooz-ME-net*	*mooz-MAN*

The feminine singular form of *hoof'al* ends in *E-et*, as in almost all other *beenyaneem* (*heef'eel* is the one exception):

mooz-ME-net	מוּז-מֶ-נֶת ◄

In the plural forms, the stress moves to the ending:

מוּז-מָ-נוֹת	מוּז-מָ-נִים ◄
mooz-ma-NOT	*mooz-ma-NEEM*

---

3 Many *hoof'al* present tense forms serve as adjectives. For more details see the chapter "Adjectives Resulting from an Action Taken and Completed," pp. 159-169.

The *ah* vowel of מוּזְמָן does **not** change when the plural endings are added. This is also the case in *beenyan neef'al* (נִכְנָסִים) and in *beenyan poo'al* (מְצוּלָמִים).

Want to see if you've understood?
Write the correct present tense form of the underlined verb.

1. העיתון <u>מודפס</u> בלילה. החוברת _____. החוברות _____.

2. התמונה <u>מוגדלת</u> כדי שתוכלו לראות את כל הפרטים הקטנים. התמונות _____.

Answers:[4]

1. מוּדְפֶּסֶת, מוּדְפָּסוֹת   2. מוּגְדָּלוֹת

• *Past tense* (הוּזְמַן)

Here are the past tense forms of the verb הוּזְמַן:

	plural				singular	
hooz-MA-noo/hool-BASH-noo	הוּזְמַנּוּ[5]/הוּלְבַּשְׁנוּ	אנחנו:		hooz-MAN-tee	הוּזְמַנְתִּי	אני:
hooz-MAN-tem[6]	הוּזְמַנְתֶּם	אתם:		hooz-MAN-ta	הוּזְמַנְתָּ	אתה:
hooz-MAN-ten	הוּזְמַנְתֶּן	אתן:		hooz-MANT	הוּזְמַנְתְּ	את:
hooz-me-NOO	הוּזְמְנוּ	הם, הן		hooz-MAN	הוּזְמַן	הוא
				hooz-me-NA	הוּזְמְנָה	היא

Q: What prefix is shared by all these verbs?

A: They all begin with הוּ- (*hoo*).

---

4 It is not necessary for you to write vowel signs in your answers. We have added vowel signs to the answers in the chapters on verbs only in order to make clear how the forms are pronounced.

5 In this specific verb the נ of the root and the נ of אנחנו become one. Therefore, instead of הוּזְמַנְנוּ*, the form is הוּזְמַנּוּ with one נ. (We see this same phenomenon in the *heef'eel* אנחנו הִזְמַנּוּ). We have added the verb הוּלְבַּשְׁנוּ in order to show a regular *hoof'al* verb. Note: In full spelling, the forms for אנחנו and הם look the same (הוזמנו), but are pronounced differently.

6 Most speakers today stress the next to the last syllable, as indicated here. According to the rules of grammar, the stress is on the **last** syllable: *hooz-man-TEM, hooz-man-TEN*.

Now let's look at the bottom of the chart where the endings הָ- and ו- are added.

Q: What happens to the *ah* vowel in הוּזְמַן when these endings are added?

A: It "reduces" to *eh* (the reduced vowel is written ◌ in texts with vowel signs):

הוּזְ-מְ-נָה, הוּזְ-מְ-נוּ
hooz-me-NA *hooz-me-NOO*

In all other forms (i.e., those in the upper part of chart), the vowel in the syllable before the endings is a stressed *AH*:

הוּזְ-מַנְ-תִי, הוּזְ-מַנְ-תָ, הוּזְ-מַנְתְ...
hooz-MAN-tee *hooz-MAN-ta* *hooz-MANT*

Want to see if you've understood?
Write the correct past tense form of the underlined verb.

1. השם של המנהל הקודם <u>הוזכר</u> בישיבת המורים אתמול. גם את _____ בישיבה.

   גם אתם _____.

2. האותיות בספר לכיתה א' <u>הוגדלו</u>. גם התמונה בעמוד הראשון _____.

Answers:

1. הוּזְכַּרְתְ, הוּזְכַּרְתֶם   2. הוּגְדְלָה

• *Future tense* (יוּזְמַן)

Here are the future tense forms of the verb הוּזְמַן:

	prefixes and endings		*only prefixes*	
אני:			אוּזְמַן	*'ooz-MAN*
אתה:			תוּזְמַן	*tooz-MAN*
את:	תוּזְמְנִי	*tooz-me-NEE*		
הוא:			**יוּזְמַן**	*yooz-MAN*
היא:			תוּזְמַן	*tooz-MAN*
אנחנו:			נוּזְמַן	*nooz-MAN*
אתם, אתן:	תוּזְמְנוּ	*tooz-me-NOO*		
הם, הן:	יוּזְמְנוּ	*yooz-me-NOO*		

As in all other tenses in *hoof'al*, here, too, the *oo* sound (written ו) comes **before** the first root letter. In the forms in the right-hand column above, only the prefix changes:

תוּזְמַן...   אוּזְמַן,   ◄
tooz-MAN   *'ooz-MAN*

As in all *beenyaneem* except for *heef'eel*, in the forms with an ending (in the left-hand column above), the stress moves to the ending, and the preceding vowel "reduces" to *eh* (and is written as a ▢ in texts with vowel signs):

יוּזְ-מְ-נוּ   תוּזְ-מְ-נוּ,   תוּזְ-מְ-נִי,   ⇐   יוּזְמַן   ◄
yooz-me-NOO   *tooz-me-NOO*   *tooz-me-NEE*   *yooz-MAN*

Be careful! Note that **no** *hoof'al* verb form contains an *ee* sound in the middle. Therefore, **none** of them is written with a י. In contrast, many *heef'eel* verbs, including the infinitive form (לְהַזְמִין) and all the base forms (הִזְמִין, מַזְמִין, יַזְמִין), contain a י.

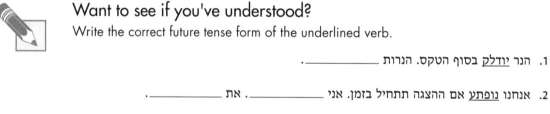

Want to see if you've understood?
Write the correct future tense form of the underlined verb.

1. הנר <u>יודלק</u> בסוף הטקס. הנרות _____.

2. אנחנו <u>נופתע</u> אם ההצגה תתחיל בזמן. אני _____. את _____

הם _____.

Answers:

1. יוּדְלְקוּ   2. אוּפְתַּע, תּוּפְתְּעִי, יוּפְתְּעוּ

Chapter summary

♦ These are the base forms (the past, present and future הוא forms) of regular *beenyan hoof'al* verbs:

future	present	past	
יוּזְמַן	מוּזְמָן	הוּזְמַן	◄
yooz-MAN	*mooz-MAN*	*hooz-MAN*	

Want to see if you've understood this chapter?

Write the correct form of the underlined verb (past, present, future or infinitive).

.1 <u>הוזמנתי</u> לחתונה של נירית וגלעד. גם אַת _____ _____? שמעתי שבקרוב (אנחנו)

_____ לחתונה של אורלי ורון.

.2 בישיבה אתמול <u>הוחלטו</u> כמה החלטות בקשר לפרויקט החדש. אבל רק מחר _____
(הוא=it)
מתי הפרויקט יתחיל.

.3 ביום שלישי שעבר _____ ישיבת המורים בשעה. אולי גם בשבוע הבא <u>תוקדם</u> הישיבה.
(past)

.4 המורה אמרה: "רוב הפתרונות לתרגילים _____ בסוף הספר. התרגילים הקשים
(present)
יותר <u>יוסברו</u> בשיעור".

Answers:

.1 הוּזְמַנְתְּ, נוּזְמַן   .2 יוּחְלַט   .3 הוּקְדְּמָה   .4 מוּסְבָּרִים

8. Regular Verbs in All *Beenyaneem*: Summary

Preview

• *Chart of regular verbs in all seven* beenyaneem

• *The base form as a "hyperlink" to other forms*

• *Chart of regular verbs in all seven* beenyaneem

The chart on the following page contains the forms of *regular* verbs in all seven *beenyaneem*. We have included here all three tenses and the infinitive. Forms of the imperative can be found in the chapter "Command Forms" (pp. 567-577).

The הוא form of each tense is highlighted.

The numbers on the right refer to phenomena that are discussed following the chart.

הופעל	הפעיל	התפעל	פועל	פיעל	נפעל	פעל	
hoof'al	*heef'eel*	*heetpa'el*	*poo'al*	*pee'el*	*neef'al*	*pa'al*	
							past עבר
הוּזְמַנְתִּי	הִרְגַּשְׁתִּי	הִתְלַבַּשְׁתִּי	צוּלַּמְתִּי	דִּבַּרְתִּי	נִכְנַסְתִּי	כָּתַבְתִּי¹	אני
הוּזְמַנְתָּ	הִרְגַּשְׁתָּ	הִתְלַבַּשְׁתָּ	צוּלַּמְתָּ	דִּבַּרְתָּ	נִכְנַסְתָּ	כָּתַבְתָּ	אתה
הוּזְמַנְתְּ	הִרְגַּשְׁתְּ	הִתְלַבַּשְׁתְּ	צוּלַּמְתְּ	דִּבַּרְתְּ	נִכְנַסְתְּ	כָּתַבְתְּ	את
הוּזְמַנּוּ / הוּלְבַּשְׁנוּ	הִרְגַּשְׁנוּ	הִתְלַבַּשְׁנוּ	צוּלַּמְנוּ	דִּבַּרְנוּ	נִכְנַסְנוּ	כָּתַבְנוּ	אנחנו
הוּזְמַנְתֶּם	הִרְגַּשְׁתֶּם	הִתְלַבַּשְׁתֶּם	צוּלַּמְתֶּם	דִּבַּרְתֶּם	נִכְנַסְתֶּם	כָּתַבְתֶּם / כְּתַבְתֶּם²	אתם
הוּזְמַנְתֶּן	הִרְגַּשְׁתֶּן	הִתְלַבַּשְׁתֶּן	צוּלַּמְתֶּן	דִּבַּרְתֶּן	נִכְנַסְתֶּן	כָּתַבְתֶּן / כְּתַבְתֶּן	אתן
הוּזְמַן	הִרְגִּישׁ	הִתְלַבֵּשׁ	צוּלַּם	דִּבֵּר	נִכְנַס	כָּתַב	הוא
הוּזְמְנָה	הִרְגִּישָׁה	הִתְלַבְּשָׁה	צוּלְּמָה	דִּבְּרָה	נִכְנְסָה	כָּתְבָה	היא
הוּזְמְנוּ	הִרְגִּישׁוּ	הִתְלַבְּשׁוּ	צוּלְּמוּ	דִּבְּרוּ	נִכְנְסוּ	כָּתְבוּ	הם/הן
							present הווה
מוּזְמָן	מַרְגִּישׁ	מִתְלַבֵּשׁ	מְצוּלָּם	מְדַבֵּר	נִכְנָס	כּוֹתֵב	אני, אתה, הוא
מוּזְמֶנֶת	מַרְגִּישָׁה	מִתְלַבֶּשֶׁת	מְצוּלֶּמֶת	מְדַבֶּרֶת	נִכְנֶסֶת	כּוֹתֶבֶת	אני, את, היא
מוּזְמָנִים	מַרְגִּישִׁים	מִתְלַבְּשִׁים	מְצוּלָּמִים	מְדַבְּרִים	נִכְנָסִים	כּוֹתְבִים	אנחנו, אתם, הם
מוּזְמָנוֹת	מַרְגִּישׁוֹת	מִתְלַבְּשׁוֹת	מְצוּלָּמוֹת	מְדַבְּרוֹת	נִכְנָסוֹת	כּוֹתְבוֹת	אנחנו, אתן, הן
							future עתיד
אוּזְמַן	אַרְגִּישׁ	אֶתְלַבֵּשׁ	אֲצוּלַּם	אֲדַבֵּר	אֶכָּנֵס	אֶכְתּוֹב	אני
תּוּזְמַן	תַּרְגִּישׁ	תִּתְלַבֵּשׁ	תְּצוּלַּם	תְּדַבֵּר	תִּכָּנֵס	תִּכְתּוֹב	אתה
יוּזְמַן	יַרְגִּישׁ	יִתְלַבֵּשׁ	יְצוּלַּם	יְדַבֵּר	יִיכָּנֵס	יִכְתּוֹב / יִלְמַד	הוא
תּוּזְמַן	תַּרְגִּישׁ	תִּתְלַבֵּשׁ	תְּצוּלַּם	תְּדַבֵּר	תִּכָּנֵס	תִּכְתּוֹב	היא
נוּזְמַן	נַרְגִּישׁ	נִתְלַבֵּשׁ	נְצוּלַּם	נְדַבֵּר	נִיכָּנֵס	נִכְתּוֹב	אנחנו
תּוּזְמְנִי	תַּרְגִּישִׁי	תִּתְלַבְּשִׁי	תְּצוּלְּמִי	תְּדַבְּרִי	תִּיכָּנְסִי	תִּכְתְּבִי	את
תּוּזְמְנוּ	תַּרְגִּישׁוּ	תִּתְלַבְּשׁוּ	תְּצוּלְּמוּ	תְּדַבְּרוּ	תִּיכָּנְסוּ	תִּכְתְּבוּ	אתם/אתן
יוּזְמְנוּ	יַרְגִּישׁוּ	יִתְלַבְּשׁוּ	תְּצוּלְּמוּ	יְדַבְּרוּ	יִיכָּנְסוּ	יִכְתְּבוּ	הם/הן
							infinitive שם הפועל
(לְהַזְמִין – סָבִיל)	לְהַרְגִּישׁ	לְהִתְלַבֵּשׁ	(לְצַלֵּם – סָבִיל)³	לְדַבֵּר	לְהִיכָּנֵס	לִכְתּוֹב	
to be invited	to feel	to get dressed	to be photographed	to speak	to enter	to write	

---

1 In the chapter on *beenyan pa'al*, we used סגר as our model in order not to deal with the presence and absence of the weak *dagesh* in כתב. Here we use כתב, the usual model verb of *pa'al*.

2 The forms כְּתַבְתֶּם / כְּתַבְתֶּן reflect the pronunciation used by most Hebrew speakers today: *ka-TAV-tem/ten*. According to the rules of grammar, the correct form is כְּתַבְתֶּם / כְּתַבְתֶּן (when used today, these are usually pronounced *ktav-TEM, ktav-TEN* or *ke-tav-TEM, ke-tav-TEN*). Note: According to the rules of grammar, the תֶּם– and תֶּן– endings in the past tense of all the *beenyaneem* are stressed.

3 *Beenyan poo'al* and *beenyan hoof'al* have no infinitive of their own.

1   *Past tense, first and second persons*

In the past tense of regular verbs in all *beenyaneem*, there is always a stressed *AH* sound in the syllable before the endings that begin with a consonant (*-tee, -ta, -t, -noo, -tem, -ten*): כָּתַבְתִּי (*ka-TAV-tee*), דִּיבַּרְתִּי (*dee-BAR-tee*)…

2   *Past tense, third person*

In the past tense of regular verbs in all *beenyanaeem* (except for *heef'eel*), when endings begin with a vowel (ה‪ָ‬ -*AH* and ו‪ּ‬- -*OO*), the stress moves to the ending, and the vowel before it "reduces." In texts with vowel signs, a *shva* (◻) is written under the middle root letter: כָּתְבָה (*kat-VA*), דִּיבְּרָה (*deeb-RA*).

3   *Present tense, feminine singular*

The feminine singular form in the present tense of all but *heef'eel* regular verbs ends in תʼ: כּוֹתֶבֶת, מְדַבֶּרֶת… In *heef'eel*, the feminine ending is ה‪ָ‬-: מַרְגִּישָׁה.

4   *Present tense, plural forms*

The same change that is described in **2** above ("vowel reduction") takes place in the present tensebefore endings that begin with vowels (ים‪ִ‬- -*EEM*, ות- -*OT*), but only when there is an *eh* (◻) vowel in the last syllable of the הוא form (כּוֹתֵב, מְדַבֵּר, מִתְלַבֵּשׁ). In these forms, the *eh* "reduces": it is usually not pronounced by today's speakers and is written as *shva* (◻). This change takes place in *pa'al* (כּוֹתְבוֹת / כּוֹתְבִים), *pee'el* (מְדַבְּרוֹת / מְדַבְּרִים) and *heetpa'el* (מִתְלַבְּשׁוֹת / מִתְלַבְּשִׁים).

5   *Future tense forms with endings*

Here, too, the same change as is described in **2** and **4** ("vowel reduction") takes place. In the future tense this "reduction" takes place before the vowel endings י‪ִ‬- (-*EE*) and ו‪ּ‬- (-*OO*). This happens in all *beenyaneem* except for *heef'eel*. In the future tense, the *shva* (◻) sometimes indicates an *eh* vowel (e.g., תִּכְתְּבִי *teech-te-VEE*) and sometimes a "zero" vowel (e.g., תְּדַבְּרִי *te-dab-REE*).

6   *Infinitive and future tense forms*

There is a striking resemblance between the infinitive and the future tense base form. If we know the infinitive, we arrive at the future tense base form in the following way:

- In *beenyaneem* that do **not** have a הʼ in the infinitive (*pa'al* and *pee'el*), we simply change the prefix ל- to י-,[4] e.g., לִכְתוֹב ⇐ יִכְתּוֹב.

- When there is a הʼ in the infinitive (*neef'al*, *heef'eel*, *heetpa'el*), we eliminate לה- and add יʼ (of the הוא base form) with the vowel of the הʼ, e.g., לְהִיכָּנֵס ⇐ יְהִ‪ּ‬יכָּנֵס ⇐ יִיכָּנֵס.

---

4   In *pa'al*, this is true of verbs with "ו" in the future: לִכְתּוֹב ⇐ יִכְתּוֹב.

• *The base form as a "hyperlink" to other forms*

Once you have learned all the verb tenses and forms listed in the chart above, the base form of a particular verb can serve as a kind of "hyperlink" to all its other forms. Let's see how this works:

Let's say you encounter the הוא past tense form of a new verb: שיתף. In order to know its other forms, you would ask: Which form in the chart does this verb resemble? The answer is: שיתף resembles דִּיבֵּר in the third column of the chart (*beenyan pee'el*).

This determination leads you from שִׁיתֵּף (which is like דִּיבֵּר) – as a "hyperlink" – to the other base forms: מְשַׁתֵּף (which is like מְדַבֵּר) and יְשַׁתֵּף (which is like יְדַבֵּר). It also leads you to the infinitive לְשַׁתֵּף (which is like לְדַבֵּר).

The base forms שִׁיתֵּף, מְשַׁתֵּף, יְשַׁתֵּף also act as "hyperlinks" and lead you to all other forms in each tense. Thus, from the future tense הוא form יְשַׁתֵּף (which is like יְדַבֵּר), you can easily arrive at the אני form אֲשַׁתֵּף (which is like אֲדַבֵּר), the אתה form תְּשַׁתֵּף (which is like תְּדַבֵּר) and so on.

This method can be used with any form of the verb that we encounter.

Here are the base forms and the infinitives of regular verbs in the seven *beenyaneem*:

הופעל *hoof'al*	הפעיל *heef'eel*	התפעל *heetpa'el*	פועל *poo'al*	פיעל *pee'el*	נפעל *neef'al*	פעל *pa'al*	
הוּזְמַן	הִרְגִּישׁ	הִתְלַבֵּשׁ	צוּלַם	דִּיבֵּר	נִכְנַס	כָּתַב	עבר *past*
מוּזְמָן	מַרְגִּישׁ	מִתְלַבֵּשׁ	מְצוּלָם	מְדַבֵּר	נִכְנָס	כּוֹתֵב	הווה *present*
יוּזְמַן	יַרְגִּישׁ	יִתְלַבֵּשׁ	יְצוּלַם	יְדַבֵּר	יִיכָּנֵס	יִכְתּוֹב / יִלְמַד	עתיד *future*
(לְהַזְמִין – סביל)	לְהַרְגִּישׁ	לְהִתְלַבֵּשׁ	(לְצַלֵם – סביל)	לְדַבֵּר	לְהִיכָּנֵס	לִכְתּוֹב	שם הפועל *infinitive*

IV. Verbs with Guttural Consonants (א׳, ה׳, ח׳, ע׳)

Introduction

Read the following sentences out loud paying special attention to the verbs:

1. ⟵ בשיעורי עברית לפעמים הסטודנטים **עוֹבְדים** בזוגות. הם **קוֹרְאים** טקסטים **ושוֹאֲלים** זה את זה
                   sho-'a-LEEM   *kor-'EEM*   *'ov-DEEM*   שאלות.

    In Hebrew lessons, the students sometimes work in pairs. They read texts and ask each other questions.

2. לפני שדני **יִמְכּוֹר** את המכונית שלו, הוא **יִבְדּוֹק** מחירים באינטרנט ואז **יִשְׁלַח** מודעה לעיתון
               yeesh-LACH   *yeev-DOK*   *yeem-KOR*   המקומי.

    Before Danny sells his car, he'll check prices on the internet and will then send an ad to the local newspaper.

3. תומר רוצה **לִלְמוֹד לִכְתוֹב** ביפנית, והוא מחפש מישהו שיוכל **לַעֲזוֹר** לו.
               la-'a-ZOR   *leech-TOV* *leel-MOD*

    Tomer wants to learn to write in Japanese, so he is looking for someone who can help him.

4. כשסבא **בִּיקֵּר** אצל הנכדים, הוא **סִיפֵּר** להם סיפורים **ותֵיאֵר** להם את החיים בעיר שלו כשהוא
           te-'ER   *see-PER*   *bee-KER*   היה ילד.

    When Grandpa visited his grandchildren, he told them stories and described life in the city he lived in (lit.: in his city) when he was a boy.

In each sentence, the vowels of the **third** verb are **different** from the vowels of the first two. Why is this?

In each case, the changes are due to the presence of a *guttural consonant* – ע׳ ,ח׳, ה׳, א׳.[1] These consonants can cause different types of changes, both in verbs and in other parts of speech.[2] Here are the basic changes we will discuss:[3]

---

1   ע׳ ,ח׳ ,ה׳, א׳ are actually letters (written symbols) that **represent** guttural consonants (sounds). For simplicity's sake, we often refer to these letters as consonants.

2   For examples of changes in nouns, see the chapter "Segolate Nouns," pp. 92, 94.

3   In order to simplify our explanation, in the following discussion also we are deliberately not making a clear distinction between **phonetic** phenomena and the indication of these phenomena in **writing**. Thus, we allow ourselves to speak of a guttural consonant's not "liking" a *shva* – which is a graphic sign – rather than saying that gutturals don't "like" being followed by *eh* or by no vowel sound at all.

1. Instead of a shva (◌ְ), gutturals "like" *ah* (or sometimes *eh*).
    Thus, in sentence 1 above, instead of עוֹבְדִים and קוֹרְאִים, we get שׁוֹאֲלִים, with an *ah* vowel
    after the 'א.

2. Gutturals like to be preceded by an *ah* vowel (or sometimes by *eh*).
    Thus, in sentence 2 above, instead of יִמְכּוֹר and יִבְדּוֹק, we get an *ah* before the 'ח in יִשְׁלַח.

3. Most gutturals like "matching vowels."
    Thus, in sentence 3, לַעֲזוֹר begins not only with *ah* before the 'ע, but also with a matching *ah*
    after it.

4. Gutturals can't take a *strong dagesh*[4] – and sometimes this affects the vowel before them.
    Thus, in sentence 4 above, the *ee* vowel of בִּיקֵּר (*bee-*) and סִיפֵּר (*see-*), which comes before a
    strong *dagesh*, changes to *eh* in תֵיאֵר (*te-*) because the 'א after it can't take a strong *dagesh*.

In the following three chapters, we will look at each *beenyan* and will see how the presence of
gutturals makes verb forms containing them **different** from *regular* verbs.

Note: Roots with a final 'א are included in these chapters when they behave like roots with a
final 'ח or 'ע. A more in-depth discussion of the differences between final 'א verbs and all other
verbs is presented in a separate chapter: "Verbs Whose Third Root Letter Is 'א" (pp. 557-566).

We have divided our discussion of gutturals in the seven *beenyaneem* as follows:

1. Guttural Consonants: *Beenyan Pa'al*
2. Guttural Consonants: *Beenyaneem Heef'eel, Hoof'al* and *Heetpa'el*
3. Guttural Consonants and 'ר: *Beenyaneem Pee'el, Poo'al* and *Neef'al*

---

4   That is, they can't be "doubled." See the chapter "The Pronunciation of 'ב, כ, פ and the *Dagesh*," p. 631 for an
    explanation of the *strong dagesh* as an indicator of a "doubled" consonant.

1. Guttural Consonants (א', ה', ח', ע'): *Beenyan Pa'al*

> ### *Preview*
>
> - Beenyan pa'al *and middle gutturals* (שָׁאַל, נָהַג, צָחַק, כָּעַס)
> - Beenyan pa'al *and initial gutturals* (חָזַר, עָמַד, הָרַס, אָסַף)
> - Beenyan pa'al *and final gutturals* (שָׁמַע, שָׁלַח, קָרָא)

In this and the following chapters, we will deal only with the tenses and forms in which guttural consonants cause changes.

• **Beenyan pa'al** *and middle gutturals*
(שָׁאַל, נָהַג, צָחַק, כָּעַס)[1]

Present tense forms with middle gutturals

Read the following out loud:

◄ בשיעורי עברית לפעמים הסטודנטים **עוֹבְדִים** בזוגות. הם **קוֹרְאִים** טקסטים ו**שׁוֹאֲלִים** זה את זה
        sho-'a-LEEM   *kor-'EEM*   *'ov-DEEM*   שאלות.

In Hebrew lessons, the students sometimes work in pairs. They read texts and ask each other questions.

In these sentences we see that the second vowel in שׁוֹאֲלִים is different from that in עוֹבְדִים and קוֹרְאִים. The reason for this change is:[2] Instead of a *shva* – gutturals "like" *ah* (and sometimes *eh*).

---

1   In grammar books, this group is also called "ע' גְרוֹנִית". This means that the second root letter (called ע' since this is the second letter in פ-ע-ל) is a *guttural* (גרונית). For an explanation of the Hebrew names for root groups, see the introduction to the unit "Special Root Groups," pp. 488-489.

2   See the introduction to this unit (pp. 448-449) for a list of the changes caused by gutturals.

Look now at all the present tense forms of verbs with middle gutturals compared with the *regular* verb סוגר (to close):

	f.pl.	m.pl.	f.s.	m.s.	root (שורש)
regular verb:	סוֹגְרוֹת	סוֹגְרִים	סוֹגֶרֶת	סוֹגֵר	ס-ג-ר ◄
	⇓	⇓			
to ask	שוֹאֲלוֹת	שוֹאֲלִים	שוֹאֶלֶת	שוֹאֵל	ש-א-ל
to drive	נוֹהֲגוֹת	נוֹהֲגִים	נוֹהֶגֶת	נוֹהֵג	נ-ה-ג
to laugh	צוֹחֲקוֹת	צוֹחֲקִים	צוֹחֶקֶת	צוֹחֵק	צ-ח-ק
to be angry	כּוֹעֲסוֹת	כּוֹעֲסִים	כּוֹעֶסֶת	כּוֹעֵס	כ-ע-ס

Q: In which forms are the vowels of the verbs with a middle guttural different from the vowels of the forms of סוגר?

A: In the **plural** forms, for example: שוֹאֲלוֹת ,שוֹאֲלִים (sho-'a-LEEM, sho-'a-LOT). In these forms there is an *ah* sound after the א′ (written ⬚), while the corresponding regular verb forms סוֹגְרוֹת ,סוֹגְרִים (sog-REEM, sog-ROT), are pronounced today with **no vowel** after the middle root consonant (here: *g*).

Past and future tense forms with middle gutturals

Now let's look at **past tense** forms:

	הם/הן	היא	הוא	אני...	root (שורש)
regular verb:	סָגְרוּ	סָגְרָה	סָגַר	סָגַרְתִּי...	ס-ג-ר ◄
	⇓	⇓			
	שָׁאֲלוּ	שָׁאֲלָה	שָׁאַל	שָׁאַלְתִּי...	ש-א-ל
	נָהֲגוּ	נָהֲגָה	נָהַג	נָהַגְתִּי...	נ-ה-ג
	צָחֲקוּ	צָחֲקָה	צָחַק	צָחַקְתִּי...	צ-ח-ק
	כָּעֲסוּ	כָּעֲסָה	כָּעַס	כָּעַסְתִּי...	כ-ע-ס

Notice that in the היא and הם/הן forms, the *shva* (⬚) that appears in regular verbs in the syllable before the ending becomes ⬚ (*ah*) when a guttural appears in the middle of the root.

The same change takes place in **future tense** forms with endings:

root (שורש)	את	אתם/אתן	הם/הן	
ס-ג-ר	תִּסְגְּרִי	תִּסְגְּרוּ	יִסְגְּרוּ	*regular verb*:
	⇓	⇓	⇓	
ש-א-ל	תִּשְׁאֲלִי	תִּשְׁאֲלוּ	יִשְׁאֲלוּ	
נ-ה-ג	תִּנְהֲגִי	תִּנְהֲגוּ	יִנְהֲגוּ	
צ-ח-ק	תִּצְחֲקִי	תִּצְחֲקוּ	יִצְחֲקוּ	
כ-ע-ס	תִּכְעֲסִי	תִּכְעֲסוּ	יִכְעֲסוּ	

Here, too, in the regular verb, a *shva* appears in the syllable before the endings, whereas an *ah* vowel (◌ֲ) takes its place when a guttural appears in the middle of the root.

The rest of the future tense conjugation of middle guttural verbs – i.e., the forms **without endings** (יִשְׁאַל, יִכְעַס, יִצְחַק, יִנְהַג) – are also different from regular verbs (יִסְגּוֹר). We will explain this difference below (p. 458).

• Beenyan pa'al *and initial gutturals*
(חָזַר, עָמַד, הָרַס, אָסַף)[3]

Future tense and infinitive forms with initial gutturals

Initial gutturals ח', ע', ה'

Read these sentences containing **future tense** verbs out loud:

אחרי שדני יִגְמוֹר את הספר וְיִכְתּוֹב עליו חיבור, הוא יַחְזוֹר לספרייה ויחזיר את הספר.

        yach-ZOR   *yeech-TOV*   *yeeg-MOR*

After Danny finishes the book and writes a composition about it, he'll go back to the library and return the book.

אם האיש יִפְרוֹץ לדירה וְיִגְנוֹב משם תכשיטים, השוטר יַעֲצוֹר אותו.

        ya-'a-TSOR   *yeeg-NOV*   *yeef-ROTS*

If the man breaks into an apartment and steals jewelry from it, the policeman will arrest him.

---

3   Also called "פ' גרונית" in grammar books, since the first root letter ('פ stands for the first root letter) is a גרונית – a guttural.

IV. Verbs with Guttural Consonants / 1. Guttural Consonants: Beenyan Pa'al

In the third verb in each of these sentences, we again see the influence of the gutturals on the vowels of the word. This time the guttural doesn't like the *ee* vowel that is supposed to **precede** it (we see *ee* in the regular verbs יִגְמוֹר *yeeg-MOR* and יִכְתוֹב *yeech-TOV*). The ח׳ in יַחְזוֹר causes the vowel **before** it to become *ah* (*yach-ZOR*). The reason for this change is: Gutturals like to be preceded by an *ah* vowel (or sometimes by *eh*).

The change in יַחְזוֹר also takes place before the ע׳ in יַעֲצוֹר (*ya-'a-TSOR*).

Q: What additional change takes place in יַעֲצוֹר (that does not take place in יַחְזוֹר)?

A: A second *ah* vowel is added **after** the ע׳ as well, creating **three** syllables, with an *ah* vowel in the first two: יַ-עֲ-צוֹר (*ya-'a-TSOR*).[4] The reason for this change is: Gutturals often like "matching vowels."

The changes we saw in יַחְזוֹר and יַעֲצוֹר take place not only in the **future tense** forms of these verbs, but also in the **infinitive**. Here are some examples:

	שם הפועל	*future* (עתיד)		שורש
	infinitive	הם	הוא	*root*
regular verb:	לִסְגוֹר	יִסְגְרוּ	יִסְגוֹר	ס-ג-ר
to return	לַחְזוֹר[5]	יַחְזְרוּ	יַחְזוֹר	ח-ז-ר
to stand	לַעֲמוֹד	יַעַמְדוּ	יַעֲמוֹד	ע-מ-ד
to destroy	לַהֲרוֹס	יַהַרְסוּ	יַהֲרוֹס	ה-ר-ס

Now let's look at the אני form of the future tense:

	future (עתיד)		שורש	
	הוא	אני	*root*	
regular verb:	יִסְגוֹר	אֶסְגוֹר	ס-ג-ר	.1
	יַחְזוֹר	אֶחְזוֹר	ח-ז-ר	.2
	יַעֲמוֹד	אֶעֱמוֹד	ע-מ-ד	.3
	יַהֲרוֹס	אֶהֱרוֹס	ה-ר-ס	.4

---

4 Forms with a *shva* also exist but are far less common, e.g., יַהֲרוֹס/יַהְרוֹס, יַעֲמוֹד/יַעְמוֹד. Note: Forms such as יַחְזוֹר, whose first root letter is ח׳, also have two possible pronunciations: יַחְזוֹר *yach-ZOR* and יַחֲזוֹר *ya-cha-ZOR*.

5 According to rules of grammar, this form may also be pronounced לַחֲזוֹר *la-cha-ZOR*. In addition, the future tense הם/הן form יַחְזְרוּ may also be pronounced יַחֲזְרוּ *ya-chaz-ROO*.

Q: In line 1, what is the difference between the אני form and the הוא form?

A: The -א of the אני form shows a **preference** for the vowel *eh*. Thus, we say אֶסְגּוֹר (*'es-GOR*) with *eh* instead of the *ee* in יִסְגּוֹר (*yees-GOR*). In line 2, אֶחֱזוֹר is just like אֶסְגּוֹר, while the forms in lines 3 and 4 – אֶעֱמוֹד, אֶהֱרוֹס – again demonstrate the tendency of gutturals to take "matching vowels": *eh-eh*.

Initial guttural 'א

Now let's look at verbs whose first root letter is 'א.

	שם הפועל	future (עתיד)			שורש
	infinitive	הם	הוא	אני	*root*
regular verb:	לִסְגּוֹר	יִסְגְּרוּ	יִסְגּוֹר	אֶסְגּוֹר	ס-ג-ר
	⇓	⇓	⇓	⇓	
to collect	לֶאֱסוֹף	יַאַסְפוּ⁶	יֶאֱסוֹף	אֶאֱסוֹף	א-ס-פ
to eat	לֶאֱכוֹל				א-כ-ל

Q: What happens to the vowels at the beginning of the words when 'א is the first root letter?

A: Here, too, we see the tendency of 'א to prefer the vowel *eh*: יֶאֱסוֹף (*ye-'e-SOF*), לֶאֱסוֹף (*le-'e-SOF*). The **future tense** and **infinitive** forms of verbs with an initial 'א like לאסוף begin with *eh-eh*, as opposed to *ah-ah* in initial guttural verbs like יַעֲמוֹד, לַעֲמוֹד.

The verb לֶאֱכוֹל in the last line of the chart has totally different future tense forms (e.g., יֹאכַל, יֹאכְלוּ). For details, see "Did you know?" below.

Did you know?
Verbs like יֹאכַל

A small number of *pa'al* verbs whose root begins with 'א have a special future form, as in:

Michael will eat at our place this evening.   מיכאל יֹאכַל אצלנו הערב.
yo-CHAL

---

6   The Hebrew Language Academy has decided that when verbs like אסף take an ending in the future tense, the recommended pronunciation is תֶּאֶסְפִי, תֶּאֶסְפוּ and יֶאֶסְפוּ, instead of תַּאַסְפִי, תַּאַסְפוּ and יַאַסְפוּ.

Verbs of this type have an *'ef'al* future form, like יִלְמַד and יִלְבַּשׁ.[7] In addition, their **first** vowel is *oh*. Here are all the future tense forms of the verb לֶאֱכוֹל (note that the infinitive form is **not** similar to the future):

	prefixes and endings	only prefixes	
אני:		אוֹכַל	
אתה:		תֹאכַל	
את:	תֹאכְלִי		
הוא:		**יֹאכַל**	
היא:		תֹאכַל	
אנחנו:		נֹאכַל	
אתם, אתן:	תֹאכְלוּ		
הם, הן:	**יֹאכְלוּ**		

Notice the special spelling of these verbs. In all but the אני form, a ו is **not** written, even when there are no vowel signs: יאכל.

The silent א of the root remains in all but the אני form, where it **drops out** and a ו is written in its stead:

אני: *אֹאכַל ⇐ אוֹכַל

The most common verbs whose future tense forms are like יֹאכַל are:

	root	future	
to like, love	א-ה-ב	יֹאהַב	
to say	א-מ-ר	יֹאמַר	

In all *pa'al* verbs whose roots begin with א, the infinitive is like לֶאֱהוֹב, לֶאֱסוֹף, לֶאֱכוֹל).

The one **exception** is לוֹמַר (root: א-מ-ר), which is similar to the אני future form אוֹמַר.

---

7   On *'ef'ol* (אפעול) and *'ef'al* (אפעל) forms in the future tense of *beenyan pa'al*, see the chapter "*Beenyan Pa'al*," pp. 398-401.

• Beenyan pa'al *and final gutturals* (שָׁמַע, שָׁלַח, קָרָא)

Present tense and infinitive forms with final gutturals

Read the following sentences out loud:

כשאורי **יושֵב** בחדר שלו, הוא תמיד **סוגֵר** את הדלת ומיד אחר כך **פותֵחַ** את החלון. ◄

po-TE-ach   *so-GER*   *yo-SHEV*

When Uri sits in his room, he always closes the door and opens the window immediately afterwards.

כשחנה רוצה **לִלְמוד** בחדר שלה, היא נוהגת **לִסְגּור** את הדלת ו**לִפְתוחַ** את החלון.

leef-TO-ach   *lees-GOR*   *leel-MOD*

When Hannah wants to study in her room, she makes it a habit to close the door and to open the window.

כשחנה **יושֶבֶת** בחדר שלה, היא **סוגֶרֶת** את הדלת ומיד אחר כך **פותַחַת** את החלון.

po-TA-chat   *so-GE-ret*   *yo-SHE-vet*

When Hannah sits in her room, she closes the door and opens the window immediately afterwards.

In all of the sentences above, the **third** verb differs from the **first two** because of the presence of a guttural.

Q: What vowel comes **before** the guttural (ח׳) in the third verb in each sentence?

A: In each case, an *ah* vowel precedes the guttural: פותֵחַ (*po-TE-ach*),[8] לִפְתוחַ (*leef-TO-ach*) and פותַחַת (*po-TA-chat*).

These are more examples of the fact that gutturals like to be preceded by *ah*, as we saw above in initial guttural forms like יַחֲזור (instead of the regular verb יִסְגּור).

Now let's take a closer look at the **present tense** and **infinitive** forms that change when a guttural appears at the end of the root.

---

8   Even though the vowel sign ◻ is written **under** the ח׳ in פותֵחַ, it is pronounced **before** the *ch*: *po-TE-ach*.

root שורש		present (הווה)				infinitive שם הפועל
	m.s.	f.s.	m.pl.	f.pl.		

		present (הווה)				שם הפועל
	root שורש	m.s.	f.s.	m.pl.	f.pl.	infinitive
regular verb: ⫸	ס-ג-ר	סוֹגֵר	סוֹגֶרֶת	סוֹגְרִים	סוֹגְרוֹת	לִסְגּוֹר
		⇓	⇓			⇓
to hear	ש-מ-ע	שׁוֹמֵעַ	שׁוֹמַעַת	שׁוֹמְעִים	שׁוֹמְעוֹת	לִשְׁמוֹעַ
to open	פ-ת-ח	פּוֹתֵחַ	פּוֹתַחַת	פּוֹתְחִים	פּוֹתְחוֹת	לִפְתוֹחַ
to read, call	ק-ר-א	קוֹרֵא	קוֹרֵאת	קוֹרְאִים	קוֹרְאוֹת	לִקְרוֹא

Q: In which present tense forms do the gutturals cause changes?

A: Only in the singular forms. Notice that in the plural forms, the gutturals cause no change.[9]

> ***Be careful!*** Even though we don't always hear ע׳ and א׳, they are always present and must not be omitted in writing.

Masculine singular and infinitive forms

When the guttural is ח׳, as in פּוֹתֵחַ (*po-TE-ach*), there is an extra *ah* sound (often called a "helping vowel") **before** the final consonant. (In texts with vowel signs, the *patach* – ◌ – is written **under** the final ח׳, even though it is pronounced **before** it.)[10] When the guttural is ע׳, as in שׁוֹמֵעַ, speakers who pronounce the ע׳ pronounce the extra *ah* sound **before** the ע׳: *sho-ME-a'*. Speakers who don't pronounce the ע׳ end the word with the extra vowel *ah*.

This same *ah* "helping vowel" appears also in the **infinitives** of these verbs: לִשְׁמוֹעַ (*leesh-MO-a'* / *leesh-MO-a*) and לִפְתוֹחַ (*leef-TO-ach*).

Notice that when the final guttural is א׳, there is **no** added *ah*: לִקְרוֹא (like לִסְגּוֹר). (We mention final א׳ verbs here, but will discuss these verbs in more depth in the chapter "Verbs Whose Third Root Letter Is א׳," pp. 557-566.)

---

9   The final root letter of verbs like בונה is actually י׳; therefore, these verbs are discussed in the chapter "Verbs Whose Third Root Letter Is י׳," pp. 532-544. The few verbs whose final root letter is ה (such as ג-ב-ה to get taller), are similar in behavior to ש-מ-ע:

⇐ אֲנִי גָּבַהְתִּי, הוּא גָּבַהּ, הִיא גָּבְהָה / הוּא גּוֹבֵהַּ (גָּבֵהַּ), הִיא גּוֹבַהַת // הֵם גּוֹבְהִים, הֵן גּוֹבְהוֹת // לִגְבּוֹהַּ

10   In traditional grammar, this is called a פַּתָח גָּנוּב (*furtive patach*).

Feminine singular forms

While the regular feminine singular form – סוֹגֶרֶת – has matching *eh* vowels before the end (*E-et*), the forms with ע׳ or ח׳ prefer matching *ah* vowels: שׁוֹמַעַת (*sho-MA-'at*) and פּוֹתַחַת (*po-TA-chat*).

Verbs with a final א׳ have a different feminine singular form. To arrive at this form, we can begin with the masculine form קוֹרֵא (*ko-RE*) and simply add a final ת׳: קוֹרֵאת (*ko-RET*).

Future tense forms with final gutturals

Read these sentences containing **future tense** verbs out loud:

⤸ אם רינה **תִּפְתּוֹר** את כל תרגילי המתמטיקה, **תִּגְמוֹר** לקרוא מאמר לשיעור בהיסטוריה **וְתִקְרָא** עוד
teek-RA' [11] *teeg-MOR* *teef-TOR*
פרק בגאוגרפיה, היא תוכל לצאת לטיול בסוף השבוע.

If Rina solves all the math problems, finishes reading an article for her history class and reads another chapter in geography, she will be able to go away this weekend.

Now let's look at the **future tense** forms with final gutturals. As we noted above, these forms all prefer an *ah* vowel before the final ע׳, ח׳, א׳.[12]

root שורש	future (עתיד) הוא
ס-ג-ר regular verb:	**יִסְגּוֹר**
	⇓
ש-מ-ע	**יִשְׁמַע**
פ-ת-ח	**יִפְתַּח**
ק-ר-א	**יִקְרָא**

Also when the **middle** root letter is a guttural, we get similar forms:

root שורש	future (עתיד) הוא
ס-ג-ר regular verb:	**יִסְגּוֹר**
	⇓
ש-א-ל	**יִשְׁאַל**
נ-ה-ג	**יִנְהַג**
צ-ח-ק	**יִצְחַק**
כ-ע-ס	**יִכְעַס**

---

11 For reasons of clarity, in this chapter we have transcribed the final א׳ even though it is not pronounced.
12 The few verbs with a final consonantal ה׳ (such as ג-ב-ה) also prefer an *ah* vowel: הוא יִגְבַּהּ (he will get taller).

Chapter summary

◆ In the following chart you can see all of the changes in *beenyan pa'al* caused by gutturals.

final gutturals ל' גרונית		middle gutturals ע' גרונית	initial gutturals פ' גרונית				regular verbs שלמים	
final א'	final ע', ח'	middle א', ה', ח', ע'	initial א' (אהב, אכל, אמר)	initial א'	initial ע', ה'	initial ח'	regular root	
								עבר *past*
קָרָאתִי	שָׁמַעְתִּי	שָׁאַלְתִּי	אָכַלְתִּי	אָסַפְתִּי	עָמַדְתִּי	חָזַרְתִּי	**סָגַרְתִּי**	אני
קָרָאתָ	שָׁמַעְתָּ	שָׁאַלְתָּ	אָכַלְתָּ	אָסַפְתָּ	עָמַדְתָּ	חָזַרְתָּ	**סָגַרְתָּ**	אתה
קָרָאת	שָׁמַעְתְּ	שָׁאַלְתְּ	אָכַלְתְּ	אָסַפְתְּ	עָמַדְתְּ	חָזַרְתְּ	**סָגַרְתְּ**	את
קָרָאנוּ	שָׁמַעְנוּ	שָׁאַלְנוּ	אָכַלְנוּ	אָסַפְנוּ	עָמַדְנוּ	חָזַרְנוּ	**סָגַרְנוּ**	אנחנו
קְרָאתֶם	שְׁמַעְתֶּם	שְׁאַלְתֶּם	אֲכַלְתֶּם	אֲסַפְתֶּם	עֲמַדְתֶּם	חֲזַרְתֶּם	**סְגַרְתֶּם**[13]	אתם
קְרָאתֶן	שְׁמַעְתֶּן	שְׁאַלְתֶּן	אֲכַלְתֶּן	אֲסַפְתֶּן	עֲמַדְתֶּן	חֲזַרְתֶּן	**סְגַרְתֶּן**	אתן
קָרָא	שָׁמַע	שָׁאַל	אָכַל	אָסַף	עָמַד	חָזַר	**סָגַר**	הוא
קָרְאָה	שָׁמְעָה	שָׁאֲלָה	אָכְלָה	אָסְפָה	עָמְדָה	חָזְרָה	**סָגְרָה**	היא
קָרְאוּ	שָׁמְעוּ	שָׁאֲלוּ	אָכְלוּ	אָסְפוּ	עָמְדוּ	חָזְרוּ	**סָגְרוּ**	הם/הן
								הווה *present*
קוֹרֵא	שׁוֹמֵעַ	שׁוֹאֵל	אוֹכֵל	אוֹסֵף	עוֹמֵד	חוֹזֵר	**סוֹגֵר**	אני, אתה, הוא
קוֹרֵאת	שׁוֹמַעַת	שׁוֹאֶלֶת	אוֹכֶלֶת	אוֹסֶפֶת	עוֹמֶדֶת	חוֹזֶרֶת	**סוֹגֶרֶת**	אני, את, היא
קוֹרְאִים	שׁוֹמְעִים	שׁוֹאֲלִים	אוֹכְלִים	אוֹסְפִים	עוֹמְדִים	חוֹזְרִים	**סוֹגְרִים**	אנחנו, אתם, הם
קוֹרְאוֹת	שׁוֹמְעוֹת	שׁוֹאֲלוֹת	אוֹכְלוֹת	אוֹסְפוֹת	עוֹמְדוֹת	חוֹזְרוֹת	**סוֹגְרוֹת**	אנחנו, אתן, הן
								עתיד *future*
אֶקְרָא	אֶשְׁמַע	אֶשְׁאַל	אוֹכַל	אֶאֱסוֹף	אֶעֱמוֹד	אֶחֱזוֹר[14]	**אֶסְגּוֹר**	אני
תִּקְרָא	תִּשְׁמַע	תִּשְׁאַל	תֹּאכַל	תֶּאֱסוֹף	תַּעֲמוֹד	תַּחֲזוֹר	**תִּסְגּוֹר**	אתה
יִקְרָא	יִשְׁמַע	יִשְׁאַל	יֹאכַל	יֶאֱסוֹף	יַעֲמוֹד	יַחֲזוֹר	**יִסְגּוֹר**	הוא
תִּקְרָא	תִּשְׁמַע	תִּשְׁאַל	תֹּאכַל	תֶּאֱסוֹף	תַּעֲמוֹד	תַּחֲזוֹר	**תִּסְגּוֹר**	היא
נִקְרָא	נִשְׁמַע	נִשְׁאַל	נֹאכַל	נֶאֱסוֹף	נַעֲמוֹד	נַחֲזוֹר	**נִסְגּוֹר**	אנחנו

13 According to the rules of grammar, the stress is on the ending of אתם and אתן forms in all verbs. In *beenyan pa'al* this causes the first vowel to "reduce" (it is written as a *shva*): סְגַרְתֶּם, סְגַרְתֶּן (pronounced *sgar-TEM*, *sgar-TEN* or *se-gar-TEM*, *se-gar-TEN*). When there is an initial guttural, we get עֲמַדְתֶּם (*'a-mad-TEM*) and עֲמַדְתֶּן (*'a-mad-TEN*).

14 According to rules of grammar, the following pronunciations are also acceptable:

לַחֲזוֹר	תַּחֲזְרִי	תַּחֲזוֹר	אֶחֱזוֹר ◄
la-cha-ZOR	*ta-chaz-REE*	*ta-cha-ZOR*	*'e-che-ZOR*

final gutturals ל׳ גרונית		middle gutturals ע׳ גרונית	initial gutturals פ׳ גרונית				regular verbs שלמים	
final א׳	final ע׳, ח׳	middle א׳, ה׳, ח׳, ע׳	initial א׳ (אהב, אכל, אמר)	initial א׳	initial ע׳, ה׳	initial ח׳	regular root	
								future עתיד
תִקְרְאִי	תִשְׁמְעִי	תִשְׁאֲלִי	תֹּאכְלִי	תֶּאֶסְפִי[15]	תַעַמְדִי	תַחְזְרִי	**תִּסְגְּרִי**	את
תִקְרְאוּ	תִשְׁמְעוּ	תִשְׁאֲלוּ	תֹּאכְלוּ	תֶּאֶסְפוּ	תַעַמְדוּ	תַחְזְרוּ	**תִּסְגְּרוּ**	אתם/אתן
יִקְרְאוּ	יִשְׁמְעוּ	יִשְׁאֲלוּ	יֹאכְלוּ	יֶאֶסְפוּ	יַעַמְדוּ	יַחְזְרוּ	**יִסְגְּרוּ**	הם/הן
לִקְרוֹא	לִשְׁמוֹעַ	לִשְׁאוֹל	לֶאֱכוֹל	לֶאֱסוֹף	לַעֲמוֹד	לַחֲזוֹר	**לִסְגּוֹר**	שם פועל
to read	to hear	to ask	to eat	to collect	to stand	to return	to close	*infinitive*

◆ Here is a summary of the changes highlighted in the chart above. All are caused by gutturals:

- Instead of a *shva* (◌ְ), gutturals like *ah* (or sometimes *eh*). Thus:

יִסְגֹּר	לִסְגֹּר	יִסְגְּרוּ	סָגְרָה	סוֹגְרִים ◄
⇓	⇓	⇓	⇓	⇓
יַעֲמֹד	לַעֲמֹד	יִשְׁאֲלוּ	שָׁאֲלָה	שׁוֹאֲלִים
יֶאֱסֹף	לֶאֱסֹף			

- Gutturals like to be preceded by an *ah* vowel (or sometimes *eh*). Thus:

יִסְגֹּר	יִסְגּוֹר	יִסְגּוֹר	סוֹגֶרֶת	סוֹגֵר	לִסְגּוֹר ◄
⇓	⇓	⇓	⇓	⇓	⇓
יַחֲזֹר	יִשְׁמַע	שׁוֹמַעַת	שׁוֹמֵעַ	לִשְׁמוֹעַ	
יַעֲמֹד	יִפְתַּח	פּוֹתַחַת	פּוֹתֵחַ	לִפְתוֹחַ	
יֶאֱסֹף	יִקְרָא				

- Most gutturals like "matching vowels." Thus:

יִסְגּוֹר	לִסְגּוֹר	סוֹגֶרֶת ◄
⇓	⇓	⇓
יַעֲמֹד	לַעֲמֹד	שׁוֹמַעַת
יֶאֱסֹף	לֶאֱסֹף	פּוֹתַחַת

---

15 The Hebrew Language Academy has decided that when verbs beginning with א׳ take endings in the future tense, the recommended pronunciation is תֶּאֶסְפִי, תֶּאֶסְפוּ and יֶאֶסְפוּ, instead of the traditional יַאַסְפוּ, תַּאַסְפוּ and תַּאַסְפִי.

Want to see if you've understood?

Read the underlined verbs out loud, paying attention to the changes caused by the gutturals. For help you can refer to the chart above.

1. דני <u>כותב</u> מכתב. / דני <u>שולח</u> מכתב.
2. הרופאים <u>בודקים</u> את החולים. / הרופאים <u>שואלים</u> שאלות.
3. יובל <u>ירקוד</u> עם דינה במסיבה. / יובל <u>ישאל</u> את דינה על העבודה שלה.
4. יוסי צריך <u>לשמור</u> בשער היום. / יוסי צריך <u>לעבוד</u> היום.
5. למה את <u>סוגרת</u> את הדלת? / למה את <u>פותחת</u> את הדלת?
6. אתה רוצה <u>ללמוד</u> פיזיקה באוניברסיטה? / אתה רוצה <u>לאכול</u> ארוחת צוהריים בקפטריה?
7. התלמיד <u>יזכור</u> את מה שהמורה אמר. / התלמיד <u>יחשוב</u> על מה שהמורה אמר.
8. דני <u>יכתוב</u> את המכתב היום. / הוא <u>ישלח</u> את המכתב מחר.
9. אתה <u>תמכור</u> את המכונית שלך בשבוע הבא. / אתה <u>תעבוד</u> קשה בשבוע הבא.

Answers:

1. כּוֹתֵב (ko-TEV), שׁוֹלֵחַ (sho-LE-ach)   2. בּוֹדְקִים (bod-KEEM), שׁוֹאֲלִים (sho-'a-LEEM)
3. יִרְקוֹד (yeer-KOD), יִשְׁאַל (yeesh-'AL)   4. לִשְׁמוֹר (leesh-MOR), לַעֲבוֹד (la-'a-VOD)
5. סוֹגֶרֶת (so-GE-ret), פּוֹתַחַת (po-TA-chat)   6. לִלְמוֹד (leel-MOD), לֶאֱכוֹל (le-'e-CHOL)
7. יִזְכּוֹר (yeez-KOR), יַחְשׁוֹב (yach-SHOV) / יַחֲשׁוֹב (ya-cha-SHOV)
8. יִכְתּוֹב (yeech-TOV), יִשְׁלַח (yeesh-LACH)   9. תִּמְכּוֹר (teem-KOR), תַּעֲבוֹד (ta-'a-VOD)

2. Guttural Consonants (אʹ, הʹ, חʹ, עʹ): *Beenyaneem Heef'eel, Hoof'al* and *Heetpa'el*

Preview

- Beenyan heef'eel   (הֶעֱבִיר, הִשְׁפִּיעַ)
- Beenyan hoof'al   (הוּפְעַל, הוּעֲבַר/הוֹעֲבַר, הוּשְׁפַּע)
- Beenyan heetpa'el   (הִתְנַהֵג, הִתְפַּתֵּחַ)

In the three chapters on guttural consonants, we discuss only the tenses and forms in which gutturals cause changes.

• Beenyan heef'eel (הֶעֱבִיר, הִשְׁפִּיעַ)

Beenyan heef'eel *and initial gutturals*

Read the following sentence out loud:

◄ רמי הִזְמִין את מירה לטיול, אבל היא הֶחְלִיטָה לא לבוא, כי היא הֶעֲדִיפָה לנסוע לחוף הים.

      he-'e-DEE-fa   *hech-LEE-ta*   *heez-MEEN*

Rami invited Mira to go on a day-trip, but she decided not to go (lit.: come) because she preferred to go to the beach.

In the last two **past tense** forms in this sentence, there is a *guttural* at the beginning of the root.

Q: To what vowel does the first *ee* of הִזְמִין change?

A: The first vowel becomes *eh*: הֶחְלִיטָה and הֶעֲדִיפָה. The reason for this change is that gutturals do not like to be preceded by *ee*, but rather prefer *ah* (as in יַחְזוֹר in *beenyan pa'al*) or *eh* (as in יֶאֱסוֹף in *beenyan pa'al* and here).

Here are more examples of past tense forms with initial gutturals:

	הם/הן	היא	הוא	אני ...	root שורש	
regular verb:	הִרְגִּישׁוּ	הִרְגִּישָׁה	הִרְגִּישׁ	הִרְגַּשְׁתִּי...	ר-ג-שׁ	.1 ◄
	⇓	⇓	⇓	⇓		
to decide	הֶחְלִיטוּ	הֶחְלִיטָה	הֶחְלִיט	הֶחְלַטְתִּי...[1]	ח-ל-ט	.2
to prefer	הֶעֱדִיפוּ	הֶעֱדִיפָה	הֶעֱדִיף	הֶעֱדַפְתִּי...	ע-ד-פ	.3
to believe	הֶאֱמִינוּ	הֶאֱמִינָה	הֶאֱמִין	הֶאֱמַנְתִּי...	א-מ-נ	

As you can see, the **first** vowel in lines 2-3 changes to *eh* no matter which guttural follows it (הֶחְלִיט, הֶעֱדִיף, הֶאֱמִין). With ע and א (line 3), an additional change takes place: the vowel **after** the guttural also changes to match the first vowel (הֶעֱדִיף *he-'e-DEEF*, הֶאֱמִין *he-'e-MEEN*).[2] As we mentioned in the preceding chapter, the reason for this change is the fact that most gutturals like "matching vowels" (compare לֶאֱכוֹל in *pa'al*).

We see this penchant for "matching vowels" with initial ע and א in the **other tenses and forms** as well:

	שם הפועל *infinitive*	future (עתיד) הם/הן	הוא	אני	present (הווה) m.pl.	f.s.	m.s	root שורש	
regular verb:	לְהַרְגִּישׁ	יַרְגִּישׁוּ	יַרְגִּישׁ...	אַרְגִּישׁ...	מַרְגִּישִׁים...	מַרְגִּישָׁה	מַרְגִּישׁ	ר-ג-שׁ	◄
	⇓	⇓	⇓	⇓	⇓	⇓	⇓		
	לְהַעֲדִיף	יַעֲדִיפוּ	יַעֲדִיף...	אַעֲדִיף...	מַעֲדִיפִים...	מַעֲדִיפָה	מַעֲדִיף	ע-ד-פ	
	לְהַאֲמִין	יַאֲמִינוּ	יַאֲמִין...	אַאֲמִין...	מַאֲמִינִים...	מַאֲמִינָה	מַאֲמִין	א-מ-נ	

In today's pronunciation, matching vowels do not usually occur with an initial ח (מַחְלִיט, יַחְלִיט, לְהַחְלִיט).

Note: Roots with an initial ה are rare in *heef'eel* and therefore, are not discussed here.

---

1   In certain verbs, the following forms with matching vowels also exist, but are less common in today's spoken Hebrew:

◄   הֶחֱזַרְתִּי, הֶחֱזִיר... / מַחֲזִיר... / יַחֲזִיר... / לְהַחֲזִיר

2   Forms with a *shva* also exist (in all tenses), but are less common, e.g., הֶעְדִּיפָה.

Beenyan heef'eel *and final gutturals*

Read the following sentence out loud:

השחקן **הִרְגִּיש** לא טוב, אבל **הִצְלִיחַ** לשחק עד סוף ההצגה.

heets-LEE-ach   heer-GEESH

The actor was feeling ill, but he managed to act until the end of the performance.

In הִצְלִיחַ, as opposed to הִרְגִּיש, we hear an *ah* sound before the last root letter (*heets-LEE-ach*). This is because gutturals "like" to be preceded by *ah*. Note: The *ah* is pronounced **before** the ח (*ch*) even though – in texts with vowel signs – it is written **under** it. Let's look at more examples of *heef'eel* verbs – in **all tenses** – with a final guttural:

שם הפועל *infinitive*	*future* (עתיד) הם/הן	 הוא...	*present* (הווה) *m.pl.*	 *f.s.*	 *m.s*	*past* (עבר) היא	 הוא	 אני...	שורש *root*
לְהַבְטִיחַ to promise	יַבְטִיחוּ	יַבְטִיחַ...	מַבְטִיחִים	מַבְטִיחָה	מַבְטִיחַ	הִבְטִיחָה	הִבְטִיחַ	הִבְטַחְתִּי...	ב-ט-ח
לְהַפְרִיעַ to disturb	יַפְרִיעוּ	יַפְרִיעַ...	מַפְרִיעִים	מַפְרִיעָה	מַפְרִיעַ	הִפְרִיעָה	הִפְרִיעַ	הִפְרַעְתִּי...	פ-ר-ע

Q: In which forms is this *ah* added?

A: Wherever ח and ע are the **last** letter in the form:[3]

1. In the masculine singular (הוא) forms of the **past** and the **present** tenses:

	present (הווה)		*past* (עבר)	
מפריע *maf-REE-a*	מבטיח *mav-TEE-ach*		הפריע *heef-REE-a*[4]	הבטיח *heev-TEE-ach*

---

3   This *ah* also appears in the rare roots that end in a consonantal ה, such as ג-ב-ה:
   to make taller, to raise אני הִגְבַּהְתִּי, הוא הִגְבִּיהַּ, היא הִגְבִּיהָה // הוא מַגְבִּיהַּ // הוא יַגְבִּיהַּ // לְהַגְבִּיהַּ
 The roots of much more common verbs that end in ה, such as הוא הִפְנָה (he referred), actually end in י (פ-נ-י) and are listed in the chart on p. 556.

4   We have not transcribed the ע in these forms. The transcription of these forms with the ע is: *heef-REE-a'* and *maf-REE-a'*.

2. In all forms of the **future** that do **not** have an ending:

יבטיח...	תבטיח,	אבטיח,
yav-TEE-ach	*tav-TEE-ach*	*'av-TEE-ach*
יפריע...	תפריע,	אפריע,
yaf-REE-a	*taf-REE-a*	*'af-REE-a*

3. And in the **infinitive**, too:

להפריע	להבטיח
le-haf-REE-a	*le-hav-TEE-ach*

This is the same *ah* "helping vowel" that we saw in some forms of *beenyan pa'al* (פּוֹתֵחַ / שׁוֹמֵעַ, לִפְתּוֹחַ / לִשְׁמוֹעַ) when ח' or ע' appear at the end of a word.

> ***Be careful!*** In the **past tense**, the הוא and היא forms of roots that end in ע' are written differently even though they are pronounced the same.[5]
>
> | | |
> |---|---|
> | He disturbed us when we were working. | הוא הִפְרִיעַ לנו כשעבדנו. |
> | | *heef-REE-a* |
> | She disturbed us when we were working. | היא הִפְרִיעָה לנו כשעבדנו. |
> | | *heef-REE-a*[6] |

For a discussion of the special behavior of *heef'eel* verbs with a final א' (e.g., לְהַמְצִיא to invent), see the chapter "Verbs Whose Third Root Letter Is א'," pp. 557-566.

Middle gutturals (as in לְהַכְעִיס to make someone angry) do not cause changes in *beenyan heef'eel*; therefore, we have not discussed them here.

---

5   They are pronounced the same by speakers who don't pronounce the ע'.

6   Throughout this book, in order to indicate the presence of ע' and א' as root letters, we have transcribed both of them as " ' " when they are followed by a vowel. Thus, the היא form is usually transcribed *heef-REE-'a* in this book, even though the ע' is not pronounced by many speakers.

Want to see if you've understood?

Read the underlined verbs out loud, paying attention to the changes caused by the highlighted gutturals. (For help you can refer to the tables at the end of this chapter.)

1. גלי <u>הזמינה</u> את נועה לסרט. / נועה <u>החליטה</u> ללכת למסעדה. / נועה <u>העדיפה</u> ללכת למסעדה.
2. השכן <u>הזמין</u> אותנו למסיבה. / השכן <u>הפריע</u> לנו לישון.
3. את <u>מצליחה</u> בכל מה שאת עושה. / אני <u>מאמינה</u> לכל מה שאת אומרת.
4. אתה תמיד מצליח <u>להצחיק</u> אותי. / אתה תמיד מצליח <u>להפתיע</u> אותי.

Answers:

1. הִזְמִינָה (heez-MEE-na), הֶחְלִיטָה (hech-LEE-ta), הֶעֱדִיפָה (he-'e-DEE-fa)
2. הִזְמִין (heez-MEEN), הִפְרִיעַ (heef-REE-a)   3. מַצְלִיחָה (mats-lee-CHA), מַאֲמִינָה (ma-'a-mee-NA)
4. לְהַצְחִיק (le-hats-CHEEK), לְהַפְתִּיעַ (le-haf-TEE-a)

• Beenyan hoof'al (הוּפְעַל, הוּעֲבַר/הוּעְבַר, הוּשְׁפַע)

Beenyan hoof'al *and middle gutturals*

Read the following sentence out loud:

> לאחר שההכנות האחרונות **הוּשְׁלְמוּ**, המכונות החדשות **הוּפְעֲלוּ**.
>   *hoof-'a-LOO*   *hoosh-le-MOO*

After the final preparations were completed, the new machines were turned on.

In the **second** highlighted verb in this sentence, we again see the preference of gutturals for *ah* instead of a *shva* (which in הוּשְׁלְמוּ indicates the vowel sound *eh*). This change occurs in middle guttural verbs in all the **past** and **future tense** forms that have an ending that begins with a **vowel** (*-a, -oo, -ee*):

	future (עתיד)			past (עבר)		שורש
	הם/הן	אתם/אתן	את	הם/הן	היא	root
regular verb:	**יוּזְמְנוּ**	**תוּזְמְנוּ**	**תוּזְמְנִי**	**הוּזְמְנוּ**	**הוּזְמְנָה**	**ז-מ-נ**
	⇓	⇓	⇓	⇓	⇓	
to be operated, turned on	יוּפְעֲלוּ	תוּפְעֲלוּ	תוּפְעֲלִי	הוּפְעֲלוּ	הוּפְעֲלָה	פ-ע-ל
to be left	יוּשְׁאֲרוּ	תוּשְׁאֲרוּ	תוּשְׁאֲרִי	הוּשְׁאֲרוּ	הוּשְׁאֲרָה	ש-א-ר
to be warned	יוּזְהֲרוּ	תוּזְהֲרוּ	תוּזְהֲרִי	הוּזְהֲרוּ	הוּזְהֲרָה	ז-ה-ר
to be sent away	יוּרְחֲקוּ	תוּרְחֲקוּ	תוּרְחֲקִי	הוּרְחֲקוּ	הוּרְחֲקָה	ר-ח-ק

Beenyan hoof'al *and initial gutturals*

When the **first** root letter is ע׳ or א׳, a similar change (*shva* to *ah*) occurs, as in:

> לאחר שהדו״ח **הוּשְׁלַם**, הוא **הוּעֲבַר** לכל חברי הוועדה לאישור.
>
> *hoo-'a-VAR   hoosh-LAM*
>
> After the report was completed, it was handed over to all the committee members for approval.

Here the *ah* in הוּעֲבַר replaces a *shva* that represents **no vowel sound**, so that when the *ah* is added, **three** syllables result (הוּ-עֲ-בַר *hoo-'a-VAR*). We have seen this change in many other verbs (e.g., סוֹגְ-רִים ⇐ סוֹ-גְ-רִים in *pa'al*). The change to *ah* occurs in all forms of the verb when the initial guttural is ע׳ or א׳ (line 3 below), but – in today's pronunciation – not with ח׳ (line 2). Roots with an initial ה׳ are rare in *hoof'al* and are not treated here.

	future (עתיד)		*present* (הווה)			*past* (עבר)			*root*
	הם/הן	הוא...	m.pl.	f.s.	m.s	היא	הוא	אני...	שורש
regular verb:	יוּזְמְנוּ	יוּזְמַן...	מוּזְמָנִים	מוּזְמֶנֶת	מוּזְמָן	הוּזְמְנָה	הוּזְמַן	הוּזְמַנְתִּי...	1. ז-מ-נ
	⇓	⇓	⇓	⇓	⇓	⇓	⇓	⇓	
to be returned	יוּחְזְרוּ	יוּחְזַר...	מוּחְזָרִים	מוּחְזֶרֶת	מוּחְזָר	הוּחְזְרָה	הוּחְזַר	הוּחְזַרְתִּי / הוּחְזַרְתִּי...	2. ח-ז-ר
to be moved	יוּעֲבְרוּ	יוּעֲבַר...	מוּעֲבָרִים	מוּעֲבֶרֶת	מוּעֲבָר	הוּעֲבְרָה	הוּעֲבַר	הוּעֲבַרְתִּי / הוּעֲבַרְתִּי...	3. ע-ב-ר
to be fed	יוּאֲכְלוּ	יוּאֲכַל...	מוּאֲכָלִים	מוּאֲכֶלֶת	מוּאֲכָל	הוּאֲכְלָה	הוּאֲכַל	הוּאֲכַלְתִּי / הוּאֲכַלְתִּי...	4. א-כ-ל

As you can see, an alternative pronunciation – הוֹעֲבַר *ho-'o-VAR*, מוֹעֲבָר *mo-'o-VAR* and the like – also exists, but it is heard less in today's spoken Hebrew. The pronunciation with *ho / mo / yo* instead of *hoo / moo / yoo* is possible with all initial gutturals in all tenses.

Beenyan hoof'al *and final gutturals*[7]

Read the following sentences out loud:

> רונית **מוּזְמֶנֶת** למסיבה שלנו.
>
> *mooz-ME-net*
>
> Ronit is invited to our party.

> ישראל נקראת ״הארץ **המוּבְטַחַת**״.
>
> *moov-TA-chat*
>
> Israel is called "the Promised Land."

---

7   On the changes caused by a final א׳, see the chapter "Verbs Whose Third Root Letter Is א׳," pp. 557-566.

In these cases, we hear that instead of the two *eh* vowels in the regular verb (מוּזְמֶנֶת *mooz-ME-net*), the guttural (ח׳) in מוּבְטַחַת causes a change to two *ah* vowels: *moov-TA-chat*. This happens also with a final ע׳: מוּשְׁפַּעַת (*moosh-PA-'at*).[8] This same change takes place in *beenyan pa'al* (סוֹגֶרֶת ⇐ שׁוֹמַעַת, פּוֹתַחַת) and occurs because gutturals like to be preceded by *ah* and they also like "matching vowels."

In all other forms in the **present** and in **other tenses**, verbs with a final ע׳ or ח׳ act like regular verbs.

Want to see if you've understood?
Read the underlined verbs out loud, paying attention to the changes caused by the highlighted gutturals. For help you can refer to the tables at the end of this chapter.

1. ההודעה הוקלטה אתמול וכבר הועברה לכולם.
2. הילדה הולבשה בבגדי חג והונעלה בנעליים החדשות.
3. המוסיקה שמוקלטת עכשיו מהרדיו מושמעת בקול רם מדיי.
4. הנערים המפריעים לא יוכנסו למועדון. הם יורחקו ממנו גם בשבועות הקרובים.

Answers:

1. הוּקְלְטָה (*hook-le-TA*), הוּעַבְרָה (*hoo-'av-RA*) (הוֹעֲבְרָה *ho-'ov-RA*)
2. הוּלְבְּשָׁה (*hool-be-SHA*), הוּנְעֲלָה (*hoon-'a-LA*)
3. מוּקְלֶטֶת (*mook-LE-tet*), מוּשְׁמַעַת (*moosh-MA-'at*) 4. יוּכְנְסוּ (*yooch-ne-SOO*), יוּרְחֲקוּ (*yoor-cha-KOO*)

• Beenyan heetpa'el (הִתְפַּתֵּחַ, הִתְנַהֵג)
Beenyan heetpa'el *and middle gutturals*

Read this sentence out loud:

השמרטפית (הבייביסיטר) אמרה שהילדה הִתְלַבְּשָׁה לבד וְהִתְנַהֲגָה יפה כל היום. ◄
heet-na-ha-GA   heet-lab-SHA

The babysitter said that the girl had gotten dressed by herself and had behaved nicely all day.

---

8   Also rare roots with ה׳ at the end act this way: היא מוּגְבַּהַת (It/she is being raised or made higher).

In the **second** highlighted verb in this sentence, we again see the preference of gutturals for *ah* instead of a *shva* (here, indicating **no vowel sound**). This change occurs in *beenyan heetpa'el* in the following forms, all of which have a **vowel ending** (*-a, -oo, -ee*):

	future (עתיד)			*present* (הווה)		*past* (עבר)		שורש
	הם/הן	אתם/אתן	את	*f.pl.*	*m. pl.*	הם/הן	היא	*root*
regular verb:	יִתְלַבְּשׁוּ	תִּתְלַבְּשׁוּ	תִּתְלַבְּשִׁי	מִתְלַבְּשׁוֹת	מִתְלַבְּשִׁים	הִתְלַבְּשׁוּ	הִתְלַבְּשָׁה	ל-ב-ש
	⇓	⇓	⇓	⇓	⇓	⇓	⇓	
to behave	יִתְנַהֲגוּ	תִּתְנַהֲגוּ	תִּתְנַהֲגִי	מִתְנַהֲגוֹת	מִתְנַהֲגִים	הִתְנַהֲגוּ	הִתְנַהֲגָה	נ-ה-ג
to wash oneself	יִתְרַחֲצוּ	תִּתְרַחֲצוּ	תִּתְרַחֲצִי	מִתְרַחֲצוֹת	מִתְרַחֲצִים	הִתְרַחֲצוּ	הִתְרַחֲצָה	ר-ח-צ
to be sorry	יִצְטַעֲרוּ	תִּצְטַעֲרוּ	תִּצְטַעֲרִי	מִצְטַעֲרוֹת	מִצְטַעֲרִים	הִצְטַעֲרוּ	הִצְטַעֲרָה	צ-ע-ר
to boast	יִתְפָּאֲרוּ	תִּתְפָּאֲרוּ	תִּתְפָּאֲרִי	מִתְפָּאֲרוֹת	מִתְפָּאֲרִים	הִתְפָּאֲרוּ	הִתְפָּאֲרָה	פ-א-ר

Beenyan heetpa'el *and final gutturals*[9]

Read the following sentences containing verbs in the **present tense**:

אבי **מִתְקַדֵּם** בלימודיו וּ**מִתְפַּתֵּחַ** יפה מבחינה חברתית.

meet-pa-TE-ach   meet-ka-DEM

Avi is progressing in his studies and – socially – is developing nicely.

יעל **מִתְקַדֶּמֶת** בלימודיה וּ**מִתְפַּתַּחַת** יפה מבחינה חברתית.

meet-pa-TA-chat   meet-ka-DE-met

Yael is progressing in her studies and – socially – is developing nicely.

The "helping vowel" *ah* that precedes the final ח' in מִתְפַּתֵּחַ and the vowel change in the feminine singular form (מִתְקַדֶּמֶת ⇐ מִתְפַּתַּחַת) are the same changes that we saw in *beenyan pa'al* (e.g., פּוֹתֵחַ, פּוֹתַחַת) and in some of the other *beenyaneem*. These changes also take place with a final ע' (מִשְׁתַּגֵּעַ, מִשְׁתַּגַּעַת) and are explained in the chapter "Guttural Consonants: *Beenyan Pa'al*" (pp. 456-458).[10]

In *beenyan heetpa'el,* the "helping vowel" *ah* (found in מִתְפַּתֵּחַ) occurs in **all the tenses and forms** when ח' or ע' appear at the end of a word.[11] Here are all the places in which it occurs, presented together with the feminine singular present tense form:

---

9   On verbs that end in א', see the chapter "Verbs Whose Third Root Letter Is א'," pp. 557-566.

10   This change also takes place in rare roots that end in ה', for example: מִתְמַהְמֵהַּ, מִתְמַהְמַהַת (to tarry).

11   A different (and much less commonly used) pronunciation of the past and future tense הוא forms is also regarded by the Hebrew Language Academy as acceptable: הִתְפַּתַּח (*heet-pa-TACH*), יִתְפַּתַּח (*yeet-pa-TACH*).

	infinitive		future (עתיד)					present (הווה)		past (עבר)	שורש
	שם הפועל	אנחנו	היא	הוא	אתה	אני	f.s	m.s	הוא	root
regular verb:	לְהִתְלַבֵּשׁ	נִתְלַבֵּשׁ	תִּתְלַבֵּשׁ	יִתְלַבֵּשׁ	תִּתְלַבֵּשׁ	אֶתְלַבֵּשׁ	מִתְלַבֶּשֶׁת	מִתְלַבֵּשׁ	הִתְלַבֵּשׁ	ל-ב-שׁ ◄
to develop	לְהִתְפַּתֵּחַ	נִתְפַּתֵּחַ	תִּתְפַּתֵּחַ	יִתְפַּתֵּחַ	תִּתְפַּתֵּחַ	אֶתְפַּתֵּחַ	מִתְפַּתַּחַת	מִתְפַּתֵּחַ	הִתְפַּתֵּחַ	פ-ת-ח
to go crazy	לְהִשְׁתַּגֵּעַ	נִשְׁתַּגֵּעַ	תִּשְׁתַּגֵּעַ	יִשְׁתַּגֵּעַ	תִּשְׁתַּגֵּעַ	אֶשְׁתַּגֵּעַ	מִשְׁתַּגַּעַת	מִשְׁתַּגֵּעַ	הִשְׁתַּגֵּעַ	ש-ג-ע

An **initial** guttural (as in לְהִתְחַתֵּן to marry) does not cause any changes in the forms of verbs in *heetpa'el*.

Want to see if you've understood?

Read the underlined verbs out loud, paying attention to the changes caused by the gutturals. (For help you can refer to the tables at the end of this chapter.)

1. מיכל ורון <u>התנגדו</u> לדברים שאמרנו./ רונית ומירי <u>הצטערו</u> על הדברים שהם אמרו.

2. דודי <u>יתרחץ</u> ראשון. / דני <u>יתקלח</u> אחרון.

3. יעל <u>מתפטרת</u> היום מן העבודה. / תמר <u>מתווכחת</u> הרבה בעבודה.

Answers:

1. הִתְנַגְדוּ (*heet-nag-DOO*), הִצְטַעֲרוּ (*heets-ta-'a-ROO*) 2. יִתְרַחֵץ (*yeet-ra-CHETS*), יִתְקַלֵּחַ (*yeet-ka-LE-ach*)
3. מִתְפַּטֶּרֶת (*meet-pa-TE-ret*), מִתְוַוכַּחַת (*meet-va-KA-chat*)

Chapter summary

Here are the most common forms of verbs with gutturals in *beenyaneem heef'eel, hoof'al* and *heetpa'el*:

◆ *Beenyan heef'eel* הפעיל

final gutturals ל' גרונית *final* 'ע ,'ח ב-ט-ח	middle gutturals ע' גרונית *initial* 'ע ,'א ע-ד-פ	initial gutturals פ' גרונית *initial* 'ח ח-ל-ט	regular verbs שלמים *regular root* ר-ג-ש	
				עבר *past*
הִבְטַחְתִּי	הֶעֱדַפְתִּי	הֶחֱלַטְתִּי	הִרְגַּשְׁתִּי	אני
הִבְטַחְתָּ	הֶעֱדַפְתָּ	הֶחֱלַטְתָּ	הִרְגַּשְׁתָּ	אתה
הִבְטַחְתְּ	הֶעֱדַפְתְּ	הֶחֱלַטְתְּ	הִרְגַּשְׁתְּ	את
הִבְטַחְנוּ	הֶעֱדַפְנוּ	הֶחֱלַטְנוּ	הִרְגַּשְׁנוּ	אנחנו
הִבְטַחְתֶּם	הֶעֱדַפְתֶּם	הֶחֱלַטְתֶּם	הִרְגַּשְׁתֶּם	אתם
הִבְטַחְתֶּן	הֶעֱדַפְתֶּן	הֶחֱלַטְתֶּן	הִרְגַּשְׁתֶּן	אתן
הִבְטִיחַ	הֶעֱדִיף	הֶחֱלִיט	הִרְגִּישׁ	הוא
הִבְטִיחָה	הֶעֱדִיפָה	הֶחֱלִיטָה	הִרְגִּישָׁה	היא
הִבְטִיחוּ	הֶעֱדִיפוּ	הֶחֱלִיטוּ	הִרְגִּישׁוּ	הם/הן
				הווה *present*
מַבְטִיחַ	מַעֲדִיף	מַחְלִיט	מַרְגִּישׁ	אני, אתה, הוא
מַבְטִיחָה	מַעֲדִיפָה	מַחְלִיטָה	מַרְגִּישָׁה	אני, את, היא
מַבְטִיחִים	מַעֲדִיפִים	מַחְלִיטִים	מַרְגִּישִׁים	אנחנו, אתם, הם
מַבְטִיחוֹת	מַעֲדִיפוֹת	מַחְלִיטוֹת	מַרְגִּישׁוֹת	אנחנו, אתן, הן
				עתיד *future*
אַבְטִיחַ	אַעֲדִיף	אַחְלִיט	אַרְגִּישׁ	אני
תַּבְטִיחַ	תַּעֲדִיף	תַּחְלִיט	תַּרְגִּישׁ	אתה
יַבְטִיחַ	יַעֲדִיף	יַחְלִיט	יַרְגִּישׁ	הוא
תַּבְטִיחַ	תַּעֲדִיף	תַּחְלִיט	תַּרְגִּישׁ	היא
נַבְטִיחַ	נַעֲדִיף	נַחְלִיט	נַרְגִּישׁ	אנחנו
תַּבְטִיחִי	תַּעֲדִיפִי	תַּחְלִיטִי	תַּרְגִּישִׁי	את
תַּבְטִיחוּ	תַּעֲדִיפוּ	תַּחְלִיטוּ	תַּרְגִּישׁוּ	אתם/אתן
יַבְטִיחוּ	יַעֲדִיפוּ	יַחְלִיטוּ	יַרְגִּישׁוּ	הם/הן
לְהַבְטִיחַ	לְהַעֲדִיף	לְהַחְלִיט	לְהַרְגִּישׁ	שם הפועל
to promise	to prefer	to decide	to feel	*infinitive*

◆ *Beenyan hoof'al* הוּפעל

final gutturals ל' גרונית	middle gutturals ע' גרונית	initial gutterals פ' גרונית		regular verbs שלמים	
final 'ע ,'ח ש-פ-**ע**	*middle* 'ע,'ח,'ה,'א ר-**ח**-ק	*initial* 'ע,'א ע-**ב**-ר	*initial* 'ח **ח**-ז-ר	*regular root* ל-ב-ש	
					past עבר
הוּשְׁפַּעְתִּי	הוּרְחַקְתִּי	הוּעֲבַרְתִּי	הוּחְזַרְתִּי[12]	**הוּלְבַּשְׁתִּי**	אני
הוּשְׁפַּעְתָּ	הוּרְחַקְתָּ	הוּעֲבַרְתָּ	הוּחְזַרְתָּ	**הוּלְבַּשְׁתָּ**	אתה
הוּשְׁפַּעַתְּ	הוּרְחַקְתְּ	הוּעֲבַרְתְּ	הוּחְזַרְתְּ	**הוּלְבַּשְׁתְּ**	את
הוּשְׁפַּעְנוּ	הוּרְחַקְנוּ	הוּעֲבַרְנוּ	הוּחְזַרְנוּ	**הוּלְבַּשְׁנוּ**	אנחנו
הוּשְׁפַּעְתֶּם	הוּרְחַקְתֶּם	הוּעֲבַרְתֶּם	הוּחְזַרְתֶּם	**הוּלְבַּשְׁתֶּם**	אתם
הוּשְׁפַּעְתֶּן	הוּרְחַקְתֶּן	הוּעֲבַרְתֶּן	הוּחְזַרְתֶּן	**הוּלְבַּשְׁתֶּן**	אתן
הוּשְׁפַּע	הוּרְחַק	הוּעֲבַר	הוּחְזַר	**הוּלְבַּשׁ**	הוא
הוּשְׁפְּעָה	הוּרְחֲקָה	הוּעֲבְרָה	הוּחְזְרָה	**הוּלְבְּשָׁה**	היא
הוּשְׁפְּעוּ	הוּרְחֲקוּ	הוּעֲבְרוּ	הוּחְזְרוּ	**הוּלְבְּשׁוּ**	הם/הן
					present הווה
מוּשְׁפָּע	מוּרְחָק	מוּעֲבָר	מוּחְזָר	**מוּלְבָּשׁ**	אני, אתה, הוא
מוּשְׁפַּעַת	מוּרְחֶקֶת	מוּעֲבֶרֶת	מוּחְזֶרֶת	**מוּלְבֶּשֶׁת**	אני, את, היא
מוּשְׁפָּעִים	מוּרְחָקִים	מוּעֲבָרִים	מוּחְזָרִים	**מוּלְבָּשִׁים**	אנחנו, אתם, הם
מוּשְׁפָּעוֹת	מוּרְחָקוֹת	מוּעֲבָרוֹת	מוּחְזָרוֹת	**מוּלְבָּשׁוֹת**	אנחנו, אתן, הן
					future עתיד
אוּשְׁפַּע	אוּרְחַק	אוּעֲבַר	אוּחְזַר	**אוּלְבַּשׁ**	אני
תּוּשְׁפַּע	תּוּרְחַק	תּוּעֲבַר	תּוּחְזַר	**תּוּלְבַּשׁ**	אתה
יוּשְׁפַּע	יוּרְחַק	יוּעֲבַר	יוּחְזַר	**יוּלְבַּשׁ**	הוא
תּוּשְׁפַּע	תּוּרְחַק	תּוּעֲבַר	תּוּחְזַר	**תּוּלְבַּשׁ**	היא
נוּשְׁפַּע	נוּרְחַק	נוּעֲבַר	נוּחְזַר	**נוּלְבַּשׁ**	אנחנו
תּוּשְׁפְּעִי	תּוּרְחֲקִי	תּוּעֲבְרִי	תּוּחְזְרִי	**תּוּלְבְּשִׁי**	את
תּוּשְׁפְּעוּ	תּוּרְחֲקוּ	תּוּעֲבְרוּ	תּוּחְזְרוּ	**תּוּלְבְּשׁוּ**	אתם/אתן
יוּשְׁפְּעוּ	יוּרְחֲקוּ	יוּעֲבְרוּ	יוּחְזְרוּ	**יוּלְבְּשׁוּ**	הם/הן
to be influenced	to be sent away	to be moved	to be returned	to be dressed (by…)	**שם הפועל** *infinitive*

---

12 Forms with an *oh* vowel in the first (and sometimes second) syllable also exist in verbs with an initial guttural, e.g., הוּחְזַרְתִּי (*hoch-ZAR-tee*), הוּעֲבַרְתִּי (*ho-'o-VAR-tee*). See the chapter above for an explanation.

התפעל ◆ *Beenyan heetpa'el*

final gutturals ל׳ גרונית	middle gutturals ע׳ גרונית	regular verbs שלמים	
final ח׳, ע׳ פ-ת-ח	*middle* א׳,ה׳,ח׳,ע׳ נ-ה-ג	*regular root* ל-ב-ש	
			עבר *past*
הִתְפַּתַּחְתִּי	הִתְנַהַגְתִּי	הִתְלַבַּשְׁתִּי	אני
הִתְפַּתַּחְתָּ	הִתְנַהַגְתָּ	הִתְלַבַּשְׁתָּ	אתה
הִתְפַּתַּחְתְּ	הִתְנַהַגְתְּ	הִתְלַבַּשְׁתְּ	את
הִתְפַּתַּחְנוּ	הִתְנַהַגְנוּ	הִתְלַבַּשְׁנוּ	אנחנו
הִתְפַּתַּחְתֶּם	הִתְנַהַגְתֶּם	הִתְלַבַּשְׁתֶּם	אתם
הִתְפַּתַּחְתֶּן	הִתְנַהַגְתֶּן	הִתְלַבַּשְׁתֶּן	אתן
הִתְפַּתֵּחַ	הִתְנַהֵג	הִתְלַבֵּשׁ	הוא
הִתְפַּתְּחָה	הִתְנַהֲגָה	הִתְלַבְּשָׁה	היא
הִתְפַּתְּחוּ	הִתְנַהֲגוּ	הִתְלַבְּשׁוּ	הם/הן
			הווה *present*
מִתְפַּתֵּחַ	מִתְנַהֵג	מִתְלַבֵּשׁ	אני, אתה, הוא
מִתְפַּתַּחַת	מִתְנַהֶגֶת	מִתְלַבֶּשֶׁת	אני, את, היא
מִתְפַּתְּחִים	מִתְנַהֲגִים	מִתְלַבְּשִׁים	אנחנו, אתם, הם
מִתְפַּתְּחוֹת	מִתְנַהֲגוֹת	מִתְלַבְּשׁוֹת	אנחנו, אתן, הן
			עתיד *future*
אֶתְפַּתֵּחַ	אֶתְנַהֵג	אֶתְלַבֵּשׁ	אני
תִּתְפַּתֵּחַ	תִּתְנַהֵג	תִּתְלַבֵּשׁ	אתה
יִתְפַּתֵּחַ	יִתְנַהֵג	יִתְלַבֵּשׁ	הוא
תִּתְפַּתֵּחַ	תִּתְנַהֵג	תִּתְלַבֵּשׁ	היא
נִתְפַּתֵּחַ	נִתְנַהֵג	נִתְלַבֵּשׁ	אנחנו
תִּתְפַּתְּחִי	תִּתְנַהֲגִי	תִּתְלַבְּשִׁי	את
תִּתְפַּתְּחוּ	תִּתְנַהֲגוּ	תִּתְלַבְּשׁוּ	אתם/אתן
יִתְפַּתְּחוּ	יִתְנַהֲגוּ	יִתְלַבְּשׁוּ	הם/הן
לְהִתְפַּתֵּחַ	לְהִתְנַהֵג	לְהִתְלַבֵּשׁ	שם הפועל *infinitive*
to develop	to behave	to get dressed	

3. Guttural Consonants (ע', ח', ה', א') and ר': *Beenyaneem Pee'el, Poo'al* and *Neef'al*

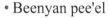

Preview

- Beenyan pee'el   (תֵּיאֵר, פִּיתֵּחַ/פִּיתַּח)
- Beenyan poo'al   (תֹּואַר, פֹּתַּח)
- Beenyan neef'al   (נֶעֱצַר, נִשְׁאַל, נִשְׁלַח)

In the three chapters on *guttural consonants*, we deal only with the tenses and forms in which gutturals cause changes.

Note: In this chapter, we often include ר' in our discussion of the gutturals (ע', ח', ה', א'). This is because under certain conditions (to be described below) ר' causes the same changes as gutturals.

• Beenyan pee'el (תֵּיאֵר, פִּיתֵּחַ/פִּיתַּח)

Beenyan pee'el *and middle gutturals*

In the introduction to the chapters on gutturals, the following sentence appeared:

◄   כשסבא **בִּיקֵר** אצל הנכדים, הוא **סִיפֵּר** להם סיפורים ו**תֵּיאֵר** להם את החיים בעיר שלו כשהוא היה ילד.

                   te-'ER   *see-PER*   *bee-KER*

When Grandpa visited his grandchildren, he told them stories and described life in the city he lived in (lit.: in his city) when he was a boy.

Q: In what way are the vowels of the third verb (תֵּיאֵר) different from those of the first two?

A: Instead of the initial *ee* vowel in בִּיקֵר and סִיפֵּר, the first vowel in תֵּיאֵר is *eh*.

Look at the representative **past tense** forms in the following chart.

		אני...	הוא...	אנחנו...		שורש / *root*	
			past (עבר)				
regular verb:		דִּיבַּרְתִּי...	דִּיבֵּר...	דִּיבַּרְנוּ...		ד-ב-ר	.1 ◄
		⇓	⇓	⇓			
to describe		תֵּיאַרְתִּי...	תֵּיאֵר...[1]	תֵּיאַרְנוּ...		ת-א-ר	.2
to bless		בֵּירַכְתִּי...	בֵּירֵךְ...	בֵּירַכְנוּ...		ב-ר-כ	.3
to play		שִׂיחַקְתִּי...	שִׂיחֵק...	שִׂיחַקְנוּ...		ש-ח-ק	.4
to manage		נִיהַלְתִּי...	נִיהֵל...	נִיהַלְנוּ...		נ-ה-ל	
to imagine, suppose		שִׁיעַרְתִּי...	שִׁיעֵר...	שִׁיעַרְנוּ...		ש-ע-ר	

Q: In which past tense verbs is the first vowel *eh* (◌) instead of *ee* (◌)?

A: In **all** the past tense forms of תֵּיאֵר (line 2) and בֵּירֵךְ (line 3), i.e., in verbs with an 'א or a 'ר in the middle.

Why does this happen?

The answer to this question has to do with the fact that, historically, the pattern of *beenyan pee'el* requires that the middle root consonant be "**doubled**" in all tenses and forms. Today we do not pronounce this doubling, but when vowel signs are written, we **see** that the middle root letter has a *strong dagesh* (the sign of historical doubling).[2] As you can see, in the chart above only the *regular* verb דִּיבֵּר has a *dagesh* in the middle root letter. All the rest, which all have either a middle guttural ('א, 'ה, 'ח, 'ע) – in lines 2 and 4 – or a 'ר in the middle (line 3), cannot "take" a *dagesh*. When this is the case, the **preceding** vowel is **sometimes** affected.[3] In *beenyan pee'el*, it is only before 'א and 'ר (lines 2 and 3) that there is a change in the preceding vowel. We hear this change only in the past tense.

Note that when we write without vowel signs, we write a 'י in all the past tense forms – whether the vowel is *ee* or *eh*: דיבר, תיאר, בירך.

---

1 An alternative הוא form also exists and is often used in formal Hebrew speech (for example, on the news), especially with middle gutturals and 'ר (תֵּיאַר *te-'AR* and בֵּירַךְ *be-RACH*) and final gutturals (see below, p. 477, note 6).

2 See the chapter "The Pronunciation of ב', כ', פ' and the *Dagesh*," p. 631 ("Did you know?").

3 This phenomenon is called *compensatory lengthening* (תַּשְׁלוּם דָּגֵשׁ).

The other noteworthy changes that take place in *pee'el* (in all its tenses and forms) are the same changes we saw in the other *beenyaneem*. Here is an example of one of these changes:

מיכל **סִיפְּרָה** לחברים שלה על הטיול שלה בסלובניה וְתֵיאֲרָה להם את הנופים היפים שראתה. ◄

te-'a-RA   *seep-RA*

Michal told her friends about her trip to Slovenia and described to them the beautiful scenery she had seen.

In the second verb – תֵיאֲרָה (*te-'a-RA*) – there is an *ah* sound instead of the *shva* that appears in a regular verb like סִיפְּרָה (*seep-RA*). Since in today's speech this *shva* is not pronounced, when *ah* (◌ֲ) takes its place, an **extra syllable** is created.

This change takes place in the **past** and **future tense** forms that have a vowel ending (*-a, -oo, -ee*) and in the **present tense** plural forms:

	future (עתיד)			present (הווה)		past (עבר)		שורש
	הם/הן	אתם/אתן	את	f.pl.	m.pl.	הם/הן	היא	root
regular verb:	יְדַבְּרוּ	תְדַבְּרוּ	תְדַבְּרִי	מְדַבְּרוֹת	מְדַבְּרִים	דִיבְּרוּ	דִיבְּרָה	ד-ב-ר ◄
	⇓	⇓	⇓	⇓	⇓	⇓	⇓	
	יְתָאֲרוּ	תְתָאֲרוּ	תְתָאֲרִי	מְתָאֲרוֹת	מְתָאֲרִים	תֵיאֲרוּ	תֵיאֲרָה	ת-א-ר
	יְשַׂחֲקוּ	תְשַׂחֲקוּ	תְשַׂחֲקִי	מְשַׂחֲקוֹת	מְשַׂחֲקִים	שִׂיחֲקוּ	שִׂיחֲקָה[4]	ש-ח-ק
	יְנַהֲלוּ	תְנַהֲלוּ	תְנַהֲלִי	מְנַהֲלוֹת	מְנַהֲלִים	נִיהֲלוּ	נִיהֲלָה	נ-ה-ל
	יְשַׂעֲרוּ	תְשַׂעֲרוּ	תְשַׂעֲרִי	מְשַׂעֲרוֹת	מְשַׂעֲרִים	שִׂיעֲרוּ	שִׂיעֲרָה	ש-ע-ר

Beenyan pee'el *and final gutturals*

Read the following sentences containing verbs in the **present tense**:

כל יום המורה **מְסַפֵּר** להורי הילד על התקדמותו בלימודים וּמְשַׁבֵּחַ אותו. ◄

me-sha-BE-ach   *me-sa-PER*

Every day the teacher (*m.*) tells the boy's parents about his progress in his studies and praises him.

כל יום המורה **מְסַפֶּרֶת** להורי הילד על התקדמותו בלימודים וּמְשַׁבַּחַת אותו.

me-sha-BA-chat   *me-sa-PE-ret*

Every day the teacher (*f.*) tells the boy's parents about his progress in his studies and praises him.

---

4   In spoken Hebrew today, many speakers tend to pronounce these words – in all the tenses – with no vowel after the ח': *seech-KA, me-sach-KEEM*, etc.

The changes that take place in מְשַׁבֵּחַ and in מְשַׁבַּחַת are the same changes that we saw in פּוֹתֵחַ and פּוֹתַחַת in *beenyan pa'al* and in some of the other *beenyaneem*. These changes also take place with a final 'ע (מְבַצֵּעַ, מְבַצַּעַת) and are explained in the chapter "Guttural Consonants: *Beenyan Pa'al*," pp. 456-458.[5]

Here are all the forms in which these changes take place:

	infinitive שם הפועל	אנחנו	היא	הוא	אתה	אני	f.s.	m.s.	הוא	root שורש
			future (עתיד)				*present* (הווה)		*past* (עבר)	
regular verb:	לְדַבֵּר	נְדַבֵּר	תְּדַבֵּר	יְדַבֵּר	תְּדַבֵּר	אֲדַבֵּר	מְדַבֶּרֶת	מְדַבֵּר	דִּיבֵּר	ד-ב-ר
to develop	לְפַתֵּחַ	נְפַתֵּחַ	תְּפַתֵּחַ	יְפַתֵּחַ	תְּפַתֵּחַ	אֲפַתֵּחַ	מְפַתַּחַת	מְפַתֵּחַ	פִּיתֵּחַ[6]	פ-ת-ח
to carry out, execute	לְבַצֵּעַ	נְבַצֵּעַ	תְּבַצֵּעַ	יְבַצֵּעַ	תְּבַצֵּעַ	אֲבַצֵּעַ	מְבַצַּעַת	מְבַצֵּעַ	בִּיצֵּעַ	ב-צ-ע

Initial gutturals (as in לְחַפֵּשׂ to look for) do not cause a change in *beenyan pee'el* and, therefore, are not discussed here.

Want to see if you've understood?

Read the underlined verbs out loud, paying attention to the changes caused by the gutturals. For help you can refer to the tables at the end of this chapter.

1. הילדים דיברו במשך שעות. הם גם שיחקו במשך שעות.
2. אנחנו מכבסים את החולצות. דורון ויונתן מגהצים אותן.
3. מי שיחק במשחק? מי ניצח במשחק?
4. המורה מלמדת את התלמידה החדשה. היא גם משבחת אותה.

Answers:

1. דִּיבְּרוּ (deeb-ROO), שִׂיחֲקוּ (see-cha-KOO). 2. מְכַבְּסִים (me-chab-SEEM), מְגַהֲצִים (me-ga-ha-TSEEM)
3. שִׂיחֵק (see-CHEK), נִיצֵּחַ (nee-TSE-ach) :or נִיצַּח (nee-TSACH)
4. מְלַמֶּדֶת (me-la-ME-det), מְשַׁבַּחַת (me-sha-BA-chat)

---

5   On verbs with a final 'א see the chapter "Verbs Whose Third Root Letter Is 'א," pp. 557-566.
6   Alternative forms (used especially in formal pronunciation) are: the הוא form in the past tense (הוא פִּיתַּח *pee-TACH* and בִּיצַּע *bee-TSA*) and all the future tense forms that end in 'ח or 'ע (e.g., יְפַתַּח *ye-fa-TACH* and יְבַצַּע *ye-va-TSA*).

• Beenyan poo'al (פּוּתַּח, תּוֹאַר)

Beenyan poo'al *and middle gutturals*

Read the following sentence out loud:

המכשיר החדש שפּוּתַּח במכון ויצמן **תּוֹאַר** בכתבה בעיתון סוף השבוע. ◄

to-'AR   *poo-TACH*

The new instrument that was developed at the Weizman Institute was described in a feature story in the weekend newspaper.

Q: In what way do the vowels of the **second** verb תּוֹאַר differ from those of the **first** verb פּוּתַּח?

A: The *oo* vowel of פּוּתַּח, which is one of the tell-tale signs of *beenyan poo'al*, has been replaced in תּוֹאַר by the vowel *oh*. As you can see in line 2 in the chart below, this change takes place in all forms in **all three tenses**:

	future (עתיד)		*present* (הווה)		*past* (עבר)		שורש
	הוא...	אני	*f.s*	*m.s*	הוא	...אני	*root*
regular verb:	יְצוּלַם...	אֲצוּלַם	מְצוּלֶמֶת...	מְצוּלָם	צוּלַם	...צוּלַמְתִּי	צ ל מ .1 ◄
	⇓	⇓	⇓	⇓	⇓	⇓	
to be described	יִתוֹאַר...	אֲתוֹאַר	מְתוֹאֶרֶת...	מְתוֹאָר	תוֹאַר	...תוֹאַרְתִּי	ת א ר .2
to be managed	יְנוֹהַל...		מְנוֹהֶלֶת...	מְנוֹהָל	נוֹהַל		נ ה ל [7]
to be documented	יְתוֹעַד...		מְתוֹעֶדֶת...	מְתוֹעָד	תוֹעַד		ת ע ד
to be banished	יְגוֹרַש...		מְגוֹרֶשֶת...	מְגוֹרָש	גוֹרַש		ג ר ש .3
to be unified	יְאוּחַד...		מְאוּחֶדֶת...	מְאוּחָד	אוּחַד		א ח ד .4

The reason for this change is the fact that the middle root letter in *beenyan poo'al* is "expected" to take a strong *dagesh* (the sign of historical doubling, as in the regular verb צוּלַם to be photographed). But, as we saw above in *beenyan pee'el*, when the middle root letter is either a guttural or a 'ר, it cannot "take" a *dagesh* and **sometimes** the preceding vowel is affected. In *beenyan poo'al*, the vowel change (from *oo* to *oh*) occurs not only before 'א and 'ר (as in *pee'el*), but rather before **all** gutturals (line 2) – **except** for 'ח (line 4) – and before 'ר (line 3).[8]

---

7   This and other passive verbs are used mainly in the *third person*; therefore, we have not listed other forms.

8   Since verbs in *beenyan heetpa'el* belong to the same "family" as verbs in *pee'el* and *poo'al*, and they also "take" a strong *dagesh* in the middle root letter, we would expect a change in the vowel before a middle guttural in *heetpa'el* verbs as well. This change sometimes takes place, as in מִתְפָּאֵר vs. מִתְלַבֵּשׁ (from ◌ to ◌ָ), but it does not affect the pronunciation of these verbs. For this reason, we did not point out this change in our discussion of *heetpa'el* above.

The other change in *poo'al* verbs with a middle guttural is the appearance of an *ah* sound instead of a *shva*, for example:

צוּלְּמָה	⇐	תוֹאֲרָה	תוֹעֲדָה	נוֹהֲלָה	אוּחֲדָה[9]
tsool-MA		to-'a-RA	to-'a-DA	no-ha-LA	'oo-cha-DA

Notice that this creates an **extra syllable** in these forms: they have **three** syllables instead of the **two** in צוּלְּמָה (*tsool-MA*).

An *ah* (◌ֲ) appears instead of a *shva* in the **past** and **future tenses** in all the forms that have a **vowel ending** (-*a*, -*ee*, -*oo*):

	future (עתיד)				*past* (עבר)		שורש
	הם/הן	אתם/אתן	את		הם/הן	היא	*root*
regular verb:	יְצוּלְּמוּ	תְּצוּלְּמוּ	תְּצוּלְּמִי		צוּלְּמוּ	צוּלְּמָה	צ-ל-מ
	⇓	⇓	⇓		⇓	⇓	
	יְתוֹאֲרוּ	תְּתוֹאֲרוּ	תְּתוֹאֲרִי		תוֹאֲרוּ	תוֹאֲרָה	ת-א-ר
	יְנוֹהֲלוּ	תְּנוֹהֲלוּ	תְּנוֹהֲלִי		נוֹהֲלוּ	נוֹהֲלָה	נ-ה-ל
	יְתוֹעֲדוּ	תְּתוֹעֲדוּ	תְּתוֹעֲדִי		תוֹעֲדוּ	תוֹעֲדָה	ת-ע-ד
	יְאוּחֲדוּ	תְּאוּחֲדוּ	תְּאוּחֲדִי		אוּחֲדוּ	אוּחֲדָה	א-ח-ד

Beenyan poo'al *and final gutturals*[10]

Read the following sentences out loud:

בדיסק שקניתי הקונצ׳רטו של מוצרט **מנוּגָּן** על ידי יצחק פרלמן. הוא **מבוּצָּע** בצורה מאוד מרגשת.
On the disc that I bought, Mozart's concerto is played by Yitzhak Perlman. It is performed very movingly.

מוסיקה קאמרית בדרך כלל **מנוּגֶּנֶת** על ידי קבוצת נגנים קטנה. היא תמיד **מבוּצַּעַת** בלי מנצח.
Chamber music is usually played by a small group of musicians. It is always performed without a conductor.

Look first at the second sentence above. In verbs with a final ע׳ or ח׳, the endings of the feminine singular forms in the **present tense** are the same as in *pa'al* and most of the other *beenyaneem*: מבוּצַּעַת and, similarly, מנוּתַּחַת (is being operated on) (compare: שׁוֹמַעַת, פּוֹתַחַת). For an explanation, see the chapter "Guttural Consonants: *Beenyan Pa'al*," pp. 456-458.

---

9   Many Hebrew speakers today pronounce *poo'al* verbs with a middle ח׳ with no vowel after the ח׳: *'ooch-DA*. This is true of forms in the past and future tenses, for example: יאוחדו is pronounced *ye-'ooch-DOO*. These are not considered correct forms according to the rules of grammar.

10   On the changes caused by a final א׳ you can read in the chapter "Verbs Whose Third Root Letter Is א׳," pp. 557-566.

All other forms of *poo'al* verbs with a final 'ע or 'ח – in **all tenses** – act like regular *poo'al* verbs. Compare, for example, מְבוּצָע and the regular verb מְנוּגָּן in the first sentence above.

Want to see if you've understood?

Read the underlined verbs out loud, paying attention to the changes caused by the highlighted gutturals and 'ר. For help you can refer to the tables at the end of this chapter.

1. החולה הַמְטוּפֶּלֶת בבית חולים בתל אביב מְנוּתַחַת עכשיו.

2. לאחר שההבקשה של הילדה אוּשְׁרָה, היא צוֹרְפָה לכיתה.

3. השחקנית צוּלְמָה לעיתון סוף השבוע. היא תוֹאֲרָה בכתבה כמצחיקה ומבריקה.

4. קירות הדירה מְקוּשָּׁטִים בציורים, והחדרים מְרוֹהָטִים בסגנון מודרני.

Answers:

1. מְטוּפֶּלֶת (me-too-PE-let), מְנוּתַּחַת (me-noo-TA-chat)   2. אוּשְׁרָה ('oosh-RA), צוֹרְפָה (tsor-FA)
3. צוּלְמָה (tsool-MA), תוֹאֲרָה (to-'a-RA)
4. מְקוּשָּׁטִים (me-koo-sha-TEEM), מְרוֹהָטִים (me-ro-ha-TEEM)

• Beenyan neef'al (נֶעֱצַר, נִשְׁאַל, נִשְׁלַח)

Beenyan neef'al *and initial gutturals*

Read the following sentences out loud:

1. אחרי שהאסיר נִמְלַט מהכלא, הוא נִתְפַּס וְנֶחְקַר על ידי המשטרה. גם מי שהסתיר אותו נֶעֱצַר.   ◄
   ne-'e-TSAR   nech-KAR neet-PAS   neem-LAT

   After the convict escaped from prison, he was caught and questioned by the police. The person who hid him was also arrested.

2. אם האסיר יִּמָּלֵט שוב, הוא יִּתָּפֵס וְיֵיחָקֵר עוד פעם. ייתכן שגם מי שיעזור לו יֵיעָצֵר.
   ye-'a-TSER   ye-cha-KER yee-ta-FES yee-ma-LET

   If the convict escapes again, he will again be caught and questioned. Whoever helps him will probably also be arrested.

The last two verbs in each of these sentences contain initial gutturals. Look again at the first sentence, which is in the past tense.

Q: What happens to the *ee* vowel of נִמְלַט and נִתְפַּס when there is an initial guttural?

A: It changes to *eh*: נֶחְקַר (*nech-KAR*), נֶעֱצַר (*ne-'e-TSAR*).

As you can see, this change in the first vowel(s) of the *neef'al* past tense forms is similar to the change that takes place in *heef'eel* verbs with an initial guttural: הִזְמִין (*heez-MEEN*) ⇒ הֶחְלִיט (*hech-LEET*), הֶעֱבִיר (*he-'e-VEER*). In *neef'al* (and *heef'eel*), when the first root letter is ח', in the speech of many speakers today only one change takes place: the *ee* vowel (נִמְלַט, נִתְפַּס) changes to *eh*: נֶחְקַר.[11] When the root begins with one of the other gutturals, an additional change takes place: the second vowel **matches** the first one (e.g., נֶעֱצַר).[12]

These changes take place in all the **past** and **present tense** forms of *beenyan neef'al*:

	present (הווה)			*past* (עבר)			שורש
	m.pl.	*f.s.*	*m.s.*	היא	הוא	אני...	*root*
regular verb:	נִכְנָסִים	נִכְנֶסֶת	נִכְנָס	נִכְנְסָה	נִכְנַס	נִכְנַסְתִּי...	כ נ ס .1
	⇓	⇓	⇓	⇓	⇓	⇓	
to be interrogated	נֶחְקָרִים	נֶחְקֶרֶת	נֶחְקָר	נֶחְקְרָה	נֶחְקַר	נֶחְקַרְתִּי...	ח ק ר .2
to disappear	נֶעֱלָמִים	נֶעֱלֶמֶת	נֶעֱלָם	נֶעֶלְמָה	נֶעֱלַם	נֶעֱלַמְתִּי...	ע ל ם .3
to be said	נֶאֱמָרִים	נֶאֱמֶרֶת	נֶאֱמָר	נֶאֶמְרָה	נֶאֱמַר		א מ ר
to be destroyed	נֶהֱרָסִים	נֶהֱרֶסֶת	נֶהֱרָס	נֶהֶרְסָה	נֶהֱרַס		ה ר ס

Now look at sentence 2 at the beginning of this section, in which the verbs appear in the **future tense**.

Q: What happens to the initial *ee* vowel found in regular verbs like יִמָּלֵט (*yee-ma-LET*) and יִתָּפֵס (*yee-ta-FES*) when there is an initial guttural?

A: It also changes to *eh*: יֵחָקֵר (*ye-cha-KER*), יֵעָצֵר (*ye-'a-TSER*).

This change takes place not only in the future tense, but also in the **infinitive** (לְהֵחָקֵר, לְהֵעָצֵר). The reason for this change is **different** from the reason for the change to *eh* in the past and present tenses (נֶחְקַר, נֶעֱצַר) and is connected to the fact that **regular** *neef'al* verbs have a strong *dagesh* in the first root letter of the future and infinitive: יִכָּנֵס and לְהִכָּנֵס. As we saw in our discussion of *beenyan pee'el* above: Gutturals – and ר' – can't "take" a strong *dagesh* – and sometimes this affects the vowel before them.

---

11 In certain verbs, forms with an *eh* after the ח' in the past and present tense also exist but are less common in today's spoken Hebrew:

  ◁ נֶחֱלַשְׁתִּי, נֶחֱלַשׁ... / נֶחְלַשׁ...

12 Forms with a *shva* (e.g., נֶעְצַר) also exist, but they are less common.

Just as the *ee* in דִּבֵּר (*dee-*) became *eh* in תֵּיאֵר (*te-*) in *pee'el*, so, too, *ee* becomes *eh* in the future and infinitive of *neef'al*. Look in the middle and left-hand columns of the following chart to see before **which** gutturals this change takes place:

	שם הפועל		*future* (עתיד)		שורש
	infinitive	הם/הן	הוא	אני	root
regular verb:	לְהִיכָּנֵס	יִיכָּנְסוּ	יִיכָּנֵס	אֶכָּנֵס	1. כ נ ס ◄
	⇓	⇓	⇓	⇓	
	לְהֵיחָקֵר	יֵיחָקְרוּ	יֵיחָקֵר	אֵיחָקֵר	2. ח ק ר
	לְהֵיעָלֵם	יֵיעָלְמוּ	יֵיעָלֵם	אֵיעָלֵם	3. ע ל מ
	לְהֵיאָמֵר	יֵיאָמְרוּ	יֵיאָמֵר		א מ ר
	לְהֵיהָרֵס	יֵיהָרְסוּ	יֵיהָרֵס		ה ר ס
to fall asleep	לְהֵירָדֵם	יֵירָדְמוּ	יֵירָדֵם	אֵירָדֵם	4. ר-ד-מ

As you can see, the change from *ee* to *eh* occurs before **all** gutturals (lines 2-3) and also before ר׳ (לְהֵירָדֵם and יֵירָדֵם line 4). Since ר has no problem with *shva*, it is like a regular verb in the past and present tenses: נִרְדַּם.

Note that in the above chart we have included the אני form in the future tense: אֵיעָלֵם, אֵיחָקֵר. Though the regular אני future tense form has no י (אֶכָּנֵס), when the first root letter is a guttural, in *full spelling* we **do** write a י (אֵיעָלֵם, אֵיחָקֵר).

Beenyan neef'al *and middle gutturals*

Read the following sentence aloud:

לאחר שהחשודים נִתְפְּסוּ, הם נִשְׁאֲלוּ על מעשיהם.

neesh-'a-LOO neet-pe-SOO

After the suspects were caught, they were asked about what they had done (lit: their deeds).

In נִשְׁאֲלוּ (*neesh-'a-LOO*) there is an *ah* sound instead of a *shva* (נִתְפְּסוּ *neet-pe-SOO*). As in other *beenyaneem*, this change takes place in the **past** and **future tenses** in all forms that have a vowel ending.

		future (עתיד)		*past* (עבר)		שורש
	הם/הן	אתם/אתן	את	הם/הן	היא	root
regular verb:	יִיכָּנְסוּ	תִּיכָּנְסוּ	תִּיכָּנְסִי	נִכְנְסוּ	נִכְנְסָה	כ נ ס ◄
	⇓	⇓	⇓	⇓	⇓	
to be asked	יִישָׁאֲלוּ	תִּישָׁאֲלוּ	תִּישָׁאֲלִי	נִשְׁאֲלוּ	נִשְׁאֲלָה	ש א ל
to be frightened	יִיבָּהֲלוּ	תִּיבָּהֲלוּ	תִּיבָּהֲלִי	נִבְהֲלוּ	נִבְהֲלָה	ב ה ל
to be chosen	יִיבָּחֲרוּ	תִּיבָּחֲרוּ	תִּיבָּחֲרִי	נִבְחֲרוּ	נִבְחֲרָה	ב ח ר
to be locked	יִינָּעֲלוּ	תִּינָּעֲלוּ	תִּינָּעֲלִי	נִנְעֲלוּ	נִנְעֲלָה	נ ע ל

Note that in the **future tense**, the addition of *ah* results in an extra syllable, for example: תִּיכָּנְסִי (*tee-kan-SEE*) versus תִּישָּׁאֲלִי (*tee-sha-'a-LEE*).

Beenyan neef'al *and final gutturals*

Read the following sentences out loud:

◄ לְאַחַר שֶׁהַגַּנָּב יִישָּׁפֵט, הוּא בְּוַדַּאי יִישָּׁלַח לַכֶּלֶא.
               yee-sha-LACH   *yee-sha-FET*

After the thief is tried, he will certainly be sent to jail.

הַגַּנָּב פּוֹחֵד לְהִישָּׁפֵט, מִכֵּיוָן שֶׁאֵינוֹ רוֹצֶה לְהִישָּׁלַח לַכֶּלֶא.
        le-hee-sha-LACH   *le-hee-sha-FET*

The thief is afraid to be tried because he doesn't want to be sent to jail.

In the **future tense** and **infinitive** forms, the *eh* vowel in יִישָּׁפֵט and לְהִישָּׁפֵט is replaced by an *ah* vowel: יִישָּׁלַח, לְהִישָּׁלַח. This is because ח' and also ע' (e.g., יִישָּׁמַע, לְהִישָּׁמַע to be heard) prefer to be preceded by an *ah* vowel. We saw this preference in the future tense of *pa'al* verbs, for example: יִשְׁלַח and יִשְׁמַע versus the regular verb יִסְגּוֹר.

Here are all the forms in which this change occurs:

root שורש	אני	אתה	הוא	היא	אנחנו	infinitive שם הפועל	
			future (עתיד)				
regular verb: כ-נ-ס ►	אֶכָּנֵס	תִּיכָּנֵס	יִיכָּנֵס	תִּיכָּנֵס	נִיכָּנֵס	לְהִיכָּנֵס	
	⇓	⇓	⇓	⇓	⇓	⇓	
to be sent ש-ל-ח	אֶשָּׁלַח	תִּישָּׁלַח	יִישָּׁלַח	תִּישָּׁלַח	נִישָּׁלַח	לְהִישָּׁלַח	
to be heard; to obey ש-מ-ע	אֶשָּׁמַע	תִּישָּׁמַע	יִישָּׁמַע	תִּישָּׁמַע	נִישָּׁמַע	לְהִישָּׁמַע	

Read the following sentences in the **present tense**:

◄ לָמָּה אַתְּ לֹא נִכְנֶסֶת לַמְּכוֹנִית? הַדֶּלֶת לֹא נִפְתַּחַת?
        neef-TA-chat   *neech-NE-set*

Why aren't you getting into the car? Doesn't the door open?

The feminine singular (נִפְתַּחַת) is the only present tense form of verbs with a final ח' or ע' that differs from regular verbs: Instead of *E-e* (נִכְנֶסֶת *neech-NE-set*), the vowels are *A-a* (נִפְתַּחַת *neef-TA-chat*).[13]

---

13 On the changes caused by a final א', see the chapter "Verbs Whose Third Root Letter Is א'," pp. 557-566.

Want to see if you've understood?

Read the underlined verbs out loud, paying attention to the changes caused by the highlighted gutturals and ר'. For help you can refer to the tables at the end of this chapter.

1. הקשר בין מספר שעות השינה לבין ההצלחה בלימודים <u>נבדק</u> <u>ונחקר</u> פעמים רבות.

2. הגנבים <u>נתפסו</u> על ידי בעלי הבית <u>ונעצרו</u> זמן קצר אחר כך על ידי השוטרים.

3. החברים <u>נפגשו</u> עם גילי לפני מסיבת ההפתעה לכבודה <u>ונזהרו</u> לא לספר לה על המסיבה.

4. כל הדברים שייאמרו בישיבה <u>ייכתבו</u> בפרוטוקול.

5. החלון הגדול <u>ייסגר</u> ברוח, והחלון הקטן <u>ייפתח</u>.

6. רק אחרי שהרכבת <u>נכנסת</u> לתחנה ועוצרת, הדלת <u>נפתחת</u>.

Answers:

1. נִבְדַּק (neev-DAK), נֶחְקַר (nech-KAR)   2. נִתְפְּסוּ (neet-pe-SOO), נֶעֶצְרוּ (ne-'ets-ROO)
3. נִפְגְּשׁוּ (neef-ge-SHOO), נִזְהֲרוּ (neez-ha-ROO)   4. יֵיאָמְרוּ (ye-'am-ROO), יִיכָּתְבוּ (yee-kat-VOO)
5. יִיסָּגֵר (yee-sa-GER), יִיפָּתַח (yee-pa-TACH)   6. נִכְנֶסֶת (neech-NE-set), נִפְתַּחַת (neef-TA-chat)

Chapter summary

◆ Beenyan pee'el פיעל

final gutturals ל׳ גרונית		middle gutturals ע׳ גרונית		regular verbs שלמים	
final ח׳, ע׳ פ-ת-ח	middle ר׳ ב-ר-כ	middle א׳ ת-א-ר	middle ח׳, ע׳, ה׳ ש-ח-ק	regular root ד-ב-ר	past עבר
פִּיתַּחְתִּי	בֵּירַכְתִּי	תֵּיאַרְתִּי	שִׂיחַקְתִּי	דִּיבַּרְתִּי	אני
פִּיתַּחְתָּ	בֵּירַכְתָּ	תֵּיאַרְתָּ	שִׂיחַקְתָּ	דִּיבַּרְתָּ	אתה
פִּיתַּחְתְּ	בֵּירַכְתְּ	תֵּיאַרְתְּ	שִׂיחַקְתְּ	דִּיבַּרְתְּ	את
פִּיתַּחְנוּ	בֵּירַכְנוּ	תֵּיאַרְנוּ	שִׂיחַקְנוּ	דִּיבַּרְנוּ	אנחנו
פִּיתַּחְתֶּם	בֵּירַכְתֶּם	תֵּיאַרְתֶּם	שִׂיחַקְתֶּם	דִּיבַּרְתֶּם	אתם
פִּיתַּחְתֶּן	בֵּירַכְתֶּן	תֵּיאַרְתֶּן	שִׂיחַקְתֶּן	דִּיבַּרְתֶּן	אתן
פִּיתַּח[15]	בֵּירֵךְ	תֵּיאֵר[14]	שִׂיחֵק	דִּיבֵּר	הוא
פִּיתְּחָה	בֵּירְכָה	תֵּיאֲרָה	שִׂיחֲקָה	דִּיבְּרָה	היא
פִּיתְּחוּ	בֵּירְכוּ	תֵּיאֲרוּ	שִׂיחֲקוּ	דִּיבְּרוּ	הם/הן
					present הווה
מְפַתֵּחַ	מְבָרֵךְ	מְתָאֵר	מְשַׂחֵק	מְדַבֵּר	אני, אתה, הוא
מְפַתַּחַת	מְבָרֶכֶת	מְתָאֶרֶת	מְשַׂחֶקֶת	מְדַבֶּרֶת	אני, את, היא
מְפַתְּחִים	מְבָרְכִים	מְתָאֲרִים	מְשַׂחֲקִים	מְדַבְּרִים	אנחנו, אתם, הם
מְפַתְּחוֹת	מְבָרְכוֹת	מְתָאֲרוֹת	מְשַׂחֲקוֹת	מְדַבְּרוֹת	אנחנו, אתן, הן
					future עתיד
אֲפַתֵּחַ	אֲבָרֵךְ	אֲתָאֵר	אֲשַׂחֵק	אֲדַבֵּר	אני
תְּפַתֵּחַ	תְּבָרֵךְ	תְּתָאֵר	תְּשַׂחֵק	תְּדַבֵּר	אתה
יְפַתֵּחַ[16]	יְבָרֵךְ	יְתָאֵר	יְשַׂחֵק	יְדַבֵּר	הוא
תְּפַתֵּחַ	תְּבָרֵךְ	תְּתָאֵר	תְּשַׂחֵק	תְּדַבֵּר	היא
נְפַתֵּחַ	נְבָרֵךְ	נְתָאֵר	נְשַׂחֵק	נְדַבֵּר	אנחנו
תְּפַתְּחִי	תְּבָרְכִי	תְּתָאֲרִי	תְּשַׂחֲקִי	תְּדַבְּרִי	את
תְּפַתְּחוּ	תְּבָרְכוּ	תְּתָאֲרוּ	תְּשַׂחֲקוּ	תְּדַבְּרוּ	אתם/אתן
יְפַתְּחוּ	יְבָרְכוּ	יְתָאֲרוּ	יְשַׂחֲקוּ	יְדַבְּרוּ	הם/הן
לְפַתֵּחַ to develop	לְבָרֵךְ to bless	לְתָאֵר to describe	לְשַׂחֵק to play	לְדַבֵּר to speak	שם הפועל *infinitive*

---

14 An alternative הוא form with an *ah* vowel in the second syllable also exists and is often used in formal Hebrew speech in verbs with middle and final gutturals, for example: תֵּיאַר, בֵּירַךְ, פִּיתַּח and בִּיצַע.

15 See note 14.

16 An alternative form with an *ah* vowel in the second syllable (e.g., יְפַתַּח *ye-fa-TACH* and יְבַצַּע *ye-va-TSA*) also exists and is often used in formal Hebrew speech in all the future tense forms that end in ח׳ or ע׳ (i.e., forms that do not have an ending).

◆ *Beenyan poo'al* פועל

final gutturals ל' גרונית	middle gutturals ע' גרונית			regular verbs שלמים	
final ח', ע' **נ-ת-ח**	middle ר' **ג-ר-ש**	middle א', ה', ע' **ת-א-ר**	middle ח' **ש-ח-ד**	regular root **צ-ל-מ**	**past עבר**
נוּתַּחְתִּי	גּוֹרַשְׁתִּי	תּוֹאַרְתִּי	שׁוּחַדְתִּי	**צוּלַמְתִּי**	אני
נוּתַּחְתָּ	גּוֹרַשְׁתָּ	תּוֹאַרְתָּ	שׁוּחַדְתָּ	**צוּלַמְתָּ**	אתה
נוּתַּחְתְּ	גּוֹרַשְׁתְּ	תּוֹאַרְתְּ	שׁוּחַדְתְּ	**צוּלַמְתְּ**	את
נוּתַּחְנוּ	גּוֹרַשְׁנוּ	תּוֹאַרְנוּ	שׁוּחַדְנוּ	**צוּלַמְנוּ**	אנחנו
נוּתַּחְתֶּם	גּוֹרַשְׁתֶּם	תּוֹאַרְתֶּם	שׁוּחַדְתֶּם	**צוּלַמְתֶּם**	אתם
נוּתַּחְתֶּן	גּוֹרַשְׁתֶּן	תּוֹאַרְתֶּן	שׁוּחַדְתֶּן	**צוּלַמְתֶּן**	אתן
נוּתַּח	גּוֹרַשׁ	תּוֹאַר	שׁוּחַד	**צוּלַם**	הוא
נוּתְּחָה	גּוֹרְשָׁה	תּוֹאֲרָה	שׁוּחֲדָה	**צוּלְמָה**	היא
נוּתְּחוּ	גּוֹרְשׁוּ	תּוֹאֲרוּ	שׁוּחֲדוּ	**צוּלְמוּ**	הם/הן
					present הווה
מְנוּתָּח	מְגוֹרָשׁ	מְתוֹאָר	מְשׁוּחָד	**מְצוּלָם**	אני, אתה, הוא
מְנוּתַּחַת	מְגוֹרֶשֶׁת	מְתוֹאֶרֶת	מְשׁוּחֶדֶת	**מְצוּלֶמֶת**	אני, את, היא
מְנוּתָּחִים	מְגוֹרָשִׁים	מְתוֹאָרִים	מְשׁוּחָדִים	**מְצוּלָמִים**	אנחנו, אתם, הם
מְנוּתָּחוֹת	מְגוֹרָשׁוֹת	מְתוֹאָרוֹת	מְשׁוּחָדוֹת	**מְצוּלָמוֹת**	אנחנו, אתן, הן
					future עתיד
אֲנוּתַּח	אֲגוֹרַשׁ	אֲתוֹאַר	אֲשׁוּחַד	**אֲצוּלַם**	אני
תְּנוּתַּח	תְּגוֹרַשׁ	תְּתוֹאַר	תְּשׁוּחַד	**תְּצוּלַם**	אתה
יְנוּתַּח	תְּגוֹרַשׁ	יְתוֹאַר	יְשׁוּחַד	**יְצוּלַם**	הוא
תְּנוּתַּח	תְּגוֹרַשׁ	תְּתוֹאַר	תְּשׁוּחַד	**תְּצוּלַם**	היא
נְנוּתַּח	נְגוֹרַשׁ	נְתוֹאַר	נְשׁוּחַד	**נְצוּלַם**	אנחנו
תְּנוּתְּחִי	תְּגוֹרְשִׁי	תְּתוֹאֲרִי	תְּשׁוּחֲדִי	**תְּצוּלְמִי**	את
תְּנוּתְּחוּ	תְּגוֹרְשׁוּ	תְּתוֹאֲרוּ	תְּשׁוּחֲדוּ	**תְּצוּלְמוּ**	אתם/אתן
יְנוּתְּחוּ	יְגוֹרְשׁוּ	יְתוֹאֲרוּ	יְשׁוּחֲדוּ	**יְצוּלְמוּ**	הם/הן
to be operated on	to be expelled, deported	to be described	to be bribed	to be photographed	

◆ *Beenyan neef'al* נפעל

final gutturals ל' גרונית	middle gutturals ע' גרונית	initial gutturals פ' גרונית			regular verbs שלמים	
final	*middle*	*initial*	*initial*	*initial*	*regular*	
ח', ע'	א', ה', ח', ע'	ר'	א', ה', ע'	ח'	*root*	
ש-ל-ח	**ש-א-ל**	**ר-ד-מ**	**ע-צ-ר**	**ח-ק-ר**	**כ-נ-ס**	
						עבר *past*
נִשְׁלַחְתִּי	נִשְׁאַלְתִּי	נִרְדַּמְתִּי	נֶעֱצַרְתִּי	נֶחְקַרְתִּי	**נִכְנַסְתִּי**	אני
נִשְׁלַחְתָּ	נִשְׁאַלְתָּ	נִרְדַּמְתָּ	נֶעֱצַרְתָּ	נֶחְקַרְתָּ	**נִכְנַסְתָּ**	אתה
נִשְׁלַחְתְּ	נִשְׁאַלְתְּ	נִרְדַּמְתְּ	נֶעֱצַרְתְּ	נֶחְקַרְתְּ	**נִכְנַסְתְּ**	את
נִשְׁלַחְנוּ	נִשְׁאַלְנוּ	נִרְדַּמְנוּ	נֶעֱצַרְנוּ	נֶחְקַרְנוּ	**נִכְנַסְנוּ**	אנחנו
נִשְׁלַחְתֶּם	נִשְׁאַלְתֶּם	נִרְדַּמְתֶּם	נֶעֱצַרְתֶּם	נֶחְקַרְתֶּם	**נִכְנַסְתֶּם**	אתם
נִשְׁלַחְתֶּן	נִשְׁאַלְתֶּן	נִרְדַּמְתֶּן	נֶעֱצַרְתֶּן	נֶחְקַרְתֶּן	**נִכְנַסְתֶּן**	אתן
נִשְׁלַח	נִשְׁאַל	נִרְדַּם	נֶעֱצַר	נֶחְקַר	**נִכְנַס**	הוא
נִשְׁלְחָה	נִשְׁאֲלָה	נִרְדְּמָה	נֶעֶצְרָה	נֶחְקְרָה	**נִכְנְסָה**	היא
נִשְׁלְחוּ	נִשְׁאֲלוּ	נִרְדְּמוּ	נֶעֶצְרוּ	נֶחְקְרוּ	**נִכְנְסוּ**	הם/הן
						הווה *present*
נִשְׁלָח	נִשְׁאָל	נִרְדָּם	נֶעֱצָר	נֶחְקָר	**נִכְנָס**	אני, אתה, הוא
נִשְׁלַחַת	נִשְׁאֶלֶת	נִרְדֶּמֶת	נֶעֱצֶרֶת	נֶחְקֶרֶת	**נִכְנֶסֶת**	אני, את, היא
נִשְׁלָחִים	נִשְׁאָלִים	נִרְדָּמִים	נֶעֱצָרִים	נֶחְקָרִים	**נִכְנָסִים**	אנחנו, אתם, הם
נִשְׁלָחוֹת	נִשְׁאָלוֹת	נִרְדָּמוֹת	נֶעֱצָרוֹת	נֶחְקָרוֹת	**נִכְנָסוֹת**	אנחנו, אתן, הן
						עתיד *future*
אֶשָּׁלַח	אֶשָּׁאֵל	אֵירָדֵם	אֵיעָצֵר	אֵיחָקֵר	**אֶכָּנֵס**	אני
תִּשָּׁלַח	תִּשָּׁאֵל	תֵּירָדֵם	תֵּיעָצֵר	תֵּיחָקֵר	**תִּכָּנֵס**	אתה
יִשָּׁלַח	יִשָּׁאֵל	יֵירָדֵם	יֵיעָצֵר	יֵיחָקֵר	**יִכָּנֵס**	הוא
תִּשָּׁלַח	תִּשָּׁאֵל	תֵּירָדֵם	תֵּיעָצֵר	תֵּיחָקֵר	**תִּכָּנֵס**	היא
נִשָּׁלַח	נִשָּׁאֵל	נֵירָדֵם	נֵיעָצֵר	נֵיחָקֵר	**נִכָּנֵס**	אנחנו
תִּשָּׁלְחִי	תִּשָּׁאֲלִי	תֵּירָדְמִי	תֵּיעָצְרִי	תֵּיחָקְרִי	**תִּכָּנְסִי**	את
תִּשָּׁלְחוּ	תִּשָּׁאֲלוּ	תֵּירָדְמוּ	תֵּיעָצְרוּ	תֵּיחָקְרוּ	**תִּכָּנְסוּ**	אתם/אתן
יִשָּׁלְחוּ	יִשָּׁאֲלוּ	יֵירָדְמוּ	יֵיעָצְרוּ	יֵיחָקְרוּ	**יִכָּנְסוּ**	הם/הן
לְהִשָּׁלַח	לְהִשָּׁאֵל	לְהֵירָדֵם	לְהֵיעָצֵר	לְהֵיחָקֵר	**לְהִיכָּנֵס**	שם הפועל *infinitive*
to be sent	to be asked	to fall asleep	to be arrested, to be stopped, to stop	to be interrogated, investigated	to enter	

V. Special Root Groups גְּזָרוֹת

Introduction

Thus far, we have discussed verb forms in which all three (or four) root letters appear (שְׁלֵמִים and מְרוּבָּעִים). The following chapters are devoted to the conjugation of verbs from *special root groups* (גְּזָרוֹת).[1] These include roots containing one of the letters נ, ו, י, א in the positions indicated in the chart below. In certain forms, these letters may disappear or cause significant changes. Roots that contain the same letter in the second and third positions (e.g., פ-ר-ר, ח-ג-ג) also cause certain changes.[2]

Roots with *gutturals* (א, ה, ח, ע), are presented as a group in a separate unit called "Verbs with Guttural Consonants," pp. 448-487. Because of the special behavior of א, we have devoted a special chapter in the present unit to verbs with a final א (*lamed-'alef* verbs). Even though verbs with an initial א (*pe-'alef*, e.g., א-כ-ל) are also considered a *special root group* (גְּזָרָה), we have not included them here, but rather in the chapter "Guttural Consonants: *Beenyan Pa'al*," pp. 454-455.

Naming the special root groups

In order to indicate where in the root the letters נ, ו, י, א appear, we give a special name to each root letter, based on the word פָּעַל (verb), whose root is פ-ע-ל. The **first** root letter is called פ' הַפּוֹעַל (*pe hapo'al*), the **second** is called ע' הַפּוֹעַל (*'ayeen hapo'al*) and the **third** is called ל' הַפּוֹעַל (*lamed hapo'al*).

Take a look at the following chart:

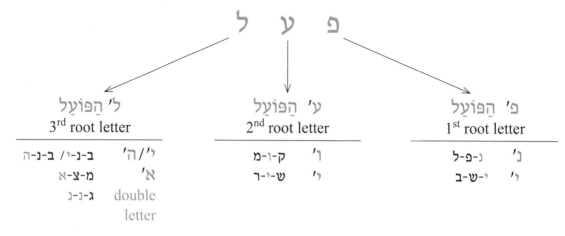

---

1   The Hebrew term for *special root groups* is actually גְּזָרוֹת עֲלוּלוֹת.
2   These roots, called גְּזֶרֶת הַכְּפוּלִים, will not be examined in this book, since they are usually learned at the advanced level of Hebrew study.

How do we name each root group (גְזְרָה)?

When the **first** letter of the roots in a root group is 'נ, as in נ-פ-ל and נ-ס-ע, we call this group גִזְרַת פ"נ (*geezrat pe-noon*) – which means that in the first (פ') position there is a 'נ. Similarly, when 'י is in the first position, as in י-ש-ב and י-ר-ד, we say that these roots belong to גִזְרַת פ"י (*geezrat pe-yod*). When 'י is in the **second** (ע') position, as in ש-י-ר and ש-י-מ, we call the root group גִזְרַת ע"י (*geezrat 'ayeen-yod*), and so on.

Want to see if you've understood?
Match the roots and the name of their root group.

name of root group	sample roots
a. ע"ו	1. י-ל-ד, י-ש-ב
b. פ"נ	2. ר-ו-צ, ל-ו-נ
c. פ"י	3. נ-ט-ל, נ-ש-א
d. מרובעים	4. ל-מ-ד, ב-ד-ק
e. ל"י	5. ר-צ-י, צ-פ-י
f. שלמים	6. פ-ר-ס-מ, ט-ל-פ-נ

Answers:

1. c (פ"י) 2. a (ע"ו) 3. b (פ"נ) 4. f (שלמים) 5. e (ל"י) 6. d (מרובעים)

In the chapters that follow, we will deal with the following root groups:

1. **Verbs Whose First Root Letter Is 'נ**   (*Pe-Noon* גִזְרַת פ"נ)
2. **Verbs Whose First Root Letter Is 'י**   (*Pe-Yod* גִזְרַת פ"י)
3. **Verbs Whose Middle Root Letter Is 'ו or 'י**   (*'Ayeen-Vav / 'Ayeen-Yod* ע"י / ע"ו גִזְרַת)
4. **Verbs Whose Final Root Letter Is 'י (or 'ה)**   (*Lamed-Yod / Lamed-He* ל"ה / ל"י גִזְרַת)
5. **Verbs Whose Final Root Letter Is 'א**   (*Lamed-'Alef* ל"א גִזְרַת)

1. Verbs Whose First Root Letter Is נ

גְּזְרַת פ"נ

Preview

• Beenyan pa'al	(נָפַל, נָסַע)
• Beenyan heef'eel	(הִפִּיל)
• Beenyan hoof'al	(הוּפַּל)
• Beenyaneem pee'el, poo'al *and* heetpa'el	(נִיגֵּן, נוּגַּן, הִתְנַגֵּד)[1]

Introduction

The נ' in verbs whose first root letter is נ' – i.e., *pe-noon* verbs – "likes" to play hide-and-seek. In this chapter, we will see in which forms we **see** (and **hear**) the נ' at the beginning of the root and in which forms it "hides" from us. Our discussion will be limited mainly to verbs that are usually taught at the beginning through intermediate levels of Hebrew study and will focus on the *beenyaneem* in which *pe-noon* verbs are significantly different from *regular* verbs (שְׁלֵמִים).

In each *beenyan* we will present the *base forms* (the הוא forms) of each tense. The changes in the rest of the forms in each tense follow the same general rules that we have seen in the regular verbs.[2] At the end of the chapter we have included a chart with full conjugations of the *pe-noon* verbs discussed.

• Beenyan pa'al (נָפַל, נָסַע)

If we look at **all** the *pe-noon* verbs that exist in *beenyan pa'al* (not just those usually learned at the beginning and intermediate levels of Hebrew study), we will find that **most** of them behave just like regular verbs, i.e., their נ' appears in all forms. For example, the verb לִנְשׁוֹם (to breathe) behaves just like לִכְתּוֹב:

---

1   Verbs in *beenyan neef'al* (e.g., נִיתַּן/לְהִינָּתֵן), some of whose forms are different from regular verbs, are beyond the scope of this book.

2   See the chapter "Regular Verbs in All *Beenyaneem*: Summary," pp. 444-447.

	שם הפועל *infinitive*	עתיד *future*	הווה *present*	עבר *past*	
regular verb ('ef'ol):[3]	לִכְתּוֹב	יִכְתּוֹב	כּוֹתֵב	כָּתַב	◄
pe-noon ('ef'ol):	לִנְשׁוֹם	יִנְשׁוֹם	נוֹשֵׁם	נָשַׁם	

The verb לִנְעוֹל (to lock; to wear shoes), which has a *guttural* (ע') as its second root letter and, therefore, takes the *'ef'al* form in the future tense, behaves just like the regular verb לִלְמוֹד:[4]

regular verb ('ef'al):	לִלְמוֹד	יִלְמַד	לוֹמֵד	לָמַד	◄
pe-noon ('ef'al):	לִנְעוֹל	יִנְעַל	נוֹעֵל	נָעַל	

Similarly, all other *pe-noon* verbs that have a middle guttural (e.g., נהג to drive, נאם to give a speech) act like regular verbs in all their forms.

So why are we discussing *pe-noon* verbs in *beenyan pa'al* at all?

As mentioned above, there are a number of *pe-noon* verbs in which the נ' tends to "go into hiding" in certain forms. Many of these verbs happen to be very common (e.g., נפל to fall, נסע to travel, נתן to give), and – since there are no hard and fast rules for the behavior of the נ' – we must learn each verb and its particular behavior.

Verbs in which the נ' does not appear in the future

Let's start with the verb נָפַל. Here are its forms in the three tenses compared with those of לִכְתּוֹב:

	עתיד *future*	הווה *present*	עבר *past*	
regular verb ('ef'ol):	יִכְתּוֹב	כּוֹתֵב	כָּתַב	◄
pe-noon ('ef'ol):	יִפּוֹל	נוֹפֵל	נָפַל	

Q: In which of the forms of נפל are **all three** root letters present?

A: In the past and present tenses: נָפַל and נוֹפֵל. The past and present tenses of *pe-noon* verbs in *pa'al* act exactly like regular verbs.[5] This is because whenever the נ' has a vowel sound **right after** it – here *ah* (נָפַל *na-FAL*) and *oh* (נוֹפֵל *no-FEL*) – the נ' remains stable and **no change** takes place.

---

3   For an explanation of *'ef'ol*, see the chapter "*Beenyan Pa'al*," pp. 398-399.
4   For more on *'ef'al*, see the chapter "*Beenyan Pa'al*," pp. 400-401.
5   Except for the past tense forms of נָתַן. See below p. 496.

In the **future tense**, on the other hand, the three root letters are **not** always present. Here, for example, is the future tense form of נָפַל:

The boy will fall if he isn't careful.   הילד ייפול אם הוא לא ייזהר.   ◄

yee-POL

We would expect this form to be יִנְפּוֹל* (*yeen-POL*), like יִכְתּוֹב (*veech-TOV*), but instead we get יִיפּוֹל. The נ "goes into hiding" since it is **not** followed by a vowel.[6]

When the נ does not appear, several additional changes take place. In *full spelling*, for example, we write a י instead of the hiding נ in all forms of the future tense whose first vowel sound is *ee*:...יִיפּוֹל, תִּיפּוֹל.[7] Only the אני form – אֶפּוֹל – has an *eh* vowel and, therefore, is **not** written with י. In addition, when the second root letter is ב, כ, פ, it is pronounced as a *hard* sound (*b, k, p*), e.g., יִיפּוֹל (*yee-POL*).[8]

Of all the *pe-noon* verbs whose נ does not appear in the future tense, the following are usually learned at the beginning and intermediate levels:[9]

לָקַח	נָתַן	נָשָׂא	נָטַע	נָגַע	נָסַע	נָפַל	◄
to take	give	carry, marry (a woman)	plant	touch	travel	fall	

Note: Even though לקח begins with a ל, its behavior is the same as that of the other verbs listed here.

Now let's look at the *base forms* of these verbs in the future tense. First, let's divide them into two main groups: *'ef'ol* (like יִכְתּוֹב) and *'ef'al* (like יִלְמַד).

---

6   We can also express this in other terms: When נ appears at the end of a *closed syllable* ("נם"), it tends to "go into hiding." This same phenomenon occurs in the future tense of *neef'al*: instead of יִנְכָּנֵס*, the future form of נִכְנַס is יִיכָּנֵס.

7   In *standard spelling* we write יפל – with no added י.

8   When we write with vowel signs, the second root letter has a *strong dagesh* in it as if to **compensate** for the hiding נ. Grammar books describe the consonant *n* as *assimilating* to (=becoming the same as) the consonant that follows it (*yeen-POL* ⇒* *yeep-POL*). This is called *full assimilation* (הִידָּמוּת מְלֵאָה). The following consonant is considered to be "doubled" (*yeep-POL*) and, in standard spelling, a strong *dagesh* (דָּגֵשׁ חָזָק) appears in the letter that represents the "doubled" consonant (יפל). In today's Hebrew, we pronounce this simply as *p*, without special doubling or lengthening. See the chapter "The Pronunciation of ב, כ, פ and the *Dagesh*," pp. 635-637 for examples.

9   There are some verbs usually learned at the advanced level that have **two** possible future tense forms – one **with** the נ and one **without** the נ (for example: יִיקּוֹם/יִנְקּוֹם – to take revenge, יִיבּוֹל/יִנְבּוֹל – to wilt). There is a tendency today to use the form **with** the נ, making the forms of these verbs just like those of regular verbs.

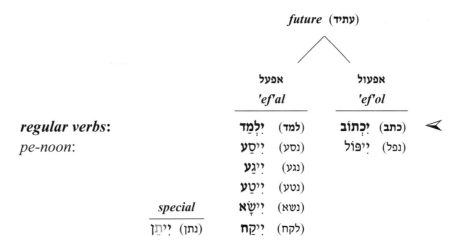

		אפעל 'ef'al	אפעול 'ef'ol	
regular verbs:		(למד) יִלְמַד	(כתב) יִכְתוֹב	◄
pe-noon:		(נסע) יִסַּע	(נפל) יִפּוֹל	
		(נגע) יִגַּע		
		(נטע) יִטַּע		
	special	(נשא) יִשָּׂא		
	(נתן) יִתֵּן	(לקח) יִקַּח		

Q: How many of these *pe-noon* verbs belong to the *'ef'ol* group?

A: Only one: יִפּוֹל (נפל).[10] All the rest, except for one – יִתֵּן (נתן) – belong to *'ef'al*. Notice that these verbs all end in ע׳, ח׳ or א׳ (gutturals), and this is the reason they belong to *'ef'al,* just like verbs without an initial נ׳, such as יִשְׁמַע, יִשְׁלַח and יִקְרָא.

The verb נָתַן has a unique future tense form – with an *eh* vowel in the second syllable: יִתֵּן (*yee-TEN*).

Note: In full spelling, all the forms of the verbs in the chart above are written with a י׳ in place of the נ׳ that disappears (תִּיפּוֹל, נִיפּוֹל... / תִּיסַּע, נִיסַּע...) except for the אני form (אֶפּוֹל, אֶסַּע), whose first vowel is *eh*.

Imperatives (Command forms) (קַח, סַע)

Read the following instructions, which are addressed to guests at a men's dormitory and are written in formal Hebrew:

אורח יקר! כשאתה יוצא מן החדר, אנא נְעַל את הדלת, קַח את המפתח ותֵן אותו לפקיד הקבלה. ◄

Dear Guest! When you leave your room, please lock the door, take the key and give it to the receptionist.

The verbs highlighted in this sentence are all *imperatives*. The use of imperatives is typical of formal Hebrew. Some short imperatives – like קַח and תֵן (and סַע shown below) – are commonly used in informal Hebrew as well, including in everyday speech.

---

10 Other examples exist (e.g., יִטוֹל – he will wash his hands, he will take), but are usually taught at advanced levels.

As discussed in the chapter "Command Forms" (pp. 569-571), we derive the imperative forms of verbs in *beenyan pa'al* from their future tense forms, for example:

	imperative		future	
◄	נְעַל!	⇐	תִּנְעַל	
	קַח!	⇐	תִּ/קַח	
	תֵן!	⇐	תִּ/תֵן	

Notice that when נ does **not** appear in the future tense of a given verb, it usually does **not** appear in the imperative (e.g., תֵן, קַח).

Here are examples of all three forms (אתה, את, אתם/אתן) of *pe-noon* imperatives whose initial נ disappears:[11]

m.s.:	תֵן!	קַח!	סַע!	◄
f.s.:	תְּנִי!	קְחִי!	סְעִי!	
m.pl. / f.pl.:	תְּנוּ!	קְחוּ!	סְעוּ!	
	Give!	Take!	Go!	
			(to a driver)	

Infinitives (לִיפּוֹל, לִנְסוֹעַ)

As mentioned at the beginning of the section on *pe-noon* verbs in *beenyan pa'al*, the majority of verbs keep their נ in **all** forms. Indeed, all the verbs that **keep** their נ in the future tense also keep it in the infinitive (e.g., יִנְעַל/לִנְעוֹל, יִנְשׁוֹם/לִנְשׁוֹם).

Now we will concentrate on the verbs that **do lose** their נ in the future tense, since there is a **chance** that the נ in these verbs will also "go into hiding" in their infinitive form.

Here are some examples showing the three types of infinitive forms of these verbs:

Where do you want to go?	(*root*: נ-ס-ע)	◄ לאן אתם רוצים לִנְסוֹעַ?
Be careful not to fall!	(*root*: נ-פ-ל)	תיזהר לא לִיפּוֹל!
It is forbidden to touch the paintings in the museum.	(*root*: נ-ג-ע)	אסור לָגַעַת בציורים במוזאון.

Q: Does the נ of the root appear in **any** of these infinitives?

A: Yes, it appears in לִנְסוֹעַ. This infinitive contains all of its root letters, just like a regular verb.

---

11 The imperative of verbs whose future tense forms do not have a נ and belong to the *'ef'ol* group (e.g., תִיפּוֹל) also may have no נ, as in פּוֹל, פְּלִי, פְּלוּ.

However, in the other two infinitives – לִיפּוֹל and לָגַעַת – the נ' is nowhere in sight. The first of these – לִיפּוֹל – is quite similar to the form of a regular verb, except that in place of its "hiding נ'", we write a י' in *full spelling*: לִיפּוֹל. As in the future tense, when ב', כ', פ' are the second root letter, they take a *strong dagesh* when written with vowel signs and are pronounced as *hard* sounds (*b, k, p*): לִיפּוֹל.

In contrast, the form לָגַעַת is totally different from the infinitive form of regular verbs. Here, too, only the last **two** root letters (ג-ע) are present. However, this *pe-noon* verb seems to have gotten a bit "confused" about its identity and has adopted the infinitive pattern used by verbs in the *pe-yod root group*, such as לָדַעַת (whose *root* is י-ד-ע).[12] This infinitive form has the same ending as the verb's feminine singular present tense form:

פ"נ *pe-noon*	פ"י *pe-yod*	
נוֹגַעַת / לָגַעַת	יוֹדַעַת / לָדַעַת	(אני / את / היא) ◄

In the following chart you can see which verbs take which of these infinitive forms:

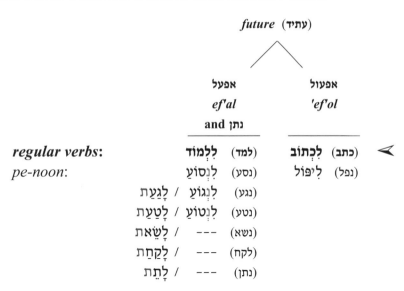

	אפעל *ef'al* and נתן	אפעול *'ef'ol*	
regular verbs:	(למד) **לִלְמוֹד**	(כתב) **לִכְתּוֹב** ◄	
pe-noon:	(נסע) לִנְסוֹעַ	(נפל) לִיפּוֹל	
	(נגע) לִנְגּוֹעַ / לָגַעַת		
	(נטע) לִנְטוֹעַ / לָטַעַת		
	(נשא) --- / לָשֵׂאת		
	(לקח) --- / לָקַחַת		
	(נתן) --- / לָתֵת		

Notice that לִיפּוֹל – in the *'ef'ol* column – is the **only** infinitive of its type here.[13] In the *'ef'al* column, there are **three** infinitives that retain their נ' – and all of them happen to end in ע': לִנְסוֹעַ, לִנְטוֹעַ, לִנְגּוֹעַ (this can help you remember them). The last two of these (לִנְטוֹעַ and לִנְגּוֹעַ) have an alternative form similar to *pe-yod* infinitives: לָגַעַת and לָטַעַת. In today's Hebrew, the forms לָגַעַת (rather than לִנְגּוֹעַ) and לָטַעַת (rather than לִנְטוֹעַ) are more common.

---

12 For all the variations of this pattern (לָצֵאת, לָדַעַת, לָשֶׁבֶת), see the chapter "Verbs Whose First Root Letter Is י'", pp. 504-507.

13 Among verbs that are usually studied at the advanced level, many infinitives of verbs in the *'ef'ol* group retain their נ', for example: לִנְשוֹם (to breathe) and לִנְטוֹש (to abandon).

The rest of the verbs in the chart have only **one** form. The infinitives לָקַחַת and לָשֵׂאת have the same pattern as *pe-yod* infinitives. The infinitive לָתֵת is somewhat different. In this form, of its three root letters (נ-ת-נ), only the middle root letter – ת' – remains.

The special verb נָתַן

The present tense of נתן is just like a regular verb:

נוֹתֵן, נוֹתֶנֶת, נוֹתְנִים, נוֹתְנוֹת ◄

Here are the past tense forms:

	plural				singular		
na-TA-noo	נָתַנּוּ	אנחנו:		na-TA-tee	נָתַתִּי	אני:	◄
na-TA-tem / ne-ta-TEM	נָתַתֶּם / נְתַתֶּם[14]	אתם:		na-TA-ta	נָתַתָּ	אתה:	
na-TA-ten / ne-ta-TEN	נָתַתֶּן / נְתַתֶּן	אתן:		na-TAT	נָתַתְּ	את:	
nat-NOO	נָתְנוּ	הם, הן		na-TAN	נָתַן	הוא	
				nat-NA	נָתְנָה	היא	

Notice that only the third person (הוא, היא, הם/הן) forms are like regular verbs, with all three root letters present. In the other forms, the second נ' of the root disappears.[15]

Now look at the אנחנו and הם/הן forms. When written **without** vowel signs, these forms are both spelled the same, but they are pronounced differently:

הם/הן	אנחנו	
נתנו	נתנו	◄
nat-NOO	na-TA-noo	

The future tense forms (e.g., יִיתֵּן), the imperative (e.g., תֵּן) and the infinitive (לָתֵת) have already been discussed in the sections above.

---

14 According to the rules of grammar, the correct pronunciation is נְתַתֶּן, נְתַתֶּם (*ne-ta-TEM, ne-ta-TEN*).

15 When all the vowel signs are written, a strong *dagesh* appears in the letter after the place where the נ' disappears, e.g., נָתַתִּי ⇐ *נתנתי.

Let's review

♦ In today's Hebrew, most *pa'al* verbs whose first root letter is נ keep their נ and behave like regular verbs, e.g.: נָשַׁם, נוֹשֵׁם, יִנְשׁוֹם, לִנְשׁוֹם, נְשׁוֹם!.

♦ In the following verbs, the נ does **not** appear in the future tense and imperative forms. The infinitives of these verbs vary, as follows:

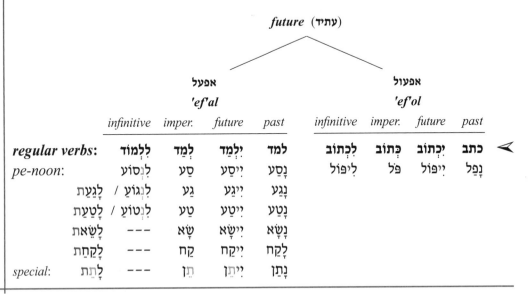

| | | | | future (עתיד) | | | | |

| | אפעל
'ef'al | | | | אפעול
'ef'ol | | | |
	infinitive	imper.	future	past	infinitive	imper.	future	past
regular verbs:	לִלְמוֹד	לְמַד	יִלְמַד	למד	לִכְתּוֹב	כְּתוֹב	יִכְתּוֹב	כתב
pe-noon:	לִנְסוֹעַ	סַע	יִיסַּע	נָסַע	לִיפּוֹל	פֹּל	יִיפּוֹל	נָפַל
	לִנְגּוֹעַ / לָגַעַת	גַּע	יִיגַּע	נָגַע				
	לִנְטוֹעַ / לָטַעַת	טַע	יִיטַּע	נָטַע				
	לָשֵׂאת	---	שָׂא	יִישָּׂא	נָשָׂא			
	לָקַחַת	---	קַח	יִיקַּח	לָקַח			
special:	לָתֵת	---	תֵּן	יִיתֵּן	נָתַן			

Want to see if you've understood?

Write the missing forms of the underlined verbs.

1. הוריי <u>נסעו</u> לטבריה בשבוע שעבר, ובשבוע הבא הם _____ לחיפה.

   חבל שאני לא יכולה _____ איתם.

2. מיכל אומרת שהמנהל <u>נתן</u> לה אישור לצאת מוקדם היום, והיא מקווה שהוא _____ לה
   אישור כזה גם מחר.

3. המוכר לדויד: "כמה כסף <u>נתת</u> לי?"

   דויד: "_____ לך מאה שקלים".

   המוכר: "בסדר. אז אני צריך _____ לך 35 ₪ עודף!"

4. הילד הלך בזהירות ולא <u>נפל</u>. אם גם אתה תלך בזהירות, אני בטוחה שלא _____.

Answers:

1. יִיסְעוּ, לִנְסוֹעַ   2. יִיתֵּן   3. נָתַתִּי, לָתֵת   4. תִּיפּוֹל

• Beenyan heef'eel (הִפְּיל)

Read the following sentence:

◄ המלצר כמעט נָפַל אבל, למזלו, הוא לא הִפִּיל אף אחת מהצלחות שהיו בידו.

The waiter almost fell but, luckily, he didn't drop even one of the plates that were in his hand.

The two verbs highlighted in this sentence share the same root: נ-פ-ל. The first verb (נָפַל) belongs to *beenyan pa'al* and means *to fall*. The second (הִפִּיל) belongs to *beenyan heef'eel* and means *to drop, to cause something to fall*. In this verb we see only **two** of the root letters: פ-ל. The נ at the beginning of the root has "gone into hiding." Compare:

◄ הִרְגִּיש   ***regular verb*:**

הִנְפִּיל ⇐ הִפִּיל*   *pe-noon*:

Here, again, the נ is **not** followed by a vowel (i.e., it is at the end of a *closed* syllable "נְם"), thus it tends to disappear, just as it did in יִפּוֹל ⇐ יִנְפּוֹל. When the second root letter is ב', כ', פ', it is pronounced with a *hard* sound (b, k, p), as in all the following words: [16]

◄ הִפִּיל*   הִבִּיעַ*   הִבִּיט[17]*   הִכִּיר[18]*

⇓   ⇓   ⇓   ⇓

הַכִּיר   הַבִּיט   הַבִּיעַ   הַפִּיל

to know,   look (at)   express   drop
recognize

A special note about full spelling: According to rules of full spelling, we would expect past tense forms like הכיר and הכרתי to be spelled with a י after their initial ה (as in יִפּוֹל and יִכָּנֵס – where a י is written in place of the נ that is "hiding"). However, this does **not** happen in the past tense of *heef'eel*. Why not? Because by **not** adding a י after the ה, we ensure that forms like הִכִּיר and הִכַּרְתִּי resemble regular *heef'eel* forms, none of which have a י after their initial ה (e.g., הרגיש).

---

16 As was the case in יִפּוֹל, when vowel signs are written, the letter following the missing נ gets a strong *dagesh*: הִפִּיל. This is the same phonetic process (called *full assimilation*) that was described in footnote 7 above.

17 The verb הִנְבִּיט **with** a נ exists as well and means *to make a seed germinate, sprout*.

18 The *dagesh* in these theoretical forms is a *weak dagesh*, while the *dagesh* in the forms without the נ is a strong *dagesh*. Both are written the same and, today, both indicate the same hard pronunciation of ב', כ', פ'. For the difference between them, see the chapter "The Pronunciation of ב', כ', פ' and the *Dagesh*," pp. 624-639.

The prefixes of *pe-noon heef'eel* verbs in all tenses and forms are the same as regular verbs, for example:

	infinitive	future	present	past	
regular verb:	לְהַרְגִּישׁ	יַרְגִּישׁ	מַרְגִּישׁ	הִרְגִּישׁ	◄
pe-noon:	לְהַפִּיל	יַפִּיל	מַפִּיל	הִפִּיל	
	le-ha-PEEL	ya-PEEL	ma-PEEL	hee-PEEL	

As you can see, the נ is not present in any of the *pe-noon heef'eel* forms.

Here are some more examples of *pe-noon heef'eel* verbs. Some have roots that are known to us from *beenyan pa'al* or other *beenyaneem* where we can see all three root letters.

root:	(נ-צ-ל)	(נ-ג-שׁ)	(נ-ס-ע)	(נ-ג-ע)	(נ-כ-ר)
past tense:	הִצִּיל	הִגִּישׁ	הִסִּיעַ	הִגִּיעַ	הִכִּיר	◄
	to save	serve (tea…),	drive	arrive,	know	
		hand in	(someone)	reach	(a person or place)	

Sometimes the נ remains

In most *pe-noon heef'eel* verbs learned at the beginning and intermediate levels, the נ tends to "go into hiding," as we saw in the verbs above. There are, however, some verbs in *heef'eel* that retain their נ in all forms, for example:

הִנְמִיךְ	הִנְשִׁים	הִנְהִיג	◄
heen-MEECH	heen-SHEEM	heen-HEEG	
to make lower	resuscitate,	lead	
	put someone on a respirator		

הִנְהִיג is an example of a verb whose middle root letter (ה) is a guttural (א׳, ה׳, ח׳, ע׳). In such verbs (most of which are learned at the advanced level), the נ always remains.

• Beenyan hoof'al (הוּפַּל)

Read the following sentence:

השׁוֹדֵד הוּפַּל עַל יְדֵי שׁוֹמֵר הבנק.   ◄   The robber was knocked down by the bank guard.

The past tense base form הוּפַּל begins with -הוּ (*hoo-*) like regular *hoof'al* verbs (e.g., הוּלְבַּשׁ), but the -הוּ in הוּפַּל is followed by only **two** root letters (פ-ל). The נ of the root (נ-פ-ל) is not present in any of the forms of this verb, for example:

	future	present	past
to be knocked down, dropped	יוּפַּל	מוּפָּל	הוּפַּל
	yoo-PAL	moo-PAL	hoo-PAL

As in *heef'eel*, whenever ב', כ', פ' are the **second** letter of the root, they have a hard pronunciation – *b, k, p* – as in: הוּפַּל and הוּכַּר (was recognized).

Verbs that keep their נ' in *heef'eel* do so in *hoof'al*, too, for example:

הוּנְמַךְ	הוּנְשַׁם	הוּנְהַג
hoon-MACH	hoon-SHAM	hoon-HAG
to be made lower	to be resuscitated, put on a respirator	to be lead

Did you know?

There are several verbs in *heef'eel* and *hoof'al* that have the same pattern as *pe-noon* verbs, yet their first root letter is not נ', but rather י'. Here are some examples:

root:	(י-צ-ת)	(י-צ-ע)	(י-צ-ג)
heef'eel:	הִצִּית	הִצִּיעַ	הִצִּיג
	hee-TSEET	hee-TSEE-a	hee-TSEEG
	to light (a cigarette), ignite	offer	present
hoof'al:	הוּצַּת	הוּצַּע	הוּצַּג
	hoo-TSAT	hoo-TSA	hoo-TSAG
	to be lit, ignited	to be offered	to be presented

These are often called *pe-yod-tsadee* (פי"צ) verbs since, as you might have noticed, the second root letter of all of them is צ'. In all tenses and forms, they are just like *pe-noon* verbs:[19]

	infinitive	future	present	past
to present	לְהַצִּיג	יַצִּיג	מַצִּיג	הִצִּיג
	le-ha-TSEEG	ya-TSEEG	ma-TSEEG	hee-TSEEG
to be presented		יוּצַּג	מוּצַּג	הוּצַּג
		yoo-TSAG	moo-TSAG	hoo-TSAG

---

19 In standard spelling with vowel signs, there is a strong *dagesh* in the צ' (הִצִּיג, הֻצַּג), as in all *pe-noon* verbs.

Let's review

◆ In many *heef'eel* and *hoof'al* verbs whose first root letter is נ' (*pe-noon*), the נ'
is missing in all tenses and forms, as in:

	infinitive	future	present	past	
heef'eel:	לְהַכִּיר	יַכִּיר	מַכִּיר	הִכִּיר	◄
hoof'al:		יוּכַּר	מוּכָּר	הוּכַּר	

◆ In some verbs, the נ' appears, as in:

	infinitive	future	present	past	
heef'eel:	לְהַנְשִׁים	יַנְשִׁים	מַנְשִׁים	הִנְשִׁים	◄
hoof'al:		יוּנְשָׁם	מוּנְשָׁם	הוּנְשָׁם	

Want to see if you've understood?

A. Write the missing forms of the underlined *heef'eel* verbs.

1. בדרך כלל אבא של יונתן לא <u>מַסִיע</u> אותו לבית הספר, אבל אתמול בבוקר הוא _____ אותו.

2. אני צריכה _____ למוזאון, אבל אני לא יודעת איך <u>מגיעים</u> לשם.

3. ביקשתי שתַנמיכו את המוזיקה. למה לא _____ אותה קודם?

Answers:

1. הִסִיעַ   2. לְהַגִיעַ   3. הִנְמַכְתֶּם

B. Write the missing forms of the underlined *hoof'al* verbs.

1. החולה <u>מונשם</u> כרגע. הוא _____ עד שיוכל לנשום בכוחות עצמו.
   (future)

2. אתה <u>מוכר</u> לי ואת לא _____ לי.
   (present)

Answers:

1. יוּנְשָׁם   2. מוּכֶּרֶת

• Beenyaneem pee'el, poo'al *and* heetpa'el (נִיגֵן, נוּגַן, הִתְנַגֵּד)

In *beenyaneem pee'el*, *poo'al* and *heetpa'el*, the נ' appears in all tenses and forms since it is always followed by a vowel, for example:

		infinitive	future	present	past
pee'el:	to play (an instrument)	לְנַגֵּן	יְנַגֵּן	מְנַגֵּן	נִיגֵן ◄
poo'al:	to be played		יְנוּגַן	מְנוּגָן	נוּגַן
heetpa'el:	to be opposed to	לְהִתְנַגֵּד	יִתְנַגֵּד	מִתְנַגֵּד	הִתְנַגֵּד

Chapter summary

Here are the forms of *pe-noon* verbs in *beenyaneem pa'al*, *heef'eel* and *hoof'al*:

◆ *Hoof'al* הוּפְעַל	◆ *Heef'eel* הִפְעִיל	◆ *Pa'al* פָּעַל		past עבר
הוּפַּלְתִּי	הִכַּרְתִּי	נָפַלְתִּי		אני
הוּפַּלְתָּ	הִכַּרְתָּ	נָפַלְתָּ		אתה
הוּפַּלְתְּ	הִכַּרְתְּ	נָפַלְתְּ		את
הוּפַּלְנוּ	הִכַּרְנוּ	נָפַלְנוּ		אנחנו
הוּפַּלְתֶּם	הִכַּרְתֶּם	נָפַלְתֶּם / נְפַלְתֶּם [19]		אתם
הוּפַּלְתֶּן	הִכַּרְתֶּן	נָפַלְתֶּן / נְפַלְתֶּן		אתן
הוּפַּל הוּנְשַׁם	הִכִּיר הֻנְשַׁם	נָפַל		הוא
הוּפְּלָה	הִכִּירָה	נָפְלָה		היא
הוּפְּלוּ	הִכִּירוּ	נָפְלוּ		הם/הן

				present הווה
מוּפָּל מוּנְשָׁם	מַכִּיר מֻנְשָׁם	נוֹפֵל		אני,אתה, הוא
מוּפֶּלֶת	מַכִּירָה	נוֹפֶלֶת		אני, את, היא
מוּפָּלִים	מַכִּירִים	נוֹפְלִים		אנחנו, אתם, הם
מוּפָּלוֹת	מַכִּירוֹת	נוֹפְלוֹת		אנחנו, אתן, הן

				'ef'ol אֶפְעַל	*'ef'al* אֶפְעוֹל	future עתיד
אוּפַּל		אַכִּיר		אֶגַּע	אֶפּוֹל	אני
תוּפַּל		תַּכִּיר		תִּיגַּע	תִּיפּוֹל	אתה
יוּפַּל יוּנְשַׁם		יַכִּיר יֻנְשַׁם		יִיגַּע יִנְהַג	יִיפּוֹל יִנְשֹׁם	הוא
תוּפַּל		תַּכִּיר		תִּיגַּע	תִּיפּוֹל	היא
נוּפַּל		נַכִּיר		נִיגַּע	נִיפּוֹל	אנחנו
תוּפְּלִי		תַּכִּירִי		תִּיגְעִי	תִּיפְּלִי	את
תוּפְּלוּ		תַּכִּירוּ		תִּיגְעוּ	תִּיפְּלוּ	אתם/אתן
יוּפְּלוּ		יַכִּירוּ		יִיגְעוּ	יִיפְּלוּ	הם/הן

						שם הפועל
to be dropped, knocked down to be resuscitated	לְהַכִּיר לְהַנְשִׁים	לִנְגוֹעַ לִנְהוֹג לָגַעַת		לִנְשֹׁם לִיפּוֹל		*infinitive*
	to resuscitate know, recognize	to drive touch		fall breathe		

The imperative forms of *beenyan pa'al* are discussed in the chapter.

---

[20] On the right we have noted the pronunciation used by most Hebrew speakers today. According to the rules of grammar, the correct pronunciation is נְפַלְתֶּן, נְפַלְתֶּם (*ne-fal-TEM, ne-fal-TEN*).

2. Verbs Whose First Root Letter Is י

גְּזָרַת פ"י

> ### Preview
>
> • Beenyan pa'al   (יָשַׁב)
>
> • Beenyan heef'eel   (הוֹרִיד)
>
> • Beenyan hoof'al   (הוּרַד)
>
> • Beenyaneem pee'el, poo'al *and* heetpa'el   (יִשֵּׁב, יֻשַּׁב, הִתְיַישֵּׁב)
>
> • *The special verb* יָכוֹל

Introduction

Now you see it (the י), now you don't! Sometimes it's written as a single letter (י), sometimes it's doubled ("יי") – and sometimes it wears a different guise (ו). In this chapter we will examine *pe-yod* verbs, i.e., verbs whose first root letter is י. We will limit our discussion mainly to verbs that are usually taught at the beginning through intermediate levels of Hebrew study and will look only at the *beenyaneem* in which *pe-yod* verbs are significantly different from *regular* verbs (שְׁלֵמִים).[1]

In each *beenyan* we will present the *base forms* (the הוא forms) of each tense. The changes in the rest of the forms in each tense follow the same general rules that we have seen in the regular verbs.[2] We have included a chart with all the forms at the end of the chapter.

• Beenyan pa'al (יָשַׁב)

The past and present *pe-yod* forms in *beenyan pa'al* are exactly the same as regular verbs:

	הווה *present*	עבר *past*	
regular verb:	כּוֹתֵב	כָּתַב	◄
pe-yod:	יוֹשֵׁב	יָשַׁב	

---

1   Verbs in *beenyan neef'al* (e.g., נוֹלַד / לְהִיוָּלֵד) are beyond the scope of this book.

2   See the chapter "Regular Verbs in All *Beenyaneem*: Summary," pp. 444-447.

The following are the *pe-yod* verbs usually learned in the beginning and intermediate levels. All of these verbs behave like יָשַׁב (to sit):

הָלַךְ[3]	(היא) יָלְדָה	יָדַע	יָצָא	יָרַד ◄
to go, walk	to give birth	to know	to go out	to go down, descend

The unique features of these *pe-yod* verbs – which make them **different** from regular verbs – are found in the future tense, imperative (command) and infinitive forms.

Future tense (יָשַׁב)

As we saw in the chapter "*Beenyan Pa'al*" (pp. 398-401), the future tense of **regular** *pa'al* verbs is usually expressed in one of two forms:

	'ef'al	'ef'ol
	יִלְמַד	יִכְתּוֹב ◄

The future tense forms of the *pe-yod* verbs mentioned above are totally different:

דָּנִיאֵל יֵלֵךְ לבנק.	רִינָה תֵּלֵד בעוד חודש.	אוּרִי יֵדַע[4] את התשובה.	רוֹן יֵצֵא מהדירה וְיֵרֵד במדרגות.	דָּן יֵשֵׁב במטבח. ◄
ye-LECH	te-LED	ye-DA	ye-RED ye-TSE	ye-SHEV
Daniel will go to the bank.	Rina will give birth in a month.	Uri will know the answer.	Ron will leave the apartment and go down the stairs.	Dan will sit in the kitchen.

Q: How many root letters do you see in these future tense verbs?

A: Two. The י in יֵשֵׁב is the *future prefix* for הוא. The only root letters here are שׁ-ב. Likewise, in יֵצֵא, צ-א are the only root letters present, in יֵרֵד we see only ר-ד, and so on. The **first** root letter י, which was present in the past and present tense forms, is **missing** in all these forms.[5] In addition, the vowel in **both** syllables (when no ending is added) is *eh*:[6]

		with endings			without endings				
	הם/הן	אתם/אתן	את	אנחנו	היא	הוא	אתה	אני	
standard spelling:	יֵשְׁבוּ	תֵּשְׁבוּ	תֵּשְׁבִי	נֵשֵׁב	תֵּשֵׁב	יֵשֵׁב	תֵּשֵׁב	אֵשֵׁב	◄
full spelling:[7]	ישבו	תשבו	תשבי	נשב	תשב	ישב	תשב	אשב	
	yesh-VOO	tesh-VOO	tesh-VEE	ne-SHEV	te-SHEV	ye-SHEV	te-SHEV	'e-SHEV	

---

3   The verb הָלַךְ is also included among פ"י verbs even though it begins with ה and not י, since, as we will see below, in the future, imperative and infinitive forms, the verb הָלַךְ behaves as if its root were י-ל-כ.

4   The final ע causes a change in the second vowel of this verb:...אֶדַע, תֵּדַע, יֵדַע, נֵדַע.

5   For this reason, these roots are grouped together and called "חַסְרֵי פ"י" (=lacking an initial י).

6   On the forms of יֵדַע (ye-DA), see footnote 4 above.

7   See the chapter "Hebrew Spelling," pp. 660-662 for the rules of full spelling (when the vowel signs are omitted).

Notice that in the full spelling of these verbs, **no י** is added after the first letter (i.e., after the future prefix).[8]

Imperative (Command) (שֵׁב)

The imperative forms of verbs whose first root letter is י are frequently used both in speaking and in writing.[9] Here are the imperative forms of the verb יָשַׁב:

שְׁבוּ!	שְׁבִי!	שֵׁב! ◄
SHVOO	SHVEE	SHEV

The imperative forms of יָדַע (to know) are slightly different because of the final ע:

דְּעוּ!	דְּעִי!	דַּע! ◄
D'OO[10]	D'EE	DA

Infinitive (לָשֶׁבֶת)

The six verbs mentioned above – הלך, ילדה, ידע, יצא, ירד, ישב – share the same basic infinitive pattern as well. Here are four of them:

root:	(כ-ל-ה)	(י-ל-ד)	(י-ר-ד)	(י-ש-ב)
infinitive:	לָלֶכֶת	לָלֶדֶת	לָרֶדֶת	לָשֶׁבֶת ◄
	la-LE-chet	la-LE-det	la-RE-det	la-SHE-vet

Q: What do these infinitives have in common?

A: The first root letter י is **missing** in all of them. They all begin with "לָ" and have an extra ת at the end. The last two syllables of the infinitive (ת-- E-et) are the same as those found on the feminine singular forms in the present tense:

הוֹלֶכֶת	יוֹלֶדֶת	יוֹרֶדֶת	יוֹשֶׁבֶת ◄

You can think of the ending added to these infinitives as a kind of compensation for the missing י: the ת adds length to the word that would otherwise look very short.

---

8   Some people add a י to the הוא and הם/הן forms – יישב (ye-SHEV) and יישבו (yesh-VOO) – in order to make them different from the past tense forms: ישב (ya-SHAV) and ישבו (yash-VOO). According to the current guidelines of the Hebrew Language Academy, a י is not to be added.

9   For more on imperatives, see the chapter "Command Forms," pp. 567-577.

10 Some speakers pronounce these words de-'EE, de-'OO.

When the root ends in א' (יצ-א) or ע' (יד-ע), the vowels are the same as those found in the present tense feminine singular form. Compare:

	infinitive		present f.s.	
	לָצֵאת	⇔	יוֹצֵאת	◄
	la-TSET		yo-TSET	
	לָדַעַת	⇔	יוֹדַעַת	◄
	la-DA-'at		yo-DA-'at	

Let's review

- *Beenyan pa'al* verbs whose first root letter is י' – יָשַׁב, יָרַד, יָצָא, יָדַע, יָלְדָה – and the verb הלך, as well, have the same forms as regular verbs in the past and present tenses:

	present	past	
	יוֹשֵׁב	יָשַׁב	◄

- In the future tense, imperative and infinitive forms, they lose their first root letter, as in:

	infinitive	imperative	future	
	לָשֶׁבֶת	שֵׁב!	יֵשֵׁב	◄

  - In the future tense, the vowels are *e-E* in forms without an ending, as in:

	תֵּשֵׁב ...	אֵשֵׁב,	◄
	te-SHEV	'e-SHEV	

  - The infinitive forms have "לְ" at the beginning and have the same vowels and ending as feminine singular verbs in the present tense. Compare: יוֹשֶׁבֶת and לָשֶׁבֶת.

Want to see if you've understood?
Write the missing forms of the underlined verb.

‏1.‏   <u>יְרַדְתֶּם</u> לאילת בשבוע שעבר. גם מחר (אתם) _____ לאילת.

גם אנחנו רוצים _____ לאילת.

‏2.‏   מירי <u>יָדְעָה</u> את התשובה לשאלה של המורה. אם היא לא _____ , מישהו אחר בכיתה

_____ . כל התלמידים רוצים _____ את התשובה הנכונה.

‏3.‏   מתי את <u>יוֹצֵאת</u> מהבית כל בוקר? מתי (את) _____ מחר? את צריכה _____ מוקדם?

Answers:[11]

‏1. תֵּרְדוּ, לָרֶדֶת   2. תֵּדַע, יֵדַע, לָדַעַת   3. תֵּצְאִי, לָצֵאת

Did you know?

The forms of other *pe-yod* verbs in *beenyan pa'al*, which are generally taught at more advanced levels, are similar to regular *pa'al* verbs. In full spelling, the י in these verbs does **not** drop out.[12] Here are some examples:

		infinitive	future	present	past	root
regular 'ef'ol verb:		לִכְתּוֹב	יִכְתּוֹב	כּוֹתֵב	כָּתַב	כ-ת-ב
pe-yod 'ef'ol verb:	to create	לִיצוֹר	יִיצוֹר	יוֹצֵר	יָצַר	י-צ-ר
regular 'ef'al verb:		לִלְמוֹד	יִלְמַד	לוֹמֵד	לָמַד	ל-מ-ד
pe-yod 'ef'al verb:	to spit	לִירוֹק	יִירַק	יוֹרֵק	יָרַק	י-ר-ק
regular 'ef'al + pa'el[13] *verb:*		לִגְדוֹל	יִגְדַל	גָּדֵל	גָּדַל	ג-ד-ל
pe-yod 'ef'al + pa'el verb:	to sleep	לִישוֹן	יִישַן	יָשֵן	יָשַן	י-ש-ן

---

11   It is not necessary for you to write vowel signs in your answers. We have added vowel signs to the answers in the chapters on verbs in order to make clear how the forms are pronounced.

12   In standard spelling, the situation is more complex (sometimes the י drops, as in יָצַר, and sometimes it doesn't, as in יִישַן). The root group of words like יָצַר is called חַסְרֵי פי״צ; while the root group of verbs like יִישַן is called נְחֵי פ״י.

13   See the chapter "*Beenyan Pa'al*," pp. 393-395, 401.

• Beenyan heef'eel (הוֹרִיד)[14]

Read the following:

הַנוֹסֵעַ בְּמָטוֹס הוֹרִיד אֶת הַתִּיק שֶׁלוֹ מֵהַתָּא הָעֶלְיוֹן וְהוֹצִיא מִמֶּנוּ סֵפֶר. ◄

The passenger on the plane took his bag down from the upper compartment and took a book out of it.

The verbs highlighted in this sentence belong to *beenyan heef'eel*. Let's compare them to the regular verb הִרְגִּישׁ:

	regular verb:	הוּא הִ רְ גִּ י שׁ	◄
		הוֹ רִ י ד	
		הוֹ צִ י א	

Q: What is the first root letter of הוֹרִיד and הוֹצִיא?

A: It appears here as 'ו. Notice that these verbs are related in meaning (and "genetically") to *pe-yod* verbs that we saw in *beenyan pa'al*:

	heef'eel הפעיל			*pa'al* פעל	
	to take down	הוֹרִיד	⇔	to go down	יָרַד	◄
(=to cause something / someone to go down)					
	to take out	הוֹצִיא	⇔	to go out	יָצָא	◄
(=to cause something / someone to go out)					

Today we consider the first root letter of verbs like הוֹרִיד and הוֹצִיא to be 'י: י-ר-ד and י-צ-א. However, the original root letter of many *pe-yod* verbs was actually 'ו (which was probably pronounced *w*).[15] At a certain stage in the development of Hebrew, this original *w* (ו') turned into *y* (י') when it appeared at the **beginning** of the word, as in the past tense form of *pa'al* (יָרַד). However, in *heef'eel*, where *w* (ו') was not at the very beginning of the word, it remained ו' (הוֹרִיד). We see this in other words as well, for example: הוּא נוֹלַד (ל-ד-', *beenyan neef'al*, he was born), מוֹשָׁב (י-ש-ב a cooperative settlement or a seat), תּוֹשָׁב (י-ש-ב a resident).[16]

The "ו" (*oh*) of the root appears in all tenses and forms of *beenyan heef'eel*:

infinitive	*future*	*present*	*past*	
לְהוֹרִיד	יוֹרִיד	מוֹרִיד	הוֹרִיד	◄
le-h*o*-REED	y*o*-REED	m*o*-REED	h*o*-REED	

---

14 A small number of *heef'eel* verbs whose first root letter is 'י behave like verbs whose first root letter is נ' and, therefore, are discussed in the chapter "Verbs Whose First Root Letter Is נ'," p. 500 ("Did you know?"). The second root letter of most of these verbs is צ, for example: לְהַצִּיעַ (to suggest, offer), לְהַצִּיג (to present).

15 For this reason some grammar books call this *root group* פו"י (*pe-vav-yod*), i.e., verbs beginning with ו' or with י'.

16 For more on this historical development, see Joüon and Muraoka, 1996, vol. I, pp. 94 and 191.

• Beenyan hoof'al (הוּרַד)

Read the following sentence:

◄ החתול הוּרַד מהעץ.   The cat was taken down from the tree.

The past tense *base form* הוּרַד begins with וּ-הו (*hoo*) like regular *hoof'al* verbs (e.g., הוּלבש), but, unlike in regular *hoof'al* verbs, the וּ-הו in הורד is followed by only **two** root letters (ר-ד).[17]

Here are the base forms of the verb הוּרַד:

past	present	future
◄ הוּרַד	מוּרָד	יוּרַד
hoo-RAD	*moo-RAD*	*yoo-RAD*

As you can see, in all the tenses, the prefix is followed by **two** root letters only (ר-ד).

Let's review

♦ These are the *base forms* of *pe-yod* verbs in *beenyaneem heef'eel* and *hoof'al*:

	שם הפועל	עתיד	הווה	עבר	שורש
	infinitive	*future*	*present*	*past*	*root*
beenyan heef'eel:	לְהוֹרִיד	יוֹרִיד	מוֹרִיד	הוֹרִיד	י-ר-ד ◄
beenyan hoof'al:		יוּרַד	מוּרָד	הוּרַד	י-ר-ד

Want to see if you've understood?
Write the missing forms of the underlined verb.

1.   יונתן הוֹצִיא את הכלב לטיול אתמול. כל יום הוא _____ את הכלב. גם מחר הוא

_____ את הכלב. הוא אוהב _____ את הכלב.

2.   הודיעו לכם מתי יוצאים לטיול מחר? בדרך כלל _____ לנו שבוע קודם.

אם לא _____ לנו עד שמונה בערב, נתקשר למדריך.

---

17 For ease of learning, we have described these forms as having two root letters. The "וּ" here is actually a remnant of the original root letter *w* and is also present in standard spelling, as in הוּרַד.

3. הילדים של שרה ושמואל <u>הושבו</u> ליד השולחן. כשהילדים של יעל ויוסי יגיעו,

הם _____ לידם.

Answers:

1. מוֹצִיא, יוֹצִיא, לְהוֹצִיא   2. מוֹדִיעים, יוֹדִיעוּ   3. יוֹשְׁבוּ

• Beenyaneem pee'el, poo'al *and* heetpa'el (יִישֵׁב, יוּשַׁב, הִתְיַישֵׁב)

The forms of *pe-yod* verbs in *pee'el*, *poo'al* and *heetpa'el* are like regular verbs. We have included them here because the **spelling** of these forms warrants attention.

Let's look at the base forms of verbs with the root י-שׁ-ב in *pee'el* and *heetpa'el*.

		infinitive	*future*	*present*	*past*	
pee'el:	to settle a place or a dispute	לְיַישֵׁב	יְיַישֵׁב	מְיַישֵׁב	יִישֵׁב	◄
heetpa'el:	to settle/live in a place	לְהִתְיַישֵׁב	יִתְיַישֵׁב	מִתְיַישֵׁב	הִתְיַישֵׁב	

As you can see, in these two *beenyaneem*, there is a **double** י ("יי") in **all** forms. Remember: We only write a maximum of **two** י, never three.[18]

The situation in *poo'al* is different. Here are the base forms:

poo'al:	to be settled	יְיוּשַׁב	מְיוּשָׁב	יוּשַׁב	◄

Because of the spelling rule (mentioned in the chapter "Hebrew Spelling," p. 664) that says that we do **not** add an extra י before or after "ו", we never add an extra י in *poo'al*. Thus, in full spelling we write יושב and מיושב with one י only. In the future tense, the two forms that have a י prefix (הוא יְיוּשַׁב, הם/הן יְיוּשְׁבוּ) naturally have two י at the beginning: One is the prefix and one is part of the root; neither of them is an **added** י. For this reason, the forms ייושב and ייושבו are the same in standard spelling and full spelling.

---

18 There is one exception: the plural adjective ניסויִים (experimental). See the chapter "Hebrew Spelling," pp. 657-665 for an explanation of why and where we add an extra י.

• *The special verb* יָכוֹל

The verb יכול (to be able), whose root is י-כ-ל, belongs to *beenyan pa'al*. It has no infinitive form and its conjugation is unique.[19]

Present tense (יָכוֹל)

Read the following sentence:

דניאל יָכוֹל לעזור לכם לצבוע את הדירה.   ◄

Daniel can help you paint the apartment.

As you can see, the word יכול (*ya-CHOL*) has an *ah* sound in the **first** syllable and an *oh* sound in the **second** syllable. Now let's take a look at the other present tense forms of יכול:

ya-CHOL	יָכוֹל	:(m.s.)	אני, אתה, הוא ◄
ye-cho-LA	יְכוֹלָה	:(f.s.)	אני, את, היא
ye-cho-LEEM	יְכוֹלִים	:(m.pl.)	אנחנו, אתם, הם
ye-cho-LOT	יְכוֹלוֹת	:(f.pl.)	אנחנו, אתן, הן

The *ah* sound that we hear in יָכוֹל changes to *eh* at the beginning of the other forms.[20] The "וֹ" (*oh*) remains in the second syllable of all the forms (as in the adjective גָדוֹל, גְדוֹלָה...).

Past tense (יָכוֹלְתִי...)

Read the following sentence in which the **past tense** form of יכול appears:

אתמול דניאל לא יָכוֹל לעזור לכם לצבוע את הדירה.   ◄

Yesterday Daniel couldn't help you paint the apartment.

As you've probably noticed, the past tense (הוא) base form – יָכוֹל – **sounds** just like the base form of the present tense and – in full spelling – it also **looks** the same.[21] For this reason, we tend to add היה either before or after יכול when it indicates the past tense, for example:[22]

דניאל לא היה יכול לבוא למסיבה.   ◄
דניאל לא יכול היה לבוא למסיבה.

Daniel couldn't come to the party.

---

19 In order to express "to be able to," we often use "להיות מסוגל".

20 For an explanation, see the chapter "Reduction of Vowels and the *Shva*," pp. 640-644.

21 In standard spelling, the past tense forms are: יָכֹלְתִי...יָכֹל – with no ו – and in the present tense they contain a ו: יָכוֹל, יְכוֹלָה... Thus in **standard** spelling there **is** a difference in spelling between past tense יָכֹל and present tense יָכוֹל.

22 When we add היה, we are not actually adding היה to the past tense form (this is impossible in Hebrew), but rather to the form used in the present tense.

Here are all the past tense forms:

plural			singular		
ya-CHOL-noo	יָכֹלְנוּ	אנחנו:	ya-CHOL-tee	יָכֹלְתִּי	אני: ◄
ya-CHOL-tem / ye-chol-TEM	יָכֹלְתֶּם / יְכוֹלְתֶּם [23]	אתם:	ya-CHOL-ta	יָכֹלְתָּ	אתה:
ya-CHOL-ten / ye-chol-TEN	יָכֹלְתֶּן / יְכוֹלְתֶּן	אתן:	ya-CHOLT	יָכֹלְתְּ	את:
yach-LOO	יָכְלוּ	הם, הן	ya-CHOL	יָכֹל (היה)	הוא
			yach-LA	יָכְלָה	היא

Q: Which forms in the chart contain the base form יָכֹל complete with all its vowels?

A: All of the forms at the top of the chart:

◄ יָכֹלְתִּי / -תָּ / -תְּ / -נוּ / -תֶּם / -תֶּן

The base form and these forms are all different from regular *pa'al* verbs (כָּתַב, כָּתַבְתִּי... *ka-TAV, ka-TAV-tee*...) in that they contain an *oh* ("וֹ") in the second syllable.

The forms of היא and הם/הן have the same pattern as regular *pa'al* verbs:

regular verb:	כָּתְבָה,	כָּתְבוּ	◄
will be able	יָכְלָה,	יָכְלוּ	

Future tense (יוּכַל)

Read the following sentence:

◄ מחר דניאל יוּכַל לעזור לכם לצבוע את הדירה.

Tomorrow Daniel will be able to help you paint the apartment.

As you can see, the future tense form of יכול is unlike any other *pa'al* verb. There is an *oo* sound as part of the prefix -יוּ (*yoo-*). This *oo* sound is maintained throughout the future tense conjugation, as you can see in the following table:

prefixes and suffixes		only prefixes		
		'*oo-CHAL*	אוּכַל	אני: ◄
		too-CHAL	תוּכַל	אתה:
tooch-LEE	תוּכְלִי			את:
		yoo-CHAL	יוּכַל	הוא:

---

23 The formal pronunciation is יְכוֹלְתֶּם / יְכוֹלְתֶּן (*ye-chol-TEM / ye-chol-TEN*), with the stress on the last syllable and an *eh* sound after the י.

	prefixes and suffixes		only prefixes		
			too-CHAL	תּוּכַל	היא:
			noo-CHAL	נוּכַל	אנחנו:
tooch-LOO	תּוּכְלוּ				אתם/אתן:
yooch-LOO	יוּכְלוּ				הם/הן:

The י of the root יכ־ל does not appear in any of the future tense forms. The ו in these forms is probably the original root letter *w* (which became י when it appeared at the beginning of the word).[24]

Want to see if you've understood?
Write the correct forms of יכול.

1. לא <u>יכולנו</u> להגיע לפגישה אתמול. גם היום אנחנו לא _____ להגיע,

    (present)

    אבל מחר _____ להגיע.

2. מירי ומתן לא <u>יוכלו</u> לצלצל אליי בערב. גם אתמול הם לא _____ לצלצל אליי. חבל!

3. אתמול (אני) לא _____ להיפגש איתך, אבל היום אני <u>יכולה</u> להיפגש איתך,

    וגם מחר _____ להיפגש איתך.

Answers:

1. יְכוֹלִים, נוּכַל   2. יָכְלוּ   3. יָכוֹלְתִּי, אוּכַל

---

24 One widely-held theory sees the future tense forms of יכול as belonging to *beenyan hoof'al*. Compare יוּרַד (י־ר־ד) in the section on *hoof'al* above. See Joüon and Muraoka, vol. I, pp. 195-196.

Chapter summary

Here are the forms of *pe-yod* verbs in *beenaneem pa'al*, *heef'eel* and *hoof'al*:

◆ *Hoof'al* הופעל	◆ *Heef'eel* הפעיל		◆ *Pa'al* פעל			
		ישׁן, ירק...		יצר...	ישׁב, ירד, יצא, ידע, הלך, ילד	**past** עבר
הוּרַדְתִּי	הוֹרַדְתִּי	יָשַׁנְתִּי		יָצַרְתִּי	יָשַׁבְתִּי	אני
הוּרַדְתָּ	הוֹרַדְתָּ	יָשַׁנְתָּ		יָצַרְתָּ	יָשַׁבְתָּ	אתה
הוּרַדְתְּ	הוֹרַדְתְּ	יָשַׁנְתְּ		יָצַרְתְּ	יָשַׁבְתְּ	את
הוּרַדְנוּ	הוֹרַדְנוּ	יָשַׁנּוּ[26]		יָצַרְנוּ	יָשַׁבְנוּ	אנחנו
הוּרַדְתֶּם	הוֹרַדְתֶּם	יְשַׁנְתֶּם		יְצַרְתֶּם	יְשַׁבְתֶּם[25]	אתם
הוּרַדְתֶּן	הוֹרַדְתֶּן	יְשַׁנְתֶּן		יְצַרְתֶּן	יְשַׁבְתֶּן	אתן
הוּרַד	**הוֹרִיד**	יָשַׁן		יָצַר	יָשַׁב	הוא
הוּרְדָה	הוֹרִידָה	יָשְׁנָה		יָצְרָה	יָשְׁבָה	היא
הוּרְדוּ	הוֹרִידוּ	יָשְׁנוּ		יָצְרוּ	יָשְׁבוּ	הם/הן
						present הווה
מוּרַד	**מוֹרִיד**	יָשֵׁן / יוֹרֵק		יוֹצֵר	יוֹשֵׁב	אני, אתה, הוא
מוּרֶדֶת	מוֹרִידָה	יְשֵׁנָה / יוֹרֶקֶת		יוֹצֶרֶת	יוֹשֶׁבֶת	אני, את, היא
מוּרָדִים	מוֹרִידִים	יְשֵׁנִים / יוֹרְקִים		יוֹצְרִים	יוֹשְׁבִים	אנחנו, אתם, הם
מוּרָדוֹת	מוֹרִידוֹת	יְשֵׁנוֹת / יוֹרְקוֹת		יוֹצְרוֹת	יוֹשְׁבוֹת	אנחנו, אתן, הן
		'ef'al אפעל		*'ef'ol* אפעול		**future** עתיד
אוּרַד	אוֹרִיד	אִישַׁן		אֶצוֹר	אֵשֵׁב	אני
תּוּרַד	תּוֹרִיד	תִּישַׁן		תִּצוֹר	תֵּשֵׁב	אתה
יוּרַד	**יוֹרִיד**	יִישַׁן		יִצוֹר	יֵשֵׁב	הוא
תּוּרַד	תּוֹרִיד	תִּישַׁן		תִּצוֹר	תֵּשֵׁב	היא
נוּרַד	נוֹרִיד	נִישַׁן		נִצוֹר	נֵשֵׁב	אנחנו
תּוּרְדִי	תּוֹרִידִי	תִּישְׁנִי		תִּצְרִי	תֵּשְׁבִי	את
תּוּרְדוּ	תּוֹרִידוּ	תִּישְׁנוּ		תִּצְרוּ	תֵּשְׁבוּ	אתם/אתן
יוּרְדוּ	יוֹרִידוּ	יִישְׁנוּ		יִצְרוּ	יֵשְׁבוּ	הם/הן
	לְהוֹרִיד	לִישׁוֹן / לִירוֹק		לִיצוֹר	לָשֶׁבֶת	**שם הפועל** **infinitive**
to be taken down, lowered	to take down, lower	to spit / to sleep		to create	to sit	

---

25 We have presented the form used by most Hebrew speakers today. According to the rules of grammar, the stress is on the ending of the אתם and אתן forms. This is true of all the אתם and אתן forms in the table above. In *beenyan pa'al* verbs, the stress on the final syllable causes the first vowel to "reduce" and be written as *shva*, e.g.: יְשַׁבְתֶּם (*ye-shav-TEM*), יְצַרְתֶּם (*ye-tsar-TEM*), etc.

26 In the אנחנו form, the נ of the root combines with the נ of the ending (יָשַׁנְנוּ*) to form: יָשַׁנּוּ – with **one** נ.

◆ *Pe-yod* verbs in *beenyaneem pee'el, poo'al* and *heetpa'el* have the same forms as regular verbs. Note how they are spelled (details are provided in the chapter above):

heetpa'el	*poo'al*	*pee'el*	
הִתְיַישֵׁב	יוּשַׁב	יִישֵׁב	◄

◆ For the forms of יכול, see above – before the exercise.

3. Verbs Whose Middle Root Letter Is ו׳ or י׳

גְּזֶרַת ע"ו-ע"י

Preview

- Beenyan pa'al (קָם)
- Beenyan heef'eel (הֵבִין)
- Beenyan hoof'al (הוּבָן)
- Beenyaneem pee'el, poo'al *and* heetpa'el (קֵיֵם, קוֹיַם, הִתְקַיֵּם; כִּיֵּון, כּוּיַן, הִתְכַּוֵּון)[1]

Introduction

Verbs whose middle root letter is either ו׳ or י׳ – *'ayeen-vav* and *'ayeen-yod* verbs – often put on a good disappearing act. In forms like לָקוּם (to get up) and לָשִׁיר (to sing), the middle root letters appear, but in the past and present tenses – קָם and שָׁר – they seem to have disappeared into thin air. The ו׳ and י׳ appear and disappear in different tenses and *beenyaneem*, as we will see below. In addition, when they appear, they often represent vowels (*oo, ee* or *oh*) – not consonants, as root letters normally do.

There is no doubt that we are dealing here with **unusual** roots, perhaps roots that originally consisted only of **two** letters.[2] The forms of the verbs in this group are different from *regular* verbs in **all** *beenyaneem*. In this chapter we will limit our discussion mainly to the *beenyaneem* that are usually taught in the beginning through intermediate levels of Hebrew study.

In places where the conjugation rules of *'ayeen-vav / 'ayeen-yod* verbs (which we will also call *'ayeen vav/yod* verbs) are **different** from those of regular verbs, we will present the full conjugation of the verb. However, in places where the conjugation of *'ayeen-vav/yod* verbs is formed according to the same rules as regular verbs, we will provide only the *base forms*.[3] A chart with full conjugations of the verbs discussed here is included at the end of the chapter.

---

1 In order to avoid confusion, we have not written the *strong dagesh* in the middle root letters י׳ and ו׳ in these verbs.

2 See Joüon and Muraoka, vol. I, pp. 212-224 and Yehoshua Blau, 1972, pp. 188-192.

3 See the chapter "Regular Verbs in All *Beenyaneem*: Summary," p. 447.

• Beenyan pa'al (קָם)

Present tense (קָם)

Read the following sentences:

> כל בוקר יובל קָם מוקדם וְרָץ קילומטר. תוך כדי ריצה הוא מקשיב למוסיקה וְשָׁר את השירים שהוא שומע. ◄
>
> Every morning Yuval gets up early and runs a kilometer. While running he listens to music and sings the songs that he hears.

The words highlighted in these sentences are the present tense base forms of *'ayeen-vav* and *'ayeen-yod* verbs.

Q: How many root letters appear in these forms?

A: Only two. These two-letter forms are the base upon which all four present tense forms are built. Unlike the base form of regular verbs in *pa'al*, this two-letter form does **not** change when endings are added. Compare:

	f.pl. אנחנו, אתן, הן	m.pl. אנחנו, אתם, הם	f.s. אני, את, היא	m.s. אני, אתה, הוא
regular verb:	כּוֹתְבוֹת kot-VOT	כּוֹתְבִים kot-VEEM	כּוֹתֶבֶת ko-TE-vet	כּוֹתֵב ◄ ko-TEV
'ayeen-vav:	קָמוֹת ka-MOT	קָמִים ka-MEEM	קָמָה KA-ma[4]	קָם KAM

As discussed in the chapter "Signs of Tenses and Forms" (pp. 369-371), the plural present tense endings on *'ayeen-vav/yod* verbs (-ִים and -וֹת) are the same as those on regular verbs, but the feminine singular ending (-ָה) is **different**. Thus, when the subject of the above sentence is changed to feminine singular, we say:

> כל בוקר רותי קָמָה מוקדם וְרָצָה קילומטר. תוך כדי ריצה היא מקשיבה למוסיקה וְשָׁרָה את השירים שהיא שומעת. ◄
> SHA-ra   RA-tsa   KA-ma
>
> Every morning Ruthie gets up early and runs a kilometer. While running she listens to music and sings the songs that she hears.

---

4   Most Hebrew speakers today place the stress on the **first** syllable of the feminine singular form (קָ-מָה KA-ma), pronouncing it the same as the past tense form. However, according to rules of grammar, the stress in the present tense is on the **second** syllable (just as in the plural forms קָ-מוֹת and קָ-מִים):
>   Every day Rina gets up early.   כל יום רינה קָ-מָה מוקדם. ◄
>   ka-MA

Note: One verb – מֵת (*MET* to die) – has a different *vowel* (*eh*) in the present tense:[5]

מֵתוֹת	מֵתִים,	מֵתָה,	מֵת, ◄
me-TOT	*me-TEEM*	*ME-ta*[6]	*MET*

Past tense (קָם)

Now read the same sentences in the past tense:

◄ בקיץ שעבר יובל קָם מוקדם כל בוקר וְרָץ קילומטר. תוך כדי ריצה הוא הקשיב למוסיקה וְשָׁר את השירים שהוא שמע.

Last summer Yuval got up early every morning and ran a kilometer. While running he listened to music and sang the songs that he heard.

◄ גם רותי קָמָה מוקדם וְרָצָה קילומטר. תוך כדי ריצה היא הקשיבה למוסיקה וְשָׁרָה את השירים שהיא

SHA-ra   *RA-tsa*   *KA-ma.*   שמעה.

Ruthie, too, got up early every morning and ran a kilometer. While running she listened to music and sang the songs that she heard.

Q: Are these past tense forms **different** from those in the present tense shown above?

A: No. Strangely, the הוא and היא forms in both tenses – as pronounced by most speakers today – are exactly the **same**.

Now let's look at the whole past tense conjugation:

	plural			*singular*	
KAM-noo	קַמְנוּ	אנחנו:	*KAM-tee*	קַמְתִי	אני: ◄
KAM-tem[7]	קַמְתֶם	אתם:	*KAM-ta*	קַמְתָ	אתה:
KAM-ten	קַמְתֶן	אתן:	*KAMT*	קַמְתְ	את:
KA-moo	קָמוּ	הם, הן	*KAM*	קָם	הוא
			KA-ma	קָמָה	היא

---

5   The root of this word is מ-ו-ת. Its future tense and infinitive forms – יָמוּת and לָמוּת – are like the verb לָקוּם. Its past and present tense forms are not.

6   We have indicated the pronunciation used by most speakers today. As with קמה, here too – according to rules of grammar – the stress should be on the **second** syllable: *me-TA*.

7   This is the pronunciation of the אתם and אתן forms of most Hebrew speakers today. According to the rules of grammar, the stress is on the last syllable: קַמְתֶם *kam-TEM* and קַמְתֶן *kam-TEN*.

As you can see, the entire past tense conjugation of *'ayeen-vav/yod* verbs is based on a **two-letter** base form (קָם- *KAM*). In the היא and הם/הן forms, there is no vowel reduction before the ending, as there is in regular *pa'al* verbs (e.g., כָּתְ-בָה, כָּתְ-בוּ).

The verb מֵת has a different vowel (*eh*) in the following forms:

הם / הן	היא	הוא
מֵתוּ[8]	מֵתָה	מֵת
ME-too	*ME-ta*	*MET*

Infinitive (לָקוּם)

Here are the infinitive forms of the verbs in the sentences above:

יובל ורותי אוהבים לָקוּם מוקדם ולָרוּץ קילומטר. שניהם אוהבים לָשִׁיר תוך כדי ריצה.
Yuval and Ruthie like to get up early and run a kilometer. They both like to sing while running.

While the present and past tense forms of all the highlighted verbs are the **same** (קָם, רָץ, שָׁר), the infinitive forms of these verbs do not all have the same pattern. All have the same *prefix* -לָ (*la*), but the *v*owel after the first root letter **differs**:

verbs with ee (י-)	*verbs with oo* ("ו")	
לָשִׁיר	לָרוּץ	לָקוּם
la-SHEER	*la-ROOTS*	*la-KOOM*

In these infinitive forms, we see the full **three-letter root** of each verb (ר-ו-צ, ק-ו-מ and ש-י-ר). By looking at the present or past tense two-letter forms of a given verb, it is impossible to tell whether its middle root letter is ו or י. Since the great majority of verbs in this group have *oo* (ו), not *ee* (י), if you learn the *ee* (י) verbs, you can assume the rest have *oo* (ו). Here are the *ee* (י) verbs usually learned at the beginning and intermediate levels:

---

8   The other forms of מֵת have an *ah* vowel like קַמְתִּי, קַמְתָּ ... and, when their third root letter ת comes before an ending that begins with ת, the two ת ("תת") combine into one ת, as in:

אתן	אתם	אנחנו	את	אתה	אני	
מַתֶּן	מַתֶּם	מַתְנוּ	מַת	מַת	מַתָּ	מַתִּי
MA-ten	*MA-tem*	*MAT-noo*	*MAT*	*MA-ta*	*MA-tee*	

(When written in *standard spelling* with vowel signs, the ת in these forms takes a *strong dagesh*, as in: מַתִּי* ⇐ מַתְּי*). Note: Most speakers today do not use these forms. They do not combine the "תת" into one ת, as called for by the rules of grammar, but rather write and pronounce these verbs like this: מַתְתִּי (*MA-te-tee*), מַתְתָ (*MA-te-ta*)...

לָרִיב   לָשִׂים   לָשִׁיר   ◄

to argue, fight   to put   to sing

One verb – הוּא בָּא (he came / is coming) – is **different** from the rest: only in this verb does the infinitive have an *oh* vowel – rather than *oo* or *ee* – in the middle:

la-VO   לָבוֹא   ◄

Future tense (יָקוּם)

As is the case with most Hebrew verbs, the future tense forms of *'ayeen-vav/yod* verbs are very similar to the infinitive form. Compare the infinitives and the future tense base forms highlighted in the following sentences:

יוּבל אוֹהב לָקוּם מוּקדם כּדי לָרוּץ. מחר הוּא יָקוּם מוּקדם וְיָרוּץ כּמו בּכל בּוֹקר. ◄

Yuval likes to get up early in order to run. Tomorrow he will get up early and will run as he does every morning.

ארז אוֹהב לָשִׁיר שירי אוֹפּרה. בּמסיבת יום ההוֹלדת של אשתו הוּא יָשִׁיר לפני כל המשפּחה.

Erez likes to sing arias. At his wife's birthday party he will sing in front of the whole family.

מנהל בּית הספר הוֹדיע: מי שלא יכוֹל לָבוֹא לטיוּל בּיום ראשוֹן הזה יָבוֹא בּיום ראשוֹן הבּא.

The principal announced: Whoever can't come on the trip this Sunday will come next Sunday.

As you can see, once we know the infinitive form, we can easily arrive at the future tense base form by substituting -יְ for -לְ.

The future tense of *'ayeen-vav/yod* verbs is different from regular verbs in *beenyan pa'al* in that the three-letter root with its vowel **remains the same** throughout – and so does the place of the stress – even when endings are added (this is not the case in verbs like תִכְתְּבִי ⇐ תִכְתּוֹב).

	prefixes and endings			only prefixes					
הם, הן	אתם, אתן	את		אנחנו	היא	הוא	אתה	אני	
יָקוּמוּ	תָקוּמוּ	תָקוּמִי		נָקוּם	תָקוּם	יָקוּם	תָקוּם	אָקוּם	◄
		... ta-KOO-mee						*...'a-KOOM*	
יָשִׁירוּ	תָשִׁירוּ	תָשִׁירִי		נָשִׁיר	תָשִׁיר	יָשִׁיר	תָשִׁיר	אָשִׁיר	
		... ta-SHEE-ree						*... 'a-SHEER*	
יָבוֹאוּ	תָבוֹאוּ	תָבוֹאִי		נָבוֹא	תָבוֹא	יָבוֹא	תָבוֹא	אָבוֹא	
		... ta-VO-'ee						*... 'a-VO*	

Imperative (**קום**)

Imperatives of *'ayeen-vav/yod* verbs are commonly used in everyday speech. They are formed by removing the תָּ- from the future tense forms, for example:

m.s.:	imperative		future	imperative		future	imperative		future
	בּוֹא!	⇐	תָּבוֹא	שִׁיר!	⇐	תָּשִׁיר	קוּם!	⇐	תָּקוּם	◄
f.s.:	בּוֹאִי!	⇐	תָּבוֹאִי	שִׁירִי!	⇐	תָּשִׁירִי	קוּמִי!	⇐	תָּקוּמִי
m.pl. / f.pl.:	בּוֹאוּ!	⇐	תָּבוֹאוּ	שִׁירוּ!	⇐	תָּשִׁירוּ	קוּמוּ!	⇐	תָּקוּמוּ
	Come!			Sing!			Get up!		

See the chapter "Command Forms" (pp. 567-577) for more details.

Let's review

♦ In the present and past tense forms of *'ayeen-vav / 'ayeen-yod* verbs, the middle root letter – ו or י – does not appear:

present tense: קָם, שָׁר (קָמָה, שָׁרָה...) ◄
past tense: קָם, שָׁר (קַמְתִּי, שַׁרְתִּי...)

♦ In the infinitive, future tense and imperative forms, most verbs have "ו" (*oo*) in the middle and some have ִי- (*ee*):

	'ayeen-yod (י)			*'ayeen-vav* (ו)		
	imper.	future	inf.	imper.	future	inf.
	שִׁיר!	יָשִׁיר	לָשִׁיר	קוּם!	יָקוּם	לָקוּם	◄

Only the verb בָּא has "וֹ" (*oh*):

				בּוֹא!	יָבוֹא	לָבוֹא	◄

Want to see if you've understood?
Write the missing forms of the underlined verbs.

1. בשנה שעברה דן גָּר עם שני חברים, ובשנה הבאה הוא _____ לבד.

2. הזמרת אמרה: עד עכשיו _____ שירים בעברית, אבל השירים הבאים שאָשִׁיר יהיו באנגלית.

3. ‫מתי <u>טסתם</u> לצרפת? גם בשנה הבאה _____ לשם?‬

4. ‫אחותי _____ לבקר אותי בכל יום שלישי. היא <u>תבוא</u> אליי גם מחר.‬
   (present)

5. ‫מירה, איפה <u>שמת</u> את התיק שלי? ביקשתי ממך _____ אותו בחדר שלי, והוא לא שם.‬

6. ‫דויד, _____, מהר! אם לא <u>תרוץ</u> מהר, לא תגיע לאוטובוס בזמן.‬

Answers:

‫1. יָגוּר   2. שֵׁרַתִּי   3. טַסְתֶּם   4. בָּאָה   5. לָשִׂים   6. רוּץ‬

• Beenyan heef'eel (‫הֵבִין‬)

Read the following sentence:

◄ ‫נשיא ארה"ב <u>טָס</u> בחודש שעבר ללונדון. הטייס האישי שלו <u>הֵטִיס</u> את מטוסו.‬
The President of the U.S. flew last month to London. His personal pilot flew his plane.

The two verbs highlighted in the above sentences share the same three-letter root: ‫ט-ו-ס‬. The first verb – ‫טָס‬ – is in *beenyan pa'al*, and we know its root from forms such as ‫לָטוּס‬ and ‫יָטוּס‬. The second verb – ‫הֵטִיס‬ (=to **cause** a plane to fly, to fly a plane) – contains the tell-tale signs of a past tense verb in *beenyan heef'eel*: ‫הַ _ _ י _‬, as in a regular verb like ‫הִרְגִּישׁ‬ (with certain differences that we will discuss below). All of the forms of ‫הֵטִיס‬ contain the signs of *heef'eel*, but **none** of them contains the full three-letter root. Compare:

		שם הפועל *infinitive*	עתיד *future*	הווה *present*	עבר *past*	
regular verb:	(*root:* ‫ר-ג-ש‬)	‫לְהַרְגִּישׁ‬ le-har-GEESH	‫יַרְגִּישׁ‬ yar-GEESH	‫מַרְגִּישׁ‬ mar-GEESH	‫הִרְגִּישׁ‬ heer-GEESH	◄
'ayeen-vav:	(*root:* ‫ט-ו-ס‬)	‫לְהָטִיס‬ le-ha-TEES	‫יָטִיס‬ ya-TEES	‫מֵטִיס‬ me-TEES	‫הֵטִיס‬ he-TEES	

This same pattern is found in the verb ‫הֵבִין‬ (to understand), whose root is ‫ב-י-נ‬:[9]

'ayeen-yod:	(*root:* ‫ב-י-נ‬)	‫לְהָבִין‬ le-ha-VEEN	‫יָבִין‬ ya-VEEN	‫מֵבִין‬ me-VEEN	‫הֵבִין‬ he-VEEN	◄

---

9   On the basis of forms in Biblical Hebrew that are regarded as belonging to *beenyan pa'al*, we see that the *root* of ‫הֵבִין‬ is ‫ב-י-נ‬. See, for example, Proverbs 23:1 (‫"בִּין תָּבִין אֶת-אֲשֶׁר לְפָנֶיךָ"‬) and Daniel 10:1 (‫"וּבִין אֶת-הַדָּבָר"‬).

In these forms, too, we see only **two** root letters: ב-נ. As mentioned at the beginning of this chapter, it is possible that all of these verbs originally had only two root letters.

Note: In order to conjugate *'ayeen-vav/yod* verbs in *beenyan heef'eel* correctly, it is not important to know whether the middle root letter is ו or י (the overwhelming majority of roots have a ו), but only that a verb belongs to the *'ayeen-vav/yod root group*.

Now let's look at the **differences** between regular verbs in *heef'eel* and *'ayeen-vav/yod* verbs.

Past tense (הֵבִין)

Let's take another look at the past tense base forms shown above: הֵבִין, הֵטִיס and הִרְגִּיש. These forms all begin with ה.

Q: What vowel sound follows the *h* (ה) in each verb?

A: While the regular verb begins with *hee* (הרגיש), the two *'ayeen-vav/yod* verbs begin with *heh* (הֵטִיס, הֵבִין).

Notice that when ב, כ, פ follow this prefix – as in הֵבִין (*he-VEEN*) – they are pronounced with a *soft* sound (*v, ch, f*). Here are more examples:

	הֵכִין	הֵבִיא	(הוא) ◁
	he-CHEEN	*he-VEE*	
	he prepared	he brought	

These are the past tense forms of *'ayeen-vav/yod heef'eel* verbs:[10]

	הם, הן	היא	הוא		אתה...	אני	
	הֵבִינוּ	הֵבִינָה	הֵבִין		הֵבַנְתָּ...	הֵבַנְתִּי	◁
	he-VEE-noo	*he-VEE-na*	*he-VEEN*		*he-VAN-ta*	*he-VAN-tee*	

---

10 The past tense forms of הֵבִיא are slightly different because the third root letter is א: הֵבֵאתָ..., הֵבֵאתִי. For more, see the chapter "Verbs Whose Third Root Letter Is א," pp. 561-562.

Present tense (מֵבִין)

Read the following sentence:

אורי לא הֵבִין את השיר החדש כשהוא שמע אותו ברדיו, אבל עכשיו – אחרי שהוא קרא את המילים
של השיר באינטרנט – הוא מֵבִין כל מילה.

Ori didn't understand the new song when he heard it on the radio, but now – after reading it (lit.: the words of the song) on the internet – he understands every word.

As you can see (and hear), the prefix of the present tense base form מֵבִין (*me-VEEN*) has the **same** vowel sound as the past tense base form הֵבִין (*he-VEEN*). It is different from the regular *heef'eel* base form, which begins with *ma*, as in: מַרְגִּישׁ (*mar-GEESH*).

Here are all present tense forms of מֵבִין (contrasted with a regular *heef'eel* verb):

	f.pl.	*m.pl.*	*f.s.*	*m.s.*
	אנחנו, אתן, הן	אנחנו, אתם, הם	אני, את, היא	אני, אתה, הוא
regular verb:	מַרְגִּישׁוֹת	מַרְגִּישִׁים	מַרְגִּישָׁה	מַרְגִּישׁ
	mar-gee-SHOT	*mar-gee-SHEEM*	*mar-gee-SHA*	*mar-GEESH*
'ayeen-vav/yod:	מְבִינוֹת	מְבִינִים	מְבִינָה	מֵבִין
	me-vee-NOT	*me-vee-NEEM*	*me-vee-NA*	*me-VEEN*

Notice that in **all** the *'ayeen vav/yod* present tense forms, the vowel of the prefix -מ is pronounced *eh* (the vowel sign changes from "מֵ" to "מְ", but today both are pronounced the same).

Be careful! *Pe-noon* verbs in *beenyan heef'eel*, such as הִפִּיל (he knocked over) and הִכִּיר (he knew, recognized) also contain only **two** root letters. However, these verbs have the **same** prefixes as regular verbs (-הִ, -מַ, -יַ), and when ב', כ', פ' follow the prefix, they have a **hard** sound (*b, k, p*): הִכִּיר (*hee-KEER*), מַכִּיר (*ma-KEER*), יַכִּיר (*ya-KEER*).[11]

---

11 See the chapter "Verbs Whose First Root Letter Is נ'," pp. 498-499 for an explanation.

Future tense and infinitive forms (יָבִין, לְהָבִין)

Compare the following:

	infinitive (שם הפועל)	*future* (עתיד)	
regular verb:	לְהַרְגִּיש	יַרְגִּיש	◄
	le-har-GEESH	*yar-GEESH*	
'ayeen-vav/yod:	לְהָבִין	יָבִין	
	le-ha-VEEN	*ya-VEEN*	

The prefixes of the future tense and infinitive forms of *'ayeen-vav/yod* verbs sound the same as regular *heef'eel* verbs (the vowel signs are slightly different, but are pronounced the same). The second vowel – *ee* (indicated by י) – is also the same.

The major difference between the two verbs shown above is that the regular verb (לְהַרְגִּיש) has a **three-letter** root and the forms of לְהָבִין have only **two** of the root letters. The conjugation of the future tense follows the same rules as regular verbs. (See the end of this chapter for a chart with all the forms.)

Did you know?
Verbs whose middle ו or י do not disappear

There are some verbs whose second root letter is ו or י – but, rather than disappearing, these root letters **remain** in all forms and are pronounced as the consonants *v* and *y*, for example: לְהַרְוִויחַ (to earn, make money) and לְהַחֲיוֹת (to resuscitate).

• Beenyan hoof'al (הוּבַן)

The following sentence contains the past tense base form of a regular *hoof'al* verb and a verb from the *'ayeen-vav/yod* root group:

החוק החדש נגד עישון הוּסְבַּר שוב לכל התושבים לאחר שהתברר שהוא לא הוּבַן בצורה נכונה. ◄

The new law against smoking was explained again to all the residents after it turned out that it was not understood correctly.

As was the case in *heef'eel*, here, too, the *'ayeen-vav/yod* form – הוּבַן – contains only **two** root letters (נ-ב), as opposed to the **three** in הוּסְבַּר. This is the case in all three tenses. Compare:

	עתיד	הווה	עבר
	future	*present*	*past*
regular verb:	יוּסְבַּר	מוּסְבָּר	הוּסְבַּר
'ayeen-vav/yod:	יוּבַן	מוּבָן	הוּבַן

Notice that – as in *heef'eel* – when ב, כ', פ' come at the beginning of the second syllable, they are pronounced as *soft* sounds (*v, ch, f*): הוּ-בַן, as opposed to הוּסְ-בַּר. (See the explanation in *heef'eel* above.)

Be careful! The *'ayeen-vav/yod* forms have only **two** root letters, just like *pe-noon hoof'al* verbs such as הוּפַּל (it was dropped) and הוּכַּר (he/it was recognized); however, when ב, כ', פ' follow the prefix in *pe-noon* verbs, they are pronounced with a *hard* sound – הוּפַּל, הוּכַּר[12] – as opposed to הוּבַן and הוּכַּן.

The conjugations of *'ayeen-vav/yod* verbs in *hoof'al* follow the same rules as regular *hoof'al* verbs (see the chapter "*Beenyan Hoof'al*," pp. 438-443). We have included a chart with all the forms at the end of this chapter.

Note: In the present tense forms (which are often considered adjectives),[13] we say:

f.s.	*m.s.*
המילה מוּבֶנֶת.	המשפט מוּבָן.
The word is understood.	The sentence is understood.

The feminine singular ending here is the same as that on most regular verbs such as:

גם דינה מוזמֶנֶת.	רמי מוזמָן למסיבה.
Dina is also invited.	Rami is invited to the party.

---

12 The *dagesh* in these letters is a *strong dagesh*. For an explanation, see the chapter "Verbs Whose First Root Letter Is נ'," pp. 498-500. On the strong *dagesh*, see "The Pronunciation of ב, כ', פ' and the *Dagesh*," pp. 635-637.

13 See the chapter "Adjectives Resulting from an Action Taken and Completed," pp. 159-169.

The feminine forms above end in ־ֶת (E-et). One blatant exception to this is the feminine singular form of מוּכָן (prepared, ready), which ends in ה־ָ (a-A):

> גם דינה מוכָנה.   רמי מוכָן לצאת עכשיו. ◄
>
> Dina is also ready.   Rami is ready to go out now.

Let's review

- In *heef'eel* and *hoof'al* *'ayeen-vav* and *'ayeen-yod* verbs, we see only **two** (the first and last) of the root letters. There is no trace of the middle root letter ו or י.

- The vowels of the prefixes of the *heef'eel* past and present tense forms (הֵבִין and מֵבִין) are different from those of regular verbs (הִרְגִּיש and מַרְגִּיש).

- When ב׳, כ׳, פ׳ are the first root letter in *heef'eel* and *hoof'al*, they are pronounced in all forms as *soft* sounds (*v, ch, p*): הֵבִין, הוּבַן...

- These are the base forms of *heef'eel* and *hoof'al* *'ayeen-vav* and *'ayeen-yod* verbs:

	שם הפועל *infinitive*	עתיד *future*	הווה *present*	עבר *past*	
heef'eel:	לְהָבִין	יָבִין	מֵבִין	הֵבִין	◄
hoof'al:		יוּבַן	מוּבָן	הוּבַן	

Want to see if you've understood?

A. Write the missing forms of the underlined *heef'eel* verbs.

1.   אורי, יש משהו שלא _____ אתמול? אם אתה לא <u>מבין</u> משהו, אסביר שוב ואולי

      (אתה) _____.

2.   שרה, למה <u>הערת</u> אותי כל כך מוקדם? אני לא אוהבת שאת _____ אותי ב-6 בוקר.

                       (present)

       בבקשה, אל _____ אותי מחר ב-6:00!

3.   <u>תזיזו</u> את השולחן קצת ימינה, בבקשה. חבל שלא _____ אותו לפני שהאורחים הגיעו.

4. ‏אני יודעת שאת אוהבת _____ מרק. אולי תכַינִי מרק ירקות לארוחת הערב?

Answers:

‏1. הֵבַנְתָּ, תָבִין   2. מְעִירָה, תָעִירִי   3. הֵזַזְתֶם   4. לְהָכִין

B. Write the missing forms of the underlined *hoof'al* verbs.

1. ‏האורחים החשובים הוטסו במטוס מיוחד מירושלים לאילת. בשבוע הבא הם

_____ מאילת לתל אביב.

2. ‏בנגב הוקם יישוב חדש. אני מקווה שבעתיד _____ עוד הרבה יישובים חדשים בנגב.

Answers:

‏1. יוטסו   2. יוקמו

• Beenyaneem pee'el, poo'al *and* heetpa'el
‏(קִיֵּם, קוּיַּם, הִתְקַיֵּם; כִּיֵוֵן, כּוּוַן, הִתְכַּוֵּון)

Some *'ayeen-vav* and *'ayeen-yod* verbs in *pee'el, poo'al* and *heetpa'el* have a consonantal ו (pronounced *v*) or י (pronounced *y*) in the middle of the root and behave just like regular verbs.[14] Here are some examples:[15]

Pee'el (‏פִּיֵעל)

The man set his new watch.	‏האיש כִּיוֵון את השעון החדש שלו.
The girl drew (painted) a house, trees and flowers.	‏הילדה צִייְרָה בית, עצים ופרחים.

Poo'al (‏פּוּעַל)

The clock was set again after it stopped.	‏השעון כּוּוַן שוב אחרי שהוא נעצר.
The picture was painted in water color.	‏התמונה צוּיְרָה בצבעי מים.

---

14 For more on how to spell verbs with a middle ו or י, see the chapter "Hebrew Spelling," pp. 655, 663-667.

15 In order to avoid confusion, we have not written the *strong dagesh* in the middle root letters י and ו in these verbs.

Heetpa'el (הִתְפַּעֵל)

I hadn't intended to get home late.	לא הִתְכַּוַונְתִי להגיע הביתה מאוחר. ◄

אתמול הִתְקַיְימָה פגישה של תלמידי כיתה י"ב עם חבר כנסת.
A meeting of twelfth grade students and a Knesset member was held yesterday.

Many other *'ayeen-vav/yod* verbs such as לְעוֹדֵד (*root*: ע-ו-ד) (to encourage) in *pee'el*, מְעוּדָד[16] (*root*: ע-ו-ד) (to be encouraged) in *poo'al* and לְהִתְכּוֹנֵן (*root*: כ-ו-נ) (to prepare oneself, to get ready) in *heetpa'el* have a special kind of conjugation which is beyond the scope of this book.

---

16 The vowel signs indicated above have been accepted by the Hebrew Language Academy. Traditionally, the
     vowel signs are מְעוֹדָד.

Chapter summary

◆ Hoof'al הוּפְעַל		◆ Heef'eel הִפְעִיל		◆ Pa'al פָּעַל		
'ayeen-vav / yod		'ayeen-vav / yod		'ayeen-yod	'ayeen-vav	
ב-י-נ	כ-ו-נ	ב-י-נ	כ-ו-נ	ש-י-ר	ק-ו-מ	
						past עבר
	הוּבַנְתִּי		הֲכִינוֹתִי	שַׁרְתִּי	קַמְתִּי	אני
	הוּבַנְתָּ		הֲכִינוֹתָ	שַׁרְתָּ	קַמְתָּ	אתה
	הוּבַנְתְּ		הֲכִינוֹתְ	שַׁרְתְּ	קַמְתְּ	את
	הוּבַנּוּ		הֲבַנּוּ, הֲרֵמְנוּ[17]	שַׁרְנוּ	קַמְנוּ	אנחנו
	הוּבַנְתֶּם		הֲבַנְתֶּם	שַׁרְתֶּם	קַמְתֶּם	אתם
	הוּבַנְתֶּן		הֲבַנְתֶּן	שַׁרְתֶּן	קַמְתֶּן	אתן
הוּבַן /	**הוּכַן**	**הֵבִין** /	**הֵכִין**	**שָׁר**	**קָם**	הוא
	הוּבְנָה		הֵבִינָה	שָׁרָה	קָמָה	היא
	הוּבְנוּ		הֵבִינוּ	שָׁרוּ	קָמוּ	הם/הן
						present הווה
מוּבָן /	**מוּכָן**[18]	**מֵבִין** /	**מֵכִין**	**שָׁר**	**קָם**	אני, אתה, הוא
	מוּבֶנֶת		מְבִינָה	שָׁרָה	קָמָה	אני, את, היא
	מוּבָנִים		מְבִינִים	שָׁרִים	קָמִים	אנחנו, אתם, הם
	מוּבָנוֹת		מְבִינוֹת	שָׁרוֹת	קָמוֹת	אנחנו, אתן, הן
						future עתיד
	אוּבַן		אָבִין	אָשִׁיר	אָקוּם	אני
	תּוּבַן		תָּבִין	תָּשִׁיר	תָּקוּם	אתה
יוּבַן /	**יוּכַן**	**יָבִין** /	**יָכִין**	**יָשִׁיר**	**יָקוּם**	הוא
	תּוּבַן		תָּבִין	תָּשִׁיר	תָּקוּם	היא
	נוּבַן		נָבִין	נָשִׁיר	נָקוּם	אנחנו
	תּוּבְנִי		תָּבִינִי	תָּשִׁירִי	תָּקוּמִי	את
	תּוּבְנוּ		תָּבִינוּ	תָּשִׁירוּ	תָּקוּמוּ	אתם/אתן
	יוּבְנוּ		יָבִינוּ	יָשִׁירוּ	יָקוּמוּ	הם/הן
		לְהָבִין /	לְהָכִין	לָשִׁיר	לָקוּם	**שם הפועל** *infinitive*
/ to be understood to be prepared		/ to understand to prepare		to sing	to get up	

---

17 In verbs whose final root letter is נ – e.g., הֲכַנּוּ, הֲבַנּוּ and הוּבַנּוּ – the נ of the root and the נ of אנחנו ending combine and are written as one נ (with a *dagesh* in texts written with vowel signs).

18 The feminine singular form of מוּכָן happens to be מוּכָנָה; however, the usual *f.s.* form of 'ayeen-vav verbs is like מוּבֶנֶת.

4. Verbs Whose Third Root Letter Is י
גְּזֶרֶת ל"י / ל"ה (ה' or)

Preview
- Beenyan pa'al   (קָנָה)
- Beenyan pee'el   (שִׁינָה)
- Beenyan heetpa'el   (הִתְכַּסָּה)

Introduction

Lamed-yod / lamed-he verbs, i.e., verbs whose third root letter is י or ה (e.g.,קָנִיתִי, I bought and קָנָה he bought), march to a different drummer in all *beenyaneem*.[1] Verbs in this *root group* have their own private conjugation rules, which are applied in every *beenyan*. Since these rules are somewhat different from those of *regular* verbs, we will examine the entire conjugation of verbs in this group, not only the *base forms*.

Lamed-yod *or* lamed-he: *What is the third root letter?*

Read the following sentence:

> ◄ גיא כָּתַב לנו שהוא קָנָה מכונית חדשה.   Guy wrote us that he bought a new car.
> ka-NA   ka-TAV

The two verbs highlighted in the above sentence are both past tense הוא forms in *beenyan pa'al* – and both share the same vowel pattern: *a-A* (כָּתַב and קָנָה). Since the three root letters of כָּתַב are כ-ת-ב, we might conclude that the three root letters of קָנָה are ק-נ-ה. Some grammar books do present ה' as the third root letter, as do various dictionaries that list verbs according to roots.[2] However, linguistic research teaches us that the third root letter of verbs like קָנָה was originally י'. We distinctly hear this original consonant *y* in the *verbal noun* קְנִיָּה (knee-YA – buying) and in the adjective קָנוּי (ka-NOOY – bought).[3] This same י' appears in all the *beenyaneem* in past tense

---

1   By *lamed-he* (ל"ה) here we mean verbs like קָנִיתִי / קָנָה and **not** verbs like גָּבַהּ / גָּבַהְתִּי (to get taller), whose ה' is consonantal and appears in all of the verb's forms. There are very few verbs of this latter type, and most of them are taught at the advanced level.

2   For example, Reuven Alcalay, 1965 and Avraham Even-Shoshan, 2003.

3   For more on adjectives like קָנוּי, see the chapter "Adjectives Resulting from an Action Taken and Completed," pp. 159-169, especially p. 163 ("Did you know?").

forms such as the following:

יוני, אני קָנִיתִי לאימא ספר ליום ההולדת שלה. מה אתה קָנִיתָ?

ka-NEE-ta   *ka-NEE-tee*

Yoni, I bought Mom a book for her birthday. What did you buy?

Q: Do we still **hear** the original *y* sound of the י in these forms?

A: No. The י no longer denotes the consonant *y*; however, it is **always written** in the *first* and *second person* past tense forms – before the endings תִי-, תָ- etc. – as a kind of reminder of its "glorious past" as a consonant. As we will see below, this is the case in **all** *beenyaneem*.

In sum, we can say that those who call this root group "*lamed-yod*" choose to emphasize the historic root of these verbs, whose presence is still seen and heard in some forms. Those who use the term "*lamed-he,*" on the other hand, choose to name the group in accordance with the three letters that appear in the הוא past tense base form.

In this chapter we will discuss *lamed-yod / lamed-he* verbs in *beenyaneem pa'al*, *pee'el* and *heetpa'el* (these are the *beenyaneem* usually taught at the beginning and intermediate levels).

A chart of *lamed-yod* verbs in all the *beenyaneem* is found at the end of the chapter.

• Beenyan pa'al (קָנָה)

Past tense (קָנָה)

In regular *pa'al* verbs, the הוא form (כָּתַב) is the base form upon which other forms are built. In *lamed-yod* verbs, the situation is **different**. First let's look at the הוא form: קָנָה. This form was originally קְנִי* (**kanaya*),[4] but its *y* (י) disappeared and the form became קָנ* (*ka-NA*). Only later was the letter ה added to indicate the vowel sound *ah*: קנה.

 Be careful! This added ה can be a bit confusing since it creates a **masculine** form that ends in *ah* (ה-ָ)!

---

4   See Yehoshua Blau, 1972, p. 181. For a different explanation, see Joüon and Muraoka, 1996, p. 204 §c, p. 205 §d footnote 1.

Now let's see how the first and second person forms are built.

Their base is actually the original קני*. It is to this base that the endings are added:

	plural			singular		
ka-NEE-noo	קָנִינוּ	:אנחנו	ka-NEE-tee	קָנִיתִי	:אני	◄
ka-NEE-tem / knee-TEM	קָנִיתֶם / קְנִיתֶם[5]	:אתם	ka-NEE-ta	קָנִיתָ	אתה:	
ka-NEE-ten / knee-TEN	קָנִיתֶן / קְנִיתֶן	:אתן	ka-NEET	קָנִית	:את	

The presence of the vowel sound *ee* before the endings תי-, ת- etc. is unique to *lamed-yod* verbs. As you may recall, in all regular verbs in all *beenyaneem*, the vowel sound that always precedes these endings is *ah*, for example:

	heef'eel	pee'el	pa'al
◄	הִרְגַּשְׁתִּי ...	דִּיבַּרְתִּי	כָּתַבְתִּי
	heer-GASH-tee	dee-BAR-tee	ka-TAV-tee

Here are some more examples of *lamed-yod* verbs:

את בָּנִית ...	אתה בָּנִיתָ ...	גם אני בָּנִיתִי ...	⇐	◄ דני בָּנָה ארמון בחול.
ba-NEET	ba-NEE-ta	ba-NEE-tee		ba-NA

Danny built a castle in the sand.

את רָצִית ...	אתה רָצִיתָ ...	גם אני רָצִיתִי ...	⇐	אורי רָצָה גלידה.
ra-TSEET	ra-TSEE-ta	ra-TSEE-tee		ra-TSA

Ori wanted ice cream.

Now let's look at the היא form. Read the following sentence:

Dalit wrote to us that she, too, bought a new car.	◄ דלית כָּתְבָה לנו שגם היא קָנְתָה מכונית חדשה.
	kan-TA kat-VA

Both the regular verb in this sentence (כָּתְבָה) and the *lamed-yod* verb (קָנְתָה) end in the feminine singular ending הָ-.

---

5 The pronunciation used by most Hebrew speakers today is קָנִיתֶם / קָנִיתֶן (ka-NEE-tem, ka-NEE-ten). It should be noted that according to the rules of grammar, the stress is on the **ending** of the אתם and אתן forms, and this causes the first vowel to "reduce" (it is written as a *shva*): קְנִיתֶם / קְנִיתֶן (knee-TEM, knee-TEN or ke-nee-TEM, ke-nee-TEN). See the chapter "Reduction of Vowels and the *Shva*," pp. 640-645.

Q: What letter do we see in קָנְתָה immediately **before** the feminine ending הָ-?

A: The letter ת'. We can actually regard both letters **together** – תָה- (-*TA*) – as the היא ending of *lamed-yod* verbs.[6] Only **two** of the original root letters of this form remain (the original י' has disappeared).

Now let's take a look at the הם/הן form of *lamed-yod* verbs:

≺ השכנים שלנו קָנוּ דירה חדשה בתל אביב וְעָבְרוּ לשם לפני שבוע.

   'av-ROO   ka-NOO

Our neighbors bought a new apartment in Tel Aviv and moved there a week ago.

If we compare the regular verb עָבְרוּ to the *lamed-yod* verb קָנוּ, we see that both verbs end in וּ-; however, in קָנוּ there are only **two** root letters (ק-נ) before the ending, while עָבְרוּ has **three**. None of the third person *lamed-yod* forms retains the original third root letter י':

≺ הוא: קָנָה
   היא: קָנְתָה
   הם, הן: קָנוּ

Be careful! The past tense forms of היה (to be) require special attention. The original root letters of this verb are ה-י-י. In *full spelling*, a double י' ("יי") appears in all forms except הָיָה and הָיוּ:[7]

	plural				*singular*		
	ha-YEE-noo	הָיִינוּ	אנחנו:		*ha-YEE-tee*	הָיִיתִי	אני:	≺
	ha-YEE-tem	הָיִיתֶם[8]	אתם:		*ha-YEE-ta*	הָיִיתָ	אתה:	
	ha-YEE-ten	הָיִיתֶן	אתן:		*ha-YEET*	הָיִית	את:	
	ha-YOO	הָיוּ	הם, הן		*ha-YA*	הָיָה	הוא	
					hay-TA	הָיְתָה	היא	

---

6   Actually this ת' was probably the original feminine ending. The *ah* (הָ-) at the end of the word (קנתה) was presumably added later on to make the *lamed-yod* היא form resemble the היא form of a regular verb (כתבה, for example). Thus קנתה actually has two feminine signs: the ת' and the ה'. See Blau, 1972, p. 182.

7   For more details on the rules of full spelling, see the chapter "Hebrew Spelling," pp. 663-665. In standard spelling, the first and second person forms always have a double י' (הָיִיתִי...); the third person forms do not (הָיוּ, הָיְתָה, הָיָה).

8   This is the pronunciation used by most speakers today. According to the rules of grammar, the stress is on the ending of the אתם and אתן forms, and they are: הֱיִיתֶם and הֱיִיתֶן (*he-yee-TEM /TEN*).

The "head and tail" principle

Let's compare regular *pa'al* past tense forms and the past tense forms of *lamed-yod* verbs. We'll color two parts of the forms: the "head" and the "tail." (We have added another *lamed-yod* verb for the sake of comparison: רָצָה to want.)

	אתן	אתם	אנחנו	את	אתה	אני		הם, הן	היא	הוא	
regular verb:	כְּתַבְתֶּן	כְּתַבְתֶּם	כָּתַבְנוּ	כָּתַבְתְּ	כָּתַבְתָּ	כָּתַבְתִּי		כָּתְבוּ	כָּתְבָה	כָּתַב	◄
lamed-yod:	קְנִיתֶן	קְנִיתֶם	קָנִינוּ	קָנִית	קָנִיתָ	קָנִיתִי		קָנוּ	קָנְתָה	קָנָה	
	רְצִיתֶן	רְצִיתֶם	רָצִינוּ	רָצִית	רָצִיתָ	רָצִיתִי		רָצוּ	רָצְתָה	רָצָה	
	-EE-ten	*-EE-tem*	*-EE-noo*	*-EET*	*-EE-ta*	*-EE-tee*		*-OO*	*-TA*	*-A*	

Pay special attention to the *vowel pattern* of the "heads" and the "tails."

Q: Are the "heads" of regular *pa'al* verbs and *lamed-yod* verbs the same or different?

A: The "heads" are all the **same**: they all begin with the first root letter followed by the vowel sign ◻ (pronounced *ah*).[9]

Q: Are the "tails" the same or different?

A: The two *lamed-yod* verbs have the same "tails," but, in most cases, these "tails" are **different** from those of the regular verb.

Note: We will find the "head and tail" principle at work in all tenses and *beenyaneem* of *lamed-yod* verbs. The "heads" of *lamed-yod* verbs always resemble regular verbs in the same *beenyan*, and the "tails" of *lamed-yod* verbs in all *beenyaneem* resemble **each other**.

---

9   Unlike the other *lamed-yod* forms, the "head" of the היא form includes also the **second** root letter: קנתה, רצתה.

Let's review

- ◆ *Lamed-yod pa'al* verbs in the past tense have the same "head" as regular *pa'al* verbs: כָּתבתי versus קָניתי.

- ◆ It is the "tail" of each form that is different.

  - The "tail" of the הוא form is הָ- (*-A*): קָנָה, רָצָה. In this form ה׳ is written in place of the third root letter י׳.

  - The "tail" of the היא form is תָה- (*-TA*): קָנתָה, רָצתָה. Here, too, we do not see or hear the original י׳.

  - In the הם/הן form, as well – קָנו, רָצו – there is no trace of the original third root letter י׳. The regular ending ו- appears immediately after the first two root letters.

  - The "tail" of all other past tense *lamed-yod* forms always contains the original י׳. This י׳ indicates the vowel sound *ee* before the following endings:

קָנִיתֶן	קָנִיתֶם,	קָנִינו,	קָנִית,	קָנִיתָ,	קָנִיתִי,
ka-NEE-ten	ka-NEE-tem	ka-NEE-noo	ka-NEET	ka-NEE-ta	ka-NEE-tee

Want to see if you've understood?

Write the missing past tense forms of the underlined verbs.

1. דויד, <u>ראית</u> את ה"מונה ליזה" בפריז? רון _____ אותה? נעמה וענת _____ אותה?

2. המונית <u>פנתה</u> שמאלה בפינה. גם האוטובוס _____ שמאלה. רק אנחנו לא _____ .

3. כשהיינו בבית קפה דויד <u>שתה</u> קולה, אני _____ מיץ תפוזים, אחותי _____ קפה קר, וההורים שלי _____ מים מינרליים.

4. דניאל לא <u>היה</u> בכיתה אתמול. גם אני לא _____ בכיתה. נועה, את יודעת אם דנה _____ ?

Answers:

1. רָאָה, רָאו 2. פָּנָה, פָּנִינו 3. שָׁתִיתִי, שָׁתתָה, שָׁתו 4. הָיִיתִי, הָיתָה

Present tense (קוֹנֶה)

Read the following sentence:

◄ אתה כּוֹתֵב את השם שלך בתוך כל ספר שאתה קוֹנֶה?

Do you (*m.s.*) write your name in every book that you buy?

The same "head and tail" principle that we saw in the past tense works also in the present tense of *lamed-yod* verbs. The "head" of the regular verb (כּוֹתֵב) and that of the *lamed-yod* verb (קוֹנֶה) are the **same**: the first root letter followed by "וֹ" (pronounced *oh*). This is so in all four present tense forms:

	f.pl.		*m.pl.*		*f.s.*		*m.s.*	
	אנחנו, אתן, הן		אנחנו, אתם, הם		אני, את, היא		אני, אתה, הוא	
regular verb:	*kot-VOT*	כּוֹתְבוֹת	*kot-VEEM*	כּוֹתְבִים	*ko-TE-vet*	כּוֹתֶבֶת	*ko-TEV*	כּוֹתֵב ◄
lamed-yod:	*ko-NOT*	קוֹנוֹת	*ko-NEEM*	קוֹנִים	*ko-NA*	קוֹנָה	*ko-NE*	קוֹנֶה

Q: Do any of the *lamed-yod* forms contain the original third root letter י'?

A: No. Only the first **two** root letters (ק-נ) are present in these forms. The "tails" that characterize *lamed-yod* verbs are added to the end of the second root letter:

ko-NE	קוֹנֶה	:(*m.s.*)	אני, אתה, הוא ◄
ko-NA	קוֹנָה	:(*f.s.*)	אני, את, היא
ko-NEEM	קוֹנִים	:(*m.pl.*)	אנחנו, אתם, הם
ko-NOT	קוֹנוֹת	:(*f.pl.*)	אנחנו, אתן, הן

As you can see, the "tails" of the plural forms – יִם- and וֹת- – are the same as those of regular verbs (e.g., כּוֹתְבִים and כּוֹתְבוֹת). It is the "tails" of the singular forms of *lamed-yod* verbs that require our attention.

When written without vowel signs, the two singular *lamed-yod* forms **look** the same: they both end in ה-. However, the **pronunciation** of these two forms is **different**. The masculine form ends in *eh* (ה ֶ), which – in *beenyan pa'al* – happens to be the same vowel sound as that of a regular *pa'al* verb:[10]

ko-TEV	כּוֹתֵב ◄
ko-NE	קוֹנֶה

---

10 The vowel signs in the last syllable are written differently (◌ֵ and ◌ֶ) but sound exactly the same in today's pronunciation.

In contrast, the feminine singular form ends in *ah* (הָ-). This ending is strikingly different from that of a regular *pa'al* verb:

◄ כּוֹתֶבֶת   *ko-TE-vet*
קוֹנָה   *ko-NA*

Let's review

◆ As in the past tense, *lamed-yod* present tense verbs have the same "head" as regular *pa'al* verbs (כּוֹתֵב and קוֹנָה). The "tails" of the plural forms are the **same** as those of regular verbs (ים-, וֹת-), but the "tails" of the singular forms are **different**: both end in ה-, but they are pronounced differently (קוֹנָה *ko-NE*, קוֹנָה *ko-NA*).

| *regular verb*: | כּוֹתֵב, | כּוֹתֶבֶת, | כּוֹתְבִים, | כּוֹתְבוֹת | ◄ |
| *lamed-yod*: | קוֹנֶה, | קוֹנָה, | קוֹנִים, | קוֹנוֹת |

◆ In all present tense *lamed-yod* forms, only two of the three root letters are present (here ק-נ):

| *regular verb*: | כּוֹתֵב, | כּוֹתֶבֶת, | כּוֹתְבִים, | כּוֹתְבוֹת | ◄ |
| *lamed-yod*: | קוֹנֶה, | קוֹנָה, | קוֹנִים, | קוֹנוֹת |

Want to see if you've understood?
Write the missing present tense forms of the underlined verbs.

1.   מיכל <u>רוֹאָה</u> סרט כל שבוע. רון כמעט לא _____ סרטים,

    ומירה ורונית _____ סרט פעם בחודש.

2.   יצחק לשושנה ולאמיר: "אני תמיד <u>שׁוֹתֶה</u> תה בבוקר ואשתי _____ קפה.

    מה אתם _____ בבוקר?"

Answers:

1. רוֹאֶה, רוֹאוֹת   2. שׁוֹתָה, שׁוֹתִים

Future tense (יִקְנֶה)

Read the following sentences:

◄ אימא לענת: "אם אבא יִזְכּוֹר, הוא יִקְנֶה חלב במכולת בדרך הביתה. אם הוא יִשְׁכַּח, אבקש כוס חלב מהשכנים".

Mom to Anat: "If Dad remembers (lit.: will remember), he'll buy milk at the convenience store on his way home. If he forgets (lit.: will forget), I'll ask the neighbors for a cup of milk."

The three *pa'al* verbs highlighted above share the same "head": they all begin with -יִ (*yee*) followed by the first root letter (יִזְכּוֹר, יִקְנֶה, יִשְׁכַּח). However, their "tails" are very **different**. יִזְכּוֹר belongs to the *'ef'ol* group and יִשְׁכַּח belongs to *'ef'al*.[11] Most future tense verbs in *pa'al* are similar in form to one of these two verbs. In contrast, the *lamed-yod* verb (יִקְנֶה) has its own special "tail": it is written as a final ה- and is pronounced *eh*. As in the present tense, here, too, only **two** root letters (ק-נ) are present (יִקְנֶה); the third root letter י is nowhere to be seen.

Here are all the forms that end in ה-ֶ:

אני	אתה	הוא	היא	אנחנו
אֶקְנֶה	תִּקְנֶה	יִקְנֶה	תִּקְנֶה	נִקְנֶה
'ek-NE	*teek-NE*	*yeek-NE*	*teek-NE*	*neek-NE*

◄

Here are the אַת, אתם/אתן and הם/הן forms:

את	אתם/אתן	הם/הן
תִּקְנִי	תִּקְנוּ	יִקְנוּ
teek-NEE	*teek-NOO*	*yeek-NOO*

◄

The endings here are the same endings found on regular verbs (e.g., תִּזְכְּרִי, תִּזְכְּרוּ, יִזְכְּרוּ). In *lamed-yod* verbs, they are added after the **second** root letter, since the third root letter י is **not** present.

---

11 On *'ef'ol* and *'ef'al*, see the chapter "*Beenyan Pa'al*," pp. 398-401.

Be careful! In full spelling, the future tense forms of היה (to be) are written with only **one** י before the end even though this י is pronounced with a *y* sound.[12] (Note: we have added vowel signs to the **full spelling** in order to make the pronunciation clearer.)

	אני	אתה	הוא	היא	אנחנו
forms that end in הֶ-:	אֶהְיֶה	תִּהְיֶה	יִהְיֶה	תִּהְיֶה	נִהְיֶה

	את	אתם/אתן	הם/הן
forms with endings:	תִּהְיִי	תִּהְיוּ	יִהְיוּ

Let's review

- In the future tense, as in the past and present tenses, *lamed-yod* verbs have the same "head" as regular verbs: יִכְתּוֹב and יִקְנֶה.

- However, unlike regular verbs, the "tail" of the *lamed-yod* base form ends in הֶ- and is pronounced *-eh*. This ה comes after the **second** root letter. All future tense forms that have only a *prefix* end in הֶ-:

	אני	אתה	הוא ...
	אֶקְנֶה	תִּקְנֶה	יִקְנֶה ...

- The original third root letter י does not appear in **any** future tense form. Thus, when endings are added, they appear after the **second** root letter:

	את	אתם/אתן	הם/הן
	תִּקְנִי	תִּקְנוּ	יִקְנוּ

---

12 According to the rules of the Hebrew Language Academy, we do not write two י in these forms since the י appears either before ה, as in יהיה, before וּ-, as in יהיו, or before י, as in תהיי. For more details, see the chapter "Hebrew Spelling," pp. 663-665.

Want to see if you've understood?

Write the missing future tense forms of the underlined verbs.

1. המלצר: "אדוני, מה <u>תשתה</u>? גברתי, מה את _____ ? ומה הילדים _____ ?"

2. מחר <u>יהיה</u> יום יפה. לא _____ עננים בשמים, ולא _____ רוח חזקה.

3. מיכל, <u>תפני</u> אליי אם יהיו לך שאלות. דויד, _____ אליי גם אתה, בבקשה.

Answers:

1. תִּשְׁתִּי, יִשְׁתּוּ   2. יִהְיוּ, תִּהְיֶה   3. תִּפְנֶה

Infinitive (לִקְנוֹת)

Read the following sentences:

◄   מיכאל רוצה לִמְכּוֹר את הדירה שלו בירושלים, לִקְנוֹת אדמה ליד חיפה ולִבְנוֹת שם בית גדול.

Michael wants to sell his apartment in Jerusalem, buy land near Haifa and build a big house there.

All of the infinitives highlighted above belong to *beenyan pa'al*, and for this reason they all have the same "head" (*lee_-* -לִ□):

◄ | | | | |
|---|---|---|---|
| *regular verb*: | (*root*: | מ-כ-ר) | לִמְכּוֹר |
| *lamed-yod verbs*: | (*root*: | ק-נ-י) | לִקְנוֹת |
| | (*root*: | ר-א-י) | לִרְאוֹת |

As you can see, all of these infinitives have an *oh* vowel ("וֹ") in the last syllable – לִמְכּוֹר, לִקְנוֹת, לִרְאוֹת – however, while the regular verb ends in its third root letter, the י of the *lamed-yod* verbs does **not** appear in their infinitives.

Q: What ending is shared by both *lamed-yod* infinitives?

A: They both end in וֹת- (*-ot*): לִקְנוֹת and לִרְאוֹת.[13]

---

13 We regard the ending as וֹת- – and not just ת- – since וֹת- is the ending we find on the infinitive forms of all the other *beenyaneem* that have infinitives, e.g., לְשַׁנּוֹת in *pee'el*, לְהִתְכַּסּוֹת in *heetpa'el*, etc.

Did you know?
The verb לִחְיוֹת

The verb לִחְיוֹת (to live) also belongs to the *lamed-yod* root group. Its infinitive (לִחְיוֹת *leech-YOT*) has the same form as לִבְנוֹת (*leev-NOT*), and its root is ח-י-י. However, some of the most frequently used forms of לחיות are **different** from those of other *lamed-yod* verbs.

In the **present** tense, for example, לחיות "forgets" that it is a *lamed-yod* verb and acts almost as if it belongs to the *'ayeen-vav* group.[14] Compare:

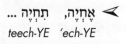

קָמוֹת	קָמִים,	קָמָה,	קָם,
ka-MOT	ka-MEEM	KA-ma[15]	KAM
חָיוֹת	חַיִּים,	חַיָּה,	חַי,
cha-YOT	cha-YEEM	CHA-ya[16]	CHAI

'ayeen-vav:

The **past** tense הוּא form is also "irregular": it is the same as the form used in the present tense (it, too, looks and sounds like קָם):

מוֹצַרְט חַי בַּמֵּאָה הַ-18.   Mozart lived in the eighteenth century.
CHAI

One other past tense form – the plural הם/הן form – acts like an *'ayeen-vav* verb (קָמוּ):

בָּאךְ וְהֶנְדֶל חָיוּ מִסּוֹף הַמֵּאָה הַ-17 עַד אֶמְצַע הַמֵּאָה הַ-18.
CHA-yoo

Bach and Handel lived from the end of the 17th century to the middle of the 18th century.

All the rest of the past tense forms of this verb are like other *lamed-yod* verbs:

חֲיִיתֶן	חֲיִיתֶם,[17]	חָיִינוּ,	(הִיא) חָיְתָה,	חָיִית,	חָיִיתָ,	חָיִיתִי,
cha-YEE-ten	cha-YEE-tem	cha-YEE-noo	chai-TA	cha-YEET	cha-YEE-ta	cha-YEE-tee

The **future** tense forms all behave like *lamed-yod* verbs, for example:

אֶחְיֶה, תִּחְיֶה ...
'ech-YE teech-YE

---

14 In actuality, the forms חַיָּה, חַיִּים, חָיוֹת have a *strong dagesh* in the middle root letter; therefore, the forms are really like verbs with a double root letter (none of which are usually taught at the beginning and intermediate levels).

15 This is the pronunciation used by most speakers today. According to the rules of grammar, the stress is on the last syllable: *ka-MA*.

16 This is the pronunciation used by most speakers today. According to the rules of grammar, the stress is on the last syllable: *cha-YA*.

17 This is the pronunciation used by most speakers today. According to the rules of grammar, the stress is on the ending of the אתם and אתן forms and they are: חֲיִיתֶם and חֲיִיתֶן (*cha-yee-TEM /TEN*).

Let's review

◆ The "head" of *lamed-yod* infinitives in *pa'al* is the same as that of regular *pa'al* verbs.

regular verb: לִכְתוֹב ◄

lamed-yod: לִקְנוֹת, לִרְאוֹת

◆ *Lamed-yod* infinitives contain only the first **two** root letters, and always end in תֹ-:

לִקְנוֹת, לִרְאוֹת ◄

Want to see if you've understood?

Write the missing infinitive forms of the underlined verbs.

1. מה שֶׁקָּרָה למיכל יכול _____ לכל אחד.

2. שָׁתִית מספיק מים היום? חשוב _____ הרבה מים במיוחד בימים חמים.

Answers:

1. לִקְרוֹת   2. לִשְׁתּוֹת

See the end of the chapter for a full conjugation of *lamed-yod* verbs in *pa'al*.

• Beenyan pee'el (שִׁינָּה)

The "head and tail" principle described in the preceding section works simply and beautifully in *beenyan pee'el*. In all tenses and forms, the "heads" of *pee'el lamed-yod* verbs are the same as the "heads" of regular *pee'el* verbs, while the *lamed-yod* "tails" follow the pattern of the "tails" of *lamed-yod* **pa'al** verbs described above.

Past tense (שִׁינָה)

Read the following sentences:

> ◄ אחרי שאמיר דִיבֵּר עם יוסי על התוכניות שלו לטייל בהודו, הוא שִׁינָה את דעתו והחליט לנסוע לדרום אמריקה.

After Amir spoke with Yossi about his plans to travel in India, he changed his mind and decided to go to South America.

> אחרי שדִיבַּרְתִי עם אימא שלי על התוכניות שלי לטייל בסין, שִׁינִיתִי את דעתי והחלטתי לנסוע לאוסטרליה.

After I spoke with my mother about my plans to travel in China, I changed my mind and decided to go to Australia.

All the verbs highlighted in these sentences are past tense verbs that belong to *beenyan pee'el* and, therefore, they all have the same "head" (_ee- -יﬦ):

	אני ...		הוא	
regular verbs:	*dee-BAR-tee* ... דִיבַּרְתִי		*dee-BER* דִיבֵּר	◄
lamed-yod:	*shee-NEE-tee* ... שִׁינִיתִי		*shee-NA* שִׁינָה	

The "tails" of each regular verb and its corresponding *lamed-yod* verb, on the other hand, are **different**: דִיבֵּר versus שִׁינָה and דִיבַּרְתִי versus שִׁינִיתִי. The "tails" of the *lamed-yod* verbs are the same "tails" that we saw on the *pa'al* verb קָנָה:

		אתה ...	אני	הם, הן	היא	הוא	
lamed-yod pa'al:	(*root*: ק-נ-י)	קָנִיתָ ...	קָנִיתִי	קָנוּ	קָנְתָה	קָנָה	◄
lamed-yod pee'el:	(*root*: ש-נ-י)	שִׁינִיתָ[18]...	שִׁינִיתִי	שִׁינוּ	שִׁינְתָה	שִׁינָה	
		-EE-ta	*-EE-tee*	*-OO*	*-TA*	*-A*	

Note: The י before the ending in the forms שׁינִיתי, קָנִיתי... is actually the third root letter.

---

18 The Hebrew Language Academy also regards the pronunciation שִׁינֵיתִי (*shee-NE-tee*), שִׁינֵיתָ (*shee-NE-ta*) – with an *eh* vowel in the middle – as permissible. This pronunciation is less common than the one indicated above.

Want to see if you've understood?

Write the missing past tense forms of the underlined verbs.

1. <u>חִיכִּינוּ</u> לאוטובוס במשך שעה. גם את _____ ? גם דויד _____ ?

2. מיכאל <u>נִיסָה</u> לעזור לי ללמוד למבחן במתמטיקה. גם שרה _____ לעזור לי.

   אפילו יוסי ומיקי _____ לעזור לי. אני מקווה שאני באמת אצליח...

3. אתמול בערב <u>בִּילִינוּ</u> במסיבת יום ההולדת של מיכאל. תמר, איפה את _____ ?

Answers:

1. חִיכִּית, חִיכָּה   2. נִיסְתָה, נִיסוּ   3. בִּילִית

Present tense (מְשַׁנֶּה)

Read the following sentences:

◄ כשיונתן מְדַבֵּר עם ילדים קטנים, הוא מְשַׁנֶּה את טון הדיבור הרגיל שלו.
   When Yonatan talks with small children, he changes his regular tone of voice.

כשתמר מְדַבֶּרֶת עם ילדים קטנים, גם היא מְשַׁנָּה את טון הדיבור הרגיל שלה.
   When Tamar talks with small children, she, too, changes her regular tone of voice.

All the highlighted verbs in the sentences above begin with the "head" typical of *pee'el* present tense verbs (*me-_a-* -מְ□):

	היא		הוא	
regular verb:	*me-da-BE-RET*	מְדַבֶּרֶת	*me-da-BER*	מְדַבֵּר	◄
lamed-yod:	*me-sha-NA*	מְשַׁנָּה	*me-sha-NE*	מְשַׁנֶּה	

Now let's look at the "tails" of *lamed-yod pee'el* forms as compared to regular *pee'el* forms:

	f.pl.	*m.pl.*	*f.s.*	*m.s.*	
	אנחנו, אתן, הן	אנחנו, אתם, הם	אני, את, היא	אני, אתה, הוא	
regular verb pee'el:	מְדַבְּרוֹת	מְדַבְּרִים	מְדַבֶּרֶת	מְדַבֵּר	◄
lamed-yod pee'el:	מְשַׁנּוֹת	מְשַׁנִּים	מְשַׁנָּה	מְשַׁנֶּה	

As was the case in *beenyan pa'al*, the most striking **difference** between the "tails" of the regular *pee'el* verb and those of the *lamed-yod* verb is found in the feminine singular: -E_-et versus -A. The *lamed-yod* "tails" on the *pee'el* verb מְשַׁנֶּה are the same as those found on the *pa'al* verb קוֹנֶה:

lamed-yod pa'al:	קוֹנוֹת	קוֹנִים	קוֹנָה	קוֹנֶה ◄
lamed-yod pee'el:	מְשַׁנּוֹת	מְשַׁנִּים	מְשַׁנָּה	מְשַׁנֶּה
	-OT	-EEM	-A	-E

Want to see if you've understood?

Write the missing present tense forms of the underlined verbs.

1. רונית גרה בתל אביב. כל יום שישי היא נוסעת לחוף הים וַמבלה שם עד 14:00.

   גם החברות הטובות של רונית _____ איתה בחוף היום.

2. יוסי שואל את החולים בתור לרופא: "אתם מחכים לד"ר סילמן?" "גם אתה _____ לד"ר סילמן?".

   "למי את _____?"

Answers:

1. מְבַלּוֹת   2. מְחַכֶּה, מְחַכָּה

Future tense (יְשַׁנֶּה)

Read the following sentences:

שי אמר לחברו: "אֲדַבֵּר איתך בטלפון אם אֲשַׁנֶּה את דעתי בקשר לתוכניות שלנו ללכת לסרט ביחד". ◄

Shai said to his friend: "I will speak with you on the phone if I change my mind about our plans to go to a movie together."

שי אמר לחברו שהוא יְדַבֵּר איתו אם הוא יְשַׁנֶּה את דעתו בקשר לתוכניות שלהם ללכת לסרט ביחד.

Shai told his friend that he would speak with him if he changed his mind about their plans to go to a movie together.

Compare the "heads" of the corresponding regular verbs and *lamed-yod* verbs from the above sentences:

	הוא	אני
regular verb:	יְדַבֵּר	אֲדַבֵּר ◄
lamed-yod:	יְשַׁנֶּה	אֲשַׁנֶּה

As expected, the "heads" are the same. The "tails," however, are different from one another: אֲדַבֵּר versus אֲשַׁנֶּה. The "tails" of the *pee'el lamed-yod* verbs are the same as *lamed-yod* verbs in *pa'al*:

	הם, הן	אתם, אתן	את	אתה	אני
lamed-yod pa'al:	יִקְנוּ	תִּקְנוּ	תִּקְנִי	תִּקְנֶה	אֶקְנֶה
lamed-yod pee'el:	יְשַׁנּוּ	תְּשַׁנּוּ	תְּשַׁנִּי	תְּשַׁנֶּה	אֲשַׁנֶּה
	-OO	-OO	-EE	-E	-E

Here, as in *pa'al*, the original third root letter י is nowhere to be seen.

 Be careful! When written **without** vowel signs, the future tense forms of *lamed-yod* verbs in *pa'al* and *pee'el* look (but **don't** sound) the same (e.g., יקנה and ישנה). You really have to be familiar with each *lamed-yod* verb you encounter in a text (i.e., you must know its *beenyan*) in order to know how to pronounce its future tense form.

 ## Want to see if you've understood?
Write the missing future tense forms of the underlined verbs.

1. אם אתם לא תַגלו את הסוד שלי, אני לא _____ את הסוד שלכם.

2. מי יְשנה את העולם? אולי אנחנו _____ את העולם?

3. טלי לדויד ולמירה: "אני אבוא לאסוף אתכם לארוחת ערב בשעה שמונה. דויד,

אתה תְחכה לי ליד הבית שלך, ומירה, את _____ לי בפינת הרחוב שלך".

Answers:

1. אֲגַלֶּה 2. נְשַׁנֶּה 3. תְחַכִּי

Infinitive (לְשַׁנּוֹת)

Read the following sentence:

אני רוצה לְבַקֵּשׁ מכם לְנַסּוֹת לְשַׁנּוֹת את שעת המפגש.
I want to ask you to try to change the time of the meeting.

The "heads" of the infinitives of *pee'el lamed-yod* verbs (לְשַׁנּוֹת and לְנַסּוֹת) are the same as the "head" of the regular *pee'el* infinitive (לְבַקֵּשׁ). However, the "tails" of לְנַסּוֹת and לְשַׁנּוֹת are not like that of לְבַקֵּשׁ; rather, they are exactly the same as the "tail" of *lamed-yod pa'al* infinitives, such as לִקְנוֹת and לִרְאוֹת.

When written **without** vowel signs, the infinitive of *lamed-yod pee'el* verbs **looks** (but **doesn't** sound) the same as that of *pa'al* verbs. Compare:

lamed-yod pa'al:	*leek-NOT*	לקנות
lamed-yod pee'el:	*le-sha-NOT*	לשנות

Only if you are familiar with these verbs (i.e., if you know their *beenyan*) can you know how to pronounce them.

Want to see if you've understood?
Write the missing infinitive forms of the underlined verbs.

1. חִיכִּיתי לחברה שלי ברחוב יפו, והיא לא הגיעה. לא ידעתי שהייתי צריכה _____ לה במקום אחר.

2. רון וגלי סיפרו שהם בִּילוּ שבועיים נהדרים ברומא. גם אנחנו רוצים _____ שם.

Answers:

1. לְחַכּוֹת   2. לְבַלּוֹת

Let's review

♦ The "heads" of *lamed-yod pee'el* verbs are the same as those of regular *pee'el* verbs. The "tails" are the same as those of *lamed-yod* forms in *beenyan pa'al*. Compare:

	infinitive	future הוא	future אני	present f.s.	present m.s.	past אני	past היא	past הוא
regular pee'el:	לְדַבֵּר	יְדַבֵּר	אֲדַבֵּר	מְדַבֶּרֶת	מְדַבֵּר	דִּיבַּרְתִּי	דִּיבְּרָה	דִּיבֵּר
lamed-yod pee'el:	לְשַׁנּוֹת	יְשַׁנֶּה	אֲשַׁנֶּה	מְשַׁנָּה	מְשַׁנֶּה	שִׁינִּיתִי	שִׁינְּתָה	שִׁינָּה
lamed-yod pa'al:	לִקְנוֹת	יִקְנֶה	אֶקְנֶה	קוֹנָה	קוֹנֶה	קָנִיתִי	קָנְתָה	קָנָה
	-OT	*-E*	*-E*	*-A*	*-E*	*-EE-tee*	*-TA*	*-A*

• Beenyan heetpa'el (הִתְכַּסָּה)

Heetpa'el is the third – and last – *beenyan* we will look at in this chapter. Here, too, the "head and tail" principle makes learning *lamed-yod* verbs significantly easier.

Past tense (הִתְכַּסָּה)

Read the following sentence:

◄ האַרכיאולוג הִתְרַגֵּשׁ מאוד כשבחפירות בגליל הִתְגַּלָּה בית כנסת עתיק.

The archaeologist got very excited when an ancient synagogue was discovered at the excavations in the Galilee.

Here, too, we see that the "head" of the *lamed-yod* form הִתְגַּלָּה is the same as that of the regular verb הִתְרַגֵּשׁ, whereas its "tail" (ה- ָ- -*A*) is the same "tail" that we saw in the הוא form of *lamed-yod* *pa'al* and *pee'el* verbs: קָנָה and שִׁינָּה.

The same is true of the היא and הם/הן forms. They have the same "head" as regular verbs:

	הם, הן	היא
regular heetpa'el:	הִתְרַגְּשׁוּ	הִתְרַגְּשָׁה
lamed-yod heetpa'el:	הִתְגַּלּוּ	הִתְגַּלְּתָה

◄

The "tails" of the *lamed-yod* verbs are the same as those we saw in *pa'al* and *pee'el*:

	הם, הן	היא
lamed-yod pa'al:	קָנוּ	קָנְתָה
lamed-yod pee'el:	שִׁינּוּ	שִׁינְּתָה
lamed-yod heetpa'el:	הִתְגַּלּוּ	הִתְגַּלְּתָה

◄

Now let's see what happens to the "tails" of the **other** *lamed-yod* past tense forms. Read the following:

◄ בטיול שלי במדבר יהודה ישנתי באוהל. מכיוון שהיה קר מאוד, הִתְלַבַּשְׁתִּי בבגדים חמים, נכנסתי לשק השינה שלי וגם הִתְכַּסֵּיתִי בשתי שמיכות חמות.

On my hike in the Judean Desert I slept in a tent. Since it was very cold, I put on warm clothes, got into my sleeping bag and covered myself with two warm blankets.

As expected, the "tail" of the *lamed-yod* verb הִתְכַּסֵּיתִי (*heet-ka-SE-tee*) is **different** from that of the regular verb הִתְלַבַּשְׁתִּי (*heet-la-BASH-tee*). Also as expected, the original third root letter י appears in the *lamed-yod* form – as in the other *beenyaneem*. Compare:

lamed-yod pa'al:	ka-NEE-tee	קָנִיתִי
lamed-yod pee'el:	shee-NEE-tee	שִׁינִּיתִי
lamed-yod heetpa'el:	heet-ka-SE-tee	הִתְכַּסֵּיתִי

Notice that when written **without** vowel signs, the "tails" of these verbs all **look** the same (יתי-).

Q: In what way does the "tail" of the **heetpa'el** *lamed-yod* verb differ from the "tails" of the *pa'al* and *pee'el* verbs?

A: When pronounced, the "tail" of the *heetpa'el* verb begins with the vowel sound *eh* (*heet-ka-SE-tee* הִתְכַּסֵּיתִי), whereas in *pa'al* and *pee'el* the vowel sound is *ee* (*ka-NEE-tee* קָנִיתִי, *shee-NEE-tee* שִׁינִּיתִי).

Note: In *lamed-yod* verbs, the vowel sound before the endings תִי-, תָ- etc. is *ee* **only** in *pa'al* and *pee'el*. In **all other other** *beenyaneem*, the vowel sound before these endings is *eh*, as in *beenyan heetpa'el* (*heet-ka-SE-tee* הִתְכַּסֵּיתִי). (See charts at the end of this chapter.) No matter what the pronunciation, a י is **always written** before the first and second person endings.

Want to see if you've understood?
Write the missing past tense forms of the underlined verbs.

1. אורי <u>השתנה</u> מאז שראינו אותו בפעם האחרונה. גם אשתו _____.

   אולי גם אני _____?

2. הילדה ששיחקה על חוף הים <u>התכסתה</u> בחול. גם החברים שלה _____ בחול.

   אתם _____ פעם בחול?

Answers:

1. הִשְׁתַּנְתָה, הִשְׁתַּנֵּיתִי 2. הִתְכַּסּוּ, הִתְכַּסֵּיתֶם

Present tense (מִתְכַּסֶּה)

The present tense forms of *lamed-yod heetpa'el* verbs are formed according to the same "head and tail" principle:

	f.pl. אנחנו, אתן, הן	m.pl. אנחנו, אתם, הם	f.s. אני, את, היא	m.s. אני, אתה, הוא	
regular verb:	מִתְלַבְּשׁוֹת	מִתְלַבְּשִׁים	מִתְלַבֶּשֶׁת	מִתְלַבֵּשׁ	◄
lamed-yod:	מִתְכַּסוֹת	מִתְכַּסִים	מִתְכַּסָה	מִתְכַּסֶה	

Here, too, the "heads" of the *lamed-yod* verbs are the same as those of the regular verbs: מִתְלַבֵּשׁ, מִתְכַּסֶה. The *lamed-yod* "tails" are the same as those on *pa'al* and *pee'el* present tense forms:

◄	־ֶה	־ָה	־ִים	־וֹת
	-E	*-A*	*-EEM*	*-OT*

In *heetpa'el*, another feminine singular form – מִתְכַּסֵית (*meet-ka-SET*), also exists and is sometimes used. Here the original root letter י is seen.

Want to see if you've understood?

Write the missing present tense forms of the underlined verbs.

1. בכל דור המוזיקה <u>משתנה</u>, וגם סגנון הלבוש _____ .

2. כשקר בבית רמי <u>מתכסה</u> בשמיכה חמה. גם אנחנו _____ בשמיכה.

   שרה _____ בשתי שמיכות.

Answers:

1. מִשְׁתַּנֶה   2. מִתְכַּסִים, מִתְכַּסָה

Future tense (יִתְכַּסֶּה)

The "heads" of *heetpa'el lamed-yod* verbs are the same as those of regular *heetpa'el* verbs:

	אתה ... 	אני 	
regular verbs:	תִתְלַבֵּשׁ ...	אֶתְלַבֵּשׁ	◄
lamed-yod:	תִתְכַּסֶה ...	אֶתְכַּסֶה	

The "tails" are like those of *lamed-yod* verbs in the other *beenyaneem*:

	הם/הן	אתם/אתן	את	אתה...	אני	
lamed-yod pa'al:	יִקְנוּ	תִּקְנוּ	תִּקְנִי	תִּקְנֶה...	אֶקְנֶה	◄
lamed-yod pee'el:	יְשַׁנּוּ	תְּשַׁנּוּ	תְּשַׁנִּי	תְּשַׁנֶּה...	אֲשַׁנֶּה	
lamed-yod heetpa'el:	יִתְכַּסּוּ	תִּתְכַּסּוּ	תִּתְכַּסִּי	תִּתְכַּסֶּה...	אֶתְכַּסֶּה	
	-OO	-OO	-EE	-E	-E	

Want to see if you've understood?

Write the missing future tense forms of the underlined verbs.

1. אם מזג האוויר יִשְׁתַּנֶּה ויהיה קר מדיי, גם התוכניות שלנו לטייל בטבע _____.

2. אורי הבטיח לדויד שהסודות שלו לא יִתְגַּלוּ. דויד הבטיח לאורי שגם הסוד (*m.*) שלו לא _____.

Answers:

‏1. יִשְׁתַּנּוּ   2. יִתְגַּלֶּה

Infinitive (לְהִתְכַּסּוֹת)

Read the following sentence:

הילד הקטן עדיין לא יודע לְהִתְלַבֵּשׁ לבד, והוא גם לא יכול לְהִתְכַּסּוֹת בעצמו.   ◄

The small child still doesn't know how to get dressed by himself and also can't cover himself (in bed).

As expected, the "heads" of these two verbs are the same: לְהִתְלַבֵּשׁ and לְהִתְכַּסּוֹת. The "tail" of לְהִתְכַּסּוֹת is the same as those of *lamed-yod* verbs in other *beenyaneem*: לִקְנוֹת and לְשַׁנּוֹת.

Want to see if you've understood?

Write the missing infinitive forms of the underlined verbs.

1. יוסי, <u>השתנית</u> לטובה בשנה האחרונה. לא כל אחד יכול _____. כל הכבוד לך!

2. מחלת הסוכרת <u>מתגלה</u> לפעמים בגיל צעיר. היא יכולה _____ גם בגיל מבוגר.

Answers:

1. לְהִשְׁתַּנּוֹת   2. לְהִתְגַּלּוֹת

Let's review

◆ The "heads" of *lamed-yod heetpa'el* verbs are the same as those of regular *heetpa'el* verbs.

◆ In writing, the "tails" are the same as those of *lamed-yod* forms in *pa'al* and *pee'el*, however the **pronunciation** of the "tails" in the past tense forms that begin with a consonant (תָ– ,תִי–) is **different**: instead of *EE-tee, EE-ta*..., as in קָנִיתִי, קָנִית, we say *E-tee, E-ta*.... Compare:

	infinitive	future		present		past		
		הוא	אני	*f.s.*	*m.s.*	אני...	היא	הוא
regular heetpa'el:	לְהִתְלַבֵּשׁ	יִתְלַבֵּשׁ	אֶתְלַבֵּשׁ	מִתְלַבֶּשֶׁת	מִתְלַבֵּשׁ	הִתְלַבַּשְׁתִּי...	הִתְלַבְּשָׁה	הִתְלַבֵּשׁ
lamed-yod heetpa'el:	לְהִתְכַּסּוֹת	יִתְכַּסֶּה	אֶתְכַּסֶּה	מִתְכַּסָּה	מִתְכַּסֶּה	הִתְכַּסֵּיתִי...	הִתְכַּסְּתָה	הִתְכַּסָּה
						-E-tee		
lamed-yod pee'el:	לְשַׁנּוֹת	יְשַׁנֶּה	אֲשַׁנֶּה	מְשַׁנָּה	מְשַׁנֶּה	שִׁינִּיתִי...	שִׁינְּתָה	שִׁינָּה
lamed-yod pa'al:	לִקְנוֹת	יִקְנֶה	אֶקְנֶה	קוֹנָה	קוֹנֶה	קָנִיתִי...	קָנְתָה	קָנָה
	-OT	*-E*	*-E*	*-A*	*-E*	*-EE-tee*	*-TA*	*-A*

Chapter summary

Here are the three *beenyaneem* discussed in this chapter. The differences between *lamed-yod* and regular verbs have been highlighted. Below this chart is a chart with all of the *beenyaneem*. You can see that they have the same "tails" as the *beenyaneem* we have discussed.

◆ *Heetpa'el* התפעל	◆ *Pee'el* פיעל	◆ *Pa'al* פעל	
			עבר *past*
הִתְכַּסֵּיתִי	שִׁינִּיתִי	קָנִיתִי	אני
הִתְכַּסֵּיתָ	שִׁינִּיתָ	קָנִיתָ	אתה
הִתְכַּסֵּית	שִׁינִּית	קָנִית	את
הִתְכַּסֵּינוּ	שִׁינִּינוּ	קָנִינוּ	אנחנו
הִתְכַּסֵּיתֶם	שִׁינִּיתֶם	קָנִיתֶם / קְנִיתֶם [19]	אתם
הִתְכַּסֵּיתֶן	שִׁינִּיתֶן	קָנִיתֶן / קְנִיתֶן	אתן
הִתְכַּסָּה	שִׁינָּה	קָנָה	הוא
הִתְכַּסְּתָה	שִׁינְּתָה	קָנְתָה	היא
הִתְכַּסּוּ	שִׁינּוּ	קָנוּ	הם/הן
			הווה *present*
מִתְכַּסֶּה	מְשַׁנֶּה	קוֹנֶה	אני, אתה, הוא
מִתְכַּסָּה/מִתְכַּסֵּית	מְשַׁנָּה	קוֹנָה	אני, את, היא
מִתְכַּסִּים	מְשַׁנִּים	קוֹנִים	אנחנו, אתם, הם
מִתְכַּסּוֹת	מְשַׁנּוֹת	קוֹנוֹת	אנחנו, אתן, הן
			עתיד *future*
אֶתְכַּסֶּה	אֲשַׁנֶּה	אֶקְנֶה	אני
תִּתְכַּסֶּה	תְּשַׁנֶּה	תִּקְנֶה	אתה
יִתְכַּסֶּה	יְשַׁנֶּה	יִקְנֶה	הוא
תִּתְכַּסֶּה	תְּשַׁנֶּה	תִּקְנֶה	היא
נִתְכַּסֶּה	נְשַׁנֶּה	נִקְנֶה	אנחנו
תִּתְכַּסִּי	תְּשַׁנִּי	תִּקְנִי	את
תִּתְכַּסּוּ	תְּשַׁנּוּ	תִּקְנוּ	אתם/אתן
יִתְכַּסּוּ	יְשַׁנּוּ	יִקְנוּ	הם/הן
לְהִתְכַּסּוֹת	לְשַׁנּוֹת	לִקְנוֹת	שם הפועל *infinitive*
to cover oneself	to change something/someone	to buy	

---

19 The pronunciation used by most Hebrew speakers today is קָנִיתֶם / קָנִיתֶן (*ka-NEE-tem, ka-NEE-ten*). It should be noted that according to the rules of grammar, the stress is on the **ending** of the אתם and אתן forms, and this causes the first vowel to "reduce" (it is written as a *shva*): קְנִיתֶם / קְנִיתֶן (*knee-TEM, knee-TEN* or *ke-nee-TEM, ke-nee-TEN*). See the chapter "Reduction of Vowels and the *Shva*," pp. 640-645.

Lamed-yod verbs in all the *beenyaneem*:

◆ Neef'al נפעל	◆ Hoof'al הופעל	◆ Heef'eel הפעיל	◆ Poo'al פועל	◆ Heetpa'el התפעל	◆ Pee'el פיעל	◆ Pa'al פעל	
							עבר *past*
נִבְנֵיתִי[20]	הוּפְנֵיתִי	הִפְנֵיתִי	כּוּסֵיתִי	הִתְכַּסֵּיתִי	שִׁינֵּיתִי	קָנִיתִי	אני
נִבְנֵיתָ	הוּפְנֵיתָ	הִפְנֵיתָ	כּוּסֵיתָ	הִתְכַּסֵּיתָ	שִׁינֵּיתָ	קָנִיתָ	אתה
נִבְנֵית	הוּפְנֵית	הִפְנֵית	כּוּסֵית	הִתְכַּסֵּית	שִׁינֵּית	קָנִית	את
נִבְנֵינוּ	הוּפְנֵינוּ	הִפְנֵינוּ	כּוּסֵינוּ	הִתְכַּסֵּינוּ	שִׁינֵּינוּ	קָנִינוּ	אנחנו
נִבְנֵיתֶם	הוּפְנֵיתֶם	הִפְנֵיתֶם	כּוּסֵיתֶם	הִתְכַּסֵּיתֶם	שִׁינֵּיתֶם	קָנִיתֶם[21]	אתם
נִבְנֵיתֶן	הוּפְנֵיתֶן	הִפְנֵיתֶן	כּוּסֵיתֶן	הִתְכַּסֵּיתֶן	שִׁינֵּיתֶן	קָנִיתֶן	אתן
נִבְנָה	הוּפְנָה	הִפְנָה	כּוּסָה	הִתְכַּסָּה	שִׁינָּה	קָנָה	הוא
נִבְנְתָה	הוּפְנְתָה	הִפְנְתָה	כּוּסְתָה	הִתְכַּסְּתָה	שִׁינְּתָה	קָנְתָה	היא
נִבְנוּ	הוּפְנוּ	הִפְנוּ	כּוּסוּ	הִתְכַּסּוּ	שִׁינּוּ	קָנוּ	הם/הן
							הווה *present*
נִבְנָה	מוּפְנָה	מַפְנֶה	מְכוּסֶה	מִתְכַּסֶּה	מְשַׁנֶּה	קוֹנֶה	אני, אתה, הוא
נִבְנֵית	מוּפְנָה/מוּפְנֵית	מַפְנָה	מְכוּסָה	מִתְכַּסָּה/מִתְכַּסֵּית[22]	מְשַׁנָּה	קוֹנָה	אני, את, היא
נִבְנִים	מוּפְנִים	מַפְנִים	מְכוּסִים	מִתְכַּסִּים	מְשַׁנִּים	קוֹנִים	אנחנו, אתם, הם
נִבְנוֹת	מוּפְנוֹת	מַפְנוֹת	מְכוּסוֹת	מִתְכַּסּוֹת	מְשַׁנּוֹת	קוֹנוֹת	אנחנו, אתן, הן
							עתיד *future*
אֶבָּנֶה	אוּפְנֶה	אַפְנֶה	אֲכוּסֶה	אֶתְכַּסֶּה	אֲשַׁנֶּה	אֶקְנֶה	אני
תִּיבָּנֶה	תּוּפְנֶה	תַּפְנֶה	תְּכוּסֶה	תִּתְכַּסֶּה	תְּשַׁנֶּה	תִּקְנֶה	אתה
יִיבָּנֶה	יוּפְנֶה	יַפְנֶה	יְכוּסֶה	יִתְכַּסֶּה	יְשַׁנֶּה	יִקְנֶה	הוא
תִּיבָּנֶה	תּוּפְנֶה	תַּפְנֶה	תְּכוּסֶה	תִּתְכַּסֶּה	תְּשַׁנֶּה	תִּקְנֶה	היא
נִיבָּנֶה	נוּפְנֶה	נַפְנֶה	נְכוּסֶה	נִתְכַּסֶּה	נְשַׁנֶּה	נִקְנֶה	אנחנו
תִּיבָּנִי	תּוּפְנִי	תַּפְנִי	תְּכוּסִי	תִּתְכַּסִּי	תְּשַׁנִּי	תִּקְנִי	את
תִּיבָּנוּ	תּוּפְנוּ	תַּפְנוּ	תְּכוּסוּ	תִּתְכַּסּוּ	תְּשַׁנּוּ	תִּקְנוּ	אתם/אתן
יִיבָּנוּ	יוּפְנוּ	יַפְנוּ	יְכוּסוּ	יִתְכַּסּוּ	יְשַׁנּוּ	יִקְנוּ	הם/הן
לְהִיבָּנוֹת		לְהַפְנוֹת		לְהִתְכַּסּוֹת	לְשַׁנּוֹת	לִקְנוֹת	**שם הפועל** *infinitive*
to be built	to be referred to	to refer someone to	to be covered	to cover oneself	to change (something/someone)	to buy	

---

20 This specific verb is used mainly in the third person. The forms given here are sometimes used in a metaphorical sense, as in the song by Menashe Rabina: "אנו באנו ארצה לבנות ולהיבנות" ("We've come to the Land of Israel to build it and to be built by it").

21 See above, note 19.

22 In the present tense of *heetpa'el* and *hoof'al*, an additional feminine singular form ending in ית- (-ET) is sometimes used. In *neef'al* the form ending in ית- is the **only** form used today.

5. Verbs Whose Third Root Letter Is א׳

גְּזֵרַת ל״א

Preview

• *Guidelines for pronouncing* lamed-'alef *verbs*

• Lamed-'alef *forms that are different from regular verbs*

Introduction

Even though א׳ at the end of a root in verbs is often **not pronounced** at all (see explanation below), in writing it almost always **appears**. This persistent א׳ also frequently "sees to it" that its presence is felt by affecting the vowels that **precede** it (as in הִתְפַּלֵּאתִי as opposed to הִתְלַבַּשְׁתִּי) and by causing other noticeable changes in vowels and form (e.g., אֶקְרָא rather than אֶכְתּוֹב). These changes are the focus of this chapter.

• *Guidelines for pronouncing* lamed-'alef *verbs*

Before we discuss the forms of *lamed-'alef* verbs, let's look at some guidelines for pronouncing them.

When is א׳ silent?

As a rule, when א׳ is **not** followed by a vowel, it is **not** pronounced. Here are some examples:

1. When א׳ appears at the very **end** of a word, as in:

הִקְפִּיא	מִילֵּא	לִמְצוֹא	מוֹצֵא	קָרָא
heek-PEE	*mee-LE*	*leem-TSO*	*mo-TSE*	*ka-RA*
he froze (something)	he filled	to find	is finding	he read, called out

If we were to erase the final א׳ that appears in these words (and leave the vowel signs for guidance), our pronunciation would **not change**.

Be careful! Unlike ע', a final א' is **never** preceded by a "helping *ah*." Compare:

לְהַשְׁפִּיעַ	לִשְׁמוֹעַ	שׁוֹמֵעַ	◄
le-hash-PEE-a	leesh-MO-a	sho-ME-a[1]	
to influence	to hear	he hears	
לְהַקְפִּיא	לִמְצוֹא	מוֹצֵא	
le-hak-PEE	leem-TSO	mo-TSE	

2. When א' appears at the **end** of a syllable in the middle of a word, it is not pronounced, for example:

הִקְ-פֵּא-תִי	קָ-רָא-תִי	◄
heek-PE-tee	ka-RA-tee	
I froze (something)	I read, called out	

Here, too, were we to erase the א', our pronunciation of these words would not change.

3. Also, when א' appears in the **middle** of a syllable, it is not pronounced, for example:

◄ אתמול קָרָאת שלושה מאמרים, ועכשיו את קוֹרֵאת מאמר נוסף?!

ka-RAT   ko-RET

Yesterday you (*f.s.*) read three articles, and now you are reading another one (lit.: article)?!

Here, again, if we were to erase the silent א' in these words, their pronunciation would not be affected.

Be careful! Since we don't hear or pronounce the א' in words like those mentioned above, we simply must know that their final root letter is א', and we have to write the א' in order to spell the word correctly.

---

1   We have indicated above the pronunciation used by Hebrew speakers who do not pronounce the ע' but still add the *helping ah* (*furtive patach* פַּתָח גָנוּב). The transcription with ע' is: *le-hash-PEE-a', leesh-MO-a', sho-ME-a'.*

When is 'א pronounced?

'א is pronounced as a kind of "catch" in the throat[2] whenever it is followed by a vowel. Here are some examples:

followed by ah (הָ-): עדי קָרְאָה בעיתון על מכונית גנובה שנִמְצְאָה לאחר שלוש שנים. ◄

neem-tse-'A   *kar-'A*

Adi read in the newspaper about a stolen car that was found after three years.

followed by oo ("וּ): הילדים מָצְאוּ את המתנות שהוּחְבְּאוּ בתוך הארון. ◄

hooch-be-'OO   *mats-'OO*

The children found the presents that had been hidden in the closet.

followed by ee (-י):   בכל יום שישי אנחנו קוֹרְאִים את העיתון ומְמַלְאִים את התשבץ השבועי. ◄

me-mal-'EEM   *kor-'EEM*

Every Friday we read the newspaper and fill in the weekly crossword puzzle.

followed by oh ("וֹ):

כשהתלמידות בבית הספר היסודי לבנות יוֹצְאוֹת לחצר, תמיד נִמְצָאוֹת שם שתי מורות. ◄

neem-tsa-'OT   *yots-'OT*

When the students at the elementary school for girls go out to the playground, two teachers are always there.

Let's review

- ◆ As a rule, when 'א is **not** followed by a vowel, it is **not** pronounced, as in:

הִבְרִיא	נִמְצֵאתִי	קוֹרֵאת	קָרָא	◄
heev-REE	*neem-TSE-tee*	*ko-RET*	*ka-RA*	

- ◆ 'א is **pronounced** as a kind of "catch" in the throat whenever it is followed by a vowel, as in:

הִבְרִיאוּ	נִמְצָאוֹת	קוֹרְאִים	◄
heev-REE-'oo	*neem-tsa-'OT*	*kor-'EEM*	

---

2   In books on phonetics, this is often referred to as a "glottal stop." Laufer mentions three ways in which Hebrew speakers realize (pronounce) the 'א: as a short glottal stop, as "creaky voice" or as nothing (i.e., it is not pronounced). Asher Laufer, 2008, pp. 80-81.

Want to see if you've understood?

Read the following verbs out loud. Circle the forms in which the 'א is heard.

1. מָצָאנוּ   2. הִתְפַּלֵּא   3. הִקְפִּיאוּ   4. נִמְצָאוֹת   5. תִּקְרְאִי   6. לִקְרוֹא   7. לְהַמְצִיא   8. תִּתְפַּלְּאִי

Answers:

6. leek-RO   5. neem-tsa-'OT   4. teek-re-'EE   3. heek-PEE-'oo   2. heet-pa-LE   1. ma-TSA-noo
Circled: 3, 4, 5, 8   8. teet-pal-'EE   7. le-ham-TSEE

• Lamed-'alef *forms that are different from regular verbs*

In writing, *lamed-'alef* verbs look the same as *regular* verbs. However, there are two cases in which the 'א causes a significant change in **pronunciation**:

1. *Feminine singular forms in the present tense*

Read the following sentences containing feminine singular verbs in the present.

➤ *beenyan pa'al:*   כשמיכל לומֶדֶת למבחנים, היא קוֹרֵאת את כל החומר לפחות שלוש פעמים.
                            ko-RET   lo-ME-det
When Michal studies for exams, she reads all the material at least three times.

beenyan pee'el: כששרה מְדַבֶּרֶת מהר, היא לא מְבַטֵאת את כל המילים בצורה ברורה.
                         me-va-TET   me-da-BE-ret
When Sarah speaks quickly, she doesn't pronounce all her (lit.: the) words clearly.

beenyan heetpa'el: נועה מִתְרַגֶּשֶׁת לפני כל מבחן ומִתְפַּלֵּאת שסטודנטים אחרים לא מתרגשים.
                        meet-pa-LET   meet-ra-GE-shet
Noa gets nervous before every exam and is amazed that the other students don't get nervous.

Since the verbs in each sentence belong to the same *beenyan*, they **begin** with the same *pattern*:

	lamed-'alef		*regular*
pa'al:	קוֹרֵאת	⇔	לומֶדֶת
pee'el:	מְבַטֵאת	⇔	מְדַבֶּרֶת
heetpa'el:	מִתְפַּלֵּאת	⇔	מִתְרַגֶּשֶׁת

Q: What is the difference between the way the regular verbs and the *lamed-'alef* verbs end?

A: The regular verbs end with the sounds *E-et* (לוֹמֶדֶת *lo-ME-det*, מְדַבֶּרֶת *me-da-BE-ret*, מִתְרַגֶּשֶׁת *meet-ra-GE-shet*), whereas the *lamed-'alef* verbs have only **one** *eh* vowel before their final 'ת (קוֹרֵאת *ko-RET*, מְבַטֵּאת *me-va-TET*, מִתְפַּלֵּאת *meet-pa-LET*).[3] These feminine singular forms in *beenyaneem pa'al*, *pee'el* and *heetpa'el* can actually be created simply by adding a 'ת to the masculine singular forms:

קוֹרֵאת	⇐	קוֹרֵא	◄
ko-RET		*ko-RE*	
מְבַטֵּאת	⇐	מְבַטֵּא	
me-va-TET		*me-va-TE*	
מִתְפַּלֵּאת	⇐	מִתְפַּלֵּא	
meet-pa-LET		*meet-pa-LE*	

As mentioned above, the 'א in *lamed-'alef* feminine singular forms that end in *-ET* is **not pronounced**, but it is always **written** in Modern Hebrew.

Note: In *heef'eel* there is **no difference** between the present tense feminine singular form of regular verbs (מַרְגִּישָׁה) and *lamed-'alef* verbs (מַמְצִיאָה) since it is the only *beenyan* in which the regular feminine singular form ends in *-A* (מַרְגִּישָׁה) rather than *E-et* (e.g., לוֹמֶדֶת).

2. Past tense forms with endings that begins with a consonant (-תִי, -תָ ...)

Read the following sentences containing verbs in the past tense:

beenyan pee'el: למה לא סִיפַּרְתֶם לנו שכבר מִילֵּאתֶם את הטופס לבקשת דרכון חדש? ◄
mee-LE-tem *see-PAR-tem*

Why didn't you (*m.pl.*) tell us that you already filled out the form for ordering a new passport?

beenyan heef'eel: הִרְגַּשְׁנוּ לא טוב בשבוע שעבר, אבל בינתיים הִבְרֵאנוּ.
heev-RE-noo *heer-GASH-noo*

We didn't feel well last week, but since then we've gotten better.

---

3 In addition to feminine singular forms like מְבַטֵּאת and מִתְפַּלֵּאת, present tense feminine singular forms ending in הָ (*-AH*) also exist and are often used in speech, for example:

מְבַטְּאָה, מִתְפַּלְּאָה ◄

These forms are grammatically correct. Many speakers who use these forms pronounce them as if the 'א were not present, as in *lamed-yod* verbs like מְשַׁנָּה and מִתְכַּסָּה. They say: *me-va-TA* and *meet-pa-LA*.

beenyan heetpa'el:

הִתְרַגַּשְׁתִּי כשהבת שלי קיבלה את פרס ההצטיינות, וְהִתְפַּלֵּאתִי שהיא לא התרגשה כמוני.

heet-pa-LE-tee   *heet-ra-GASH-tee*

I got excited when my daughter received a prize for excellence, and I was amazed that she didn't get as excited as I did.

Since the verbs in each sentence belong to the same *beenyan*, they **begin** with the same pattern:

	lamed-'alef		regular	
pee'el:	מִילֵּאתֶם	⇔	סִיפַּרְתֶּם	◄
heef'eel:	הִבְרֵאנוּ	⇔	הִרְגַּשְׁנוּ	
heetpa'el:	הִתְפַּלֵּאתִי	⇔	הִתְרַגַּשְׁתִּי	

Now look at the **regular** verbs only. In keeping with the conjugation rules of past tense verbs in all *beenyaneem*,[4] the vowel before endings that begin with a consonant (i.e., ‎-תִי, ‎-תָ, ‎-תְ, ‎-נוּ, ‎-תֶם, ‎-תֶן) is *ah*: סִיפַּרְתֶּם (*see-PAR-tem*), הִרְגַּשְׁנוּ (*heer-GASH-noo*), הִתְרַגַּשְׁתִּי (*heet-ra-GASH-tee*).

Q: What vowel comes before these endings in the *lamed-'alef* verbs?

A: The vowel *eh*: מִילֵּאתֶם (*mee-LE-tem*), הִבְרֵאנוּ (*heev-RE-noo*), הִתְפַּלֵּאתִי (*heet-pa-LE-tee*). The א is always written, but never pronounced.

This change from *ah* to *eh* before consonantal endings takes place in *lamed-'alef* verbs in all *beenyaneem* except for *pa'al*. Most verbs in *beenyan pa'al* keep the *ah* vowel before the consonantal endings, just like regular verbs:

כָּתַבְתִּי חיבור על הטיול שלי באירופה, ואחר כך קָרָאתִי אותו לשותפה שלי לחדר. ◄

ka-RA-tee   *ka-TAV-tee*

I wrote a composition about my trip to Europe, and afterwards I read it to my roommate.

However, there are several *pa'al* verbs that have an *eh* vowel before the consonantal endings. The most common of these verbs is לִשְׂנוֹא (to hate):

שָׂנֵאתָ,   שָׂנֵאתִי ◄

sa-NE-ta   *sa-NE-tee*

---

4   See the chapter "Regular Verbs in All *Beenyaneem:* Summary," pp. 444-446 (number 1).

Did you know?
Sometimes 'א becomes 'י

As mentioned at the beginning of this chapter, when 'א is the third root letter, it almost always appears in the written form of a word, even if it is not pronounced.

There are, however, some forms related to verbs (i.e., adjectives and *verbal nouns*) in which the 'א of the root changes to a 'י. Here are some examples:

- Adjectives of the כָּ□□וּ□ (*pa'ool*) pattern (*model form*: כָּתוּב)[5]

  Some *lamed-'alef* adjectives retain their final 'א:

		f.pl.	m.pl.	f.s.	m.s.	
frozen	(*root*: ק-פ-א)	קְפוּאוֹת	קְפוּאִים,	קְפוּאָה,	קָפוּא,	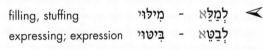
hated	(*root*: ש-נ-א)	שְׂנוּאוֹת	שְׂנוּאִים,	שְׂנוּאָה,	שָׂנוּא,	

  Others have a 'י instead:

  | found | (*root*: מ-צ-א) | מְצוּיוֹת | מְצוּיִּים, | מְצוּיָה, | מָצוּי, | |
  | called | (*root*: ק-ר-א) | קְרוּיוֹת | קְרוּיִּים, | קְרוּיָה, | קָרוּי, | |

  The adjective from the root נ-ש-א (as in the verb: משה נָשָׂא את שרה לאישה Moshe married Sarah) is special. Only the masculine singular form loses its 'א.

  | married | נְשׂוּאוֹת | נְשׂוּאִים, | נְשׂוּאָה, | נָשׂוּי, | |

- Verbal nouns of *beenyan pee'el* (*model form*: דִּיבּוּר)[6]

  The verbal nouns of most *lamed-'alef* verbs in *pee'el* lose their final 'א and have a 'י instead, for example:

  | filling, stuffing | מִילּוּי | - | לְמַלֵּא |
  | expressing; expression | בִּיטוּי | - | לְבַטֵּא |

---

5   For more on adjectives that result from verbs, see the chapter "Adjectives Resulting from an Action Taken and Completed," pp. 159-169.

6   For more on verbal nouns, see the chapter "Verbal Nouns," pp. 108-123.

Let's review

Lamed-'alef verbs **look** the same as regular verbs, but in two cases the א' causes a change in vowels and, hence, in **pronunciation**:

♦ In feminine singular forms in the present tense

Regular verbs in all *beenyaneem* except *heef'eel* end in *E-et*, while *lamed-'alef* verbs end in -*ET*, for example:

	lamed-'alef		*regular*	
pa'al:	קוֹרֵאת	⇔	חוֹשֶׁבֶת	◄
pee'el:	מְבַטֵּאת	⇔	מְדַבֶּרֶת	

In *beenyan heef'eel*, regular and *lamed-'alef* verbs are the same: מַרְגִּישָׁה, מַמְצִיאָה.

♦ In the past tense, the vowel before endings that begin with a consonant (תִי-, ...תָ-), which is *ah* in regular verbs, changes to *eh* in *lamed-'alef* verbs, as in:

	lamed-'alef		*regular*	
pee'el:	מִילֵּאתֶם	⇐	סִיפַּרְתֶּם	◄
heef'eel:	הִבְרֵאנוּ	⇐	הִרְגַּשְׁנוּ	

This does **not** usually happen in *beenyan pa'al* – e.g., קָרָאתִי, מָצָאתִי – except for in a small number of verbs like שָׂנֵאתִי (with *eh*).

Want to see if you've understood?

Write the missing forms of the underlined verbs and say it out loud.

1. אתה <u>קורא</u> ספרים באנגלית ושרה _____ ספרים בצרפתית.

2. קשה לי <u>לבטא</u> את שמך. איך את _____ אותו?
   (present)

3. יובל <u>הבריא</u> סוף סוף מהשפעת. גם אתם _____?

4. מישהו <u>מצא</u> את הספר שלי? דויד, אולי אתה _____ אותו?

Answers:

1. קוֹרֵאת (ko-RET)   2. מְבַטֵּאת (me-va-TET)   3. הִבְרֵאתֶם (heev-RE-tem)   4. מָצָאתָ (ma-TSA-ta)

Chapter summary

◆ Neef'al נפעל	◆ Hoof'al הופעל	◆ Poo'al פועל	◆ Heef'eel הפעיל	◆ Heetpa'el התפעל	◆ Pee'el פיעל	◆ Pa'al פעל	
							past עבר
נִמְצֵאתִי	הוּחְבֵּאתִי⁹	דּוּכֵּאתִי⁸	הִבְרֵאתִי	הִתְפַּלֵּאתִי	מִילֵּאתִי	קָרָאתִי⁷	אני
נִמְצֵאתָ	הוּחְבֵּאתָ	דּוּכֵּאתָ	הִבְרֵאתָ	הִתְפַּלֵּאתָ	מִילֵּאתָ	קָרָאתָ	אתה
נִמְצֵאת	הוּחְבֵּאת	דּוּכֵּאת	הִבְרֵאת	הִתְפַּלֵּאת	מִילֵּאת	קָרָאת	את
נִמְצֵאנוּ	הוּחְבֵּאנוּ	דּוּכֵּאנוּ	הִבְרֵאנוּ	הִתְפַּלֵּאנוּ	מִילֵּאנוּ	קָרָאנוּ	אנחנו
נִמְצֵאתֶם	הוּחְבֵּאתֶם	דּוּכֵּאתֶם	הִבְרֵאתֶם	הִתְפַּלֵּאתֶם	מִילֵּאתֶם	קָרָאתֶם¹⁰	אתם
נִמְצֵאתֶן	הוּחְבֵּאתֶן	דּוּכֵּאתֶן	הִבְרֵאתֶן	הִתְפַּלֵּאתֶן	מִילֵּאתֶן	קָרָאתֶן	אתן
נִמְצָא	הוּחְבָּא	דּוּכָּא	הִבְרִיא	הִתְפַּלֵּא	מִילֵּא	קָרָא	הוא
נִמְצְאָה	הוּחְבְּאָה	דּוּכְּאָה	הִבְרִיאָה	הִתְפַּלְּאָה	מִילְּאָה	קָרְאָה	היא
נִמְצְאוּ	הוּחְבְּאוּ	דּוּכְּאוּ	הִבְרִיאוּ	הִתְפַּלְּאוּ	מִילְּאוּ	קָרְאוּ	הם/הן
							present הווה
נִמְצָא	מוּחְבָּא	מְדוּכָּא	מַבְרִיא	מִתְפַּלֵּא	מְמַלֵּא	קוֹרֵא	אני, אתה, הוא
נִמְצֵאת	מוּחְבֵּאת	מְדוּכֵּאת	מַבְרִיאָה	מִתְפַּלֵּאת¹²	מְמַלֵּאת¹¹	קוֹרֵאת	אני, את, היא
נִמְצָאִים	מוּחְבָּאִים	מְדוּכָּאִים	מַבְרִיאִים	מִתְפַּלְאִים	מְמַלְאִים	קוֹרְאִים	אנחנו, אתם, הם
נִמְצָאוֹת	מוּחְבָּאוֹת	מְדוּכָּאוֹת	מַבְרִיאוֹת	מִתְפַּלְאוֹת	מְמַלְאוֹת	קוֹרְאוֹת	אנחנו, אתן, הן
							future עתיד
אֶמָּצֵא	אוּחְבָּא	אֲדוּכָּא	אַבְרִיא	אֶתְפַּלֵּא	אֲמַלֵּא	אֶקְרָא	אני
תִּימָצֵא	תּוּחְבָּא	תְּדוּכָּא	תַּבְרִיא	תִּתְפַּלֵּא	תְּמַלֵּא	תִּקְרָא	אתה
יִימָצֵא	יוּחְבָּא	יְדוּכָּא	יַבְרִיא	יִתְפַּלֵּא	יְמַלֵּא	יִקְרָא	הוא
תִּימָצֵא	תּוּחְבָּא	תְּדוּכָּא	תַּבְרִיא	תִּתְפַּלֵּא	תְּמַלֵּא	תִּקְרָא	היא
נִימָצֵא	נוּחְבָּא	נְדוּכָּא	נַבְרִיא	נִתְפַּלֵּא	נְמַלֵּא	נִקְרָא	אנחנו

7 A few verbs in *pa'al* do have an *eh* vowel in the past as in the other *beenyaneem*. One of them is the verb שָׂנָא (to hate), as in: שָׂנֵאתִי (*sa-NE-tee*), שָׂנֵאתָ (*sa-NE-ta*)…

8 These *poo'al* and *hoof'al* verbs are used in the past and future tense mainly in the *third person* (הוא, היא, הם, הן).

9 See note 8.

10 According to the rules of grammar, the stress is on the ending of the אתם and אתן forms. This is true of all the אתם and אתן forms in the table above. In *beenyan pa'al* verbs, the stress on the final syllable causes the first vowel to "reduce" and be written as *shva*, e.g.: קְרָאתֶם (*kra-TEM* or *ke-ra-TEM*).

11 In *beenyaneem pee'el* and *heetpa'el*, present tense feminine singular forms ending in הָ- (-A) are often used in speech, for example: מְבַטָּאָה, מִתְפַּלְאָה. Forms like these are grammatically correct and are also commonly used here and there in other *beenyaneem*, for example: היא קוֹרְאָה (she is reading / calling out) and היא מְדוּכָּאָה (she is depressed).

12 See note 11.

◆ Neef'al נפעל	◆ Hoof'al הופעל	◆ Poo'al פועל	◆ Heef'eel הפעיל	◆ Heetpa'el התפעל	◆ Pee'el פיעל	◆ Pa'al פעל	
תִּימָצְאִי	תּוּחְבְּאִי	תְּדוּכְּאִי	תַּבְרִיאִי	תִּתְפַּלְּאִי	תְּמַלְּאִי	תִּקְרְאִי	את
תִּימָצְאוּ	תּוּחְבְּאוּ	תְּדוּכְּאוּ	תַּבְרִיאוּ	תִּתְפַּלְּאוּ	תְּמַלְּאוּ	תִּקְרְאוּ	אתם/אתן
יִימָצְאוּ	יוּחְבְּאוּ	יְדוּכְּאוּ	יַבְרִיאוּ	יִתְפַּלְּאוּ	יְמַלְּאוּ	יִקְרְאוּ	הם/הן
לְהִימָצֵא			לְהַבְרִיא	לְהִתְפַּלֵּא	לְמַלֵּא	לִקְרוֹא	**שם הפועל**
to be found	to be hidden	to become depressed, to be oppressed, crushed (a revolt)	to become healthy, recuperate	to be amazed	to fill, to fill out	to read, to call out	*infinitive*

VI. Command Forms (Imperatives)
צִיוּוּי

Preview
- *When do we use imperative forms?*
- *Creating imperative forms*
- *Negative commands*

• *When do we use imperative forms?*

Here are some instructions commonly found in **formal** (and, in this case, written) Hebrew:

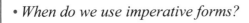

Write (*m.s.*) the correct word.	כְּתוֹב את המילה הנכונה.
Look up (*m.s.*) the new words in the dictionary.	חַפֵּשׂ את המילים החדשות במילון.

The words highlighted in these sentences are called *commands* or *imperatives* (צִיוּוּי). They are verb forms used to tell the reader or listener what to do or not to do. For this reason, they are always addressed to "you" (*s.* or *pl.*), but without the "you" pronouns: אתה, את, אתם, אתן.

In Modern Hebrew, we often ask someone to do something by using the future tense forms instead of the imperative. In most cases, the future tense forms are **less formal** than the imperative. Thus, instead of the above, we would say (or write):

Write (*m.s.*) the correct word, please. (lit.: you will write)	תִכְתּוֹב את המילה הנכונה, בבקשה.
Look up (*m.s.*) the new words in the dictionary. (lit.: you will look up)	תְחַפֵּשׂ את המילים החדשות במילון.

These future tense forms usually sound a bit less direct and harsh than imperative forms.

Even though most imperative forms are used only in **formal** Hebrew, some are also frequently used in **informal** Hebrew, including in everyday speech. For example, a parent might say to a child:

◄ בּוֹא הנה (בבקשה) וְשֵׁב ליד השולחן!   Come (*m.s.*) here (please) and sit at the table!

The imperatives used in informal Hebrew are all **short** and belong to special *root groups* (גְּזָרוֹת[1]) in **beenyan pa'al**. Here are some more examples:

1st root letter נ (פ״נ)			*1st root letter* י (פ״י)			*2nd root letter* ו or י (ע״וי)		
סַע!	קַח!	תֵּן לִי...!	לֵךְ!	צֵא!	רֵד!	שִׂים!	רוּץ!	קוּם!
Go!	Take!	Give me...!	Go!	Go out!	Go down!	Put!	Run!	Get up!
(to a driver)				Leave!				

The longer feminine singular and plural forms of these words (e.g., קוּמִי, קוּמוּ), which we will discuss below, are also used in everyday speech. The future tense forms of verbs like these (e.g., תֵּשֵׁב, תָּבוֹא) are also sometimes used in informal Hebrew.

Did you know?

1. *Please...*(אָנָא, נָא, בְּבַקָשָׁה)

In formal, especially written Hebrew, the word אָנָא (please) is sometimes added before the imperative, as in:

◄ אנא הודיעו לנו באי-מייל...   Please inform us by e-mail...

Alternatively, the form נָא is sometimes, though less frequently, used before the imperative:[2]

◄ נא כתוב לנו את דעתך.   Please send us your opinion in writing (lit.: write to us).

Another way of softening a command is by adding בְּבַקָשָׁה, which is less formal than אנא and נא, for example:

◄ קומי, בבקשה!   Please get up! (*f.s.*)

שימו לב, בבקשה!   Please pay attention! (*pl.*)

---

1   For more on special root groups, see the chapter "Special Root Groups," Introduction, pp. 488-489.

2   נא appears more frequently before an infinitive form (e.g., ...נא לכתוב). See below, p. 577.

> ## 2. *Imperatives and political correctness*
>
> In the past it was customary to use **masculine singular** imperative forms when giving instructions to all readers. This usage is still sometimes found in texts today. For example, on exams you may find instructions such as "כתוב את הפועל המתאים" (Write the appropriate verb). In cookbooks, feminine singular forms are sometimes used under the assumption that most cooks are women (!), e.g., "הוסיפי כוס חלב," (Add a cup of milk). As awareness of political correctness increases in Israeli society, these singular forms are being replaced more and more with plural forms, e.g., "כתבו את הפועל".

• *Creating imperative forms*

In today's Hebrew, three imperative forms – for אתה (*m.s.*), אַת (*f.s.*) and אתם/אתן (*pl.*) – are generally used. In *beenyaneem **pa'al*** and ***pee'el*** these forms usually resemble **future tense** forms. For example, compare:

	עתיד	ציווי
	future	*imperative*
(אתה):	תָקוּם	קוּם!
(אַת):	תָקוּמִי	קוּמִי!
(אתם/אתן):	תָקוּמוּ	קוּמוּ![3]

In these two *beenyaneem*, we usually use the future tense forms as our starting point for creating imperatives. In contrast, as we will see below, in the *beenyaneem* whose infinitive contains a ה' – להיכנס (*neef'al*), להתלבש (*heetpa'el*), להרגיש (*heef'eel*) – we use the **infinitive** (and not the future tense forms) as our starting point. The remaining *beenyaneem* – the passive *beenyaneem* ***poo'al*** and ***hoof'al*** – do not have imperative forms.

Pa'al *and* pee'el: *starting from future tense forms*

Beenyan pa'al (כְּתוֹב)

Now look again at the forms of the verb לָקוּם shown above.

---

3   In Biblical Hebrew, there is a separate form for אתן: קומנה! (קֻמְנָה). This is used today only in very formal or literary Hebrew.

Q: How do we create imperatives from their future tense forms?

A: In the case of לָקוּם, we simply take off the *prefix* תָּ-:

		imperative		future
◄	(אתה):	קוּם!	⇐	תָּקוּם
	(את):	קוּמִי!	⇐	תָּקוּמִי
	(אתם/אתן):	קוּמוּ!	⇐	תָּקוּמוּ

This method works for *pa'al* verbs that belong to **special** root groups. Here are some more examples:

(ל"י)		(פ"נ)		(פ"י)		(ע/ו"י)	
3rd root letter י		first root letter נ		1st root letter י		2nd root letter ו or י	
imperative	future	imperative	future	imperative	future	imperative	future

◄	(אתה):	קְנֵה![4] ⇐ תִּקְנֶה		סַע! ⇐ תִּ/סַע		שֵׁב! ⇐ תֵּשֵׁב		שִׂים! ⇐ תָּשִׂים	
	(את):	קְנִי! ⇐ תִּקְנִי		סְעִי! ⇐ תִּ/סְעִי		שְׁבִי! ⇐ תֵּשְׁבִי		שִׂימִי! ⇐ תָּשִׂימִי	
	(אתם/אתן):	קְנוּ! ⇐ תִּקְנוּ		סְעוּ! ⇐ תִּ/סְעוּ		שְׁבוּ! ⇐ תֵּשְׁבוּ		שִׂימוּ! ⇐ תָּשִׂימוּ	
	Buy!		Go!		Sit!		Put...!	

This is also the way we arrive at the imperative **base forms** (= אתה forms) of *regular* verbs in *beenyan pa'al*, including almost all verbs with *gutturals* (א', ה', ח', ע'):

	'ef'al (אפעל)				'ef'ol (אפעול)		
	imperative	future			imperative	future	
◄	Study! / Learn!	לְמַד! ⇐ תִּלְמַד		Write!	כְּתוֹב! ⇐ תִּכְתוֹב	
	Listen!	שְׁמַע! ⇐ תִּשְׁמַע		Stand!	עֲמוֹד! ⇐ תַּעֲמוֹד	
	Ask!	שְׁאַל! ⇐ תִּשְׁאַל		Collect!	אֱסוֹף! ⇐ תֶּאֱסוֹף	

Notice that the division into *'ef'ol* and *'ef'al* in the future forms applies also to the imperatives.[5]

Note: The imperative form of לֶאֱכוֹל is אֱכוֹל!. This verb and other *pe-'alef* verbs whose future tense forms are like those of לֶאֱכוֹל – i.e., תֹּאכַל – form their imperative by removing the -ל from the **infinitive**:

◄	לֶאֱכוֹל ⇐ אֱכוֹל!	Eat!

---

4   The vowel sign at the end of this form changes from ◌ֶ to ◌ֵ, but in today's Hebrew the pronunciation of both of these is the same: *eh*.

5   On *'ef'ol* and *'ef'al* in the future tense of verbs in *beenyan pa'al*, see the chapter "*Beenyan Pa'al*," pp. 398-401.

Now let's see what happens when the endings ‎ֹי- and ‎ו- are added to these forms:

	'ef'al		'ef'ol	
	(לְמַד!)		(כְּתוֹב!)	
(את): ◄	תִּלְמְדִי ⇐ לִמְדִי!		תִּכְתְּבִי ⇐ כִּתְבִי!	
(אתם/אתן):	תִּלְמְדוּ ⇐ לִמְדוּ!		תִּכְתְּבוּ ⇐ כִּתְבוּ!	

As you can see, as in the future forms of אַתְ and אתם/אתן, so too in the imperative forms, there is no difference between *'ef'ol* and *'ef'al*. In all of the imperative forms with endings, the **first** vowel almost always becomes *ee* (ִ) (כִּתְבִי *keet-VEE*, כִּתְבוּ *keet-VOO*…).[6]

Here are some more examples:

	(שְׁמַע!)	(אֱסוֹף!)	(עֲמוֹד!)
(את): ◄	שִׁמְעִי!	אִסְפִּי!	עִמְדִי!
(אתם/אתן):	שִׁמְעוּ!	אִסְפוּ!	עִמְדוּ!

Only the אַתְ and אתם/אתן forms of verbs with a middle guttural (e.g., שאל) are different from these forms: They have **three** syllables and their first two vowels are *a-a*:

		(שְׁאַל!)
(את): ◄	שַׁאֲלִי!	*sha-'a-LEE*
(אתם/אתן):	שַׁאֲלוּ!	*sha-'a-LOO*

Beenyan pee'el (דִּבֵּר)

In *beenyan pee'el*, we simply remove the ת׳ prefix to arrive at the three imperative forms. The first vowel of all *pee'el* imperatives is *ah*:

	3rd root letter י (ל"י)		2nd root letter ו or י (ע"י)		regular verbs	
	imperative	future	imperative	future	imperative	future
(אתה): ◄	נַסֵּה![7] ⇐ תְּנַסֶּה		תָּאֵר! ⇐ תְּתָאֵר		דַּבֵּר! ⇐ תְּדַבֵּר	
(את):	נַסִּי! ⇐ תְּנַסִּי		תָּאֲרִי![8] ⇐ תְּתָאֲרִי		דַּבְּרִי! ⇐ תְּדַבְּרִי	
(אתם/אתן):	נַסּוּ! ⇐ תְּנַסּוּ		תָּאֲרוּ! ⇐ תְּתָאֲרוּ		דַּבְּרוּ! ⇐ תְּדַבְּרוּ	
	Try!		Describe!		Speak!	

---

6 This happens for phonetic reasons. See J. Weingreen, 1959, p. 11.

7 The vowel sign at the end of this form changes from ֵ to ֶ, but in today's Hebrew the pronunciation of both of these is the same: *eh*.

8 On the use of *ah* (ֲ) after a *guttural*, see the chapter "Guttural Consonants: *Beenyan Pa'al*," pp. 450-453.

Want to see if you've understood?
Write the imperative forms of the underlined verbs.

1. ‏תשבו‎ פה! ⇐ _____ פה!

2. ‏תחפשי‎ את המפתחות בחדר שלך! ⇐ _____ את המפתחות בחדר שלך!

3. ‏תחכה‎ לי, בבקשה. ⇐ _____ לי, בבקשה.

4. ‏תבואי‎ בחמש! ⇐ _____ בחמש!

5. ‏תפנה‎ שמאלה ברמזור! ⇐ _____ שמאלה ברמזור!

6. ‏תשימו‎ לב לשלט! ⇐ _____ לב לשלט!

7. ‏תיתן‎ לי עוד הזדמנות, בבקשה. ⇐ _____ לי עוד הזדמנות, בבקשה.

8. ‏תיקחי‎ את הנעליים שלך מן הסלון, בבקשה. ⇐ _____ את הנעליים שלך מן הסלון, בבקשה.

9. ‏תשמרו‎ על עצמכם! ⇐ _____ על עצמכם!

10. ‏תעצור‎ פה! ⇐ _____ פה!

11. ‏תקראו‎ את הקטע! ⇐ _____ את הקטע!

12. ‏תחזרו‎ מיד! ⇐ _____ מיד!

Answers:[9]

1. שְׁבוּ 2. חַפְּשִׂי 3. חַכֵּה 4. בּוֹאִי 5. פְּנֵה 6. שִׂימוּ 7. תֵן 8. קְחִי 9. שִׁמְרוּ 10. עֲצוֹר 11. קִרְאוּ
12. חִזְרוּ

Neef'al, heetpa'el *and* heef'eel: *starting from infinitive forms*

The infinitives of three *beenyaneem* – *neef'al*, *heetpa'el* and *heef'eel* – contain a ‏ה׳‎ after the initial ‏-ל‎. The imperative forms of all three *beenyaneem* also begins with a ‏ה׳‎.

---

9   It is not necessary for you to write vowel signs in your answers. We have added vowel signs to the answers in the chapters on verbs in order to make clear how the forms are pronounced.

Neef'al *and* heetpa'el (הִיכָּנֵס, הִתְלַבֵּשׁ)

First let's compare the infinitive and imperative base forms of *neef'al* and *heetpa'el*:

		ציווי *imperative*		שם הפועל *infinitive*	
neef'al:	Come in!	הִיכָּנֵס!	⇐	לְהִיכָּנֵס	◄
heetpa'el:	Get dressed!	הִתְלַבֵּשׁ!	⇐	לְהִתְלַבֵּשׁ	

Q: What must we do in order to create imperative base forms from the infinitives?

A: We simply remove the initial -לְ:

הִיכָּנֵס!	⇐	לְהִיכָּנֵס	◄
הִתְלַבֵּשׁ!	⇐	לְהִתְלַבֵּשׁ	

Here is what happens when we add endings (־י and ־וּ) to the base forms:

	heetpa'el	*neef'al*	
(אתה):	הִתְלַבֵּשׁ!	הִיכָּנֵס!	◄
(את):	הִתְלַבְּשִׁי!	הִיכָּנְסִי!	
(אתם/אתן):	הִתְלַבְּשׁוּ!	הִיכָּנְסוּ!	

Notice that the same change in the vowel before the ending that took place in regular verbs in *pa'al* (כִּתְבִי) and *pee'el* (דַבְּרִי) takes place here as well: The vowel "reduces" (it is usually not pronounced and is written as *shva* when vowel signs are added), e.g., הִיכָּנְסִי (hee-kan-SEE), הִתְלַבְּשִׁי (heet-lab-SHEE).

Here are examples of verbs with gutturals (and ר'):[10]

	heetpa'el	*neef'al*		
	(לְהִתְנַהֵג)	(לְהֵירָשֵׁם)	(לְהִישָׁאֵר)	
(אתה):	הִתְנַהֵג!	הֵירָשֵׁם!	הִישָׁאֵר!	◄
(את):	הִתְנַהֲגִי!	הֵירָשְׁמִי!	הִישָׁאֲרִי!	
(אתם/אתן):	הִתְנַהֲגוּ!	הֵירָשְׁמוּ!	הִישָׁאֲרוּ!	
	Behave!	Register!	Stay!	

---

10 See the chapters "Guttural Consonants: *Beenyan Heef'eel, Hoof'al* and *Heetpa'el*," pp. 468-469 and "Guttural Consonants: *Beenyaneem Pee'el, Poo'al* and *Neef'al*," pp. 480-483 for explanations of these changes. The explanations of changes in *neef'al* future tense verbs apply to the changes in the imperatives.

Want to see if you've understood?
Write the imperative forms of the underlined verbs.

1. <u>תִתְקַשְׁרוּ</u> מחר. ⟸ _____ מחר!

2. <u>תִישָׁאֵר</u> שם. ⟸ _____ שם!

3. <u>תִתְקַלְחִי</u> מהר. ⟸ _____ מהר.

4. <u>תִיזָהֲרוּ</u> בדרך. ⟸ _____ בדרך!

Answers:

1. הִתְקַשְּׁרוּ   2. הִישָׁאֵר   3. הִתְקַלְּחִי   4. הִיזָהֲרוּ

Heef'eel (הַקְשֵׁב)

Read the following instructions:

Complete (*m.s.*) the sentence!	הַשְׁלֵם את המשפט! ⟵
Listen (*m.s.*) to the lifeguard's instructions!	הַקְשֵׁב להוראות המציל!

As you can see, the אתה form of the imperative in *beenyan heef'eel* is a bit different from the infinitive form. Compare:

		ציווי *imperative*		שם הפועל *infinitive*	
regular verb:	Order! / Invite!	הַזְמֵן!	⟸	לְהַזְמִין	⟵

When we move from the infinitive to the אתה form of the imperative, **not only** does the לְ- drop off, but also the vowel in the final syllable changes to *eh* (◌ֵ) and the י that appears in the infinitive is no longer written: הַזְמֵן!. Here are some more *heef'eel* verbs in which you can see the same change:

pe-noon:	Look!	(*root:* נ-ב-ט)	הַבֵּט!	⟸	לְהַבִּיט ⟵
'ayeen-vav/yod:	Get ready! / Prepare!	(*root:* כ-ו-נ)	הָכֵן!	⟸	לְהָכִין
pe-yod:	Take down!	(*root:* י-ר-ד)	הוֹרֵד!	⟸	לְהוֹרִיד
initial guttural:	Believe!	(*root:* א-מ-נ)	הַאֲמֵן!	⟸	לְהַאֲמִין

This vowel change takes place **only** in the אתה form. Compare the forms with endings to the אתה form:

הָאֲמֵן!	הוֹרֵד!	הָכֵן!	הַבֵּט!	הַזְמֵן!	(אתה):
הַאֲמִינִי!	הוֹרִידִי!	הָכִינִי!	הַבִּיטִי!	הַזְמִינִי!	(את):
הַאֲמִינוּ!	הוֹרִידוּ!	הָכִינוּ!	הַבִּיטוּ!	הַזְמִינוּ!	(אתם/אתן):

In order to create the אַת and אתם/אתן forms, we simply take the infinitive without its ל (...לְהַבִּיט, לְהַזְמִין) and add the endings -ִי and -ּוּ. Note that – just as in the future (תַזְמִינִי, תַזְמִינוּ) – there is **no** "reduction" here of the vowel before the ending.

When the final root letter is ע' or ח', in addition to omitting the י', the vowel in the אתה form changes to *ah*, as in:

לְהַצְבִּיעַ	לְהַבְטִיחַ	
הַצְבַּע!	הַבְטַח!	(אתה):
הַצְבִּיעִי!	הַבְטִיחִי!	(את):
הַצְבִּיעוּ!	הַבְטִיחוּ!	(אתם/אתן):
Vote!	Promise!	

Want to see if you've understood?
Write the imperative form of the underlined verb.

1. תַסְבִּיר לנו שוב! ⇐ _____ לנו שוב!

2. תַעֲבִירִי לי את המלח, בבקשה. ⇐ _____ לי את המלח, בבקשה.

3. תָרִים את הידיים למעלה! ⇐ _____ את הידיים למעלה!

4. תוֹשִׁיב את האורחים במקומותיהם! ⇐ _____ את האורחים במקומותיהם!

Answers:

1. הַסְבֵּר   2. הַעֲבִירִי   3. הָרֵם   4. הוֹשֵׁב

Let's review

◆ Imperative forms in *pa'al* and *pee'el* are very similar to future tense forms. To create the imperatives, we simply remove the prefix -תְ from the future tense forms:

	pee'el (פיעל)				*pa'al* (פעל)	
imperative		*future*		*imperative*		*future*
דַּבֵּר	⇐	תְּדַבֵּר		קוּם	⇐	תָּקוּם
דַּבְּרִי	⇐	תְּדַבְּרִי		קוּמִי	⇐	תָּקוּמִי
דַּבְּרוּ	⇐	תְּדַבְּרוּ		קוּמוּ	⇐	תָּקוּמוּ

◆ In the אַתְ and אתם/אתן forms of **regular** *pa'al* verbs, there is, in addition, a change in pronunciation (the imperative begins with *ee*):

imperative		*future*
כִּתְבִי	⇐	תִּכְתְּבִי
כִּתְבוּ	⇐	תִּכְתְּבוּ

◆ In verbs whose infinitive has a ה' (*neef'al, heetpa'el, heef'eel*), the imperative form begins with ה':

	imperative				*infinitive*	
neef'al:	הִיכָּנְסוּ	הִיכָּנְסִי,	הִיכָּנֵס,	⇐	לְהִיכָּנֵס
heetpa'el:	הִתְלַבְּשׁוּ	הִתְלַבְּשִׁי,	הִתְלַבֵּשׁ,	⇐	לְהִתְלַבֵּשׁ
heef'eel:	הַזְמִינוּ	הַזְמִינִי,	הַזְמֵן,	⇐	לְהַזְמִין

◆ In *heef'eel*, the אתה form (הַזְמֵן) has the vowel *eh* in its final syllable and there is no י'.

• *Negative commands*

Read the following negative commands:

Don't get up!	אַל תָּקוּם!	(אתה):
	אַל תָּקוּמִי!	(אַת):
	אַל תָּקוּמוּ!	(אתם/אתן):

Q: Are these the same imperative forms that we saw above?

A: No. For negative commands, we use the word אַל for negation, followed by **future tense** – not imperative – forms. Here are some more examples:

אַל תִּכָּנְסוּ!	אַל תְּדַבְּרִי!	אַל תִּכְתּוֹב! ◁
Don't come in!	Don't talk!	Don't write!
(pl.)	*(f.s.)*	*(m.s.)*

Did you know?
Using the infinitive as a "command"

Another way to ask someone to do (or not to do) something in formal Hebrew is by using the infinitive form (often preceded by נָא), for example:

Please do not disturb!	נָא לֹא להפריע! ◁
Please turn off all cell phones!	נָא לכבות פלאפונים!

When נא is omitted, the use of the infinitive as a command sounds less formal. Sometimes the word בְּבַקָשָׁה is used. For example, the bus driver might call out:

Please move further in!	בבקשה להיכנס פנימה! ◁
or:	להיכנס פנימה, בבקשה!

Want to see if you've understood?
Change to negative commands.

1. <u>דַבֵּר</u> איתו הערב! ⇐ _____ איתו הערב!

2. <u>הִישָׁאֲרוּ</u> בבית היום! ⇐ _____ בבית היום!

3. <u>הַגְדִילִי</u> את האותיות! ⇐ _____ את האותיות!

Answers:

1. אַל תְּדַבֵּר   2. אַל תִּישָׁאֲרוּ   3. אַל תַּגְדִילִי

VII. Meanings and the *Beenyaneem*

Introduction

At the beginning of this book, we discussed two of the basic building blocks of words in Hebrew: *root* and *pattern*. We saw there that roots usually have a basic meaning, and when they appear in different patterns, this meaning is modified in some way. In the following chapters, we will see how the seven basic **verb patterns** (***beenyaneem***) can modify the meaning of roots.

Here's an example of how the root כ-ת-ב, which has to do with **writing**, is modified in the five different *beenyaneem* in which it appears in Modern Hebrew:[1]

◄ עו"ד גדעון לוי מירושלים כתב מכתב לעורך דין בניו יורק.

Mr. Gidon Levy, a Jerusalem lawyer, wrote a letter to a lawyer in New York.

המכתב נכתב אתמול בערב.

The letter was written last night.

עו"ד לוי הכתיב מכתב נוסף למזכירה שלו.

Mr. Levy dictated another letter to his secretary.
=He caused his secretary to write it.

המכתב הוכתב והוקלד אתמול.

The letter was dictated and typed yesterday.

עו"ד לוי מתכתב כל הזמן עם עורכי דין בניו יורק.

Mr. Levy corresponds all the time with lawyers in New York.
=They write to each other.

Do beenyaneem *have fixed and predictable meanings?*

We **cannot** assign a fixed and predictable meaning to each *beenyan*. The meaning of two of the seven *beenyaneem* – *poo'al* and *hoof'al* – **is** predictable in that these *beenyaneem* contain only **passive** verbs. The other five *beenyaneem* tend to convey certain **kinds** of meanings. By becoming familiar with the range of meanings of each *beenyan*, we (as readers and listeners) are better able to guess the meaning of a verb whose root is known to us. As speakers and writers of Hebrew, we use our knowledge of the **possible** meanings of *beenyaneem* to make an educated guess as to which *beenyan* we should use. (Such a guess must, of course, be checked in the dictionary or by asking a native speaker).

---

1   While, theoretically, every three-letter root can fit into every *beenyan*, in reality this does **not** happen: One root may appear in all seven *beenyaneem*, while another may be found in only two or three.

In the chapters in this unit, we will examine the following categories of meanings and their connection to various *beenyaneem*: [2]

1. **Active and Passive Verbs** פָּעִיל וְסָבִיל
2. **Special Categories of Active Verbs**
   - **Causative verbs (i.e., causing something to happen or be)**
   - **Reflexive verbs (i.e., doing something to oneself)**
   - **Reciprocal verbs (i.e., doing something to or with each other)**
3. **Verbs that Are Neither Active Nor Passive**
4. **Meanings and the *Beenyaneem*: Summary**

---

2 In grammar books, these meanings are often referred to as *voice*: the *active voice*, the *passive voice*, the *causative voice*, the *reflexive voice*, the *reciprocal voice*.

1. Active and Passive Verbs פָּעִיל וְסָבִיל

> ### Preview
> - *Active verbs* פָּעִיל / אַקְטִיבִי •
> - *Passive verbs* סָבִיל / פָּסִיבִי •
> - *Active-passive pairs (pee'el-poo'al, heef'eel-hoof'al)*
> - Beenyan neef'al *also contains passive verbs*
> - Beenyan heetpa'el *also contains passive verbs*
> - *Which active verbs can be made passive?*

• *Active verbs* פָּעִיל / אַקְטִיבִי •

Read the following paragraph:

> ◄ ירון ואחותו התלבשו יפה ויצאו ביחד למסיבה. במסיבה הם רקדו, אכלו, הקשיבו ללהקה שניגנה
> ודיברו עם חברים. ב-2:00 בבוקר הם נפרדו מהחברים שלהם וחזרו הביתה.

Yaron and his sister got dressed up and went out together to a party. At the party they danced, ate, listened to the band that was playing and talked with friends. At 2 a.m., they said goodbye to (lit.: parted from) their friends and returned home.

The verbs highlighted above belong to five different *beenyaneem*:

pa'al:	יצאו, רקדו, אכלו, חזרו ◄
pee'el:	ניגנה, דיברו
heef'eel:	הקשיבו
neef'al:	נפרדו
heetpa'el:	התלבשו

All these verbs convey that some **action** has been taken. And who performs this action? The **subject** of these verbs (here: ירון ואחותו – Yaron and his sister – and הלהקה – the band).[1]

---

1 In order to simplify our discussion, we say here and elsewhere that the "subject" (a grammatical term) performs the action, when in reality it is the person (or entity) **denoted** by the subject that performs the action.

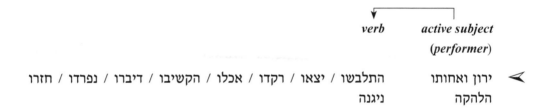

verb	active subject (*performer*)
התלבשו / יצאו / רקדו / אכלו / הקשיבו / דיברו / נפרדו / חזרו / ניגנה	ירון ואחותו ההלהקה

When the **subject** performs the action indicated by the verb, we say that the verbs are ***active verbs***.[2]

An **active verb** in Hebrew appears **only** in one of the following **five** *beenyaneem*: *pa'al*, *pee'el*, *heef'eel*, *neef'al* and *heetpa'el* – and **never** in the other two *beenyaneem*: *poo'al* and *hoof'al*.

> ***Be careful!*** All active verbs appear in one of these five *beenyaneem*; however, not **all** verbs in these *beenyaneem* are active. We will discuss the non-active meanings of verbs in each *beenyan* below and in the chapter "Verbs that Are Neither Active Nor Passive" (pp. 606-612).

Now let's ask: When we wish to express an active verb in Hebrew, can we know in **which** of these five *beenyaneem* it will appear?

In order to answer this question, let's examine the following translations of English verbs:

He ran away is in Hebrew both ברח (*pa'al*) and נמלט (*neef'al*).
He phoned is in Hebrew התקשר (*heetpa'el*) and טלפן (*pee'el*).
He threw is in Hebrew both זרק (*pa'al*) and השליך (*heef'eel*).

As you can see, each of the English verbs above is active, and each has Hebrew equivalents that appear in **more than one** *beenyan*. We **cannot** accurately **predict** into which of the five "active" *beenyaneem* a given active verb will fit. Having said this, we will see in the next chapter that sometimes there are types of meanings that allow us to narrow down our choice to fewer than five.

---

2   We are using this as our working definition of active verbs since we find it useful for learners of Hebrew, especially in explaining the transition from active to passive verbs. It should also be noted that in this book we refer to reciprocal verbs (e.g., נפרדו) and reflexive verbs (e.g., התלבשו) as active verbs. See the chapter "Special Categories of Active Verbs," pp. 593-605.

• *Passive verbs* סָבִיל / פָּסִיבִי

Read the following sentences containing passive verbs:[3]

The soup was cooked (by Dan).	1א. המרק בושל (על ידי דן).[4] ◄
The telephone was fixed (by Ron).	ב. הטלפון תוקן (על ידי רון).
Yuval was invited for dinner.	2א. יובל הוזמן לארוחת ערב.
The light was turned on (by the teacher).	ב. האור הודלק (על ידי המורה).

Here, too, the verbs indicate that an action has been performed. But these sentences are **different** from the ones with active verbs.

Q: Did the subject in these sentences perform the actions denoted by the verbs?

A: **No.** It is **not** the subject that performed the actions. Rather, the action was done **to** the subject (e.g., the soup was cooked), i.e., the subject is **passive**. The performer of the action – דן (Dan) and רון (Ron) in sentences 1א׳ and ב׳1 above and המורה (the teacher) in sentence 2ב׳ – is not always indicated or known. We call the verbs in sentences like these ***passive verbs***.

Q: To which *beenyaneem* do these passive verbs belong?

A: בושל and תוקן belong to *poo'al*.
הוזמן and הודלק belong to *hoof'al*.

Verbs in *poo'al* and *hoof'al* always have a passive meaning.[5] Notice that both *beenyaneem* have the sound *oo-ah*: *poo'al*, *hoof'al*. When you hear *oo-ah* in a verb, you immediately know that it is passive.

Be careful! As we will see below, there are passive verbs also in **other** *beenyaneem*, and they do **not** contain the sounds *oo-ah*.

---

3   We use the term *passive verbs* to refer to verbs to which "by + the performer of the action" can be added, as in the sentence המרק בושל על ידי דן (The soup was cooked by Dan). Other verbs like נגמר in השיעור נגמר ב-12:00 (The lesson ended at 12:00), which are close to passives but to which we cannot add "by + someone," are called in this book "it happened to him/her/it" verbs. For more on these verbs, see the chapter "Verbs that Are Neither Active Nor Passive," pp. 608-611.

4   In sentences like these (with passive verbs), we do not usually mention **who** performed the action. If we wish to do so, we can add a phrase that begins with עַל יְדֵי (by) (abbreviated as: ע״י).

5   We are speaking here only of the **verbs** in these *beenyaneem* and not of adjectives like מצוין (excellent) and מוצלח (successful), whose **forms** are those of present tense verbs.

• *Active-passive pairs* (pee'el-poo'al, heef'eel-hoof'al)

Now let's look at the following pairs of sentences that contain active and passive verbs:

passive		*active*	
המרק בושל (על ידי דן).	⇔	אתמול דן בישל את המרק המיוחד שלו.	1א.
The soup was cooked (by Dan).		Yesterday Dan cooked his special soup.	
הטלפון תוקן (על ידי רון).	⇔	רון תיקן את הטלפון המקולקל.	ב.
The telephone was fixed (by Ron).		Ron fixed the broken telephone.	
יובל הוזמן לארוחת ערב.	⇔	הזמינו את יובל לארוחת ערב.	2א.
Yuval was invited to dinner.		Someone invited Yuval to dinner.	
האור הודלק (על ידי המורה).	⇔	המורה הדליקה את האור.	ב.
The light was turned on (by the teacher).		The teacher turned on the light.	

The passive verbs in Set 1 (בושל and תוקן) belong to *beenyan poo'al*.

Q: To which *beenyan* do their active counterparts (בישל and תיקן) belong?

A: To *beenyan pee'el*. In Set 1 we see that *poo'al* and *pee'el* are paired together:

poo'al פועל	⇔	*pee'el* פיעל
בושל		בישל
תוקן		תיקן

These two *beenyaneem* are "genetically" related: They both have a *strong dagesh* in the middle root letter (in texts with vowel signs).[6] In order to go from one to the other, we leave the consonants of the *beenyan* the same and simply change the vowels:[7]

poo'al	⇔	*pee'el*
פוּעַל		פִּיעֵל

Now look at Set 2 above. The passive verbs in this set (הוזמן and הודלק) belong to *beenyan hoof'al*.

Q: To which *beenyan* do their active counterparts (הזמינו and הדליקה) belong?

A: To *beenyan heef'eel*. In Set 2 we see that *hoof'al* and *heef'eel* are paired together:

---

6   See the chapter "The Pronunciation of ב, כ, פ and the *Dagesh*," pp. 631-633.
7   In writing, this change in vowel sounds also involves changing the "vowel letters": י in *pee'el* and ו in *poo'al*. For an enlightening description of these changes, see Mazal Cohen-Weidenfeld, 2000, vol. I, pp. 137, 248.

	heef'eel הפעיל ◄
hoof'al הופעל ⟺	
הוזמן	הזמינו
הודלק	הדליק

These two *beenyaneem* are also "genetically" related: they both have an initial 'ה in front of their first root letter. Here, too, in order to go from one to the other, we leave the consonants of the *beenyan* the same and simply change the vowels:

hoof'al ⟺ *heef'eel* ◄
הוּפְעַל הִפְעִיל

When we change passive sentences to active sentences, the verbs change from *poo'al* to *pee'el* and from *hoof'al* to *heef'eel*. When we change from active to passive, we do the reverse: *pee'el* changes to *poo'al* and *heef'eel* changes to *hoof'al*.[8]

These four *beenyaneem* can be thought of as belonging to two distinct "families": the *pee'el-poo'al* family and the *heef'eel-hoof'al* family.

passive			active	
poo'al	פועל	⟺	*pee'el*	פיעל
hoof'al	הופעל	⟺	*heef'eel*	הפעיל

Did you know?
Converting active to passive and vice versa

In addition to learning the **active-passive pairs** of *beenyaneem*, there are several other matters that require attention when we change from active to passive sentences and vice versa.

1. The object and the subject change places
Active to Passive
When we change from an active to a passive sentence, the **object** of the active verb (here: הטלפון) becomes the subject of the passive verb:

---

8   In unusual cases, the passive of a specific *pee'el* verb is not found in *poo'al*, and the passive of a specific *heef'eel* verb is not found in *hoof'al*. Rather, the passives are found in other *beenyaneem*, for example:

neef'al		*heef'eel*	*heetpa'el*		*pee'el*	
נִיצַל	⟺	הציל	התקבל	⟺	קיבל	◄
was saved		saved	was received		received	

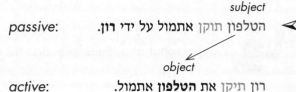

The original subject of the active sentence – רון – either disappears in the passive sentence or – much less frequently – is added as part of a phrase: על ידי רון (by Ron).

Passive to Active
When we change from **passive** to **active**, the reverse process takes place: The subject of the passive sentence (here: הטלפון) becomes the **object** of the active sentence. If the object is definite,[9] we add אֶת before it (for exceptions, see p. 591):

If the performer of the action is noted in the passive sentence (here: על ידי רון), then the performer (רון) becomes the subject of the active sentence.

But what happens when the performer of the action is **not indicated** in the passive sentence (i.e., no על ידי phrase appears in the passive sentence)?

subject

passive: הטלפון תוקן אתמול.

object

active: תיקנו את הטלפון אתמול.

---

9   The object is definite (specific) if it is preceded by ה- (the), if it is a proper noun (i.e., the name of a person or place and the like) or if it has a possessive ending (e.g., בנו his son). For more details, see the chapter "The Direct Object and the Use of אֶת," pp. 698-702.

As you can see, when we don't know who performed the action, the active sentence has **no** subject. It is an *impersonal* (סְתָמִי) sentence with a **masculine plural** (הם) form of the verb: תיקנו.[10]

2. Matching the verb to the subject

The verb of each sentence must **match** its subject (m. ⇔ m., f. ⇔ f., sing. ⇔ sing., pl. ⇔ pl.). Thus, after we change an active sentence to a passive one or a passive sentence to an active one, we must make sure the verb matches its new subject, for example:

passive		active
f.s. ⇔ *f.s.*		*m.s.* ⇔ *m.s.*
הטלוויזיה תוקנה אתמול (על ידי רון).	⇔	רון תיקן את הטלוויזיה אתמול.
m.pl. ⇔ *m.pl.*		*f.s.* ⇔ *f.s.*
האורות הודלקו (על ידי שרה).	⇔	שרה הדליקה את האורות.

The only time this matching does not take place is when the active sentence is **impersonal** and, therefore, has no subject.

Want to see if you've understood?

A. *Pee'el-poo'al*: Write the missing active or passive verb.

passive		active

1. אבי <u>שילם</u> את חשבון הטלפון בזמן. ⇐ החשבון _____ בזמן.

2. הילדים <u>יסדרו</u> את החדר שלהם. ⇐ אם החדר _____ , הם ילכו לסרט.

3. מנהל בית הספר _____ אתמול את הפגישה עם ההורים. ⇒ הפגישה עם ההורים <u>בוטלה</u>.

Answers:

1. שוּלַם   2. יְסוּדַר   3. בִּיטֵל

___

10 See the chapter "Sentences Without Subjects: Impersonal Sentences," pp. 694-696 for an explanation of impersonal sentences of this type.

B. *Heef'eel-hoof'al*: Write the missing active or passive verb.

passive	active

1. הרופאה <u>הסבירה</u> לחולה את המצב. ⇐ המצב _____ לחולה.

2. הסטודנט <u>הדפיס</u> את העבודה שלו במחשב. ⇐ העבודה _____ במחשב.

3. הגנב _____ מחר את הכסף. ⇒ הכסף <u>יוחזר</u> מחר.

Answers:

1. הוּסְבַּר   2. הוּדְפְּסָה   3. יָחְזִיר

• Beenyan neef'al *also contains passive verbs*

Now let's look at some more sentences with passive verbs:

The patient was examined (by the doctor).	החולה נבדק (על ידי הרופא).
The letter was sent yesterday (by the bank).	המכתב נשלח אתמול (על ידי הבנק).

Here, too, the subjects (החולה, המכתב) are not the performers of the actions, but rather they are **passive**: they "receive" the action (the action is performed **upon** them).

Q: To which *beenyan* do these passive verbs belong?

A: They belong to *beenyan neef'al*.

Earlier in this chapter, we saw **active** verbs in *beenyan neef'al*: נפרד (he parted) and נמלט (he escaped). Now we see that some verbs in *neef'al* (e.g., נבדק and נשלח) are **passive**. The fact that one *beenyan* contains **both** active and passive verbs is an "abnormality" that developed as a result of special circumstances. (See "Did you know?" below.)

Now let's examine the active counterparts of the above passive *neef'al* verbs:

passive		active
החולה נבדק (על ידי הרופא).	⇔	הרופא בדק את החולה.
The patient was examined (by the doctor).		The doctor examined the patient.
המכתב נשלח אתמול (על ידי הבנק).	⇔	הבנק שלח את המכתב אתמול.
The letter was sent yesterday (by the bank).		The bank sent the letter yesterday.

Q: To which *beenyan* do the active verbs (בדק, שלח) belong?

A: They belong to *beenyan pa'al*. In the majority of the cases, the active counterparts of passive verbs in *neef'al* are verbs in *pa'al* and vice versa: If you want to make a sentence with a *pa'al* verb passive, you use a verb in *neef'al*. Notice that while the passives of *pee'el* and *heef'eel* were created by a simple change of vowels to *oo-ah* (*poo'al, hoof'al*), the passive of *pa'al* doesn't have the sounds *oo-ah*. Instead, -נ is added to the front (and the vowels change).

Did you know?

Originally, *beenyan pa'al* – like *pee'el* and *heef'eel* – was paired with a passive *beenyan* that contained the vowels *oo-ah*. Remnants of this *beenyan* appear in the Bible, for example:

"because from man she was taken" ◄ "כִּי מֵאִישׁ לֻקֳחָה זֹּאת"

(Genesis 2:23) (בראשית ב, 23)

"who were born to him in the land of Canaan" "אֲשֶׁר יֻלְּדוּ-לוֹ בְּאֶרֶץ כְּנַעַן"

(Genesis 36:5) (בראשית לו, 5)

Apparently, because this *beenyan* was so similar in form to *poo'al*, it disappeared over time.[11] *Beenyan neef'al*, which originally was **not** a passive *beenyan*, "came to the rescue" and took over as the passive of *pa'al*. This is the reason why *neef'al* contains both active and passive verbs.

Want to see if you've understood?

Pa'al-neef'al: Write the missing active or passive verb.

passive	active

1. מר לוי _____ את החנות בשמונה בבוקר. ⇐ החנות נִפְתְּחָה על ידי מר לוי.

2. השומרים סָגְרוּ את השער. ⇐ השער _____ ביום שישי בבוקר (על ידי השומרים).

3. רבקה כָּתְבָה מכתב תודה לחברים שלה בחו"ל. ⇐ המכתב _____ על ידי רבקה.

Answers:

1. פָּתַח 2. נִסְגַּר 3. נִכְתַּב

---

11 Actually its "past tense" form is similar to *poo'al* and its "future tense" form is similar to *hoof'al*. For an explanation, see Joüon and Muraoka, 1996, vol. I, pp. 166-168.

Let's review

♦ Here are the three families of *beenyaneem* (I, II, III) arranged in active-passive pairs:

passive			active			
neef'al	נפעל	⇔	*pa'al*	פעל	I	
	החולה נבדק.			הרופא בדק את החולה.		
poo'al	פועל	⇔	*pee'el*	פיעל	II	
	המרק בושל.			דן בישל את המרק.		
hoof'al	הופעל	⇔	*heef'eel*	הפעיל	III	
	יובל הוזמן למסיבה.			אורי הזמין את יובל למסיבה.		

• Beenyan heetpa'el *also contains passive verbs*

As we saw at the beginning of this chapter, *beenyan heetpa'el* (e.g., התלבש got dressed, התקשר phoned) primarily contains **active** verbs. However, when it "saw" that *beenyan neef'al* had started to take on passive meanings in addition to its active ones (see "Did you know?" above), it, too, "decided" to do this.[12] But how?

Beenyan heetpa'el is actually part of the *pee'el-poo'al* family of *beenyaneem*: just like them it has a strong *dagesh* in the second root letter. In addition, *heetpa'el* verbs are often connected in meaning to verbs in *pee'el* and *poo'al*. So, when *pee'el* verbs found themselves without a *poo'al* counterpart, *heetpa'el* sometimes stepped in and took on the passive meaning. Some examples are the verbs קיבל (received) and ביקש (requested), which do not have passive verb counterparts in *beenyan poo'al*. Here are the active-passive pairs of these verbs:[13]

---

12 For a more detailed philological accounting of this process, see Abba Bendavid, 1971, vol. I, p. 125; vol. II, pp. 483, 485-486.

13 In today's Hebrew, there are also cases in which התפעל is used almost interchangeably with *poo'al* as the passive of *pee'el*. See Mazal Cohen-Weidenfeld, 2000, vol. II, p. 177.

passive		*active*
הזמר התקבל במחיאות כפיים (על ידי הקהל).	⇔	הקהל קיבל את הזמר בהתלהבות. ◄
The singer was received enthusiastically (by the audience).		The audience received the singer enthusiastically.
אבי התבקש (על ידי המנהל) לבוא למשרד.	⇔	המנהל ביקש מאבי לבוא למשרד.[14]
Avi was asked (by the principal) to come to the office.		The principal asked Avi to come to the office.

Here is an amended version of the active-passive chart:

passive			*active*		
neef'al	נפעל	⇔	*pa'al*	פעל	I ◄
	החולה נבדק.			הרופא בדק **את** החולה.	
poo'al	פועל	⇔	*pee'el*	פיעל	II
	המרק בושל.			דן בישל **את** המרק.	
heetpa'el)	(התפעל			הקהל קיבל **את** הזמר בהתלהבות.	
	הזמר התקבל בהתלהבות.				
hoof'al	הופעל	⇔	*heef'eel*	הפעיל	III
	יובל הוזמן למסיבה.			אורי הזמין **את** יובל למסיבה.	

• *Which active verbs can be made passive?*

Now look again at the **active** verbs in the chart above:

בדק, בישל, קיבל, הזמין ◄

Q: What preposition comes after them?

A: In all cases, אֶת follows these verbs (when the *direct object* is **definite**). If the direct objects in these sentences had been *indefinite*, **no** preposition would have been used after the verb (e.g., דן בישל מרק).[15]

---

14 ביקש can be made passive when the request is directed to a person (here: אבי). This person, in turn, becomes the subject of the passive verb.

15 On את and the direct object, see the chapter "The Direct Object and the Use of אֶת," pp. 697-704.

The great majority of active verbs that can be made passive are verbs that take the preposition את when their object is definite or **no** preposition when their object is indefinite.[16] Many other active verbs **cannot** be made passive. These include almost all verbs from *pa'al*, *pee'el* and *heef'eel* that require ב-, -ל, -מ, עם, על etc. and all verbs in *neef'al* and *heetpa'el*, which virtually never take את. Here are just a few examples of such active verbs:

◄ אסף קם בבוקר. הוא התקלח, התלבש ויצא מהבית. הוא הלך לתחנת האוטובוס וחיכה שם. כעבור חמש דקות האוטובוס הגיע לתחנה. אסף עלה לאוטובוס, התיישב ליד אבנר, החבר הטוב שלו, ונסע איתו עד האוניברסיטה. באוניברסיטה הוא נפרד מאבנר והלך לספרייה ללמוד.

Assaf got up in the morning. He took a shower, got dressed and left the house. He walked to the bus stop and waited there. Five minutes later, the bus arrived at the bus stop. Assaf got on the bus, sat down next to his good friend, Avner, and went with him to the university. At the university, he said goodbye to Avner and went to the library to study.

Did you know?
Active verbs with prepositions like ב-, על... that can be made passive

As mentioned above, almost all active verbs that can be made passive take אֶת. However, there are some exceptions, for example:

טיפל ב- ⇔ טופל	תמך ב- ⇔ נתמך	קרא ל- ⇔ נקרא ►
took care of	supported	called
החליט על ⇔ הוחלט	דיבר על ⇔ דובר[17]	השפיע על ⇔ הושפע מ-
decided about	spoke about	influenced

---

16 See "Did you know?" on this page for examples of active verbs with prepositions other than את that can be made passive. Note: Not all verbs that take את have a corresponding passive verb in Hebrew, for example: לשנוא את (to hate), לארח את (to host), להרוויח את (to earn).

17 When החליט על and דיבר על are made passive, we usually use דובר על/ב- and הוחלט על/ב-, as in:
► בישיבה דיברו על שינוי שיטת הבחירות. ⇔ בישיבה דובר על שינוי שיטת הבחירות.
(החליטו על)   (הוחלט על)
A change in the electoral system was discussed (decided upon) at the meeting. (Since the active sentence is impersonal, this is the translation of both the active and passive sentences above.)
The structure of these passive sentences is different from that described above in "Did you know?" ("Converting active to passive and vice versa"), pp. 584-586.

Chapter summary

♦ Active verbs can appear in five of the seven *beenyaneem*: *pa'al, pee'el, heef'eel, neef'al* and *heetpa'el*.

♦ Three of these five – *pa'al, pee'el* and *heef'eel* – have a special feature: only **these *beenyaneem*** contain verbs that take the preposition את when their object is definite. It is these verbs that can be made passive.[18]

♦ Passive verbs appear mainly in three *beenyaneem*. Two of these – *poo'al* and *hoof'al* – are **exclusively** passive. The third – *neef'al* – contains **both** passive and active verbs. A fourth *beenyan* – *heetpa'el* – contains mainly active verbs, but also has **some** passive ones.

♦ When we convert sentences with passive verbs to sentences with active verbs, and vice versa, we usually change the verb forms according to the following pairs of *beenyaneem*:

	passive			active		
	neef'al	נפעל	⇔	*pa'al*	פעל	I
(*heetpa'el* התפעל)	*poo'al*	פועל	⇔	*pee'el*	פיעל	II
	hoof'al	הופעל	⇔	*heef'eel*	הפעיל	III

Want to see if you've understood this chapter?

Write the missing active or passive verb. (The new verb should be in the same tense as the verb that is given.)

passive	active

1. המדריך _____ את הילדים. ⇐ הילדים נִסְפְרו על ידי המדריך בתחילת הטיול.

2. חילקו את הכיתה לשני חלקים. ⇐ הכיתה _____ לשני חלקים.

3. יפתחו את התמונות מחר. ⇐ אנחנו מקווים שהתמונות _____ בצורה מקצועית.

4. בעל המכולת יסגור את המכולת בשעה שבע בערב. ⇐ המכולת _____ בשעה שבע בערב.

5. אימא _____ את נרות השבת. ⇒ נרות השבת הודלקו (על ידי אימא).

6. אנחנו מזמינים אתכם למסיבה. ⇐ אתם _____ למסיבה.

Answers:

1. סָפַר 2. חוּלְקָה 3. יְפוּתְחוּ 4. תִיסָגֵר 5. הִדְלִיקָה 6. מוּזְמָנִים

---

18 See "Did you know?" above for some other verbs in *pa'al, pee'el* and *heef'eel* that take prepositions other than את and can be made passive.

2. Special Categories of Active Verbs

Preview

- *Causative verbs: causing something to happen or to be*   גּוֹרֵם / קוֹזָטִיבִי
- *Reflexive verbs: doing something to oneself*   חוֹזֵר / רֶפְלֶקְסִיבִי
- *Reciprocal verbs: doing something to or with each other*   הֲדָדִי

Introduction

In this chapter, we will look more closely at the following specialized meanings of **active** verbs in *beenyaneem pee'el, heef'eel, neef'al* and *heetpa'el: causative, reflexive* and *reciprocal.*[1] These meanings apply to only part of the active verbs in Hebrew. The many verbs that do **not fit** into any of these specialized categories may simply be regarded as active.

• *Causative verbs: causing something to happen or to be* גּוֹרֵם/קוֹזָטִיבִי

Read the following sentences:

אתמול המורה לספרות לימד את התלמידים סיפור חדש. הוא קרא את הסיפור בקול, הסביר את הקטעים הקשים ושאל את התלמידים שאלות. מכיוון שהם לא הספיקו לסיים את הסיפור, המורה ביקש להאריך קצת את השיעור ולקצר את ההפסקה. הוא הכתיב לתלמידים את שיעורי הבית במהירות. הם כתבו את השאלות של המורה במחברותיהם, ואחר כך הכניסו את המחברות לתיקים ויצאו מן הכיתה.

Yesterday the literature teacher taught the students a new story. He read the story aloud, explained the difficult passages and asked the students questions. Because they didn't manage to finish the story, the teacher asked that they stay a little longer (lit.: lengthen the lesson a bit) and shorten the break. He dictated the homework assignment to the students. They quickly wrote the teacher's questions in their notebooks and, after that, put (lit.: inserted) their notebooks in their school bags and left the classroom.

---

1 In many grammar books, *reflexive* and *reciprocal* verbs are placed in a category **separate** from *active verbs* (called "middle") because the subject of these verbs both **does** the action and **"receives"** it. For the sake of simplicity, we have labeled as *active* all verbs whose subject is active, including *reflexive* and *reciprocal* verbs.

All of the verbs highlighted in the above passage are active. In addition, they all take the preposition אֶת when the object is *definite* (= specific). When they are *indefinite*, they are **not** followed by **any** preposition, for example:

⋖ המורה לימד סיפור חדש.   The teacher taught a new story.

We have divided the highlighted verbs into two groups: blue and red. We regard the verbs highlighted in blue as *simply active*.

Now look at the verbs that are highlighted in red.

If we regard the simply active verbs as denoting the most basic actions, we can say that the verbs in red indicate a different "level" of action: they cause something. Some of the verbs in red cause someone **to do the simple actions** – for example, ללמד (to teach) is to cause someone to learn (ללמוד), להכתיב (to dictate) is to cause someone to write (לכתוב) and להכניס (to put something in) is to cause something to go in (להיכנס). The other verbs in red above cause something or someone **to be in a certain state** (which can be expressed as an adjective or as a "verb of state / change of state"):[2] להאריך (to lengthen) is to cause something to become long or longer (ארוך) and לקצר (to shorten) is to cause something to become short or shorter (קצר).[3] These verbs are called *causative verbs*.[4]

Which beenyaneem *contain causative verbs?*

Look again at the causative verbs in the above sentences.

Q: To which *beenyaneem* do these verbs belong?

A: To one of two *beenyaneem*: *pee'el* (ללמד, לקצר) or *heef'eel* (להאריך, להכניס, להכתיב).

---

2   By "verbs of state" we mean verbs such as ישב (to sit) and שוכב (to lie down), and by "verbs of change of state" we mean verbs such as עולה (to rise, go up) and יורד (to go down), as in המחירים עולים ויורדים (The prices go up and down). Verbs like these will be discussed in the next chapter.

3   For the sake of convenience, we sometimes "stretch our imagination" when defining a verb as causative. For example, we often regard a verb like גידל (e.g., ההורים גידלו את הילדים The parents raised the children) as a kind of causative, even though the parents didn't actually **cause** the children to grow or to grow up (לגדול).
    Note: Many *simply active* verbs, such as לקרוא, do indeed cause something to happen, as in: When we read a book, we cause it to be read (להיקרא). However, we do not label the active verbs in active-passive pairs (such as להיקרא – לקרוא) as causative (in relation to their passive "partners").

4   For a detailed discussion of causatives, see Mazal Cohen-Weidenfeld, 1996, vol. I, pp. 129, 237-238.

Here are some more examples of causative verbs in *pee'el* and *heef'eel*:

pee'el:

לגדל	לייבש	לחזק	לשמח ◄
to grow (vegetables), to raise (children)= to **cause** them to grow	to dry something= to **cause** it to become dry	to strengthen= to **cause** something or someone to be strong	to make someone happy= to **cause** someone to be happy

heef'eel:

להצחיק	להגדיל	להקטין	להלביש ◄
to make someone laugh= to **cause** someone to laugh	to enlarge= to **cause** something to be larger	to make something smaller= to **cause** something to be smaller	to dress someone= to **cause** someone to be dressed

There is no special reason why a specific causative verb is in *pee'el* rather than *heef'eel* or vice versa. In fact, there are even pairs of opposites, each of which appears in a different *beenyan*, for example:

heef'eel		*pee'el*
להאריך to lengthen	#	לקצר to shorten ◄
להחליש to weaken	#	לחזק to strengthen
להעציב to make sad	#	לשמח to make happy

This, of course, is not always the case (e.g., להגדיל # להקטין are both in the same *beenyan*); however, the pairs of opposites from different *beenyaneem* show that we **cannot** predict whether a causative verb will be in *pee'el* or *heef'eel*.

Comparing causative verbs in Hebrew and English

Now let's look at some pairs of simply active verbs or verbs of state and their causative partners:

simply active:	The cat ate.	.1. החתול אכל.
causative:	The boy fed the cat.	הילד האכיל את החתול.

verb of state:		.2. החברים שלנו שמחו לקבל את המתנה.
	The friends were happy to receive the gift.	
causative:		שימחנו את החברים כשנתנו להם את המתנה.
	We made our friends happy when we gave them the gift.	

simply active:	The dog returned home.	.3. הכלב חזר הביתה.
causative:		השכן החזיר את הכלב האבוד לבעליו.
	The neighbor returned the lost dog to its owners.	

Notice that in the Hebrew of each pair of sentences, when the meaning changes from simply active or state of being to causative, the same root is used, but in a **different *beenyan*.**[5] In the above examples, *beenyan pa'al* (אכל, שמחו, חזר) is used for the simple action or state of being, while either *heef'eel* (האכיל, החזיר) or *pee'el* (שימחנו) are used for the causative meaning.

Now look at the English translations of these sentences.

Q: In what way are the English translations of number 3 different from those of 1 and 2?

A: In 1 and 2, the English translations of the verbs in each sentence are **different** from each other. Each different form in Hebrew (e.g., אכל and האכיל) has a different translation in English. However, in number 3, the different Hebrew forms have the **same** English translation ("returned"). This fact makes it difficult for English speakers to translate sentences like those in 3 from English to Hebrew. In each case, we must think about what the verb *returned* means. In the first sentence above (The dog returned home), the subject (the dog) performs a simple action, whereas in the second sentence (The neighbor returned the lost dog...), the subject **causes** the dog to return to its owners. If we know that **both** חזר and החזיר exist in Hebrew, knowing that *beenyan heef'eel* is often causative helps us know to choose חזר as the translation of the simply active verb and החזיר as the translation of the causative action.

---

5   This is often the case. However, sometimes in Hebrew, just as in English, a given verb may have more than one kind of meaning. For example, משמין can be causative (to be fattening) or can denote a change of state (to gain weight). For more examples, see the chapter "Verbs that Are Neither Active Nor Passive," pp. 610-611.

Be careful! Remember that not every verb in *pee'el* and *heef'eel* is causative. Often, verbs in these *beenyaneem*, such as לדבר (to speak) and להזמין (to invite), are simply active. In addition, even when the **same root** appears in **both** *pa'al* and *pee'el* or *heef'eel*, the latter are **not** always causative, for example:

pa'al:	Yonatan opened the door.	יונתן פתח את הדלת. ◄
pee'el:	The company developed a new drug.	החברה פיתחה תרופה חדשה.
pa'al:	Sarit closed the window.	שרית סגרה את החלון.
		מקסיקו הסגירה את הפושעים לארה"ב.
heef'eel:	Mexico turned over / deported the criminals to the U.S.	

When we read texts, we have to be aware of this fact. We can guess that a verb in *pee'el* or *heef'eel* **may** be causative, but we **should not assume** that it is.

Let's review

♦ One special category of active verbs is causative verbs. Causative verbs may denote one of the following:

- the causing of an **action**:

causative:	The boy fed the cat.	הילד האכיל את החתול. ◄
simply active:	The cat ate.	החתול אכל.

- the causing of a **state**:

causative:		שימחנו את החברים כשנתנו להם את המתנה. ◄
	We made our friends happy when we gave them the gift.	
state of being:		החברים שלנו שמחו לקבל את המתנה.
	The friends were happy to receive the gift.	

♦ Causative verbs appear mainly in *beenyaneem heef'eel* and *pee'el*.

Want to see if you've understood?

In the following sentences you are given a choice of a *simply active* or *state of being* verb, on the one hand, and a *causative* verb, on the other. Choose the verb that fits the context.

1. חמישה עצי פרי _____ בגינה שלנו.
(גדלים / מגדלים)

2. _____ לדירה חדשה.
(עברנו / העברנו)

3. _____ את כל הרהיטים שלנו לדירה החדשה.
(עברנו / העברנו)

4. ההודעה על החתונה _____ אותנו מאוד.
(שמחה / שימחה)

5. אתם מאוד _____ היום.
(שמחים / משמחים)

6. המורה החדשה _____ אותנו אנגלית.
(מלמדת / לומדת)

7. תמר כל הזמן _____ אותנו.
(צוחקת / מצחיקה)

8. טליה, למה את לא _____ מהבדיחות (jokes) של תמר?
(צוחקת / מצחיקה)

9. _____ בגדים חגיגיים לכבוד המסיבה.
(לבשנו / הלבשנו)

10. _____ את אחותי הקטנה לכבוד יום ההולדת שלה.
(לבשתי / הלבשתי)

Answers:

1. גְדֵלים 2. עברנו 3. העברנו 4. שימחה 5. שמֵחים 6. מלמדת 7. מצחיקה 8. צוחקת 9. לבשנו 10. הלבשתי

• *Reflexive verbs: doing something to oneself*

חוֹזֵר / רֶפְלֶקְסִיבִי

Read the following passage:

בשעה שמונה בבוקר דפנה קמה, התקלחה, התלבשה, התאפרה ויצאה לפגישה חשובה. היא הגיעה ◄ לפגישה מוקדם וחיכתה שעה עד שכל המשתתפים נכנסו לחדר הישיבות והתארגנו לקראת הפגישה.

At 8 a.m. Dafna got up, showered, got dressed, put on makeup and left for an important meeting. She arrived at the meeting early and waited an hour until all the participants entered the conference room and got organized for the meeting.

All the verbs highlighted in the passage above are active verbs (i.e., their subjects are active). The verbs that are highlighted in blue are simply active, while those highlighted in red have a special meaning: their subjects all do the action to themselves.

להתארגן	להתאפר	להתלבש	להתקלח ◄
to get organized=	to put on makeup=	to get dressed=	to take a shower=
to organize **oneself**	to make **oneself** up	to dress **oneself**	to shower **oneself**

As you can see, these verbs may have several translations in English, but in all cases the action is done to **oneself**. These are called *reflexive verbs*.

Q: To which *beenyan* do the above verbs belong?

A: They all belong to *beenyan heetpa'el*.[6] Most reflexive verbs are found in this *beenyan*.[7] Here are some more examples:

להתחבא	להתגלח	להתרחץ ◄
to hide (oneself)	to shave (oneself)	to wash oneself,
		to get washed[8]

Knowing that one **possible** meaning of *heetpa'el* verbs is reflexive can help us guess the meaning of a *heetpa'el* verb that we may encounter in a text. This knowledge can also help us translate reflexive verbs from English to Hebrew, i.e., if we know that לבש and התלבש exist, we would choose the *heetpa'el* התלבש as a translation of the reflexive meaning. However, such a choice cannot be made automatically without consulting a dictionary or asking a Hebrew speaker.

---

6   The active counterparts of these *heetpa'el* verbs belong to a variety of *beenyaneem*, for example: להתלבש
   means להלביש את עצמו (*heef'eel*), להתקלח means לקלח את עצמו (*pee'el*).

7   *Beenyan neef'al* also contains a number of reflexive verbs, for example:
           Yoni registered (=listed himself) for the course.   יוני נרשם לקורס. ◄
         The addict is trying to get off of (=wean himself from) drugs.   הנרקומן מנסה להיגמל מסמים.
   Though a number of examples of reflexive verbs exist in *beenyan neef'al*, it is unclear whether the *reflexive* meaning is widespread enough in *neef'al* for us to view it as one of the meanings that the *beenyan* gives to roots that appear in it.

8   This is just one meaning of this verb. It is also commonly used to mean: *to go swimming / bathing* in the ocean.

Be careful! In many cases, a reflexive in English cannot be translated using a *heetpa'el* verb in Hebrew. Instead, the Hebrew might require that we use as an active verb followed by a form of the word עצמו (oneself), for example:

> The girl saw herself in the mirror.   הילדה ראתה את עצמה בראי.
>
> Not everyone likes/loves himself.   לא כל אחד אוהב את עצמו.

Comparing reflexive verbs in Hebrew and English

Now read the following pairs of sentences:

simply active:	Yoni shaved his head.	יוני גילח את ראשו.
reflexive:	Yoni shaved before he got dressed.	יוני התגלח לפני שהוא התלבש.
causative:	Anne Frank hid her diary.	אנה פרנק החביאה את היומן שלה.
reflexive:		אנה פרנק התחבאה בעליית גג באמסטרדם.
	Anne Frank hid in an attic in Amsterdam.	

Q: Do the English translations of the reflexive verbs contain a form of the word *oneself*?

A: No. The words *himself* or *herself* are **understood** but not expressed. In fact, in each pair of sentences above, the **same** verb form is used in English to express **different** meanings of the verbs *to shave* and *to hide*. In contrast, Hebrew uses **different *beenyaneem*** to express **different meanings** of related verbs. In order to translate English verbs like *shaved* and *hid* into Hebrew, we must think about the meaning of the verb and ask if it is reflexive (= is done to oneself). If it is, as in the case of the second verb in each pair above, we would tend to choose the *heetpa'el* form as the proper translation.

Note: Since verbs with a reflexive meaning already contain their own direct object (i.e., oneself, himself, herself...), they are never followed by אֶת. (Indeed, verbs in *heetpa'el* and *neef'al* are virtually never followed by אֶת.)

Let's review

- Another special category of active verbs is reflexive verbs, which denote an action done to **oneself**, as in:

  Dafna got dressed quickly.   דפנה התלבשה מהר.

  =dressed **herself**   הלבישה **את עצמה**=

- Most reflexive verbs in Hebrew appear in *beenyan heetpa'el*.

Want to see if you've understood?
Choose the correct verb.

1. דני, למה _____ אֶת הַזָּקָן שלך?
   (גילחת / התגלחת)

2. באיזה גיל דני התחיל _____?
   (לגלח / להתגלח)

3. מיכלי _____ בעצמה, או שאימא _____ אותה?
   (סירקה / הסתרקה)   (סירקה / הסתרקה)

4. _____ חבר חדש לקבוצה שלנו.
   (צירפנו / הצטרפנו)

5. עשרה סטודנטים _____ אתמול לארגון הסטודנטים באוניברסיטה.
   (צירפו / הצטרפו)

6. בשבוע שעבר המנהל _____ חמישה עובדים.
   (פיטר / התפטר)

7. מנהלת בית הספר _____ בשבוע שעבר.
   (פיטרה / התפטרה)

Answers:

1. גילחת   2. להתגלח   3. הסתרקה, סירקה   4. צירפנו   5. הצטרפו   6. פיטר   7. התפטרה

• *Reciprocal verbs: doing something to or with each other* הֲדָדִי

Read the following passage:

◄ יעל ומיכל הן חברות קרובות מאוד. הן מתכתבות כמעט כל יום באי-מייל, אבל הן לא מתראות הרבה. בשבוע שעבר הן סוף סוף מצאו זמן להיפגש בבית קפה. כשהן נפגשו, הן התחבקו והתנשקו. אחר כך הן הזמינו קפה ועוגה. יעל סיפרה על הטיול שלה להודו. הן צחקו וכרגיל גם קצת התווכחו, ובסוף הן נפרדו זו מזו בחיבוקים.

Yael and Michal are very close friends. They correspond by e-mail almost everyday, but they don't see each other very much. Last week they finally found time to meet at a café. When they met, they hugged and kissed (each other). Afterwards, they ordered coffee and cake. Yael told about her trip to India. They laughed together and, as usual, also argued a bit. In the end they hugged and said goodbye to each other (lit.: parted from each other with hugs).

All of the verbs highlighted in this passage are active, but only the verbs in red have an element of reciprocity: two people who do the same thing to or with **each other**. (Yael and Michal correspond **with each other**, they don't see **each other**, they meet **with each other**, etc.). These verbs denote actions that can't be done alone, but rather require two sides: two people or two groups of people (e.g., armies, teams, etc.).

Q: To which *beenyaneem* do these verbs belong?

A: Most belong to *heetpa'el*:[9]

	להתכתב	להתראות	להתחבק	להתנשק	להתווכח
	to correspond	to see	to hug	to kiss	to argue
	(with **each other**)	**each other**	(**each other**)	(**each other**)	(with **each other**)

The two remaining verbs with a reciprocal meaning belong to *beenyan neef'al*:[10]

	להיפגש	להיפרד
	to meet	to part
	(with **each other**)	(from **each other**)

Clearly, *heetpa'el* is the *beenyan* associated most with the reciprocal meaning. Thus, when we encounter a *heetpa'el* verb in a text and wish to guess its meaning, one educated guess would be that the verb has a reciprocal meaning. Here are some more examples of verbs with this meaning:

	להתחתן	להתחבק	להתגרש
	to get married	to hug **each other**	to get divorced
	(to **each other**)		(from **each other**)

Note: Reciprocity can be expressed in Hebrew not only with verbs like those above, but also by adding to a simply active verb a variation of the words זה את זה (each other – *formal*) or אחד את השני (each other – *informal*), just as we do in English:[11]

The people didn't hear each other.	האנשים לא שמעו זה את זה (or: אחד את השני).
They were angry at each other.	הם כעסו זה על זה (or: אחד על השני).

---

9   These verbs are not reciprocals of one particular *beenyan*. Their simply active counterparts belong to a variety of *beenyaneem*: להתכתב means לכתוב זה לזה (*pa'al*), להתחבק means לחבק זה את זה (*pee'el*). Some verbs, such as להתווכח, are reciprocal but don't have a simply active counterpart.

10   More reciprocal verbs in *neef'al* are להילחם (to fight), להיאבק (to struggle). There are varying opinions as to whether the reciprocal meaning is widespread enough in *neef'al* for us to view it as one of the meanings that the *beenyan* gives to roots that appear in it, or whether we should view the appearance of reciprocal verbs in *neef'al* as a coincidence. (For an example of the former opinion, see Mazal Cohen-Weidenfeld, 1996, vol. I, p. 208; the latter opinion was expressed by Rivka Halevy-Nemirovsky in a lecture on "Constructions of Reciprocity" that was delivered on April 27, 2010 at the Hebrew University.)

11   For more on זה את זה and the like, see the chapter "Pronouns and Pointing Words," pp. 211-214.

Comparing reciprocal ("each other") verbs in Hebrew and English

Let's look at some simply active-reciprocal pairs:

The groom kissed the bride.	החתן נישק את הכלה.
The couple kissed.	בני הזוג התנשקו.[12]
Dana hugged Anat.	דנה חיבקה את ענת.
The friends hugged.	החברות התחבקו.

Q: Do the English translations of the reciprocal verbs (התנשקו and התחבקו) contain the words *each other*?

A: No. These words can be added, but they are not always present. In order to translate English verbs like *kissed* and *hugged* into Hebrew, we must think about the meaning of the verb and ask if it is reciprocal (= is done to each other). If it is, as in the case of the second of each of the two verbs above, we would tend to choose the *heetpa'el* form as the proper translation.

Notice that – like all *heetpa'el* verbs – those with a reciprocal meaning can be followed by a variety of prepositions (-להתווכח עם, להתגרש מ), but never by אֶת.

Let's review

♦ Reciprocal verbs, in which two or more people (or groups) do the same thing to or with **each other,** constitute another special category of active verbs, as in:

The couple kissed.	בני הזוג התנשקו.
= kissed each other	= נישקו זה את זה

♦ Most reciprocal verbs in Hebrew appear in *beenyan heetpa'el.*

---

12 It is also possible to add variations of "זה __ זה" to plural reciprocal verbs, for example:
הם התנשקו זה עם זה.   הן התחבקו אחת עם השנייה.

Want to see if you've understood?
Choose the correct verb.

1. דני והבן שלו תמיד _____ כשהם _____ .
   (מחבקים / מתחבקים)   (פוגשים / נפגשים)

2. דני תמיד _____ את בנו כשהוא _____ אותו.
   (מחבק / מתחבק)   (פוגש / נפגש)

3. אל _____ את הכלב מפה!
   (תגרש / תתגרש)

4. בני הזוג _____ שלוש שנים אחרי שהם _____ .
   (גירש / התגרשו)   (חיתנו / התחתנו)

5. יוסי ורינה _____ את הבת שלהם ביום ראשון.
   (יחתנו / יתחתנו)

Answers:

1. מתחבקים, נפגשים   2. מחבק, פוגש   3. תגרש   4. התגרשו, התחתנו   5. יחתנו

Chapter summary

◆ Some of the active verbs in *beenyaneem pee'el, heef'eel, neef'al* and *heetpa'el* have specialized meanings.

◆ **Causative** verbs denote the **causing** of an action or the **causing** of something or someone to be in a certain state, as in:

The boy fed the cat.	הילד האכיל את החתול. ◄
= **caused** the cat to eat	
Vitamins strengthen the body.	ויטמינים מחזקים את הגוף.
= **cause** it to be strong	

This meaning tends to be found in *heef'eel* and *pee'el*.

◆ **Reflexive** verbs denote doing something to **oneself**, as in:

Dafna got dressed quickly.	דפנה התלבשה מהר. ◄
= dressed **herself**	

This meaning is found mainly in *heetpa'el*.

◆ **Reciprocal** verbs tell about two or more people (or groups) who do the same thing to or with **each other**, as in:

The couple kissed.   בני הזוג התנשקו.

= kissed **each other**

This meaning is also found mainly in *heetpa'el*.

◆ When we encounter **active** verbs in Hebrew, and we are familiar with the *root*, it is often helpful to know that the following *beenyaneem* may denote one of the following meanings:

- *pee'el* – simply active or causative
- *heef'eel* – simply active or causative
- *heetpa'el* – simply active or reflexive or reciprocal
- *neef'al* – simply active (with a number of blatant examples of reflexive and reciprocal verbs)

3. Verbs that Are Neither Active Nor Passive

> ### Preview
>
> • *Verbs that express a state of being*   מַצָּב
>
> • *Verbs that express "it happened to him…," a change of state ("he became…") or a process*   "זה קרה לו", שינוי מצב, תהליך

Introduction

In Chapter 1 of this section, we looked at *active* and *passive* verbs and saw that some active verbs (especially those that take אֶת) can be made passive (e.g., כתב he wrote ⟹ נכתב it was written), while others cannot (e.g., הלך he went). In the case of both kinds of active verbs, the subject of the verb **does** something – it is **active**. In sentences with passive verbs, the subject is **acted upon**, it "**receives**" the action – it is **passive**.

In the present chapter, we will look at verbs whose subjects are **neither** active **nor** passive; they can be placed between the active and passive verbs on a kind of sliding scale. We will examine two variations of these kinds of verbs and the *beenyaneem* to which they tend to belong.

• *Verbs that express a state of being* מַצָּב

Read the following passage:

> כשהמורה נכנסה לכיתה אחרי ההפסקה, רוב הילדים ישבו במקומותיהם. שלושה ילדים עדיין עמדו
> בצד, אבל כשהם ראו את המורה, הם מיד התיישבו במקומותיהם. ילד אחד שכב על הרצפה וישן.
> המורה לא אמרה מילה. היא לא כעסה, אבל היא גם לא שָׂמחה לראות את מצב הכיתה.

When the teacher went into the classroom after recess, most of the children were sitting in their places. Three children were still standing on the side, but when they saw the teacher, they sat down in their seats right away. One child was lying on the floor asleep (lit.: and sleeping). The teacher didn't say a word. She was not angry, but she also was not happy to see the situation in the classroom.

The verbs highlighted in blue are active (i.e., their subjects **do** something).

Q: Are the verbs highlighted in red also active?

A: No. The subjects of these verbs are in a kind of **non-active state**: in the state of sitting, standing, lying down, sleeping, being angry and being happy. These are often called *stative verbs* or *verbs of state*.

Verbs that denote emotion, like כעס above, and also verbs of cognition (e.g., ידע he knew) and of perception (e.g., שמע he heard), are often considered to be verbs of state.[1]

Q: To which *beenyan* do the verbs of state (in red above) belong?

A: They all happen to belong to *beenyan pa'al*.

Did you know?

Verbs of state in *beenyan pa'al* have regular past tense forms (they are like כָּתַב); however, in the present tense they may appear in one of the following two forms:

- a form like the active verb כּוֹתֵב (with "וֹ"), as in: עכשיו הוא יוֹשֵׁב (Now he is sitting.)
- a form like the adjective שָׁמֵן (called *pa'el*),[2] as in: עכשיו הוא יָשֵׁן (Now he is sleeping.)

Note: Many, but not **all** verbs whose present tense form is *pa'el* are "verbs of state." As we will see in the next section, some – e.g., גָּדֵל he is growing up – are verbs that describe a **process** or **change** of state.

While a great many verbs that denote a state of being belong to *beenyan pa'al*, there are verbs of state in other *beenyaneem* as well, for example: לחכות ל- (to wait – *pee'el*), להצטיין (to excel – *heetpa'el*).[3]

---

1   It may be convincingly argued that when we are angry or when we think or when we sleep (and the like), our mind and body are actually **active** and that there is not always a clear distinction between active and stative verbs. Be that as it may, recognizing that many verbs are clearly stative heightens our awareness of the fact that not all verbs are **either** active **or** passive. Rather, there is a sliding scale of "activeness": from active verbs to less active, to non-active and – ultimately – to passive verbs (and subjects).

2   See the chapter "*Beenyan Pa'al*," p. 383.

3   While many verbs of state have objects (e.g., דני כועס על יוסי Danny is angry at Yossi), including objects with את (e.g., דליה זוכרת את יוסי Dalia remembers Yossi), not many of them can be made passive in Hebrew (e.g., זכר את he remembered, רצה את he wanted – cannot be made passive). An example of a verb of state that can be made passive is להבין את (to understand):

הסטודנט הבין את התרגיל.   ➤   ⇐   התרגיל הובן על ידי הסטודנט.

The student understood the exercise.   The exercise was understood by the student

Be careful! Because verbs of state describe a state and not an action, they are close in meaning to adjectives. Thus, when translating from English to Hebrew, sometimes an adjective in English will be expressed as a **verb** (of state) in Hebrew, for example:

➤ The teacher was angry.   המורה כעסה.

The teacher was happy to receive the interesting stories that the students wrote.
המורה שָׂמְחָה לקבל את הסיפורים המעניינים שהתלמידים כתבו.

Let's review

- Verbs of state (stative verbs) denote the subject's state of being. The subject of these verbs is not considered to be active, for example:

הוא שמח.	הוא ישב.	הוא עמד.	◄
He was happy.	He was sitting.	He was standing.	

- Many verbs of state belong to *beenyan pa'al*.

• *Verbs that express "it happened to him...," a change of state ("he became...") or a process*
"זה קרה לו", שינוי מצב, תהליך

Read the following sentences containing more verbs in *beenyan pa'al*:

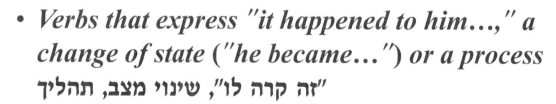

הפער בין מחירי המכוניות קטן בשנה האחרונה.	מחיר הלחם עלה.	הילד גדל בירושלים.	◄
The difference (gap) between the prices of cars got smaller in the last year.	The price of bread went up.	The boy grew up in Jerusalem.	

These verbs (and their subjects) are **neither** active nor passive. They are also not verbs of state, such as ישן and ישב; rather, in these sentences something **happens to** the subjects, they undergo a **process**, they **become** different (their state **changes**): the boy grew up (גדל) – it happened to him, he underwent a change; the price of bread went up (עלה) – it changed.[4]

Verbs in the "it happened to him" / change of state / process category are found in other *beenyaneem*, too. For example, here are verbs with this meaning in *beenyan neef'al*:[5]

הקונצרט נמשך שעתיים ונגמר ב-22:00.	האישה נפצעה בתאונה.	הילדה נרדמה. ◄
The concert lasted two hours and ended at 10 p.m.	The woman was injured in the accident.	The girl fell asleep.

Many verbs in this category of meaning belong to *beeyaneem heetpa'el*, for example:[6]

השיעור הסתיים ב-12:00.	הנערה השתנתה מאוד.	המרק התבשל במשך שעתיים. ◄
The lesson ended at 12:00.	The girl changed a lot.	The soup cooked for two hours.

The meaning of some verbs in this category (such as נפצעה she was injured = this happened to her) is **close to** that of passive verbs, but they are different from passive verbs in that there is no one in the background who **performed** (performs or will perform) the actions denoted by these verbs.

---

4 a. There are actually some *change of state* verbs that may be seen as active (e.g., התיישב he took a seat, or perhaps התגייר he converted – became Jewish – which requires that the subject be active). Since we are defining *change of state* verbs as **neither** active nor passive, we do not include verbs like התיישב here. Rather, we categorize them as active *heetpa'el* verbs as mentioned in Chapter 1 above ("Active and Passive Verbs," pp. 580-581).

b. Here are some more examples of *pa'al* verbs with this meaning:

נפל	אבד	גבה	ירד	צמח	פחת	גבר ◄
fell	was lost	got tall(er)	went down	(he/it) grew	lessened	grew stronger
			(e.g., the price went down)			

5 Here are some more examples of *neef'al* verbs:

נפסק	נעלם	נבהל	נפתח	נסגר ◄
(he/it) ceased	disappeared	was frightened	opened	closed
			(the door opened)	(the window closed)

6 Here are more examples of *heetpa'el* verbs:

השתפר	התקדם	התפוצץ	הזדקן	התבגר	התקצר	התארך ◄
(he/it) improved	progressed	exploded	aged	matured	got shorter	got longer

Did you know?
Roots that appear in pee'el, poo'al *and* heetpa'el

In some cases, the root of *heetpa'el* verbs in this category appears also in the related *beenyaneem pee'el* and *poo'al* (with the same basic meaning). When this is the case, the *pee'el* verb is active, the *poo'al* verb is passive and the *heetpa'el* verb often has the meaning "it happened to him"/ change of state / process.

"it happened to him"/ change of state / process	*passive*	*active*
המרק התבשל במשך חצי שעה. The soup cooked for half an hour.	המרק **בושל** בסיר לחץ. The soup **was cooked** in a pressure cooker.	דניאל בישל מרק בסיר לחץ. Daniel cooked soup in a pressure cooker.
העיר התפתחה מאוד בשנתיים האחרונות. The city has developed a lot in recent years.	תרופה חדשה **פותחה.** A new drug **was developed.**	חברה ישראלית פיתחה תרופה חדשה. An Israel company developed a new drug.

Notice that in these examples, Hebrew expresses the different meanings by using **different** *beenyaneem* (i.e., different forms). This is not necessarily the case in English.[7] Thus, when you translate sentences like these from English to Hebrew, you have to think about what the English verb really means in its context. (Is it active or not? Causative? etc.) Asking and answering these questions can help you decide in which *beenyan* the Hebrew verb is **likely** to appear.

In addition to the verbs in *pa'al*, *neef'al* and *heetpa'el*, there are also verbs in *beenyan heef'eel* in this category of meaning, for example:[8]

השיער שלו הלבין. His hair turned white.	החולה הבריא. The patient got well.	הילד השמין. The boy got heavier / gained weight.	המצב החמיר. The situation worsened.

---

7   It is, of course, not always the case in Hebrew either. For example, as we saw above, עלה can be either active (הוא עלה במדרגות He went up the stairs) or stative (המחיר עלה The price went up). The verb נסגר can be either stative (החנות נסגרה ב-13:00 The store closed at 1 p.m.) or passive (המסעדה נסגרה על ידי משרד הבריאות The restaurant was closed by the Department of Health).

8   Here are some more examples of verbs in *beenyan heef'eel*:

הפרי הבשיל. The fruit ripened.	המצב החריף. The situation worsened.	הפנים של האיש האדימו. The man's face turned red.

Some of these verbs may be used to express **both** the "it happened to him…" meaning and an active-causative meaning. For example, compare the following:

"it happened to him / her / it"	*active-causative*
המצב הכלכלי החמיר.	העלייה בערך הדולר החמירה את המצב. ⤴
The economic situation worsened / got worse.	The rise in the value of the dollar made the situation worse.
השיער של האיש הלבין.	משחת השיניים הזאת יכולה להלבין את שיניך.
The man's hair turned white.	This toothpaste can whiten your teeth.

In these sentences (and in others like them), only the **context** and the use of אֶת (with causative verbs) tells us what the verb's meaning is.

Note that the **change** or **process** indicated by many of the verbs mentioned in this section can take place over an extended period of time, as in התפתח (developed) and השמין (gained weight, got "heavy"), or they can be sudden and quick, as in נגמר/הסתיים (ended) and נרדם (fell asleep). The action denoted by some of these verbs can be likened to what happens to a balloon: it expands (more and more) or shrinks (little by little) or bursts.

We have grouped together the meanings "it happened to him…," change of state ("he became…") and process since they sometimes overlap. The important point here is that verbs with one or more of these meanings are neither active nor passive. They are never followed by אֶת and cannot be made passive.

Let's review

◆ Another category of non-active verbs is verbs that denote "it happened to him…" / change of state / process, for example:

The lesson ended at 12:00.	השיעור הסתיים ב-12:00. ⤴
The girl fell asleep.	הילדה נרדמה.
The price of bread went up.	מחיר הלחם עלה.
The patient got well.	החולה הבריא.

◆ These verbs are found mainly in *beenyaneem heetpa'el*, *neef'al* and *pa'al*. Some are found in *heef'eel*.

Want to see if you've understood?
Choose the correct verb.

1. הייתה רוח חזקה והדלת _____.
(פתחה / נפתחה)

2. הבשר _____ כבר שלוש שעות על האש.
(מבשל / מתבשל)

3. יופי! _____ את הציונים שלכם!
(שיפרתם / השתפרתם)

4. המורה לספורט אמר לי: מאוד _____ בריצה. כל הכבוד!
(שיפרת / השתפרת)

5. לפני שבוע _____ את השם של הרחוב שלנו.
(שינו / השתנו)

6. משהו באחותי _____, אבל אני לא יודע מה בדיוק.
(שינה / השתנה)

7. באיזו שעה השיעור _____?
(גומר / נגמר)

8. יונתן _____ את התיק שלו בכיתה ביום שישי. התיק _____ שם עד יום ראשון.
(נשאר / השאיר)

Answers:

1. נפתחה   2. מתבשל   3. שיפרתם   4. השתפרת   5. שינו   6. השתנה   7. נגמר   8. השאיר, נשאר

4. Meanings and the *Beenyaneem*: Summary

Preview

- *Chart I: Meanings of verbs arranged from active to passive*
- *Chart II: Meanings of verbs arranged according to* beenyaneem

In the chapters in this unit, we have tried to see how the *beenyaneem* are used to modify the basic meaning of roots. For example, the root כ-ת-ב, whose basic meaning is connected with **writing**, has the following specialized meanings in different *beenyaneem*:

active:

simply active:	(pa'al)	עו"ד גדעון לוי מירושלים כתב מכתב לעורך דין בניו יורק.

Mr. Gidon Levy, a Jerusalem lawyer, wrote a letter to a lawyer in New York.

active-causative:	(heef'eel)	עו"ד לוי הכתיב את המכתב למזכירה שלו.

Mr. Levy dictated the letter to his secretary.
= He caused his secretary to write it.

active-reciprocal:	(heetpa'el)	עו"ד לוי ועורך הדין האמריקאי מתכתבים כל הזמן.

Mr. Levy and the American lawyer correspond all the time.
= They write to each other.

passive:

	(neef'al)	המכתב נכתב אתמול בערב (על ידי מר לוי).

The letter was written last night (by Mr. Levy).

	(hoof'al)	המכתב הוכתב אתמול (על ידי מר לוי).

The letter was dictated yesterday (by Mr. Levy).

Below you will find two charts. The first presents specialized **meanings** like these, beginning with active meanings, continuing down through meanings that are neither active nor passive and ending with the passive. In the active category we have included *simply active, causative, reflexive* and *reciprocal* verbs.[1] In the "neither active nor passive" category, we have included

---

1   In many grammar books, *reflexive* and *reciprocal* verbs are placed in a category **separate** from *active verbs* (called "middle") because the subject of these verbs both **does** the action and "**receives**" it. For the sake of simplicity, we have labeled as *active* all verbs whose subject is active, including *reflexive* and *reciprocal* verbs.

verbs of state and verbs expressing *"it happened to him" / change of state / process*. Next to the meanings, we have listed the *beenyaneem* **typically** used to express them.

The second chart presents the same information, but it is arranged according to the ***beenyaneem***. Here we see each *beenyan* and the meanings it typically denotes. The verbs in the second chart are taken from the sentences in the first chart. We have put parentheses around the meanings that exist in a given *beenyan* and are often noted in grammar books as typical of this *beenyan*, but are not commonly found. This chart is intended to give you an **overall** view as to the connection between the *beenyaneem* and the different meanings. It is not exhaustive.

Remember: Except for *poo'al* and *hoof'al*, which are always passive,[2] the *beenyaneem* **do not have fixed and predictable meanings**. Therefore, when we list a *beenyan* as having a particular meaning, this does not mean that all verbs in the *beenyan* have this meaning.

Note: The footnotes for the chart on the next page are found at the bottom of this page.

---

2   We are speaking here only of the **verbs** in these *beenyaneem* and not of adjectives like מצוין (excellent) and
    מוצלח (successful), whose **forms** are those of present tense verbs.
3   אֶת is used when the direct object is *definite* (= specific), as in דן כתב את המכתב (Dan wrote **the** letter); when
    the direct object is *indefinite*, no preposition is used: דן כתב מכתב (Dan wrote **a** letter). The great majority of
    active verbs that can be made passive are verbs that take את (and not a different preposition). However, there
    are some verbs that take a different preposition and can be made passive, such as: טיפל ב-⇐טופל, תמך ב-⇐נתמך.
    For more examples, see the chapter "Active and Passive Verbs," p. 591.
4   Some of these verbs can appear without any preposition, and some can appear with a preposition such as
    ב-, ל-, על or the like, but none take אֶת.
5   There are not many examples of *neef'al* verbs with this meaning.
6   There are not many examples of *neef'al* verbs with this meaning.
7   See note 4.

• *Chart I: Meanings of verbs arranged from active to passive*

◆ Active	Simply active	take אֶת;[3] can be made passive	*pa'al*:	wrote	דן כתב את המכתב.
			pee'el:	fixed	רון תיקן את המחשב.
			heef'eel:	invited	אורי הזמין את האורחים.
	Causative		*pee'el*:	shortened	גדי קיצר את הסיפור.
			heef'eel:	lengthened	רן האריך את הסיפור.
	Simply active[4]	don't take אֶת; cannot be made passive	*pa'al*:	went	גיל הלך למכולת.
			pee'el:	traveled	יוני טייל לבד.
			heef'eel:	arrived	קובי הגיע לפגישה.
			neef'al:	entered	יוסי נכנס לבנק.
			heetpa'el:	looked at	אלעד הסתכל בתמונה.
	Reflexive ("oneself")		*heetpa'el*:	got dressed	אריאל התלבש מהר.
			neef'al:[5]	registered	גלעד נרשם לקורס.
	Reciprocal ("each other")		*heetpa'el*:	corresponded	החברים התכתבו.
			neef'al:[6]	separated	בני הזוג נפרדו לאחר שלוש שנות נישואין.
◆ Neither Active Nor Passive	Verbs of State	take אֶת; some can be made passive, some cannot	various *beenyaneem*: can be made passive:		
				understood	הסטודנט הבין את ההרצאה.
			cannot be made passive:		
				wanted	הילד רצה את הגלידה.
				liked	רוני תמיד חיבב את שרה.
	Verbs of State	don't take אֶת;[7] cannot be made passive	*pa'al*:	sat	נדב ישב בחדר שלו.
			other *beenyaneem*:		
				waited	רון חיכה לאוטובוס.
				believed	השופט האמין לדברי הנאשם.
				meant	הוא לא התכוון לפגוע בך.
	"It happened to him" / change of state / process	cannot be made passive	*heetpa'el*:	developed	הילד התפתח.
			neef'al:	fell asleep	הבחור נרדם.
			pa'al:	went up	המחיר עלה.
			heef'eel:	worsened	המצב החמיר.
◆ Passive			*neef'al*:	was written	המכתב נכתב (על ידי דן).
			poo'al:	was fixed	המחשב תוקן (על ידי רון).
			hoof'al:	was invited	האורח הוזמן (על ידי אורי).
			heetpa'el:	was received	המכתב התקבל אתמול (על ידי עדי).

615

• *Chart II: Meanings of verbs arranged according to beenyaneem*

	Active					Neither Active Nor Passive			Passive
	Simply active	Causative	Simply active	Reflexive ("oneself")	Reciprocal ("each other")	Verbs of State		"It happened to him"/ change of state / process	
	take את; can be made passive	don't take את; cannot be made passive				take את; some can be made passive; some cannot	don't take את; cannot be made passive	cannot be made passive	
◆ *pa'al*	כָּתַב		הָלַךְ			רָצָה[8]	יָשַׁב	המחיר עלה.	
◆ *pee'el*	תִּיקֵן	קִיצֵר	טִיֵּיל			(חִיבֵּב)	חִיכָּה		
◆ *heef'eel*	הִזְמִין	הֶאֱרִיךְ	הִגִּיעַ			הֵבִין	הֶאֱמִין	המצב החמיר.	
◆ *heetpa'el*			הִסְתַּכֵּל	הִתְלַבֵּשׁ	הִתְכַּתְבוּ		הִתְכַּוֵּון	הִתְפַּתַּח	(הִתְקַבֵּל)
◆ *neef'al*			נִכְנַס	(נִרְשַׁם)	(נִפְרְדוּ)			נִרְדַּם	נִכְתַּב
◆ *poo'al*									תוּקַן
◆ *hoof'al*									הוּזְמַן

---

8   רצה and חיבב cannot be made passive.

Here are a few points worthy of attention:

There are verbs that can have **more than one meaning** and thus will appear in more than one place in the chart above. In such cases we can determine the meaning of the verb by looking at the context, for example:

➤ העשן **השחיר** את קירות הבית.   *active-causative*:
The smoke blackened the walls of the house.

קירות הבית **השחירו**.   *"it happened to them" / change of state*:
The walls of the house **turned black**.

➤ האיש עלה במדרגות.   *active*:
The man went up the stairs.

המחיר **עלה**.   *"it happened to it" / change of state*:
The price **went up**.

Note: In this example and others, looking at whether the subject is **animate** or not helps us determine the verb's meaning. Here is another example:

➤ הילדה התכסתה בשמיכה.   *active-reflexive*:
The girl covered herself with a blanket.

המכונית **התכסתה** בחול.   *"it happened to it" / change of state*:
The car **became / got covered** with sand.

Also, sometimes the meaning can be interpreted or understood in more than one way, for example:

➤ האישה **התקרבה** לטלוויזיה כדי לראות יותר טוב.
The woman **got closer** to the television in order to see better.

The verb **התקרבה** can be understood here as *reflexive* – "brought herself closer" – or as a *change of state* or *process* – "got closer."

In addition, sometimes verbs in different *beenyaneem* may have the **same** – or a very **similar** – meaning, as in:

➤ בני הדודים של יוני **גרים** בלונדון.   Yoni's cousins live in London.
בני הדודים של יוני **מתגוררים** בלונדון.[9]

הילד **פוחד** מכלבים.   The boy is afraid of dogs.
הילד **מפחד** מכלבים.

---

9   מתגוררים is more formal than גרים.

PART THREE:
PRONUNCIATION AND SPELLING

I. Basic Concepts: Sounds and Syllables

Preview

• *Vowels and consonants*

• *Open and closed syllables*

• *Syllable stress (accent)*

In this chapter we will examine basic concepts that are important for the understanding of the next two chapters.

• *Vowels and consonants*

The terms vowel and consonant refer to the two basic **sounds** in all languages, including Hebrew. The vowels in Israeli Hebrew are: *ah, eh, ee, oh* and *oo*. In Hebrew a vowel is called a תְּנוּעָה (lit.: movement), since when we pronounce vowels, the air **moves** quite **freely** out of our mouth. If you had enough air (and perhaps operatic training), you could sing the vowels forever: *aaaaaaa...,* *eeeeeeee..., ooooooo...*

The consonants are the sounds that are **not** vowels, for example: *b, d, f, g* and so on. In Hebrew a consonant is called an עִיצוּר (from the root ע-צ-ר to stop), since when we pronounce consonants, we **stop** or **limit** the flow of air out of our mouth. For example, when we say *b*, we stop the flow of air completely; when we say *s*, we limit the flow significantly.

Want to see if you've understood?

Read the following list of sounds and write each sound under the proper heading.

ee   d   f   eh   sh   oo   s   ah   t   v   oh   r   k

consonants עיצורים   *vowels* תנועות

_____   _____

Answers:

consonants: d, f, sh, s, t, v, r, k   vowels: ee, eh, oo, ah, oh

• *Open and closed syllables*

As a rule, a syllable in Hebrew begins with a consonant[1] and contains one vowel.[2] In most cases, the number of syllables in the word is equal to the number of vowels in the word. This means that if there is **one** vowel in a word, the word has only **one** syllable. If there are **two** vowels, the word has **two** syllables and so on.

one syllable:	YAD	יָד ◄
three syllables:	har-ga-SHA	הַרְגָּ-שָׁה

Read the following words, which are divided into syllables:

לִי-מוֹן	תֵּ-שֵׁב	דָּ-בָר ◄
lee-MON	te-SHEV	da-VAR

Q: Does the first syllable in the above words **end** in a vowel or a consonant?

A: The first syllable ends in a vowel: *ah* in *da-VAR*, *eh* in *te-SHEV*, *ee* in *lee-MON*.

A syllable that ends in a vowel is called an *open syllable* (i.e., the airway is **open**).

Q: Does the second syllable in the above words end in a vowel or a consonant?

A: The second syllable ends in a consonant: *da-VAR*, *te-SHEV*, *lee-MON*.

A syllable that ends in a consonant is called a *closed syllable* (i.e., the airway is either completely or partially **closed**).[3] Any one of the syllables in a word can be open (*o*) or closed (*c*):

c o c	*o o*	*c c*
מַחְ-בֶּ-רֶת	שִׁי-רָה	מִשְׂ-חָק ◄
mach-BE-ret	shee-RA	mees-CHAK
notebook	singing, poetry	game

---

1   The one blatant exception is when, for phonetic reasons, the word "וְ" (and) changes to "וּ" (*oo*). In such a case, the syllable begins with a vowel (*oo*). In addition, speakers who do not pronounce 'ע or 'א at the beginning of a word actually begin a syllable with a vowel sound. Another case in which a syllable begins with a vowel is in words like רוּחַ (*ROO-ach*), in which the helping vowel *ah* begins the final syllable. Note: The division into syllables presented in this book is based on today's spoken Hebrew. It does not always correspond to the division into syllables presented in classical Hebrew grammar books.

2   This is the general rule. However, there are cases in which two vowels (i.e., a vowel and a semi-vowel) can appear in one syllable (as a *diphthong*), as in: בָּנַי (*ba-NAI* my sons).

3   There are syllables that end in two consonants, such as: כָּתַבְתְּ (*ka-TAVT*).

Want to see if you've understood?

A. Read the following words and divide them into syllables.

Example: ת וֹ-דָ ה   ◄

4. אֲ נִ י   3. דִ י רָ ה   2. תַ לְ מִ י ד   1. יֶ לֶ ד

6. שִׂ מְ לָ ה   5. שָׁ ל וֹ ם

B. Write above the syllable if it is open ("o") or closed ("c").

$$\overset{o \quad o}{\text{ת וֹ-דָ ה}}$$

Example: ◄

Answers:

$$\overset{o \ c}{\text{6. שִׂמְ-לָה}} \quad \overset{c \ o}{\text{5. שָׁ-לוֹם}} \quad \overset{o \ o}{\text{4. אֲ-נִי}} \quad \overset{o \ o}{\text{3. דִי-רָה}} \quad \overset{c \ o}{\text{2. תַלְ-מִיד}} \quad \overset{c \ o}{\text{1. יֶ-לֶד}}$$

• *Syllable stress (accent)*

A word usually has one *stressed* syllable. If you tap out each syllable on the table with your hand, you will make a louder tap where the stress is. The *stress* in Hebrew is usually either on the **last** syllable of the word or on the syllable **before** the last.[4]

the stress is on the last syllable:	*mees-PAR*	מִסְ-פָּר ◄
the stress is on the syllable before last:	*SE-ret*	סֶ-רֶט
	mach-BE-ret	מַחְ-בֶּ-רֶת

---

4   In some – especially foreign – words, the stress is two syllables before the last syllable, as in אוֹטוֹבּוּס ('*O-to-boos*).

II. The Pronunciation of 'פ ,'כ ,'ב and the *Dagesh*

Preview

- *Two possible pronunciations of* 'פ ,'כ ,'ב
- *The weak* dagesh   דָּגֵשׁ קַל[1]
- *The strong* dagesh   דָּגֵשׁ חָזָק

• *Two possible pronunciations of* 'פ ,'כ ,'ב

Each of the letters 'פ ,'כ ,'ב has two possible pronunciations: hard and soft.[2]

	soft		*hard*
ב	*v*	ב	*b*
כ	*ch*	כ	*k*
פ	*f*	פ	*p*

Here are examples of words with the hard pronunciation (*b, k, p*):

לִשְׁבּוֹר	בּוֹדֵק	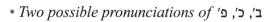
leesh-BOR	*bo-DEK*	
to break	is checking	
לִשְׁכַּב	כּוֹתֵב	
leesh-KAV	*ko-TEV*	
to lie down	is writing	
מִסְפָּר	פּוֹגֵשׁ	
mees-PAR	*po-GESH*	
number	is meeting	

---

1   In grammar books דָּגֵשׁ קַל is also called *dagesh lene*. דָּגֵשׁ חָזָק is also called *dagesh forte*.

2   We say here that the letters are "pronounced." Properly stated, letters – the graphic representation of consonants and some vowels – are "realized"; consonants and vowels are "pronounced." In books on phonetics, hard sounds are called *stops* or *plosives*; soft sounds are called *fricatives*.

When a text has vowel signs, a dot (*dagesh*) inside the letters בּ, כּ, פּ indicates that they are to be pronounced with the hard pronunciation. When there is **no** *dagesh*, the soft pronunciation is used. Here are some examples of the soft pronunciation (*v, ch, f*):

אוֹהֵב	עוֹבֵד ◄
'o-HEV	*'o-VED*
likes	is working
שׁוֹפֵךְ	שׁוֹכֵב
sho-FECH	*sho-CHEV*
is pouring	is lying down
אֶלֶף	קוֹפֵץ
'E-lef	*ko-FETS*
a thousand	is jumping

But when we read texts **without** vowel signs – and in everyday speech – how do we know when to pronounce בּ, כּ, פּ as *b, k, p* (hard) and when to pronounce them as *v, ch, f* (soft)?

In this chapter we will examine when בּ, כּ, פּ are pronounced as hard sounds, i.e., when we write a *dagesh* in these (and other) letters in a text with vowel signs. It should be noted that there are actually two different **kinds** of *dagesh* (a *weak dagesh* and a *strong dagesh*), and each appears for different reasons. Both kinds of *dagesh* **look** the same and – today – both indicate the same hard pronunciation when they appear in בּ, כּ, פּ.[3]

After you learn when the pronunciation of בּ, כּ, פּ should be hard, you can assume that in all other cases it will be soft.

---

3 In the sections below, we have not merely pointed out where בּ, כּ, פּ are pronounced as hard sounds, but also we have divided our discussion according to the types of *dagesh* that are used to indicate this sound. Knowing **which kind** of *dagesh* causes the hard pronunciation is essential for understanding the rules of pronunciation.

• *The weak dagesh* דָּגֵשׁ קַל

Where do we find a weak dagesh?

There are two places in which the hard pronunciation of פ׳ כ׳, ב׳, is indicated by a weak *dagesh*: [4]

1. *At the beginning of a word*

When פ׳ כ׳, ב׳, appear at the beginning of the word, they are almost always pronounced *b, k, p* (hard), as in:

	p		*k*		*b*	
	פָּתַח	פֹּה	כָּתַב	כֶּלֶב	בִּיקֵשׁ	בַּיִת
	pa-TACH	*PO*	*ka-TAV*	*KE-lev*	*bee-KESH*	*BA-yeet*
	opened	here	wrote	dog	requested	house

Some exceptions

There are very few exceptions to this rule. One exception is the word כֵן in the following expressions:

לִפְנֵי כֵן	אַחֲרֵי כֵן	אַף עַל פִּי כֵן
leef-nei CHEN	*'a-cha-rei CHEN*	*'af-'al-pee CHEN*
beforehand	afterwards	despite this

In all these expressions, כ׳ comes at the beginning of the word but is pronounced *chen* (with a soft *ch*). This is because in these expressions כן is **not** regarded as a **separate** word, but rather as part of one long word.[5]

Another exception to the rule regarding the hard pronunciation of פ׳ כ׳, ב׳, at the beginning of a word concerns foreign words that have entered Hebrew, including foreign place names. These words maintain their original soft pronunciation, for example:

פְּלוֹרִידָה	פֶסְטִיבָל	פִילוֹסוֹפְיָה
FLO-ree-da	*fes-tee-VAL*	*fee-lo-SOF-ya*
Florida	festival	philosophy

---

4   a. We are dealing here only with the rules that are relevant for the pronunciation of Israeli Hebrew. For a more complete treatment of the weak *dagesh*, see a grammar of Biblical Hebrew, for example: J. Weingreen, 1959, pp. 14-17.

　　b. In texts written with vowel signs, the weak *dagesh* appears not only in פ׳ כ׳, ב׳, but also in ת׳ ד׳, ג׳, (called in traditional grammar *beged kefet* or *begad kefat*: ת׳ פ׳, כ׳, ד׳, ג׳, ב׳,). In Modern Hebrew, only in פ׳ כ׳, ב׳, does the presence or absence of the *dagesh* indicate a difference in pronunciation.

5   In the middle of a word after a vowel, פ׳ כ׳, ב׳, have a soft pronunciation. See the next section for an explanation.

Want to see if you've understood?

Add a weak *dagesh* to פ׳ ,כ׳ ,ב where they are pronounced as *b, k, p*:

1. בּוֹקֶר 2. כַּרְטִיס 3. פִּתְאוֹם 4. פִּילוֹסוֹפְיָה 5. כּוֹתֵב 6. שׁוֹכֵב 7. פּוֹגֵשׁ 8. בִּיטָחוֹן
9. פֶסְטִיבָל

Answers:

There is a weak *dagesh* in the following words:

1. בּוֹקֶר 2. כַּרְטִיס 3. פִּתְאוֹם 5. כּוֹתֵב 7. פּוֹגֵשׁ 8. בִּיטָחוֹן

2. *In the middle of a word – after a closed syllable*

When פ׳ ,כ׳ ,ב appear in the middle of a word, they may be pronounced either as hard or soft sounds. When they are pronounced as hard sounds, the *dagesh* that indicates the hard pronunciation may be one of two kinds: either a *weak dagesh* or a *strong dagesh*. First we will learn when a *weak dagesh* appears in the middle of the word. Afterwards, we will learn the rules for the *strong dagesh*.

Read the following examples in which פ׳ ,כ׳ ,ב are pronounced as hard sounds:

	לִשְׁ־פּוֹט	מַס־כִּים	מִד־בָּר	◄
	leesh-POT	*mas-KEEM*	*meed-BAR*	
	to judge	agrees	desert	

Q: What kind of syllable appears before פ׳ ,כ׳ ,ב in these words – an *open* or a *closed* syllable?[6]

A: They appear immediately after a **closed** syllable: *meed-BAR, mas-KEEM, leesh-POT.*

In the middle of the word, whenever פ׳ ,כ׳ ,ב appear after a closed syllable, they are pronounced as hard sounds and, thus, in texts with vowel signs, they get a weak *dagesh*.

---

6   On open and closed syllables, see the preceding chapter.

When is there no weak dagesh *in* ב׳, כ׳, פ׳?

When ב׳, כ׳, פ׳ are **not** at the beginning of a word and are **not** in the middle after a closed syllable, they do **not** take a weak *dagesh*, for example:

1. *After a vowel*

at the beginning of a syllable:

שׁוֹ-פֵט	רֶ-כֶב	שָׁ-בַר
sho-FET	*RE-chev*	*sha-VAR*
judge	vehicle	broke

at the end of a syllable:

תַּפְ-קִיד	מִכְ-תָּב	טַבְ-לָה
taf-KEED	*meech-TAV*	*tav-LA*
position (job), function	letter	chart, table

at the end of a word:

דַף	מֶלֶךְ	חָשׁוּב
DAF	*ME-lech*	*cha-SHOOV*
sheet (of paper)	king	important

2. *After an initial* shva[7]

שְׁכִיבָה	כְּפָר	קְבוּצָה
shchee-VA	*KFAR*	*kvoo-TSA*
lying down	village	group

Some exceptions

Many words of foreign origin maintain their foreign pronunciation no matter where ב׳, כ׳, פ׳ appear, for example:

סְנוֹב	טֵיפּ	פִּילִיפּ	סְטֵרֵאוֹטִיפּ
SNOB	*TEYP*	*FEE-leep*	*ste-re-'o-TEEP*
snob	tape player	Philip	stereotype

---

7 This initial *shva* was originally a vowel; thus, ב׳, כ׳, פ׳ following this *shva* behave as if they still follow a vowel (whether the *shva* is pronounced as *eh* or is not pronounced at all).

Did you know?

בּ׳, כּ׳, פּ׳ in the following verbs **seem** to appear after a closed syllable, and yet they are pronounced as soft sounds:

> יְ-קַלְ-פוּ / תְ-קַלְ-פוּ / תְ-קַלְ-פִּי   הוֹלְ-כִים / הוֹלְ-כוֹת   כָּתְ-בוּ / כָּתְ-בָה ◄
> ye-kal-FOO te-kal-FOO te-kal-FEE   hol-CHOT   hol-CHEEM   kat-VOO   kat-VA
>   will peel   are going   wrote

In order to understand why they are pronounced like this, let's look at their masculine singular forms:

> יְ-קַ-לֵף   הוֹ-לֵךְ   כָּ-תַב ◄
> ye-ka-LEF   ho-LECH   ka-TAV

In all the masculine singular forms of these verbs, בּ׳, כּ׳, פּ׳ come immediately after a vowel. Thus, they are pronounced with a soft sound. The other forms **in the same tense**, such as those listed above (הוֹלְכִים/הוֹלְכוֹת, כָּתְבָה/כָּתְבוּ, etc.), maintain this same pronunciation of בּ׳, כּ׳, פּ׳.[8]

Let's review

◆ בּ׳, כּ׳, פּ׳ are pronounced as hard sounds *b, k, p* (and have a weak *dagesh* in texts with vowel signs) in the following circumstances:

- At the beginning of a word: בַּיִת, כּוֹתֵב, פְּגִישָׁה

- Immediately after a closed syllable (=a syllable that ends in a consonant):

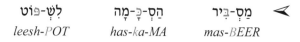

> לִשְׁ-פּוֹט   הַסְ-כָּ-מָה   מַסְ-בִּיר ◄
> leesh-*P*OT   has-*k*a-MA   mas-*B*EER

◆ In all other cases, בּ׳, כּ׳, פּ׳ do not have a weak *dagesh*.

---

8   In addition, it should be noted that while the syllables that precede בּ׳, כּ׳, פּ׳ in forms like כָּתְבָה, הוֹלְכִים and תְקַלְפִּי are pronounced in today's Hebrew as **closed** syllables (and, therefore, we have called them *closed* in this book), the traditional syllable division of these words is כָּ-תְ/בָה (*ka-te/VA*) and הוֹ-לְ/כִים (*ho-le/CHEEM*). According to this division, בּ׳, כּ׳, פּ׳ do not stand at the beginning of a new syllable and, therefore, there is no reason for them to be pronounced with a hard sound.

Want to see if you've understood?

Divide the following words into syllables and add the weak *dagesh* to ב׳, כ׳, פ׳ wherever they are pronounced *b, k, p*.

Example: לִשְׁ-פֹּךְ ◄

‎5. פָּ גַ שׁ ‎4. מִ שְׁ פָּ טִ י ם ‎3. מַ זְ כִּ י רָ ה ‎2. נִ כְ נַ ס ‎1. הִ תְ כַ תֵ ב

‎10. מִ סְ פָּ ר ‎9. כָ פָ ר ‎8. הִ סְ בִּ י ר ‎7. הַ שְׁ פָּ עָ ה ‎6. הֵ בִ י ן

‎14. בּ ו קֶ ר ‎13. הֶ בְ דֵ ל ‎12. שׁ ו כֵ ב ‎11. לְ שׁ ב ו ר

Answers:

There is a weak *dagesh* in the following words:

‎10. מִסְ-פָּר ‎9. כָּפָר ‎8. הִסְ-בִּיר ‎7. הַשְׁ-פָּ-עָה ‎5. פָּ-גַשׁ ‎4. מִשְׁ-פָּ-טִים ‎3. מַז-כִּי-רָה ‎1. הִתְ-כַּ-תֵב

‎14. בּו-קֶר ‎11. לִשְׁ-בּור

• *The strong* dagesh דָּגֵשׁ חָזָק

We said above that ב׳ ,כ׳ ,פ׳ in the middle of a word take a weak *dagesh* only after a closed syllable, and in this position they are pronounced as hard sounds (*b, k, p*). Now look at the following examples in which ב׳ ,כ׳ ,פ׳ are pronounced as hard sounds:

עִי-פָּ-רוֹן	הַ-כֶּ-סֶף	לְ-דַ-בֵּר ◄
'ee-pa-RON	*ha-KE-sef*	*le-da-BER*
pencil	the money	to speak

Q: What kind of syllable appears before ב׳ ,כ׳ ,פ׳ in these words – an open or a closed syllable?

A: They appear after an open syllable (i.e., after a vowel).[9]

If so, why are ב׳ ,כ׳ ,פ׳ pronounced as hard sounds (*b, k, p*) in these words?

The answer is that the reason for **this** hard sound is **different** from the reason for the hard sounds discussed above and indicated by the weak *dagesh* (see "Did you know?" below). The *dagesh* that indicates the hard sound in words like לְדַבֵּר is also called by a different name: the *strong dagesh*.

---

9   This is so according to Modern Hebrew pronunciation, which we are using as our guide for syllable division. In traditional grammar this is not regarded as an open syllable. This will be explained below.

> ## Did you know?
> The following background information will help you understand the reason for the hard sound in such words as לְדַבֵּר:
>
> In the distant past, consonants in certain forms were "doubled" in pronunciation (perhaps pronounced with more emphasis or length). Much later, when vowel signs were added to the written text in an attempt to indicate the traditional pronunciation more clearly, a *dagesh* was added to a letter as a sign of "doubling." Thus, *ledabber* was written לְדַבֵּר. Because this *dagesh* indicated a "doubled" consonant, it was called a *strong dagesh*.
>
> Today, however, speakers of Modern Hebrew do **not** pronounce letters in which a strong *dagesh* appears (including ב׳, כ׳, פ׳) as a "doubled" (emphasized or lengthened) consonant. And, though the strong *dagesh* may appear in any letter in a text with vowels except for א׳, ה׳, ח׳, ע׳, ר׳,[10] only in ב׳, כ׳, פ׳ does it indicate a difference in pronunciation: these are pronounced as single, but hard consonants – *b, k, p*.[11]

We will now see where a strong *dagesh* appears in texts with vowel signs so that we will know where else to pronounce ב׳, כ׳, פ׳ as hard consonants.

A strong *dagesh* appears in words for one of the following three reasons:

1. *When a* dagesh *is part of a pattern*

As explained in the chapter "Pattern" (pp. 9-16), words in Hebrew are often formed according to a *pattern* (מִשְׁקָל). Sometimes this pattern includes a strong *dagesh* in one of the root letters.[12]

---

10 Because א׳, ה׳, ח׳, ע׳ (which represent the *guttural* consonants) and often ר׳ were not "doubled" in ancient times (and thus do not take a strong *dagesh*), these consonants cause irregularities in the pronunciation of certain words. See the end of this chapter, pp. 637-638.

11 In this chapter, as in the rest of the book, we do not write a *dagesh* in letters other than ב׳, כ׳, פ׳ except for when it is important for the point being made.

12 When a strong *dagesh* is part of a pattern, it is called דָּגֵשׁ חָזָק תַּבְנִיתִי (*characteristic strong dagesh*).

For example, three verb patterns (*beenyaneem*) have a strong *dagesh* in the **second** root letter as part of their pattern.[13] When the second root letter happens to be ב׳, כ׳, פ׳, it is pronounced *b*, *k*, *p*. Here are some examples (the form in parentheses shows the strong *dagesh* in a letter other than ב׳, כ׳, פ׳):

pee'el:	(צִילֵם)	סִכֵּם	סִפֵּר	דִּבֵּר ◄
	photographed	summarized	told	spoke
poo'al:	(צוּלַם)	סוּכַּם	סוּפַּר	דוּבַּר
	was photographed	was summarized	was told	was spoken about
heetpa'el:	(הִתְרַגֵּשׁ)	הִסְתַּכֵּל	הִסְתַּפֵּר	הִתְלַבֵּשׁ
	got excited	looked at	had his hair cut	got dressed

The *noun patterns* associated with these *beenyaneem* also have a *dagesh* in the **second** root letter.

◯ִ◯וּ◯ (*pee'el*):	(צִילוּם)	לִכּוּד	סִפּוּר	דִּבּוּר ◄
	photography	consolidation	story	speaking
◯ָ◯ָ◯ָה (*pee'el*):	(בַּקָּשָׁה)		סַכָּנָה	קַבָּלָה
	request		danger	acceptance; receipt
הִתְ◯ַ◯◯וּת (*heetpa'el*):	(הִתְרַגְּשׁוּת)	הִתְמַכְּרוּת	הִתְנַפְּלוּת	הִתְאַבְּדוּת
	excitement	addiction	attacking	suicide

There are some other noun patterns that have a *dagesh*, for example:

◯ַ◯ָ◯:	(גַּנָּב)		סַפָּר	טַבָּח ◄
	thief		barber	cook
◯ִ◯ָ◯וֹן:	(שִׁיגָּעוֹן)		עִיפָּרוֹן[14]	זִיכָּרוֹן
	craziness		pencil	memory
◯ַ◯ַ◯ֶת:	(כַּלֶּבֶת)	טַבַּעַת[15]	שַׁפַּעַת	רַכֶּבֶת
	rabies	ring	influenza	train

---

13 This is so when there are **three** root letters, as is usually the case. For words with four root letters, see the chapter "*Beenyan Pee'el*," pp. 389-390.

14 Note that the plural forms of this pattern do **not** have a *dagesh*, for example: עֶפְרוֹנוֹת, זִכְרוֹנוֹת.

15 The vowels in שַׁפַּעַת and טַבַּעַת change because of the ע׳.

In the following adjective pattern (used for many colors and other common words), there is a *dagesh* in the **third root letter** when an ending is added:

סָמוּם / סָמוֹם‏ ‏‎:סָמוֹם   yellow   צָהֹב – צְהֻבָּה, צְהֻבִּים, צְהֻבּוֹת ◄

long   אָרֹךְ – אֲרֻכָּה, אֲרֻכִּים, אֲרֻכּוֹת

red   ‏(אָדֹם – אֲדֻמָּה, אֲדֻמִּים, אֲדֻמּוֹת)‏

Note the change in the vowel from *oh* to *oo* when there is a *dagesh* (i.e., in all but the *base form*).[16]

Whenever the consonants פ׳ ,כ׳ ,ב׳ appear where a word's pattern requires a *dagesh*, they are pronounced as **hard** sounds: *b, k, p*.

Want to see if you've understood?

The following chart contains examples of patterns that require a strong *dagesh*.

noun	noun	heetpa'el verbal noun	pee'el verbal noun	heetpa'el	poo'al	pee'el
שִׁיגָּעוֹן	גַּנָּב	הִתְרַגְּשׁוּת	צִילוּם	מִתְרַגֵּשׁ	מְצוּלָּם	מְצֻלָּם

Write the following words in the appropriate place in the chart above, and add a strong *dagesh* to פ׳ ,כ׳ ,ב׳ where required.

מְקוּבָּל   סַבָּל

דִּיכָאוֹן   שָׁכַב   שִׁיפּוּר   טַבָּח

מְסוּכָּן   מְסַפֵּר   מִתְחַפֵּשׂ

מְדַבֵּר   זִיכָּרוֹן

הִתְחַבְּרוּת

מִתְלַבֵּשׁ   טִיפּוּל   שׁוֹבֵר   הִתְנַפְּלוּת

Answers:

שִׁיגָּעוֹן	גַּנָּב	הִתְרַגְּשׁוּת	צִילוּם	מִתְרַגֵּשׁ	מְצוּלָּם	מְצֻלָּם
זִיכָּרוֹן	סַבָּל	הִתְחַבְּרוּת	שִׁיפּוּר	מִתְלַבֵּשׁ	מְסוּכָּן	מְסַפֵּר
דִּיכָאוֹן	טַבָּח	הִתְנַפְּלוּת	טִיפּוּל	מִתְחַפֵּשׂ	מְקוּבָּל	מְדַבֵּר

16   This pattern is different from the פָּעוּל pattern, in which **all** forms have an *oo* sound and no *dagesh,* for example: כָּתוּב, כְּתוּבָה, כְּתוּבִים, כְּתוּבוֹת.

2. Dagesh *after* -הַ, *after prepositions containing* -הַ (-בַּ, -לַ, -כַּ) *and after* -שֶׁ *and* -מִ

As a rule, the letter after -הַ (the), -שֶׁ (that, which, who) and -מִ (from, than) always has a strong *dagesh*.[17] Thus, whenever 'פ, כ', ב appear after them, they are pronounced as **hard** sounds: *b, k, p.*

Here are some examples of the strong *dagesh*:

1. After -הַ:

⟵	הַבַּיִת	הַכַּדוּר	הַפְּרחים	(הַמִשׁפחה)
	the house	the ball	the flowers	the family

When -הַ follows the prepositions "בְּ, לְ, כְּ" and thus is joined to them to form "-בַּ, -לַ, -כַּ", a strong *dagesh* comes in the following letter.

⟵	בַּבַּיִת	כַּכַּדוּר	לַפְּרָחִים[18]	(בַּמִשׁפחה)

2. After -שֶׁ:

⟵	הַילד שֶׁבָּכה	הפרח שֶׁפָּרח	התלמידה שֶׁכָּתבה	(הילדה שֶׁנָּפלה)
	the boy who cried	the flower that bloomed	the student who wrote	the girl who fell

3. After -מִ:

⟵	מִבְּאר שבע	מִפֶּתח תקווה	מִכְּפר סבא	(מִלונדון)
	from Be'er Sheva	from Petach Tikva	from Kfar Sava	from London

In the next section you can read **why** there is a *dagesh* after -מִ.

---

17 Except, of course, for 'ר and ע', ח', ה', א'.

18 According to the rules of grammar, when the prepositions -ב, -כ, -ל do **not** contain -הַ, the letter after them does **not** have a *dagesh*. Thus, we hear on the news and in formal Hebrew:

⟵ התיירים נסעו לְבֵית לחם. הם ילונו בְּכַרמיאל.
　　　　be-char-mee-'EL　　　*le-veit*

Many speakers today, especially in informal Hebrew, do not follow these grammar rules and say: לְבֵּית לחם (*le-beit LE-chem*) and בְּכַּרמיאל (*be-kar-mee-'EL*).

Want to see if you've understood?

Write a *dagesh* in ב׳, כ׳, פ׳ wherever it is required, and read the sentence out loud.

1. זֹאת הַבַּחוּרָה שֶׁכָּתְבָה אֶת הַפֶּתֶק הַמְצַחִיק.
2. שַׂמְתֶּם לֵב לַפְּרָחִים בַּפִּינָה שֶׁל הַגִּינה?
3. תֵּן לִי, בְּבַקָשָׁה, אֶת הַכּוֹס הַכְּחוּלָה.
4. אַתֶּם מִפֹּה?
5. אַתֶּם־רוֹצִים לְבַקֵּר בַּכְּנֶסֶת?

Answers:

1. זֹאת הַבַּחוּרָה שֶׁכָּתְבָה אֶת הַפֶּתֶק המצחיק.   2. שַׂמְתֶּם לֵב לַפְּרָחִים בַּפִּינָה שֶׁל הגינה?
3. תֵּן לִי, בְּבַקָשָׁה, אֶת הַכּוֹס הַכְּחוּלָה.   4. אַתֶּם מִפֹּה?   5. אַתֶּם רוֹצִים לְבַקֵּר בַּכְּנֶסֶת?

3. *When a consonant is missing*[19]

A missing נ׳

Read the following sentence:

◄ אִמָּא לְדָנִי: "תִּזָּהֵר! הַשָּׁכְנָה שֶׁלָּנוּ נָפְלָה אֶתְמוֹל בַּמַּדְרֵגוֹת לְיַד הַבַּיִת. אִם אַתָּה לֹא רוֹצֶה לִפֹּל (לִיפּוֹל)
כָּמוֹהָ, תֵּלֵךְ בִּזְהִירוּת!"

Mother to Danny: "Be careful! Our neighbor fell yesterday on the steps next to the house. If you don't want to fall like she did, walk carefully!"

The root of both the past tense נָפְלָה and the infinitive לִפֹּל (לִיפּוֹל) is the same: נ-פ-ל. In the past tense, all three root letters are visible. However, in the infinitive, the נ׳ of the root נ-פ-ל has disappeared.[20] When this happens, a strong *dagesh* is written in the following letter (here: פ׳).[21]

Other examples of a strong *dagesh* that is caused by the disappearance of a נ׳ are found in the infinitive and future tense forms of *beenyan neef'al*, for example:

---

19 In grammar books this *dagesh* is called דָּגֵשׁ חָזָק מַשְׁלִים (*compensative strong dagesh*).
20 On the disappearing נ׳, see the chapter "Verbs Whose First Root Letter Is נ׳," pp. 490-503.
21 Here are some more examples of verbs in which the initial root letter נ׳ disappears and causes the appearance of a strong *dagesh*:

heef'eel:	הִגִּיעַ (נ-ג-ע)	הִכִּיר (נ-כ-ר)	◄ הִפִּיל (נ-פ-ל)
	arrived	knew, recognized	dropped
hoof'al:		הוּכַּר (נ-כ-ר)	הוּפַּל (נ-פ-ל)
		was known, recognized	was dropped

◄ להיפֵָּגש	להִיכָּנֵס	להיבָּחֵן	(להיגָּמֵר)
ייפֵָּגש	ייכָּנֵס	ייבָּחֵן	(ייגָּמֵר)
to meet with	to enter	to take a test	to be finished

In these forms, the נ׳ of the *beenyan*, which appears in the past and present tense forms (e.g., נפגש, נכנס, נבחן, נגמר), has disappeared. As was the case in ליפול, the letter following the missing נ׳ in the above infinitives and future tense forms has a *dagesh*.

Still another example of this phenomenon appears in the preceding section, where we saw that after the preposition מ- there is always a strong *dagesh* (unless that letter is א׳, ה׳, ח׳, ע׳, ר׳). This *dagesh* is actually the result of a missing נ׳, since מ- is a short form of מן.

For exercises on the verbs mentioned above, see the chapters "Verbs Whose First Root Letter Is נ׳" (pp. 497, 501) and "*Beenyan Neef'al*" (pp. 426-427).

Did you know?

The נ׳ does not simply disappear; rather, it "assimilates to" (becomes the same as) the consonant that follows it: לִפּוֹל* ⇐ לִנְפּוֹל*. A similar process occurs in the English *inlegal* ⇒ illegal, *inregular* ⇒ irregular.[22]

In Hebrew, the double "פפ" of לפפול* is written as a **single** letter with a *dagesh*: לִפּוֹל. When we write without vowel signs, a י׳ is usually written in place of the נ׳ when the preceding vowel is *ee*: ליפול.[23] Here is the whole process:

◄ *לנפול ⇐ *לפפול ⇐ לפּול ⇐ ליפול

A missing twin consonant

In some roots the second and third letter are identical. But many times only **one** of the two letters is written. This one letter has a *dagesh* in it indicating that it represents a double consonant. Here are some examples (the roots are in parentheses):

22 For more examples, see Edward Horowitz, 1960, pp. 32-34.

23 a. One blatant exception is past tense verbs in *beenyan heef'eel*, such as: הכיר (*hee-KEER* he knew, recognized), which comes from the form *הנכיר. Verbs like הכיר are not written with a י׳ after the initial ה׳ in order that they not be written differently from regular *heef'eel* verbs, such as הרגיש (*heer-GEESH* he felt), which also do not have a י׳ after the initial ה׳.

b. We have written the *dagesh* in ליפול (the form without vowel signs) for the sake of clarity. Usually in a text without vowel signs, this *dagesh* is not written.

(ס-כ-כ)	(ט-פ-פ)	(ס-ב-ב)	(ס-ב-ב)
⌄	⌄	⌄	⌄
סִיכָּה	טִיפָּה	מְסִיבָּה	סִיבָּה
pin	drop	party	reason

When the double letter is at the **end** of the word, it has **no** *dagesh*, as in:

(ל-ב-ב)	(ד-ב-ב)	(כ-פ-פ)	(ד-פ-פ)	(ר-כ-כ)	(ר-ב-ב)
⌄	⌄	⌄	⌄	⌄	⌄
לֵב	דוֹב	כַּף	דַף	רַך	רַב
heart	bear	tablespoon	sheet of paper	soft	many, much

But when it isn't last, as in the following plural, feminine and possessive forms, the *dagesh* appears:

רַבָּה, רַבִּים, רַבּוֹת   רַכָּה, רַכִּים, רַכּוֹת   דַפִּים   כַּפּוֹת   דוּבִּים   לִבִּי, לִבְּם

Did you know?

As mentioned above, the consonants represented by א׳, ה׳, ח׳, ע׳, ר׳ were almost never doubled in ancient Hebrew and, therefore, these letters do **not** take a strong *dagesh*. In the past, when א׳, ה׳, ח׳, ע׳, ר׳ appeared in a place where doubling (a strong *dagesh*) was required – as in *beenyan pee'el* (לדבר) and after -הַ (הבית) – the vowel before them often **changed**,[24] as follows:

- An *ee* vowel (◌) became *eh* (◌), for example:
Instead of תִּיאֵר* (*tee-'ER*) – which should have a *dagesh* in the middle like דִּבֵּר – we get תֵּיאֵר (*te-'ER*) (described).

Instead of פִּירוּשׁ* (*pee-ROOSH*) – which should have a *dagesh* in the middle like דִּיבּוּר – we get פֵּירוּשׁ (*pe-ROOSH*) (interpretation).

Instead of יִיעָלֵם* (*yee-'a-LEM*) – which should have a *dagesh* in the **first** root letter like יִיכָּנֵס – we get יֵיעָלֵם (*ye-'a-LEM*) (will disappear).

---

24 Traditional grammarians refer to this change as *lengthening* and call this phenomenon *compensatory lengthening* (תַּשְׁלוּם דָּגֵשׁ). In phonetics, this change is referred to as *vowel lowering* (הַנְמָכַת תְּנוּעָה).

- An *oo* vowel (וּ) becomes *oh* (וֹ), for example:
Instead of תֻּאַר* (**too-'AR*) – which should have a *dagesh* in the middle like דֻּבַּר – we get תֹּאַר (*to-'AR*) (was described).

Instead of שֻׁחוֹרִים* (**shchoo-REEM*) – which should have a *dagesh* in the third root letter like צָהֻבִּים – we get שְׁחוֹרִים (*shcho-REEM*) (black).

See more on א׳, ה׳, ח׳, ע׳, ר׳ in the chapter "Guttural Consonants and ר׳: *Beenyaneem Pee'el, Poo'al* and *Neef'al*" (pp. 474-484).

Chapter summary

- ◆ A *dagesh* appears in many letters in texts written with vowel signs. However, only when it appears in ב׳, כ׳, פ׳ does it indicate a difference in pronunciation in today's Hebrew.

  - When there is a *dagesh* in ב׳, כ׳, פ׳ they are pronounced as hard sounds: *b, k, p.*

  - When there is no *dagesh* they are pronounced as soft sounds: *v, ch, f.*

- ◆ Here are the circumstances under which the pronunciation of ב׳, כ׳, פ׳ is hard:
  - At the beginning of a word: בַּיִת, כּוֹתֵב, פְּגִישָׁה (weak *dagesh*)

  - Immediately after a closed syllable (= a syllable that ends in a consonant): לִשְׁפּוֹט, הַסְכָּמָה, מַסְבִּיר (weak *dagesh*)

  - In certain verb and noun patterns, for example: דִּיבֵּר, סוּפַּר, שַׁפַּעַת (strong *dagesh*)

  - After -הַ (and prepositions including -הַ: "בַּ, כַּ, לַ-") and after -שֶׁ and -מִ, for example: הַבַּיִת, בַּכּוֹס, לַכְּפָר, כַּפֶּרַח / זֶה הַיֶּלֶד שֶׁבָּרַח. / הוּא בָּרַח מִפֹּה. (strong *dagesh*)

  - In cases where a consonant is missing, for example:
    ◄ לִנְפּוֹל* ⇐ לִיפּוֹל   *יִנְכְנֵס ⇐ יִיכָּנֵס   *דוּבְבִים ⇐ דוּבִּים (strong *dagesh*)

- ◆ In all cases other than those mentioned in this chapter, ב׳, כ׳, פ׳ are pronounced as soft sounds: *v, ch, f.*

Want to see if you've understood this chapter?

Write a *dagesh* in פ׳ ,כ׳ ,ב׳ wherever it is required, and read the words out loud.

1. המורים כבר בדקו את כל הבחינות.
2. קיבלתם את כל מה שביקשתם.
3. מה כתוב במשפט הבא?
4. אל תשכחו להביא כלי כתיבה לטיול.
5. ניפגש כשתחזרו מבית הספר.
6. דני שבר כוס. אם לא תיזהרי, גם את תשברי משהו.

Answers:

1. הַמוֹרִים כְּבָר בָּדְקוּ את כָּל הַבְּחִינוֹת.   2. קִיבַּלְתֶם את כָּל מה שֶׁבִּיקַשְׁתֶם.   3. מה כָּתוּב בַּמִשְׁפָּט הַבָּא?
4. אל תִשְׁכְּחוּ לְהָבִיא כְּלֵי כְּתִיבָה לטיול.   5. נִיפָּגֵש כְּשֶׁתַחְזְרוּ מִבֵּית הַסֵפֶר.
6. דני שָׁבַר כּוֹס. אם לא תיזהרי, גם את תִשְׁבְּרִי משהו.

III. Reduction of Vowels and the *Shva*

Preview

- *What is "vowel reduction"?* (גָּדוֹל ⟸ גְּדוֹלָה)
- *Vowel reduction two syllables before the stress*
- *What causes the stress to move to a different syllable?*
- *When do vowels not reduce?*
- *Vowel reduction one syllable before the stress*
- *Vowel reduction and* א׳, ה׳, ח׳, ע׳ *(gutturals)*

• *What is "vowel reduction"?*

Read the forms of the following two words out loud:

	f.pl.	m.pl.	f.s.	base form m.s.	
big	גְּדוֹלוֹת	גְּדוֹלִים	גְּדוֹלָה ⟸	גָּדוֹל	⟵
	gdo-LOT	*gdo-LEEM*	*gdo-LA*	*ga-DOL*	
short (in stature), low	נְמוּכוֹת	נְמוּכִים	נְמוּכָה ⟸	נָמוּךְ	
	ne-moo-CHOT	*ne-moo-CHEEM*	*ne-moo-CHA*	*na-MOOCH*	

In the *base forms* – גָּדוֹל and נָמוּךְ – the vowel *ah* appears in the first syllable (it is indicated by the vowel sign ◌ָ).

Q: Do we hear this *ah* sound in the other forms?

A: No. In the other forms of גָּדוֹל there is **no vowel sound** at all after the ג׳ (*g*): *gdo-LA, gdo-LEEM, gdo-LOT*.[1] The *ah* has totally *"reduced"* – in this case **disappeared** –

---

1   This is the regular pronunciation today. Only in **formal** pronunciation of Modern Hebrew – for example in some news broadcasts – and in the reading of Biblical Hebrew, do we hear the *shva* at the beginning of a word like גְּדוֹלָה pronounced as *eh* (*ge-do-LA*). Note: The division into syllables in this book (e.g., *gdo-LA*) is based on the pronunciation of spoken Hebrew and, therefore, does not always correspond to the syllable division in traditional grammar.

and is written with a ְ ‎ □ – called a *shva*.[2] In the forms of נְמוּךְ, too, we see that a *shva* (□) is written where the □ (*kamats*) was, but because it is difficult to pronounce a word like נְמוּכָה with no vowel after the 'נ, we pronounce an *eh* sound: *ne-moo-CHA, ne-moo-CHEEM, ne-moo-CHOT*.

This change in vowels when we move from a base form to other forms of the same word isn't unique to Hebrew. It happens in English, too, in words like *pronounce* and *pronunciation*, *supreme* and *supremacy*.

In order fully to understand when vowel reductions do and do not take place, you must have a good knowledge of **traditional** Hebrew grammar. The information covered in this chapter gives you a "feel" for when reductions do and do not occur and will enable you to learn Hebrew pronunciation with heightened awareness.

Did you know?

Most Hebrew speakers today tend **not** to pronounce the *shva* at the beginning of a word (as in the case of גְּדוֹלָה *gdo-LA*).[3] However, in the following cases speakers **do** tend to pronounce the *shva* as *eh*:

1. When the first consonant is "לְ, מְ, נְ, רְ, יְ", as in:

יְשָׁנָה	רְחָבָה	נְמוּכָה	מְקוֹמוֹת	לְשׁוֹנוֹת ◄
ye-sha-NA	*re-cha-VA*	*ne-moo-CHA*	*me-ko-MOT*	*le-sho-NOT*
old	wide	short (in stature), low	places	tongues, languages

2. When the consonant **after** the *shva* is 'א, 'ה, 'ע:

צְעִירָה	צְהוּבָּה	כְּאוּבָה ◄
tse-'ee-RA	*tse-hoo-BA*	*ke-'oo-VA*
young (f.s.)	yellow (f.s.)	painful (f.s.)

---

2   In grammar books this is called *vowel reduction* or *vowel shortening* (חִיטוּף הַתְּנוּעָה or הֵיחָטְפוּת הַתְּנוּעָה), and this *shva* is called a *mobile* or *vocal shva* (שְׁוָוא נָע), though today we do not always pronounce it, as we see in גְּדוֹלָה (*gdo-LA*).

3   Properly stated, we do not "pronounce," but rather "realize" the vowel sign (*shva*).

3. After the prepositions -לְ, -כְּ, -בְּ and after -וְ (and), as in:

וְרָחֵל	כְּתִינוֹק	בִּרִיצָה
ve-ra-CHEL	*ke-tee-NOK*	*be-ree-TSA*
and Rachel	like a baby	while running

Compare the following, in which the first letter is **not** added on, but rather is part of the **word itself**. In these cases the *shva* is **not pronounced**:

וְרָדִים	כְּתִיבָה	בְּרִית
vra-DEEM	*ktee-VA*	*BREET*
roses	writing	alliance, covenant

• *Vowel reduction two syllables before the stress*

Before reading the following explanation of when vowels tend to reduce, it is recommended that you read the chapter "Sounds and Syllables" (pp. 621-623), in which the terms used here (such as *vowels, consonants, open* and *closed syllables* and *stress*) are introduced.

Now let's look at the base form דָּבָר (thing) and its plural form דְּבָרִים (things, also: words).

In the word דָּ-בָר (*da-VAR*), the first syllable (*da*) is *open* (i.e., ends in a vowel), and the stress is on the second syllable (*VAR*). When we add the plural ending -ים (-*EEM*), we expect the following plural form: *da-va-REEM.[4] In *da-va-REEM, the first syllable is still open, but the stress has moved **away** from it. It is no longer on the second syllable, but rather on the **third** syllable -רים (*REEM*). In the newly created form *דָּ-בָ-רִים (*da-va-REEM), the stress is actually **two syllables away** from the open syllable *da*. This is exactly the situation in which the vowel ָ (*ah*) often reduces to a *shva*:

דְּבָ-רִים	⇐	(דָּ-בָ-רִים*)	⇐	דָּ-בָר
dva-REEM		*da-va-REEM*		*da-VAR*

---

4 a. An asterisk (*) indicates that the form does not exist.

   b. Remember: As a rule, a syllable in Hebrew begins with a consonant; therefore, when the ending -*EEM* is added, the *R* of *da-VAR* "moves" to the beginning of the third syllable in *da-va-REEM so that the new syllable will begin with a consonant.

The vowel ◻ (*eh*) sometimes reduces in the same way:

שְׁמוֹ-תָיו ⇐ (שְׁ-מוֹ-תָיו*) ⇐ שְׁ-מוֹת ≺

shmo-TAV   she-mo-TAV   she-MOT

his names   names

As was the case in גְדוֹלָה (*gdo-LA*), the *shva* in the words דְּבָרִים (*dva-REEM*) and שְׁמוֹתָיו (*shmo-TAV*) is not pronounced at all in everyday speech. The original *ah* vowel of דָּבָר (*da-VAR*) and *eh* of שְׁמוֹת (*she-MOT*) have reduced **completely**.

> ***Be careful!*** Not every vowel in an open syllable at the beginning of a word reduces when it is two syllables before the stress. Usually, when the vowel is indicated by ◻, the vowel reduces, and also – though much less frequently – when it is ◻. However, when the vowel is indicated by "וֹ", "וּ" or "◻ִי", the vowel does **not** reduce, for example:

דּוֹ-דוֹ-תָיו ⇐	דּוֹ-דוֹת ≺	his aunts
צוּ-רוֹ-תָיו ⇐	צוּ-רוֹת	its forms
קִי-רוֹ-תָיו ⇐	קִי-רוֹת	its walls

Did you know?

The reduction of the vowel in an open syllable two syllables before the stress can also occur in the middle of the word, as in:

חַבְרֵיהֶם ⇐ (חַ-בֵ-רֵי-הֶם*) ⇐ חַ-בֵ-רִים ≺

their friends   chav-rei-HEM   *cha-ve-rei-HEM   cha-ve-REEM

friends

אַרְצוֹת-הַבְּרִית⁵ ⇐ (אַ-רָ-צוֹת-) ⇐ אַ-רָ-צוֹת ≺

the United States   'ar-tsot-   *'a-ra-tsot-   'a-ra-TSOT

lands, countries

---

5   In these words, there is also a change from ◻ to ◻. For an explanation, see J. Weingreen, p. 11.

• *What causes the stress to move to a different syllable?*

1. *Endings*

The main reason for the shift of stress is the adding of endings. Endings that are added onto base forms usually **attract** the stress to them. Here are some examples:

a. Plural endings:

thing(s)	דְּבָרִים *dva-REEM*	⟸ (*דְּ-בָ-רִים) *da-va-REEM*	⟸ דָּ-בָר ◄ *da-VAR*
place(s)	מְקוֹמוֹת *me-ko-MOT*	⟸ (*מָ-קוֹ-מוֹת) *ma-ko-MOT*	⟸ מָ-קוֹם *ma-KOM*

b. The feminine ending הָ-:

big	גְּדוֹלָה *gdo-LA*	⟸ (*גָּ-דוֹ-לָה) *ga-do-LA*	⟸ גָּ-דוֹל ◄ *ga-DOL*

c. Possessive endings:[6]

your (*f.s.*) welfare (in the expression מַה שְׁלוֹמֵךְ?)	שְׁלוֹמֵךְ *shlo-MECH*	⟸ (*שְׁ-לוֹ-מֵךְ) *sha-lo-MECH*	⟸ שָׁ-לוֹם ◄ *sha-LOM* peace
his names	שְׁמוֹתָיו *shmo-TAV*	⟸ (*שְׁ-מוֹ-תָיו) *she-mo-TAV*	⟸ שֵׁ-מוֹת *she-MOT* names

d. Other endings (e.g., the abstract ending וּת-, the adjective ending י-):

health	בְּרִיאוּת *bree-'OOT*	⟸ (*בָּ-רִי-אוּת) *ba-ree-'OOT*	⟸ בָּ-רִיא ◄ *ba-REE* healthy
my place	מְקוֹמִי *me-ko-MEE*	⟸ (*מָ-קוֹ-מִי) *ma-ko-MEE*	⟸ מָ-קוֹם *ma-KOM* place

---

6 See the chapter "Nouns with Possessive Endings," pp. 60-77.

2. Smeechoot

Another situation in which the stress shifts and causes vowel reduction is when one noun is added to the end of another noun to form a *smeechoot* phrase.[7] In *smeechoot* phrases, the main stress **moves away** from the first word and is placed on the **last** word.[8] As a result, the vowels in the first word reduce, as in:

			smeechoot		base form	
extrapolation of a Torah passage	דְּבַר-תּוֹרה	⇐	(-דָּ-בַר*)	⇐	דָּ-בָר	◄
	dvar-		**da-var-*		*da-VAR*	
					thing; in certain contexts: word	
place of birth	מְקוֹם-לידה	⇐	(-מָ-קוֹם*)	⇐	מָ-קוֹם	
	me-kom-		**ma-kom-*		*ma-KOM*	
					place	
hibernation	שְׁנַת-חוֹרף[9]	⇐	(-שֶׁ-נַת*)	⇐	שֵׁ-נָה (שינה)	
	shnat-		**she-nat-*		*she-NA*	
					sleep	

Q: What happens to ◌ָ and ◌ֶ in the first syllable of the first word of the above *smeechoot* phrases?

A: They change to ◌ְ (*shva*), just as they did in דְברים and שְׁמוֹתיו above. This reduction occurs since the vowels *ah* and *eh* are both in an **open** syllable **two syllables** before the final **word** of the these *smeechoot* phrases. (The final **word** is considered to be stressed regardless of exactly which syllable in that word is stressed). Thus, in דָּ-בַר-תּוֹרה*, the syllable "דָּ" (*da*) is considered to be two syllables before the stress, and its vowel reduces as shown above.[10]

---

7 The first word is not always a noun (e.g., it may be a number). Also, a *smeechoot* phrase may contain more than two words. For more on *smeechoot,* see the chapter "Smeechoot," pp. 170-199.

8 In today's pronunciation of *smeechoot* phrases, the stress sometimes may be found on the first word(s) as well. Nevertheless, the vowel reductions in the first word(s) of *smeechoot* phrases – which are shown in the examples that follow – usually still take place in today's pronunciation.

9 The vowel that reduces here is ◌ַ – as it is written in standard spelling – and not ◌ִי, as it is written in full spelling.

10 If the *smeechoot* has more than two words, vowel reductions may take place in **each** of the words preceding the last word (as if each is the first word of a two-word *smeechoot*), for example:

the president of South Africa	נשיא דְּרום אפריקה	⇐	אפריקה	+	דְּרום	+	נשיא	◄
	ne-see drom 'AF-ree-ka				*da-ROM*		*na-SEE*	

• *When do vowels not reduce?*

As we saw above, vowels reduce to *shva* only in open syllables. Thus, the vowel in the first syllable of a word like תַלְמִידִים, which is **closed** (*tal-mee-DEEM*), never reduces. In addition, as we mentioned above, certain vowels, especially those written with a 'ו or 'י, do **not** reduce (e.g., מוֹכֵר נעליים shoe salesman).

There are also additional cases in which vowels do not reduce:

1. When a syllable **sounds** open, but in traditional grammar is considered closed. For example, let's look at the word טַבָּח (chef) and its plural טַבָּחִים. You might expect this word to act like דָּבָר ⇐ דְּבָרִים, but it doesn't. Why not?

   The 'ב in the word טַבָּח (cook) has a *strong dagesh*, which – as we saw in the preceding chapter – represents what once was a **double consonant**: טבבח*.[11] Thus, in traditional grammar, the syllable division is טב-בח in the singular and טב-ב-חים in the plural. According to this division, the first syllable is **closed**, so the vowel in it does **not** reduce. Here are some more examples, all of which contain a strong *dagesh*:

   > *no reduction*:   גַּנָּבִים ⇐   (traditional syllable division: גַּנ-נָ-בִים) ⇐   גַּנָּב + ־ים ⋖
   >   thief

   > *no reduction*:   מַכִּירִים ⇐ (traditional syllable division: מַכ-כִּי-רִים) ⇐   מַכִּיר + ־ים
   >   know, recognize

2. Exceptional cases
   Here are some examples:[12]

   > *no reduction*:   לְקוֹחוֹת ⇐   (we would expect: לְ־) לְ-קוֹ-חוֹת ⇐   לָקוֹחַ + ־וֹת ⋖
   >   customer

   > *no reduction*:   רָהִיטִים ⇐   (we would expect: רְ־) רָ-הִי-טִים ⇐   רָהִיט + ־ים
   >   piece of furniture

> ## Let's review
>
> ◆ When ◌ (*ah*) or ◌ (*eh*) appear in an **open** syllable **two** syllables before the stress, they tend to "reduce" to *shva* (◌), as in גָּדוֹל ⇐ גְּדוֹלָה and נָמוּךְ ⇐ נְמוּכָה.

---

11 See the chapter "The Pronunciation of ב', כ', פ' and the *Dagesh*," pp. 630-637.
12 The vowel that remains in these words is called a קָמָץ קַיָּים (irreducible *kamats*).

♦ This *shva* tends not to be pronounced in speech today (*gdo-LA*), but sometimes – depending on the consonants involved – it **is** pronounced as *eh*, as in *ne-moo-CHA*.

♦ Vowel reduction is triggered by the shift of stress **away** from a given syllable. This shift takes place when endings are added to a base form or when a noun is added to the end of another noun to create a *smeechoot* phrase:

the plural endings ־ים and ־וֹת:	דְּבָרִים ⇐	דָּבָר ◄
the feminine ending ־ָה:	גְּדוֹלָה ⇐	גָּדוֹל
possessive endings:	שְׁלוֹמֶךָ ⇐	שָׁלוֹם
other endings:	בְּרִיאוּת ⇐	בָּרִיא
adding a noun to form a smeechoot *phrase*:	נְשִׂיא המדינה ⇐	נָשִׂיא

♦ There are cases in which a first syllable **sounds** open, but is considered **closed** in traditional grammar because of the presence of a *strong dagesh*. Such syllables do not reduce:

גַּנָּבִים ⇐ גַּנָּב ◄

Want to see if you've understood?
Write the vowel sign in the first syllable of the form after the arrow.
Circle the words whose first vowel is *shva*.

Example: (דְּבָרִים) ⇐ דָּבָר ◄

11. דָּרוֹם + אמריקה ⇐ דְּרוֹם אֲמֶרִיקָה	6. מוֹרֶה ⇐ מוֹרִים	1. צָעִיר ⇐ צְעִירִים
12. נָשִׂיא + צרפת ⇐ נְשִׂיא צָרְפַת	7. קָטָן ⇐ קְטַנִּים	2. יָרֹק ⇐ יְרוּקָה
13. שִׂמְלָה + כלה ⇐ שִׂמְלַת כַּלָּה	8. שִׁיר ⇐ שִׁירִים	3. עוּגָה ⇐ עוּגוֹת
14. שָׂדֶה + תעופה ⇐ שְׂדֵה תְעוּפָה	9. צָהֹב ⇐ צְהוּבָּה	4. בָּרוּר ⇐ בְּרוּרִים
	10. גָּבֹהַּ ⇐ גְבוֹהִים	5. תַּלְמִיד ⇐ תַּלְמִידִים

Answers:
The following words have a reduced vowel (*shva*) in the first syllable:
1. צְעִירִים 2. יְרוּקָה 4. בְּרוּרִים 7. קְטַנִּים 9. צְהוּבָּה 10. גְבוֹהִים 11. דְּרוֹם 12. נְשִׂיא־ 14. שְׂדֵה־

• *Vowel reduction one syllable before the stress*

In the sections above, we saw that a shift in syllable stress often causes the reduction to *shva* of an *ah* vowel and sometimes of an *eh* vowel in an **open** syllable **two** syllables before the stressed syllable. We will now examine cases in which a change in syllable stress causes a reduction of a vowel **one** syllable before the stress.[13]

Read the following words:

	with endings		base form	
	לָמְדוּ	⇐	לָמַד	◄
	lam-DOO		la-MAD	
	they studied		he studied	
	יִלְמְדוּ	⇐	יִלְמַד	
	yeel-me-DOO		yeel-MAD	
	they will study		he will study	

The **second** (final) syllable in the base forms לָ-מַד and יִלְ-מַד contains the vowel *ah* (indicated by the vowel sign ▢).

Q: Do we hear this *ah* sound when an ending is added (לָמְדוּ, יִלְמְדוּ)?

A: No. When the ending is added to לָמַד to form לָמְדוּ, the *ah* vowel completely reduces, and there is **no vowel sound** at all after the 'מ (lam-DOO).[14] When the ending is added to יִלְמַד to form יִלְמְדוּ, again the *ah* vowel reduces, but this time we hear the sound *eh* (yeel-me-DOO).[15] Here is the process that takes place:

לָמְדוּ	⇐	(לָ-מַ-דוּ*)	⇐	לָ-מַד	◄
lam-DOO		*la-ma-DOO		la-MAD	
יִלְמְדוּ	⇐	(יִלְ-מַ-דוּ*)	⇐	יִלְ-מַד	
yeel-me-DOO		*yeel-ma-DOO		yeel-MAD	

Now look closely at the forms in parentheses. Notice that once the ending is added, the syllable preceding it becomes open, and thus its vowel can reduce to *shva*.

---

13 In grammar books, the reduction that takes place two syllables before the stress is called *propretonic reduction*. The reduction that takes place one syllable before the stress is called *pretonic reduction*.

14 Only in the reading of Biblical Hebrew is this *shva*, which is the result of a reduced vowel, pronounced *eh* (la-me-DOO).

15 You may have noticed that the word יִלְמְדוּ has **two** *shva'eem*. The first *shva* is simply a graphic sign marking the end of a closed syllable – called a *resting, quiescent* or *silent shva* (שְׁוָא נָח). It is **not** the result of a vowel reduction, as is the second *shva*.

Here are some more examples:

כּוֹתְבִים ⇐ (כּוֹ-תְ-בִים*) ⇐ כּוֹ-תֵב ◄
kot-VEEM   *ko-te-VEEM   ko-TEV

יִשְׁמְרוּ ⇐ (יִשְׁ-מוֹ-רוּ*) ⇐ יִשְׁ-מוֹר
yeesh-me-ROO   *yeesh-mo-ROO   yeesh-MOR

As you can see, a variety of vowels can reduce to *shva* when the reduction takes place **one** syllable before the stress (*ah* ◌, *eh* ◌ and *oh* ◌).[16]

The reduction one syllable before the stress frequently takes place in verbs, as you can see above. It also takes place in some words that are not verbs, for example:

מַחְשְׁבִים ⇐ מַחְשֵׁב   טִפְּשִׁי ⇐ טִפֵּשׁ ◄
mach-she-VEEM [17]   mach-SHEV   teep-SHEE   tee-PESH
           computer   stupid   a stupid
                         (adj.)   person

Be careful! The reduction of *ah* **one** syllable before the stress takes place when the *ah* vowel is written with ◌ (*patach*) (as in לָמַד ⇐ לָמְדוּ) **not** with ◌ (*kamats*). Thus, the *ah* vowel in מִכְתָּב (letter), for example, does **not** reduce when an ending is added: מִכְתָּבִים (meech-ta-VEEM). Since both *ah* vowels (◌ and ◌) **sound** the same, only if you know its vowel sign is it possible to predict when an *ah* vowel will or will not reduce one syllable before the stress. Knowing noun patterns is also helpful (i.e., if you know that the *ah* in מִכְתָּבִים does not reduce, you know that the *ah* in words with the same pattern – e.g., מִטְבָּחִים (kitchen) and מִגְדָּלִים (tower) – does not reduce).

---

16   The "וֹ" that appears in ישמור is **not** written with a "ו" (*vav*) in standard spelling with vowel signs: יִשְׁמֹר. We mention this fact since, as a rule, vowels indicated by **letters** in addition to vowel signs, i.e., "וֹ", "וּ" or "ִים", do **not** reduce. The reduction in יִשְׁמְרוּ (ישמור) is of ◌ not of "וֹ".

17   When the *shva* is pronounced, as in *mach-she-VEEM*, it sounds the same as the *eh* vowel in the base form (*mach-SHEV*).

Did you know?

The following are cases in which – in today's Hebrew – we **do** pronounce the *shva* that results from the reduction of a vowel **one** syllable before the stress:

- When this *shva* follows a *silent shva*, as in:

מַחְשְׁבִים	נִבְדְּקוּ	יִלְמְדוּ ◄
mach-she-VEEM	neev-de-KOO	yeel-me-DOO

- When this *shva* comes after the first of two identical consonants, as in:

מִתְפַּלְּלִים	יְבָרְרוּ	מְחַמְּמִים ◄
meet-pa-le-LEEM	ye-va-re-ROO	me-cha-me-MEEM

Let's review

◆ In certain cases, when an ending is added to a word, the stress shifts to the ending, and the syllable before the ending **becomes open**. Vowels that appear in such a syllable (**one** syllable before the stress) sometimes reduce. These include *ah* ☐, *eh* ☐ and *oh* ☐), as in:

יִלְמְדוּ	⇐	יִל-מַד ◄
yeel-me-DOO		yeel-MAD

כּוֹתְבִים	⇐	כּוֹ-תֵב
kot-VEEM		ko-TEV

יִשְׁמְרוּ	⇐	יִשְׁ-מוֹר
yeesh-me-ROO		yeesh-MOR

◆ The *shva* that results from a vowel reduction is sometimes pronounced as *eh* (e.g., יִלְמְדוּ *yeel-me-DOO*) and sometimes is not pronounced at all, as in כּוֹתְבִים (*kot-VEEM*).

Want to see if you've understood?

Write the vowel sign in the syllable before the final syllable.
Circle the words whose vowel sign is a *shva*.

Example: הוא שָׁמַר ⇐ הם שָׁמְרוּ

הוא לָמַד ⇐ היא לָמְדָה .1
הוא שָׁמַע ⇐ הם שָׁמְעוּ .2
הוא מִתְרַגֵּשׁ ⇐ היא מִתְרַגֶּשֶׁת .3
הוא טִיפֵּל ⇐ הן טִיפְּלוּ .4

הוא יִבְדוֹק ⇐ הם יִבְדְּקוּ .5
הוא יְסַפֵּר ⇐ הם יְסַפְּרוּ .6
הוא הִלְבִּישׁ ⇐ היא הִלְבִּישָׁה .7
הוא יִתְלַבֵּשׁ ⇐ הם יִתְלַבְּשׁוּ .8

Answers:

The following words should be circled. They have a reduced vowel (*shva*) one syllable before the stress:

‏1. לָמְדָה   2. שָׁמְעוּ   4. טִיפְּלוּ   5. יִבְדְּקוּ   6. יְסַפְּרוּ   8. יִתְלַבְּשׁוּ

• *Vowel reduction and* א׳, ה׳, ח׳, ע׳ *(gutturals)*

Look at the following set of words:

	vowel reduces		ending added, stress moves		base form	
model form:	ktoo-VEEM	כְּתוּבִים ⇐	(*כְּ-תוּ-בִים) ⇐	ka-TOOV	כָּ-תוּב	⤡
forbidden	'a-soo-REEM	אֲסוּרִים ⇐	(*אֲ-סוּ-רִים) ⇐	'a-SOOR	אָ-סוּר	
destroyed	ha-roo-SEEM	הֲרוּסִים	(*הֲ-רוּ-סִים)	ha-ROOS	הָ-רוּס	
sour	cha-moo-TSEEM	חֲמוּצִים	(*חֲ-מוּ-צִים)	cha-MOOTS	חָ-מוּץ	
sad	'a-tsoo-VEEM	עֲצוּבִים	(*עֲ-צוּ-בִים)	'a-TSOOV	עָ-צוּב	

In the model form, when the ending is added, the stress moves to it and the *ah* vowel in "כָּ",
which is **two** syllables before the stress, reduces and is written with a *shva* ("כְּ").

Q: Does the same change take place in the words that begin with א׳, ה׳, ח׳, ע׳?

A: Not exactly. We do **see** a change in the vowel sign at the beginning of the plural forms – ָ
has changed to ֲ (*chataf patach*), which is a variation of *shva*. For phonetic reasons, א׳, ה׳, ח׳,
ע׳ (gutturals) cannot take a *shva* when their vowel reduces and instead are followed by one

of three variations of the *shva*: ◻, ◻, ◻.[18] The fact that we **see** ◻ in the plural forms above shows that a reduction has taken place. However, in today's pronunciation we do not **hear** any difference between the sound at the beginning of the singular אָסוּר and the plural אֲסוּרִים. What we **do** hear is the difference between the beginning of כְּתוּבִים and the beginnings of all the words listed underneath it in the chart above: הֲרוּסִים, אֲסוּרִים and so on.

Here are some more examples in which ◻ appears instead of ◻. This time the reduction takes place **one** syllable before the stress:

		vowel reduces			ending added, stress moves		base form		
model form:	wrote	kat-VA	כָּתְבָה	⇐	(*כָּ-תְ-בָה)	⇐	ka-TAV	כָּ-תַב	◄
	asked	sha-'a-LA	שָׁאֲלָה	⇐	(*שָׁ-אֲ-לָה)	⇐	sha-'AL	שָׁ-אַל	
	drove	na-ha-GA	נָהֲגָה		(*נָ-הֲ-גָה)		na-HAG	נָ-הַג	
model form:		kot-VEEM	כּוֹתְבִים	⇐	(*כּוֹ-תְ-בִים)	⇐	ko-TEV	כּוֹ-תֵב	◄
		sho-'a-LEEM	שׁוֹאֲלִים	⇐	(*שׁוֹ-אֲ-לִים)	⇐	sho-'EL	שׁוֹ-אֵל	
		no-ha-GEEM	נוֹהֲגִים		(*נוֹ-הֲ-גִים)		no-HEG	נוֹ-הֵג	

You can read more about these changes in verbs in the unit "Verbs with Guttural Consonants" (pp. 448-487).

Let's review

♦ In a text with vowel signs, when vowel reduction is expected after guttural consonants (א',ה',ח',ע'), instead of *shva*, we see one of the variants of the *shva*: ◻, ◻, ◻. Here are some examples:

	reduction one syllable before stress			reduction two syllables before stress		
model forms:	כָּתְבָה	⇐	כָּתַב	כְּתוּבִים	⇐	כָּתוּב	◄
	kat-VA		ka-TAV	ktoo-VEEM		ka-TOOV	
	שָׁאֲלָה	⇐	שָׁאַל	אֲסוּרִים	⇐	אָסוּר	
	sha-'a-LA		sha-'AL	'a-soo-REEM		'a-SOOR	

---

18 a. Properly stated, gutturals are followed by vowels that are represented in writing by the *chatafeem* ◻, ◻, ◻.
   b. ◻ (*chataf patach*) is pronounced *ah*; ◻ (*chataf segol*) is pronounced *eh*; ◻ (*chataf kamats*) is pronounced *oh*.

Chapter summary

In order fully to understand vowel reduction, a basic knowledge of traditional Hebrew grammar is necessary. In this chapter, we have tried to give you a "feel" for when reductions do and do not occur.

- We have seen above that when endings are added to a base form, or when a noun is added to the end of another noun to create a *smeechoot* phrase, the stress moves to the ending (or to the last word in *smeechoot*). This shift **may** trigger the reduction of vowels to *shva*.

- Reduction of vowels to *shva* may take place in one of two places:
  - in an open syllable **two** syllables before the stress, as in: דָּבָר ⇐ דְּבָרִים
  - in an open syllable **one** syllable before the stress, as in: יָלְמַד ⇐ יָלְמְדוּ

- In an open syllable that is **two** syllables before the stress, only the vowels *ah* (◌ָ) and *eh* (◌ֶ) reduce. In an open syllable that is **one** syllable before the stress, the vowels *ah* (◌ָ), *eh* (◌ֶ) and *oh* (◌ֹ) reduce.

- A reduced vowel is written as a *shva*. This *shva* either is not pronounced at all (as in גְּדוֹלָה *gdo-LA* and לָמְדוּ *lam-DOO*) or is pronounced as *eh* (as in נְמוּכָה *ne-moo-CHA* and יִלְמְדוּ *yeel-me-DOO*).

- Gutturals (ע׳ ,ח׳ ,ה׳ ,א׳) generally are not followed by a *shva*. Often – in texts with vowel signs – instead of a *shva*, we find ◌ֲ, ◌ֱ, ◌ֳ written under them. These are pronounced *ah*, *eh* and *oh*, respectively.

IV. Hebrew Spelling: Selected Issues

Preview

- *Full spelling: When do we add a י or ו?*   כְּתִיב מָלֵא
- *Spelling foreign words: selected problems*

• *Full spelling: When do we add a י or ו?*   כְּתִיב מָלֵא

Read the following two versions of the same sentences:

◄ 1. יוּבָל הִזְמִין מִשְׂחַק מַחְשֵׁב מְיֻחָד מֵחֲנוּת בְּחוּ"ל. הוּא קִבֵּל אוֹתוֹ בַּדֹּאַר לִפְנֵי שְׁבוּעַיִם וּמְשַׂחֵק בּוֹ כָּל לַיְלָה.

2. יובל הזמין משחק מחשב מיוחד מחנות בחו"ל. הוא קיבל אותו בדואר לפני שבועיים ומשחק בו כל לילה.

Yuval ordered a computer game from a store abroad. He received it in the mail two weeks ago and plays it every night.

In the **first** version of these sentences, vowel *sounds* (*ah, eh, ee, oh, oo*) are indicated by vowel *signs* (mainly above and beneath the letters).[1] Some vowel sounds are indicated not only by vowel signs, but **also** by the letters ה, ו and י, as in the words הוּא, לַיְלָה and הִזְמִין.[2] This, however, is not always the case. For example, the *oo* in הוּא is spelled with the letter ו, but in מְיֻחָד it isn't. The second *ee* in the word הִזְמִין is spelled with the letter י, but the first *ee* isn't. This system of spelling may, indeed, **seem** to be inconsistent but, in actuality, it does have fixed rules (which are beyond the scope of this book). We will call the spelling in the first version above *standard spelling*.[3] This term refers not to the presence or absence of vowel signs, but rather to spelling in which **no extra** *yodeem* and *vaveem* are added to make reading easier. In Hebrew today, we find standard spelling almost exclusively in texts written **with** vowel signs (in poetry, children's books and the like).

---

1   These signs are called סִימָנֵי נִיקוּד.

2   The letters י, ו, ה and also א can function as letters that represent vowel sounds (called *vowel letters* אִמּוֹת קְרִיאָה).

3   The Hebrew term is כְּתִיב חָסֵר, usually translated with the unfortunate term *defective spelling*.

It is important to be aware of the fact that standard spelling reflects certain developments that took place in Hebrew over the course of its long history. For this reason, there is not always an exact correspondence between the way we pronounce Hebrew today and the way it is spelled. For example, you may guess that the word *hoo* (English: he) would be written הו, but, in fact, it is written הוא – with a silent (and, thus, superfluous) 'א on the end. This spelling, which reflects a pronunciation of this word that had already gone out of use by Biblical times (i.e., *HOO-'a*), simply has to be memorized. This is the case with many Hebrew words.

Now look at the **second** version of the Hebrew sentences presented above. The spelling used in this version is the system used in most books and articles written today. This system, called *full spelling*, uses standard spelling as its base, but usually does **not** use vowel signs.[4] Instead, 'ו and 'י are **added** in many places in order to make the recognition and pronunciation of words clearer to readers.

According to the rules of full spelling, generally speaking, 'י is added to indicate *ee*, and sometimes also *eh*; 'ו is added to indicate *oh* and *oo*. In addition, "וו" (a double 'ו) in the middle of a word tells us to read *v* (e.g., קווים *ka-VEEM*), while "יי" is used to indicate a *y* sound (e.g., קיים *ka-YAM*). These are **general** guidelines; however, in order to spell correctly and to understand the spelling of words, it is necessary to learn the rules of full spelling in more detail.

In this chapter we will present the main rules for full spelling according to the latest version published by the Hebrew Language Academy.[5]

Note: Names of people and places (*proper nouns*) are not necessarily written according to the rules of full spelling. For example, the names יעקב (*ya-'a-KOV*) and משה (*mo-SHE*) are usually spelled **without** a 'ו.

Writing 'ו *for* oo

The simplest of the spelling rules is this: Whenever you hear an *oo* sound, write 'ו. Here are some examples:

הוזמן ◁	דובר	מיוחד	בול	קופה	סיפור
hooz-MAN	*doo-BAR*	*me-yoo-CHAD*	*BOOL*	*koo-PA*	*see-POOR*
was invited	was spoken about	special	stamp	ticket counter	story

---

4   In this book, we use full spelling as our base – but often, rather than leaving it completely without vowel signs and other *diacritical marks* like *dagesh,* we **add** some of them in order to make a word's pronunciation clearer. In most publications in Modern Hebrew, when full spelling is used, vowel signs are not added.

5   The rules given here were published by the Hebrew Language Academy in *Leshonenu La'am*. See: The Academy of the Hebrew Language, 1994a, pp. 31-43. Any updates may be found on the internet site of the Academy: http://hebrew-academy.huji.ac.il/decision1.html

Obviously, since וֹ is used to indicate both *oo* and *oh*, only the context and your knowledge of Hebrew tell you how to pronounce these words. The וֹ narrows down the possibilities to one of these two vowel sounds.

Writing וֹ *for* oh

Almost every *oh* sound is written with וֹ:

זול	בקושי	עיתון	ארוך	יכול	דואר	לומד	שלום ◄
ZOL	*be-KO-shee*	*'ee-TON*	*'a-ROCH*	*ya-CHOL*	*DO-'ar*	*lo-MED*	*sha-LOM*
cheap	with difficulty	newspaper	long	can, is able	mail	is studying	peace

However, a small number of words with an *oh* sound are **not** written with וֹ. This means that in order to read these words correctly (with an *oh* sound), you have to **learn** them and their correct pronunciation. These words include the following:

1. Some words that end in ה':

שלמה	איפה	פה ◄
shlo-MO	*'EI-fo*[6]	*PO*
Shlomo	where	here

2. Some words in which a silent א' comes after the *oh*, for example:

צאן	שמאל	ראש	זאת	לא ◄
TSON	*SMOL*	*ROSH*	*ZOT*	*LO*
flock	left	head	this (*f.*)	no

The silent א' is present in the standard spelling of these words and is, therefore, kept in their full spelling.

This category includes some verbs whose first *root letter* is א', for example:

יאהב	יאכל	יאמר ◄
yo-HAV	*yo-CHAL*	*yo-MAR*
he will love	he will eat	he will say

---

6   Most speakers stress the first syllable of this word. In formal pronunciation, the **second** syllable is stressed: *'ei-FO.*

Chapter summary

3. Some words that have an *oh* vowel in the first syllable:[7]

תכנית ◄	חכמה	צהריים	אנייה	אמנם	אמן
toch-NEET	*choch-MA*	*tso-ho-RA-yeem*	*'o-nee-YA*	*'om-NAM*	*'o-MAN*
program	wisdom	noon	ship	it is true that	artist

In this book we have chosen to write some of these words **with** a ו in order to make their pronunciation clearer, for example:

◄ תוכנית חוכמה אונייה אומן

The word כל (*kol*) always has an *oh* vowel. It is spelled **without** a ו when it is the **first** part of a **phrase**, as in:

כל היום	כל לילה	כל הילדים ◄
kol	*kol*	*kol*
all day	every night	all the children

It is spelled **with** a ו when it is **not** the first part of a phrase, as in זה הכול! (That's all!).

Writing י for *ee*

The most "fickle" of the vowel sounds is *ee*. In full spelling, י is often added to indicate *ee* – but this is **not always** the case. When an *ee* sound is **not** indicated by י, we are left to rely on our knowledge of Hebrew to guide us in our reading, understanding and pronunciation of the word. For example, in sentence 2 at the beginning of this chapter, we saw the following words containing the sound *ee*:

לפני	קיבל	משחק	הזמין ◄
leef-NEI	*kee-BEL*	*mees-CHAK*	*heez-MEEN*

Look closely at the transcription that appears under these words.

Q: In which of these words does *ee* appear in the **last** syllable?

A: In the word הזמין (*heez-MEEN*), and – as you can see – it is written with י.

When *ee* appears in the **final** syllable, it almost always likes its presence to be "announced" by י. The problem arises when *ee* appears in the **first** syllable. As you can see, in both הזמין

---

7 When written **with** vowel signs, the *oh* sound in these words is indicated by either a *kamats katan* (e.g., תָכְנִית) or a *chataf kamats* (e.g., אֳנָיָה).

(*heez-MEEN*) and משחק (*mees-CHAK*), and also in the word לפני (*leef-NEI*), the *ee* in the first syllable is **not** noted by י. On the other hand, in the following word it **is**:

◄ קיבל   *kee-BEL*

The question is: When is *ee* that appears in the **first** syllable indicated by י and when is it not?

In order to answer this question, we need to know whether the first syllable is **open** or **closed**.[8]

When ee *appears in a first syllable that is open*

When we hear the sound *ee* in an open first syllable, we almost always write י.[9] Here are some examples:

◄ די-בור	שי-טה	תי-נוק	לי-מד	תי-כ-נס
dee-BOOR	*shee-TA*	*tee-NOK*	*lee-MED*	*tee-ka-NES*
speaking, speech	system	baby	he taught	you/she will enter

Two blatant exceptions are:

1. After the preposition מ- (*mee-*) (from, than), we never add י:

    ◄ יוסי מתל אביב.   Yossi is from Tel Aviv.
    mee-tel

2. In past tense *heef'eel* verbs like הגיע (*hee-GEE-a*) and הכיר (*hee-KEER*), we never add י after the ה even though the *ee* is in an open syllable. By not adding a י after the ה, we spell these verbs (whose root begins with a נ that "drops out" in all its forms) the same as we do *regular heef'eel* verbs, such as הרגיש (*heer-GEESH*) and הזמין (*heez-MEEN*).[10]

    On the spelling of these words, see the next section.

When ee *appears in a first syllable that is closed*

In the following examples, *ee* appears in the first syllable of each word, and that syllable is closed:

---

8   See the chapter "Basic Concepts: Sounds and Syllables," p. 622, for an explanation of *open* and *closed syllables*.

9   As explained in the chapter "Basic Concepts: Sounds and Syllables," p. 622, note 1, we are defining *open* and *closed syllables* according to their pronunciation in today's Hebrew, and not according to standard rules of syllable division.

10   On *heef'eel* verbs like הגיע and הכיר, see the chapter "Verbs Whose First Root Letter Is נ," pp. 498-499.

מג-דל   אר-גון   תז-מו-רת   הת-רג-שות   הת-ל-בש   נכ-נס   תש-מור   הת-חיל

heet-CHEEL   teesh-MOR   neech-NAS   heet-la-BESH   heet-rag-SHOOT   teez-MO-ret   'eer-GOON   meeg-DAL

When written with vowel signs, the first syllable in each of these words looks like this: ־ְמַם (it ends with a *shva*). When a closed syllable like this appears at the beginning of a word, the rules of full spelling tell us **not** to add a י, as you can see in the above examples. There are however some exceptions.

Exceptions

1. *Words whose base form has a* י

In some words whose **first** syllable is closed, a י **is** written in full spelling, for example: זיכרונות (*zeech-ro-NOT*). This is because, according to the rules of spelling, if the singular or *base form* of a word is written in full spelling **with** a י (as is זיכרון *zee-ka-RON*), so are the forms based on it (plural or *smeechoot* forms in nouns and verb forms with endings), for example:

related forms				base form	
initial *closed* syllable	(but spelled like base form)			initial *open* syllable – with י	
ניסיון חיים	זיכרונו	זיכרונות	⇐	ניסיון	1. זיכרון
nees-YON cha-YEEM	zeech-ro-NO	zeech-ro-NOT		nee-sa-YON	zee-ka-RON
life experience	his memory	memories		experience, attempt	memory
	הם סיפרו	היא דיברה	⇐	הוא סיפר	2. הוא דיבר
	seep-ROO	deeb-RA		see-PER	dee-BER
	they told	she spoke		he told	he spoke
	הם ייתנו	את תיפלי	⇐	הוא ייתן	3. אתה תיפול
	yeet-NOO	teep-LEE		yee-TEN	tee-POL
	they will give	you will fall (*f.s.*)		he will give	you will fall (*m.s.*)

2. *Words of foreign origin*

Words of foreign origin that have an *ee* sound in their first syllable are always written with י in full spelling, even when the first syllable is closed, for example:

אינטרנט   היסטוריה   מיליון

internet   history   million

3. *When* ee *appears in one-syllable words*

Most one-syllable words that contain an *ee* sound are written with a י (even in standard spelling), for example:

	שיר	גיל	שים!
◄	*SHEER*	*GEEL*	*SEEM*
	song, poem;	age	Put...!
	Sing! (*m.s.*)		(*m.s.*)

However, the following words do **not** contain a י in standard spelling, and we do **not** add a י to them in full spelling either:

	עם	אם	מן
◄	*'EEM*	*'EEM*	*MEEN*
	with	if	from

Want to see if you've understood?

The following words are written in standard spelling with vowel signs. Rewrite them in full spelling, adding a י where required. (Write the words without vowel signs.)

4. סֵפֶר _____   3. גִּנָּה _____   2. מִסְפָּר _____   1. סִפּוּר _____
see-PER   gee-NA   mees-PAR   see-POOR

8. נִגְנָה _____   7. הִכִּיר _____   6. הִסְבִּיר _____   5. הִתְנַגֵּד _____
neeg-NA   hee-KEER   hees-BEER   heet-na-GED

10. נִשְׁאַר _____   9. תִּכָּנֵס _____
neesh-'AR   tee-ka-NES

Answers:
In the following words, a י is required: 1. סיפור   3. גינה   4. סיפר   8. ניגנה   9. תיכנס
All the other words are spelled the same in standard spelling and in full spelling (i.e., no י is added).

Writing י *for* eh *(often pronounced* ei*)*

In standard spelling with vowel signs, we often see cases of an *eh/ei* vowel written with י. This י, of course, is written in full spelling as well. Here are some examples (we have given two common pronunciations):

	חֵיל אוויר	בֵּית חולים	בֵּין	אֵיךְ	אֵיפֹה
◄	air force	hospital	between	How?	Where?
	cheil- / chel-	*beit- / bet-*	*bein / ben*	*'ECH*	*'El-fo / 'E-fo*

The last two words – בֵּית- and חֵיל- – are *smeechoot* forms of בַּיִת (BA-yeet) and חַיִל (CHA-yeel). These words maintain the י (*y*) that is present in their non-*smeechoot* forms. The reason for the appearance of י in the other words listed here has to do with the development of Hebrew and the evolution of its vowels (we will not go into this here). This י always appears in these words – in standard and in full spelling.

Here are some more examples of words that always have a י in standard spelling – and also in full spelling:

בָּתֵי ספר	סְפְרֵי קודש	לְפְנֵי השיעור
schools	holy books	before class
ba-TEI- / ba-TE-	seef-REI- / seef-RE-	leef-NEI- / leef-NE-

Forms like these with *eh / ei*) at the end of the word are usually plural *smeechoot* forms. The words בָּתֵי and סְפְרֵי, for example, are *smeechoot* forms of the plural nouns בָּתִים and סְפָרִים. The preposition לְפְנֵי – and also אַחֲרֵי – are also based on plural forms.[11]

When eh is not the end of a word

We will now look at cases in which *eh* is **not** indicated by י in standard spelling. Here are some examples:

	eh *in the first syllable*				eh *in the middle of a word*	
תֵּאָבוֹן	יֵעָלֵם	תֵּאוּר	בֵּרֵךְ	שְׂרֵפָה	בְּרֵכָה	שְׁאֵלָה
te-'a-VON	ye-'a-LEM	te-'OOR	be-RECH	sre-FA	bre-CHA	she-'e-LA
appetite	he will disappear	description	he blessed	fire	pool	question

The question is: When we write in full spelling, when do we add י to indicate *eh*?

The official rules of full spelling tell us, generally, **not** to **add** י to indicate *eh*. According to these rules, in full spelling we write the first three words in the list above **without** י:[12]

שאלה	ברכה	שרפה

---

11 Sometimes *eh* at the end of a word is written in standard spelling with ה, as in:

הוא בּוֹנֶה	פֶּה	קָשֶׁה	הַרְבֵּה
bo-NE	PE	ka-SHE	har-BE
he is building	mouth	hard (*m.s.*)	many, much

   Most of these words are **singular** forms of verbs, nouns or adjectives.

12 In practice, many writers of Hebrew do not adhere to the rules of correct spelling and, for example, they write a י in ברירה (in this way it is distinguished from בְּרָכָה – blessing).

In contrast, when we write the words on the left (and other words like them), according to the rules of the Hebrew Language Academy, we **do** add a ־י in full spelling:

בירך   תיאור   ייעלם   תיאבון   ⯇

The reason why ־י **is** added to these words has to do with their **patterns**. For example, the verb בירך belongs to *beenyan pee'el* and is formed according to the pattern of דיבר (*dee-BER*) and סיפר (*see-PER*): ◻◻ִי◻ֵ (_*ee-_ E_). However, the vowel in the model verbs דיבר and סיפר is *ee* (and is indicated by ־י), while the first vowel in בירך is *eh* (*be-RECH*). This variation in pronunciation is caused by the presence of ־ר in the middle of the root (בֵּיְרַךְ).[13] But, despite the fact that the vowel is now *eh*, we still write ־י after the first letter in the past tense (בירך) in order to maintain the verb's identity as a verb in *beenyan pee'el*.

The change from *ee* to *eh* is common and is often caused by the presence of ־ר or one of the *gutturals*: ע, ח, ה, א (e.g., תֵּיאֵר he described). In all cases, the principle is the same: If there is a ־י indicating *ee* in the *model form*, this ־י **is still written** – even when the vowel changes to *eh* – in order to maintain the identity of the word pattern.

Now let's look at the rest of the words on the left side of the list above:

- תיאור (*te-'OOR*) is the *verbal noun* of the verb תֵּיאֵר (*te-'ER*) in *beenyan pee'el*. Its model form is דיבור (*dee-BOOR*), which is the verbal noun of דיבר (*dee-BER*). Because of the guttural ־א in the middle of תיאור, the vowel changes to *eh*, but we still write ־י as in the model form. Here are some more examples: פירוש (*pe-ROOSH* interpretation, meaning), שירות (*she-ROOT* service).

- ייעלם (*ye-'a-LEM*) and להיעלם (*le-he-'a-LEM*), the future tense and infinitive forms of *neef'al*, are modeled after ייכנס (*yee-ka-NES* he will enter) and להיכנס (*le-hee-ka-NES* to enter). Because of the presence of ־ע, the *ee* changes to *eh*, but the ־י is still added. Here are some more examples: ייאמר (*ye-'a-MER* it will be said), ייהרס (*ye-ha-RES* it will be destroyed).

- תיאבון (*te-'a-VON*), whose model form is a word like זיכרון (*zee-ka-RON* memory), is written with ־י even though its first vowel is *eh* because of the presence of ־א. Here are some more examples: ריאיון (*re-'a-YON* interview), היריון (*he-ra-YON* pregnancy).

---

13   This happens when a strong *dagesh* is expected (here as part of the pattern), but it cannot appear because of the ־ר. For more details, see the chapter "Guttural Consonants and ־ר: *Beenyaneem Pee'el, Poo'al* and *Neef'al*," pp. 475, 478, 482.

Spelling words with a y sound

Read the following sentence, written first with standard spelling and then with full spelling. Note: As in the rest of the book, at the **end** of words and syllables, we have used *ai* (and not *ay*) to transcribe the sounds found in the English "lie," "my" and "buy." The *i* in *ai* actually represents the consonant *y*.

standard spelling:	שֶׁל הוֹרַי.	הַבִּנְיָן	לְיַד	יְלָדַי	עִם	לְטַיֵּל	עָלַי ◄
	ho-RAI	ha-been-YAN	le-YAD	ye-la-DAI		le-ta-YEL	'a-LAI

full spelling:	של הוריי.	הבניין	ליד	ילדיי	עם	לטייל	עליי

I have to take a walk with my children next to my parents' building.

As you can see, in full spelling sometimes the sound *y* is written with one ' and sometimes with two ' (יי). We will now see when we write one ' and when two (יי).

The sound y at the beginning of a word

When we hear the consonant *y* at the **beginning** of a word, we write only **one** ':

יד	ילדים ◄
YAD	ye-la-DEEM
hand	children

This remains the case also when one-letter words (e.g., -ה, -ו, -ש, -מ, -ל, -ב, -כ) are added to the front of such words, as in:

מיד	ליד	היד ◄
mee-YAD	le-YAD	ha-YAD
immediately	next to	the hand

The sound y in the middle and end of a word

There are two general guidelines for indicating the presence of the consonant *y* in the **middle** or at the **end** of a word:

1. Generally speaking, when we hear *y* in the middle or at the end of a word, we add a ' to create a double ' (יי).[13]

ידיים	שבועיים	אלייך	דודייך	עליי	דודותיי	דודיי ◄
ya-DA-yeem	shvoo-'A-yeem	'e-LA-yeech	do-DA-yeech	'a-LAI	do-do-TAI	do-DAI
hands	two weeks	to you (*f.s.*)	your (*f.s.*) uncles	on me	my aunts	my uncles

---

13 However, we do **not** add an extra ' if it results in the appearance of **three** *yodeem* in a row. Thus, for example, no ' is added to the future tense form יְיַצֵּא (*ye-ya-TSE* he will export).

Included in this group are words that contain the sound *ee-YA*, for example:[14]

	words with the ending ייה-			verbal nouns		
עוגייה	ספרדייה	ספרייה		עלייה	בנייה	קנייה ◁
'oo-gee-YA	*sfa-ra-dee-YA*	*seef-ree-YA*		*'a-lee-YA*	*bnee-YA*	*knee-YA*
cookie	Spanish woman, Sephardic woman	library		immigration to Israel; ascent	building	buying

However:

2. When the consonant *y* appears next to the vowel letters **א, ה', ו'**, we write only **one** **י'** to indicate the consonant *y* in the **middle** or **end** of a word. The one exception is words with *ee-YA* mentioned above, in which we write two *yodeem* (יי) before ה.

Here are some examples:

next to **ו'**:	היו	ציור	מצוין	בנוי	קניות ◁	
	ha-YOO	*tsee-YOOR*	*me-tsoo-YAN*	*ba-NOOY*	*knee-YOT*	
	were	drawing	excellent	built	shopping	
next to **ה'**:		ביולוגיה	היה	הפניה	בעיה[15]	
		bee-yo-LOG-ya	*ha-YA*	*haf-na-YA*	*be-'a-YA*	
		biology	was	referral; reference	problem	
next to **א'**:				בוודאי	חקלאי	
				be-va-DAI	*chak-LAI*	
				certainly	farmer; agriculturist	

The following **special cases** follow neither of the guidelines stated above. The *y* sound in them is indicated by only **one** **י'** (when we would expect two). These cases must simply be learned:

---

14 The three words on the right belong to the same pattern as verbal nouns like כְּתִיבָה (writing). The third root letter in the words above is **י'** (their roots are ע-ל-י, ק-נ-י, ב-נ-י), thus:

	pattern:	קְ מִ יָ ה ◁
		בְּ נִ יָ ה

The three words on the left in the list above all have *ee-YA* (ייה-) tacked onto the end.

15 Note: In the *smeechoot* form of words like בעיה and הפניה, where **י'** no longer comes before the vowel letter **ה'** (i.e., it is replaced by **ת'** to form -בְּעָיַת), we write a **double** **י'** (יי) – in accordance with the first guideline:

הפניית הרופא	בעיית למידה ◁
haf-na-YAT-	*be-'a-YAT-*
the doctor's referral	learning problem

1. The words מים (*MA-yeem* water) and שמים (*sha-MA-yeem* sky, heavens) end in ‏יִם‎- but are spelled with one ‏י‎ only.[16]

2. Words whose pattern is that of בית (*BA-yeet* house) and זית (*ZA-yeet* olive), called *segolates*,[17] are written with **one** ‏י‎ in the middle.

3. Two common words related to the segolates – לילה (*LAI-la* night) and הביתה (*ha-BAI-ta* home, as in "to go home") – are spelled with only **one** ‏י‎.

4. The words אולי (*'oo-LAI* perhaps), מתי (*ma-TAI* When?) and חי (*CHAI* he lives / lived) are written with only one ‏י‎.

Want to see if you've understood?

Write in full spelling. (Add ‏י‎ wherever it is needed.)

‏1. רַגְלַיִם   2. רַגְלֶיךָ   3. רַגְלַיִךְ   4. שְׁתִיָּה   5. הַיּוֹם   6. סוֹצְיוֹלוֹגְיָה   7. אֵלַי   8. מַיִם   9. צִיּוּר‎
‏10. עַגְבָנִיּוֹת‎

Answers:

‏1. רגליים   2. רגליך   3. רגלייך   4. שתייה   5. היום   6. סוציולוגיה   7. אליי   8. מים   9. ציור   10. עגבניות‎

Spelling words with a ‏ו‎ that is pronounced v

The sound v *at the beginning and end of a word*

At the **beginning** of words whose ‏ו‎ is pronounced *v*, we write one ‏ו‎ in full spelling, for example:[18]

standard spelling:	וִכּוּחַ	וַעַד	וֶרֶד ◄
	vee-KOO-ach	VA-'ad	VE-red
full spelling:	ויכוח	ועד	ורד
	argument	council	Rose

---

16 Proper nouns like ירושלים (*ye-roo-sha-LA-yeem* Jerusalem) and מצרים (*meets-RA-yeem* Egypt) are also spelled with only one ‏י‎. As noted at the beginning of the chapter, rules of full spelling do not necessarily apply to names of people and places.

17 On *segolates*, see the chapter "Segolate Nouns," pp. 89-107.

18 A double ‏ו‎ (וו) at the beginning of a word is used to indicate the sound *w* (e.g., וושינגטון Washington). See below, p. 669.

Also at the **end** of a word only one 'ו is written, as in:

standard spelling:	סְתָו	עַכְשָׁו ◄
	STAV	'ach-SHAV
full spelling:	סתיו	עכשיו
	autumn	now

Q: What is added **before** the consonantal 'ו in these words?

A: The letter 'י. This 'י does **not** represent a sound; rather, it tells us that the final 'ו is to be pronounced as the consonant *v* and not as the vowel *oo* or *oh*.

When a word has only **one** syllable, we do not add a 'י, for example: קו (*KAV* – line) and תו (*TAV* – a musical note).

The sound *v* in the middle

In the **middle** of a word, when 'ו represents the consonant *v* – and not the vowels *oo* or *oh* – we write a **double** 'ו (וו) in full spelling, for example:

standard spelling:	הַוִּילוֹן	לְהִתְכַּוֵּן	הַשְׁוָאָה	מָוֶת	תִּקְוָה ◄
	ha-vee-LON	le-heet-ka-VEN	hash-va-'A	MA-vet	teek-VA
full spelling:	הוווילון	להתכוון	השוואה	מוות	תקווה
	the curtain	to mean, intend	comparison	death	hope

As you can see in הוווילון, when we add the *definite article* (-ה) to a word that begins with one 'ו, the 'ו is doubled (וו). This is true whenever one-letter words (e.g., -ב, -ש) are added before a 'ו, as in:

standard spelling:	אֲנִי מַאֲמִינָה שֶׁוִּיטָמִינִים עוֹזְרִים לַגּוּף לְהִלָּחֵם בַּוִּירוּסִים. ◄
	be-VEE-roo-seem *she-vee-ta-MEE-neem*
full spelling:	אני מאמינה שוויטמינים עוזרים לגוף להילחם בווירוסים
	I believe that vitamins help the body fight viruses.

As we saw above, this is **not** the case with the consonant *y*: הילד, where only **one** 'י is written after -ה and other one-letter words added before it.

Note: We do **not** double the ו when it comes before the vowel letters "וֹ" and "וּ", so as not to write **more than** two ו in full spelling, thus:

standard spelling:	הֵן מְקַוּוֹת שֶׁ- תִּקְווֹת ◄
	me-ka-VOT teek-VOT
full spelling:	מקוות תקוות
	they (*f.s.*) hope that hopes

Want to see if you've understood?

Write in full spelling. (Add ו wherever it should be added.)

1. הַוְּרָדִים   2. קַוִּים   3. עִיּוּר   4. לַוֶטֶרִינָר   5. וִיטָמִין   6. מְכֻוָּן

Answers:

1. הוורדים   2. קווים   3. עיוור   4. לווטרינר   5. ויטמין   6. מכוון

• *Spelling foreign words: selected problems*

There are quite a few words of foreign origin in Hebrew. In this section we will deal with questions concerning the way some of the consonants in these words are represented in Hebrew spelling.

The sounds s *and* k

We use the Hebrew letter ס (not שׂ) to spell foreign words that contain the sound *s*, for example:

סולו	סוציולוגיה ◄
SO-lo	*sots-yo-LOG-ya*
solo	sociology

The Hebrew letter ק (not כּ) is used for the sound *k*, whether it be spelled with *k* or *c* (or with a different letter) in the foreign language, for example:

מקסיקו	ארקטי	קינטי ◄
MEK-see-ko	*ARK-tee*	*kee-NE-tee*
Mexico	Arctic	kinetic

Spelling foreign words with **t** *and* **th**

As you probably know, the sound *th* in foreign words like *theater* and *mathematics* does **not** exist in Modern Hebrew. Hebrew speakers pronounce the Hebrew versions of these words with a *t* sound identical to the *t* sound in the second part of these words: *te-'a-TRON* and *ma-te-MA-tee-ka*. However, when we spell these foreign words in Hebrew, we use **two** different Hebrew letters for the **one** sound *t*: 'ט and 'ת. The choice of which of these letters to use is usually based on the spelling (and pronunciation) of these words **in the foreign language**: We use 'ט when the foreign spelling is *t* and 'ת when the foreign spelling is *th*. Here are some examples:

תאטרון	מתמטיקה	דוקטור	טקסט ◄
te-'at-RON	*ma-te-MA-tee-ka*	*DOK-tor*	*TEKST*
theater	mathematics	doctor	text

Note: The spelling of the word תה (*TE* – tea) is apparently based on the French spelling *thé*.

The sound v

The sound *v* is usually written with 'ו at the **beginning** of a word – e.g., ונטילטור (*ven-tee-LA-tor* ventilator, fan) – and "וו" in the **middle** – e.g., טלוויזיה (*te-le-VEEZ-ya* television).

Exception: In the **middle** of a word, when the vowel *oo* or *oh* – written with a 'ו – appears next to the *v* sound, we write the *v* with a 'ב, as in:

לבוב	נובמבר ◄
le-VOV	*no-VEM-ber*
Lvov	November
(city in Ukraine)	

At the **end** of a word, *v* is written with a 'ב:

נרטיב ◄
na-ra-TEEV
a narrative

In order to maintain uniformity, it is also common practice to write the adjective based on this word – נרטיבי (*na-ra-TEE-vee* = narrative) – with a 'ב.[19] The spelling of this and other similar adjectives derived from nouns ending in "ive" has led to the common practice of spelling all words that end in "ive" with a 'ב, for example:

---

19 At this point in time, the Hebrew Language Academy has not made an official ruling in this matter. What we have written here is based on information provided by Ms. Ruth Almagor-Ramon and Ms. Ronit Gadish, both of the Hebrew Language Academy.

נאיבי	פסיבי	אקטיבי ◄
na-'EE-vee	*pa-SEE-vee*	*'ak-TEE-vee*
naive	passive	active

In addition, some words are spelled with 'ב because Hebrew speakers are so used to spelling them this way that the spelling has been maintained, for example:

אוניברסלי	אוניברסיטה ◄
'oo-nee-ver-SA-lee	*'oo-nee-VER-see-ta*
universal	university

Words that begin with w

Foreign words that begin with the sound *w* are usually written with a double 'ו (וו), as in:

וואו	וולבי	וושינגטון ◄
WAW	*WA-la-bee*	*WA-sheeng-ton*
Wow!	wallaby	Washington

Want to see if you've understood?

Translate using the Hebrew versions of the highlighted foreign words.

1. Prof. Mira Cohen teaches **mathematics** at **Washington University**, and her husband, Dr. Rafi Cohen, is a **cardiologist**.

   _____

2. In November we saw two performances (הצגות) at the Jerusalem **Theater**.

   _____

3. The new medicine is very **effective**.

   _____

Answers:

1. פרופ' מירה כהן מלמדת מתמטיקה באוניברסיטת וושינגטון, ובעלה ד"ר רפי כהן הוא קרדיולוג.
2. בנובמבר ראינו שתי הצגות בתאטרון ירושלים.   3. התרופה החדשה אפקטיבית מאוד.